ELECTRONIC INSTRUMENTATION FUNDAMENTALS

ELECTRONIC INSTRUMENTATION FUNDAMENTALS

Albert Paul Malvino

Foothill College, Los Altos Hills, California
Consultant, Varian Associates, Palo Alto, California

McGraw-Hill Book Company

New York • St. Louis • San Francisco • Dallas
London • Toronto • Sydney

ELECTRONIC INSTRUMENTATION FUNDAMENTALS

Library of Congress Catalog Card Number: 67-14893

39847

1 2 3 4 5 6 7 8 9 10 (MP) 7 4 3 2 1 0 6 9 8 7

To Joanna and the children

without whose help this book would
have been finished five years earlier.

Preface

A vast number of textbooks have been written on electronics; but I feel that there is still a great need for a book that gives the electronics technician a solid foundation in the theory behind electronic instruments. This book, I hope, will do just that. It analyzes a number of basic electronic instruments to illustrate how they work, what they do, and what their limitations are. In the course of this analysis it reviews a considerable amount of electronics theory and introduces a good deal of material which will be quite new to most technicians.

This book was specifically written for an electronics technician in his second year of study in a junior college or technical institute. Algebra and trigonometry are the only mathematical prerequisites. A number of worked-out examples have been included, as well as a glossary, in the hope that this book will also be suitable for home study.

I would like to express my thanks to John W. Sherman and William E. Long, of Foothill College, for their suggestions and encouragement throughout the writing of this book, and to Paul H. Chitwood, of Oregon Technical Institute, and Thomas Wong, of Ames Research Center/NASA, for their careful reviews of the final manuscript and for their many excellent suggestions. I also wish to thank Mrs. Beatrice Sanders for typing the final manuscript.

A. P. MALVINO

Contents

1 Introduction

An electric signal is a versatile quantity. It can be amplified, attenuated, modified, modulated, rectified, transmitted, measured, and controlled, to name but a few of the possibilities. This fact is of practical interest only if we can use this versatility to improve the physical environment in which we live. Fortunately, there is a way. Devices known as *transducers* can convert the nonelectrical quantities in our environment into electrical quantities. We can then indirectly manipulate the quantities in our environment with the speed and versatility that is found only in electronic instruments. As if this were not enough, we also find electronic instruments invading the domain of the mind. They are computing, manipulating, and processing information in much the same way as the mind. In some areas they are far superior to the mind. For these reasons, the importance of studying electronic instruments is clear.

In this book we examine a number of basic electronic instruments, hoping to develop a deep insight into the way that instruments work, what they do, and what their limitations are. A number of selected theoretical topics have been included because they are crucial to a clear understanding of instruments, and we will therefore be involved at times in pure theory. But rest assured that when a purely theoretical topic is encountered, the practical use of it is not far behind.

1-1 Common Prefixes and the Use of Hertz

It will be helpful to have a list of the common prefixes used throughout this book. These common prefixes are shown in Table 1-1.

Table 1-1 List of Prefixes

Prefix	Abbreviation	Meaning
Mega	M	10^6
Kilo	k	10^3
Milli	m	10^{-3}
Micro	μ	10^{-6}
Nano	n	10^{-9}
Pico	p	10^{-12}

The unit of hertz, abbreviated Hz, will be used instead of cycles per second (cps). For instance, we will speak of 1 Hz instead of 1 cps, 1 kHz instead of 1 kc, and 1 MHz instead of 1 Mc.

1-2 Ideal Sources and Linear Elements

The ideal voltage source is a source whose voltage is independent of the value of any load connected to it. Figure 1-1*a* illustrates the symbols we will use for ideal voltage sources.

Throughout this book, whenever we use the symbols of Fig. 1-1*a* we are referring to an ideal battery or a-c generator which has no internal

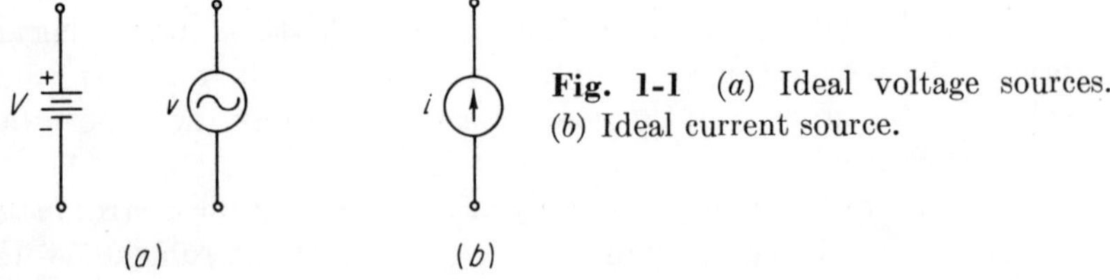

Fig. 1-1 (*a*) Ideal voltage sources. (*b*) Ideal current source.

impedance. To indicate a real battery with internal resistance, we will add a resistor in series with the ideal battery. A similar statement applies to the ideal a-c generator.

An important point to grasp about the ideal voltage source is that the voltage at its terminals will not change under any load conditions. For instance, if the ideal battery is labeled 50 volts, it will remain at 50 volts no matter how small or how large a load resistor is connected to it.

The ideal current source is shown in Fig. 1-1*b*. This is a source whose current is independent of the load attached to it. For instance, if the current source is labeled 5 amp, then 5 amp always flows into and out of its terminals, regardless of the value of load connected to it. (In all our work we will use the conventional direction of current flow, that is, opposite the direction of electron flow.)

It should be understood that the ideal sources do not exist in nature but only in our minds as ultimate or perfect sources. Nevertheless, these ideal devices can be used in solving real circuit problems whenever approximate answers are acceptable. For example, pentodes and transistors are often represented by ideal current sources as a step toward obtaining approximate gain formulas.

So much for the ideal sources.

The next concept to absorb is that of a linear circuit element. By this we simply mean a resistor, inductor, or capacitor whose value does not change as the voltage across it changes. For instance, a 5-ohm resistor which maintains this value for small or large voltages across it is a linear resistor. Ordinary composition and wire-wound resistors may be considered linear resistors for practical purposes. A diode would be an example of a nonlinear resistor, since its total voltage divided by its total current does not give a fixed value of resistance for a changing terminal voltage.

An example of a linear inductance would be an air-core coil. The inductance for this type of coil remains constant in spite of changes in the terminal voltage. On the other hand, an iron-core coil is a nonlinear inductance because the core eventually saturates, leading to a change in the inductance value.

An ordinary capacitor with a dielectric like paper, glass, or mica may be considered a linear capacitance for practical purposes. An example of a nonlinear capacitance would be a semiconductor diode biased in the reverse direction. Under this condition the diode acts as a capacitor, but the value of the capacitance changes with the value of reverse voltage.

Example 1-1

Find the value of voltage across the resistor and across the ideal current source for the circuit of Fig. 1-2*a*.

Solution

The current through the current source must be 2 ma. Therefore, the voltage across the resistor is 2 volts with the polarity shown.

To find the voltage across the current source we may apply Kirchhoff's voltage law. To do this we will go around the loop in a clockwise

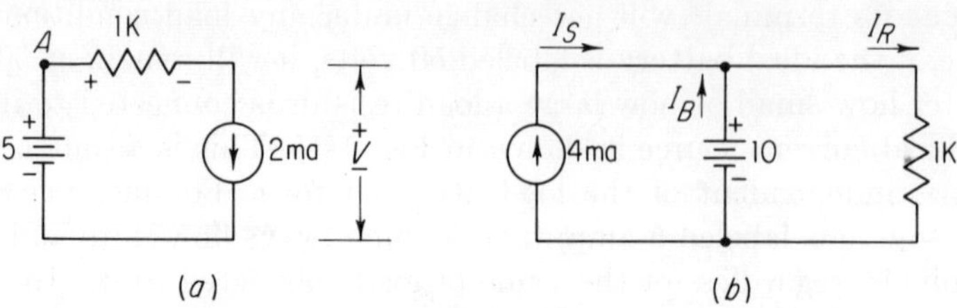

Fig. 1-2 (*a*) Example 1-1. (*b*) Example 1-2.

direction writing down the first sign (+ or −) that we encounter and the value of the voltage. Starting at point A,

$$+2 + V - 5 = 0$$

or

$$V = 5 - 2 = 3 \text{ volts}$$

Note that if we reverse the direction of the current source, the voltage across the resistor will be 2 volts of the opposite polarity. The voltage across the current source will be 7 volts. (If in doubt, apply Kirchhoff's law.)

Example 1-2

Find the current in the resistor and in the battery of Fig. 1-2*b*.

Solution

Because of the ideal battery, the voltage across the resistor must be 10 volts. Therefore, the current through the resistor is 10 ma.

From Kirchhoff's current law:

$$I_B + I_S = I_R$$

or

$$I_B = I_R - I_S = 10 - 4 \text{ ma} = 6 \text{ ma}$$

Note that if the current source is reversed, the resistor current is still 10 ma in the direction shown, but the battery current must rise to 14 ma. (Apply Kirchhoff's current law again, if in doubt.)

1-3 Thévenin's Theorem Applied to D-C Circuits

If any one theorem concerning electric circuits could be singled out as the greatest practical timesaving tool ever discovered, it would probably be the famous Thévenin theorem. Many complicated circuits which are extremely difficult to analyze by the methods of Kirchhoff's law become mere child's play if Thévenin's theorem is applicable. Since we will apply this theorem many times throughout the course of this book, a discussion at this time is essential.

We begin our study by discussing the meaning of Thévenin's theorem as it applies to d-c circuits. Assume that there is a d-c circuit enclosed in a box, as shown in Fig. 1-3. Inside the box is a circuit consisting of ideal batteries, ideal current sources, and linear resistors, connected in any one of the infinite number of combinations possible.

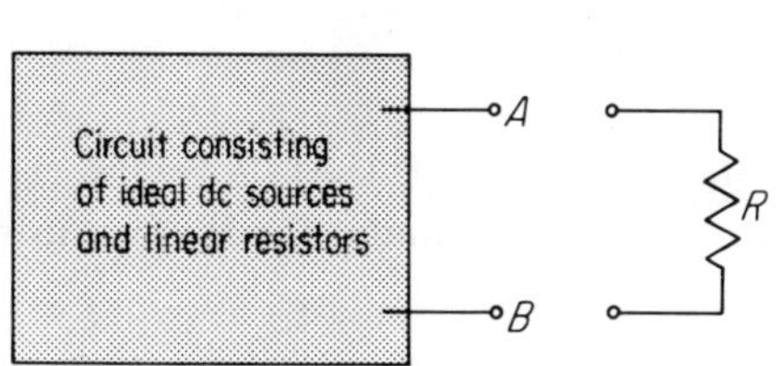

Fig. 1-3 Developing Thévenin's theorem.

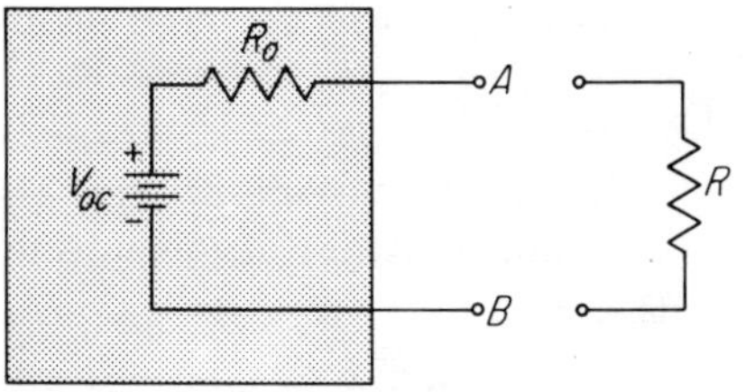

Fig. 1-4 The Thévenin equivalent circuit.

Suppose that we plan to connect an external resistor across any two points A and B in the circuit. The A and B points have been brought outside the box for convenience of discussion. Once the resistor is connected to the AB terminals, there will probably be a current flow through it. How do we find the value of this current?

In many circuit applications we are confronted with precisely the situation described. Finding the current in the resistor may be easy or difficult, depending upon the circuit that is inside the box.

In any event, Thévenin's theorem says that the circuit inside the box may be replaced by a single ideal battery and a linear resistor, as shown in Fig. 1-4.

How do we find the value of V_{oc} and R_o?

According to the Thévenin theorem, the battery voltage is the voltage across the AB terminals of the original circuit *before* connecting the external resistor. We will refer to this voltage as the open-circuit voltage and use the notation V_{oc} to aid us in remembering that the battery voltage is the open-circuit voltage at the AB terminals.

The resistance R_o, called the *Thévenin resistance,* can be obtained as follows. First, reduce all sources in the original circuit to zero. This is equivalent to replacing all batteries by short circuits and all current sources by open circuits. Second, with all sources at zero, compute the resistance that an ohmmeter would measure from A to B. This is the value of R_o. We will refer to this value as the resistance seen when looking back into the AB terminals.

The formal proof of Thévenin's theorem must be left to advanced courses in electrical engineering.

Let us summarize our rules for finding V_{oc} and R_o.

1. Find the open-circuit voltage across the AB terminals of the given circuit. This is V_{oc}.
2. Short all batteries, open all current sources, and find the net resistance between the A and B terminals. This is R_o.

The application of Thévenin's theorem to a-c circuits will be discussed in later chapters as the need arises.

Example 1-3

Given the circuit of Fig. 1-5, find the current that flows in the 1-kilohm resistor if it is connected to the AB terminals. Use Thévenin's theorem.

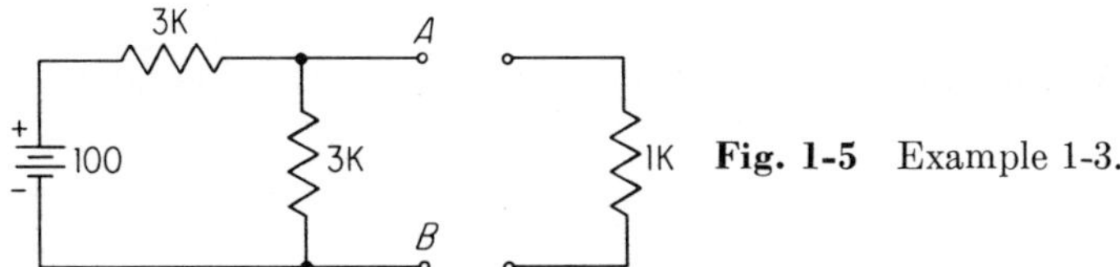

Fig. 1-5 Example 1-3.

Solution

V_{oc} is the voltage across the AB terminals before the 1-kilohm resistor is connected. Obviously, V_{oc} is 50 volts because the 100-volt ideal source is across a voltage divider of two 3-kilohm resistors.

R_o is the resistance between the AB terminals with the battery shorted as shown in Fig. 1-6a. Obviously, R_o is 1.5 kilohms because with the voltage source shorted, 3 kilohms appears in parallel with 3 kilohms as seen from AB.

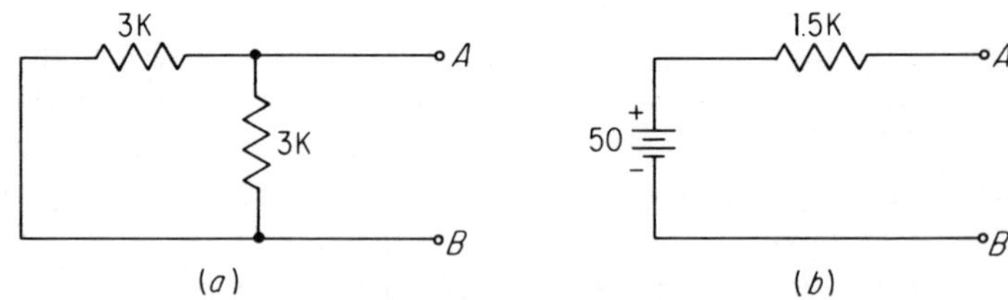

Fig. 1-6 (a) Finding the Thévenin resistance. (b) The Thévenin equivalent circuit.

The Thévenin equivalent circuit is shown in Fig. 1-6b. When the 1-kilohm resistor is connected to the AB terminals, the current flow through it will be

$$I = \frac{50}{1.5(10^3) + 10^3} = 20 \text{ ma}$$

Example 1-4

Find the Thévenin equivalent circuit for the circuit shown in Fig. 1-7*a*.

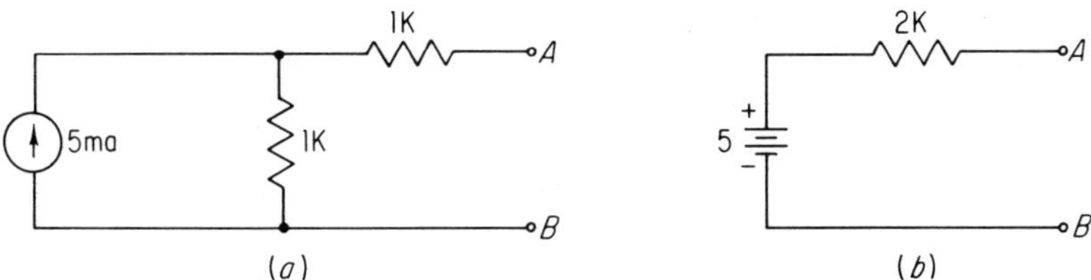

Fig. 1-7 (*a*) Example 1-4. (*b*) The Thévenin equivalent circuit.

Solution

Before connecting any load to the AB terminals, the open circuit voltage across AB is

$$V_{oc} = 5(10^{-3})(10^{3}) = 5 \text{ volts}$$

R_o is the resistance from A to B with the current source removed or open. Obviously, R_o is 2 kilohms, because 1 kilohm appears in series with 1 kilohm as seen from the AB terminals.

The Thévenin equivalent is shown in Fig. 1-7*b*.

Notice that a load resistor connected to the AB terminals of either circuit will have the same current flowing through it. For instance, let us connect a load resistor of 0 ohms across the AB terminals. In the original circuit of Fig. 1-7*a* the short would have 2.5 ma flowing through it. In the Thévenin equivalent of Fig. 1-7*b* it is clear that 2.5 ma would also flow through a shorted load.

Example 1-5

Find the current in the 1-kilohm resistor of Fig. 1-8*a*.

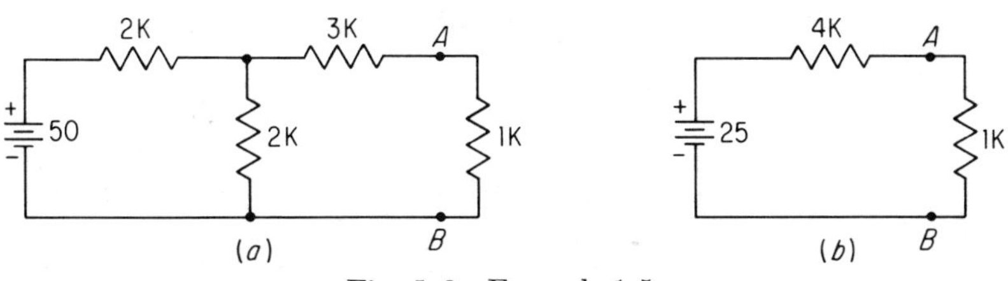

Fig. 1-8 Example 1-5.

Solution

To find the current in the 1-kilohm resistor we need to find the Thévenin equivalent at the AB terminals with the 1-kilohm resistor removed from the circuit. Visualize the 1-kilohm resistor removed and find V_{oc} and R_o. The Thévenin equivalent is shown in Fig. 1-8*b* with the 1-kilohm resistor connected. The circuit to the left of the *AB* terminals is the Thévenin equivalent for the original circuit to the left of the *AB* terminals.

Clearly, the current through the 1-kilohm resistor is 5 ma.

Example 1-6

Find the current in the 4-kilohm resistor of Fig. 1-9.

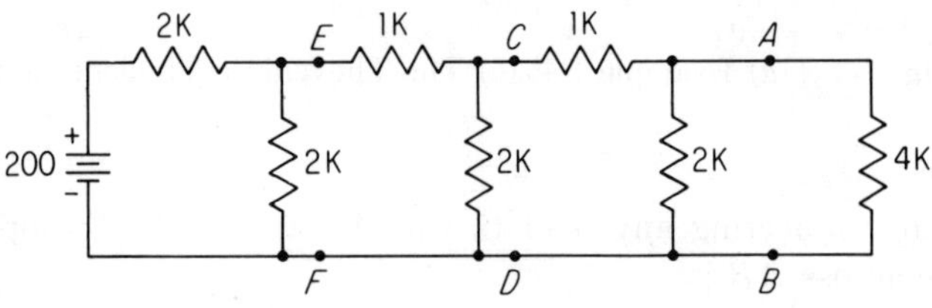

Fig. 1-9 Example 1-6.

Solution

We can use Thévenin's theorem several times during the course of a problem. Referring to the given circuit, notice that the Thévenin equivalent of that part of the circuit to the left of the *EF* terminals is that shown in Fig. 1-10*a*.

We can connect this to the remainder of the original circuit to obtain Fig. 1-10*b*.

In the new circuit of Fig. 1-10*b* we can apply Thévenin's theorem to the circuit to the left of the *CD* terminals, obtaining Fig. 1-10*c*.

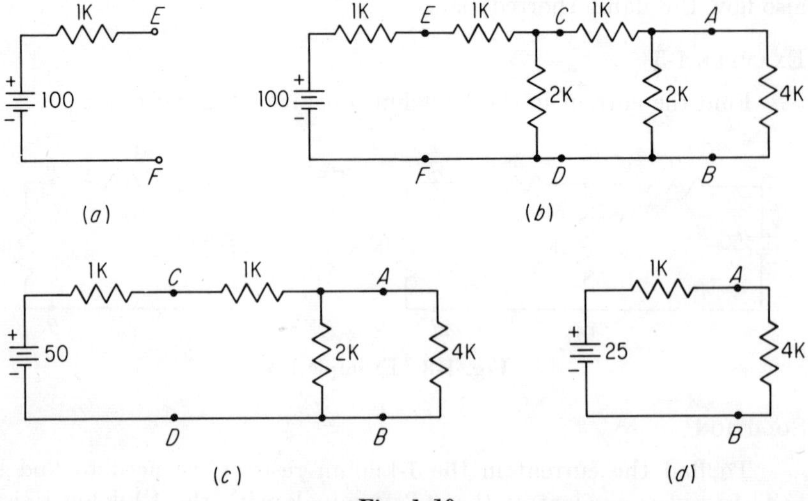

Fig. 1-10

Finally, we can apply Thévenin's theorem to the AB terminals to arrive at the single-loop circuit shown in Fig. 1-10d.

The current in the 4-kilohm resistor is 5 ma, the same result that we would find by applying methods derived from Kirchhoff's law to the original given circuit of Fig. 1-9.

Note that this type of problem can be solved by the use of Thévenin's theorem in a matter of minutes, whereas using Kirchhoff's law involves four simultaneous equations, whose solution would take considerable time.

The successive application of Thévenin's theorem several times within a given circuit provides us with an unusually powerful tool for reducing a multiloop circuit into a single-loop circuit. The advantages of a single loop are obvious.

Example 1-7

Find the input voltage across the grid resistor in Fig. 1-11a.

Solution

Imagine that we have removed the 200-kilohm resistor and the grid connection. All that remains is the voltage divider shown in Fig. 1-11b.

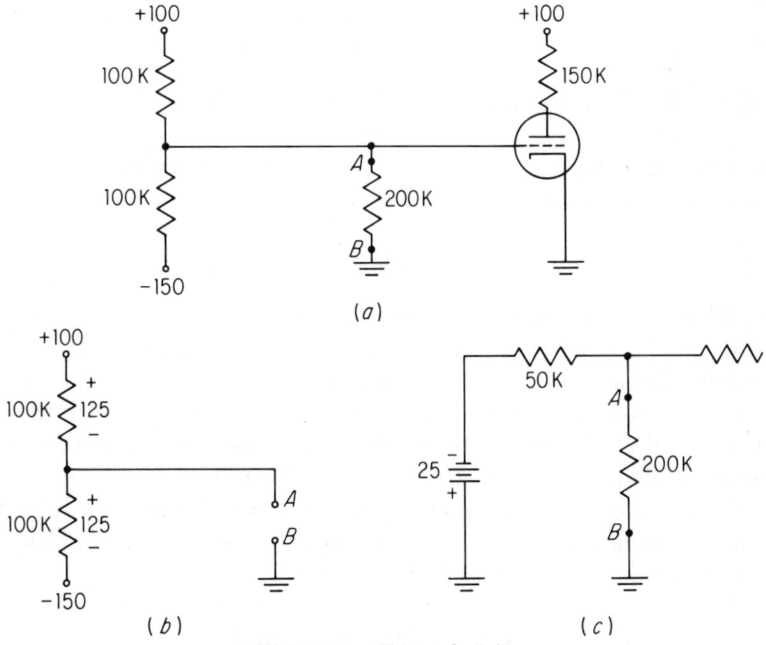

Fig. 1-11 Example 1-7.

The voltage across each resistor is the same, so that each resistor drops one-half of the total voltage (250 volts) across the divider.

Hence, V_{oc} is -25 volts $(-150 + 125)$.

Furthermore, the resistance from A to B with the power supplies shorted to ground is 50 kilohms (100 kilohms in parallel with 100 kilohms).

The Thévenin equivalent for the voltage divider with the grid resistor reconnected is shown in Fig. 1-11c. From this figure it is clear that the voltage across the grid resistor is

$$\frac{200(10^3)}{250(10^3)}(-25) = -20 \text{ volts}$$

1-4 The Unit Exponential Function

A function which often arises in electronics is the exponential function. Specifically, we are referring to an equation of the form

$$y = \epsilon^{-x} \tag{1-1}$$

We will call this equation the unit exponential function.

Recall the meaning of a negative exponent. The foregoing equation may be rewritten as

$$y = \frac{1}{\epsilon^x}$$

In either form the value of y is the same. The first expression is more commonly used since it is easier to write.

The Greek letter ϵ is the base of natural logarithms. In calculus it is shown that ϵ is an irrational number which equals

$$\epsilon = 2.71828 \ldots$$

For slide-rule purposes, we will use $\epsilon \cong 2.72$.

The unit exponential function is essential for analyzing any kind of *transient behavior*, which refers to those changes in voltage or current that occur in an electric circuit whenever a switch is thrown. Since the next section will deal with transients in RC circuits, as a preparation, we must become familiar with the unit exponential function.

It should be clear from Eq. (1-1) that y is a function of x, meaning that for each value of x chosen, one corresponding value of y can be calculated. As an example, if x equals 1, then

$$y = \epsilon^{-1} = 2.72^{-1} = \frac{1}{2.72} = 0.368$$

As another example, if x equals 2, then

$$y = \epsilon^{-2} = \frac{1}{2.72^2} = 0.135$$

If we continue in this fashion, computing the different y values corresponding to the x values, eventually there will be enough pairs of x and y to tabulate, as shown in Table 1-2. This partial table of values will be useful to us in our later discussion of peak detectors, clamping circuits, oscilloscope circuits, and differentiating circuits.

Table 1-2 The Unit Exponential Function

x	ϵ^{-x}
0	1
1	0.368
2	0.135
3	0.0498
4	0.0183
5	0.00674
6	0.00248
7	0.00091
8	0.00034
9	0.00012
10	0.00005

The data of Table 1-2 may be presented pictorially by means of an xy graph, as shown in Fig. 1-12. This is a graph of the unit exponential function (we use the words "unit exponential" simply because the graph starts at unity). We could include negative values of x, but this is unnecessary for our later work.

The shape of this graph is classical in electric-circuit theory. Note how the graph starts at unity and decreases rapidly, getting closer and closer to the x axis. Theoretically, the graph never touches the x axis. For practical purposes, however, we may arbitrarily say that it is approximately zero for x greater than 5.

Example 1-8

Sketch the graph of $v = \epsilon^{-t}$.

Solution

The given equation is still of the form $y = \epsilon^{-x}$. Therefore, the relation between v and t is the same as the relation between y and x. Table 1-2 still applies, as does Fig. 1-12, except that the letter y becomes v, and the letter x becomes t. Hence, the sketch is that of Fig. 1-12.

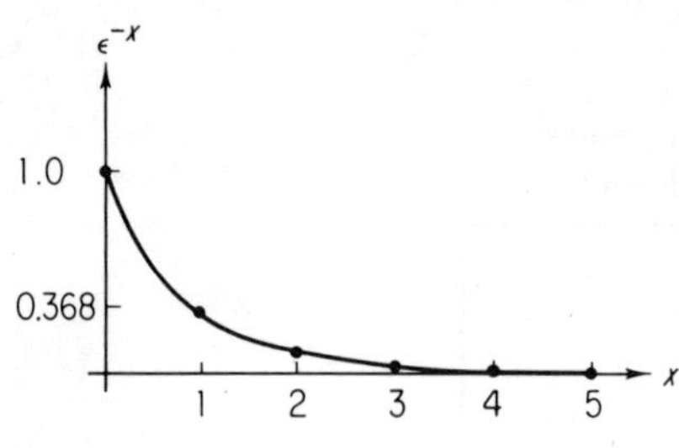

Fig. 1-12 The unit exponential function.

Example 1-9

Sketch $v = 5\epsilon^{-t}$.

Solution

For any value of t, v is simply five times the value of the unit exponential function. In other words, the graph of Fig. 1-12 has every y value multiplied by five.

The correct sketch for $v = 5\epsilon^{-t}$ is shown in Fig. 1-13*a*.

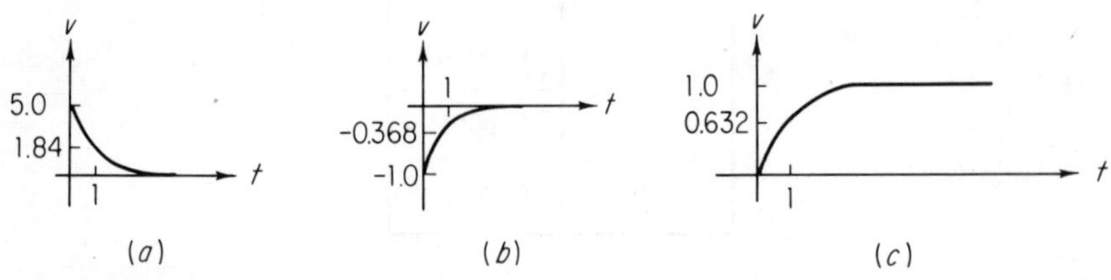

Fig. 1-13 (*a*) Example 1-9. (*b*) Example 1-10. (*c*) Example 1-11.

Example 1-10

Sketch $v = -\epsilon^{-t}$.

Solution

For any value of t that we pick, the value of v is simply minus the value of the unit exponential function. In other words, our graph starts at minus unity, so that we can sketch as shown in Fig. 1-13*b*.

EXAMPLE 1-11

Sketch $v = 1 - \epsilon^{-t}$.

SOLUTION

If we pick a value for t, then v is simply 1 minus the value of the unit exponential. For example,

When $t = 0$ $\quad v = 1 - \epsilon^{0} = 0$
When $t = 1$ $\quad v = 1 - \epsilon^{-1} = 1 - 0.368 = 0.632$
When $t = 2$ $\quad v = 1 - \epsilon^{-2} = 1 - 0.135 = 0.865$
When $t = \infty$ $\quad v = 1 - \epsilon^{-\infty} = 1 - 0 = 1$

Thus, the graph starts at zero and approaches unity. The sketch is shown in Fig. 1-13*c*.

1-5 The Transient Response of *RC* Circuits

A powerful equation for analyzing the transients of an *RC* circuit driven by d-c sources is given by

$$v = v_f + (v_i - v_f)\epsilon^{-t/RC} \tag{1-2}$$

where v is the instantaneous voltage across any part of the *RC* circuit
v_i is the initial voltage across that part
v_f is the final voltage across that part
t is the time elapsed after a switch is opened or closed
RC is the time constant of a single-loop equivalent circuit

To bring out the meaning of each quantity in Eq. (1-2), let us consider the circuit of Fig. 1-14. This is an *RC* circuit driven by an ideal battery. The part of the circuit we have chosen for analysis is the capacitor. In Eq. (1-2), v is the voltage across the capacitor at any instant in time after the switch is closed.

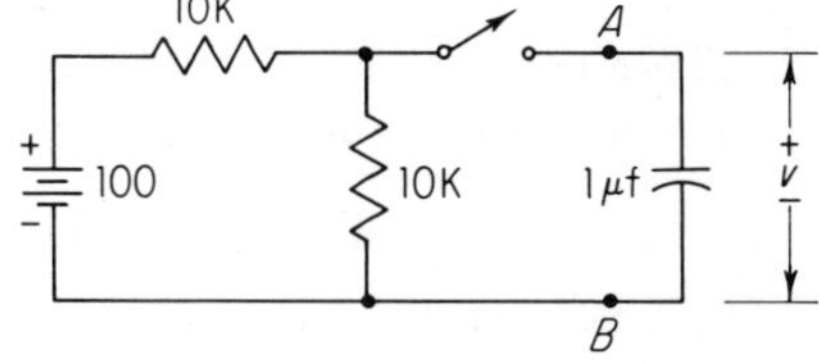

Fig. 1-14 An *RC* transient problem.

The voltage v_i is the initial voltage of the capacitor. For instance, if the capacitor is initially charged to 20 volts just before the switch closes, then just after the switch closes, the capacitor voltage is still 20 volts. We know this to be true simply because a capacitor cannot change its voltage instantaneously. It takes time in any real circuit to remove or add charge.

The voltage v_f is the value of v after the switch has been closed for a long time. In this case, our knowledge of capacitors indicates that charge flows into a capacitor until it becomes fully charged, at which time no more current flows. The capacitor then resembles an open circuit. In any event, v_f is the final voltage.

The value of t in Eq. (1-2) is simply the time that has elapsed after the switch closes.

The value of RC to use in Eq. (1-2) is the time constant of an RC equivalent single-loop circuit. How do we obtain this equivalent single-loop circuit from the given circuit of Fig. 1-14? Very simply. We apply Thévenin's theorem to the AB terminals. The capacitor is considered the load, and we find the Thévenin equivalent for the circuit to the left of the AB terminals. The resulting single-loop circuit is shown in Fig. 1-15a.

For purposes of numerical illustration, let us assume that initially the capacitor is uncharged. Therefore, at the instant that the switch is closed, $v_i = 0$.

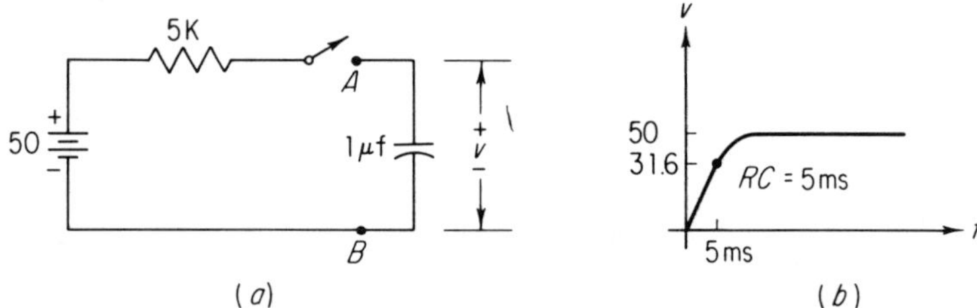

Fig. 1-15 (a) Reduction to a single loop. (b) The transient response.

After the switch has been closed for a long time, our reasoning tells us that the capacitor becomes fully charged to 50 volts, so that $v_f = 50$.

The RC time constant of the single loop is

$$RC = 5(10^3)(10^{-6}) = 5(10^{-3}) = 5 \text{ msec}$$

These three, v_i, v_f, and RC, are all we need to find.

The next step is merely to substitute into Eq. (1-2):

$$v = 50 + (0 - 50)\epsilon^{-t/5 \text{ msec}} = 50(1 - \epsilon^{-t/5 \text{ msec}}) \qquad (1\text{-}3)$$

Equation (1-3) completely describes the voltage across the capacitor after the switch is closed. For any value of t that we pick, the value of v can be calculated. For instance,

When $t = 0$

$$v = 50(1 - \epsilon^0) = 0$$

When $t = 5$ msec

$$v = 50(1 - \epsilon^{-1}) = 50(0.632) = 31.6 \text{ volts}$$

When $t = 25$ msec

$$v = 50(1 - \epsilon^{-5}) = 50(0.993) = 49.6 \text{ volts}$$

How can we graph Eq. (1-3) easily and quickly?

The graph of v vs. t will simply be an exponential graph starting at the initial voltage $v_i = 0$ and approaching the final voltage $v_f = 50$ (see Fig. 1-15*b*).

In general, for any *RC* circuit driven by d-c voltage sources the following procedure may be used to find the transient response.

1. Determine the initial voltage v_i across the component of interest. It is helpful to remember that capacitor voltages cannot change instantaneously. Therefore, uncharged capacitors resemble short circuits at the instant that a switch is thrown. Charged capacitors resemble batteries at the instant that a switch is thrown.
2. Determine the final voltage v_f across the component of interest. It is helpful to remember that capacitors become open circuits after enough time has elapsed, because eventually no more current can flow into or out of a capacitor.
3. Compute the value of the *RC* time constant for the circuit. If there is more than one loop in the circuit, it is necessary to reduce the given circuit to a single loop. Thévenin's theorem and the various rules for combining resistors and capacitors may be used to obtain a single loop. The *RC* time constant is the product of the total series resistance and the total series capacitance.
4. Substitute into Eq. (1-2) and simplify. If only a sketch of the transient response is desired, skip this step, and go directly to step 5.
5. Sketch the transient response by drawing an exponential that starts at the initial voltage v_i and approaches the final voltage v_f.

The following examples illustrate some of the details involved in applying these steps.

Example 1-12

Sketch the voltage v after the switch is closed in the circuit of Fig. 1-16*a*. The capacitor is initially uncharged.

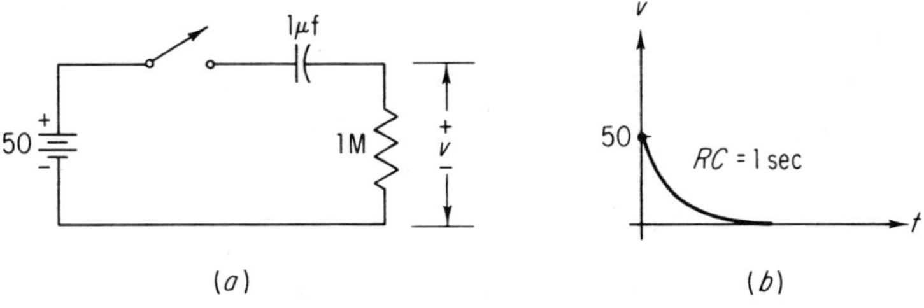

Fig. 1-16 Example 1-12.

SOLUTION

Step 1: At the first instant the switch is thrown, the capacitor resembles a short circuit because it has no initial charge. Therefore, all the battery voltage appears across the 1-megohm resistor, and $v_i = 50$.

Step 2: After enough time has elapsed, the capacitor becomes fully charged and acts like an open circuit. Therefore, no more current is flowing in the 1-megohm resistor, and $v_f = 0$.

Step 3: The circuit is already in single-loop form, so that the RC value is simply $10^{-6}(10^6)$, or 1 sec.

Step 4: Since we are after a sketch, we can skip this step.

Step 5: We now draw the transient response starting at an initial voltage of 50 volts and approaching 0 volts. The exponential curve is shown in Fig. 1-16*b*.

EXAMPLE 1-13

Sketch v in the circuit of Fig. 1-17*a* after the switch is closed. The capacitor is initially charged to 50 volts with the polarity shown.

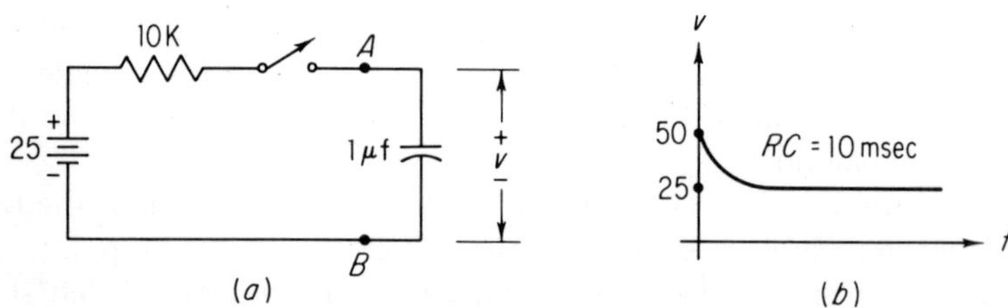

Fig. 1-17 Example 1-13.

SOLUTION

Step 1: At the instant that the switch is thrown the capacitor voltage is still 50 volts. Hence, $v_i = 50$ volts.

Step 2: Given enough time, the capacitor acts like an open circuit, and no more current flows. With no current flowing in the 10-kilohm resistor the battery voltage must appear across the capacitor. Hence, $v_f = 25$ volts.

Step 3: The RC time constant is $10^4(10^{-6})$, or 10 msec. The sketch of the transient response is shown in Fig. 1-17*b*.

EXAMPLE 1-14

In the circuit of Fig. 1-18*a* find the equation of v and sketch the transient. The capacitor is initially uncharged.

SOLUTION

We can simplify this problem by observing that the Thévenin equivalent to the left of the switch is a 100-volt battery in series with a 25-kilohm resistor. Thus, the given circuit can be replaced by the single-loop equivalent shown in Fig. 1-18*b*.

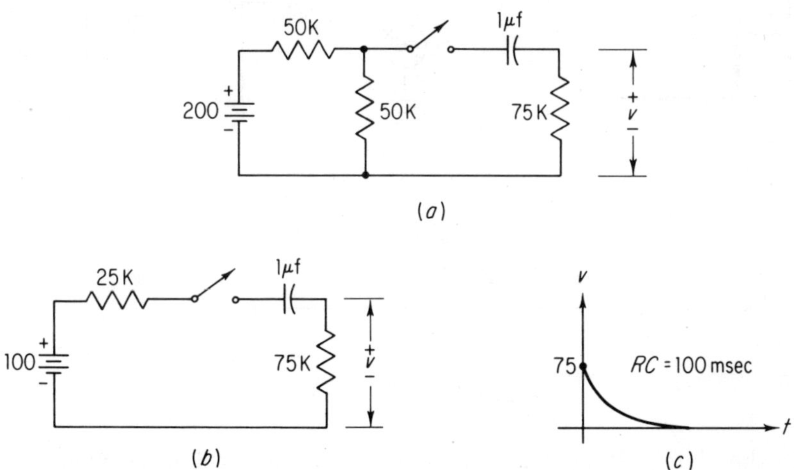

Fig. 1-18 (*a*). Example 1-14. (*b*) Reduction to a single loop. (*c*) The transient response.

At the instant of switch closure, the capacitor is initially uncharged and therefore resembles a short. The current in the circuit must be 1 ma at this first instant, and it follows that the voltage across the 75-kilohm resistor is 75 volts. Hence, $v_i = 75$.

The final voltage v_f must equal zero, because given enough time, the capacitor becomes fully charged, implying that no more current is in the circuit. Hence, $v_f = 0$.

The *RC* time constant is the product of the effective resistance in the circuit and the effective capacitance. In this case, it is the product of 100-kilohms and 1 μf. Hence, $RC = 0.1$ sec.

Substituting into Eq. (1-2), we obtain

$$v = 0 + (75 - 0)\epsilon^{-t/0.1} = 75\epsilon^{-t/0.1}$$

The sketch for the transient is shown in Fig. 1-18*c*. It starts at v_i and approaches v_f.

EXAMPLE 1-15

At point *A* in time a large negative-going signal is applied to the grid of the circuit in Fig. 1-19*a*. This signal is large enough to cut off the tube current. Before point *A* in time, the capacitor is fully charged

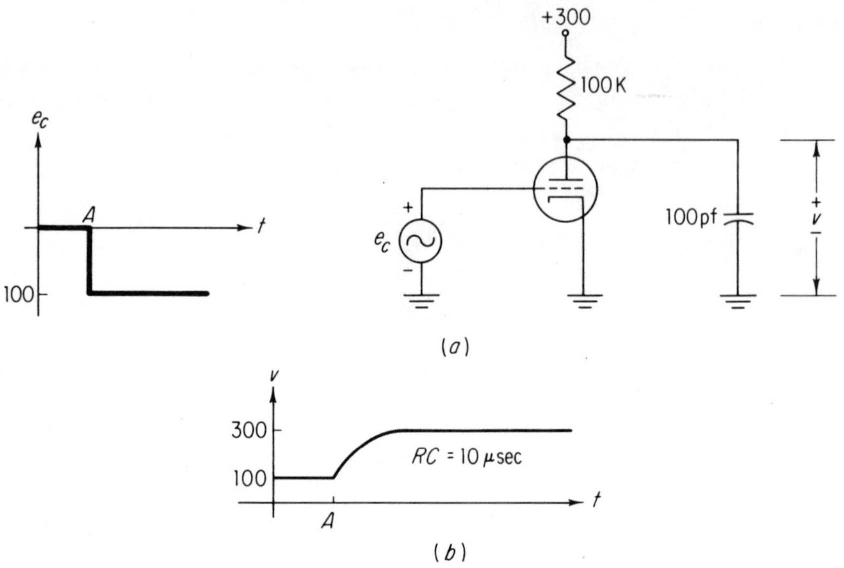

Fig. 1-19 Example 1-15.

to the plate voltage, and a d-c current of 2 ma is flowing. Sketch the voltage v.

SOLUTION

The initial voltage $v_i = 100$ volts, because before point A in time, there is a 200-volt drop across the plate resistor (2 ma times 100 kilohms). This means that the voltage appearing across the tube and capacitor is 100 volts, so that $v_i = 100$ volts.

After point A in time the tube current is cut off. With no plate current we may visualize the tube as completely removed from the circuit. The capacitor must therefore charge to the full power-supply voltage of 300 volts. Thus, $v_f = 300$ volts.

The RC time constant involved in the capacitor charging is the product of the plate resistor (100 kilohms) and the capacitor value (100 pf). Hence, $RC = 10\ \mu$sec.

We can now sketch the transient response showing an exponential curve starting at v_i and approaching v_f, as illustrated by Fig. 1-19*b*.

1-6 Decibel Conversions

The use of decibels is widespread throughout the electronics industry. Many electronic instruments are calibrated in decibels, and it is common for data sheets describing various instruments and devices to give the specifications in terms of decibels. For these reasons a study of their use is essential.

Let us begin by considering the situation depicted by Fig. 1-20. A voltage generator is driving an amplifier. The input resistance of the amplifier

Fig. 1-20 Developing the decibel concept.

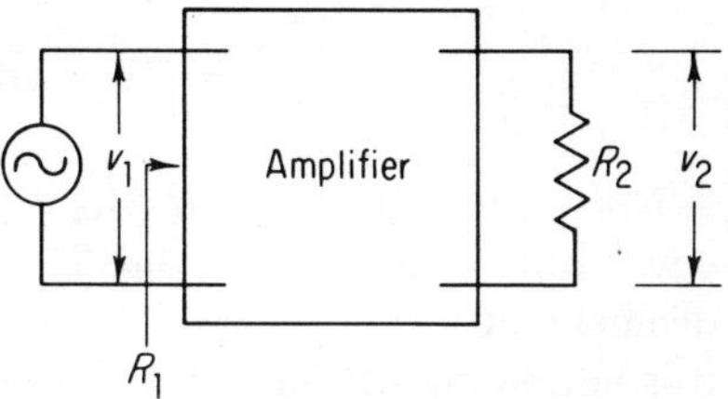

is R_1. The amplifier delivers an output voltage v_2 to a load resistor whose value is R_2. In describing the gain of the amplifier we may speak of either the power gain or the voltage gain. The power gain G is defined as the power delivered to R_2 divided by the power delivered to the amplifier resistance R_1. That is,

$$G = \frac{p_2}{p_1} = \frac{v_2^2/R_2}{v_1^2/R_1} = \left(\frac{v_2}{v_1}\right)^2 \frac{R_1}{R_2} \tag{1-4}$$

The voltage gain A is defined simply as the output voltage v_2 divided by the input voltage v_1. That is,

$$A = \frac{v_2}{v_1} \tag{1-5}$$

It will be recalled from basic electronics courses that the power gain in decibels is defined as

$$G_{db} = 10 \log G \tag{1-6}$$

where G is the power gain and, G_{db} is the decibel equivalent of G. Note that the base 10 is used in Eq. (1-6).

If we like, we can obtain an alternate formula for G_{db} by substituting Eq. (1-4) into Eq. (1-6) to obtain

$$G_{db} = 10 \log G = 10 \log \left(\frac{v_2}{v_1}\right)^2 \frac{R_1}{R_2}$$

The properties of logarithms allow us to rewrite this equation as

$$G_{db} = 20 \log \frac{v_2}{v_1} + 10 \log \frac{R_1}{R_2} \tag{1-7}$$

Historically, decibels were defined strictly for use with power ratios. However, modern usage of decibels has developed to the point where it is now common to speak of either the power gain in decibels or the voltage gain in decibels. The voltage gain in decibels is the first term of Eq.

(1-7), that is,

$$A_{db} = 20 \log A \tag{1-8}$$

where A is the voltage gain, v_2/v_1, and A_{db} is the decibel equivalent of A.

Thus, we can rewrite Eq. (1-7) simply as

$$G_{db} = A_{db} + 10 \log \frac{R_1}{R_2} \tag{1-9}$$

Note carefully that if R_1/R_2 is unity, then $G_{db} = A_{db}$. If R_1/R_2 does not equal unity, then $G_{db} \neq A_{db}$. It is very important, therefore, when using decibel equivalents to specify voltage gain or power gain. In other words, it is not enough to say that the gain is so many decibels. We must specify that the voltage gain is so many decibels or that the power gain is so many decibels, whichever the case may be.

Let us summarize the use of decibels up to this point. In the modern usage of decibels we may speak of either the decibel equivalent of a power ratio or the decibel equivalent of a voltage ratio. The decibel equivalent of a power ratio is given by

$$G_{db} = 10 \log G \tag{1-10}$$

where G is the ratio of two powers, p_2/p_1. The decibel equivalent of a voltage ratio is given by

$$A_{db} = 20 \log A \tag{1-11}$$

where A is the ratio of two voltages, v_2/v_1. In speaking of the gain of an amplifier, $G_{db} = A_{db}$ only if the load resistance R_2 equals the input resistance R_1. If the two resistances are not equal, it is essential to specify whether the gain in decibels is for the voltage gain or for the power gain.

In the remainder of this section we develop some shortcuts that allow rapid conversion between ordinary numbers and decibel equivalents. Consider Eq. (1-11). A_{db} is a function of A, meaning that for each value of A selected, only one value of A_{db} can be calculated. For instance,

When $A = 1$ $\quad A_{db} = 20 \log 1 = 0$ db
When $A = 2$ $\quad A_{db} = 20 \log 2 = 20(0.3) = 6$ db
When $A = 4$ $\quad A_{db} = 20 \log 4 = 20(0.6) = 12$ db
When $A = 10$ $\quad A_{db} = 20 \log 10 = 20(1) = 20$ db

We can continue in this fashion until there are enough pairs of A and A_{db} to tabulate as shown in Table 1-3.

To bring out certain properties of decibels more clearly, let us graph the data of Table 1-3, using semilogarithmic paper to compress the A values (see Fig. 1-21).

What are the important properties of decibels implied in the graphs of Fig. 1-21?

Table 1-3 Voltage Gain and Its Decibel Equivalent

A	A_{db}
$1/100$	-40
$1/10$	-20
$1/8$	-18
$1/4$	-12
$1/2$	-6
1	0
2	6
4	12
8	18
10	20
100	40
1000	60

First, note in Fig. 1-21*a* that each time A is increased by a factor of two

$$A = 1, 2, 4, 8, \ldots$$

A_{db} increases by 6 db

$$A_{db} = 0, 6, 12, 18, \ldots$$

Conversely, each time that A decreases by a factor of two

$$A = 1, 1/2, 1/4, 1/8, \ldots$$

A_{db} decreases by 6 db

$$A_{db} = 0, -6, -12, -18, \ldots$$

Second, note in Fig. 1-21*b* that each time A is increased by a factor of ten

$$A = 1, 10, 100, 1000, \ldots$$

A_{db} increases by 20 db

$$A_{db} = 0, 20, 40, 60, \ldots$$

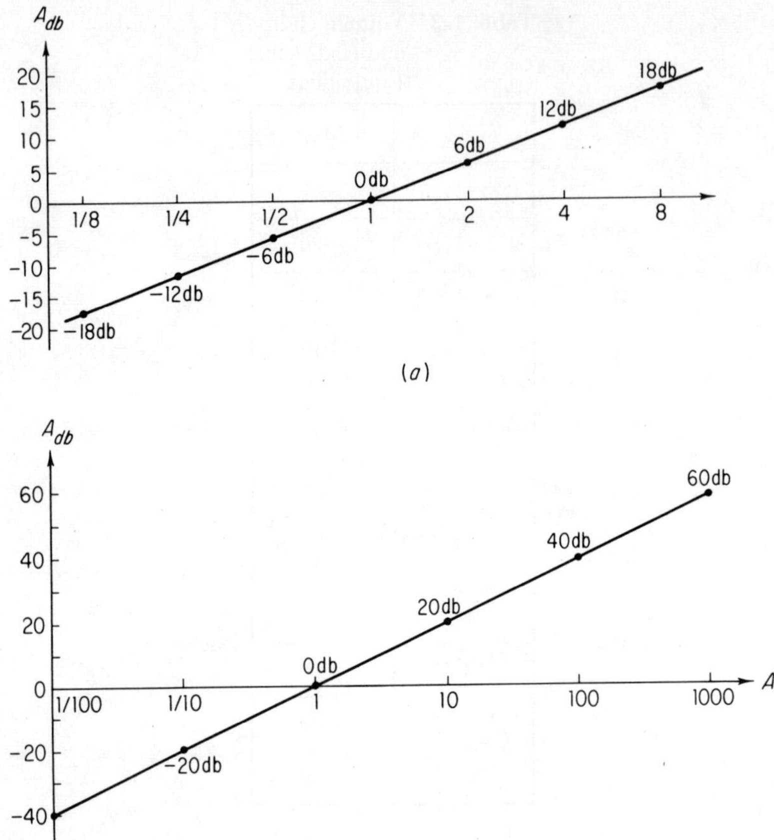

Fig. 1-21 Graphs of A_{db} vs. A.

Conversely, each time A is decreased by a factor of ten

$$A = 1, \tfrac{1}{10}, \tfrac{1}{100}, \tfrac{1}{1000}, \ldots$$

A_{db} decreases by 20 db

$$A_{db} = 0, -20, -40, -60, \ldots$$

These properties of decibels make the conversion from ordinary numbers into decibels a simple matter. We need only express the ordinary number in factors of two and ten and convert according to the decibel properties described. As an example, let us convert $A = 4000$ into its decibel equivalent.

$$A = 4000 = 2 \cdot 2 \cdot 10 \cdot 10 \cdot 10$$
$$A_{db} = 6 + 6 + 20 + 20 + 20 = 72 \text{ db}$$

We have factored A into twos and tens and added 6 or 20 db for each factor of two or ten to obtain the total of 72 db.

As another example, consider $A = 0.004$. We write this as a fraction and then factor into twos and tens

$$A = 0.004 = \frac{4}{1000} = \frac{2 \cdot 2}{10 \cdot 10 \cdot 10}$$
$$A_{db} = 6 + 6 - 20 - 20 - 20 = -48 \text{ db}$$

In this case we add 6 db for the numerator factors and subtract 20 db for each denominator factor.

When the value of A is not exactly factorable into twos and tens, we can obtain an approximate answer by interpolation. For instance, if $A = 60$, we observe that this is a number between $A = 40$ and $A = 80$. Hence,

Since $A = 40 = 2 \cdot 2 \cdot 10$ $\quad A_{db} = 32$ db
Since $A = 80 = 2 \cdot 2 \cdot 2 \cdot 10$ $\quad A_{db} = 38$ db

$A = 60$ is halfway between 40 and 80, so that $A_{db} \cong 35$ db. We have interpolated to find the approximate decibel equivalent of $A = 60$. Using the exact formula $A_{db} = 20 \log 60$, yields a value of $A_{db} = 35.56$ db. The error in our approximate answer is only about 0.5 db. Usually, errors of less than 1 db are acceptable in practice. Only in those situations where the greatest accuracy is required must we use the exact formula,

$$A_{db} = 20 \log A$$

Let us summarize our procedure for finding decibel equivalents.

1. For any ratio A of voltages or currents, express the number in factors of two and ten. If the number is not exactly factorable into twos and tens, bracket it between the next lower and higher numbers that are factorable into twos and tens.
2. Add 6 db for every factor of two in the numerator and 20 db for every factor of ten. Subtract 6 db for every factor of two in the denominator and 20 db for every factor of ten.
3. Interpolate, if necessary, to obtain the decibel equivalent.
4. When dealing with a power ratio G, proceed as in steps 1 to 3 but divide the result by 2 to obtain G_{db}.

EXAMPLE 1-16

Find the decibel equivalent of $A = 2000$.

SOLUTION

$$A = 2000 = 2 \cdot 10 \cdot 10 \cdot 10$$
$$A_{db} = 6 + 20 + 20 + 20 = 66 \text{ db}$$

Example 1-17

Find the decibel equivalent of $A = 3000$.

Solution

This number is not factorable into twos and tens, but it lies between 2000 and 4000, numbers which are so factorable.

$$A = 2000 = 2 \cdot 10 \cdot 10 \cdot 10$$
$$A_{db} = 6 + 20 + 20 + 20 = 66 \text{ db}$$

$A = 4000$ implies that we add 6 db to obtain $A_{db} = 72$ db.

For $A = 3000$, we interpolate to obtain $A_{db} = 69$ db.

(The exact answer is 69.5 db. Whenever we interpolate, the maximum error possible is about 0.5 db.)

Example 1-18

Find the decibel equivalent of $p_2/p_1 = 2000$.

Solution

This is a ratio of two powers. The decibel equivalent of a power ratio is one-half the decibel equivalent of a voltage ratio of the same numerical value. We need only proceed in our usual manner and divide the answer by 2.

$$2000 = 2 \cdot 10 \cdot 10 \cdot 10$$
$$6 + 20 + 20 + 20 = 66 \text{ db}$$

Hence,

$$G_{db} = 33 \text{ db}$$

Example 1-19

An amplifier has an input voltage of 1 mv and an output voltage of 1.6 volts. Express the voltage gain of the amplifier in decibels.

Solution

The voltage gain of the amplifier is the output voltage divided by the input voltage.

$$A = \frac{1.6}{10^{-3}} = 1600 = 2 \cdot 2 \cdot 2 \cdot 2 \cdot 10 \cdot 10$$
$$A_{db} = 6 + 6 + 6 + 6 + 20 + 20 = 64 \text{ db}$$

Example 1-20

Find the decibel equivalent of $A = \frac{1}{200}$.

Solution

$$A = \frac{1}{200} = \frac{1}{2 \cdot 10 \cdot 10}$$
$$A_{db} = -6 - 20 - 20 = -46 \text{ db}$$

Example 1-21

Find the decibel equivalent of $A = 0.002$.

Solution

$$A = 0.002 = \frac{2}{10 \cdot 10 \cdot 10}$$

$$A_{db} = 6 - 20 - 20 - 20 = -54 \text{ db}$$

Example 1-22

Voltages are often expressed in decibel equivalents by comparing their value to a reference voltage. In Fig. 1-22*a*, suppose that we use a reference voltage of 0.5 volt. Form the ratio of each given voltage to 0.5 volt and find the decibel equivalent of these ratios.

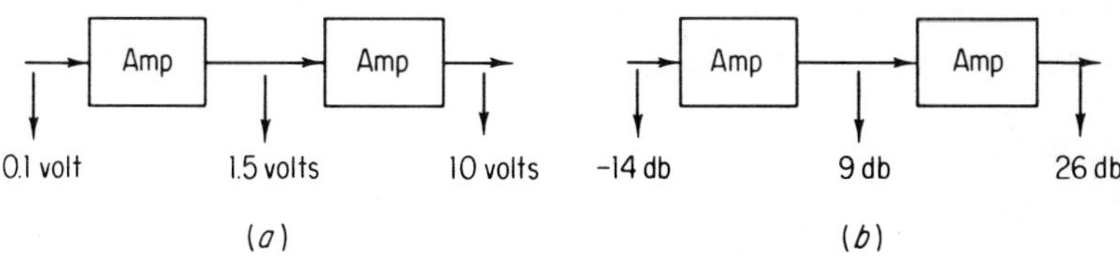

Fig. 1-22 Example 1-22.

Solution

For 0.1 volt, we have

$$\frac{0.1}{0.5} = \frac{2}{10}$$

which has a decibel equivalent of -14 db. Hence, we would say that the first voltage, 0.1 volt, is -14 db with respect to 0.5 volt.

In a similar way, the ratio of the second voltage to the reference voltage is

$$\frac{1.5}{0.5} = 3$$

which has a decibel equivalent of about 9 db.

Finally, the ratio of 10 volts to 0.5 volt is

$$\frac{10}{0.5} = 20$$

which has a decibel equivalent of 26 db.

Hence, our system can be labeled with the decibel equivalents as shown in Fig. 1-22*b*. It is important to realize that these decibel values have the correct meaning only for a reference voltage of 0.5 volt. Had we chosen a different reference voltage, the decibel equivalents would all be different from those shown.

1-7 Decibel Gain of a System

One important reason for the use of decibels is that for a system consisting of many stages, the overall gain in decibels is the sum of the stage gains expressed in decibels. To prove this, consider Fig. 1-23.

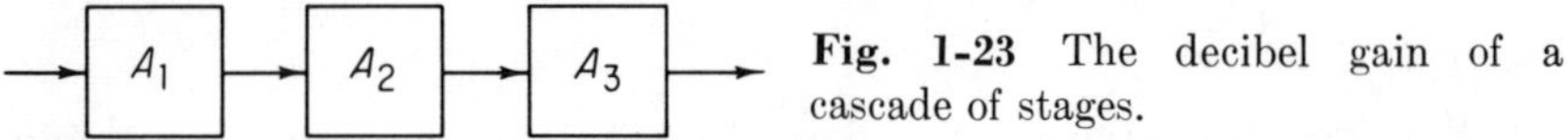

Fig. 1-23 The decibel gain of a cascade of stages.

A_1, A_2, and A_3 are the voltage gains of each stage expressed in ordinary numbers, that is, as ratios. For instance, the first stage may have a voltage gain of 100, so that A_1 is 100, meaning that the output voltage divided by the input voltage is 100.

To find the ordinary voltage gain of the entire system we already know that the gains are multiplied

$$A = A_1 A_2 A_3$$

where A is the overall gain.

Let us find the decibel equivalent of the overall gain.

$$A_{db} = 20 \log A = 20 \log A_1 A_2 A_3$$

Recall that the logarithm of a product of numbers is equal to the sum of the logarithms of each number.

$$\begin{aligned} A_{db} &= 20(\log A_1 + \log A_2 + \log A_3) \\ &= 20 \log A_1 + 20 \log A_2 + 20 \log A_3 \end{aligned}$$

Each term on the right-hand side of the last equation is merely the decibel gain of each stage. Hence,

$$A_{db} = A_{1(db)} + A_{2(db)} + A_{3(db)} \tag{1-12}$$

Equation (1-12) tells us that the overall decibel gain is the sum of the decibel gains of the individual stages. This property is another reason for the popularity of decibels. If we work with decibel gains, we add the stage gains to find the overall gain. This is considerably easier than working with ordinary gains, where it is necessary to multiply to find the overall gain.

In practice, we will find that voltmeters often have a decibel scale, so that the gain of a stage can be measured in decibels. For instance, on some voltmeters a reference voltage of 0.775 volt is used. A decibel scale is provided on the meter face, so that all voltages can be read in decibels with respect to 0.775 volt. We might find, for example, that the input to a stage reads -10 db and the output reads $+20$ db. The gain of the stage is the algebraic difference between these two values, or 30 db. In this way, the decibel gains of different stages are easily found. Once they are known, they can be added to find the overall gain of a system in decibels.

EXAMPLE 1-23

Find the overall gain for the system of Fig. 1-24.

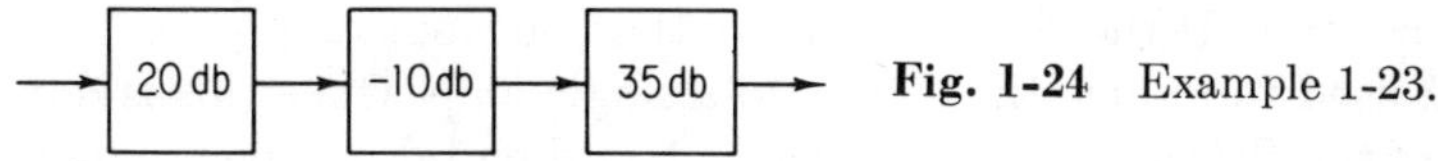

Fig. 1-24 Example 1-23.

SOLUTION

$$A_{db} = 20 - 10 + 35 = 45 \text{ db}$$

EXAMPLE 1-24

A data sheet for an amplifier specifies that the voltage gain is 40 db. If we cascade three amplifiers of this type, what is the overall gain expressed as an ordinary number?

SOLUTION

$$A_{db} = 40 + 40 + 40 = 120 \text{ db}$$

For every 20 db we know that there is a factor of ten in A. Hence,

$$A_{db} = 20 + 20 + 20 + 20 + 20 + 20$$
$$A = 10 \cdot 10 \cdot 10 \cdot 10 \cdot 10 \cdot 10 = 10^6$$

EXAMPLE 1-25

A voltmeter is calibrated in decibels with a reference voltage of 0.775 volt. What does the voltmeter read in decibels for a voltage of 3.1 volts?

SOLUTION

$$\frac{v}{v_{\text{ref}}} = \frac{3.1}{0.775} = 4$$

The voltmeter will read 12 db, meaning that given voltage is four times greater than the reference of 0.775 volt.

SUMMARY

Ideal voltage and current sources do not exist in nature, but they do exist in our minds as the ultimate in perfect sources. Their great use is that real devices can be approximated by ideal sources in order to obtain answers more easily.

Linear circuit elements refer to resistors, inductors, and capacitors that do not change in value for different voltage levels.

Thévenin's theorem is one of the most powerful analytical tools ever discovered. The fundamental idea is that the current flowing in any resistance of a complex circuit can be found by using an equivalent circuit consisting of a single battery and a single resistance to represent the circuit driving the load resistance.

The unit exponential function is basic to all study of transients.

Transients in *RC* circuits can be handled by means of the general transient equation. If the circuit has more than one loop, Thévenin's theorem can be used to reduce the circuit to a single loop. Once this is done, the value of the *RC* time constant is easily found by taking the product of the total series resistance and the total capacitance.

Decibels are widely used. In finding the decibel equivalent of voltage gain, the gain is expressed in factors of two and ten. Factors of two correspond to 6 db, and factors of ten correspond to 20 db.

GLOSSARY

decibel equivalent An alternate way of specifying a power ratio or a voltage ratio based upon logarithms of the base 10.

hertz (*Hz*) Cycles per second.

ideal current source (*constant current source*) A source that fixes the current flowing out of its terminals at a value which is independent of the load resistance connected to its terminals.

ideal voltage source (*constant voltage source*) A source whose terminal voltage is independent of the value of load resistance connected to its terminals.

linear circuit element Generally refers to a resistance, inductance, or capacitance whose value does not depend upon the size of the applied voltage.

power gain In reference to an amplifier or other device, this is the ratio of the output power to the input power.

semilogarithmic paper Graph paper which has a linear scale along one axis and a logarithmic scale along the other axis.

transient A temporary change in circuit voltages and currents usually caused by closing a switch or some similar abrupt change in the circuit configuration.

unit exponential An exponential function whose initial value is one, and whose final value is zero.

voltage gain The ratio of the output voltage to the input voltage.

REVIEW QUESTIONS

1. What is true about the voltage at the terminals of an ideal voltage source?

2. What is a linear circuit element?
3. What is Thévenin's theorem?
4. What is the unit exponential function?
5. What is a transient?
6. In applying the general RC transient equation, how do you find the effective RC time constant for a multiloop circuit?
7. What is the definition for power gain in decibels? For voltage gain in decibels?
8. In finding the decibel equivalent for a voltage gain, how many decibels correspond to a factor of two? To a factor of ten?
9. In a cascade of stages how is the overall decibel gain found?
10. What is a hertz? What does kHz stand for? What does MHz mean?

PROBLEMS

1-1 In the circuit of Fig. 1-25*a*:

(*a*) Find the Thévenin equivalent to the left of the AB terminals.

(*b*) If $R = 0$, how much current flows through R?

(*c*) If $R = 5$ kilohms, how much current flows through R?

1-2 Find the current through the 25-kilohm load resistor of Fig. 1-25*b* by using Thévenin's theorem.

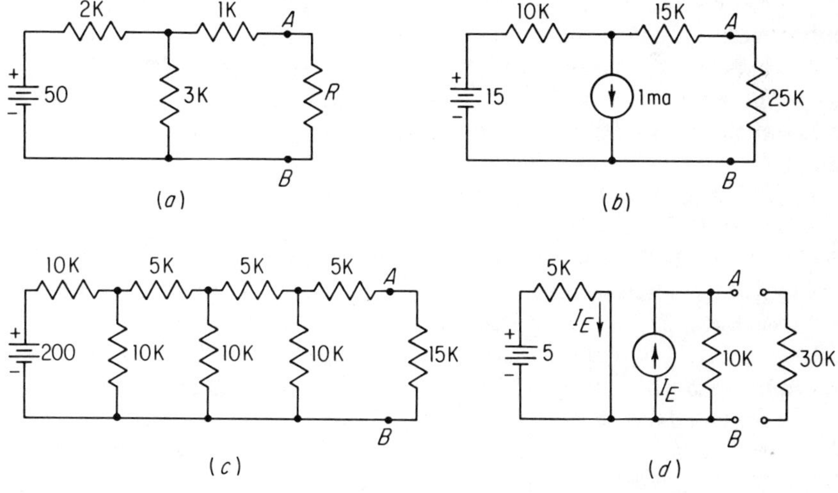

Fig. 1-25

1-3 In Fig. 1-25*c* find the current through the 15-kilohm load resistor. Use Thévenin's theorem.

1-4 Find the Thévenin equivalent at the AB terminals of the circuit shown in Fig. 1-25*d*. If the 30-kilohm resistor is connected to the AB terminals, how much current flows through it, and what is the voltage across it?

1-5 In Fig. 1-26a find the Thévenin equivalent of the circuit at the AB terminals. If the 15-kilohm load is connected to the AB terminals, what is the voltage across it?

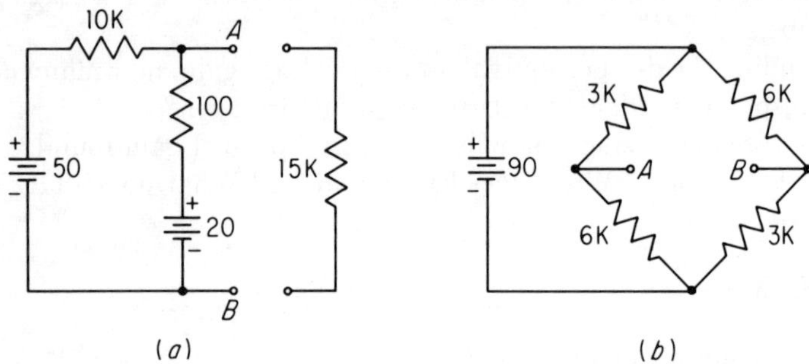

Fig. 1-26

1-6 If a 4-kilohm resistor is connected to the AB terminals of Fig. 1-26b, how much current will flow through it? Use Thévenin's theorem.

1-7 A real battery has an open-circuit voltage of 10 volts. If a 10-ohm resistor is connected to the battery, the voltage across it is found to be only 9 volts. What is the Thévenin resistance of the battery?

1-8 A d-c power supply has an open-circuit voltage of 100 volts. If a 1-kilohm resistor is connected to the power supply, the current through it is found to be only 90 ma. What is the Thévenin resistance of the power supply?

1-9 Sketch $v = 50(1 - \epsilon^{-t/1\ \text{msec}})$.

1-10 Sketch $v = 75\epsilon^{-t/75\ \text{msec}}$.

1-11 In Fig. 1-27a the capacitor is initially uncharged. Find the equation of the voltage across the capacitor after the switch is closed. Also, sketch the waveform of this voltage versus time.

1-12 In Fig. 1-27a the capacitor is initially charged to 75 volts. Find the equation of the voltage v after the switch is closed, and sketch v vs. t.

1-13 In Fig. 1-27a the capacitor is initially charged to 150 volts. Find the equation for v and sketch v vs. t.

1-14 The capacitor in Fig. 1-27b is initially uncharged. The switch is closed. What is the voltage across the capacitor after 1 msec?

1-15 If the capacitor of Fig. 1-27b is initially charged to 10 volts, what is the capacitor voltage after the switch has been closed for one time constant?

1-16 In Fig. 1-27c the capacitor is initially charged to 50 volts. The switch is closed. Find the equation of v and sketch the waveform.

1-17 Before point A in time, e_g equals 0 volts in Fig. 1-27d. The current in the 10-kilohm plate resistor is 20 ma, and the capacitor voltage is not changing. After point A in time, e_g equals -50 volts, enough to cut off the tube current. Sketch the capacitor voltage waveform after point A in time.

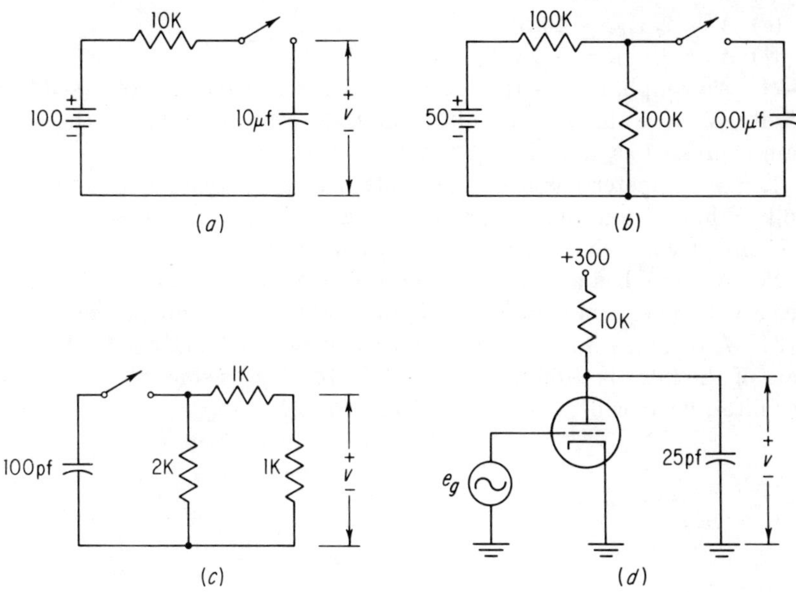

Fig. 1-27

1-18 In Fig. 1-28a the capacitor is initially uncharged. The left switch is closed. Sketch the voltage waveform across the capacitor.

The left switch is now opened, and the right switch is closed. Sketch the voltage waveform across the capacitor.

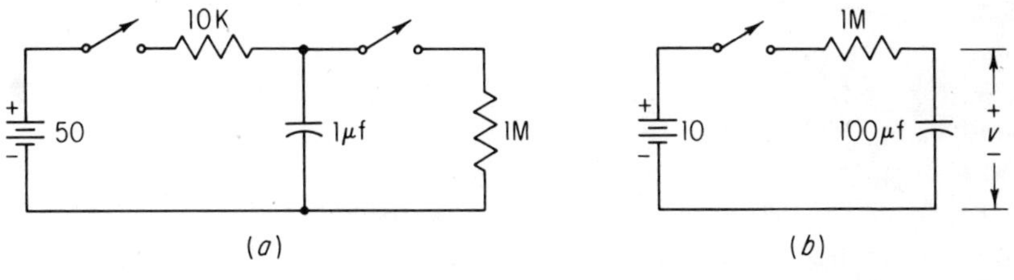

Fig. 1-28

1-19 The capacitor in Fig. 1-28b is an electrolytic capacitor with a leakage resistance of 2 megohms. Sketch the waveform of the capacitor voltage after the switch is closed. The capacitor is initially uncharged. (*Hint:* The leakage resistance is in parallel with 100 μf.)

1-20 Perform the following decibel conversions using the approximate methods of this chapter.

(*a*) $A = 400$, $A_{db} = ?$
(*b*) $A = 22{,}000$, $A_{db} = ?$
(*c*) $A = 0.005$, $A_{db} = ?$
(*d*) $A = ?$, $A_{db} = 46$ db
(*e*) $A = ?$, $A_{db} = -23$ db

1-21 An amplifier has three stages with voltage gains of 20, 32, and 15 db. What is the overall voltage gain in decibels? What is the overall gain expressed as an ordinary number?

1-22 A voltmeter has a decibel scale with a reference voltage of 0.775 volt. What would the following voltages read in decibels: 7.75 volts, 7.75 mv, 4 volts, and 0.1 volt? (Approximate.)

1-23 A mixer has a conversion gain of -12 db. If the incoming signal has a voltage of 1 mv rms, what is the voltage of the output signal?

1-24 A bandpass filter has a center frequency of 1 MHz. At 5 MHz the gain of the filter is -66 db. If a 5-MHz 1-volt rms sine wave is put into the filter, what will the output voltage equal?

2 D-C Meters

In this chapter we discuss, first, the elementary methods for measuring current, voltage, and resistance and, second, the errors that are encountered when making measurements. Our emphasis will be upon the limitations of simple d-c meters in typical measurements.

2-1 The Ideal Ammeter

We already know that a d-c ammeter is a device that indicates the amount of direct current flowing through it. The D'Arsonval ammeter is the most common type, consisting of a moving coil, a spring, and a permanent magnet. As current passes through the coil, a magnetic torque causes the coil to move. The amount of movement is determined by the size of the current. By attaching a needle to the coil, an indication of the size of the current is obtained.

There are other types of simple ammeters, but the basic idea remains the same. A needle deflection is obtained corresponding to the amount of current through the ammeter.

Let us consider the concept of an ideal ammeter, which has two basic properties. First, the resistance of the ideal ammeter is zero. Second, the needle deflection in the ideal ammeter is directly proportional to current, which implies that the meter face of the ideal ammeter is marked off with uniform spacing between the divisions.

The current readings obtained with an ideal ammeter are perfect. Since it has no resistance, it will not disturb the current in any circuit in which it is connected. Furthermore, because of the perfectly marked meter face, the readings are 100 percent accurate.

Naturally, the ideal ammeter cannot be built. Any real ammeter must have some resistance. Furthermore, in any real ammeter the amount of needle deflection is not exactly proportional to the amount of current. Nevertheless, real d-c ammeters may approach the properties of the ideal ammeter. The resistance is made as low as possible, and the needle deflection is almost linear.

We will use the concept of the ideal ammeter as the perfect ammeter with which to compare the performance of real ammeters.

2-2 Calibration Error

One type of error encountered in a real ammeter is calibration error. It arises from the fact that the meter face may not be accurately marked. Inexpensive ammeters have a meter face marked off in uniform divisions. Since needle deflection is not exactly proportional to the amount of current, the needle will usually indicate an incorrect value of current.

Figure 2-1 brings this type of error out more clearly. An ideal ammeter (perfect readings) is in series with a real ammeter. The ideal ammeter correctly reads the values of current source, whereas the real ammeter has a meter face that is incorrectly marked, resulting in slightly erroneous readings.

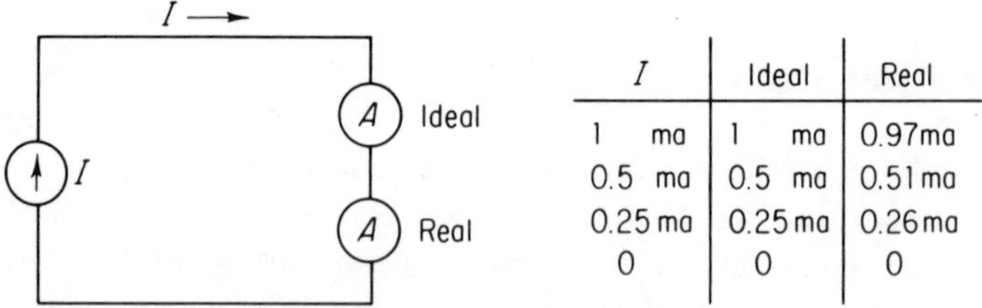

I	Ideal	Real
1 ma	1 ma	0.97 ma
0.5 ma	0.5 ma	0.51 ma
0.25 ma	0.25 ma	0.26 ma
0	0	0

Fig. 2-1 Calibration error.

In the construction of an expensive ammeter it is possible to minimize this type of error. The following method is employed. An ammeter with an unmarked meter face is placed in series with an ammeter (called a standard) whose face is accurately marked. Different values of current are introduced, and for each value the blank meter face is marked to agree with the standard.

In any event, whenever an ammeter is used, one should be aware of calibration error. The size of the calibration error for a specific ammeter may be obtained from the manufacturer's data sheet. Typical values for calibration error are around 3 percent of full-scale current. Since the specification for this error is in terms of full-scale current, the greatest inaccuracy will occur for small deflection. For instance, for a 1-ma movement the calibration error would typically be about ± 0.03 ma, so that for 1 ma of current the ammeter would read between 0.97 and 1.03 ma. On the other hand, if the current through the ammeter is only 0.25 ma, the ammeter can read anywhere between 0.22 and 0.28 ma. Thus, the percent error can be as large as 12 percent at 0.25 ma, compared to 3 percent at 1 ma. This is why good measurement practice calls for obtaining up-scale readings whenever possible.

2-3 Ammeter Loading Effects

The second major type of error encountered in the use of an ammeter (and one often overlooked) is the error caused by its resistance. A real ammeter placed in the branch of a circuit will add resistance to the branch. This added resistance always reduces the current in any real circuit. The question we wish to answer in this section is how much reduction actually takes place. We will find that the reduction in current may be negligibly small or perhaps quite large, depending upon the relation between the ammeter resistance and the resistance of the circuit under test.

Consider the situation shown in Fig. 2-2a. There is a d-c circuit with sources and resistors inside the box. Part of the branch whose current

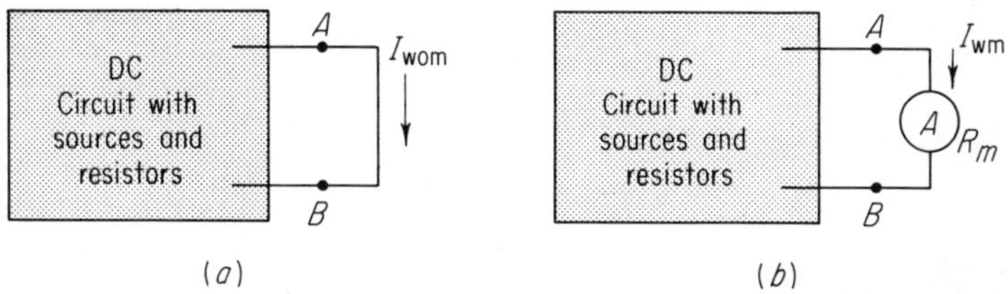

Fig. 2-2 (a) Current without the meter. (b) Current with the meter.

we wish to measure has been brought outside the box for convenience of discussion. The current in the branch labeled I_{wom} is the true current in the branch without the meter connected. This is the current we wish to measure.

In Fig. 2-2b we have connected the ammeter in series with the branch. Because of the ammeter resistance, the original current in the branch has been disturbed. A new value of current I_{wm} is flowing. This is the current in the branch with the meter connected. This is the current the ammeter actually measures.

What is the mathematical relation between the current we actually are measuring and the original current?

One way of finding such a relation is by use of Thévenin's theorem. In Fig. 2-2*a* the load on the *AB* terminals is a short. This is what an ideal ammeter would present. In Fig. 2-2*b* the load on the *AB* terminals is the meter resistance R_m.

If we visualize the circuit inside the box as being replaced by its Thévenin equivalent, we will have the situation illustrated in Fig. 2-3.

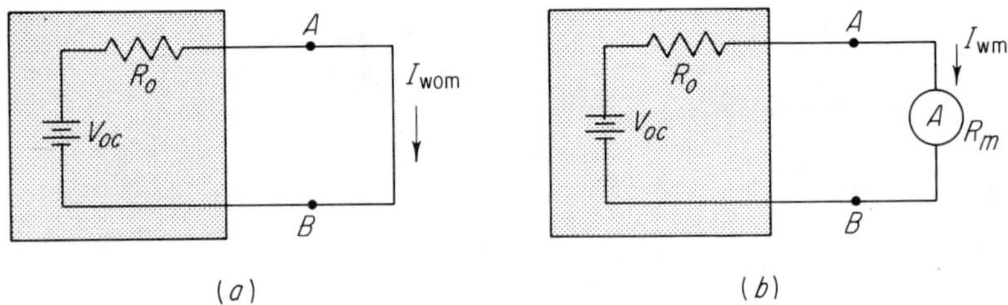

Fig. 2-3 Thévenin equivalent circuits.

The true current we wish to measure is

$$I_{wom} = \frac{V_{oc}}{R_o}$$

The current we actually measure is

$$I_{wm} = \frac{V_{oc}}{R_o + R_m}$$

Dividing I_{wm} by I_{wom} yields

$$\frac{I_{wm}}{I_{wom}} = \frac{R_o}{R_o + R_m} \tag{2-1}$$

Equation (2-1) is very useful. It compares the current with the meter to the current without the meter and indicates that this ratio depends only upon the Thévenin resistance and the meter resistance.

As an example, suppose we have a circuit as illustrated in Fig. 2-4. We wish to measure I_{wom}, the true current through the 500-ohm resistor. The ammeter is placed in series with the 500-ohm resistor. Once this is done, the current through the 500-ohm resistor is reduced to a new value I_{wm}.

To use Eq. (2-1) we must find R_o, the Thévenin resistance looking back into the AB terminals. R_o is merely 500 ohms plus the value of the two 1-kilohm resistors in parallel. Hence, using Eq. (2-1), we obtain

$$\frac{I_{wm}}{I_{wom}} = \frac{R_o}{R_o + R_m} = \frac{1000}{1100} = 0.91 = 91\%$$

Solving for I_{wm}, we obtain

$$I_{wm} = 0.91 I_{wom}$$

The current that is actually measured is 91 percent of the true current in the original circuit. In the circuit of Fig. 2-4 the true current is 1 ma. When the meter is connected, the new current I_{wm} is 0.91 ma.

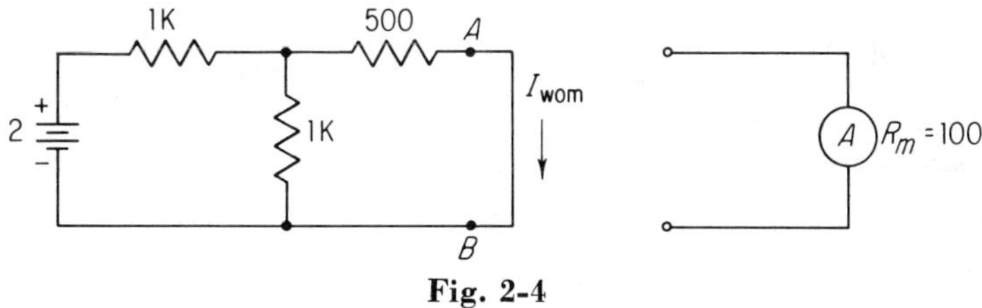

Fig. 2-4

Equation (2-1) may be interpreted as an accuracy equation. In other words, it is a measure of how accurate the reading is. For instance, a perfect reading would correspond to

$$\text{Accuracy} = \frac{I_{wm}}{I_{wom}} = 1 = 100\%$$

From now on, we will speak of Eq. (2-1) as the accuracy equation of an ammeter. Remember that this accuracy refers only to loading effects. Calibration error is not included in the accuracy equation since it is a distinctly different type of error bearing no relation whatever to loading effects. To obtain the total error, the calibration error is added or subtracted from the loading error, depending upon whether it aids or opposes the loading error.

The percent of loading error, that is, the percent error in the ammeter reading due to loading effects, is

$$\text{Percent loading error} = (1 - \text{accuracy}) \times 100\%$$

This should make sense. A reading which is 100 percent accurate means that the loading error is 0 percent. A 99 percent accurate reading means that the loading error is 1 percent.

EXAMPLE 2-1

In the circuit of Fig. 2-5, find the true current and the current that the ammeter reads when connected. Assume no calibration error.

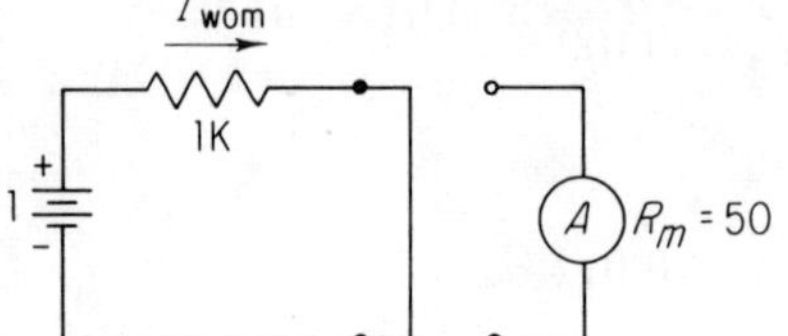

Fig. 2-5 Example 2-1.

SOLUTION

The true current is 1 ma by inspection. When the ammeter is connected in series, it reads

$$I_{wm} = \frac{R_o}{R_o + R_m} I_{wom} = \frac{1000}{1050} 1 \text{ ma} = 0.952 \text{ ma}$$

EXAMPLE 2-2

In the circuit of Example 2-1, approximately what value of resistance is required to produce a 99 percent accurate reading?

SOLUTION

$$\text{Accuracy} = \frac{R_o}{R_o + R_m}$$

$$0.99 = \frac{1000}{1000 + R_m}$$

Solving for R_m, or by inspection, R_m equals 10 ohms.

EXAMPLE 2-3

An ammeter with a resistance of 1000 ohms is used to measure I_{wom} in the circuit of Fig. 2-6. The ammeter reads 40 μa. Find the value of I_{wom}. Assume no calibration error.

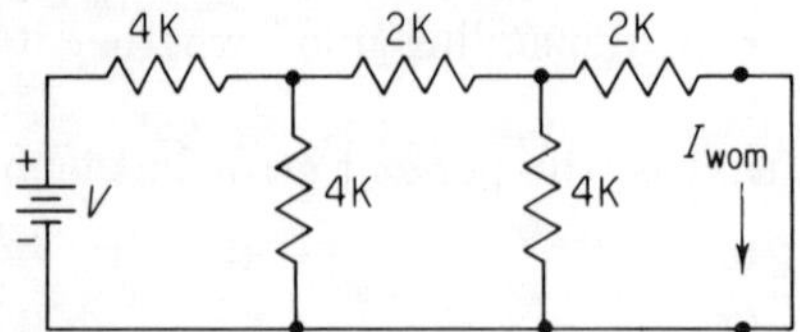

Fig. 2-6 Example 2-3.

SOLUTION

$$\frac{I_{wm}}{I_{wom}} = \frac{R_o}{R_o + R_m}$$

R_m and I_{wm} are given. R_o is 4 kilohms by inspection. Substituting, we obtain

$$\frac{40(10^{-6})}{I_{wom}} = \frac{4(10^3)}{5(10^3)} = \frac{4}{5}$$

$$I_{wom} = \tfrac{5}{4}(40)\mu a = 50\ \mu a$$

EXAMPLE 2-4

Find the accuracy and the percent loading error for the ammeter and circuit of the preceding example.

SOLUTION

$$\text{Accuracy} = \frac{R_o}{R_o + R_m} = \frac{4(10^3)}{5(10^3)} = 0.8 = 80\%$$

$$\text{Percent loading error} = 1 - \text{accuracy} = 1 - 0.8 = 0.2 = 20\%$$

The accuracy value of 80 percent tells us that the ammeter reading is 80 percent of the true current. Alternatively, the loading error indicates that the ammeter reads 20 percent lower than the true value.

2-4 Some Practical Observations

As we have seen in the preceding section, an ammeter may load the circuit under test to the point of producing significant error. A few practical observations, therefore, are pertinent at this time.

The size of R_m compared to R_o determines the accuracy of the reading insofar as loading effects are concerned. For 99 percent accuracy R_o must be greater than $100R_m$. This can be proved by substituting $R_o = 100R_m$ into Eq. (2-1).

$$\text{Accuracy} = \frac{R_o}{R_o + R_m} = \frac{100R_m}{100R_m + R_m} = \frac{100R_m}{101R_m} = 0.99 = 99\%$$

By a similar proof we can show that for a 95 percent accurate reading, R_o must be greater than $20R_m$.

The foregoing rules are very helpful guides in the use of ammeters. Occasionally, the circuit under test may be too complicated to allow rapid calculation of R_o. For example, we may be confronted with a circuit such as shown in Fig. 2-7.

In a complicated circuit like that of Fig. 2-7, finding the Thévenin resistance R_o would be difficult and time-consuming. Yet, we need some assurance that when the ammeter is connected, accurate readings will be obtained.

What rule can we find that guarantees 99 percent accurate readings?

The following rule will be our guide for those circuits which are too complicated to allow calculation of R_o: for 99 percent accurate readings R must be greater than $100R_m$, and for 95 percent accurate readings R must be greater than $20R_m$. Note that R is the total resistance of the branch in which the ammeter is placed.

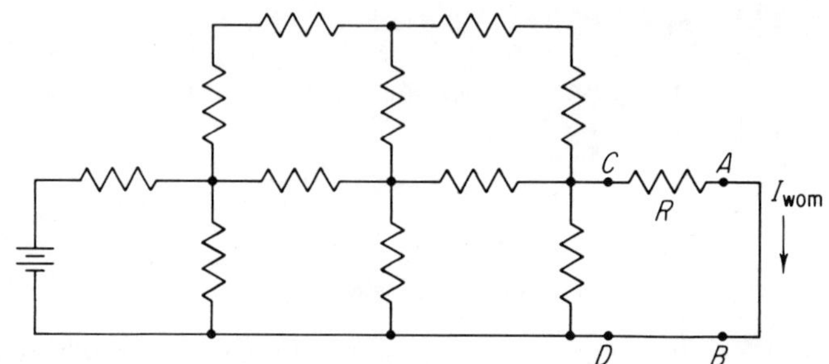

Fig. 2-7 A circuit whose Thévenin resistance is difficult to find.

The foregoing rule is more conservative than the rule involving R_o, as can be seen by realizing that R_o is the sum of R and the resistance looking back into the CD terminals. Hence R is smaller than R_o, and the use of the latter rule results in a smaller value of R_m. This means that we are perfectly safe in using the latter rule.

Example 2-5

The Thévenin resistance of a circuit under test is 20 kilohms. What is the largest value of meter resistance permissible if 99 percent accuracy is desired? Assume no calibration error.

Solution

$$R_o = 100R_m$$

$$20 \text{ kilohms} = 100R_m$$

or

$$R_m = 200 \text{ ohms}$$

Example 2-6

In Fig. 2-7 all resistors are 1 kilohm. What is the largest permissible ammeter resistance if 95 percent accuracy is desired?

Solution

Since it is too difficult to compute R_o, we use the more conservative rule as our guide.

$$R = 20R_m$$

$$1 \text{ kilohm} = 20R_m$$

or

$$R_m = 50 \text{ ohms}$$

2-5 Ammeter Shunts

An ammeter with a full-scale current of I_{fs} can be shunted by a resistor in order to measure currents greater than I_{fs}. Figure 2-8 illustrates a shunted ammeter. As indicated, at full-scale deflection a total current of I_t flows into the circuit. Part of this current is shunted through R_{sh}.

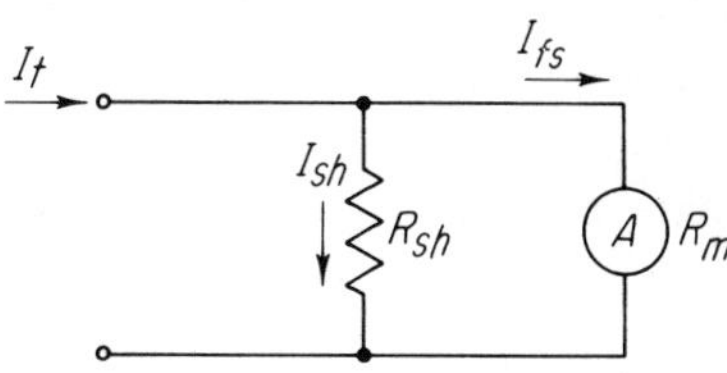

Fig. 2-8 Shunting an ammeter.

To find the formula for the shunt resistor, we need an equation involving the various circuit quantities. Such an equation can be obtained by noting that the voltage across the shunt resistor must equal the voltage across the ammeter.

$$I_{sh}R_{sh} = I_{fs}R_m$$

or

$$R_{sh} = \frac{I_{fs}}{I_{sh}} R_m \tag{2-2}$$

Normally, we will be given R_m, I_{fs}, I_t and will be required to find R_{sh}. Equation (2-2) can be modified to a more useful form by noting that

$$I_t = I_{sh} + I_{fs}$$

or

$$I_{sh} = I_t - I_{fs} \tag{2-3}$$

Substituting Eq. (2-3) into (2-2) yields a convenient formula for the calculation of the shunt resistor.

$$R_{sh} = \frac{I_{fs}}{I_t - I_{fs}} R_m \tag{2-4}$$

Another quantity of interest is the input resistance of a shunted ammeter. By inspection of Fig. 2-8 we can see that a shunted ammeter has an input resistance of

$$R'_m = R_m \| R_{sh} = \frac{R_m R_{sh}}{R_m + R_{sh}} \tag{2-5}$$

where R'_m is the resistance of a shunted ammeter.

Note the vertical parallel lines in Eq. (2-5), which will be used throughout this book to indicate that two resistors are in parallel.

Another useful expression for R'_m can be obtained by the following approach.

$$R'_m = \frac{V_{\text{in}}}{I_{\text{in}}}$$

where V_{in} is the voltage across the terminals of a shunted ammeter and I_{in} is the total current into the input terminals.

This equation may be rewritten in terms of I_{fs} and I_t as

$$R'_m = \frac{V_{\text{in}}}{I_{\text{in}}} = \frac{I_{fs}}{I_t} R_m \tag{2-6}$$

Equation (2-6) is very useful. It tells us that if the total current is greater than I_{fs} by a given factor, the resistance of the shunted ammeter will be decreased by that factor. For instance, if $R_m = 50$, $I_{fs} = 1$ ma, and we wish to measure a total of $I_t = 10$ ma, then we will be extending the current range by a factor of ten. Therefore, the shunted ammeter resistance R'_m will be one-tenth of R_m, or 5 ohms.

Note that when computing the accuracy, Eq. (2-1), for a shunted ammeter, we must use R'_m instead of R_m.

Example 2-7

An ammeter with a meter resistance of 50 ohms and a full-scale deflection current of 1 ma is to be shunted so as to allow a total current of 3 ma. Find the value of the shunt resistor and the value of the input resistance of the shunted ammeter.

Solution

$$R_{sh} = \frac{I_{fs}}{I_t - I_{fs}} R_m = \frac{1 \text{ ma}}{3 - 1 \text{ ma}} 50 = 25 \text{ ohms}$$

$$R'_m = \frac{I_{fs}}{I_t} R_m = \frac{1 \text{ ma}}{3 \text{ ma}} 50 = 16.7 \text{ ohms}$$

Note that the total current was extended from 1 to 3 ma by shunting. This is a factor of three, hence the ammeter resistance effectively is reduced by a factor of three.

Example 2-8

The ammeter in Example 2-7 is shunted as required to obtain a total current of 1 amp. Find the value of shunt resistor and the input resistance of the shunted ammeter.

Solution

$$R_{sh} = \frac{1 \text{ ma}}{1000 - 1 \text{ ma}} 50 = \tfrac{1}{999}\, 50 \cong 0.05 \text{ ohm}$$

$$R'_m = \frac{1 \text{ ma}}{1000 \text{ ma}} 50 = 0.05 \text{ ohm}$$

In this case the shunt resistor is so small compared to the meter resistance that the parallel combination produces a resistance approximately equal to the shunt resistance.

Example 2-9

An ammeter with a meter resistance of 2000 ohms and a full-scale current of 50 μa is shunted as shown in Fig. 2-9*a*. The various current ranges are 5, 50, and 500 ma. Find the input resistance of the shunted ammeter on each range.

Solution

5-ma range $\quad R'_m = \frac{50(10^{-6})}{5(10^{-3})} 2000 = 20 \text{ ohms}$

50-ma range $\quad R'_m = 2 \text{ ohms}$

500-ma range $\quad R'_m = 0.2 \text{ ohm}$

Note that the circuit of Fig. 2-9*a* has a serious pitfall. There is a real danger of ruining the meter movement, because as we switch from one

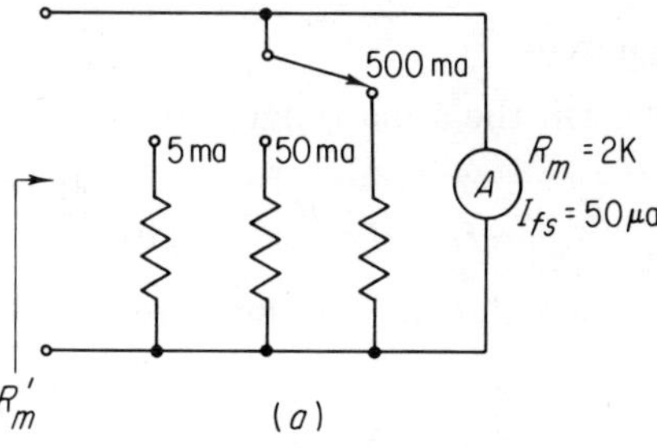

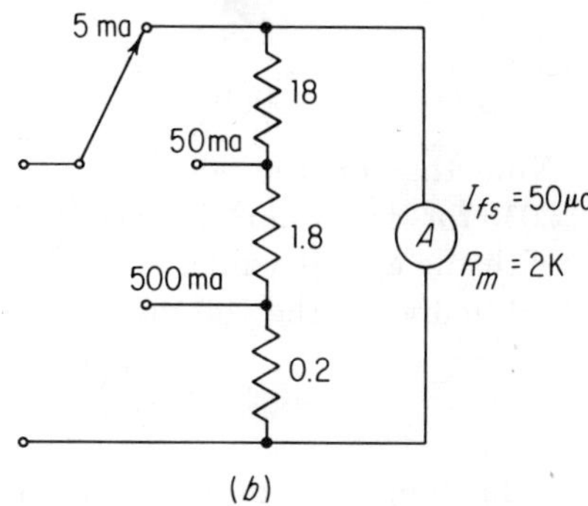

Fig. 2-9 (*a*) An ammeter with different ranges. (*b*) Ayrton shunt.

range to another, the switch is momentarily open. This means that the ammeter is not shunted during the switching time. For instance, suppose that the switch is in the 500-ma position and the current reading is around 50 ma. Naturally, we would switch to a lower range in order to obtain an up-scale reading. As we switch to the 50-ma range, the ammeter is momentarily unshunted, so that the entire 50 ma passes through the 50-μa movement. This will burn out the meter movement.

To avoid this possibility, we can use a special switch which makes before it breaks. The contact with a given position remains until the adjacent position has been connected. Only then is the original position disconnected. Hence, there is never a danger of passing the total current through the ammeter when changing ranges.

In Example 2-9 the shunting arrangement must use a make-before-break switch to protect the meter movement. An alternative to this type of switch is the Ayrton shunt, shown in Fig. 2-9*b*. This circuit uses an ordinary switch, but the total current is interrupted between positions, thus preventing any possible meter damage due to switching. (The meter movement can still be damaged if the total current far exceeds the capacity of the shunted ammeter.)

EXAMPLE 2-10

Show that the total current capacity is 5, 50, and 500 ma as indicated for each position of the range switch for the circuit of Fig. 2-9*b*.

SOLUTION

On the 5-ma range, the correct value of R_{sh} would be

$$R_{sh} = \frac{I_{fs}}{I_t - I_{fs}} R_m = \frac{50(10^{-6})}{5(10^{-3}) - 50(10^{-6})} 2000 = 20.2 \cong 20 \text{ ohms}$$

The value of 20 ohms agrees with that shown:

$$18 + 1.8 + 0.2 = 20 \text{ ohms}$$

On the 50-ma range

$$R_{sh} = \frac{50(10^{-6})}{50(10^{-3}) - 50(10^{-6})} 2018 \cong 2.02 \cong 2 \text{ ohms}$$

Note that on the 50-ma position, 18 ohms is added to 2000 to give 2018 for the total resistance in that branch. The value of 2 ohms agrees with the circuit value.

Finally, on the 500-ma position

$$R_{sh} \cong \frac{50(10^{-6})}{500(10^{-3})} 2019.8 \cong 0.2 \text{ ohm}$$

The approximations made for the values of R_{sh} are within 1 percent of the exact values, which is adequate for most cases. If necessary, all shunt resistors may be increased by 1 percent to remove this small approximation error.

2-6 Converting the Ammeter to a Voltmeter

A simple d-c voltmeter can be constructed by placing a resistor in series with an ammeter and marking the meter face to read the voltage across the resistor and ammeter (see Fig. 2-10).

If a voltage V is impressed across the input terminals, a current I flows through the ammeter. The relation between V and I is obtained from Ohm's law:

$$V = (R_s + R_m)I \tag{2-7}$$

This equation indicates that V is a function of I, meaning that for a given value of I, there must be a voltage V across the terminals which is $R_s + R_m$ times larger than the current. For instance, if $R_s + R_m$ equals 10 kilohms and I equals 1 ma, the applied voltage V must be 10 volts.

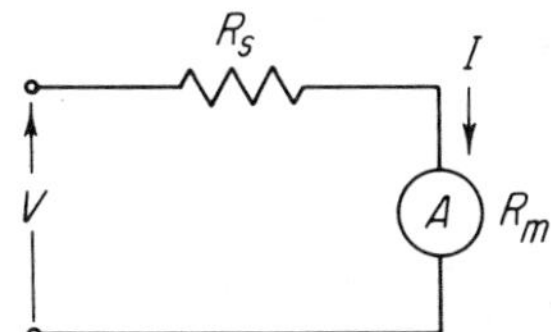

Fig. 2-10 Simple d-c voltmeter.

The final step in converting the ammeter to a voltmeter is to mark the meter face in volts rather than amperes. Equation (2-7) specifies how this marking is to be done.

For a given value of full-scale current, the series resistor will determine the maximum voltage we can measure. Let us find a formula for this series resistor. For full-scale current, Eq. (2-7) becomes

$$V_{fs} = (R_s + R_m)I_{fs}$$

where V_{fs} is the voltage that produces full-scale current.

We solve this equation for R_s to obtain

$$R_s = \frac{V_{fs}}{I_{fs}} - R_m \tag{2-8}$$

This equation is in a convenient form for finding the value of R_s, given I_{fs}, R_m, and V_{fs}. Usually the value of R_m is negligibly small compared to V_{fs}/I_{fs}, and Eq. (2-8) reduces to

$$R_s \cong \frac{V_{fs}}{I_{fs}} \tag{2-9}$$

Example 2-11

An ammeter with $I_{fs} = 1$ ma and $R_m = 50$ ohms is to be converted to a voltmeter. Compute the size of the series resistor required to measure a full-scale voltage of 50 volts.

Solution

$$R_s = \frac{V_{fs}}{I_{fs}} - R_m = \frac{50}{10^{-3}} - 50 \cong 50 \text{ kilohms}$$

EXAMPLE 2-12

Convert an ammeter with $I_{fs} = 50\ \mu a$ and $R_m = 2000$ ohms to a voltmeter with a full-scale voltage of 100 volts.

SOLUTION

$$R_s = \frac{V_{fs}}{I_{fs}} - R_m = \frac{100}{50(10^{-6})} - 2(10^3) \cong 2 \text{ megohms}$$

EXAMPLE 2-13

Show the schematic of a voltmeter with the following ranges: 5, 15, 50, and 150 volts. The ammeter has a full-scale current of 50 μa and a resistance of 2 kilohms.

SOLUTION

For $V_{fs} = 5$

$$R_s = \frac{5}{50(10^{-6})} - 2000 \cong 98 \text{ kilohms}$$

For $V_{fs} = 15$

$$R_s = \frac{15}{50(10^{-6})} - 2000 \cong 300 \text{ kilohms}$$

For $V_{fs} = 50$

$$R_s = \frac{50}{50(10^{-6})} - 2000 \cong 1 \text{ megohm}$$

For $V_{fs} = 150$

$$R_s = \frac{150}{50(10^{-6})} - 2000 \cong 3 \text{ megohms}$$

A voltmeter with the correct ranges is shown in Fig. 2-11.

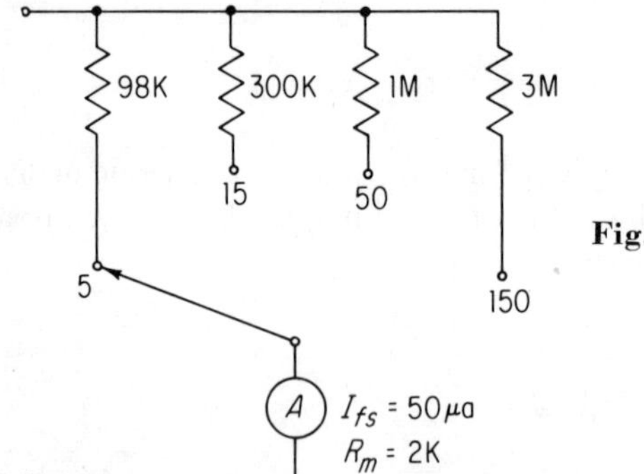

Fig. 2-11 Example 2-13.

2-7 The Input Resistance of a Voltmeter

For the simple voltmeter of Fig. 2-10 the input resistance is merely the sum of the series resistance and the meter resistance.

$$R_{\text{in}} = R_s + R_m$$

Given the schematic, we would merely add the given values of R_s and R_m to find the input resistance of the voltmeter. On the other hand, lacking the schematic but given a commercial voltmeter in its instrument case, how do we find the input resistance?

Refer to Fig. 2-10. It should be clear that the input resistance can be found from

$$R_{\text{in}} = \frac{V}{I}$$

Since R_{in} is constant for any voltage-current condition, it certainly can be expressed by

$$R_{\text{in}} = \frac{V_{fs}}{I_{fs}} \tag{2-10}$$

R_{in} is the full-scale voltage divided by the full-scale current. Thus, if a voltmeter has a 1-ma movement, on the 100-volt scale it has an input resistance of 100 kilohms. If the range is changed to 10 volts, the input resistance becomes 10 kilohms.

Hence, with a commercial instrument we could quickly compute the input resistance of a voltmeter on its different ranges by dividing the full-scale voltage by the full-scale current of the meter movement. This would be a straightforward procedure if the value of I_{fs} were printed on the meter face. However, such is not the case. The value of I_{fs} is not normally on the meter face. Instead, a different number, called the *sensitivity*, generally appears. It is defined as

$$S \triangleq \frac{1}{I_{fs}} \tag{2-11}$$

where S is the sensitivity of the voltmeter and I_{fs} is the full-scale current of the meter movement.

Equation (2-11) cannot be derived from other equations. It is a pure definition, meaning that someone invented the word "sensitivity" and said that it was equal to the reciprocal of the full-scale current. As long as we all use this definition, there will be no misunderstanding about the meaning of sensitivity. Whenever someone speaks of the sensitivity of a voltmeter, he means the reciprocal of the full-scale current of the meter movement. The entire situation is analogous to the use of the word "tree." We all know what a tree is. Someone invented the word, and it has been widely accepted ever since. However, the inventor originally could have chosen a different word like "teer" instead of tree. If such had been the case, we would now be using the word "teer" and would be completely comfortable in its use. The crucial point is that we do not try to probe definitions. We accept them *arbitrarily*. Whenever an equation is a definition, we will use the small triangle over the equal sign to mean just that. We will realize that any such equations are nonderivable, and we need only memorize them to get in step with the rest of the world, which has already agreed to use them as definitions.

The sensitivity of a voltmeter has the dimensions of 1 divided by amperes, or ohms per volt.

$$S = \frac{1}{I_{fs}} = \frac{1}{\text{amperes}} = \frac{1}{\text{volts/ohm}} = \frac{\text{ohms}}{\text{volt}}$$

Thus, for a voltmeter with a basic movement of 1 ma, the sensitivity would be

$$S = \frac{1}{1\text{ ma}} = 1000 \text{ ohms per volt}$$

Notice how the definition for sensitivity may be used to modify Eq. (2-10).

$$R_{\text{in}} = \frac{V_{fs}}{I_{fs}} = SV_{fs} \tag{2-12}$$

Equation (2-12) tells us that the input resistance of a voltmeter on any range equals the sensitivity times the full-scale voltage of that range.

The value of S is generally printed on the meter face, and with this value a rapid mental calculation can be made for the input resistance of a voltmeter.

Why are we so interested in the input resistance of voltmeter? Any voltmeter, when connected to a circuit under test, will reduce the voltage we are trying to measure. This means that we will have loading error in the reading. The size of this error depends upon the input resistance of the voltmeter compared to the circuit resistance. This will be discussed more fully in the next section.

Example 2-14

A voltmeter uses a 1-ma movement. Find the input resistance on the 5-, 50-, and 500-volt ranges.

Solution

$$S = \frac{1}{1\text{ ma}} = 1000 \text{ ohms per volt}$$

For $V_{fs} = 5$ $\quad R_{\text{in}} = 1000(5) = 5$ kilohms

For $V_{fs} = 50$ $\quad R_{\text{in}} = 1000(50) = 50$ kilohms

For $V_{fs} = 500$ $\quad R_{\text{in}} = 500$ kilohms

Example 2-15

A voltmeter with a 50-μa movement has ranges of 5, 50, and 500 volts. Find the input resistance on each range.

SOLUTION

$$S = \frac{1}{50(10^{-6})} = 20 \text{ kilohms per volt}$$

For $V_{fs} = 5$ $\quad R_{\text{in}} = 100$ kilohms
For $V_{fs} = 50$ $\quad R_{\text{in}} = 1$ megohm
For $V_{fs} = 500$ $\quad R_{\text{in}} = 10$ megohms

2-8 Voltmeter Loading Error

Recall from Sec. 2-3 that whenever an ammeter is placed in series with a circuit branch, the current is reduced in that branch. The reduction may be small or large, depending upon the ammeter resistance compared to the Thévenin resistance of the circuit.

In a similar way, placing a voltmeter across any part of a circuit reduces the voltage across that part, and the size of this reduction depends upon the input resistance of the voltmeter compared to the Thévenin resistance of the circuit.

Figure 2-12*a* illustrates a typical measurement situation. There is a d-c circuit with sources and resistors inside the box. A resistor R, whose voltage is to be measured, has been shown outside the box for convenience. There is a voltage across R labeled V_{wom}, the voltage without the meter connected. This is the true voltage that we wish to measure.

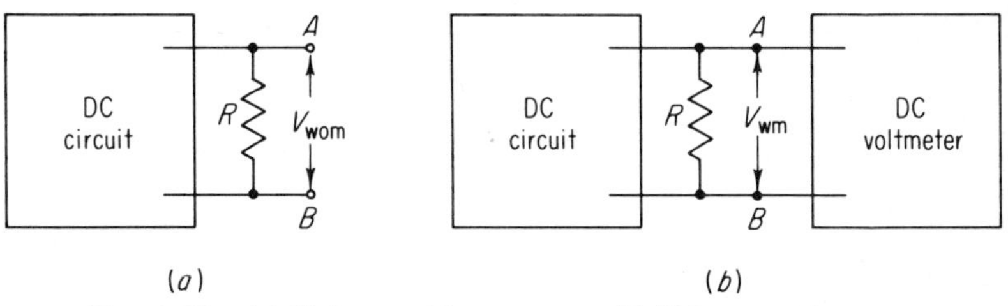

Fig. 2-12 (*a*) Voltage without meter. (*b*) Voltage with meter.

In Fig. 2-12*b* we have connected the voltmeter across R in order to measure the voltage. Because of the voltmeter input resistance the original circuit has been disturbed. A new value of voltage appears across R labeled V_{wm}. This is the voltage with the meter connected and is the voltage that is actually impressed across the voltmeter input terminals.

In order to find the relation between V_{wm} and V_{wom} we replace the d-c circuit by its Thévenin equivalent, as shown in Fig. 2-13. R_o is the Thévenin resistance of the circuit of Fig. 2-12*a* and consists of R shunted by the remainder of the circuit.

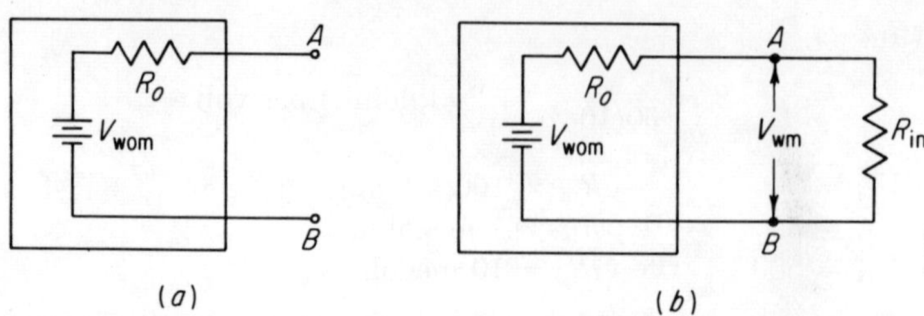

Fig. 2-13 Developing the accuracy formula for a voltmeter.

Applying Ohm's law to Fig. 2-13*b*, we find

$$V_{wm} = \frac{R_{in}}{R_{in} + R_o} V_{wom} \tag{2-13}$$

or

$$\frac{V_{wm}}{V_{wom}} = \frac{R_{in}}{R_{in} + R_o} \triangleq \text{accuracy} \tag{2-14}$$

Equation (2-14) is the dual of ammeter accuracy, Eq. (2-1). In other words, Eq. (2-14) represents the voltmeter accuracy insofar as loading effects are concerned. Calibration error is still a distinct kind of error not included in Eq. (2-14).

As with the ammeter, we can write an expression for the percent loading error:

$$\text{Percent loading error} = (1 - \text{accuracy}) \times 100\%$$

EXAMPLE 2-16

The voltmeter is on the 50-volt range. Find the accuracy of the voltmeter reading and the voltage actually measured across AB for the circuit of Fig. 2-14. Assume no calibration error.

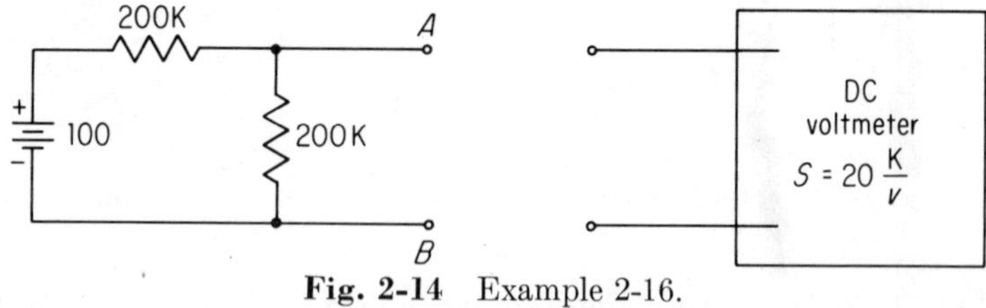

Fig. 2-14 Example 2-16.

SOLUTION

Without the voltmeter connected, the true voltage across AB is 50 volts by inspection. This is the value of V_{wom}. Also, R_o is 100 kilohms by inspection.

On the 50-volt range the voltmeter has an input resistance of

$$R_{in} = SV_{fs} = 20(10^3)(50) = 1 \text{ megohm}$$

Hence, the accuracy is

$$\frac{V_{wm}}{V_{wom}} = \frac{R_{in}}{R_{in} + R_o} = \frac{10^6}{10^6 + 100(10^3)} = \frac{1}{1.1} = 91\%$$

The accuracy is 91 percent, meaning that the voltmeter reading is 91 percent of the true voltage. Thus,

$$V_{wm} = 0.91V_{wom} = 0.91(50) = 45.5 \text{ volts}$$

Example 2-17

To demonstrate how serious loading effects can become, consider the measurement situation depicted in Fig. 2-15. Find the voltmeter reading on the 50-volt range and on the 5-volt range.

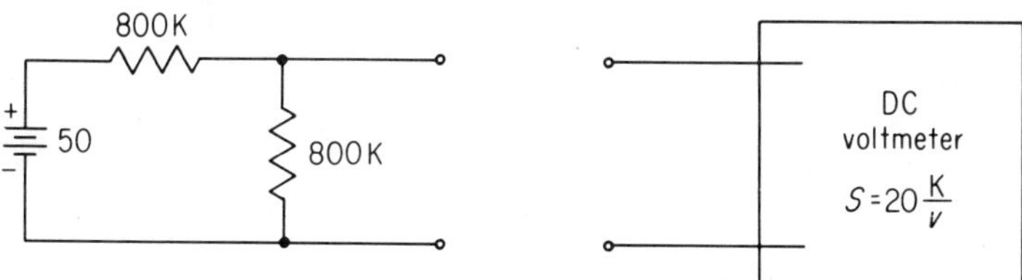

Fig. 2-15 Example 2-17.

Solution

Notice that the V_{wom} is 25 volts and R_o is 400 kilohms by inspection. On the 50-volt range, $R_{in} = 1$ megohm. Thus,

$$V_{wm} = \frac{10^6}{10^6 + 400(10^3)} 25 = 17.9 \text{ volts}$$

Next, we change the range switch to 5 volts. Does this peg the meter? Not at all! Since R_{in} has been reduced to 100 kilohms, we have

$$V_{wm} = \frac{100(10^3)}{100(10^3) + 400(10^3)} 25 = 5 \text{ volts}$$

We have obtained two different readings. Both readings are incorrect, since the true voltage is 25 volts. Whenever we obtain different voltage readings as we change ranges, we immediately know that the voltmeter is loading the circuit excessively, and therefore the readings are erroneous.

On the other hand, if we can change ranges without obtaining contradictory readings, we may rest assured that negligible loading has occurred.

2-9 Guides for Avoiding Loading Effects

The accuracy equation for a voltmeter is given by Eq. (2-14). If we wish to obtain 99 percent accuracy, R_{in} should be greater than $100R_o$. The proof is to substitute $100R_o$ for R_{in} in Eq. (2-14).

$$\frac{V_{wm}}{V_{wom}} = \frac{100R_o}{100R_o + R_o} = \frac{100}{101} = 0.99 = 99\%$$

In a similar way, we can prove that for a 95 percent accurate reading, R_{in} must be greater than $20R_o$.

Ideally, we would like to avoid loading effects completely. This is impossible. Any voltmeter must have some input resistance and therefore must load the circuit under test. Special electronic voltmeters, to be discussed in a later chapter, do have very high input resistances, so that little loading occurs for typical circuits. However, even these special high-input-resistance voltmeters may load the circuit under test if the Thévenin resistance is not small enough compared to the input resistance of the voltmeter. In any event, the guides developed are useful criteria for minimizing loading effects.

If the circuit being tested is extremely complicated, finding R_o may be difficult and time-consuming. Figure 2-16 illustrates such a circuit. R_o is

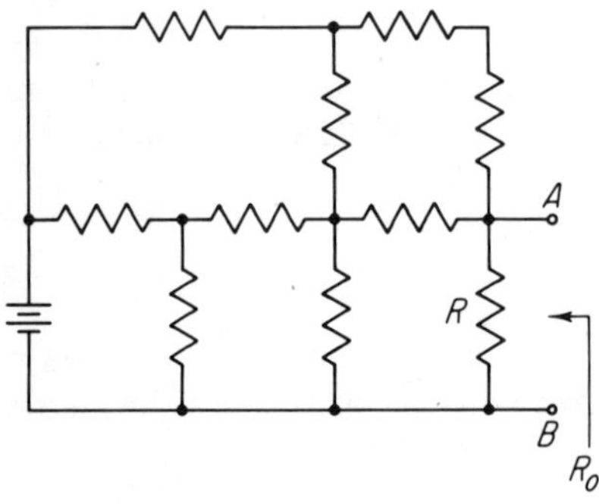

Fig. 2-16 A circuit whose Thévenin resistance is difficult to find.

the value of R shunted by the remainder of the circuit. Thus, R_o is smaller than R, and our guides may be safely changed to the following: for 99 percent accurate readings, R_{in} must be greater than $100R$, and for 95 percent accurate readings, R_{in} must be greater than $20R$.

Experimentally, we may be assured that the readings are correct if it is possible to change ranges and not obtain contradictory readings (see Example 2-17). This statement applies only to the simple d-c voltmeters that we have been discussing in this chapter; it does not apply to vacuum-tube voltmeters.

EXAMPLE 2-18

A single-loop circuit consists of a battery and three 100 kilohms resistors in series. If the voltage across one of these resistors is to be measured with 99 percent accuracy, what is the minimum permissible value of R_{in}?

SOLUTION

The Thévenin resistance is 100 kilohms shunted by 200 kilohms, or $R_o \cong 67$ kilohms. Therefore, the input resistance of the voltmeter must be at least 6.7 megohms.

EXAMPLE 2-19

In the circuit of Fig. 2-16 all resistors are 1 kilohm. Find the minimum permissible value of R_{in} that guarantees 95 percent accurate readings.

SOLUTION

We naturally will use the simple guide, since R_o is too difficult to find. R_{in} must be greater than $20R$. Therefore, $R_{in} = 20$ kilohms.

2-10 The Ohmmeter

A simple ohmmeter can be made by using a battery, an ammeter, and a resistor, as shown in Fig. 2-17. R_o is the Thévenin resistance of the ohmmeter, so that it includes the meter resistance R_m. V_{oc} is the open-circuit voltage of the ohmmeter at the measuring terminals AB.

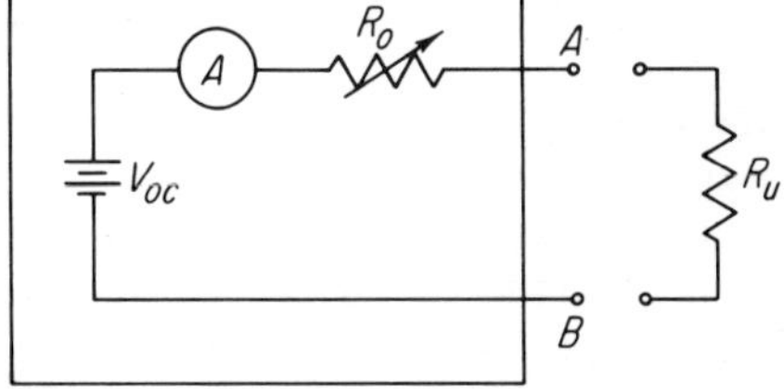

Fig. 2-17 A simple ohmmeter.

R_o is shown as an adjustable resistor because a rheostat is always included in an ohmmeter to correct for aging of the battery. Normally, an ohmmeter is first zeroed before trying to measure the unknown resistor R_u. Zeroing means that we must short the AB terminals and adjust R_o to produce full-scale current through the ammeter. This means that

$$I_{fs} = \frac{V_{oc}}{R_o} \tag{2-15}$$

To measure R_u we connect it to the AB terminals. This results in a current of

$$I = \frac{V_{oc}}{R_o + R_u} \tag{2-16}$$

A concise equation relating the meter deflection and the value of the unknown resistor can be obtained by taking the ratio of these last two equations

$$\frac{I}{I_{fs}} = \frac{R_o}{R_o + R_u} \tag{2-17}$$

or

$$D = \frac{R_o}{R_o + R_u} \tag{2-18}$$

where D is the meter deflection, I/I_{fs}.

Equation (2-18) is very useful in that it tells us how the meter face must be marked in order to indicate the value of R_u. Table 2-1 contains some

Table 2-1

R_u	D
0	1
$R_o/3$	¾
R_o	½
$3R_o$	¼
$7R_o$	⅛
∞	0

values for R_u and D. In it we see that a value of zero for the unknown resistor produces a deflection of 1, or full-scale deflection. This makes sense, since a zeroed ohmmeter implies full-scale current. We would therefore mark 0 ohms at full scale.

For an infinite value of R_u, or an open circuit, no current can flow, so that the deflection is zero. We therefore would mark infinity at the zero-current point on the meter face.

For R_u equal to R_o, half-scale deflection occurs, so that we mark the value of R_o at midscale on the meter face. Continuing in this fashion, the entire meter can be correctly marked to read ohms. A partially marked meter face is shown in Fig. 2-18. Note the nonlinearity, or crowding effect, that takes place on the ohms scale. This is common to all ohmmeters.

As a numerical example, let us assume that the ohmmeter of Fig. 2-17 has a 10-volt battery and a 1-ma movement. To zero the ohmmeter, R_o

must be adjusted to 10 kilohms in order to allow a full-scale current of 1 ma to flow. With R_o equal to 10 kilohms the meter face must be marked as shown in Fig. 2-19 for a correct reading of the value of an unknown resistor.

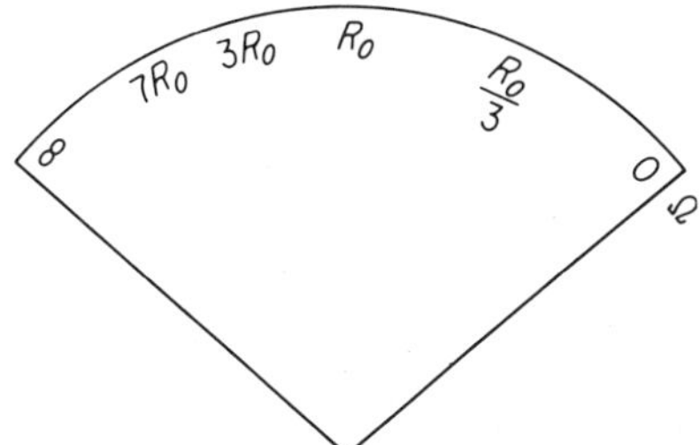

Fig. 2-18 Marking the ohmmeter scale.

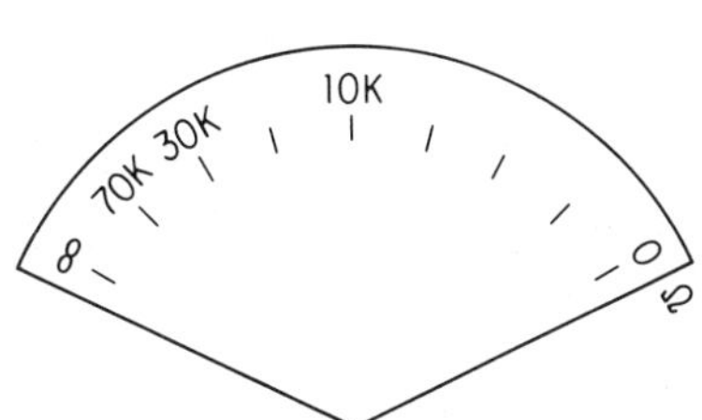

Fig. 2-19 An ohmmeter scale for an internal resistance of 10 kilohms.

Occasionally, there may be a need for an equation for R_u in terms of D and R_o. Equation (2-18) can be rearranged to obtain

$$R_u = R_o \frac{1 - D}{D} \tag{2-19}$$

As already indicated, the actual ohmmeter circuitry may be as simple as the circuit of Fig. 2-17 or may be considerably more complicated in order to have different ohmmeter ranges. Obtaining these different ranges implies the use of switches to change the value of ammeter shunts and the value of R_o. On any one range, however, Fig. 2-18 and Eqs. (2-18) and (2-19) apply. For instance, in order to have a range for measuring small resistors, an R_o of possibly 15 ohms would be desirable. In this case, the midscale value of ohms would be 15. In order to accomplish this change in R_o, a suitable switching arrangement is needed for changing the ammeter shunt to an appropriate value.

Another worthwhile observation is that as the ohmmeter battery ages, some error will result in the readings. For instance, assume the ohmmeter of Fig. 2-17 has $V_{oc} = 10$ and $I_{fs} = 1$ ma. After zeroing, R_o must equal 10 kilohms, and the meter face of Fig. 2-19 applies. If a 10-kilohm resistor is measured, the current will be one-half the full-scale current. Thus the correct reading of 10 kilohms is indicated.

Suppose that the battery then ages to 9 volts. The ohmmeter is rezeroed, but now R_o must be 9 kilohms in order to produce a full-scale current of 1 ma. If a 9-kilohm resistor is measured, exactly midscale deflection occurs. The meter face shown in Fig. 2-19 would indicate that the unknown has a resistance of 10 instead of 9 kilohms.

To avoid the battery-aging error just described, the adjustable range of R_o must be restricted to prevent gross errors.

Example 2-20

The ohmmeter of Fig. 2-17 has a meter movement of 50 μa and 2000 ohms resistance. The open-circuit voltage is 6 volts. The ohmmeter is zeroed, and then an unknown resistor is measured, which produces quarter-scale deflection. What is the value of the unknown resistor?

Solution

$$R_o = \frac{V_{oc}}{I_{fs}} = \frac{6}{50(10^{-6})} = 120 \text{ kilohms}$$

$$R_u = R_o \frac{1-D}{D} = 120(10^3)\frac{1-\frac{1}{4}}{\frac{1}{4}} = 120(10^3)(3) = 360 \text{ kilohms}$$

Example 2-21

The ohmmeter of Example 2-20 has its meter movement shunted by 20 ohms. Approximately what value of R_u produces half-scale deflection?

Solution

$$R'_m = \frac{I_{fs}}{I_t} R_m$$

The meter has been heavily shunted, so that the effective meter resistance has become 20 ohms. Hence, all quantities in the foregoing equation are known except I_t. Solving for I_t, we obtain

$$I_t = \frac{R_m}{R'_m} I_{fs} = \frac{2000}{20} 50(10^{-6}) = 5 \text{ ma}$$

Since the total current through the ohmmeter terminals is 5 ma, we can compute the value of R_o

$$R_o = \frac{V_{oc}}{I_t} = \frac{6 \text{ volts}}{5 \text{ ma}} = 1.2 \text{ kilohms}$$

For midscale deflection to occur the unknown resistor must equal the Thévenin resistance of the ohmmeter. Therefore, $R_u = 1.2$ kilohms.

2-11 The Volt-Ohm-Milliammeter

In this chapter we have discussed the simple methods used for measuring voltage, resistance, and current. It should be obvious that by means of a suitable switching arrangement a single instrument capable of measuring all three quantities can be produced. Such an instrument is commercially known as a volt-ohm-milliammeter, abbreviated VOM.

A typical VOM has a meter movement with a full-scale current of 50 μa, or a sensitivity of 20 kilohms per volt when used as a d-c voltmeter.

Typically, the voltage ranges extend from about 1.5 volts on the lowest range to about 5000 volts on the highest range, so that the input resistance of the voltmeter section may be as low as 30 kilohms or as high as 100 megohms.

When used as an ohmmeter, the VOM generally has three ranges, $R \times 1$, $R \times 100$, and $R \times 10$ kilohms. On the lowest range, $R \times 1$, the midscale value is around 15 ohms, making this range suitable for measuring small resistance. On the highest range, $R \times 10$ kilohms, the midscale value is 15×10 kilohms, or 150 kilohms, making this range suitable for high-resistance measurements.

When used as a milliammeter, the VOM typically has ranges of about 150 μa to 15 amp. (The lowest range is 150 μa instead of 50, because of the use of an Ayrton shunt.)

A-c voltage measurements are also possible with the VOM by using diode rectifiers. The sensitivity on these a-c ranges is usually only 5 kilohms per volt. The reason for this is discussed in a later chapter dealing with a-c voltmeters.

In conclusion, the VOM is a useful instrument. It offers the advantage of being portable and not requiring a source of external voltage. If the limitations of calibration error and loading error are kept in mind, this instrument can be used to obtain reasonably accurate measurements.

SUMMARY

The ideal ammeter has no calibration error and no input resistance. The real ammeter has both a calibration error and a resistance. This resistance disturbs the circuit in which the ammeter is placed, resulting in a loading error. The smaller the meter resistance, compared to the Thévenin resistance of the circuit, the more accurate the readings of the ammeter. The calibration error of the ammeter can be virtually eliminated by carefully marking the meter face to agree with a standard.

An ammeter may be shunted in order to extend its range. The resistance of a shunted ammeter is the meter resistance in parallel with the shunting resistor. If an ammeter has been shunted so as to increase the total current capacity by a factor of N, the input resistance of the shunted ammeter will be the meter resistance divided by N.

A simple d-c voltmeter is made by placing an ammeter in series with a resistor. The ammeter face is then marked to indicate the voltage across the series combination.

The simple voltmeter has a calibration error and a loading error. The higher the input resistance of the voltmeter compared to the Thévenin resistance of the circuit being measured, the more accurate the reading.

The sensitivity of a voltmeter refers to the reciprocal of the full-scale current of the ammeter. If the ammeter is shunted, the sensitivity is the reciprocal of the total current. If we multiply the sensitivity by the full-range voltage, the input resistance for that range is obtained.

A simple ohmmeter is made by placing a battery, a resistor, and an ammeter in series. After zeroing the ohmmeter, external resistors can be placed in series with the ohmmeter to produce different amounts of deflection. The meter face can be calibrated to read ohms. The sources of error are the calibration error and the battery-aging error.

A volt-ohm-milliammeter (VOM) is an instrument that combines the various simple instruments into one unit. By means of switches, different values of shunt and multiplier resistances can be selected to provide various ranges. The VOM is portable and requires no external power source.

GLOSSARY

Ayrton shunt A special kind of ammeter shunt arrangement which avoids having the ammeter in the circuit without a shunt.

calibration error Error that arises because the marking of the meter face is not correct.

D'Arsonval meter The most common type of ammeter movement, it consists of a permanent magnet and a moving coil whose deflection depends upon the size of the current through the coil.

deflection (D) The amount of needle displacement, usually expressed as a fraction of full scale.

ideal ammeter An ammeter with zero internal resistance and with a deflection directly proportional to the current.

loading error The error produced by placing an ammeter in a circuit. The ammeter resistance causes the branch current to decrease.

sensitivity (S) In reference to a simple voltmeter this is the reciprocal of the full-scale current of the ammeter used in the voltmeter.

VOM Abbreviation for volt-ohm-milliammeter.

zeroing an ohmmeter The initial step in using an ohmmeter: adjusting the internal resistance so that the shorted ohmmeter terminals produce a full-scale current.

REVIEW QUESTIONS

1. What is an ideal ammeter?
2. What is calibration error?
3. Why are down-scale readings generally less accurate than up-scale readings?

4. How can calibration error be reduced in expensive ammeters?
5. Why does an ammeter produce loading error?
6. What relation should exist between the ammeter resistance and the Thévenin resistance of the circuit under test if accurate readings are desired?
7. How is the percent of loading error defined?
8. For 99 percent accurate readings insofar as loading is concerned, how big should the Thévenin circuit resistance be compared to the ammeter resistance?
9. How can the current capacity of an ammeter be increased?
10. What is a make-before-break switch?
11. What is an Ayrton shunt?
12. How is an ammeter converted to a voltmeter?
13. What is the sensitivity of a voltmeter?
14. How do you find the input resistance of a voltmeter using the sensitivity?
15. Describe voltmeter loading error.
16. If the voltmeter loading error is to be less than 1 percent, what relation must exist between the input resistance of the voltmeter and the Thévenin resistance of the circuit under test?
17. How is a simple ohmmeter constructed?
18. What does zeroing the ohmmeter mean in terms of the amount of current through the ammeter?
19. On any ohmmeter range the value of the internal ohmmeter resistance corresponds to what amount of deflection?
20. What is a VOM?

PROBLEMS

2-1 An ammeter with a full-scale deflection of 1 ma has a calibration error of ± 5 percent of the full-scale current. If the ammeter reads 0.35 ma, what is the possible range in the true current through the ammeter?

2-2 In Fig. 2-20*a* the ammeter has a resistance of 200 ohms. Assuming no calibration error, what does the ammeter read? If the ammeter is ideal, what will it read?

2-3 In Fig. 2-20*a* the ammeter has a resistance of 50 ohms and a full-scale current of 1 ma. If the calibration error is ± 3 percent of the full-scale reading, what is the possible range of ammeter readings?

2-4 The ammeter of the circuit in Fig. 2-20*b* has a meter resistance of 100 ohms. What is the percent loading error?

2-5 If the percent loading error is to be less than 1 percent in the circuit of Fig. 2-20*b*, what should the ammeter resistance be?

2-6 If the percent loading error in the circuit of Fig. 2-20*b* is to be less than 5 percent, what should the ammeter resistance be?

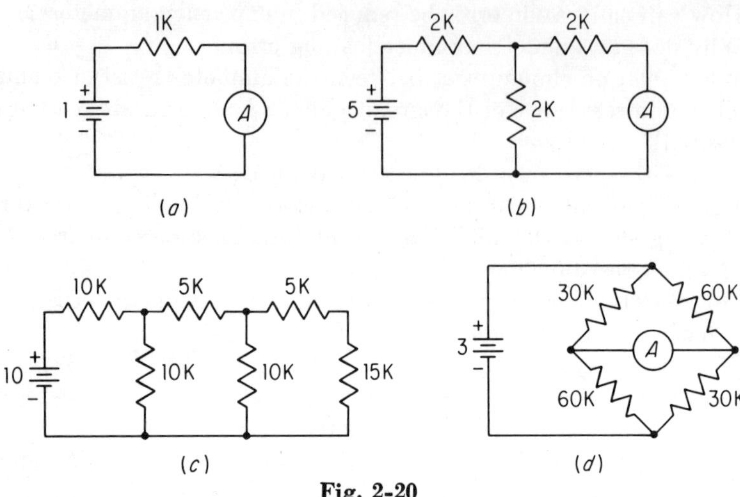

Fig. 2-20

2-7 What is the true current in the 15-kilohm resistor of Fig. 2-20*c*? If an ammeter with a meter resistance of 2 kilohms is used to measure the current in the 15-kilohm resistor, what will it read? If a loading accuracy of 99 percent is desired in measuring the current, what should the ammeter resistance be?

2-8 If an ideal ammeter is connected across the bridge circuit of Fig. 2-20*d*, what will it read?

2-9 A 50-μa 2-kilohm meter movement is to be shunted so as to allow a total current measurement of 0.5 ma. What size should the shunt resistor be? What is the resistance of the shunted ammeter?

2-10 In Fig. 2-20*a* the ammeter has a full-scale current of 1 ma. If this ammeter is replaced by a 50-μa 2-kilohm ammeter which has been shunted to allow a total current of 1 ma, what is the percent loading error?

2-11 If a 1-ma 50-ohm ammeter is shunted by a 1-ohm resistor, what is the effective input resistance of the shunted ammeter? What is the total current capacity of the shunted ammeter? How much voltage appears across the ammeter for full-scale deflection?

2-12 A 0.1-ma 1-kilohm meter movement is converted to a simple d-c voltmeter by adding a series resistance. For a full-scale voltage of 100 volts, what should the value of the series resistance be?

2-13 Find the values of multiplier resistances needed to provide the following voltage ranges: 1.5, 5, 15, 50, 150, and 500 volts. The meter is a 20-μa 5-kilohm movement.

2-14 A meter movement with a sensitivity of 5 kilohms per volt has a calibration error of ± 3 percent of the full-scale value. If this movement is used in a simple d-c voltmeter, what is the possible range in true voltage if the voltmeter reads 50 volts on the 100-volt scale?

2-15 What is the half-scale current of an ammeter with a sensitivity of 10 kilohms per volt?
2-16 A VOM has a sensitivity of 20 kilohms per volt. What is the input resistance of the voltmeter on the 2.5-volt range? On the 5000-volt range?
2-17 The true voltage across the 500-kilohm resistor of Fig. 2-21*a* is obviously 10 volts. What would a voltmeter with a sensitivity of 20 kilohms per volt read on the following ranges: 50, 15, and 5 volts?
2-18 A d-c voltmeter with a sensitivity of 20 kilohms per volt is used to measure the voltage across the *AB* terminals of Fig. 2-21*b*. What is the percent loading error and accuracy on the 30-volt range?

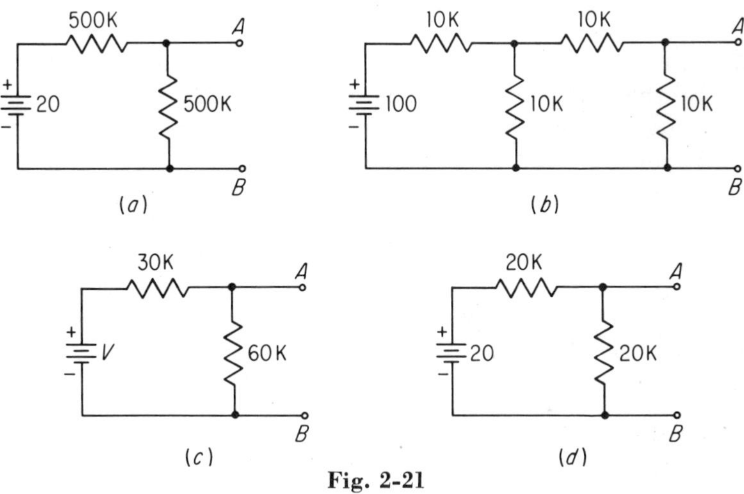

Fig. 2-21

2-19 A d-c voltmeter with a sensitivity of 20 kilohms per volt is connected to the *AB* terminals of Fig. 2-21*c*. If it reads 5 volts on the 5-volt range, what is the value of the battery voltage?
2-20 In Fig. 2-21*d* a d-c voltmeter with a sensitivity of 1 kilohm per volt is connected to the *AB* terminals. The voltmeter reads 5 volts. It has the following ranges: 1, 3, 5, 10, 30, 100, and 300 volts. What range is the voltmeter on?
2-21 In order to measure the voltage across the *AB* terminals of Fig. 2-21*a* with a loading accuracy of 99 percent, what is the minimum voltmeter input resistance permissible?
2-22 If the voltage across the *AB* terminals of Fig. 2-21*b* is to be measured with less than 5 percent loading error, what is the minimum allowable voltmeter resistance?
2-23 For the simple ohmmeter of Fig. 2-22*a*, which uses a 1-ma 50-ohm meter movement, what is the value of R_s that produces full-scale current?

2-24 If a 50-μa movement is used in Fig. 2-22a, what value of ohms is marked at midscale? At quarter scale?

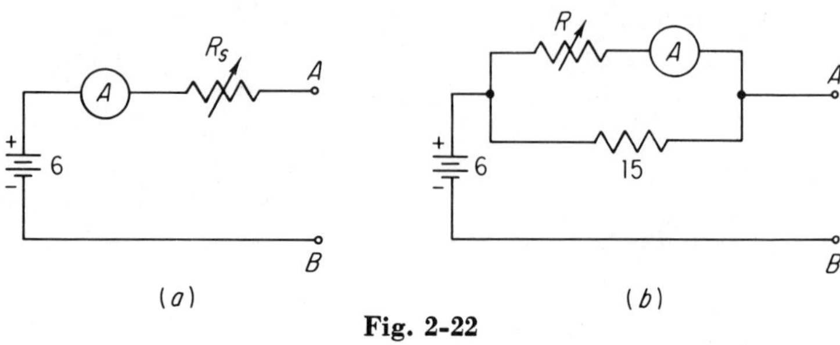

Fig. 2-22

2-25 In Fig. 2-22a the meter movement has a full-scale current of 1 ma; therefore, the midscale value of ohms is 6 kilohms. If the battery ages down to 5 volts, what will a 6-kilohm resistor actually read?

2-26 Figure 2-22b is the circuit of an ohmmeter. If the meter is a 50-μa 2-kilohm movement, what is the value of R after zeroing the ohmmeter? What is the Thévenin resistance of the ohmmeter? If the battery ages down to 5 volts, what will a 15-ohm resistor read?

2-27 In the circuit of Fig. 2-22a, what is the deflection as a percent of full scale if a resistance of 20 kilohms is measured? (Use a meter movement of 1 ma.)

3 Diodes

Diodes are devices of the greatest importance to electronic instrumentation. They are widely used in a-c voltmeters, in clipping and clamping circuits, in voltage regulators, in computer applications, and so on into an endless list. It is assumed that the reader already has a basic knowledge of vacuum-tube diodes. As a result, the emphasis will be upon semiconductor diodes. Since we lack the time to examine the solid-state physics behind diode operation, we examine instead the diode as a circuit device, that is, in terms of its voltage-current characteristics. The background theory developed in this chapter will make it easier to analyze the many diode circuits that will be encountered throughout this book.

3-1 Real Diodes

A diode is a device that passes current more easily in one direction than in the other. The schematic symbol for a semiconductor diode is shown in Fig. 3-1*a*. Note that conventional current passes easily from the anode to the cathode in any rectifier diode. To help remember this, note that the *triangle* points in the easy direction of conventional current.

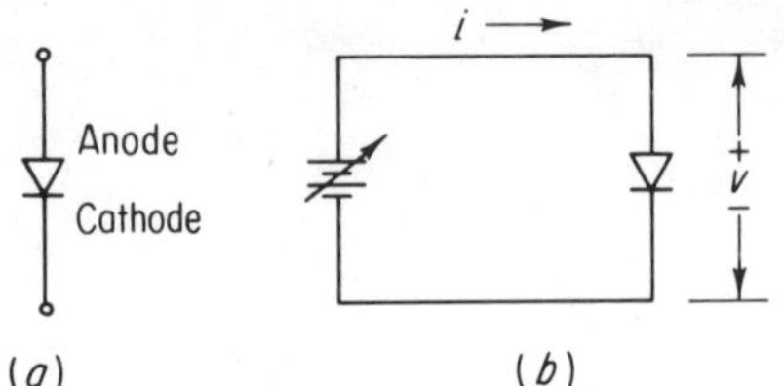

Fig. 3-1 (*a*) Schematic symbol for a semiconductor diode. (*b*) Obtaining the *iv* characteristics.

Imagine that we connect the circuit of Fig. 3-1*b*. The power supply is adjustable, so that different values of current can be produced. The diode in the figure may be any typical semiconductor junction diode. As we increase the battery voltage from zero to higher values, a current begins to flow through the diode. The current will rise very slowly at first, but after the battery has been increased to a few tenths of a volt, the current will increase quite rapidly, as shown in Fig. 3-2*a*. The knee of this curve will depend upon the material used in the diode. Common materials are germanium and silicon. For a germanium diode we find that the voltage V_K at the knee of the curve is approximately 0.3 volt, whereas for a silicon diode it is approximately 0.7 volt. These numbers are intended only as guides, indicating that for a germanium diode at least 0.3 volt must be dropped across it before any appreciable current can flow, whereas for silicon at least 0.7 volt is required for significant current flow.

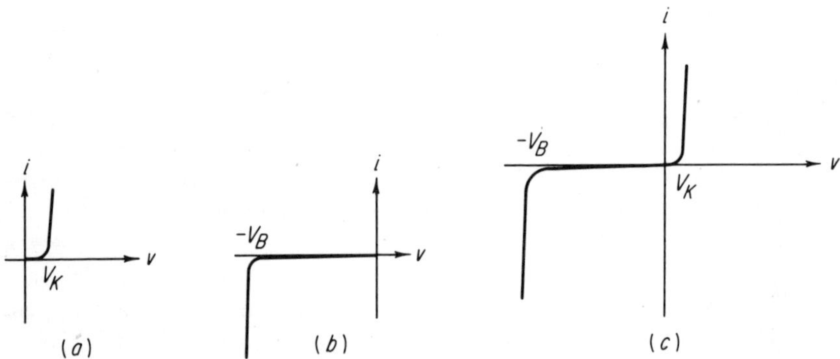

Fig. 3-2 (*a*) The forward *iv* characteristic. (*b*) The reverse *iv* characteristic. (*c*) The composite *iv* characteristic.

Suppose we now reverse the direction of the battery from that shown in Fig. 3-1*b*. As we increase the battery from zero to higher values, we discover that very little current flows through the diode. In fact, the battery voltage could be increased to a very large value before any appreciable current flow would occur, as indicated by Fig. 3-2*b*. Note that the graph has been shown to the left of the origin since the value of v is negative as a result of reversing the battery. Similarly, i is shown as negative because current is flowing in the opposite direction from that shown in

Fig. 3-1*b*. The approximate value of reverse voltage where current flow begins to become large is called the *breakdown voltage*. This value varies from one type of diode to another, taking on values from a few volts to hundreds of volts.

In Fig. 3-2*c* the graphs for the forward and reverse characteristics have been combined into a single graph. This overall picture agrees with our notion of what a diode should do, namely, the current flows more easily in one direction than in the other. Note that a typical semiconductor diode is not perfect, since a small voltage drop occurs in the forward direction, and a small reverse current flows in the reverse direction. Furthermore, if too much voltage is applied in the reverse direction, the diode breaks down. This breakdown voltage is analogous to the peak inverse voltage of a vacuum-tube diode.

We might think that germanium diodes, having a lower knee voltage than silicon diodes, would always be preferred. They are not. One important advantage of silicon over germanium is that the reverse current is generally much smaller. The importance of this advantage depends upon the specific circuit application. The point is that both diodes are commonly used.

3-2 Ideal Diodes

The current-voltage characteristics of vacuum tubes are published in various manuals. With these graphs it is possible to apply graphical techniques, such as load lines, to obtain information on how the vacuum tube will behave in a circuit.

The current-voltage characteristics of semiconductor diodes are not generally published in the form of graphs. As a result, the load-line approach is not practical for semiconductor diodes. Furthermore, the use of graphical techniques is difficult and time-consuming, usually not worth the effort since much easier and faster methods of analysis are available.

In this section we want to develop an approximation for the real diode. Consider Fig. 3-2*c*. What characteristics of this graph make the real diode imperfect? Certainly the reverse current and the breakdown are undesirable. Also, the small voltage drop in the forward direction is an imperfection. If we had a diode with none of these obvious defects, that diode would be ideal.

The graph of an ideal-diode characteristic is shown in Fig. 3-3*a*. Note that there is no voltage drop in the forward direction and no reverse current or breakdown in the reverse direction.

The circuit equivalent of the ideal diode is shown in Fig. 3-3*b*. Note that the ideal diode is equivalent to a switch. The switch is closed whenever the diode is forward-biased. In other words, if the ideal diode is in

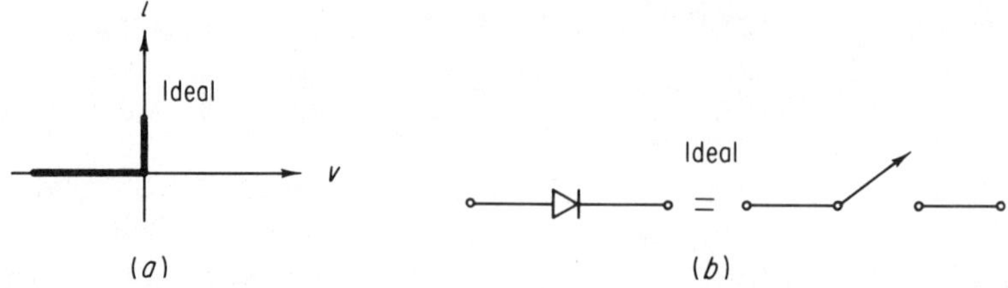

Fig. 3-3 (*a*) Ideal-diode characteristic. (*b*) Circuit equivalent of an ideal diode.

a circuit where the conventional current is trying to flow in the direction of the triangle, the switch is closed. If the conventional current is trying to flow against the direction of the triangle, the switch is open.

Of course, the ideal diode does not exist. It is merely a convenient and simple approximation of the behavior of a real diode. We will use the ideal-diode approximation whenever we wish to obtain a basic idea of how diode circuits operate. Occasionally the answers we obtain by using the ideal diode in the place of a real diode will be grossly inaccurate. However, we will find that in many typical diode circuits, mentally replacing all real diodes by ideal diodes permits a rapid and reasonably accurate insight into the circuit operation. In any event, succeeding sections will deal with improved approximations of real diodes, so that if there is some doubt as to the answers obtained by the ideal-diode approach, the answers can be refined by better approximations of the real diode.

EXAMPLE 3-1

In Fig. 3-4*a* we have replaced a real diode by an ideal diode. Sketch the output voltage across the resistor.

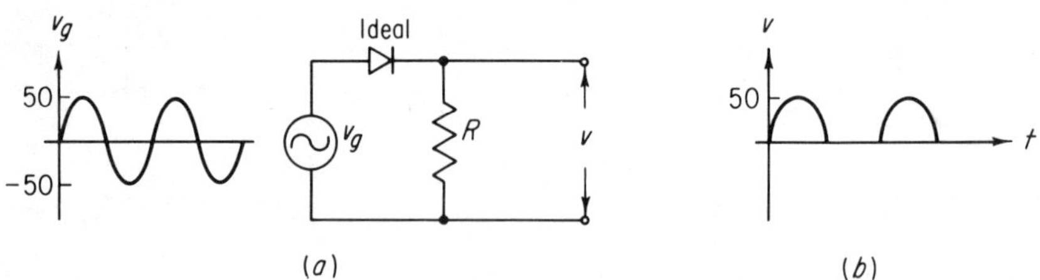

Fig. 3-4 Example 3-1.

SOLUTION

During the positive half cycle of input voltage, the current is trying to flow in the direction of the triangle. Therefore, the diode acts as a closed switch, and the output voltage equals the input voltage.

During the negative half cycle of input voltage, the current is trying to flow against the direction of the triangle. As a result, the diode acts as an open switch. With no current flow, the voltage across the resistor must be zero.

The sketch for the output voltage is shown in Fig. 3-4*b*. This is the standard half-wave-rectified sine wave.

EXAMPLE 3-2

In Fig. 3-5*a* sketch the output voltage using the ideal-diode approximation. The generator signal is a sine wave with a peak value of 50 volts.

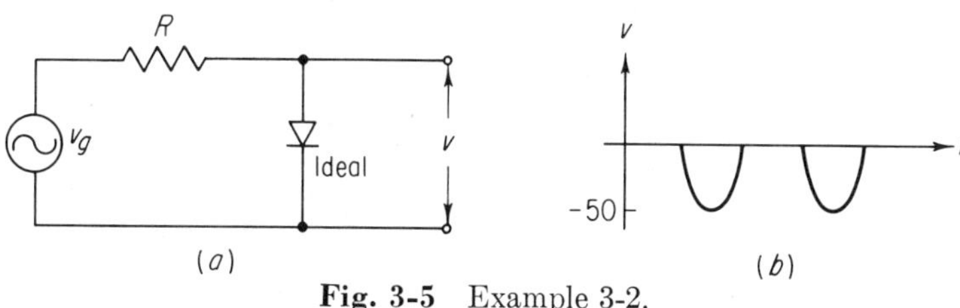

Fig. 3-5 Example 3-2.

SOLUTION

During the positive half cycle, the current is trying to flow in the direction of the triangle. Therefore, the diode acts as a closed switch. The voltage across a closed switch is zero. Therefore, during the entire positive half cycle, the output voltage is zero.

During the negative half cycle, the current is trying to flow against the direction of the triangle. As a result, the diode acts as an open switch. If the switch is open, no current can flow through the resistor. Therefore, there can be no voltage drop across the resistor, and the generator signal must appear at the output terminals.

The sketch of output voltage is illustrated in Fig. 3-5*b*.

The circuit of Fig. 3-5 is commonly known as a positive clipper, simply because it clips off the positive parts of the input signal. Any waveshape input may be used with the same result, namely, all positive parts of the input signal will be clipped off.

EXAMPLE 3-3

Sketch the output voltage for the circuit of Fig. 3-6*a*. The generator signal is a sine wave with a 100-volt peak.

SOLUTION

As the input signal increases from 0 to 25 volts, the battery voltage is larger than the input, with the result that current is trying to flow against the triangle. Therefore, as long as the input is less than 25 volts, the diode is open, and no current flows through the resistor.

With no current flow through the resistor the generator voltage appears at the output terminals.

Whenever the generator signal is greater than 25 volts, the current is in the direction of the triangle, so that the diode is shorted. With the diode shorted, the output terminals are directly across the battery. Therefore, the output voltage must be 25 volts. The difference between the generator voltage and the 25-volt output is dropped across the resistor. For instance, at the peak the input voltage is 100, the output is 25, and the remaining 75 volts appear across the resistor.

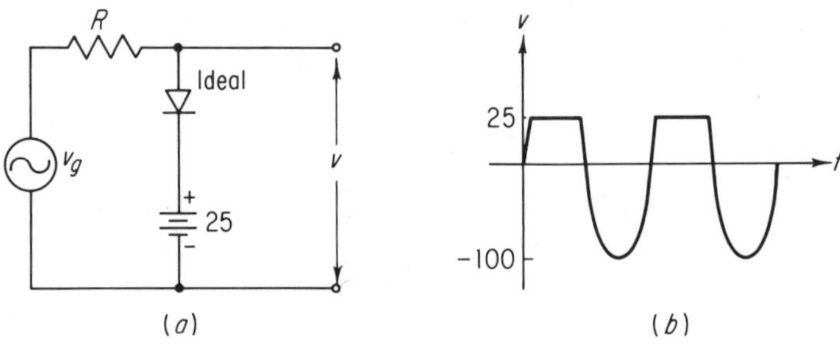

Fig. 3-6 Example 3-3.

The sketch of output voltage is shown in Fig. 3-6*b*. Note that this is a modified form of the positive clipper of Example 3-2. By using a battery in series with the diode, we have moved the clipping level up to 25 volts. If the battery voltage is changed to 40 volts, the output will be clipped at the 40-volt level.

Once again, we can generalize the operation of this circuit by saying that it clips off all positive parts above the clipping level. The clipping level is equal to the battery voltage.

Example 3-4

Sketch the output voltage for the circuit of Fig. 3-7*a*. The generator signal is a sine-wave signal with a peak value of 75 volts.

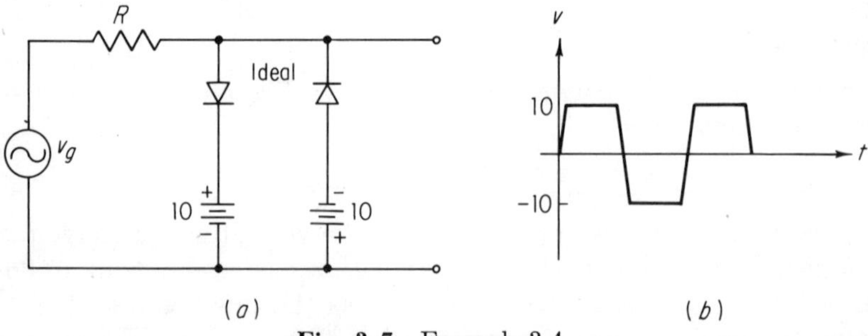

Fig. 3-7 Example 3-4.

SOLUTION

The diode-battery combination on the left is a positive clipper with a clipping level of 10 volts. The diode-battery combination on the right is a negative clipper with a clipping level of −10 volts. Therefore, the output will be a sine-wave signal with all positive parts above 10 volts and all negative parts below −10 volts clipped off. The sketch is shown in Fig. 3-7*b*.

3-3 The Second Approximation of a Real Diode

In general, the ideal-diode approximation yields reasonably good answers if the generator signal driving the circuit is large compared to the small drop in the forward direction that takes place in a real diode. In the examples of preceding section, the generator voltage was on the order of 50 volts or more, so that intuitively we feel it is reasonable to neglect the small drop in the forward direction.

As a refinement, we can improve on the ideal-diode approximation by making some allowance for the forward voltage drop. Figure 3-8*a* indicates a simple refinement. For a germanium diode we will allow 0.3 volt

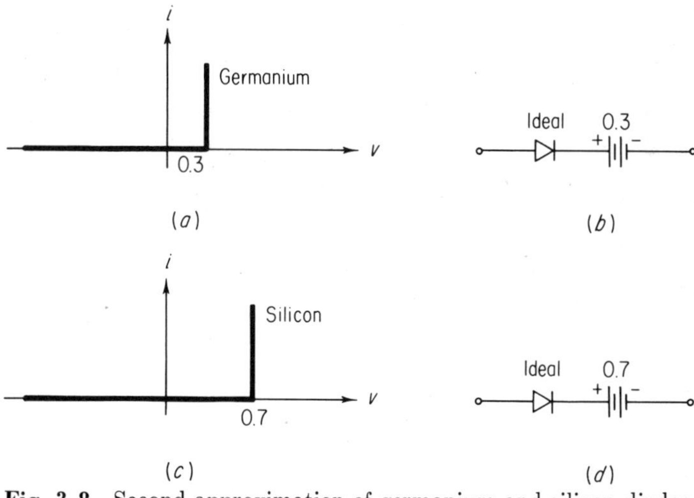

Fig. 3-8 Second approximation of germanium and silicon diodes.

for the forward voltage drop. The circuit interpretation is that of an ideal diode in series with a 0.3-volt battery, as shown in Fig. 3-8*b*. This refinement merely means that we now view the real diode as a switch that closes whenever 0.3 volt is applied across it. In other words, the combination of an ideal diode and a battery shown in Fig. 3-8*b* indicates that whenever the current is trying to flow in the direction of the triangle, the ideal diode is shorted and the combination becomes a 0.3-volt battery. On the other hand, if current is trying to flow against the triangle, the ideal diode is open and the combination becomes an open circuit.

Similar statements may be made of the silicon diode, except that we allow 0.7 volt for the forward voltage drop, as shown in Fig. 3-8*c* and *d*.

Example 3-5

Sketch the output waveshape for the circuit of Fig. 3-9*a*. The generator signal is a sine wave with a 5-volt peak. Use the second approximation of the real diode.

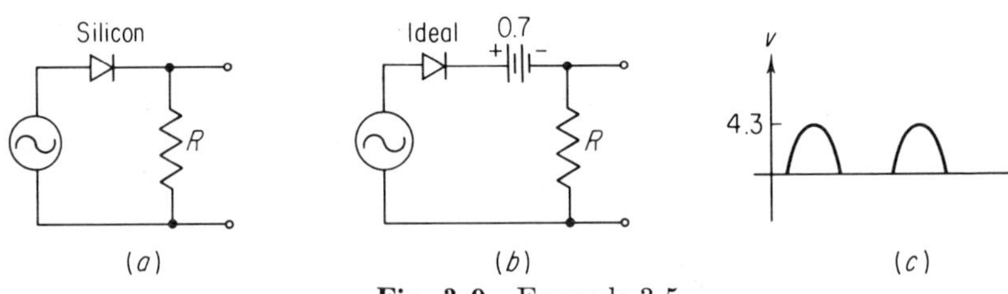

Fig. 3-9 Example 3-5.

Solution

We replace the real diode by the ideal diode–battery combination shown in Fig. 3-9*b*.

As the generator signal builds up from 0 to 0.7 volt, the 0.7-volt battery is larger than the input signal. Therefore, the current is trying to flow against the triangle, and the diode is open. Hence, the output is 0 volts. Once the generator signal exceeds 0.7 volt, the current flows in the direction of the triangle, and therefore the diode is shorted. The output voltage will then be equal to the input minus 0.7 volt.

Once the generator voltage drops below 0.7 volt, the diode opens, and the output voltage is zero. The sketch for the output waveshape is shown in Fig. 3-9*c*.

Example 3-6

A silicon diode is used in the positive clipper of Fig. 3-10*a*. Sketch the output waveshape if the input is:

(*a*) a sine wave with a peak value of 5 volts.

(*b*) a square wave with a peak value of 5 volts.

Solution

Visualize the silicon diode as an ideal diode in series with a 0.7-volt battery. It should be clear that the diode is shorted for any value of input above 0.7 volt and open for any value of input below 0.7 volt. In other words, the circuit is a positive clipper with a clipping level of 0.7 volt. The waveshapes for each type of input signal are shown in Fig. 3-10*b* and *c*.

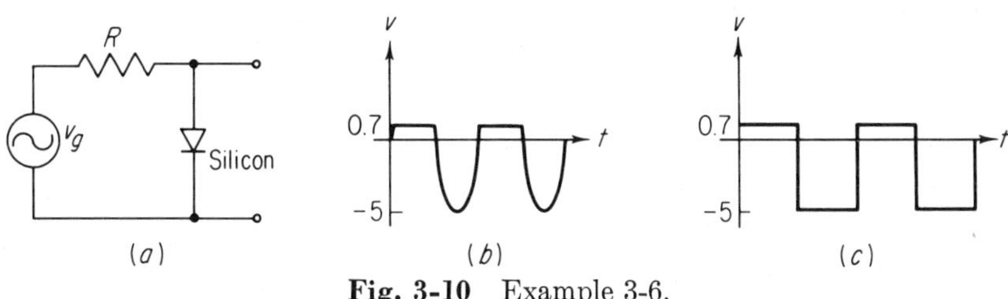

Fig. 3-10 Example 3-6.

3-4 The Third Approximation of a Real Diode

Still another approximation can be made for a real diode to account more accurately for its forward voltage drop. Referring to Fig. 3-2*c*, we see that the forward characteristic is not a vertical line. It has a slope, which implies the presence of resistance in the diode, so that as more current occurs in the forward direction, more voltage drop appears across the diode.

The graph in Fig. 3-11*a* more closely resembles the real-diode characteristic in the forward direction and means that the diode turns on

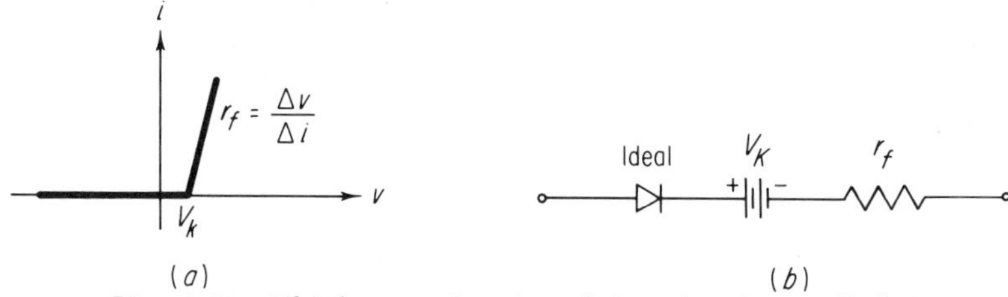

Fig. 3-11 Third approximation of a semiconductor diode.

above the value of V_K (0.3 or 0.7 volt). Once the diode is on, it acts like a resistor with a value of r_f. The value r_f is obtained by choosing any two points on the line and calculating the ratio of the change in voltage between the two points divided by the change in current. For instance, a manufacturer's data sheet generally gives the value of forward current I_F for a 1-volt drop. A typical data sheet might indicate a forward current I_F of 20 ma at 1 volt for a germanium diode. In this case, we could pick the knee of the curve as one point and use the data at 1 volt for the other point, obtaining

$$r_f = \frac{\Delta v}{\Delta i} = \frac{1 - 0.3}{20(10^{-3})} = 35 \text{ ohms}$$

This value of r_f can now be used as a guide in determining how much additional voltage drop occurs across the diode as the current in the diode increases.

Figure 3-11*b* illustrates our circuit representation. If current is trying to flow in the direction of the triangle, the ideal diode is a short. The combination becomes simply a battery and a resistor in series. For small currents, the net drop across the combination is around the knee-voltage value. As the current increases, additional voltage drop occurs across the resistor. This is not surprising, since it dovetails with the information contained in the graph of Fig. 3-11*a*.

EXAMPLE 3-7

Sketch the output for the circuit of Fig. 3-12*a*. The generator signal is a sine wave with a 10-volt peak. The diode is germanium and has a forward resistance r_f of 25 ohms.

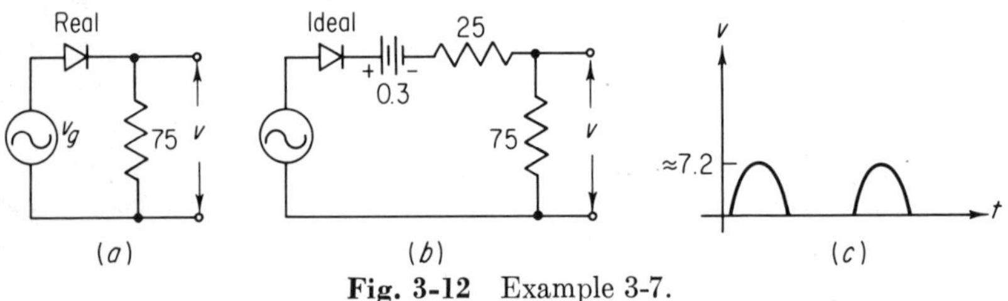

Fig. 3-12 Example 3-7.

SOLUTION

We have replaced the real germanium diode by its third approximation, as shown in Fig. 3-12*b*. The ideal diode will not turn on until the generator voltage is greater than 0.3 volt. Current begins to flow in the circuit, and it should be clear that the 25- and 75-ohm resistors form a voltage divider. At the instant the input reaches its peak of 10 volts, the output will be

$$v \cong 10 - 0.3 - 2.5 = 7.2 \text{ volts}$$

In other words, at the peak value of input 0.3 volt is accounted for by the battery (knee of curve), and about 2.5 volts are dropped across the forward resistance (slope of diode graph). Hence, only 7.2 volts are delivered to the output as shown in Fig. 3-12*c*.

Note that had we immediately used the ideal-diode approximation instead of the third approximation, we simply would have said that the output was a half-wave-rectified sine wave with a peak value of 10 volts. The error in our answer by the ideal-diode approach would have been appreciable, but still it can be argued that even though the ideal-diode approach is crude and produces significant error in some circuits, we still would have had approximately the correct waveshape, which in troubleshooting is all we generally require.

3-5 Some Perspective on the Three Diode Approximations

Perhaps it is already clear that the first approximation (ideal diode only) is adequate if the external driving voltages are much greater than the value of the knee voltage and if the diode resistance is much smaller than the circuit resistance. This is precisely the point. If the external voltages are in tens of volts, then certainly a 0.3- or 0.7-volt drop in the diode is negligible. Similarly, if the net circuit resistance in series with a diode is in kilohms, while the diode resistance is in tens of ohms, then the latter resistance is negligible.

Let us summarize the use of the three approximations.

1. In analyzing any diode circuit, start with the ideal-diode approximation. This allows a rapid determination of what the circuit does. The ideal-diode approximation is adequate for many situations.
2. If the answers obtained by the use of the ideal diode indicate that 0.3 or 0.7 volt may be significant, reanalyze the circuit using the second approximation.
3. If the circuit resistance in series with the diode is not large compared to the forward resistance of the diode, use the third approximation.

3-6 Approximating the Reverse Current

In obtaining a basic idea of how a diode circuit operates we generally disregard the reverse current entirely. For a more refined answer, however, we must make some allowance for the fact that reverse current can flow in the back direction. We will use a very *simple* approximation for this reverse current, merely viewing the diode as a large resistance whose value can be obtained by dividing any given reverse voltage by the corresponding current. For instance, if a data sheet indicates that the reverse current I_R is 50 μa at -50 volts, we compute a back resistance of 1 megohm.

It must be remembered that the back resistance is applicable up to the breakdown voltage. Once the diode is in the breakdown region, we will use a better approximation to describe its behavior.

Example 3-8

In Fig. 3-13*a* the generator signal is a sine wave with a 10-volt peak. The diode is germanium and has the following characteristics: breakdown voltage $V_B = 80$ volts, $I_F = 30$ ma at 1 volt, and $I_R = 50\ \mu$a at -50 volts.

Sketch the output waveshape, taking reverse current into account.

Solution

Immediately, from the ideal-diode approach we see that the output will resemble a half-wave-rectified sine wave. We now proceed to make small corrections by taking into account the forward resistance, the knee voltage drop, and the reverse-current effects.

First, we compute the forward resistance.

$$r_f = \frac{1 - 0.3}{30(10^{-3})} = 23 \text{ ohms}$$

This value of r_f is so small compared to the circuit resistance of 10 kilohms that we may neglect it.

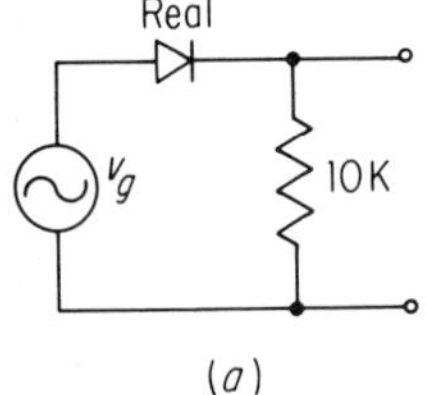

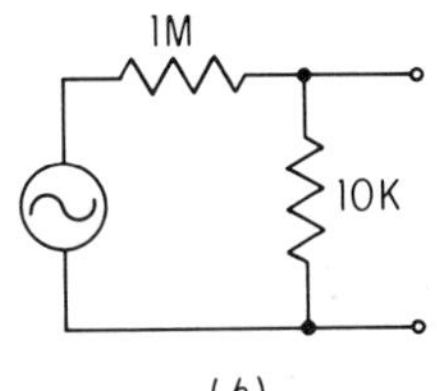

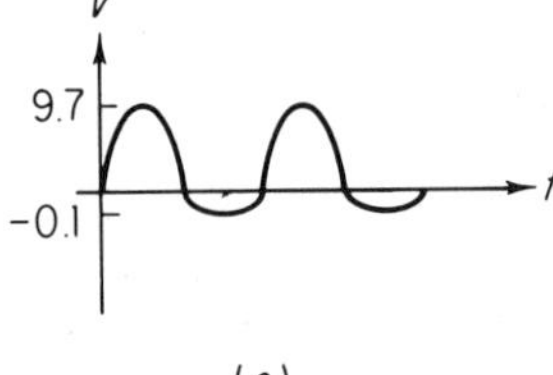

Fig. 3-13 Example 3-8.

Second, we correct for the knee voltage drop by subtracting 0.3 volt from 10 volts to obtain an output peak value of 9.7 volts.

Third, during the negative half cycle of input signal, the diode is reverse-biased. The maximum voltage across the diode in the reverse direction is 10 volts, so that there is no danger of breakdown since V_B equals 80 volts. We can replace the diode by a 1-megohm resistor, as shown in Fig. 3-13*b*. From this circuit it should be clear that the voltage across the 10-kilohm resistor is negative and equals 0.1 volt at the peak.

The final sketch is shown in Fig. 3-13*c*. If the 0.1-volt level in the negative direction is objectionable, we can change to a silicon diode, for which reverse currents are generally much smaller.

Note also that the role of reverse current becomes more important as the load-resistor value increases. In this case, for example, if the load resistor is increased to 500 kilohms, the voltage across it may become as large as 3.3 volts. This is undesirable if the circuit is intended as a half-wave rectifier. The use of a diode with a much lower reverse current is then essential.

3-7 Zener Diodes

We may be tempted to think that diodes are always used as rectifying devices and that there is no use for the breakdown phenomenon that takes place in the reverse direction. On the contrary, there is a very important use for it. By careful manufacturing techniques the breakdown can be made to have a very sharp knee. Furthermore, the graph of the breakdown portion can be made almost vertical, as shown in Fig. 3-14*a*. Such

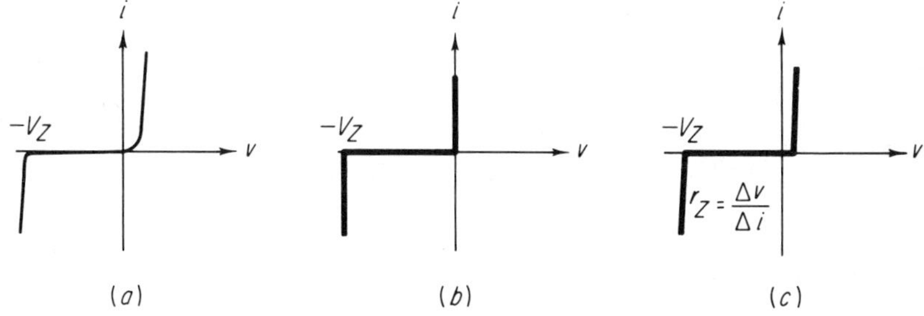

Fig. 3-14 (*a*) Zener-diode characteristic. (*b*) Ideal zener-diode characteristic. (*c*) Second approximation of zener-diode characteristic.

diodes are called *zener diodes*. The voltage V_Z is the approximate value where breakdown occurs. Note that if enough reverse voltage has been applied to cause breakdown, the diode will be operating along the almost vertical breakdown portion of Fig. 3-14*a*. The exact value of breakdown current will be dependent upon the external circuitry connected to the diode. The point is that the diode is not immediately destroyed because breakdown has occurred. If *enough* current flows so that the product of this current and the breakdown voltage exceeds the diode's power rating, then the diode will certainly burn out. We must be careful, then, to remain below the critical burnout current. If we do this, we will have a diode whose voltage is almost constant and whose current may be anywhere between zero current and the value of burnout current.

To obtain an ideal representation of the zener diode, let us replace the real graph of Fig. 3-14*a* by the ideal graph of Fig. 3-14*b*. This would be the first approximation of the zener diode. Note carefully what this graph implies: if the diode is in the breakdown region, the voltage across it is constant, whereas the current can take on any value.

What simple circuit device has the behavior described above? The ideal battery is a device whose voltage is constant whereas the current can take on any value, depending upon the external circuitry connected to the battery. Therefore, if we like, we may visualize the zener diode in the breakdown region as an ideal battery with a voltage of V_Z.

In Fig. 3-15*a* is shown the schematic symbol often used to indicate that the diode has been specially processed to have the sharp-breakdown

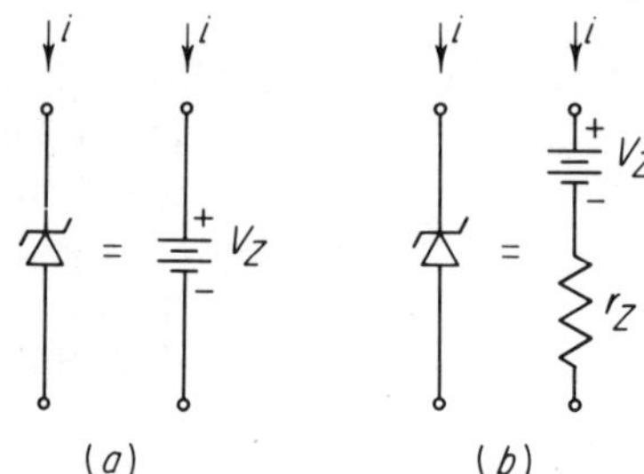

Fig. 3-15 (*a*) Circuit equivalent for ideal zener diode. (*b*) Circuit equivalent for second approximation of zener diode.

characteristic. Note carefully the polarity of the zener diode and the corresponding battery. Current flows against the triangle, since the zener diode operates in the reverse region. Furthermore, in the equivalent battery the conventional current always flows into the battery. Remember that we are not saying that the ideal zener diode is a battery. We are saying that it behaves like a battery insofar as its current-voltage characteristics are concerned. With this simple approximation we can rapidly determine what a zener-diode circuit does.

The first approximation of the zener diode is adequate for establishing the basic idea of how a zener-diode circuit operates. To improve the approximation we take the slope of the real graph into account.

Figure 3-14*c* shows the second approximation of the zener-diode graph. If the diode is operating in the breakdown region, we see that at the knee of the graph, the voltage is equal to V_Z. As current increases, the voltage across the zener diode increases slightly. To take this increase in voltage into account, we may say that the zener diode has internal resistance, so that as more current flows, more voltage appears across the diode.

The equivalent circuit for the second approximation is shown in Fig. 3-15*b*. Once again, note carefully the polarity of voltage and the direction of current. This equivalent circuit behaves as indicated by the graph of Fig. 3-14*c*. At the knee of the graph the current is zero, and the voltage is V_Z. This agrees with the equivalent circuit. If the current increases, additional voltage appears across the diode. Both the graph and the equivalent circuit indicate this. Hence, the equivalent circuit is reasonable and can be used as a second approximation of a zener diode that is in the breakdown region.

The zener diode is a very useful and important device. Typically, breakdown voltages from about 3 to 200 volts in steps of about 10 percent are available. Thus, for any circuit in which we need a constant-voltage device, we can consider using the zener diode. It is important, of course, to remember that the zener diode is not a real battery, which can deliver power to a circuit. It behaves like a battery that always absorbs power from the circuit.

The value of r_Z is normally given on the manufacturer's data sheet, as well as the value of breakdown voltage and the burnout current.

Let us summarize our procedure for dealing with zener-diode circuits.

1. First, make sure that the diode is in the breakdown region. This is done by noting whether or not the open-circuit voltage at the zener terminals is greater than the zener voltage.
2. If the zener diode is in the breakdown region, replace the diode by an ideal battery. This is the first approximation and will allow a rapid determination of how the circuit operates.
3. If necessary, use the second approximation. (Generally, if the zener resistance is much smaller than the circuit resistance in series with the zener diode, the second approximation is unnecessary.)

Example 3-9

The circuit of Fig. 3-16*a* is a zener-diode voltage regulator. Find the current through the zener diode. Also, find the Thévenin equivalent for the circuit at the *AB* terminals, using the second approximation. The burnout current of the zener diode is 30 ma.

Solution

First, we note that the zener diode must be in the breakdown region, since the 50-volt battery is larger than the zener breakdown of 30 volts. Hence, we may use the ideal zener-diode approximation (Fig. 3-16*b*) to obtain an initial idea as to how the circuit operates.

In Fig. 3-16*b* the voltage across the *AB* terminals is 30 volts. Since the power-supply voltage is 50 volts, 20 volts must appear across the 2-kilohm resistor. Hence the current through the resistor and zener diode must be equal to 10 ma. Note that this value of current is well below the burnout value of 30 ma. Hence, the zener diode behaves like a 30-volt battery with a charging current of 10 ma.

Why is this circuit a voltage regulator? Note that the voltage across the *AB* terminals remains at approximately 30 volts even if the 50-volt power supply changes value. For instance, if the power supply changes from 50 to 70 volts, the zener diode still has a breakdown voltage of 30 volts. The additional voltage is dropped across the 2-kilohm resistor. In this case, 40 volts will appear across the 2-kilohm resistor. The current increases to 20 ma, which is still below the burnout current of 30 ma. Hence, the zener diode will maintain the voltage across the *AB* terminals at about 30 volts in spite of power-supply changes.

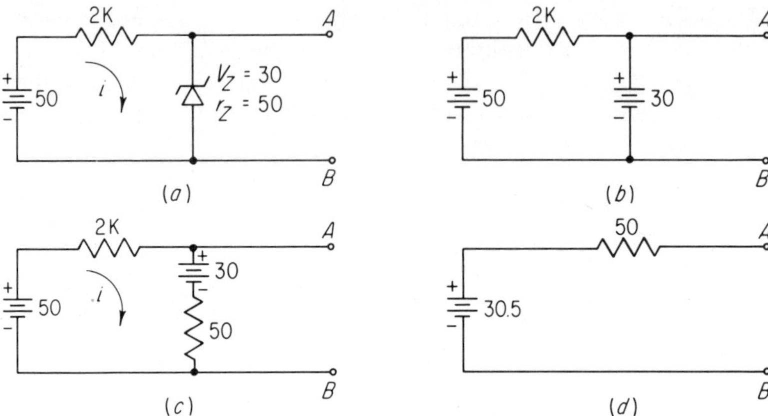

Fig. 3-16 Example 3-9.

In Fig. 3-16*c* the second approximation of the zener diode is shown. The 50-ohm resistor will account for the fact that the breakdown in a zener diode is not exactly a vertical characteristic. We observe that the current is

$$i = \frac{50 - 30}{2000 + 50} = \frac{20}{2050} = 9.75 \text{ ma}$$

Note that for practical purposes the value of current obtained by the first approximation (10 ma) is essentially correct, being in error only by 2.5 percent.

The voltage across the AB terminals is the sum of the zener voltage and the voltage across the 50-ohm resistor, or

$$v = 30 + 9.75(10^{-3})50 = 30.5 \text{ volts}$$

The voltage across the AB terminals is slightly higher than 30 volts. If the power supply changes from 50 to 70 volts, we already know that the current increases to about 20 ma. This will increase the drop across the 50-ohm resistor to 1 volt. Hence, the voltage across the AB terminals will become 31 volts. Note what this means. The power supply has changed from 50 to 70 volts, but the AB voltage has changed only from 30.5 to 31 volts. Voltage regulation is one of the major uses of the zener diode.

Finally, we obtain a Thévenin equivalent for the AB terminals. With the power supply at 50 volts, we already know that the voltage across the AB terminals is 30.5 volts. To obtain the Thévenin resistance we short all ideal batteries and compute the resistance from A to B. Clearly, this resistance is 50 ohms in parallel with 2 kilohms, which is approximately 50 ohms.

The Thévenin equivalent is shown in Fig. 3-16*d*. Note that we can use this equivalent to determine how much current would flow through an external load resistor. One word of caution is in order. The Thévenin equivalent is valid as long as the zener diode remains in the breakdown region. If the load resistor draws too much current, the zener diode will no longer remain in the breakdown region. Example 3-10 brings this point out.

EXAMPLE 3-10

A load resistor of 30 kilohms is connected to the *AB* terminals of the voltage regulator shown in Fig. 3-16*a*. Find the voltage across this resistor and the current through the zener diode.

A load resistor of 4 kilohms is connected to the *AB* terminals. Find the voltage across it and the current through the zener diode.

SOLUTION

Note in Fig. 3-16*a* that as long as the zener diode is in the breakdown region, the voltage across the 2-kilohm resistor must be 20 volts, and the current through this resistor must be 10 ma. As long as no external load resistor is connected, 10 ma of current must pass through the zener diode.

If a 30-kilohm resistor is now connected to the *AB* terminals, as shown in Fig. 3-17*a*, the voltage across it must be approximately 30 volts, and the current through it must be 1 ma. Since the current in the 2-kilohm resistor must remain at 10 ma, we conclude that the diode current must have dropped from 10 to 9 ma. This point should always be remembered, namely, the current through the 2-kilohm resistor equals the sum of the zener-diode current and the load current. As

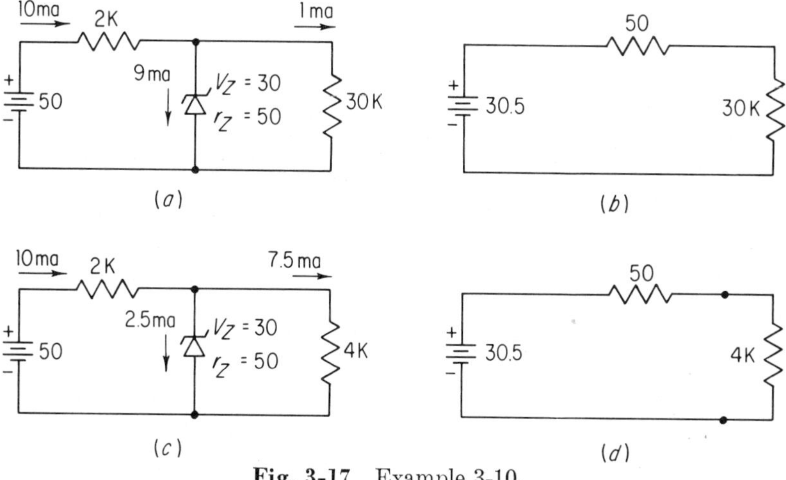

Fig. 3-17 Example 3-10.

the load current increases, the zener-diode current must decrease. In order to remain in the breakdown region, however, the zener current must be slightly greater than zero. Hence, there is a maximum amount of current that can be delivered to a load resistor before the zener diode comes out of the breakdown region.

In any event, the zener diode is still in the breakdown region, and we can use the Thévenin equivalent of Fig. 3-17*b*. The voltage across the 30-kilohm load is

$$v = \frac{30.5}{30{,}050} 30(10^3) = 30.5 \text{ volts}$$

If we now change the load to a 4-kilohm resistor, more current must flow through the load, as shown in Fig. 3-17*c*. For 30 volts across a 4-kilohm resistor, there must be 7.5 ma through it. As long as the diode is in the breakdown region, the current through the 2-kilohm series resistor must remain at 10 ma. Therefore, the diode current is 2.5 ma, as indicated.

We can now use the Thévenin equivalent to obtain a more accurate value of load voltage. Referring to Fig. 3-17*d* we see that the load voltage must be

$$v = \frac{30.5}{4050} 4(10^3) = 30.1 \text{ volts}$$

Note that the load voltage has dropped from 30.5 for a 30-kilohm resistor to 30.1 for a 4-kilohm resistor. Hence, the zener diode has held the load voltage reasonably constant in spite of changes in the load resistance.

Thus, we see that the zener-diode regulator can maintain a constant load voltage under changing power supply and changing load conditions. Of course, there are limits to its ability to correct for changes. For instance, if the load resistor in this example is lower than 3 kilohms, the zener diode will come out of the breakdown region. Furthermore, if the power-supply voltage drops too low, the zener diode will again come out of the breakdown region, and regulation will be lost. On the other hand, the power-supply voltage may become high enough to exceed the zener burnout current. In spite of all these limitations, it is usually possible to select circuit values and arrive at a voltage regulator that is satisfactory in many applications.

Example 3-11

Sketch the output waveshape of the circuit shown in Fig. 3-18*a*. Use the ideal zener-diode approximation (Fig. 3-14*b*). The generator signal is a sine wave with a peak value of 50 volts.

SOLUTION

During the positive half cycle of input signal, the upper diode is merely a short, and all that effectively remains is the lower diode. As long as the generator voltage is less than 6.8 volts, the lower diode will not break down. Hence, there is no current through the 10-kilohm resistor, and the output will equal the generator signal. However, once the generator signal exceeds 6.8 volts, the lower diode breaks down, so that the output voltage is held at 6.8 volts.

During the negative half cycle, the roles of the two diodes are reversed, so that the signal is clipped at −6.8 volts.

Figure 3-18*b* illustrates the output. Note that this circuit is a combination of a positive and negative clipper, and represents one way of obtaining approximate square waves from a sine-wave signal.

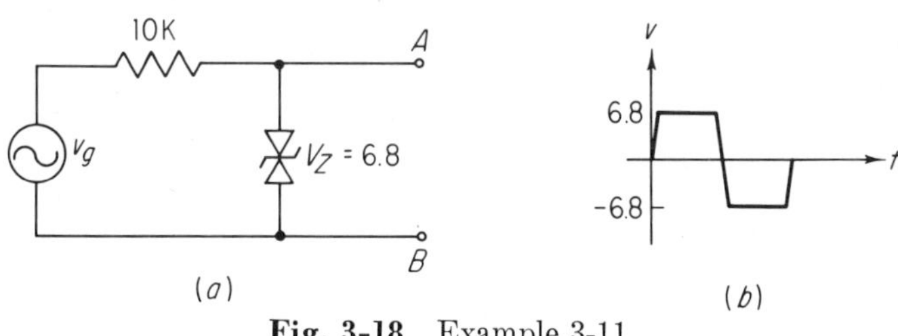

Fig. 3-18 Example 3-11.

The circuit of Fig. 3-18*a* is often used to regulate the a-c voltage applied to vacuum-tube filaments. For example, the generator signal might be an a-c voltage from a secondary transformer winding. The filament would be connected across the *AB* terminals, so that in spite of line-voltage changes, the filament voltage would remain essentially constant. In certain applications such regulation of the filament voltage is important in order to prevent large shifts in the operating point of a vacuum tube.

SUMMARY

A real diode has a small voltage drop in the forward direction and a small reverse current in the reverse direction. For a large enough reverse voltage a breakdown occurs. In order to deal with the diode efficiently, there are various approximations. The ideal diode is the simplest viewpoint, and treats the diode as an ideal switch. This viewpoint is quite useful and leads to quick insight into diode circuits. Generally, the ideal-diode approach yields excellent answers whenever the external driving voltages are much larger than the diode knee voltage.

The second approximation of the diode takes the knee voltage into account. This correction would be needed for circuits in which the driving voltages are not much larger than the knee voltage.

The third approximation takes both the knee voltage and the diode resistance into account. The diode resistance is important in those circuits where diode resistance is comparable to the circuit resistance.

The reverse current of a diode may be taken into account by approximating the diode as a resistance when back-biased. This resistance can be computed from value of reverse current and the corresponding reverse voltage. This approximation is usable up to the breakdown voltage.

Zener diodes are manufactured so as to have a very sharp breakdown characteristic. The simplest viewpoint of the zener diode is that it behaves like a battery when it is in the breakdown region. As a result, the zener diode is useful in regulating power supplies. It is also useful in providing accurate reference voltages.

The zener diode actually has some resistance, so that the second approximation of the zener diode consists of an ideal battery in series with a resistance, which is specified on data sheets. As long as the circuit resistance is much larger than the zener resistance, the zener resistance causes only a small change in the terminal voltage.

GLOSSARY

breakdown voltage The value of reverse voltage across a diode that causes a significant increase in reverse current.

clipping circuit A circuit that removes portions of the input waveform.

conventional current A mathematical concept of current that flows in the direction opposite to that of electron flow. Conventional current is normally used at all advanced levels of engineering and physics.

forward resistance (r_f) The dynamic, or a-c, resistance of a diode. The value of r_f above the knee is found by dividing a change in voltage by a change in current.

knee voltage Refers to the characteristics of a semiconductor diode. Approximately the value of forward voltage where forward current increases significantly.

reverse current The value of reverse current that flows in a back-biased diode below the breakdown voltage. Some diodes show an almost constant value of reverse current up to the breakdown voltage, whereas others have a reverse current that increases as the reverse voltage is increased.

voltage regulator A device or circuit that reduces the percentage change in a power-supply voltage caused by changes in line voltage or load current.

zener resistance (r_Z) The dynamic, or a-c, resistance of a zener diode operating in the breakdown region. The value of r_Z is found by dividing a change in voltage by a change in current.

zener voltage (V_Z) Approximately the breakdown voltage of a zener diode. Strictly speaking, the zener voltage is given for a specified value of reverse current.

REVIEW QUESTIONS

1. What is an ideal diode?
2. How does a real diode differ from an ideal diode?
3. Does the triangle of the schematic symbol point in the easy direction of electron flow or conventional-current flow?
4. How large is the knee voltage in a germanium diode? In a silicon diode?
5. Does reverse breakdown immediately destroy the diode?
6. What is a positive clipping circuit? A negative clipper?
7. How do you compute the forward resistance of a diode as defined in the third approximation?
8. What is a zener diode?
9. How can we approximate reverse-current effects in a diode?
10. What is the simplest approximation of a zener diode?
11. How is the zener resistance related to the graph of i vs. v in the breakdown region?
12. How do you compute the burnout current of a zener diode given its maximum power dissipation and its zener voltage?

PROBLEMS

3-1 In Fig. 3-19*a* the 1N100 diode is made of germanium and has a forward current of 20 ma at 1 volt.

(*a*) How much current flows if the diode is considered ideal?

(*b*) How much current flows if the diode is approximated by a battery?

(*c*) How much current flows if the battery-resistor approximation is used?

3-2 In Fig. 3-19*b* the diode is back-biased.

(*a*) If the diode is ideal, what is the voltage across it?

(*b*) If the diode is a 1N277 with a reverse current of 0.25 ma at -50 volts, what is the voltage across the diode?

(*c*) If the diode is a 1N1125 with a reverse current of 10 μa at -300 volts, what is the voltage across the diode?

3-3 In the circuit of Fig. 3-19*c*, sketch the output-voltage waveform, labeling the value of the positive and negative peaks.

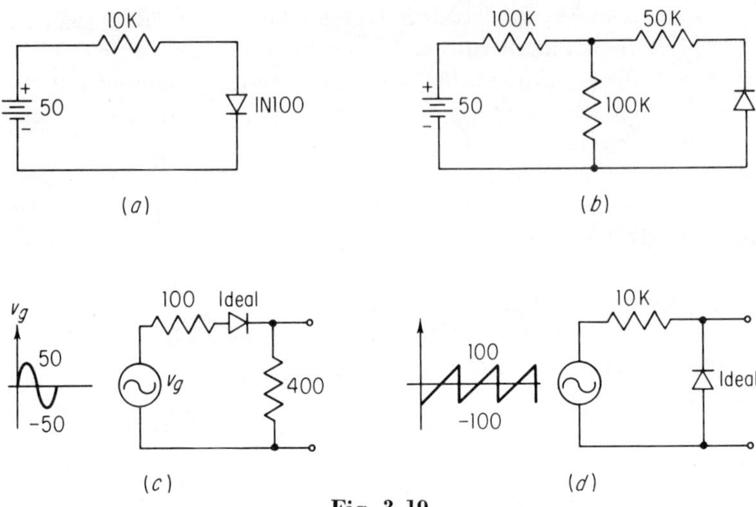

Fig. 3-19

3-4 Repeat Prob. 3-3 replacing the ideal diode by a 1N485, which has a forward current of 100 ma at 1 volt and a reverse current of 5 μa at −175 volts. The 1N485 is made of silicon.

3-5 Sketch the output-voltage waveform for the circuit of Fig. 3-19*d*.

3-6 Sketch the output-voltage waveform for Fig. 3-20*a*. What is the peak value of current through the diode?

3-7 Sketch the output-voltage waveform for the circuit of Fig. 3-20*b*.

3-8 The capacitor of Fig. 3-20*c* is initially charged to 50 volts. Sketch the output-voltage waveform before and after the switch is closed.

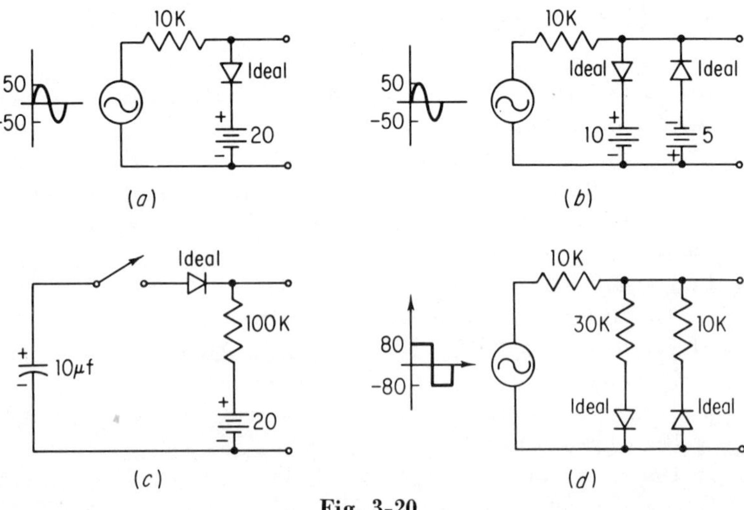

Fig. 3-20

3-9 The capacitor in Fig. 3-20*c* is initially charged to 10 volts. Sketch the output-voltage waveform.

3-10 Sketch the output-voltage waveform for the circuit of Fig. 3-20*d*. What are the positive and negative peak currents in the circuit? If the diodes were made of silicon, what changes would occur in the waveshape?

3-11 The zener diode in Fig. 3-21*a* has a breakdown voltage of 40 volts and a burnout current of 12 ma.

(*a*) What size should R be in order to have 3 ma in the diode?

(*b*) The diode will burn out if R is less than what value?

3-12 In Fig. 3-21*b* the zener voltage is 30 volts.

(*a*) Compute the current through an R_L equal to 5 kilohms.

(*b*) For what value of R_L does regulation cease?

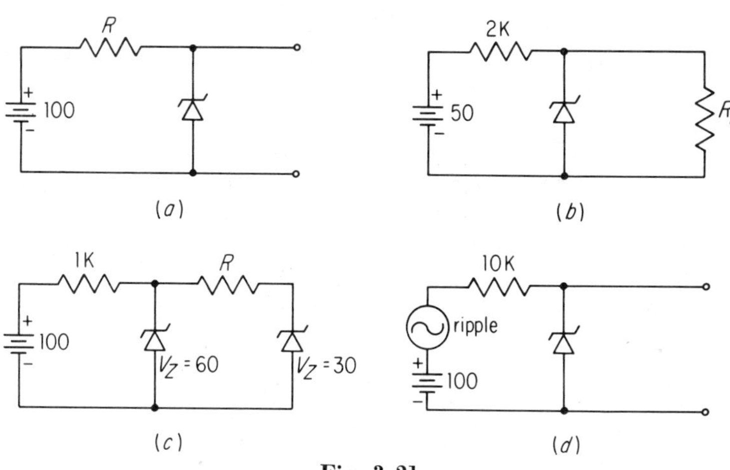

Fig. 3-21

3-13 For the circuit of Fig. 3-21*c*:

(*a*) If the current through the 30-volt zener is 5 ma, what is the value of R?

(*b*) If 5 ma flows through the 30-volt zener diode, how much current flows through the 60-volt zener diode?

3-14 In Fig. 3-21*d* the ripple is 1 volt rms. If the zener diode breaks down at 60 volts and has a zener resistance of 50 ohms, how large is the ripple at the output?

3-15 Sketch the output-voltage waveform for the circuit of Fig. 3-22*a*. What is the maximum current through the zener diode?

3-16 The back-to-back zener diodes of Fig. 3-22*b* have forward-voltage drops of approximately 0.7 volt and breakdown voltages 10 volts. Sketch the output-voltage waveform, labeling the positive and negative peaks.

3-17 If a 50-volt square wave is used instead of a sine wave in Fig. 3-22*b*, what is the output-voltage waveform?

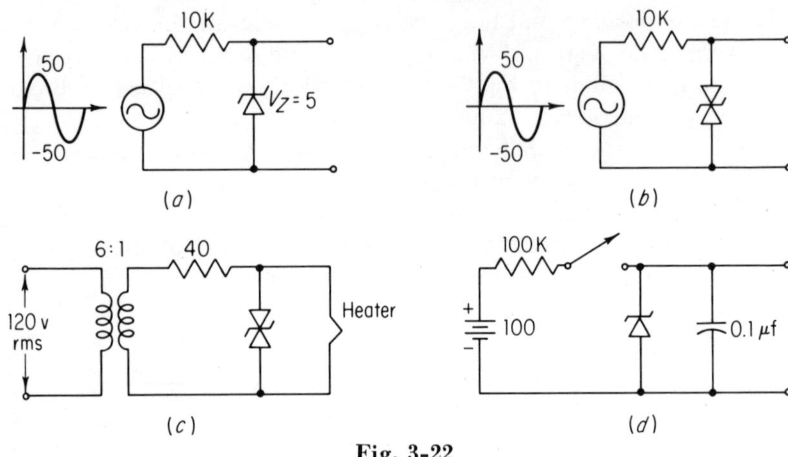

Fig. 3-22

3-18 In Fig. 3-22*c* a zener diode is used to regulate the filament voltage on a critical vacuum tube. The hot resistance of the filament is 30 ohms. The diodes have forward voltages of 0.7 and breakdown voltages of 5.6 volts.

(*a*) What is the rms value of the sine wave on the secondary winding?

(*b*) Sketch the filament-voltage waveform.

(*c*) What is the peak value of current through the zener?

3-19 The zener diode of Fig. 3-22*d* has a breakdown voltage of 60 volts. The capacitor is uncharged before the switch closes. Sketch the waveform of capacitor voltage after the switch is closed.

3-20 If the capacitor in Fig. 3-22*d* is initially charged to 30 volts and the diode has a zener voltage of 50 volts, what is the voltage waveform across the capacitor after the switch closes?

4 A-C Detection

Given an a-c signal, how do we measure its peak value or its rms value? This question often arises in electronics, and we must have an answer.

In this chapter we examine average and peak detectors. Our goal is not only to determine how a simple a-c voltmeter is made but also to acquire a knowledge of the basic detection circuits used in receivers, radar, and various measuring instruments.

4-1 The Simple Half-wave Detector

The simplest type of a-c voltmeter is the half-wave-rectifier circuit shown in Fig. 4-1*a*. The AB terminals are the measuring terminals of this simple a-c voltmeter. The signal being measured is a sine wave with a peak value of V_p. To analyze this circuit we visualize the diode as ideal, and it should then be clear that the diode is shorted during the positive half cycle and open during the negative half cycle. The resulting current through the ammeter is shown in Fig. 4-1*b*.

The half-wave-rectified sine wave of Fig. 4-1*b* has a peak value of

$$I_p = \frac{V_p}{R_s + R_m} \tag{4-1}$$

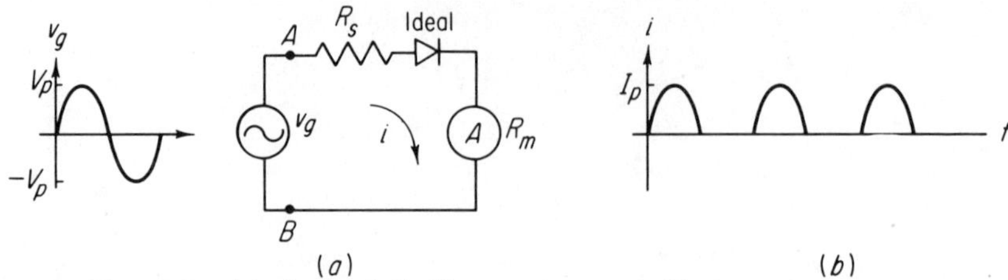

Fig. 4-1 (a) A simple half-wave detector. (b) Ammeter current.

The current of Fig. 4-1b is the actual current through the ammeter. How does a d-c ammeter respond to such a changing current? If the frequency of this current is low enough, the deflection of the d-c ammeter will actually follow the variation in current. The needle will rise to a peak value, return to zero, hold for half a cycle, and then rise again. On the other hand, if the frequency is high enough, the inertia of the moving ammeter parts will prevent the needle from following the variation in current. The needle deflection will converge upon the average value of the current variation.

The average, or d-c, value of a nonsinusoidal waveshape is more fully covered in the chapter on harmonics. For the moment, let us accept the fact that the needle will respond to an average value given by

$$I_{av} = \frac{I_p}{\pi} = 0.318I_p \tag{4-2}$$

Equation (4-2) says that the average, or d-c, value of a half-wave-rectified sine wave is equal to about 31.8 percent of the peak value. Thus, if the peak value of the current is 1 ma, the ammeter will read 0.318 ma.

Let us consider a specific example. Suppose we have the circuit shown in Fig. 4-2a. The sine wave being measured has a peak value of 100 volts. Therefore, the peak value of current will be

$$I_p = \frac{V_p}{R_s + R_m} = \frac{100}{100(10^3) + 50} \cong 1 \text{ ma}$$

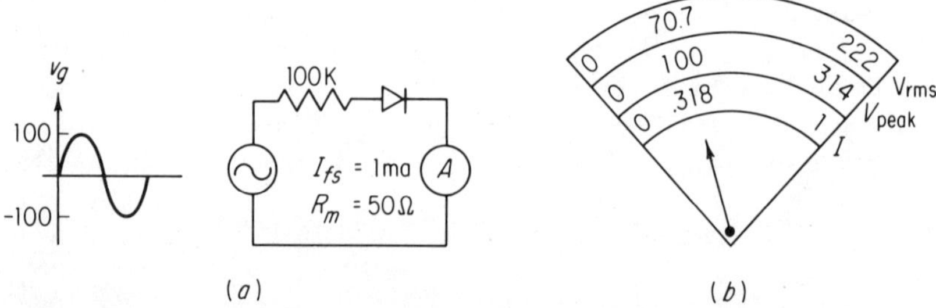

Fig. 4-2 (a) Half-wave detector. (b) Marking the meter face.

The ammeter actually indicates the average value, which is

$$I_{av} = 0.318 I_p = 0.318(1 \text{ ma}) = 0.318 \text{ ma}$$

Hence, the needle points to 0.318 ma, as shown in Fig. 4-2*b*.

Since we are interested in measuring the input voltage, we may add a scale for indicating the peak value of input voltage that produces the average value of ammeter current. This scale is shown directly above the current scale. We know that the average current of 0.318 ma is being produced by an input peak voltage of 100 volts. Therefore, we mark 100 volts directly above the 0.318 ma.

If the input voltage is raised to 314 volts peak, 3.14 ma will be the peak value of current. The average value of this is 1 ma, so that we mark 314 volts at full-scale deflection, as shown in Fig. 4-2*b*.

The rest of the peak-voltage scale can be marked off in a similar manner, resulting in a simple a-c voltmeter that responds to the average value of current but is marked off in the number of peak volts producing that average current.

Customarily, a-c voltmeters are marked off so as to indicate the rms value of the voltage being measured. This presents no problem, since we know that the rms value of a sine wave is equal to 0.707 of the peak value. Thus, to indicate rms values we need only add an rms scale above the peak-volts scale, as shown in Fig. 4-2*b*. Clearly, for a 100-volt peak sine wave, the rms value is 70.7 volts. We therefore mark 70.7 volts directly above 100 volts peak. The rest of the rms scale is marked similarly by multiplying each peak value by 0.707. Hence, at full scale we would have 0.707(314 volts), or 222 volts rms.

A word of caution is appropriate. Obviously, the rms scale is valid only for a sine-wave input. If we attempt to measure a square wave or a sawtooth, for example, the rms reading obtained is not correct. This is one of the pitfalls in the use of most a-c voltmeters. The rms scale of most a-c voltmeters assumes that the input signal is a sine wave. A safe rule is to assume automatically that the rms scale of any a-c voltmeter applies only to sine-wave inputs unless it is known that the instrument is a true rms voltmeter (see Chap. 11).

Let us determine the relation between the rms value of a sine-wave input and the corresponding value of d-c current.

$$V_{rms} = 0.707 V_p = 0.707(R_s + R_m)I_p = 0.707(R_s + R_m)\frac{I_{av}}{0.318}$$

or

$$V_{rms} = 2.22(R_s + R_m)I_{av} \tag{4-3}$$

This equation shows how the rms value of the input sine wave is related to the average current it produces in the ammeter. It applies to any half-wave rectifier of the configuration shown in Fig. 4-1*a*. This formula does not include the effects of real diodes.

EXAMPLE 4-1

In Fig. 4-1*a* R_s equals 1 megohm, and the meter movement has a full-scale current of 50 μa. The meter resistance is 2 kilohms. Find the rms value of an input sine wave that produces full-scale deflection.

SOLUTION

Equation (4-3) applies. Note that the meter resistance of 2 kilohms is negligible compared to 1 megohm.

$$V_{\mathrm{rms}} \cong 2.22(10^6)(50)(10^{-6}) = 111 \text{ volts rms}$$

Thus, we see that an input sine wave with an rms value of 111 volts produces a full-scale d-c current of 50 μa.

EXAMPLE 4-2

If the circuit of Fig. 4-1*a* is to have full-scale deflection for an input sine wave of 50 volts rms, what size should R_s be? The meter movement has $I_{fs} = 50$ μa and a meter resistance of 2 kilohms.

SOLUTION

Referring to Eq. (4-3), we see that all quantities are given except R_s. We need only solve for R_s to obtain

$$R_s = 0.45 \frac{V_{\mathrm{rms}}}{I_{\mathrm{av}}} - R_m = 0.45 \frac{50}{50(10^{-6})} - 2(10^3)$$
$$= 450(10^3) - 2(10^3) = 448 \text{ kilohms}$$

4-2 A Practical Version of the Half-wave Detector

The circuit of Fig. 4-1*a* conveys the essential theoretical ideas behind the half-wave detector. However, it has two weaknesses, which can be easily eliminated.

In our previous analysis we assumed ideal diodes. If we now consider real diodes, it should be clear that during the negative half cycle the diode in Fig. 4-1*a* will actually pass some reverse current. Furthermore, if the input signal is large enough, the real diode may break down. By adding another diode in shunt, as shown in Fig. 4-3, both these deficiencies are virtually eliminated. Clearly, during the negative half cycle, the shunt

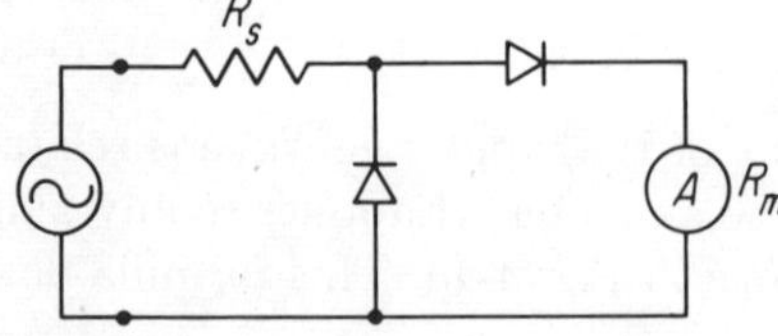

Fig. 4-3 A practical half-wave detecting voltmeter.

diode is on, so that very little voltage appears across the series diode. As a result, there is no possibility of breakdown, and the reverse current is greatly reduced.

During the positive half cycle, the shunt diode appears open. As a result, the analysis of the preceding section is still valid insofar as circuit operation is concerned during the positive half cycle. The meter current is still a half-wave-rectified sine wave, and therefore Eq. (4-3) still applies.

The circuit of Fig. 4-3 is often found in commercial instruments. Of course, this is not the only type of a-c detector. There are many other types, some of which will be considered shortly.

We will refer to the half-wave rectifier of Fig. 4-3 as an *average detector* because it responds to the average value of the current. As already indicated, the ammeter scale is marked off in rms values by using the relation of Eq. (4-3) under the assumption that only sine waves will be measured.

EXAMPLE 4-3

A simple d-c voltmeter of the type discussed in Chap. 2 uses a meter movement with a full-scale current of 50 μa and a meter resistance of 2 kilohms.

By means of a switching arrangement the same meter movement can be connected to the output of a simple half-wave rectifier.

Find the value of the multiplier resistance that is used on the 100-volt d-c range and on the 100-volt rms range.

SOLUTION

D-c voltmeter

$$R_s = \frac{100}{50(10^{-6})} - 2(10^3) \cong 2 \text{ megohms}$$

A-c voltmeter

$$R_s = 0.45\,\frac{100}{50(10^{-6})} - 2(10^3) = 900 \text{ kilohms}$$

Note that the input resistance is approximately equal to R_s. Thus, on the 100-volt d-c range, the input resistance is 2 megohms, whereas on the 100-volt rms range, it is only 900 kilohms. This reduction in input resistance is typical for all rectifier types of a-c voltmeters.

4-3 The Sensitivity of a Half-wave Detector

The input resistance of the half-wave detector shown in Fig. 4-3 is $R_s + R_m$ during the positive half cycle and R_s during the negative half cycle. Since R_m is usually much smaller than R_s in any practical design, we may say that the input resistance is essentially R_s throughout the entire cycle. Under this condition we rewrite Eq. (4-3) as

$$V_{\text{rms}} = 2.22R_{\text{in}}I_{\text{av}}$$

For full-scale deflection this equation becomes

$$V_{fs} = 2.22R_{\text{in}}I_{fs}$$

where V_{fs} is the full-scale rms value and I_{fs} is the full-scale d-c current.

We now solve for R_{in}.

$$R_{\text{in}} = 0.45\,\frac{V_{fs}}{I_{fs}} \tag{4-4}$$

Equation (4-4) tells us how to compute the value of input resistance for a half-wave detector given the full-scale rms value and the full-scale d-c current. For instance, if a half-wave detector has a full-scale voltage of 100 volts rms and uses a meter movement with a full-scale current of 1 ma, the input resistance is

$$R_{\text{in}} = 0.45\,\frac{100}{10^{-3}} = 45 \text{ kilohms}$$

There is really no reason at all why we cannot define a *sensitivity* for the half-wave rectifier as

$$S_{ac} \triangleq \frac{0.45}{I_{fs}} \tag{4-5}$$

With this definition the equation for input resistance becomes

$$R_{\text{in}} = S_{ac}V_{fs} \tag{4-6}$$

This equation is analogous to the input-resistance equation developed for a simple d-c voltmeter.

On commercial a-c voltmeters of the half-wave-rectifier type, the value of S_{ac} is printed on the meter face. As a result, it is a simple matter to find the input resistance on any rms range by multiplying the printed value of sensitivity by the full-scale rms value of the particular range.

Example 4-4

A VOM has a d-c sensitivity of 20 kilohms per volt, and an a-c sensitivity of 5 kilohms per volt. Find the input resistance of the VOM on the 10-volt d-c range and on the 10-volt rms range.

Solution

10-volt d-c range

$$R_{\text{in}} = 20\,(10^3)\,(10) = 200 \text{ kilohms}$$

10-volt rms range

$$R_{\text{in}} = 5\ (10^3)\ (10) = 50 \text{ kilohms}$$

EXAMPLE 4-5

The VOM of Example 4-4 is used to measure the voltage of a circuit with a Thévenin resistance of 10 kilohms. Find the accuracy as far as loading effects are concerned for d-c and a-c voltage measurements.

SOLUTION

For d-c measurements

$$\frac{V_{wm}}{V_{wom}} = \frac{R_{in}}{R_o + R_{in}} = \frac{200(10^3)}{210(10^3)} = 0.95 = 95\%$$

For a-c measurements

$$\frac{V_{wm}}{V_{wom}} = \frac{50(10^3)}{60(10^3)} = 0.83 = 83\%$$

This is typical. We can always expect more loading error for a-c measurements than for d-c.

4-4 Nonlinearity on the Lower RMS Ranges

Our analysis of the half-wave detector assumed that the diodes were ideal. As a result, we were able to obtain the simpler linear relation of Eq. (4-3). According to this equation, the rms value of the input voltage is directly proportional to the average current. Because of this direct proportion the meter face can be marked off uniformly.

If we now consider a real diode, we realize that a few tenths of a volt are required to turn the diode on. Because of this we can expect to find that the lower rms ranges must be nonlinearly marked. Typically, commercial VOMs attempt to go no lower than about 1.5 volt rms for the full-scale value because of nonlinearity.

One attempt at overcoming the diode nonlinearity is shown in Fig. 4-4. The meter movement is deliberately shunted, and the value of R_s is reduced in order to force the diode to operate in a more linear part of its current-voltage curve. Commercial VOMs often use the scheme of Fig. 4-4.

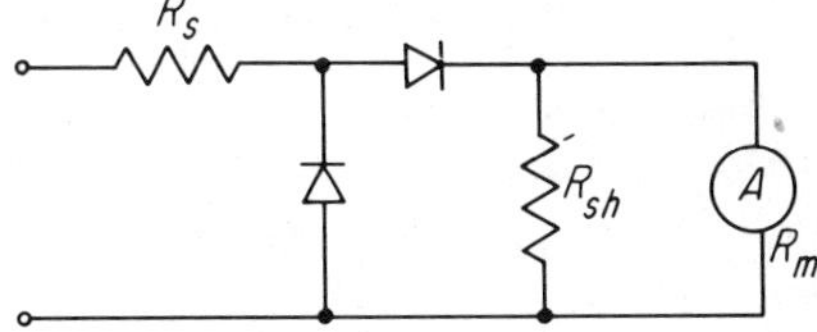

Fig. 4-4 Improving the linearity on the lower rms ranges.

EXAMPLE 4-6

A VOM uses a 50-μa 2-kilohm meter movement. On a-c voltage ranges a half-wave detector is used. Furthermore, the ammeter is shunted by 2 kilohms on a-c ranges. Find the d-c sensitivity and the a-c sensitivity of the VOM.

SOLUTION

On d-c measurements

$$S = \frac{1}{I_{fs}} = \frac{1}{50(10^{-6})} = 20 \text{ kilohms per volt}$$

On a-c measurements

$$S_{ac} = \frac{0.45}{100(10^{-6})} = 4.5 \text{ kilohms per volt}$$

Note that the correct value to use in the a-c sensitivity equation is 100 μa, the total current of the shunted ammeter at full scale. Note further that the sensitivity has been considerably reduced on a-c measurements.

4-5 Full-wave Detectors

One way of improving the sensitivity of a rectifier type of voltmeter is to use full-wave rectification. A simple full-wave rectifier is shown in Fig. 4-5. The current through the ammeter will be the familiar full-wave-rectified sine wave. This particular circuit is limited by the frequency range of the transformer.

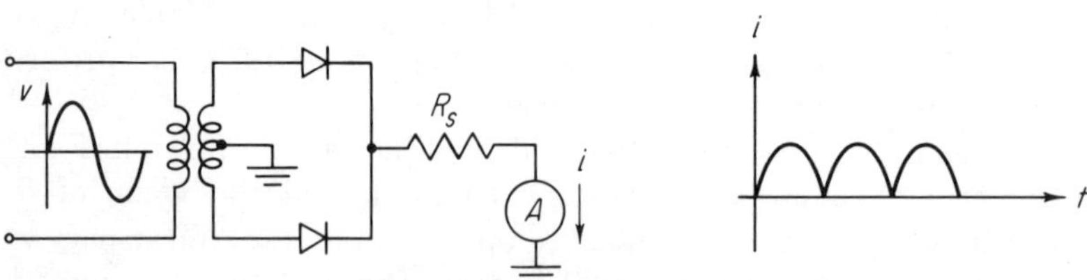

Fig. 4-5 Simple full-wave detector.

A full-wave rectifier more commonly used in broad-band applications is the full-wave bridge shown in Fig. 4-6*a*. Diodes *A* and *D* are on during the positive half cycle. During the negative half cycle, diodes *B* and *C* are on. As a result, the current flows through the ammeter from left to right throughout the entire cycle. The resulting current waveshape is shown in Fig. 4-6*b*.

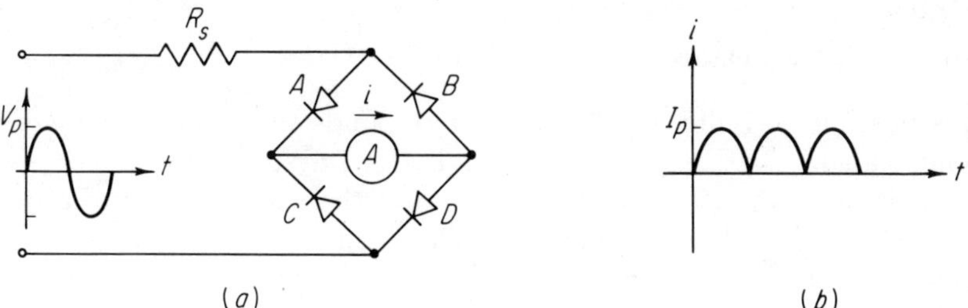

Fig. 4-6 (a) Full-wave bridge detector. (b) Ammeter current.

The average value of the ammeter current is

$$I_{av} = \frac{2I_p}{\pi} = 0.636I_p \tag{4-7}$$

We note that the average value of a full-wave-rectified sine wave is exactly double that of a half-wave-rectified sine wave. Thus, for a peak value of 1 ma, the average current is 0.636 ma for a full-wave rectifier as compared to 0.318 ma for a half-wave rectifier. An inspection of the earlier equations derived for a half-wave rectifier will show that we need only modify our earlier results by a factor of two. Hence, the equation for the series resistance R_s becomes

$$R_s = 0.9\frac{V_{fs}}{I_{fs}} - R_m \tag{4-8}$$

Similarly, the a-c sensitivity for a full-wave rectifier becomes

$$S_{ac} = \frac{0.9}{I_{fs}} \tag{4-9}$$

Example 4-7

The bridge of Fig. 4-6 uses a 1-ma movement. Find the a-c sensitivity.

Solution

$$S_{ac} = \frac{0.9}{I_{fs}} = \frac{0.9}{1 \text{ ma}} = 900 \text{ ohms per volt}$$

Example 4-8

A VOM uses an unshunted 50-μa movement. Find the input resistance on the 5-, 50-, and 500-volt rms ranges if a full-wave detector is used.

Solution

$$S_{ac} = \frac{0.9}{50(10^{-6})} = 18 \text{ kilohms per volt}$$

$$R_{in} = S_{ac}V_{fs} = 18(10^3)(5) = 90 \text{ kilohms on the 5-volt range}$$

$$R_{in} = 18(10^3)(50) = 900 \text{ kilohms on the 50-volt range}$$

$$R_{in} = 18(10^3)(500) = 9 \text{ megohms on the 500-volt range}$$

4-6 Peak Detection

It is possible to build a detector that responds to the peak value of the input signal. Consider the circuit of Fig. 4-7*a*. Assume that the signal has just been applied at t equals zero and the capacitor is initially uncharged. During the first quarter cycle the generator signal is building up to its positive peak voltage. The ideal diode is forward-biased, so that it appears as a short. Therefore, the capacitor charges immediately, and the output voltage equals the generator voltage. At the end of the first quarter cycle the capacitor is fully charged to V_p volts.

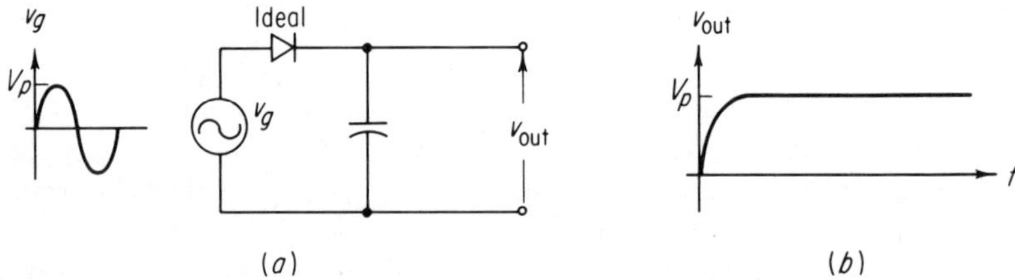

Fig. 4-7 (*a*) Unloaded peak detector. (*b*) Output voltage.

During the next quarter cycle the generator voltage drops below the peak value. Since the capacitor voltage is V_p, the current will try to flow back into the generator, that is, against the diode triangle. Therefore the diode appears open. Hence, the output voltage remains at V_p volts.

The graph of output voltage is shown in Fig. 4-7*b*. Note the overall circuit action. The capacitor charges to the peak voltage during the first quarter cycle, and then the diode opens. The capacitor stays charged to the peak value for all succeeding cycles.

Figure 4-7*a* conveys the elementary idea of capacitor charging. As it now stands, the circuit is not practical, since the input signal may be removed entirely and the capacitor will still remain charged to the peak voltage. Thus, if we try to measure the peak value of a new sine wave of smaller amplitude, the capacitor will still indicate the original V_p volts.

We may add a resistor across the capacitor as shown in Fig. 4-8*a*.

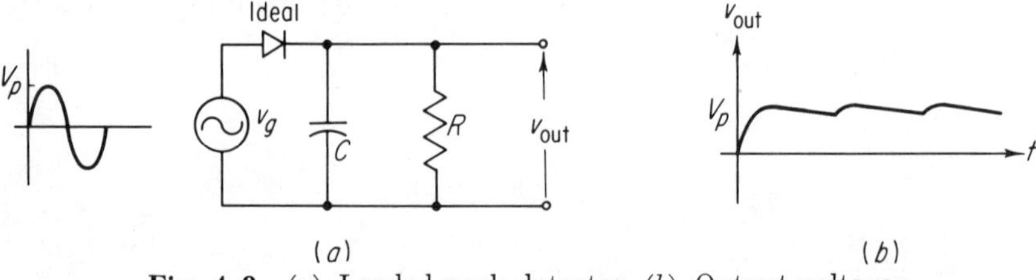

Fig. 4-8 (*a*) Loaded peak detector. (*b*) Output voltage.

Obviously, if the resistor is very large, we can expect the circuit to operate more or less as it would without a resistor. Figure 4-8*b* indicates the output voltage. Note that the capacitor charges to the peak voltage during the first quarter cycle. Then approximately at the peak the diode opens. Now the capacitor discharges through the resistor. As long as the resistor is large, we can expect a small discharge, as indicated in Fig. 4-8*b*. The diode remains off until almost the peak of the next cycle. Then it turns on momentarily allowing the capacitor to charge again to V_p volts. If the ripple on the output voltage is small, then for practical purposes we may say the circuit of Fig. 4-8*a* is a peak detector. The output is essentially a d-c voltage whose value equals the peak value of the input signal. A d-c voltmeter connected across the output terminals would read approximately V_p volts.

The circuit of Fig. 4-8*a* is widely used as a peak detector. It is very simple and easy to construct. Furthermore, the input signal is not restricted to sine waves. Square waves, sawtooths, and other nonsinusoidal signals may be used as input signals, and the output will still be a d-c voltage whose value approximately equals the peak voltage.

A simple a-c voltmeter is shown in Fig. 4-9*a*. The resistor and ammeter constitute a simple d-c voltmeter of the type studied in Chap. 2. Figure 4-9*b* illustrates that any d-c voltmeter can be used to measure the voltage across the capacitor. The input resistance of the voltmeter provides the discharge path for the capacitor.

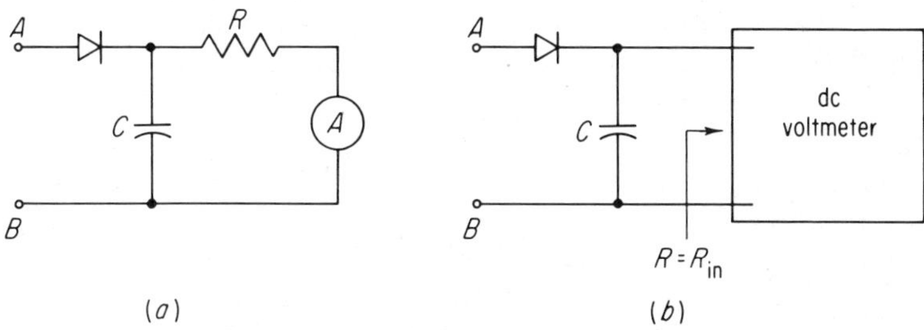

Fig. 4-9 Peak-detecting voltmeters.

It should be clear that if we remove the input signal, the capacitor can completely discharge, given enough time. The detector will then be ready to measure a new input signal.

The meter face can be marked off in peak values or in rms values. If rms values are used, all peak values are multiplied by 0.707 if we assume sine-wave input. Once again, we must be aware of the fact that an rms scale is valid only for sine-wave inputs if 0.707 is used to convert from peak to rms values.

EXAMPLE 4-9

The circuit of Fig. 4-8*a* is used to measure a sine wave with a peak value of 50 volts. The diode is made of germanium. Use the second approximation of a diode to find the approximate value of output voltage.

SOLUTION

During the first quarter cycle the diode is on and resembles a 0.3-volt battery. Hence, the capacitor will charge 50 − 0.3, or 49.7 volts. Assuming that the resistor is very large, very little discharge takes place, so that the output voltage is approximately 49.7 volts. For practical purposes, the output is 50 volts.

4-7 The Frequency Response of a Peak Detector

We now wish to come to grips with the question of how large the resistor must be in order for the capacitor voltage to remain near the peak value of input voltage. Consider the circuit of Fig. 4-8*a*. As already indicated, if R is very large, we can expect a small discharge, and the output voltage will remain near the peak voltage (see Fig. 4-10*a*). If the value of R is reduced sufficiently, a large discharge will take place, and we can expect the output voltage to resemble that shown in Fig. 4-10*b*. Finally, if R is extremely small, the capacitor effects are negligible, and the circuit reduces to a simple half-wave rectifier. In other words, if the R is very small, the capacitor may as well not even be in the circuit. The output voltage is then a half-wave-rectified sine wave, as shown in Fig. 4-10*c*.

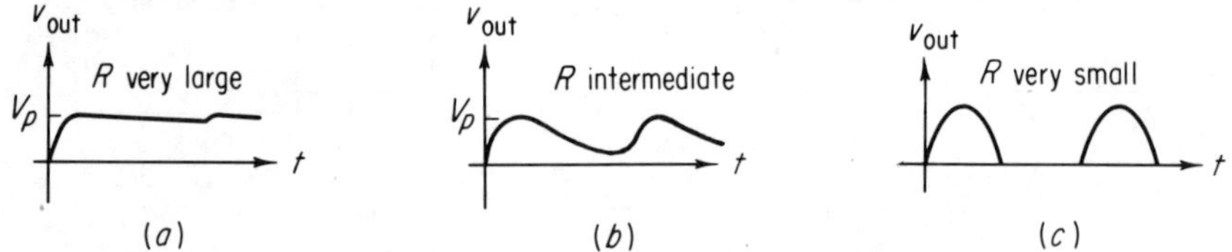

Fig. 4-10 Peak-detector output for different values of loading.

Clearly, we want the output voltage to resemble Fig. 4-10*a*. Thus, we know that a large resistor must be used in a peak detector. But there is more involved than just the size of the resistor. The size of the capacitor is also involved, as well as the frequency of the input signal. How can we relate the value of R, C, and input frequency?

Consider the circuit of Fig. 4-11*a*. When the ideal diode is off, the capacitor will discharge through the resistor. At the beginning of the discharge time, the capacitor is charged to V_p. If we have a good peak detector, the capacitor discharges for approximately T sec, the amount of time between two successive input peaks. But this is the same as the period of the input signal.

From our study of transients in Chap. 1 we may write the equation for the voltage during the discharge time

$$v = V_p \epsilon^{-t/RC} \tag{4-10}$$

where V_p is the initial capacitor voltage at the beginning of the discharge and t is the amount of time the capacitor has been discharging.

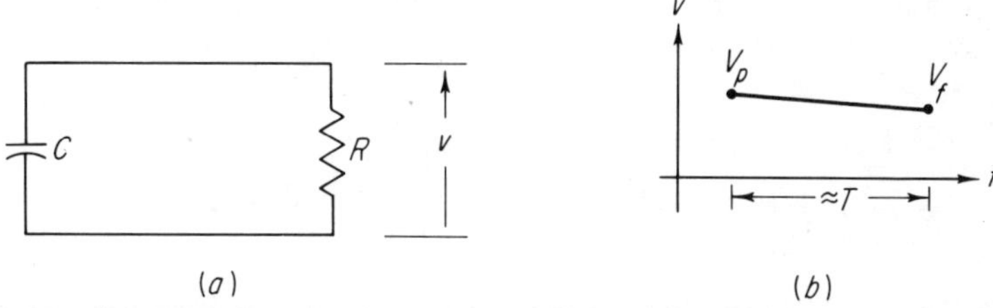

Fig. 4-11 (*a*) Peak detector during the off time of the diode. (*b*) Output voltage during the off time of the diode.

As shown in Fig. 4-11*b* the capacitor discharges for approximately T seconds and reaches a voltage of V_f. Hence, we may substitute into Eq. (4-10) by noting that for $t \cong T$, $v = V_f$.

$$V_f = V_p \epsilon^{-T/RC} \tag{4-11}$$

This equation merely tells us that the capacitor voltage at the end of the discharge equals V_f, and V_f is calculated by the expression on the right-hand side of Eq. (4-11). Remember that this equation is for a good peak detector, i.e., one in which the capacitor discharges for almost the entire period.

Let us divide both sides of Eq. (4-11) by V_p to obtain

$$\frac{V_f}{V_p} = \epsilon^{-T/RC} \triangleq \text{accuracy} \tag{4-12}$$

This is a useful equation. Basically, we may think of it as an accuracy equation, since it relates the final capacitor voltage at the end of the discharge to the peak voltage we are trying to measure. For instance, if the accuracy is 0.99, or 99 percent, the final capacitor voltage is 99 percent of the peak value, indicating a very small ripple on the output voltage.

From Eq. (4-12) one thing should be immediately evident. In order to have an accuracy approaching 100 percent, the right-hand side of the equation must be almost equal to unity. Therefore, the exponent of ϵ

must be almost zero. Symbolically

$$\frac{T}{RC} \cong 0 \qquad \text{or } T \ll RC$$

We are saying that for a good peak detector the period of the input signal must be much smaller than the RC time constant. Equation (4-12) can be put into a more convenient form by using a formula that is derived in higher mathematics.

$$\epsilon^{x} = 1 + x + \frac{x^2}{2!} + \frac{x^3}{3!} + \frac{x^4}{4!} + \cdots \tag{4-13}$$

This equation says that ϵ raised to any power can be calculated by the expression on the right-hand side. For instance, if $x = 0.1$,

$$\begin{aligned}\epsilon^{0.1} &= 1 + 0.1 + \frac{0.1^2}{2} + \frac{0.1^3}{3(2)} + \frac{0.1^4}{4(3)(2)} + \cdots \\ &= 1 + 0.1 + 0.005 + 0.000167 + 0.000004 + \cdots \\ &\cong 1.105\end{aligned}$$

Note that for small values of x, such as $x = 0.1$ or less, the values of the higher-degree terms rapidly approach zero. As a result, Eq. (4-13) is often used in the place of the exponential term whenever the exponent is almost zero. In other words, for a small x, the higher-degree terms become negligible, and we write

$$\epsilon^{x} \cong 1 + x \qquad \text{for } x \ll 1 \tag{4-14}$$

This equation is accurate to within ½ percent if x is less than 0.1.

In a good peak detector Eq. (4-12) applies. Furthermore, we already know that the exponent T/RC must be almost zero. Therefore, we can simplify Eq. (4-12) to obtain

$$\frac{V_f}{V_p} = \epsilon^{-T/RC} \cong 1 - \frac{T}{RC} = \text{accuracy} \tag{4-15}$$

This simplified equation is a useful guide in determining the relation between the RC time constant and the period. For instance, if we wish to have an accuracy of 0.99, then by inspection T/RC must equal 0.01. Similarly, if an accuracy of 0.95 is required, T/RC must be 0.05.

Since the period is the reciprocal of the frequency, we note that for a 99 percent accurate peak detector

$$T = 0.01RC \qquad \text{or} \qquad RC = 100T$$

or

$$RC = \frac{100}{f}$$

where f is the frequency of the input.

In summary, we may use the following two guides in the construction of peak detectors:

For a 99 percent accurate peak detector

$$RC = \frac{100}{f}$$

For a 95 percent accurate peak detector

$$RC = \frac{20}{f}$$

Note that we have defined accuracy as the final capacitor voltage divided by the peak value. A d-c voltmeter will actually read the average between the peak voltage and the final voltage. Thus, if we have a 95 percent accurate peak detector and the input signal is a 100-volt peak sine wave, the output voltage will vary from 100 to 95 volts. A d-c voltmeter would read about 97.5 volts.

Example 4-10

In the circuit of Fig. 4-8*a* the resistance equals 100 kilohms, and the capacitor equals 0.01 μf.

(*a*) For a 50-volt peak sine wave find the frequency at which the capacitor voltage is 49.5 volts at the end of the discharge cycle.

(*b*) Find the frequency at which the capacitor voltage is 47.5 volts.

Solution

(*a*)

$$\frac{V_f}{V_p} = \frac{49.5}{50} = 0.99 = 99\%$$

$$RC = \frac{100}{f} \quad \text{or} \quad f = \frac{100}{RC} = \frac{100}{10^5(10^{-8})} = 100 \text{ kHz}$$

Hence, we note that if the frequency is any lower than 100 kHz, the final capacitor will drop below 49.5 volts.

(*b*) In this case, the ratio of V_f to V_p is 47.5/50, which equals 0.95, or 95 percent. As a result

$$RC = \frac{20}{f} \quad \text{or} \quad f = \frac{20}{RC} = \frac{20}{10^5(10^{-8})} = 20 \text{ kHz}$$

We note that at 20 kHz the capacitor voltage decays to 47.5 volts at the end of the discharge time. If a d-c voltmeter is used to measure v_{out}, it will read the average of 50 volts and 47.5 volts, or 48.75 volts.

EXAMPLE 4-11

In the circuit of Fig. 4-9*b* the input resistance of the d-c voltmeter is 10 megohms. Choose a capacitor size so that the capacitor voltage decays no more than 1 percent from 20 Hz to 20 kHz.

SOLUTION

Obviously, the lowest frequency is the most critical as far as capacitor discharge is concerned. Thus we may write

$$RC = \frac{100}{f} \qquad \text{or} \qquad C = \frac{100}{Rf} = \frac{100}{10^7(20)} = 0.5\ \mu\text{f}$$

4-8 Effects of Source Resistance on the Peak Detector

Our previous analysis of the peak detector has used an ideal diode and a zero resistance source. In this section we wish to determine the effects of source resistance on the operation of the peak detector.

Consider Fig. 4-12*a*. We have now included a source resistor which of course is present in any real circuit. How does the source resistance change our previous analysis of the peak detector?

First, we observe that if R_o is extremely small, we can expect the peak detector to operate according to our previous discussion. If the source resistance becomes large, the capacitor must charge through an appreciable resistance. Figure 4-12*b* depicts the Thévenin equivalent circuit that

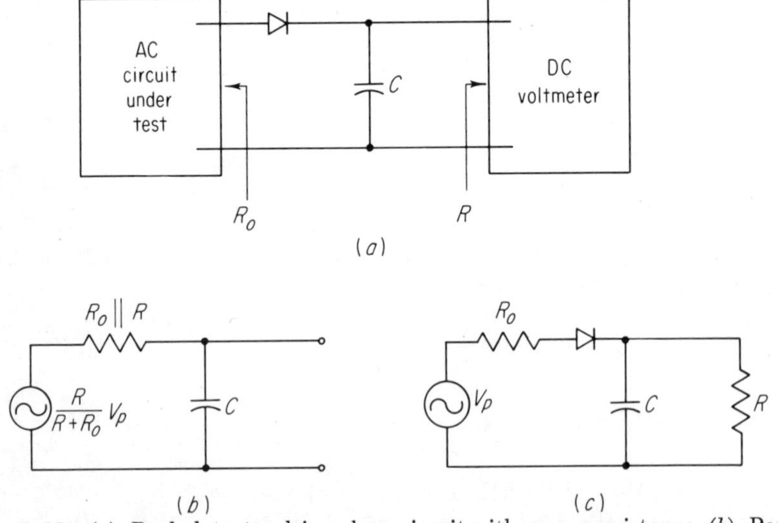

Fig. 4-12 (*a*) Peak detector driven by a circuit with source resistance. (*b*) Peak detector during the on time of the diode. (*c*) Equivalent circuit.

applies when the diode is on. From this equivalent circuit we can see that the time constant for the charging of the capacitor is

$$\text{Charging time constant} = (R_o \| R)C \tag{4-16}$$

(Recall that the parallel lines mean that R_o is in parallel with R.) Furthermore, we note that if the diode is on long enough to allow the capacitor to charge fully, the maximum possible capacitor voltage is

$$V_{max} = \frac{R}{R + R_o} V_p \tag{4-17}$$

It should be immediately clear from Eq. (4-17) that a necessary condition for good peak detection is that R_o be much smaller than R. For instance, if R_o equals 1 kilohm and R equals 100 kilohms, then V_{max} equals $0.99V_p$.

A really subtle question to answer is whether or not the capacitor has enough time during the on time of the diode to charge fully to the maximum voltage given by Eq. (4-17). A great deal depends upon the shape of the input voltage, that is, sinusoidal, square wave, sawtooth, or whatever.

In general, the capacitor will not charge to V_{max} during the first half cycle. However, during succeeding cycles the capacitor voltage will approach V_{max} if the charging time constant is much smaller than the discharging time constant.

Using Eq. (4-17), we can construct the following guides:

1. In order for the capacitor to charge to 99 percent of V_p, R should be greater than $100R_o$.
2. In order for the capacitor to reach 95 percent of V_p, R should be greater than $20R_o$.

These rules may be used as guides for any input waveshape, but they should not be taken as exact criteria.

EXAMPLE 4-12

In Fig. 4-12*a* the source resistance R_o equals 100 ohms. The lowest input frequency will be 50 Hz. Calculate values for R and C that will provide an accuracy of about 99 percent.

SOLUTION

Since $R_o = 100$, R should be greater than $100R_o$, or 10 kilohms. For an $R = 10$ kilohms, we compute C from

$$C = \frac{100}{Rf} = \frac{100}{10^4(50)} = 200\ \mu\text{f}$$

Hence, $R = 10$ kilohms, and $C = 200\ \mu$f.

Note that we are free to choose larger values of R if we wish. In this case, even though 200-μf capacitors are available in practice, we should use a smaller capacitor than this. There is no reason at all why we cannot choose $R = 100$ kilohms. In fact, the charging of the capacitor will now more closely approach the peak value. Since we have increased R by a factor of ten, we can reduce C by a factor of ten. Thus, another suitable set of design values would be $R = 100$ kilohms and $C = 20\ \mu$f.

4-9 The Loading Effects of a Peak-detector Voltmeter

If a peak-detector type of voltmeter such as shown in Fig. 4-9 is used to make voltage measurements, how much loading error appears in the measurement?

The measurement situation is depicted by Fig. 4-12*a*. The situation is analogous to our analysis of the loading effects of a d-c voltmeter discussed in Chap. 2. If the a-c circuit under test is essentially resistive, we can visualize its Thévenin equivalent as shown in Fig. 4-12*c*. We will assume that the peak detector is well designed, so that its discharging time constant is at least 100 times greater than the period of the signal being measured. Under these conditions we see that the maximum voltage that the capacitor can charge to is given by Eq. (4-17). Hence, we can rewrite Eq. (4-17) as

$$\frac{V_{\max}}{V_p} = \frac{R}{R + R_o} \tag{4-18}$$

Equation (4-18) is analogous to the accuracy equation for a d-c voltmeter measurement. It cannot be taken as an exact criterion, since a great deal depends upon the exact shape of the input signal being measured; however, Eq. (4-18) is certainly a guide in determining how much loading is taking place. For instance, if the value of R is 1 megohm, a source resistance of 10 kilohms will yield

$$\frac{V_{\max}}{V_p} = \frac{10^6}{10^6 + 10(10^3)} = 0.99$$

This result indicates that the peak detector reading will be about 99 percent of the peak value of the input voltage.

4-10 Diode Effects on Peak-detector Operation

If the signals being measured by a peak detector are large, we can expect real-diode effects to be almost negligible. As the signals being measured become smaller, however, the real diode begins to produce significant error.

In our second approximation of the diode we visualize the diode as a switch in series with a battery whose value equals the knee voltage (0.3 or 0.7 volt). Thus, we must allow for this small voltage drop across the diode. For instance, if a signal with a peak value of 100 volts is detected, then for a germanium diode we can expect to detect no more than 99.7 volts. In this case the error is quite small. On the other hand, if the peak value of the input signal is only 5 volts, then for a silicon diode we can expect to detect 4.3 volts or less. Figure 4-13*a* illustrates the effect of taking the diode knee voltage into account.

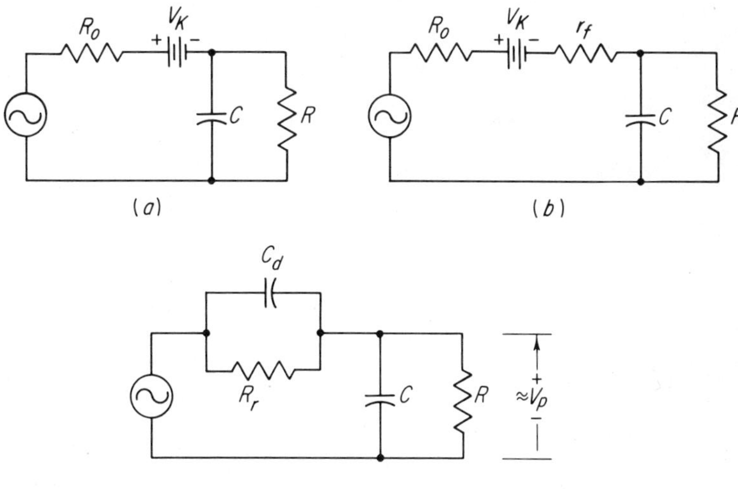

Fig. 4-13 Diode effects on peak-detector operation. (*a*) Knee-voltage effects. (*b*) Knee-voltage and forward-resistance effects. (*c*) Reverse resistance and reverse capacitance effects.

In our third approximation we also consider the diode forward resistance. By an inspection of Fig. 4-13*b* it should be clear that when the diode is on, its resistance r_f effectively becomes part of the source resistance. We therefore need only add the value of r_f to R_o in order to obtain an idea of the effect. For instance, if R_o equals 100 ohms and r_f equals 50 ohms, the effective source resistance is 150 ohms. The discharge resistor R should thus be chosen much larger than 150 ohms, say 15 kilohms or more.

In general, the diode contributes significant error for small input signals. If this error is objectionable, the signal should be amplified before peak detection.

There are two more diode effects that can produce error. During the discharge time the diode should be open. Actually, it is not, since there is a reverse current through the diode when it is back-biased. Futhermore, there is a capacitance across the diode junction.

We may visualize the back-biased diode as a resistance in shunt with a capacitance, as shown in Fig. 4-13*c*. The peak detector capacitance now has two additional paths for discharge. C can discharge through the diode reverse resistance. Hence, the reverse resistance of the diode should be much larger than R. Also, C can discharge into the diode capacitance. Hence, C_d should be kept much smaller than C.

In general, silicon diodes are available with reverse resistances in the tens and hundreds of megohms, so that reasonable sizes of R can be chosen. Furthermore, diodes with capacitances of only a few picofarads are available, so that reasonable sizes of C can be chosen.

Example 4-13

A 7-volt peak signal is to be peak-detected. If a silicon diode is used, what is the maximum possible capacitor voltage if we use the second approximation? In order to reduce the percent error by a factor of ten, how much voltage gain is required before peak detection?

Solution

If the diode is ideal, the maximum possible capacitor voltage is 7 volts. Since the diode is made of silicon, according to the second approximation we must allow 0.7 volt drop across the diode. Hence, at the peak value of input voltage, 0.7 volt appears across the diode and 6.3 volts appears across the capacitor.

The percent error is the error divided by the peak value, which is 0.7/7, or 10 percent. In order to reduce this error by a factor of ten, the peak voltage must be 70 volts. Thus, we need a voltage amplifier with a voltage gain of 10 (this is equivalent to saying a voltage gain of 20 db).

Example 4-14

A silicon diode has typical specifications as follows:

(*a*) Forward current is 10 ma at 1 volt.
(*b*) Reverse current is 0.1 μa at -50 volts.
(*c*) Diode capacity is 2 pf at -4 volts.

A source with a resistance of 100 ohms is peak-detected by a circuit using the above diode. If 1 kHz is to be the lowest frequency of operation, select reasonable values of R and C to allow good peak detection.

SOLUTION

The forward resistance of the diode according to our third approximation is

$$r_f = \frac{\Delta v}{\Delta i} = \frac{1 - 0.7}{10^{-2}} = 30 \text{ ohms}$$

During the charging time the diode resistance effectively becomes part of the source resistance, so that the total effective source resistance is 130 ohms. We must choose the value of R much larger than 130 ohms but not so large that it is comparable to the leakage resistance of the diode.

The diode reverse resistance is

$$R_r = \frac{50}{10^{-7}} = 500 \text{ megohms}$$

Obviously, there is no problem in selecting a value of R that is much greater than the effective source resistance of 130 ohms and much less than the diode resistance of 500 megohms. Arbitrarily, we may select 100 kilohms for the value of R.

We may now compute C for 99-percent accuracy

$$C = \frac{100}{Rf} = \frac{10^2}{10^5(10^3)} = 10^{-6} = 1\ \mu\text{f}$$

We should now check that this value of capacitance is much larger than the diode capacitance. Clearly, 1 μf is much larger than 2 pf, so that very little error will be produced by the diode capacitance.

Hence, our final choices of R and C are 100 kilohms and 1 μf.

4-11 The D-C Clamping Circuit

The d-c clamping circuit, also called a d-c restorer, is a well-known and widely used circuit. It is often found in radar and television, as well as a host of measuring instruments. The d-c clamping circuit is shown in Fig. 4-14. The circuit resembles the peak detector, except that the diode and the capacitor have been interchanged.

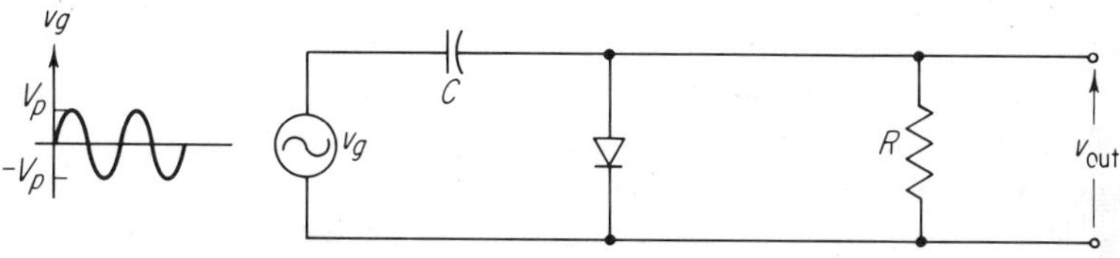

Fig. 4-14 Negative d-c clamping circuit.

The circuit operates as follows for an ideal diode. During the first quarter cycle of input voltage, the diode is shorted. The capacitor will therefore charge, and at the end of the first quarter cycle, the capacitor voltage will equal the peak voltage, as shown in Fig. 4-15*a*. After the first quarter cycle, the capacitor will try to discharge back into the generator. As a result, the diode opens. The only discharge path is through the resistor, as shown in Fig. 4-15*b*. If the resistor is large enough, the capacitor discharge will be slight, so that its voltage will remain essentially at V_p volts.

What is the output?

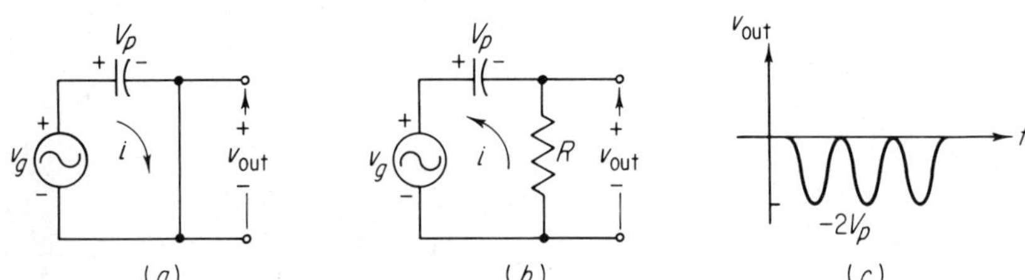

Fig. 4-15 D-c clamping circuit. (*a*) During the first quarter cycle. (*b*) During the off time of the diode. (*c*) Clamped output waveform.

From Kirchhoff's law we may add the voltages around the loop of Fig. 4-15*b* to obtain

$$v_{out} - v_g + V_p = 0$$

or

$$v_{out} = v_g - V_p \tag{4-19}$$

Equation (4-19) tells us that the output voltage is equal to the generator voltage minus a constant. In this case, the generator voltage is a sine wave with a peak value of V_p volts. To find the output voltage we must subtract V_p from the generator voltage at each instant in time. Figure 4-15*c* illustrates the result. Note that we have subtracted V_p volts from the generator voltage of Fig. 4-14.

The circuit of Fig. 4-14 is called a negative clamper because the input signal has been clamped below the zero voltage level. By turning the diode around, the circuit becomes a positive clamper, so that the input waveshape is shifted above the zero voltage level. Note clearly that the peak-to-peak value of the signal is retained and the shape is preserved. All that happens is that the signal is shifted up or down.

The choice of R and C follows the rules which were developed for the peak detector. In other words, a large RC time constant is required at the lowest frequency of operation.

Example 4-15

In the circuit of Fig. 4-16*a* the generator signal is a sine wave with a peak value of 20 volts. Sketch the output voltage under the assumption that ideal clamping action takes place.

Solution

The sine wave is negatively clamped. The shape and peak-to-peak value are preserved. Therefore, the sketch must be as shown in Fig. 4-16*b*.

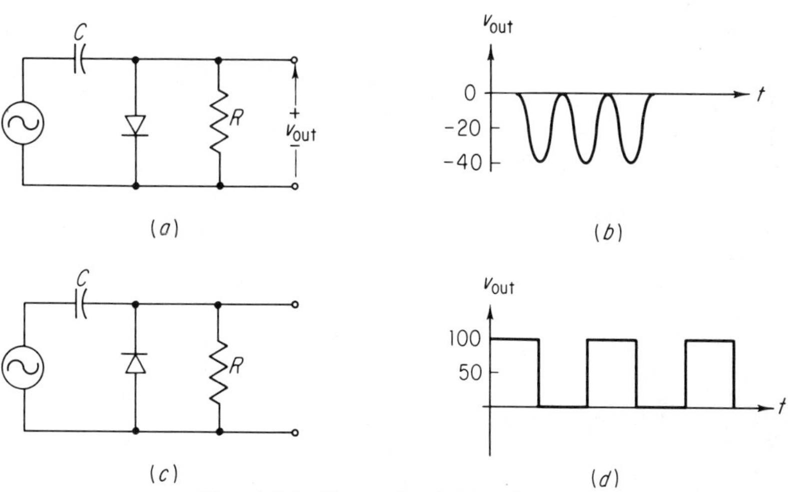

Fig. 4-16 Examples 4-15 and 4-16.

Example 4-16

A square wave with a peak voltage of 50 volts drives the clamping circuit of Fig. 4-16*c*. Sketch the output voltage.

Solution

This is a positive clamper, so that the square wave will be shifted above the 0-volt level. The sketch is shown in Fig. 4-16*d*.

4-12 A Peak-to-peak Detector

We can construct a peak-to-peak detector by cascading a clamper with a peak detector, as shown in Fig. 4-17. The operation is straightforward. The input sine wave is positively clamped above the zero level, as shown at the output of the clamper. The input to the peak detector is now a signal whose peak value is $2V_p$, which is the peak-to-peak value of the sine wave. The peak detector then has the output shown in Fig. 4-17.

The peak-to-peak detector is generally used for signals whose positive and negative half cycles are not equal. For example, if there is a square wave with a positive peak of 10 volts and a negative peak of -40 volts,

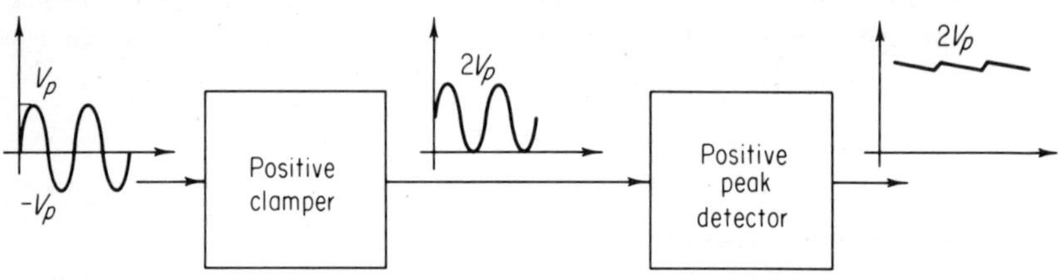

Fig. 4-17 Peak-to-peak detection.

the ordinary positive peak detector would read 10 volts, which would be misleading. The peak-to-peak detector, however, would indicate a peak-to-peak value of 50 volts, which is correct.

SUMMARY

A-c voltages can be detected by means of a half-wave rectifier. The ammeter of such a detector responds to the average, or d-c value of the half-wave rectified current. In order to indicate the rms voltage of the input signal, the meter face is marked in the number of rms volts producing the average current through the ammeter. This marking generally assumes that a sinusoidal voltage is being measured. Therefore, the rms scale of most a-c voltmeters applies only to sinusoidal signals. If other signals are measured, the readings are erroneous.

The sensitivity of an a-c voltmeter is lower than the d-c sensitivity of the same meter movement. Furthermore, the meter movement is often shunted in an attempt to improve the linearity of the lower a-c ranges. As a result, the a-c sensitivity of a voltmeter is generally lower than the d-c sensitivity by a significant factor. Therefore, the loading error becomes more of a problem with a-c voltmeters.

Full-wave detectors improve the sensitivity by a factor of two. They still respond to the average value, rather than the rms value.

A peak detector responds to the peak of the input signal. In order to indicate the rms value of the input signal, the meter face is marked in the number of rms volts producing the voltage across the charging capacitor.

A d-c clamping circuit shifts the input signal by a given amount. For the simple clamping circuits studied in this chapter the input signal is clamped positive or negative with respect to the zero voltage level.

A peak-to-peak detector consists of a clamping circuit followed by a peak detector.

GLOSSARY

amplitude The peak value of a sine wave.

clamping circuit Also known as a d-c restorer, this is a circuit that changes the average, or d-c, value of the input signal.

nonlinearity Refers to the relation between two variables which are not in direct proportion to one another.

nonsinusoidal Refers to a waveform that does not have the shape of the ordinary sine wave.

peak detector A circuit that produces a d-c voltage proportional to the peak value of the input signal.

rms value of a waveform The value of a d-c voltage or current that produces exactly the same amount of heat in a resistor as the waveform.

REVIEW QUESTIONS

1. Does the half-wave-rectifier voltmeter respond to the average value, the peak value, or the rms value? Is the meter face generally marked in average, peak, or rms values?
2. What is the average value of a half-wave-rectified signal with a peak value of I_p?
3. Why does an ordinary a-c voltmeter give erroneous rms readings for nonsinusoidal waveshapes?
4. Why is a shunt diode used in the simple two-diode half-wave rectifier?
5. Is the a-c sensitivity as high as, the same as, or lower than the d-c sensitivity of given meter movement?
6. Why do the voltage readings tend to bunch somewhat on the lower a-c voltage ranges?
7. What advantage does full-wave detection have over half-wave detection?
8. How does the sensitivity of a full-wave detector compare to a half-wave detector?
9. What is a peak detector?
10. Should the discharging time constant of a good peak detector be long or short compared to the period?

11. What effect does source resistance have upon peak-detector accuracy? Should the source resistance be very small or very large?
12. In a 99 percent accurate peak detector how large should the discharging time constant be compared to the period?
13. What is a positive d-c clamping circuit?
14. How do the design rules for a clamping circuit compare to those developed for a peak detector?
15. How can a peak-to-peak detector be made?

PROBLEMS

4-1 The current through an ammeter is a half-wave-rectified sine wave with a peak value of 15 ma. What is the d-c value of this current?

4-2 In Fig. 4-3 an input sine wave is being measured. The meter resistance is 2 kilohms, and R_s equals 48 kilohms. If the ammeter reads 30 μa, what is the rms value of the input sine wave? (Use ideal diodes.)

4-3 In Fig. 4-3, calculate the size of R_s required on the 100-volt rms range. The meter is a 50 μa, 2-kilohm movement. (Use ideal diodes.)

4-4 Compute the a-c sensitivity in Fig. 4-3 if the ammeter has a full-scale deflection current of 50 μa. What is the input resistance of the a-c voltmeter on its 5-volt range? On its 100-volt range?

4-5 An a-c voltmeter on its 10-volt range is used to measure the voltage across the 30-kilohm resistor in Fig. 4-18*a*. The sensitivity of the voltmeter is 5 kilohms per volt. If the voltmeter reads 5 volts, what is the true voltage across the 30-kilohm resistor without the voltmeter connected?

4-6 A 100-μa movement is shunted so that the total current capacity is 1 ma. What would the a-c sensitivity of this shunted ammeter be if used in a half-wave detector? In a full-wave detector?

4-7 A half-wave-rectifier type of a-c voltmeter has the usual rms scale based upon the assumption that only sine waves will be measured. If this voltmeter is used to measure a square wave, a false rms reading results. Nevertheless, if a reading of 50 volts is obtained for the square wave, what is the actual peak value of the square wave at the measuring terminals?

4-8 If a 100-μa movement with a meter resistance of 1 kilohm is used in a full-wave bridge detector, what should the size of R_s be for a 100-volt rms sine wave to produce full-scale deflection?

4-9 An a-c voltmeter has a sensitivity of 5 kilohms per volt. What is the input resistance on the 2.5-volt range? If this voltmeter is used to measure the voltage across the 30-kilohm resistor in Fig. 4-18*a*, what will the voltmeter read on its 2.5-volt range if the generator voltage is 4 volts rms?

4-10 An a-c voltmeter uses a full-wave bridge. The meter is a 1-kilohm 100-μa movement. What is the input resistance on the 50-volt range?

4-11 For the circuit of Fig. 4-18*a*, what size should the input resistance of an a-c voltmeter be in order to ensure 99 percent loading accuracy?

4-12 In the peak detector of Fig. 4-18*b*, the ammeter has a full-scale current of 1 ma and a meter resistance of 50 ohms.

(*a*) At high enough frequencies what is the peak value of the input signal that produces full-scale deflection?

(*b*) At what frequency does the capacitor discharge become 1 percent of the maximum capacitor voltage?

(*c*) If a signal with a peak voltage of 100 volts is being measured, approximately how long will it take the capacitor to discharge to 1 volt after the signal is removed?

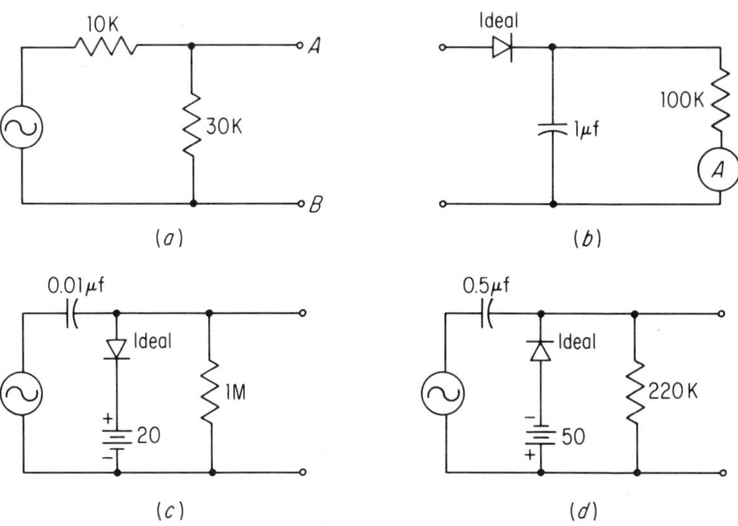

Fig. 4-18

4-13 In Fig. 4-12*a*, if the d-c voltmeter has an input resistance of 10 megohms, what size should the capacitor be in order to have a 99 percent accurate peak detector from 20 Hz to 20 kHz? (The diode is ideal and the source resistance is very small.)

4-14 In Fig. 4-12*a*, the d-c voltmeter has an input resistance of 100 kilohms. If the capacitor is to charge to 99 percent of the peak value, the effective source resistance must be less than what value? Assume ideal diode.

4-15 In Fig. 4-8*a*, a square wave is used instead of a sine wave. The resistance of 100 kilohms, and the capacitance is 1 μf. Sketch the output waveform across the capacitor if the square wave has a period of 2 msec.

4-16 The generator signal in the circuit of Fig. 4-16*a* is a square wave with a peak-to-peak value of 50 volts. Sketch the output waveform.

4-17 The generator signal in Fig. 4-16*c* is a sawtooth waveform with a peak-to-peak value of 75 volts. Sketch the output waveform.

4-18 The generator signal is a sine wave with a peak value of 50 volts. Sketch the output waveform. (Fig. 4-18*c*).

4-19 The generator signal is a square wave with a 70-volt peak value. Sketch the output waveform. (Fig. 4-18*d*).

4-20 A positive clamper is cascaded with a positive-peak detector. If the waveform of Fig. 4-19*a* is used as the input signal, sketch the waveform at the output of the clamping circuit. Also, sketch the voltage at the output of the peak detector, assuming high frequency.

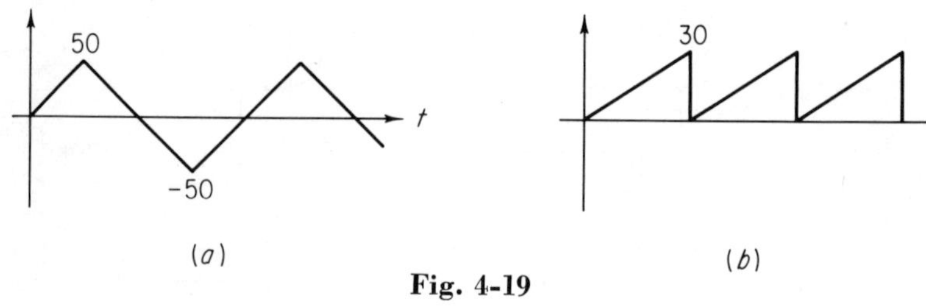

Fig. 4-19

4-21 A negative clamping circuit is cascaded with a negative-peak detector. If the waveform of Fig. 4-19*b* is used as the input to the clamper, sketch the output waveform of the clamper. Also, sketch the output waveform from the peak detector, assuming high frequency.

5 D-C Bridges

Balanced d-c bridges provide a method for making extremely accurate measurements of d-c voltage or resistance. Recall that the simple voltmeter and ohmmeter discussed in Chap. 2 had the limitations of calibration error and loading error. We shall see that a balanced d-c bridge does not have either meter-calibration error or loading error. The accuracy of the measurements is limited only by the tolerances of the internal parts of the bridge.

Unbalanced bridges are often used in control systems in order to provide a voltage which is proportional to the difference between a quantity being monitored and a reference value. The voltage out of the bridge can then be amplified and made to control the monitored quantity.

5-1 Basic Bridge Configurations

Bridge circuit generally refers to a circuit in which a load is connected between two levels of potential, much the same as a road bridge is connected between two levels of elevation.

One bridge configuration is shown in Fig. 5-1*a*. Note how the load is connected between two levels of potential. On the left side of the load there is a potential from A to ground, whereas on the right side of the load there is a potential from B to ground.

Another common form of the bridge is shown in Fig. 5-1*b*. Note that this is electrically equivalent to Fig. 5-1*a*, as will be shown later by means of Thévenin's theorem. In Fig. 5-1*b* we note that there is no current through the load if V_A equals V_B.

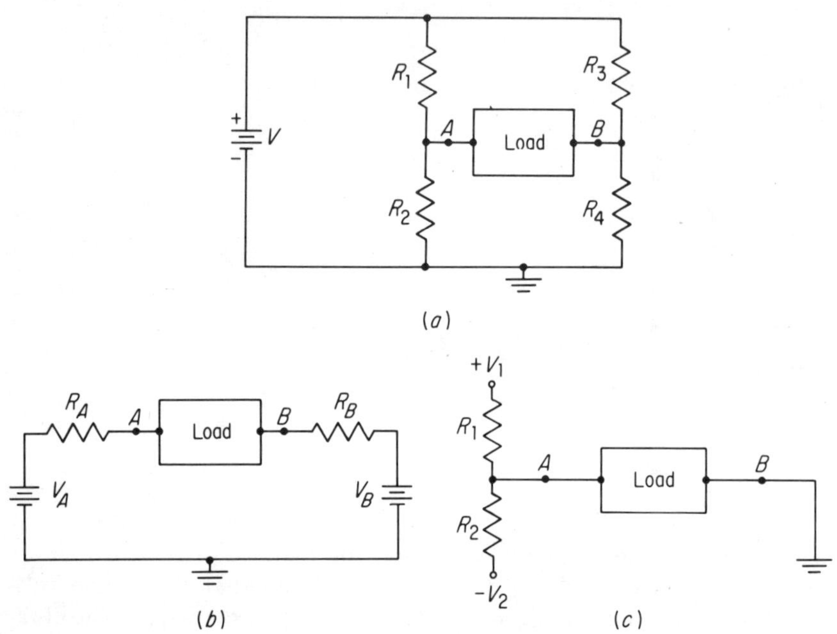

Fig. 5-1 Basic d-c bridge configurations.

Still another form of the bridge is shown in Fig. 5-1*c*. In this case the load is bridged between the potential out of the voltage divider and ground potential. Note that this form of the bridge is a special case of Fig. 5-1*b*.

5-2 The Wheatstone Bridge

The circuit of Fig. 5-1*a*, generally referred to as a *Wheatstone bridge,* is widely used for making accurate resistance measurements. Let us find the relation among resistances that produces bridge balance, that is, the condition where no current flows through the load.

First, realize that for a balanced bridge, there is no current through the load. As a result, for a balanced bridge we can remove the load shown in Fig. 5-2 without changing any of the voltages.

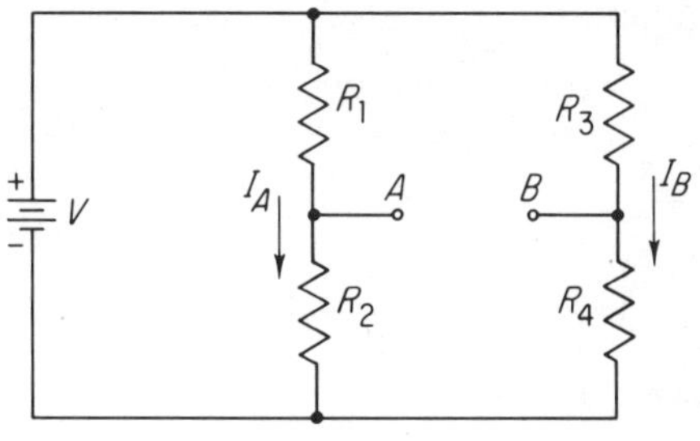

Fig. 5-2 Unloaded Wheatstone bridge.

Now let us compute the potential from A to ground.

$$V_A = I_A R_2 = \frac{V}{R_1 + R_2} R_2 = \frac{R_2}{R_1 + R_2} V \tag{5-1}$$

In a similar way, the potential from B to ground is found to be

$$V_B = I_B R_4 = \frac{V}{R_3 + R_4} R_4 = \frac{R_4}{R_3 + R_4} V \tag{5-2}$$

It should be clear that unless V_A and V_B are equal, current will flow through the load. Therefore, from an inspection of Eq. (5-1) and (5-2) it must follow that

$$\frac{R_2}{R_1 + R_2} = \frac{R_4}{R_3 + R_4} \tag{5-3}$$

From Eq. (5-3) we see what the relation among resistors must be if bridge balance has occurred. An even simpler form can be obtained by rearranging the equation as follows. Cross multiply to obtain

$$R_2R_3 + R_2R_4 = R_1R_4 + R_2R_4$$

or

$$R_2R_3 = R_1R_4$$

or

$$\frac{R_1}{R_2} = \frac{R_3}{R_4} \tag{5-4}$$

Equation (5-4), the Wheatstone-bridge balance condition, tells us that the ratio of the resistors on the left side of the bridge must equal the ratio of the resistors on the right side of the bridge at bridge balance. For instance, if $R_1 = 2$ kilohms, $R_2 = 4$ kilohms, $R_3 = 6$ kilohms, and $R_4 = 12$ kilohms, it is clear that the bridge is balanced, since the ratio on each side of the bridge is 1:2.

Example 5-1

In Fig. 5-2, $R_1 = 50$ kilohms, $R_2 = 10$ kilohms, $R_3 = 20$ kilohms, and $R_4 = 4$ kilohms. Is the bridge balanced?

SOLUTION

$$\frac{R_1}{R_2} = \frac{50(10^3)}{10(10^3)} = 5$$
$$\frac{R_3}{R_4} = \frac{20(10^3)}{4(10^3)} = 5$$

Yes, the bridge is balanced.

EXAMPLE 5-2

Is the bridge of Fig. 5-2 balanced if $R_1 = 5$ kilohms, $R_2 = 2$ kilohms, $R_3 = 10$ kilohms, and $R_4 = 3$ kilohms?

SOLUTION

$$\frac{R_1}{R_2} = \frac{5(10^3)}{2(10^3)} = 2.5$$
$$\frac{R_3}{R_4} = \frac{10(10^3)}{3(10^3)} = 3.33$$

No, the bridge is not balanced.

5-3 The Wheatstone-bridge Ohmmeter

An extremely accurate ohmmeter can be made by using an ammeter as the load across the bridge, as shown in Fig. 5-3. In this circuit, R_4

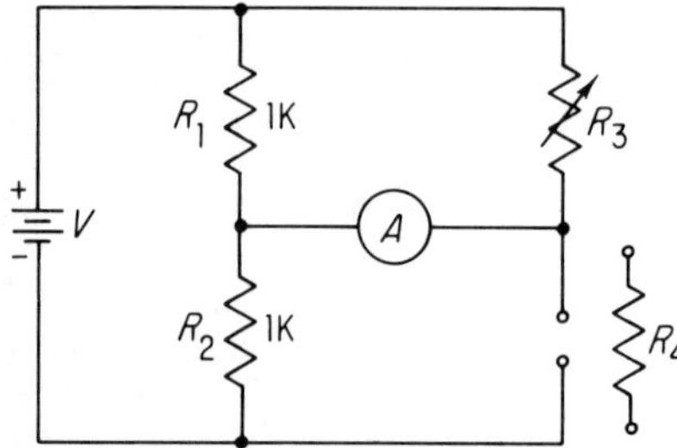

Fig. 5-3 Wheatstone bridge.

is the unknown resistor to be measured; R_3 is a variable resistor; and R_1 and R_2 are fixed resistors. The measurement is made by connecting the unknown resistor R_4 to the measuring terminals and then adjusting R_3 until the ammeter deflection goes to zero. Since the ratio of resistors on the left side of the bridge is unity, at balance the ratio of the right side is also unity. Therefore for no current through the ammeter, R_3 must equal R_4. We need only read the value of R_3 from a calibrated indicator.

Note that this type of ohmmeter does not have meter-calibration error, since the ammeter zero is exactly known. The sources of error are the tolerances of the 1-kilohm resistors, which typically would be about 0.1

percent. Furthermore, the calibration of the indicator for R_3 can also be accurate to within 0.1 percent. Hence, unknown resistors can be measured with extremely high accuracies.

Recall that the accuracy of the simple ohmmeter studied in Chap. 2 depends upon the battery voltage. The accuracy of the Wheatstone bridge, however, does not depend upon the value of the supply voltage, which is another important advantage.

Of course, the 1-kilohm resistors of Fig. 5-3 were chosen merely as examples. R_1 and R_2 may take on any values. In general, the value of the unknown resistor R_4 will equal

$$R_4 = \frac{R_2 R_3}{R_1}$$

EXAMPLE 5-3

If the bridge of Fig. 5-3 has $R_1 = 5$ kilohms and $R_2 = 50$ kilohms, what is the value of R_4 if bridge balance occurs for $R_3 = 250$ ohms?

SOLUTION

$$R_4 = \frac{50(10^3)(250)}{5(10^3)} = 2.5 \text{ kilohms}$$

5-4 The Potentiometer Bridge

The bridge of Fig. 5-1*b* is very useful for making accurate voltage measurements. If V_A is the voltage to be measured, it should be clear that by adjusting V_B, the current through the load can be made equal to zero. Under such a balance condition V_A must equal V_B. Thus, if V_B can be read from a calibrated indicator, the value of V_A will be known.

A practical version of the circuit of Fig. 5-1*b* is shown in Fig. 5-4. The voltage to be measured is applied to the input terminals. The potentiometer is then adjusted to obtain zero ammeter current. The potentiometer is of course attached to an indicator to allow a readout of V_B. Thus, the unknown voltage is quickly determined.

Note that this potentiometer bridge has no meter-calibration error, since the ammeter indicates zero, which is accurately marked on the meter face. Furthermore, this circuit introduces no loading error, since at

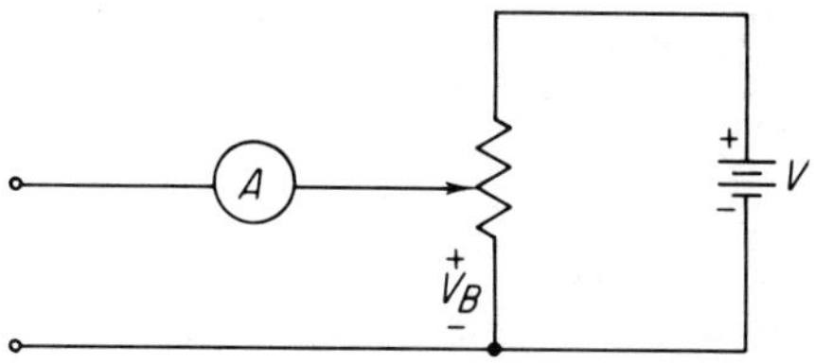

Fig. 5-4 Potentiometer bridge.

balance no current is drawn from the circuit under test. However, there are some sources of error. First, there is the calibration of the potentiometer. Second, there is the dependence upon the battery voltage. In other words, V_B varies as the battery voltage V changes. Both these sources of error can be minimized so that extremely accurate voltage measurements are possible.

5-5 Thévenin Equivalent of a Wheatstone Bridge

The Thévenin theorem can be applied to the Wheatstone bridge so as to allow easy solution of unbalanced-bridge problems. In other words, if the circuit of Fig. 5-1a is unbalanced, a current flows through the load. How can we find the value of this current? Ordinarily, an approach based on Kirchhoff's law requires three equations in three unknowns, and solving these equations is usually time-consuming and difficult.

Undoubtedly the best method of finding the load current is first to obtain a single-loop circuit by means of Thévenin's theorem. Finding the load current is then a very simple matter.

In Fig. 5-2 the load has been removed. Note that we can apply Thévenin's theorem to each side of the bridge. For instance, looking into the A terminal with respect to ground, we see a voltage of

$$V_A = \frac{R_2}{R_1 + R_2} V$$

Furthermore, the Thévenin resistance looking into the A terminal with respect to ground is

$$R_A = R_1 \| R_2$$

In a similar manner, looking into the B terminal with respect to ground yields

$$V_B = \frac{R_4}{R_3 + R_4} V \qquad \text{and} \qquad R_B = R_3 \| R_4$$

The circuit in Fig. 5-5a is an equivalent for the original bridge. Note that a load may now be connected to the AB terminals. Finding the load current in this single-loop circuit is easy.

Of course, the circuit of Fig. 5-5a may be reduced even further by applying Thévenin's theorem again. Looking into the AB terminals, we see an open-circuit voltage of $V_A - V_B$ and a Thévenin resistance of $R_A + R_B$. Thus, the Thévenin equivalent is the circuit shown in Fig. 5-5b. This equivalent circuit is very useful for solving unbalanced-bridge problems involving the current or voltage across the load.

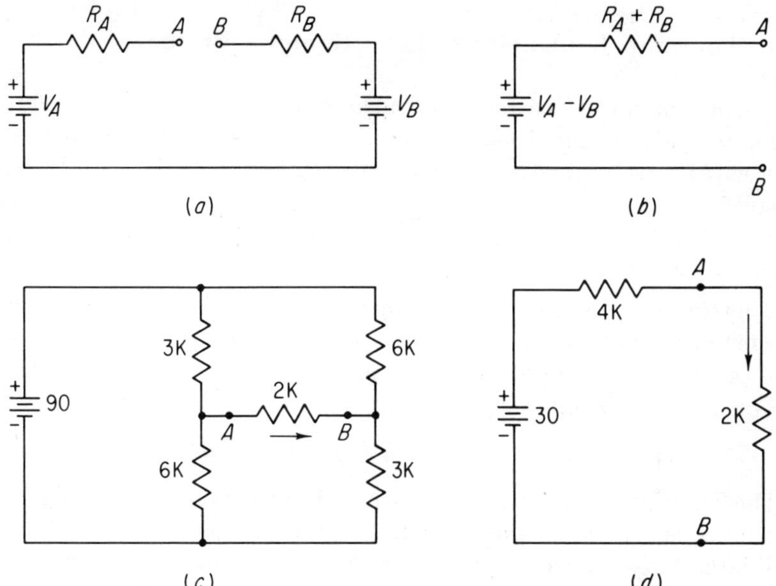

Fig. 5-5 Obtaining the Thévenin equivalent of a Wheatstone bridge.

EXAMPLE 5-4

Find the load current through the 2-kilohm resistor in the unbalanced bridge of Fig. 5-5*c*.

SOLUTION

We assume that the 2-kilohm resistor has been removed. The open-circuit voltage from A to ground is then

$$V_A = \frac{6(10^3)}{9(10^3)} 90 = 60 \text{ volts}$$

Furthermore, the Thévenin resistance from A to ground is

$$R_A = 3(10^3) \| 6(10^3) = 2 \text{ kilohms}$$

On the B side of the bridge similar results occur. We find that

$$V_B = \frac{3(10^3)}{9(10^3)} 90 = 30 \text{ volts} \quad \text{and} \quad R_B = 3(10^3) \| 6(10^3) = 2 \text{ kilohms}$$

With these results we can now draw the final Thévenin equivalent, as shown in Fig. 5-5*d*. Obviously, the load current through the 2-kilohm resistor is 5 ma.

With practice, unbalanced-bridge problems can be solved in a matter of minutes using Thévenin's theorem.

5-6 Thévenin Equivalent of Potentiometer Bridges

We wish to find the Thévenin equivalent circuits for the bridge circuits of Fig. 5-6*a* and *c*. In Fig. 5-6*a* the potentiometer has a total resistance of R. The wiper taps off a resistance equal to kR, as shown. Hence, the open-circuit voltage is

$$V_{oc} = \frac{V}{R} kR = kV \tag{5-5}$$

The letter k merely indicates how much of the total resistance is tapped. For instance, if the wiper is exactly at the middle, k equals ½. If the wiper taps off one-fourth the resistance, then k equals ¼.

The Thévenin resistance is simply

$$R_o = kR \| (1 - k)R = k(1 - k)R \tag{5-6}$$

The Thévenin equivalent is shown in Fig. 5-6*b*. Note that the Thévenin resistance is zero when the wiper is at either end of the potentiometer. The largest resistance occurs for the wiper at midposition, that is, for k equal to ½. Hence, the largest resistance possible will be $R/4$.

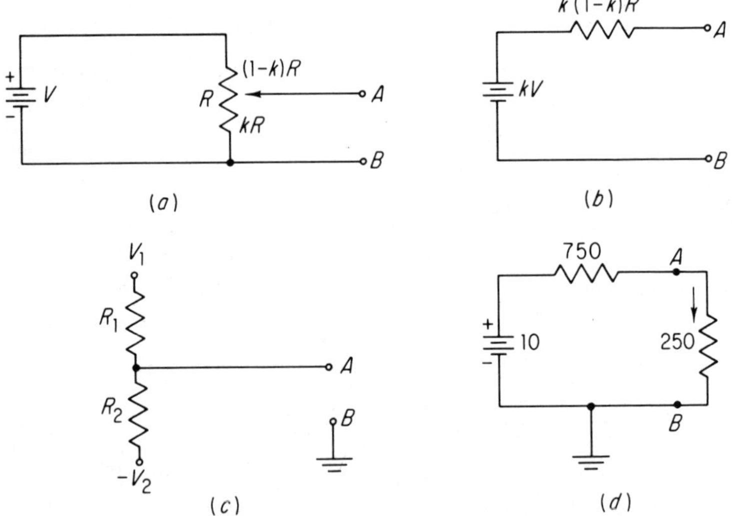

Fig. 5-6 Thévenin equivalent circuits.

As an example of finding the Thévenin equivalent, consider a situation where the value of V is 20 volts and the potentiometer has a total resistance of 10 kilohms. Then for the wiper at midposition, the Thévenin voltage will be 10 volts, and the Thévenin resistance will be 2.5 kilohms. If the wiper is now moved so that it taps off 2 kilohms, the Thévenin voltage becomes 4 volts, and the Thévenin resistance becomes 2 kilohms shunted by 8 kilohms, which is 1.6 kilohms.

The circuit of Fig. 5-6c is often used in practice as the input to an amplifier. Therefore, it will be useful to have its Thévenin equivalent circuit. It can be shown that the open-circuit voltage and the Thévenin resistance are

$$V_{oc} = V_1 - \frac{R_1}{R_1 + R_2}(V_1 + V_2) \tag{5-7}$$

$$R_o = R_1 \| R_2 \tag{5-8}$$

The use of Eqs. (5-7) and (5-8) is straightforward, as shown by the following examples.

Example 5-5

In the circuit of Fig. 5-6c the following values apply: $V_1 = 20$, $V_2 = 20$, $R_1 = 1$ kilohm, and $R_2 = 3$ kilohms. If a transistor amplifier with an input resistance of 250 ohms is connected to the AB terminals, what is the current into the amplifier?

Solution

$$V_{oc} = 20 - \frac{10^3}{4(10^3)} 40 = 10 \qquad \text{and} \qquad R_o = 10^3 \| 3(10^3) = 750$$

The Thévenin equivalent with the load connected is shown in Fig. 5-6d. Clearly, the current into the transistor amplifier is 10 ma.

Example 5-6

The circuit of Fig. 5-6a has a supply voltage of 50 volts, and the total resistance is 100 kilohms. How much current flows through a load of 75 kilohms if the wiper is set to midposition?

Solution

At midposition the open-circuit voltage is 25 volts. The Thévenin resistance is

$$R_o = k(1 - k)R = \tfrac{1}{2}(1 - \tfrac{1}{2})100(10^3) = 25 \text{ kilohms}$$

If a 75-kilohm load is connected to the AB terminals, the current will be

$$I = \frac{25}{25(10^3) + 75(10^3)} = 0.25 \text{ ma}$$

5-7 Slightly Unbalanced Bridges

From our discussion of Wheatstone bridges and potentiometer bridges, one might think that bridges were always used in the balanced condition.

Quite the contrary is true. There are many applications for bridges that are slightly unbalanced, especially in control systems. Very often the voltage out of a slightly unbalanced bridge can be amplified and then used to control the resistance of one of the bridge arms. By doing this any number of interesting applications is possible. A more complete discussion of the applications of slightly unbalanced bridges is given in Chap. 18. As a preparation, we need to find the Thévenin equivalent of bridges that are almost, but not quite, balanced.

First, let us find the Thévenin equivalent of the slightly unbalanced Wheatstone bridge shown in Fig. 5-7*a*. Note that this is a special bridge,

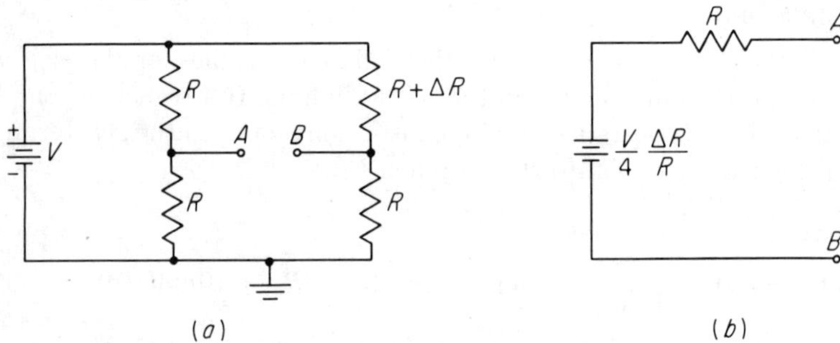

Fig. 5-7 Slightly unbalanced Wheatstone bridge. (*a*) Circuit. (*b*) Thévenin equivalent.

in which three out of the four resistors are equal. The fourth resistor differs from the others by a *small* amount, which we will designate by ΔR. For instance, the three resistors could have a value of 1 kilohm, and the fourth could have a value of 1010 ohms. Then, R equals 1 kilohm, and ΔR equals 10. If we like, we may think of the fourth resistor as being in error with respect to R by an amount of ΔR. Furthermore, the percent error can be defined as

$$\text{Percent error} \triangleq \frac{\Delta R}{R} \tag{5-9}$$

Thus, if R equals 1 kilohm and $R + \Delta R$ equals 1010, the percent error of the fourth resistor would be 1 percent.

By an inspection of Fig. 5-7*a* we can see that

$$V_A = \frac{R}{R + R} V = \frac{V}{2}$$

$$V_B = \frac{R}{2R + \Delta R} V$$

The open-circuit voltage is the difference between V_A and V_B. Hence,

$$V_{oc} = V_A - V_B = V\left(\frac{1}{2} - \frac{R}{2R + \Delta R}\right) = V\frac{\Delta R}{4R + 2\Delta R}$$

$$\cong \frac{V}{4}\frac{\Delta R}{R} \qquad \text{negligible} \uparrow \tag{5-10}$$

Equation (5-10) is obtained by noting that for slightly unbalanced bridges the value of ΔR is small compared to R. Therefore, dropping the ΔR in the denominator will cause only a small error in the value of V_{oc}. It can be shown that if $\Delta R/R$ is less than 1 percent, Eq. (5-10) is accurate to within ½ percent. If $\Delta R/R$ is less than 10 percent, Eq. (5-10) is accurate to within 5 percent. Hence, Eq. (5-10) is good approximation for slightly unbalanced bridges.

In a similar manner, the Thévenin resistance is

$$R_o = R\|R + R\|(R + \Delta R) \cong \frac{R}{2} + \frac{R}{2} = R$$

This equation is accurate to within ½ percent for $\Delta R/R$ less than 1 percent. Furthermore, the equation is accurate to within 5 percent for $\Delta R/R$ less than 10 percent.

For practical purposes, then, a slightly unbalanced bridge may be represented by the Thévenin equivalent circuit shown in Fig. 5-7*b*. This equivalent circuit is quite useful in the solution of slightly unbalanced bridges.

It will also be useful to have the Thévenin equivalent for the slightly unbalanced bridge shown in Fig. 5-8*a*. Note carefully that this is a special case with both voltages numerically equal and both resistors almost equal. We will merely indicate that the Thévenin equivalent for this bridge is the circuit shown in Fig. 5-8*b*.

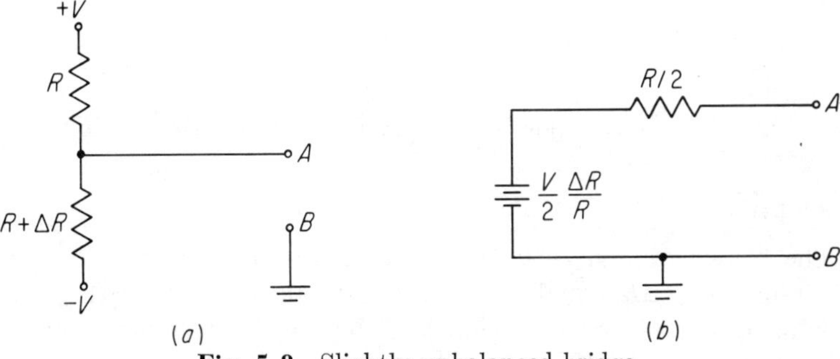

Fig. 5-8 Slightly unbalanced bridge.

EXAMPLE 5-7

In a Wheatstone bridge three out of four resistors equal 1 kilohm, and the fourth resistor equals 1010 ohms. If the battery voltage is 100 volts, what is the approximate value of the open-circuit voltage? If the output of the bridge is connected to a 4-kilohm resistor, how much current would flow through the resistor?

SOLUTION

$$V_{oc} = \frac{V}{4}\frac{\Delta R}{R} = \frac{100}{4}\frac{10}{1000} = 0.25 \text{ volts}$$

Furthermore, the Thévenin resistance is approximately 1 kilohm. The Thévenin equivalent is shown in Fig. 5-9*a*. It should be clear that the current through a 4-kilohm resistor will be

$$I = \frac{0.25}{10^3 + 4(10^3)} = 0.05 \text{ ma}$$

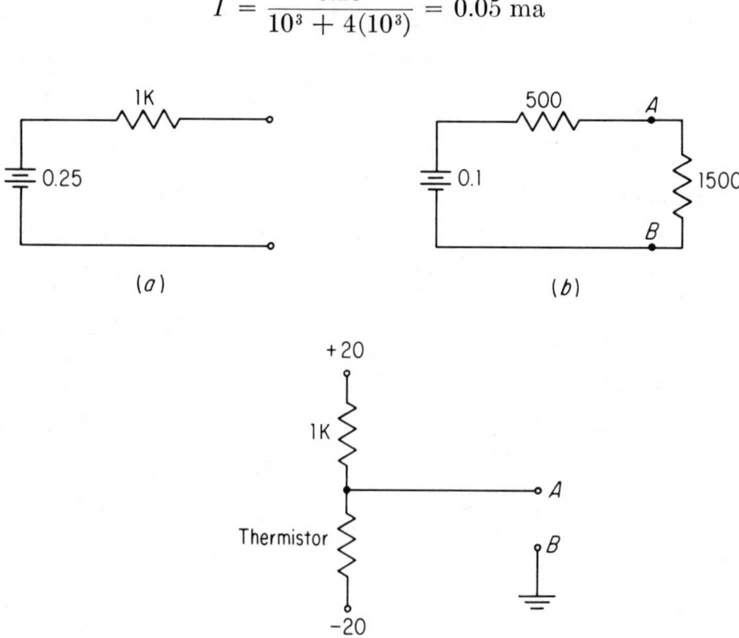

Fig. 5-9 (*a*) Example 5-7. (*b*) Example 5-8. (*c*) Example 5-9.

EXAMPLE 5-8

The bridge of Fig. 5-8*a* has V equal to 20 volts and R equal to 1 kilohm. $R + \Delta R$ equals 1010 ohms. If an amplifier with an input resistance of 1500 ohms is connected to the AB terminals, what will the input voltage to the amplifier be?

SOLUTION

$$V_{oc} \cong \frac{V}{2}\frac{\Delta R}{R} = \frac{20}{2}\frac{10}{1000} = 0.1$$

and

$$R_o \cong \frac{R}{2} = 500$$

The Thévenin equivalent circuit with the amplifier input resistance connected is shown in Fig. 5-9*b*. From this circuit it should be clear that the actual input voltage to the amplifier is

$$V = \frac{0.1}{2000} 1500 = 0.075 = 75 \text{ mv}$$

EXAMPLE 5-9

A thermistor is a resistor whose value is very sensitive to heat. At 50°C the resistance of the thermistor of Fig. 5-9*c* is 1000 ohms. As the temperature decreases, the resistance of the thermistor increases by 5 ohms for each degree drop. At what temperature is the open-circuit voltage out of the bridge equal to 50 mv?

SOLUTION

$$V_{oc} = \frac{V}{2}\frac{\Delta R}{R}$$

or

$$0.05 = \frac{20}{2}\frac{\Delta R}{1000}$$

or

$$\Delta R = 0.005(1000) = 5 \text{ ohms}$$

Hence, when the temperature drops to 49°C, the thermistor resistance will rise 5 ohms, causing the open-circuit voltage to become 50 mv.

SUMMARY

The balanced Wheatstone bridge is generally used for making very accurate resistance measurements. The potentiometer bridge is often used for making extremely accurate voltage measurements. Both bridges are based upon comparing the unknown quantity to an internal standard. As a result, the measurement is as accurate as the calibration of the standard.

A Wheatstone bridge is balanced if the ratio of resistors on one side of the bridge equals the ratio of resistors on the other side.

There are many applications for unbalanced bridges, particularly slightly unbalanced bridges. In such cases, the best procedure for finding the current and voltage across the load is to apply Thévenin's theorem.

GLOSSARY

bridge balance That condition of a bridge in which no current flows through the detector.

percent error In a slightly unbalanced bridge this refers to the deviation of a resistance value from the value required to balance the bridge. Specifically, the percent error is found by dividing the deviation in ohms by the value required to balance the bridge.

potentiometer bridge A bridge designed to measure voltages. The amount of loading error in this type of bridge is zero.

Wheatstone bridge The most basic of all bridge types. Consists of four resistors. Balance occurs only when the ratio of resistors on one side of the bridge equals the ratio of resistors on the other side of the bridge.

REVIEW QUESTIONS

1. What is a bridge circuit?
2. What is a Wheatstone bridge?
3. What limits the accuracy of a resistance measurement on a Wheatstone bridge?
4. What relation exists among the resistances of a balanced Wheatstone bridge?
5. What is a potentiometer bridge? What electrical quantity does it normally measure?
6. How much loading error does a potentiometer bridge cause when voltages are measured?
7. How is Thévenin's theorem applied to the Wheatstone bridge?
8. What does the percent error refer to in a slightly unbalanced bridge?
9. The open-circuit voltage in a slightly unbalanced bridge is proportional to what quantities?

PROBLEMS

5-1 In Fig. 5-1*a* determine whether or not the bridge is balanced for the following conditions:

(*a*) $R_1 = 3$ kilohms, $R_2 = 5$ kilohms, $R_3 = 15$ kilohms, $R_4 = 25$ kilohms

(b) $R_1 = 7$ kilohms, $R_2 = 49$ kilohms, $R_3 = 2$ kilohms, $R_4 = 14$ kilohms

(c) $R_1 = 8$ kilohms, $R_2 = 12$ kilohms, $R_3 = 3$ kilohms, $R_4 = 4$ kilohms

5-2 In Fig. 5-3 suppose the adjustable range of R_3 is from 100 ohms to 10 kilohms. In order to measure unknown resistances from 10 kilohms to 1 megohm, the value of R_2 may be changed from 1 kilohm to another value. What is this value?

5-3 In Prob. 5-2 if the unknown resistance range is to be from 1 to 100 ohms, what size should R_2 be?

5-4 In the circuit of Fig. 5-4 an unknown voltage is applied to the input terminals. If the battery voltage is 10 volts, and if the current through the ammeter equals zero for the wiper at the midposition, what is the value of the unknown voltage?

5-5 In the circuit of Fig. 5-2 find the Thévenin equivalent at the AB terminals for $V = 25$, $R_1 = 2$ kilohms, $R_2 = 5$ kilohms, $R_3 = 4$ kilohms, and $R_4 = 3$ kilohms.

5-6 For the circuit of Fig. 5-1*a* find the current through a load of 2.5 kilohms. The bridge values are: $V = 60$, $R_1 = 1$ kilohm, $R_2 = 3$ kilohms, $R_3 = 3$ kilohms, and $R_4 = 1$ kilohm.

5-7 Using the bridge values of Prob. 5-6, find the current that would flow through a load of 0 ohms.

5-8 In Fig. 5-6*a* the wiper is set to tap off 40 kilohms out of a total of 50 kilohms. If the battery voltage equals 20 volts, how much current would flow through a 4-kilohm resistor connected to the AB terminals?

5-9 If the wiper of Fig. 5-6*a* is at the midposition, what size load resistor across the AB terminals will drop the open-circuit voltage in half? The battery voltage is 20, and the total resistance R is 50 kilohms.

5-10 In Fig. 5-6*c* the values are $V_1 = 30$, $V_2 = 20$, $R_1 = 20$ kilohms, and $R_2 = 30$ kilohms. If an amplifier with an input resistance of 10 kilohms is connected to the AB terminals, what will the voltage across the AB terminals become? How much current will flow into the 10-kilohm load?

5-11 The slightly unbalanced bridge of Fig. 5-7*a* has an R value of 5 kilohms. The percent error of the fourth resistor is 2 percent. If the battery voltage is 50 volts, what is the open-circuit voltage?

5-12 The bridge of Fig. 5-7*a* has R equal to 10 kilohms and a ΔR equal to 50 ohms. The battery voltage is 30 volts. If a 20-kilohm resistor is connected across the bridge, what will the AB voltage be?

5-13 In Prob. 5-12, an amplifier is connected across the bridge instead of a 20-kilohm resistor. The voltage gain of the amplifier is 26 db. If the amplifier has an input resistance of 15 kilohms what is the output voltage of the amplifier?

5-14 The bridge of Fig. 5-8*a* has plus and minus voltages of 25 volts. If R equals 5 kilohms, what value of V_{oc} occurs for a percent error in the lower resistor of 4 percent?

5-15 The bridge of Fig. 5-8*a* has R equal to 20 kilohms, and V equal to 50 volts. What percent error in the lower resistance will produce 0.25 volts across the AB terminals?

5-16 In Fig. 5-9 what value of thermistor resistance produces an open-circuit voltage of 0.5 volts? If a 3-kilohm resistor is connected to the AB terminals, what voltage now appears across AB?

6 A-C Bridges

An a-c bridge is one that is driven by an a-c signal source. Bridges of this type may contain reactance as well as resistance. They are used to measure impedance accurately, much the same as the Wheatstone bridge is used to measure resistance accurately. Also, a-c bridges find widespread application in filters, oscillators, and other instruments. In this chapter we will examine the balance conditions for some of the most important types of a-c bridges.

6-1 Equivalent Impedances

Recall that the major concept in a-c circuit theory is that Ohm's law and Kirchhoff's laws may be extended or applied to a-c circuits if the driving signal is a sinusoidal waveshape. For sinusoidal signals we speak of the impedance of a circuit, and we use complex numbers to represent this impedance. Also, complex numbers are used to represent the sinusoidal voltages and currents in the circuits. Under these conditions, Ohm's law becomes

$$\mathbf{I} = \frac{\mathbf{V}}{\mathbf{Z}} \tag{6-1}$$

This equation is applied to a-c circuits in a manner that is completely analogous to the ordinary use of Ohm's law in d-c circuits. Also, all the rules for combining series and parallel resistances into a single equivalent resistance are applicable to the various combinations of impedances. In other words, parallel impedances combine as parallel resistances, series impedances combine as series resistances, and so on. The only difference between combining impedances instead of pure resistances is that we must use complex numbers instead of real numbers.

Now we know that the input resistance of any d-c circuit, no matter how complicated, can be represented by a single resistance. For instance, in Fig. 6-1*a* the circuit consists of pure resistances. These may be combined by the usual rules to obtain a single equivalent resistance. However, when the circuit consists of impedances, as shown in Fig. 6-1*b*, the circuit may be reduced to either a series equivalent or a parallel equivalent. Either of these basic equivalent circuits is possible, because

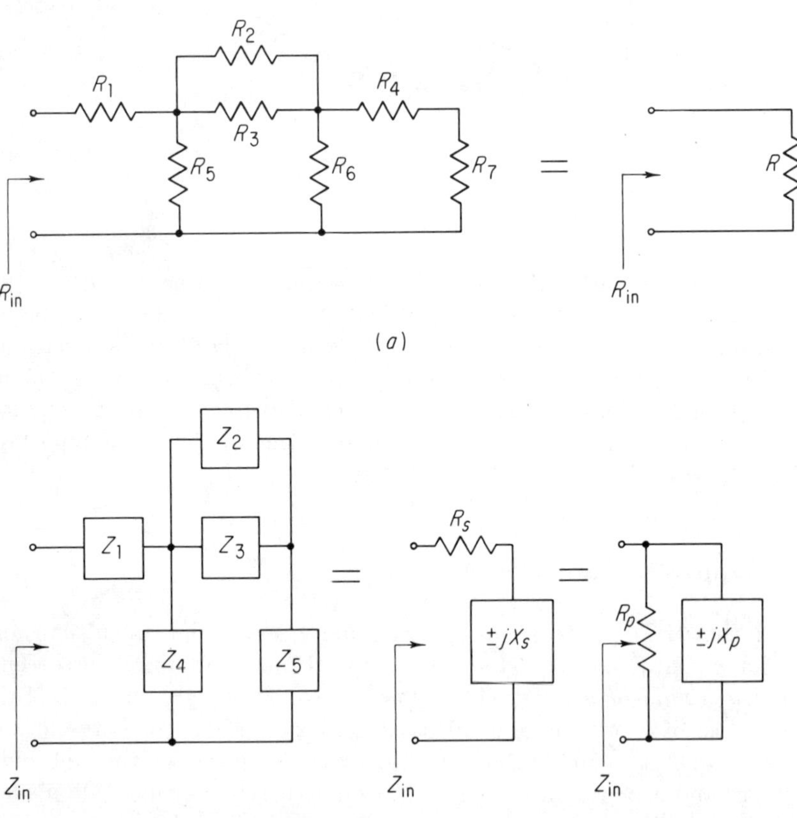

Fig. 6-1 Equivalent circuits. (*a*) Equivalent resistance. (*b*) Series and parallel equivalent impedances.

a complex number has two parts; a real part and an imaginary part. The real part represents the resistive component, and the imaginary part represents the reactive component. Because of this, either a series or a parallel equivalent is possible.

As a simple example of series and parallel equivalent circuits, let us reduce the circuit of Fig. 6-2*a*. Note that the two 20-ohm resistors combine into a 10-ohm resistor. Also, an impedance of $j50$ combines with an impedance of $-j30$ to produce a net impedance of $j20$. The result is a series equivalent circuit as shown in Fig. 6-2*b*. To obtain the parallel equivalent we must use the admittance concept as follows

$$\mathbf{Z} = 10 + j20$$

$$\mathbf{Y} = \frac{1}{\mathbf{Z}} = \frac{1}{10 + j20} = \frac{1}{10 + j20}\,\frac{10 - j20}{10 - j20} = \frac{10 - j20}{500}$$

$$\mathbf{Y} = 1/50 - j1/25$$

This tells us the admittance of the original network consists of conductance of $1/50$ mho in parallel with a susceptance of $-j1/25$ mho, as shown in Fig. 6-2*c*. Since the use of mhos is not so widespread as the use of ohms, let us convert mhos to ohms to obtain the circuit of Fig. 6-2*d*. This circuit is the parallel equivalent of the original given network. As far as the voltage and current at the terminals are concerned, the series and the parallel equivalent circuits are equally valid in representing the original given circuit. It is very important to realize this, since instruments designed to measure impedance will read either the series or the parallel

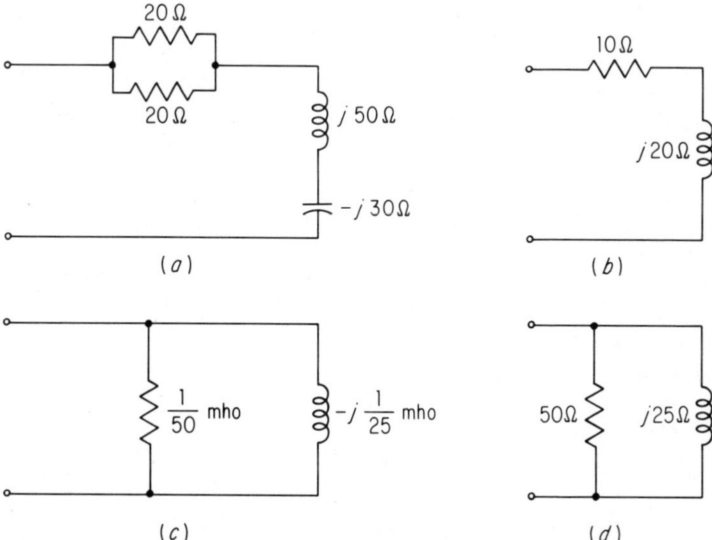

Fig. 6-2 Example of equivalent impedances. (*a*) Circuit. (*b*) Series equivalent. (*c*) Parallel equivalent in mhos. (*d*) Parallel equivalent in ohms.

equivalent impedance. In other words, if a circuit like that of Fig. 6-2*a* is measured on an a-c bridge, the a-c bridge may read either the series equivalent value or the parallel equivalent value. Thus, a bridge designed to read the series equivalent will indicate that the impedance is a 10-ohm resistor in series with an inductive reactance of 20 ohms. However, an a-c bridge designed to read the parallel equivalent would indicate a 50-ohm resistor shunted by an inductive reactance of 25 ohms. Clearly, whenever we use a bridge to measure impedances, we must know whether the bridge reads the series or the parallel equivalent of the actual impedance under test.

One very important point should be realized. The series and parallel equivalent impedances are valid only at one frequency. If the frequency is changed, we must recalculate the values of the series and parallel equivalents. For instance, in Fig. 6-2*a* the values of reactance are given for a single frequency. As long as the frequency remains constant, the series and parallel equivalent circuits of Fig. 6-2*b* and *d* are valid. If the frequency is changed, the values of reactances will change in the original circuit and in the equivalent circuits.

Example 6-1

An a-c circuit consists of a 1-ohm resistor in series with an inductive reactance of 1 ohm. Find the parallel equivalent circuit.

Solution

$$\mathbf{Z} = 1 + j1$$

$$\mathbf{Y} = \frac{1}{\mathbf{Z}} = \frac{1}{1 + j1} = \frac{1}{1 + j1}\,\frac{1 - j1}{1 - j1} = \frac{1 - j1}{2} = \frac{1}{2} - j\frac{1}{2}$$

The admittance is a ½-mho conductance shunted by an inductive susceptance of ½ mho. This is the same as a 2-ohm resistor shunted by an inductive reactance of 2 ohms.

6-2 Series-Parallel Equivalent Conversion Formulas

We now wish to develop for future reference a set of conversion formulas that will permit easy conversion from the series equivalent circuit to the parallel equivalent and vice versa.

Consider the series equivalent circuit of Fig. 6-3*a*. The input impedance is

$$\mathbf{Z} = R_s + jX_s$$

or

$$\mathbf{Y} = \frac{1}{\mathbf{Z}} = \frac{1}{R_s + jX_s} = \frac{1}{R_s + jX_s}\,\frac{R_s - jX_s}{R_s - jX_s} = \frac{R_s - jX_s}{R_s^2 + X_s^2}$$

$$\mathbf{Y} = \frac{R_s}{R_s^2 + X_s^2} - j\frac{X_s}{R_s^2 + X_s^2}$$

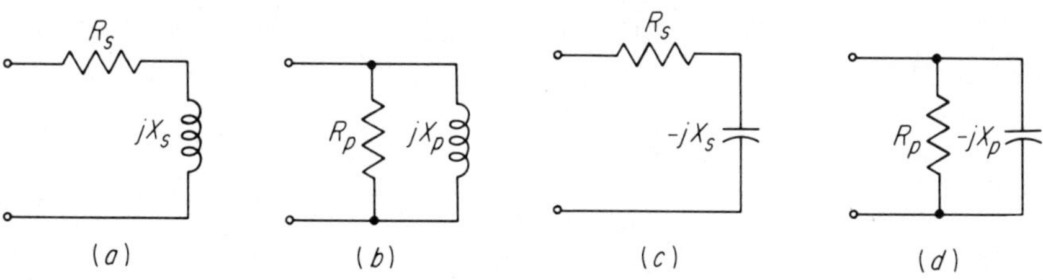

Fig. 6-3 Conversion from series to parallel equivalent. (*a*) Series *RL* circuit. (*b*) Parallel *RL* equivalent. (*c*) Series *RC* circuit. (*d*) Parallel *RC* equivalent.

The real part of this admittance is the conductance in mhos. We can convert this to ohms by inverting. In a similar manner the susceptance is in mhos and can be converted to ohms by inversion. We then will have a resistance shunted by an inductive reactance, as shown in Fig. 6-3*b*. The values for R_p and X_p are

$$R_p = \frac{R_s^2 + X_s^2}{R_s} \tag{6-2}$$

$$X_p = \frac{R_s^2 + X_s^2}{X_s} \tag{6-3}$$

These equations tell us how to convert from a given series equivalent circuit to the parallel equivalent circuit. For example, if the series equivalent impedance is $\mathbf{Z} = 1 + j1$ at 1 kHz, we would substitute into Eqs. (6-2) and (6-3) as follows:

$$R_p = \frac{1^2 + 1^2}{1} = 2 \text{ ohms}$$

$$X_p = \frac{1^2 + 1^2}{1} = 2 \text{ ohms}$$

We therefore see that a series circuit consisting of a 1-ohm resistor in series with an inductive reactance of 1 ohm may be represented or replaced by a 2-ohm resistor in shunt with an inductive reactance of 2 ohms at 1 kHz.

It can also be shown that the circuit of Fig. 6-3*c* has the parallel equivalent circuit of Fig. 6-3*d*. The values of R_p and X_p are given by the same set of equations, namely, (6-2) and (6-3).

Equations (6-2) and (6-3) are useful in making the conversion from series to parallel equivalent, but they can be changed to a simpler form by using the concept of Q. Recall that the Q of a series circuit consisting of a resistance and a reactance is

$$Q = \frac{X_s}{R_s} \tag{6-4}$$

This equation for Q applies only to a series equivalent circuit. The formula for the Q of a parallel equivalent circuit is different and will be given shortly.

From Eq. (6-4) it is clear that $X_s = QR_s$. We may now substitute into Eq. (6-2) to obtain

$$R_p = \frac{R_s^2 + X_s^2}{R_s} = \frac{R_s^2 + Q^2R_s^2}{R_s} = R_s(1 + Q^2) \tag{6-5}$$

In a similar manner we find

$$X_p = X_s\left(1 + \frac{1}{Q^2}\right) \tag{6-6}$$

Equations (6-5) and (6-6) are generally easier to use when making calculations. As an example, let us convert a series equivalent of $\mathbf{Z} = 2 + j10$. First, note that the Q equals $^{10}\!/_2$, or 5. Then,

$$R_p = R_s(1 + Q^2) = 2(1 + 5^2) = 52 \text{ ohms}$$

$$X_p = X_s\left(1 + \frac{1}{Q^2}\right) = 10\left(1 + \frac{1}{5^2}\right) = 10.4 \text{ ohms}$$

We now have a set of simple conversion formulas for obtaining the parallel equivalent circuit, given the series equivalent circuit. It is also important to be able to convert in the opposite direction. In other words, given the parallel equivalent circuit, how do we find the series equivalent?

Recall from basic electronics courses that the Q of a parallel circuit is

$$Q = \frac{R_p}{X_p} \tag{6-7}$$

In a manner analogous to what we have already used, it can be shown that the formulas for the series equivalent values are

$$R_s = \frac{R_p}{1 + Q^2} \tag{6-8}$$

$$X_s = \frac{X_p}{1 + 1/Q^2} \tag{6-9}$$

To summarize, it is often helpful, and sometimes necessary, to convert from one equivalent circuit to the other. To convert from series to parallel equivalent we use Eqs. (6-5) and (6-6). Remember that the Q to use in these equations is $Q = X_s/R_s$. To convert from parallel to series equivalent we must use Eqs. (6-8) and (6-9). The Q in these equations is

$$Q = \frac{R_p}{X_p}$$

Example 6-2

The series equivalent circuit is a 100-ohm resistor in series with a capacitive reactance of 5000 ohms. Find the parallel equivalent circuit and verify that the Q given by the parallel equivalent agrees with the Q given by the series equivalent.

SOLUTION

$$Q = \frac{X_s}{R_s} = \frac{5000}{100} = 50$$

$$R_p = R_s(1 + Q^2) = 100(1 + 50^2) \cong 250 \text{ kilohms}$$

$$X_p = X_s\left(1 + \frac{1}{Q^2}\right) = 5000\left(1 + \frac{1}{50^2}\right) \cong 5000 \text{ ohms}$$

and

$$Q = \frac{R_p}{X_p} = \frac{250(10^3)}{5(10^3)} = 50$$

Note that the Q given by each equivalent circuit is the same. We certainly would expect this to be true if the circuits are equivalent in the full sense of the word. Note also that the parallel circuit has a capacitive reactance of approximately 5000 ohms. This is the same as the value for the series circuit. It should be clear from Eq. (6-9) that for high-Q circuits, X_s and X_p are approximately equal.

One more point is that if the series circuit contains a capacitive reactance, the parallel circuit also contains a capacitive reactance. Similarly, if the series circuit is inductive, the parallel circuit is inductive.

EXAMPLE 6-3

A parallel circuit consists of a 10-kilohm resistor shunted by an inductive reactance of 100 ohms. Find the series equivalent circuit.

SOLUTION

$$Q = \frac{R_p}{X_p} = \frac{10(10^3)}{100} = 100$$

$$R_s = \frac{10(10^3)}{1 + 100^2} \cong 1 \text{ ohm}$$

$$X_s = \frac{100}{1 + 1/100^2} \cong 100 \text{ ohms}$$

The series equivalent circuit is a 1-ohm resistor in series with an inductive reactance of 100 ohms.

EXAMPLE 6-4

A vacuum tube is designed to work into a load resistance of 10 kilohms at 1 MHz. However, the input resistance of the next stage is 100 ohms. Show how this low resistance can be stepped up to 10 kilohms.

SOLUTION

One way to step 100 ohms up to 10 kilohms is by means of a transformer with a turns ratio of 10 to 1. However, we may avoid the use of a transformer by using the series equivalent circuit of Fig. 6-4*a*. Note that the Q equals 1 kilohm/100 or 10. Therefore,

$$R_p = 100(1 + 10^2) \cong 10 \text{ kilohms}$$

$$X_p = 10^3\left(1 + \frac{1}{10^2}\right) \cong 1 \text{ kilohm}$$

The parallel equivalent circuit is shown in Fig. 6-4*b*. Note that there is a 10-kilohm resistor in shunt with a reactance of 1 kilohm. If this circuit is connected to the vacuum tube, it will appear too capacitive.

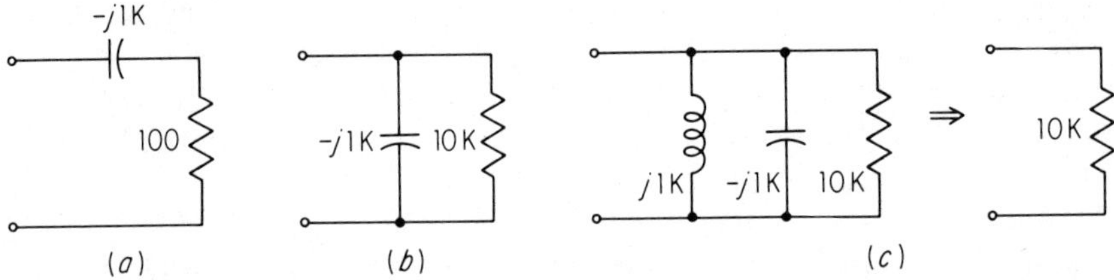

Fig. 6-4 Example 6-4. (*a*) Series circuit at 1 MHz. (*b*) Parallel equivalent at 1 MHz. (*c*) Tuning out the capacitive reactance. (*d*) Effective load on the plate at 1 MHz.

Therefore, by adding an inductive reactance of 1 kilohm we will tune out the capacitive reactance, as indicated by Fig. 6-4*c*. And so we have managed to transform a 100-ohm resistance into an effective 10-kilohm load on the vacuum tube. This method of resistance step-up is very simple and less expensive than the use of a transformer. The only restriction, of course, is that it works only at one frequency. However, there are many situations where only a single frequency is to be amplified, and this method is therefore worth remembering.

To find the actual values of inductance and capacitance, we need only use the familiar formulas for X_L and X_C. The frequency in this case is 1 MHz. The calculation is straightforward and results in $L = 0.159$ mh and $C = 159$ pf.

6-3 A-C Wheatstone-bridge Balance Conditions

Bridges used in a-c instruments often are of the form shown in Fig. 6-5*a*. An a-c signal source drives the bridge. Since this is a sinusoidal source, we can represent its voltage by a complex number $\mathbf{V}$. The arms of the bridge consist of impedances $\mathbf{Z}_1$, $\mathbf{Z}_2$, $\mathbf{Z}_3$, and $\mathbf{Z}_4$. These are complex numbers and represent the impedance of the arms to the sinusoidal signal. The output of the bridge is applied to an a-c detector. (In some cases, the signal out may first be amplified before a-c detection.)

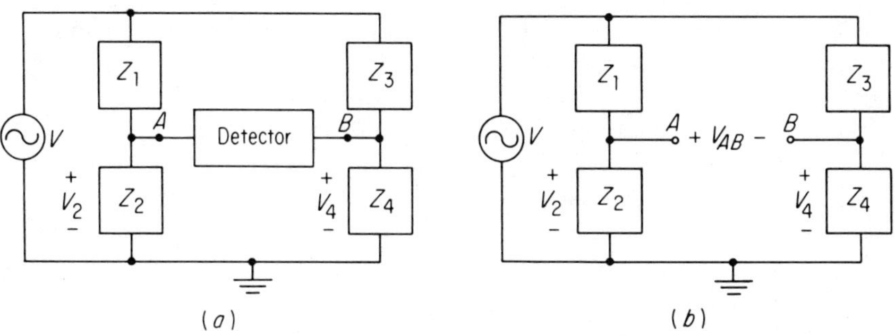

Fig. 6-5 A-c Wheatstone bridge. (*a*) Loaded bridge. (*b*) Unloaded bridge.

The configuration of this bridge is the a-c form of the Wheatstone bridge. However, the impedances may contain reactance as well as resistance. In other words, $\mathbf{Z}_1$ may contain a resistor in series with an inductive reactance. $\mathbf{Z}_2$ might be a resistor in shunt with a capacitive reactance, and so on. Nevertheless, no matter what is actually contained in each bridge arm, we can find the bridge-balance conditions in a manner completely analogous to that used for the d-c Wheatstone bridge. The only difference is that we must use complex numbers instead of real numbers.

What conditions are necessary for bridge balance? By bridge balance we mean that there is no current through the detector. If there is no current through the detector, then we can remove it, as shown in Fig. 6-5*b*. If we now compute $\mathbf{V}_2$ and $\mathbf{V}_4$, we obtain

$$\mathbf{V}_2 = \frac{\mathbf{Z}_2}{\mathbf{Z}_1 + \mathbf{Z}_2}\mathbf{V} \qquad \text{and} \qquad \mathbf{V}_4 = \frac{\mathbf{Z}_4}{\mathbf{Z}_3 + \mathbf{Z}_4}\mathbf{V}$$

It should be clear that, since we are talking about a balanced bridge, $\mathbf{V}_{AB}$ must be equal to zero. But $\mathbf{V}_{AB}$ can equal zero only if $\mathbf{V}_2 = \mathbf{V}_4$. Finally, since $\mathbf{V}_2 = \mathbf{V}_4$ we can write

$$\frac{\mathbf{Z}_2}{\mathbf{Z}_1 + \mathbf{Z}_2} = \frac{\mathbf{Z}_4}{\mathbf{Z}_3 + \mathbf{Z}_4}$$

or

$$\mathbf{Z}_1\mathbf{Z}_4 + \mathbf{Z}_2\mathbf{Z}_4 = \mathbf{Z}_2\mathbf{Z}_3 + \mathbf{Z}_2\mathbf{Z}_4$$

or

$$\mathbf{Z}_1\mathbf{Z}_4 = \mathbf{Z}_2\mathbf{Z}_3$$

$$\frac{\mathbf{Z}_1}{\mathbf{Z}_2} = \frac{\mathbf{Z}_3}{\mathbf{Z}_4} \tag{6-10}$$

This is the bridge-balance equation for any a-c bridge of the form shown in Fig. 6-5*a*. It tells us that a bridge is balanced if the ratio of impedances on one side of the bridge equals the ratio of impedances on the other side. This condition is easy to remember since it resembles the balance condition for a d-c Wheatstone bridge. Recall that for the d-c Wheatstone bridge only resistors are used in the arms of the bridge. As a result, the balance condition is the same as Eq. (6-10), except that R's instead of $\mathbf{Z}$'s are used.

Since Eq. (6-10) involves complex numbers, the left side equals the right side only if the real part of the left side equals the real part of the right side and the imaginary part of the left side equals the imaginary part of the right side. If the complex numbers are expressed in the polar form instead of the rectangular form, Eq. (6-10) is satisfied only if the magnitude of the left side equals the magnitude of the right side and the angle of the left side equals the angle of the right side.

Example 6-5

An a-c bridge is driven by a 1-kHz sinusoidal source. At this frequency the bridge arms have the following impedances: $\mathbf{Z}_1 = 2 + j2$, $\mathbf{Z}_2 = 2$, $\mathbf{Z}_3 = 1 + j1$, and $\mathbf{Z}_4 = 1$. Is the bridge balanced?

Solution

$$\frac{\mathbf{Z}_1}{\mathbf{Z}_2} \stackrel{?}{=} \frac{\mathbf{Z}_3}{\mathbf{Z}_4}$$

$$\frac{2 + j2}{2} \stackrel{?}{=} \frac{1 + j1}{1}$$

$$1 + j1 = 1 + j1$$

In the last equation it is obvious that both sides are equal, since the real part equals the real part and the imaginary part equals the imaginary part. Hence, the bridge is balanced.

Example 6-6

An a-c bridge is driven by a 1-kHz sinusoidal source. At this frequency the impedances are: $\mathbf{Z}_1 = 2$ kilohms $+ j4$ kilohms, $\mathbf{Z}_2 = 2$ kilohms, $\mathbf{Z}_3 = 5$ kilohms $- j10$ kilohms, and $\mathbf{Z}_4 = 5$ kilohms. Is the bridge balanced?

Solution

$$\frac{\mathbf{Z}_1}{\mathbf{Z}_2} \stackrel{?}{=} \frac{\mathbf{Z}_3}{\mathbf{Z}_4}$$

$$\frac{2(10^3) + j4(10^3)}{2(10^3)} \stackrel{?}{=} \frac{5(10^3) - j10(10^3)}{5(10^3)}$$

$$1 + j2 \stackrel{?}{=} 1 - j2$$

The real parts are equal, but the imaginary parts are not. Therefore, the bridge is not balanced.

Example 6-7

In the circuit of Fig. 6-6a the source is a 1-kHz sinusoid. For the given impedances, is the bridge balanced?

SOLUTION

$$\frac{\mathbf{Z}_1}{\mathbf{Z}_2} \stackrel{?}{=} \frac{\mathbf{Z}_3}{\mathbf{Z}_4}$$

Note that $\mathbf{Z}_2 = 2\|(-j2)$. We could expand this by the usual product-over-sum approach and then substitute the result into the balance equation. Then, after quite a bit of algebra, we could determine whether or not the bridge is balanced. (The reader may try this for practice if interested.)

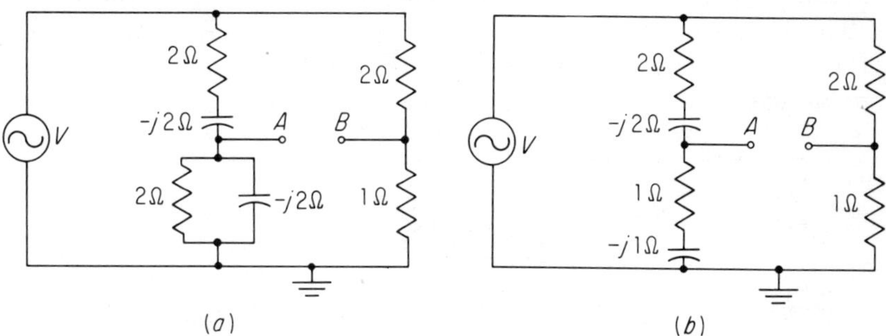

Fig. 6-6 Example 6-7. (*a*) Given bridge. (*b*) Equivalent bridge.

Let us try a different approach. Note that $\mathbf{Z}_2$ is a parallel circuit. We can convert this to a series equivalent if we like.

$$R_s = \frac{R_p}{1 + Q^2} = \frac{2}{1 + 1^2} = 1$$

$$X_s = \frac{X_p}{1 + 1/Q^2} = \frac{2}{1 + 1/1^2} = 1$$

The series equivalent circuit is shown in Fig. 6-6*b*. It may already be obvious from an inspection of this bridge that it is balanced. If there is any doubt, we can apply the balance condition to the bridge of Fig. 6-6*b*, which is the equivalent of Fig. 6-6*a*.

$$\frac{\mathbf{Z}_1}{\mathbf{Z}_2} \stackrel{?}{=} \frac{\mathbf{Z}_3}{\mathbf{Z}_4}$$

$$\frac{2 - j2}{1 - j1} \stackrel{?}{=} \frac{2}{1}$$

$$\frac{2(1 - j1)}{1 - j1} \stackrel{?}{=} 2$$

$$2 = 2$$

The bridge is obviously balanced.

The bridge of Fig. 6-6*a* is the famous Wien bridge. It is widely used in oscillators; we will study it in more detail later.

6-4 A Simple A-C Bridge

A very simple bridge can be built as shown in Fig. 6-7. The unknown impedance is connected to the measuring terminals, and we then proceed to adjust R and C. If we obtain a bridge balance, it follows that the parallel equivalent of the unknown is a resistance whose value equals the rheostat value and whose capacitance equals the value of the variable capacitance. The R and C adjustments may be ganged to dials calibrated to read the parallel equivalent resistance and capacitance of the unknown.

The bridge of Fig. 6-7 would be useful in measuring the impedance of capacitive circuits at 1 kHz. However, this bridge has a serious disadvantage. The adjustment range of variable capacitors is limited, so

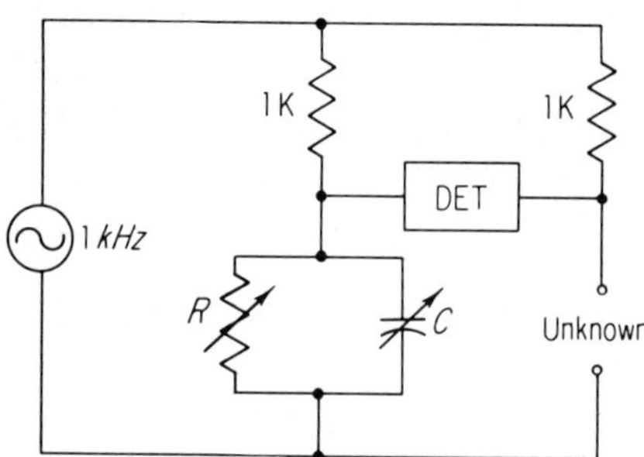

Fig. 6-7 Simple a-c bridge.

that many unknown impedances would fall outside the measurement range of this bridge. Generally, commercial bridges are designed so that both adjustments are resistive. This is better for practical purposes because larger adjustment ranges are available with resistors, plus the fact that the readout dials can be more easily calibrated when using variable resistances.

6-5 Different Forms of the A-C Wheatstone Bridge

Figures 6-8 and 6-9 illustrate some of the specific forms of the a-c Wheatstone bridge. These circuits are the more commonly used bridges. In Fig. 6-8*a* we have the simple Wheatstone bridge with all arms purely resistive. R_1, R_2, and R_3 are internal to the bridge, whereas R is an external resistor to be measured. An a-c detector (not shown) is connected across the bridge. If R_2 is adjusted to produce a null, the unknown resistance must equal

$$R = \frac{R_3}{R_1} R_2$$

Note that R_3 and R_1 are fixed resistors. Only R_2 is variable. Therefore, R is a function of R_2. Because of this, R_2 may be ganged to a dial for direct readout of the value of R. Furthermore, since there is a direct proportion, the dial calibration will be linear, that is, have uniform spacing between values. (We are assuming that the rheostat is linear and not logarithmic.) This type of bridge is used to measure the a-c resistance. (Recall from basic electronics that the a-c resistance may differ from the d-c resistance.)

If the unknown impedance to be measured contains reactance, it will be impossible to balance the bridge of Fig. 6-8*a*, and one of the other bridge forms must be used. If the unknown impedance is resistive-capacitive, a bridge like that in Fig. 6-8*b* can be used. This bridge is called a series capacitance-comparison bridge. The unknown is inside the **Z** box. We know that any impedance, no matter how complicated, can be re-

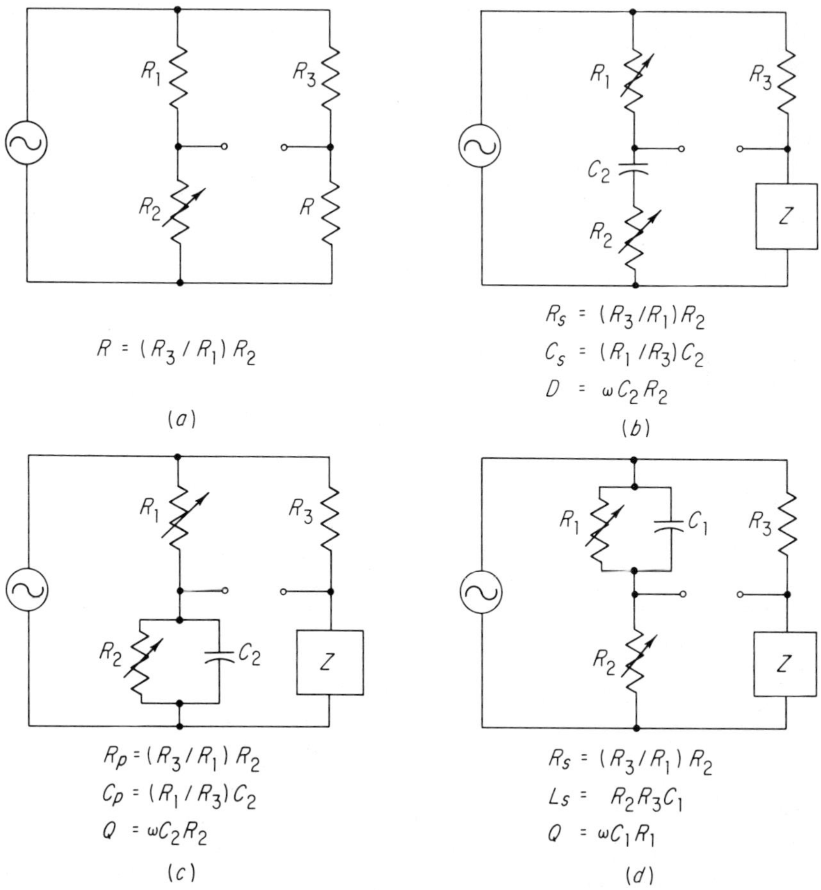

Fig. 6-8 A-c bridges. (*a*) Simple Wheatstone. (*b*) Series capacitance-comparison. (*c*) Parallel capacitance-comparison. (*d*) Maxwell.

duced to either a series equivalent or a parallel equivalent circuit. By applying the a-c balance equation (6-10) we can find the relation between the unknown impedance and the internal bridge impedances. As an example, let us apply the balance equation to Fig. 6-8*b*. We will use the series equivalent for the unknown impedance.

$$\frac{\mathbf{Z}_1}{\mathbf{Z}_2} = \frac{\mathbf{Z}_3}{\mathbf{Z}_4}$$

$$\frac{R_1}{R_2 - jX_{C2}} = \frac{R_3}{R_s - jX_{Cs}}$$

To simplify this equation we invert to obtain

$$\frac{R_2 - jX_{C2}}{R_1} = \frac{R_s - jX_{Cs}}{R_3}$$

Then, we divide to obtain

$$\frac{R_2}{R_1} - j\frac{X_{C2}}{R_1} = \frac{R_s}{R_3} - j\frac{X_{Cs}}{R_3} \tag{6-11}$$

A crucial step in dealing with any complex-number equation is to realize that the real part of the left side must equal the real part of the right side and the imaginary part of the left side must equal the imaginary part of the right side. Therefore, from Eq. (6-11) we see that

$$\frac{R_2}{R_1} = \frac{R_s}{R_3} \qquad \text{and} \qquad \frac{X_{C2}}{R_1} = \frac{X_{Cs}}{R_3}$$

We now solve for R_s to obtain

$$R_s = \frac{R_3}{R_1} R_2 \tag{6-12}$$

Also, we find C_s by rearranging the equation of the imaginary parts as follows:

$$\frac{X_{C2}}{R_1} = \frac{X_{Cs}}{R_3}$$

$$\frac{X_{C2}}{X_{Cs}} = \frac{R_1}{R_3} = \frac{\omega C_s}{\omega C_2} = \frac{C_s}{C_2}$$

Solving for C_s, we obtain

$$C_s = \frac{R_1}{R_3} C_2 \tag{6-13}$$

Equations (6-12) and (6-13) tell us how the unknown impedance is related to the internal bridge quantities. We deliberately chose the series equivalent of the unknown impedance. If we had used the parallel equivalent of the unknown at the beginning of the derivation, the results would have been more complicated. It is found with all of the remaining

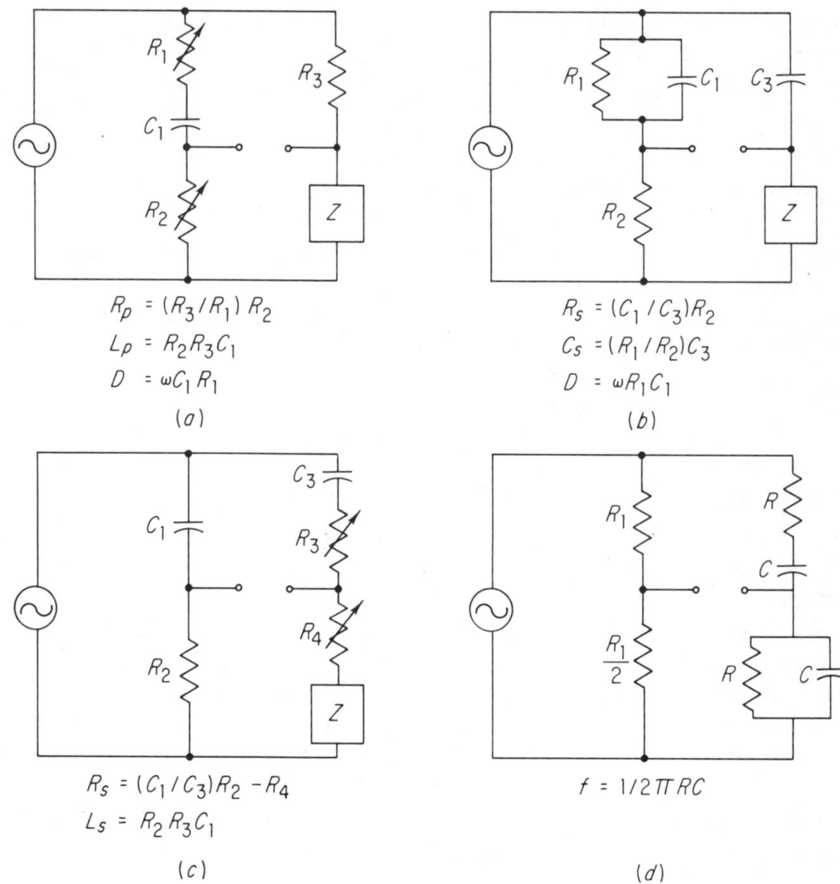

Fig. 6-9 A-c bridges. (*a*) Hay bridge. (*b*) Schering bridge. (*c*) Modified Owen. (*d*) Wien bridge, special case.

bridge forms shown in Figs. 6-8 and 6-9 that either the series or the parallel equivalent results in simpler balance formulas. As a result, some bridge formulas in these figures give the balance conditions in terms of R_s and C_s (or L_s), whereas others give the results in terms of R_p and C_p (or L_p).

Also important is the use of the quantity D shown in Fig. 6-8*b* which comes about in the following way. Referring to Eqs. (6-12) and (6-13), note that C_s is a function of R_1. (R_3 and C_2 are fixed.) Because of this, the shaft of R_1 may be ganged to a dial calibrated to read out the value of C_s. On the other hand, R_s is a function of two variables, R_1 and R_2. This implies that in order to read out the value of R_s directly, both R_1 and R_2 must somehow be ganged to a dial. This is very difficult mechanically. As a result, this type of bridge is not suitable for direct readout of R_s. Instead, such a bridge will read out the value of C_s and Q. The Q for the series equivalent circuit is

$$Q = \frac{X_{Cs}}{R_s} = \frac{1}{\omega C_s R_s} = \frac{1}{\omega (R_1/R_3) C_2 (R_3/R_1) R_2} = \frac{1}{\omega C_2 R_2}$$

Note carefully that the value of Q is a function of R_2 only, since for any given capacitance-comparison bridge C_2 is fixed, and the driving frequency is fixed. (Assume for the moment no frequency drift.) Since Q depends only upon R_2 for a given bridge, the shaft of R_2 may be ganged to a dial for direct readout of the Q. However, the relation between Q and R_2 is nonlinear, because Q is inversely proportional to R_2. If a linear relation is desired, there is no reason at all why we cannot use the reciprocal of Q. That is,

$$D \triangleq \frac{1}{Q} = \omega C_2 R_2 \tag{6-14}$$

The quantity D is called the *dissipation factor* and is defined as the reciprocal of Q. Because of this, R_2 can be ganged to a dial calibrated to read D instead of Q. One advantage of this is that the dial markings are directly proportional to the value of R_2.

We have analyzed the series capacitance-comparison bridge in detail and found the balance formulas. Note that as far as accuracy is concerned, the values read for C_s will depend upon how accurately the dial is calibrated. To simplify the calibration of the dial, precision resistors and capacitors are used. Typically, the value of C_s can be determined to within ± 1 percent. On the other hand, the value of Q depends on the frequency as well as C_2 and R_2. Generally, we can expect the signal source driving the bridge to drift both in magnitude and frequency. The magnitude drift cancels out on each side of the bridge, so that balance is independent of magnitude. However, the Q (or D) dial is calibrated on the assumption that the frequency is fixed. As a result, a drift in frequency may cause appreciable error, depending upon the exact circuit being measured. Q or D readings are typically accurate to within ± 5 percent on a commercial bridge.

The remaining bridge forms may be analyzed in the manner used to analyze the series capacitance-comparison bridge. The formulas resulting from such analysis are given in Figs. 6-8 and 6-9. Note that some of the bridges are useful for capacitance measurements, whereas others are better suited to inductance measurements. The Wien bridge is really in a class by itself. It is not normally used to measure impedance. Instead, its great uses come in those situations where oscillators and filters are required. We will discuss this bridge in more detail later. For the moment, note that this bridge balances only for the special frequency given in Fig. 6-9*d*.

As a practical matter, if the bridges of Figs. 6-8 and 6-9 are built, it will be found that perfect nulls are not possible. There will usually be a small amount of residual signal across the detector, no matter how carefully we adjust the components. The explanation for this residual signal is that there is enough stray inductance and capacitance in each circuit element to prevent perfect balance. For example, in the Maxwell bridge of Fig. 6-8*d*, the R_2 rheostat actually contains lead inductance and shunt capacity. Because of these extra reactances the bridge cannot be perfectly balanced with only two adjustments. Thus, if we actually build these bridges or use instruments containing these bridges, we cannot expect to obtain perfect balance. We can only expect the indicator to dip to some minimum value. For this condition the balance formulas shown in Figs. 6-8 and 6-9 are still reasonably accurate.

EXAMPLE 6-8

The Maxwell bridge of Fig. 6-8*d* is balanced for the following values: $R_1 = 30$ kilohms, $R_2 = 5$ kilohms, $R_3 = 1$ kilohm, and $C_1 = 1000$ pf. The driving frequency is 1 kHz. Find the values of R_s, L_s, and Q.

SOLUTION

$$R_s = \frac{10^3}{30(10^3)} 5(10^3) \cong 167 \text{ ohms}$$

$$L_s = 5(10^3)(10^3)(1000)(10^{-12}) = 5000\ \mu\text{h}$$

$$Q = 2\pi(10^3)(1000)(10^{-12})(30)(10^3) \cong 0.188$$

EXAMPLE 6-9

The Schering bridge of Fig. 6-9*b* balances under the following conditions: $R_1 = 10$ kilohms, $R_2 = 1$ kilohm, $C_1 = 100$ pf, and $C_3 = 500$ pf. The driving frequency is 1 kHz. Find the values of R_s, C_s, and D. Convert these values to parallel equivalent values.

SOLUTION

$$R_s = \frac{100(10^{-12})}{500(10^{-12})}(10^3) = 200 \text{ ohms}$$

$$C_s = \frac{10(10^3)}{10^3} 500(10^{-12}) = 5000 \text{ pf}$$

$$D = 2\pi(10^3)(10)(10^3)(100)(10^{-12}) = 0.00628$$

To find the parallel equivalent, we first note that

$$Q = \frac{1}{D} = \frac{1}{0.00628} = 159$$

We may now use Eqs. (6-5) and (6-6) to convert from series to parallel.

$$R_p = 200(1 + 159^2) = 5.12 \text{ megohms}$$

Because of the high Q, we note from Eq. (6-6) that X_p is approximately equal to X_s, which implies that C_p approximately equals C_s. Hence, we have found that the unknown impedance has a series equivalent of

$$R_s = 200 \text{ ohms} \qquad \text{and} \qquad C_s = 5000 \text{ pf}$$

The same unknown has a parallel equivalent of

$$R_p = 5.12 \text{ megohms} \qquad \text{and} \qquad C_p = 5000 \text{ pf}$$

Remember that the values obtained for the equivalent circuits are valid only at 1 kHz.

6-6 Commercial Impedance Bridges

The bridge circuits discussed in Sec. 6-5 are generally found in commercial impedance bridges. By means of switching arrangements, various bridges may be connected to allow capacitive or inductive measurements. Usually, 1 kHz is the frequency chosen for low-frequency instruments. At this frequency it is found that some bridges lead to more practical values than others. For instance, capacitive measurements are usually performed with one of the capacitance-comparison bridges. The series type leads to more practical values than the parallel type if the unknown has a low D (high Q). On the other hand, for high-D (low-Q) capacitive measurements, the parallel type of capacitance-comparison bridge is better suited because of the required bridge values.

For inductive measurements the Maxwell and Hay bridges are often used. Once again, the best compromise on available parts for the bridges occurs if the Maxwell bridge is used for low-Q (high-D) and if the Hay bridge is used for high-Q (low-D) measurements.

Once a specific type of bridge has been switched in, we can expect to be able to balance the bridge over a reasonable range of unknown values. If the unknown lies outside the range of balance, it is necessary to change the values of the fixed bridge parts. For example, suppose we are making low-Q measurements on an inductive circuit. The Maxwell bridge would then be switched into the circuit. The balance formula for L_s is $L_s = R_2R_3C_1$. For the sake of illustration, let R_2 have a range of 10 to 1000 ohms, and let R_3 equal 1 kilohm, and C_1 equal 1000 pf. The minimum value of L_s that we can measure is then 10 μh, and the maximum value is 1000 μh. As long as the unknown inductance falls in this range, we will be able to balance the bridge. However, there are many inductances outside this range. It should be clear that several ranges are needed. One easy way to obtain several ranges is by changing R_3. Thus, if the inductance falls outside the range of 10 to 1000 μh, R_3 can be changed to 10 kilohms.

Now the range on inductance is 100 to 10,000 μh. In such a way, many ranges can be obtained.

When operating a typical impedance bridge we can expect to find the following switches and adjustments. There will be a switch for selecting the type of bridge: d-c or a-c resistance, low- or high-Q inductance, low- or high-D capacitance. There will be a range switch for selecting an appropriate range of resistance, inductance, or capacitance. There will be two rheostat adjustments, one for R, L, or C, and the other for Q or D.

One more interesting feature in good commercial bridge instruments is worth mentioning. Whenever we try to find a balance for low-Q or high-D unknowns, there usually is great difficulty converging on the null. In other words, we usually find it necessary to adjust R_1 and R_2 many times before reaching a balance condition. In fact, we may even encounter several false nulls. *Orthogonal nulling* means that R_1 and R_2 are ganged together in a special way, so that rapid convergence on the null occurs. We find that turning one adjustment causes the other adjustment to track in such a way that the ratio of the two resistance values remains constant. However, the tracking is not reciprocal; that is, turning the first rheostat causes the second to track, but turning the second does not cause the first adjustment to change. With this arrangement false nulls are avoided, and the balance is quickly found.

SUMMARY

We have seen that complicated a-c networks can be represented by either a series or a parallel equivalent circuit. The conversion formulas between the two equivalent circuits are simple and easy to use. We recall that for high-Q circuits, X_p and X_s are approximately equal. Further, for high-Q circuits R_p approximately equals R_sQ^2.

There is a variety of a-c Wheatstone-bridge forms. Some are used for inductive measurements, whereas others are for capacitive measurements. The various types of bridges and their balance formulas are given in Figs. 6-8 and 6-9, which should be useful for future reference.

We recall that D (the dissipation factor) is defined as the reciprocal of Q.

For typical a-c bridges we can expect measurements on the reactive component to be within ± 1 percent, whereas the Q and D measurements are more likely to be about ± 5 percent. The main sources of error are the tolerance of the fixed parts and the calibration error of the readout dials.

Commercial instruments switch in the best bridge for the particular type of measurement. For low-Q measurements, difficulty is usually encountered in trying to find the true null. Better instruments use what is known as orthogonal nulling to converge on the true balance condition.

GLOSSARY

admittance The reciprocal of impedance.
conductance The reciprocal of resistance.
dissipation factor (D) The reciprocal of Q.
equivalent impedance Refers to either the series or parallel equivalent impedance of a circuit. Any circuit, no matter how complicated, can be reduced to an equivalent impedance insofar as the voltage and current at the terminals of the circuit are concerned.
linear rheostat An adjustable resistance whose value is directly proportional to amount of shaft rotation.
logarithmic rheostat A variable resistance whose value is logarithmically related to the amount of shaft rotation.
orthogonal nulling Refers to ganging the two adjustments of an a-c bridge together in such a way that changing one adjustment changes the other in a special way, but changing the second adjustment does not change the first.

REVIEW QUESTIONS

1. In applying Ohm's law to a-c circuits what kind of numbers must be used?
2. How are parallel impedances combined?
3. What is the series equivalent circuit for a d-c circuit? What is the parallel equivalent circuit of a d-c circuit?
4. Does an a-c bridge measure the series equivalent circuit or the parallel equivalent circuit of an unknown impedance?
5. At 1 kHz the series and parallel equivalent circuits of an impedance are calculated. If the frequency is changed to 2 kHz, do the same equivalent circuits apply?
6. What is the value of Q in a series equivalent circuit? In a parallel equivalent circuit?
7. For high-Q circuits what is the relation between X_s and X_p?
8. Is a transformer the only way of stepping up resistance at a single frequency? If not, what is one alternative?
9. What is the balance condition for an a-c bridge?
10. In order for the balance equation to hold, what must be true about the real and imaginary parts of the equation?
11. If the complex numbers are expressed in polar instead of rectangular form, what can be said about magnitudes and angles of each side of the balance equation?
12. If an a-c bridge is balanced, what must be true about $\mathbf{V}_2$ and $\mathbf{V}_4$?

13. What must be true about the real parts of $\mathbf{V}_2$ and $\mathbf{V}_4$ at balance? The imaginary parts?
14. If $\mathbf{V}_2$ and $\mathbf{V}_4$ are expressed as polar numbers, what must be true about their magnitudes and angles in a balanced a-c bridge? What does this imply about the amplitude and phase angle of the sinusoidal voltages across $\mathbf{Z}_2$ and $\mathbf{Z}_4$?
15. What are some of the disadvantages of the simple bridge of Fig. 6-7?
16. Why is the series capacitance-comparison bridge calibrated to read the series equivalent of the unknown?
17. Why is it not normal practice to read out directly the value of R_s in the series capacitance-comparison bridge?
18. How is D defined?
19. Why is it sometimes preferable to read out D instead of Q?
20. What limits the accuracy of measurements made on the capacitance-comparison bridge?
21. Why is there a small residual signal after balancing a typical a-c bridge?
22. For what type of measurements is the Hay bridge better suited than the Maxwell bridge in typical low-frequency measurements?
23. How are different ranges obtained in a given bridge type?
24. What is the advantage of orthogonal nulling? For what kind of measurements is it most useful?

PROBLEMS

6-1 Find the parallel equivalent circuit for a circuit consisting of a 50-ohm resistor in series with a capacitive reactance of 200 ohms.

6-2 Find the series equivalent circuit for a parallel combination of a 5-kilohm resistor and an inductive reactance of 100 ohms.

6-3 An electrolytic capacitor has a capacitance of 100 μf and a leakage resistance (in shunt) of 2 megohms. Find the series equivalent circuit at a frequency of 15.9 Hz. If the frequency is changed to 1.59 Hz, what is the parallel equivalent circuit?

6-4 The Q of a coil is 100 at 80 kHz. If the coil has an inductance of 0.1 mh, what is the series resistance of the coil? If the parallel equivalent circuit is calculated, what is the value of R_p?

6-5 A coil is measured on a bridge which indicates that the parallel equivalent circuit of the coil is a 10-kilohm resistor shunted by 200 ohms of reactance. Find the series equivalent circuit of the coil.

6-6 The data sheet on a capacitor indicates that it has a capacitance of 100 pf and a Q of 500 at 1 MHz. Find the value of R_p in the parallel equivalent circuit of the capacitor.

6-7 An a-c bridge indicates that the Q of a capacitor is 1000, and that the capacitance is 100 pf. What is the value of R_s in the series equivalent circuit? And what is the value of R_p in the parallel equivalent circuit? The frequency of operation is 1 MHz.

6-8 A diode is back-biased. The parallel equivalent circuit for this diode is a capacitor of 2 pf in shunt with a leakage resistance of 10 megohms. At 1 MHz what is the Q of the diode? What is the series equivalent circuit for the diode?

6-9 A coupling capacitor has a reactance of 1 ohm and a series resistance of 2 ohms. Find the parallel equivalent circuit for this capacitor.

6-10 Refer to Fig. 6-5*a*. $\mathbf{Z}_1 = 3 + j6$, $\mathbf{Z}_2 = 2$, $\mathbf{Z}_3 = 9 + j18$, and $\mathbf{Z}_4 = 4$. Is the bridge balanced? If not, what value of $\mathbf{Z}_4$ will produce bridge balance?

6-11 Refer to Fig. 6-5*a*. $\mathbf{Z}_1 = 10 + j10$, $\mathbf{Z}_2 = 10\|j10$, $\mathbf{Z}_3 = 50$, and $\mathbf{Z}_4 = 25$. Show that the bridge is balanced.

6-12 At 1 kHz a Wien bridge similar to that shown in Fig. 6-6*a* has $\mathbf{Z}_1 = 20 - j20$, $\mathbf{Z}_2 = 2\|(-j2)$, $\mathbf{Z}_3 = 5$, $\mathbf{Z}_4 = 1$. Show that this bridge is not balanced.

6-13 The Wien bridge of Fig. 6-6*a* uses 10-μf capacitors. What is the driving frequency? If this frequency is doubled, will the bridge still be balanced? Why?

6-14 If the circuit of Fig. 6-7 balances for $R = 1$ kilohm and $C = 50$ pf, what is the parallel equivalent circuit for the unknown?

6-15 A Hay bridge is driven by a 5-kHz sinusoidal source. Balance is attained for the following set of bridge values: $R_1 = 10$ kilohms, $R_2 = 2$ kilohms, $R_3 = 1$ kilohm, and $C_1 = 500$ pf. Find the value of R_p, L_p, D, and Q.

6-16 A Hay bridge has an R_3 equal to 1 kilohm and a C_1 equal to 500 pf. The driving frequency is 1 kHz. R_1 and R_2 are rheostats with a range of 100 ohms to 100 kilohms. What are the maximum and minimum values of L_p and D that can be measured on this bridge?

6-17 Derive the balance formulas shown in Fig. 6-9*b* for the Schering bridge.

6-18 The modified Owen bridge balances for: $R_2 = 1$ kilohm, $R_3 = 2$ kilohms, $R_4 = 80$, $C_1 = 200$ pf, and $C_3 = 1000$ pf. What are the values of R_s and L_s?

6-19 For the special Wien bridge shown in Fig. 6-9*d*, the value of R is 10 kilohms, and the value of C is 1000 pf. At what frequency is the bridge balanced?

7 Attenuators

Attenuators are simple but very important instruments. Unlike an amplifier, which is ordinarily used to increase a signal level by a given amount, the attenuator is used to reduce the signal level by a given amount. The use of attenuators has become so widespread that a study of their design and use is important in the study of electronic instruments. Attenuators may be constructed in many ways. We will confine our discussion to lumped-resistance attenuators.

7-1 The *L*-type Attenuator

One of the simplest types of attenuators is the *L* type, or the ordinary voltage divider (see Fig. 7-1). The voltage gain of this network is the output voltage divided by the input voltage. We can find the formula for gain in the following manner:

$$v_{\text{out}} = iR_2$$

$$v_{\text{out}} = \frac{v_{\text{in}}}{R_1 + R_2} R_2 = \frac{R_2}{R_1 + R_2} v_{\text{in}}$$

$$A = \frac{v_{\text{out}}}{v_{\text{in}}} = \frac{R_2}{R_1 + R_2} \tag{7-1}$$

Equation (7-1) should be familiar. It tells us that the voltage gain of a simple voltage divider is equal to R_2 divided by the sum of R_1 and R_2. For instance, if R_1 equals 9 kilohms and R_2 equals 1 kilohm the voltage gain equals one-tenth. As usual, to find the voltage gain expressed in decibels, we take 20 times the base 10 logarithm of A. In this case, for A equals 0.1, A_{db} equals -20 db.

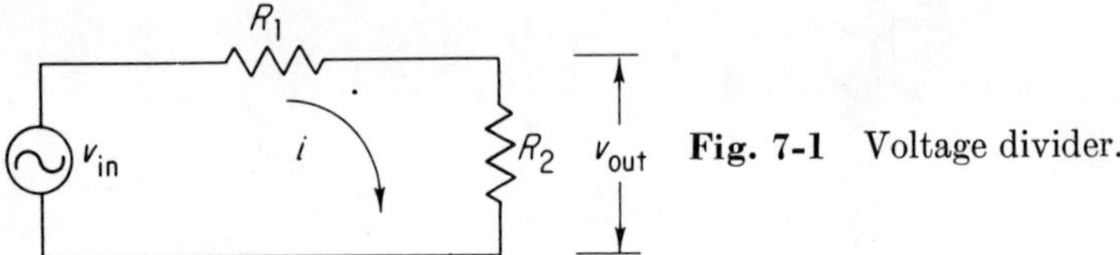

Fig. 7-1 Voltage divider.

Since attenuators always reduce the signal level, the value of A is always less than unity, and A_{db} is therefore always negative. If we like, we can use the reciprocal of A and thereby avoid values that are less than unity. In other words, let us define the attenuation as

$$a \triangleq \frac{v_{\text{in}}}{v_{\text{out}}} = \frac{1}{A} \tag{7-2}$$

For the voltage divider with R_1 equal to 9 kilohms and R_2 equal to 1 kilohm, we now say that the attenuation a is 10, or a_{db} is 20 db. The distinction between A and a is merely a detail, but it should be understood, since both terms are commonly used in practice.

EXAMPLE 7-1

In Fig. 7-1 the value of R_1 is 3 kilohms, and R_2 is 1 kilohm. Find the voltage gain in decibels and the attenuation in decibels.

SOLUTION

$$A = \frac{10^3}{10^3 + 3(10^3)} = \frac{1}{4}$$

Each factor of two in the denominator corresponds to -6 db, so that $A_{db} = -12$ db. Since a is the reciprocal of A, we have

$$a = 4 \qquad \text{and} \qquad a_{db} = 12 \text{ db}$$

7-2 Frequency Compensation of the Voltage Divider

The voltage divider is commonly used in the input stage of measuring instruments in order to prevent large signals from overdriving the instrument. Part of a typical input stage is shown in Fig. 7-2a. Note the presence of a capacitor C_2 across R_2. This capacitance is due in part to stray wiring capacitance and in part to the tube capacitance.

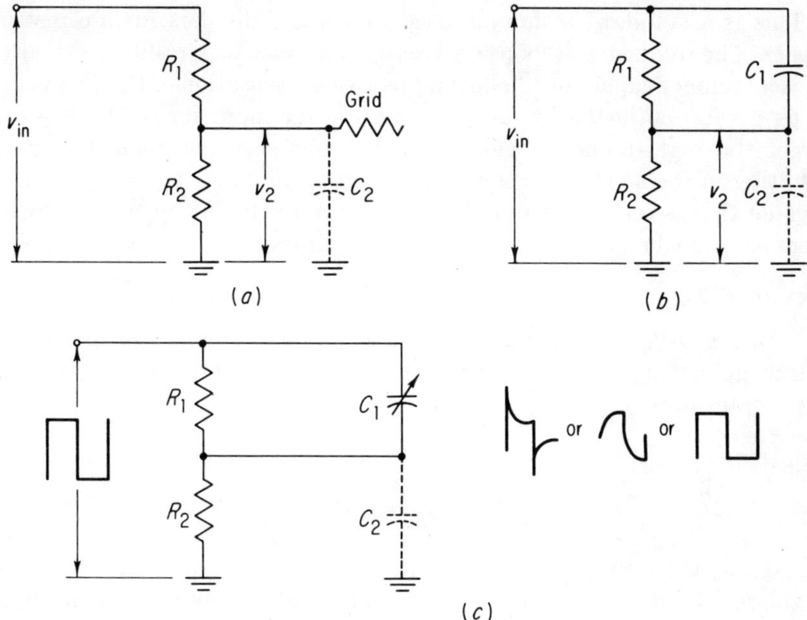

Fig. 7-2 Frequency compensation of voltage divider. (*a*) Uncompensated circuit. (*b*) Compensated circuit. (*c*) Adjusting C_1.

At very low frequencies the reactance of the capacitor is very high, so that the voltage divider behaves like the simple resistive divider discussed in the preceding section. The voltage on the grid is merely the gain of the voltage divider times the value of v_{in}.

At higher frequencies, however, the reactance of the capacitor may become small enough to reduce v_2. At infinite frequency v_2 equals zero. Clearly, the frequency range of the input stage is limited by this undesired effect.

Fortunately, there is a way to overcome the frequency-limiting effect of C_2. An external capacitor may be added, as shown in Fig. 7-2*b*. At higher frequencies both capacitors begin to shunt current around the resistors. At high enough frequencies, the network becomes predominantly capacitive, and we have a capacitive divider.

In order to make the high-frequency gain equal to the low-frequency gain we need only make sure that the ratio of the reactances equals the ratio of the resistances. That is,

$$\frac{R_1}{R_2} = \frac{X_{c1}}{X_{c2}}$$

or

$$\frac{R_1}{R_2} = \frac{\omega C_2}{\omega C_1}$$

or

$$C_1 = \frac{R_2}{R_1} C_2 \tag{7-3}$$

This is a standard technique used in voltage dividers for a-c instruments. The frequency response is greatly improved as a result. Normally, C_1 is a trimmer capacitor to allow a precise compensation of C_2. The value of C_1 is often adjusted by using a square-wave input for v_{in}. If C_1 is too large, the high-frequency gain is larger than the low-frequency gain, resulting in the spiked waveform shown in Fig. 7-2*c*. If C_1 is adjusted to a value that is too low, a rounded waveform results. The correct adjustment occurs when a square wave appears across C_2.

EXAMPLE 7-2

In Fig. 7-2*a*, the tube and stray capacitance equals 54 pf. R_1 equals 9 megohms, and R_2 equals 1 megohm. Find the value of C_1 that compensates for C_2.

SOLUTION

$$C_1 = \frac{R_2}{R_1} C_2 = \frac{10^6}{9(10^6)} 54 \text{ pf} = 6 \text{ pf}$$

Thus, if we shunt the 9-megohm resistor with a 6-pf capacitor, the voltage divider will continue to provide a 10:1 voltage division up to a much higher frequency.

7-3 The Characteristic Resistance of Symmetrical Attenuators

Usually, the term *attenuator* refers to a device that not only introduces a precise amount of attenuation but also provides an impedance match on the input and output terminals. For instance, in Fig. 7-3 an attenuator has been inserted between a source and a load. If it has been properly designed, the input resistance will be 50 ohms, thereby matching the source resistance. Further, at the output terminals, the Thévenin resistance looking back is 50 ohms, so that the load is matched.

There are many systems where impedance matching is very important. In fact, in any system using transmission lines a great deal of trouble

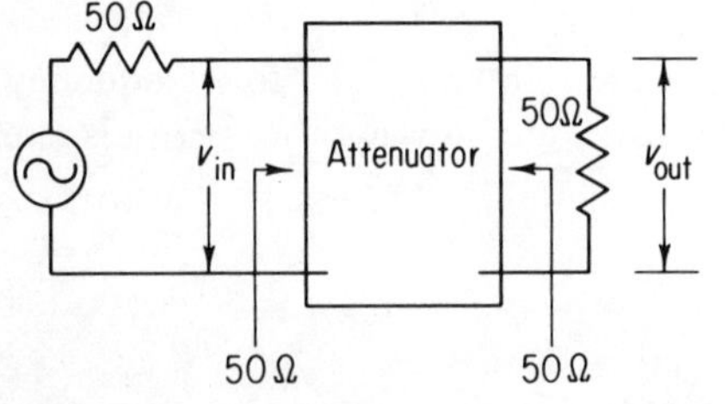

Fig. 7-3 Matched attenuator between source and load.

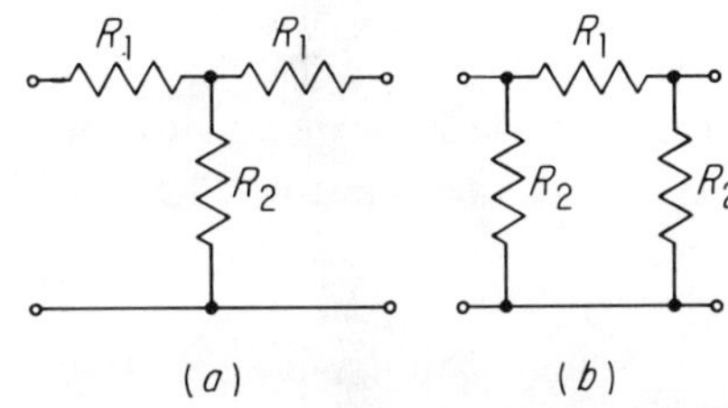

Fig. 7-4 Basic attenuators. (*a*) Symmetrical T. (b) Symmetrical π.

may be encountered unless all devices are impedance-matched. This is especially true in those situations where the wavelength associated with the signal becomes comparable to the length of the transmission line. Telephone, television, and microwave systems are examples of situations where impedance matching is normally used.

We will now be concerned with attenuators that have been designed to provide an impedance match on both the input and output side. Further, we will confine our attention to a practical class of attenuators known as *unbalanced symmetrical attenuators.* The two most basic forms in this class are shown in Fig. 7-4*a* and *b*. Note that these are symmetrical about a vertical center line. The word "unbalanced" refers to the fact that there is a common connection from input to output (the lower wire).

One extremely important property of symmetrical attenuators is what is commonly referred to as the *characteristic* (or image) *resistance.* Consider the situation in Fig. 7-5*a*. A variable-load resistor has been connected to

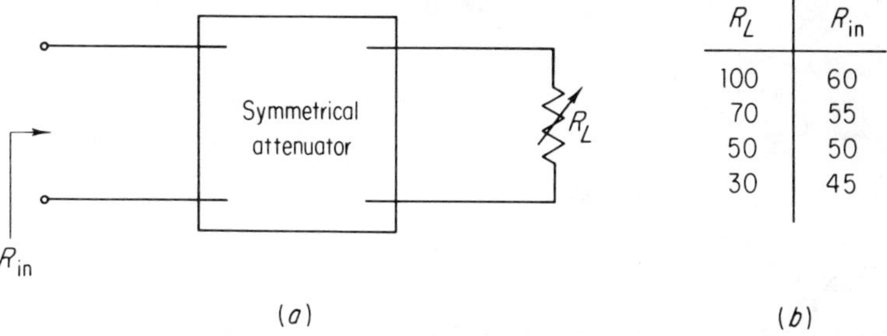

R_L	R_{in}
100	60
70	55
50	50
30	45

Fig. 7-5 Characteristic resistance of an attenuator.

the output of the attenuator. As we look into the attenuator, we see a value of input resistance that depends upon the value of load resistance. Suppose that for $R_L = 100$ ohms, $R_{in} = 60$ ohms. As we change R_L to 70 ohms, we might observe that R_{in} changes to 55 ohms. As we vary R_L again to a new value of 50 ohms, we might have an R_{in} equal to 50 ohms. Continuing in this way, we would find that R_{in} takes on different values for each value of R_L. Note one very important entry in the table of Fig. 7-5*b*. There is one entry (and only one) where R_{in} equals R_L. This value of resistance is called the characteristic resistance of the attenuator.

In general, the characteristic resistance of an attenuator is that value of load on an attenuator which produces the same value of input resistance. Every attenuator has a characteristic resistance. Under normal circumstances, attenuators should always be loaded in their characteristic resistances. If this is done, the resistance value is maintained throughout the system in which the attenuator is used. For instance, if a system uses 50-ohm load resistors and 50-ohm source resistances, using an attenuator with a characteristic resistance of 50 ohms between a load and a source will match the impedance on the source and load sides of the attenuator.

A useful formula for the characteristic resistance R_o of an attenuator is

$$R_o = \sqrt{R_{ins} R_{ino}} \tag{7-4}$$

where R_{ins} is the input resistance of the attenuator with the output terminals shorted and R_{ino} is the input resistance of the attenuator with the output terminals open. This equation can be derived by use of z parameters. We will accept it without derivation.

EXAMPLE 7-3

Find the characteristic resistance of the symmetrical T attenuator shown in Fig. 7-6*a*.

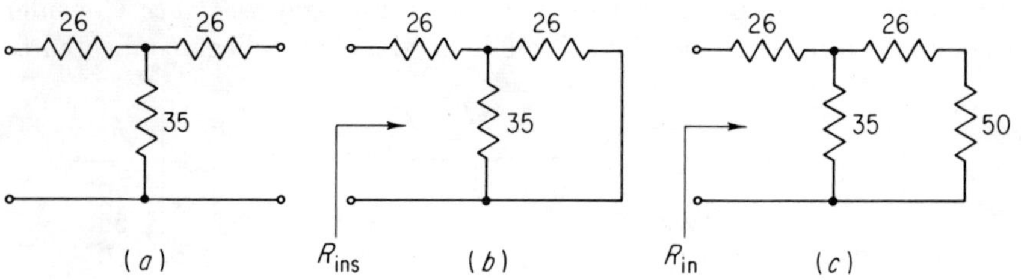

Fig. 7-6 Examples 7-3 and 7-4.

SOLUTION

Experimentally, this can be done in the laboratory by connecting a variable resistance on the output side of the attenuator. We can measure the input resistance with an ohmmeter. By varying R_L we find that there is a value of R_L such that R_{in} equals R_L. Alternately, we can use Eq. (7-4).

$$R_o = \sqrt{R_{ins} R_{ino}}$$

Referring to Fig. 7-6*b*, we note that

$$R_{ins} = 26 + 35 \| 26 = 26 + 15 = 41$$

Also, using Fig. 7-6*a*, we get

$$R_{ino} = 26 + 35 = 61$$

Then $$R_o = \sqrt{41(61)} = 50$$

Thus, the characteristic resistance is 50 ohms. This attenuator would normally be used with a source and load resistance of 50 ohms.

EXAMPLE 7-4

Prove that the input resistance of the attenuator of Example 7-3 is 50 ohms when loaded by its characteristic resistance.

SOLUTION

Referring to Fig. 7-6*c*, we note that

$$R_{in} = 26 + 35\|(26 + 50) = 26 + 35\|76$$
$$R_{in} = 26 + 24 = 50 \text{ ohms}$$

7-4 Symmetrical T Analysis Formulas

In this section we wish to find a pair of formulas that will be useful whenever we have to deal with the symmetrical T attenuator. In order to simplify the formulas it is helpful to define the ratio of R_2 to R_1 as follows:

$$m \triangleq \frac{R_2}{R_1} \tag{7-5}$$

or

$$R_2 = mR_1 \tag{7-6}$$

With this definition for m, the attenuator may be relabeled as shown in Fig. 7-7.

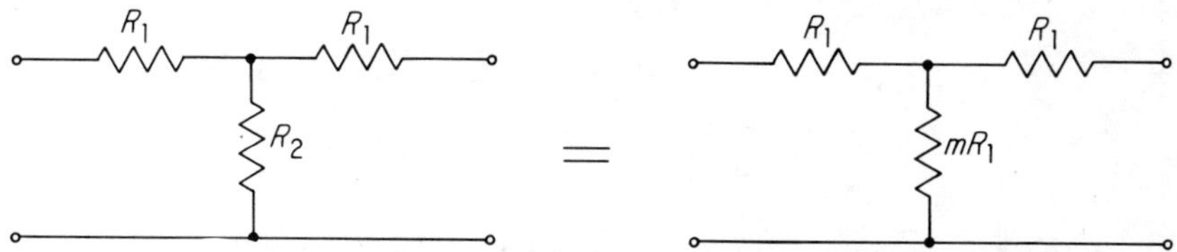

Fig. 7-7 Deriving the T attenuator formulas.

First, let us find R_o.

$$R_o = \sqrt{R_{ins}R_{ino}} = \sqrt{(R_1 + R_1\|mR_1)(R_1 + mR_1)}$$

After a few simplifying algebra steps we can obtain

$$R_o = R_1\sqrt{1 + 2m} \tag{7-7}$$

The second formula that will be useful in our work is a formula for the amount of attenuation that takes place from the input to the output terminals of an attenuator loaded in its characteristic resistance (see Fig. 7-8).

We require a formula for v_{in}/v_{out}, that is, the attenuation. There are several approaches that can be used in finding such an expression. We will merely note that after the required algebra, it can be shown that

$$a = \frac{v_{in}}{v_{out}} = \frac{1 + m + \sqrt{1 + 2m}}{m} \tag{7-8}$$

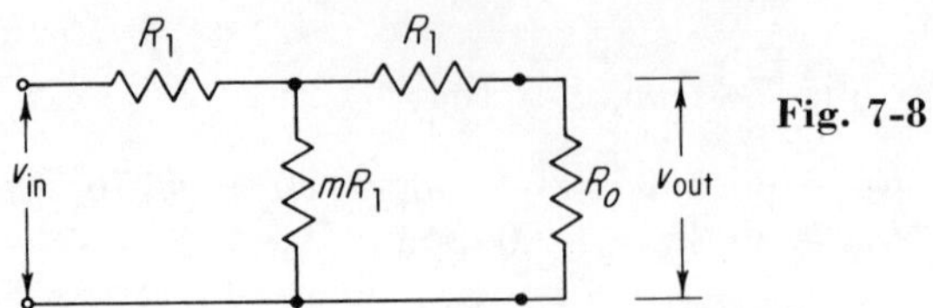

Fig. 7-8

Let us summarize. In Eqs. (7-7) and (7-8) we have the analysis formulas for a symmetrical T attenuator. Given the values of R_1 and R_2 (such as on a schematic), we can find m by taking the ratio of R_2 to R_1. Then, substituting into Eqs. (7-7) and (7-8) we can easily find the characteristic resistance and the attenuation for the T attenuator.

Example 7-5

Compute the characteristic resistance and the attenuation of a symmetrical T attenuator which has $R_1 = 409$ and $R_2 = 101$.

Solution

$$m = \frac{R_2}{R_1} = \frac{101}{409} = 0.247$$

$$R_o = R_1\sqrt{1 + 2m} = 409\sqrt{1 + 2(0.247)} = 500 \text{ ohms}$$

$$a = \frac{1 + 0.247 + \sqrt{1 + 2(0.247)}}{0.247} = 10$$

Thus, the given attenuator should be used with a 500-ohm load and source resistance. If this is done, the attenuation will be equal to 10, which is equivalent to 20 db.

Example 7-6

If the attenuator of Example 7-5 has all resistances reduced by a factor of ten, what is the value of R_o and a for the new attenuator?

Solution

We note that now $R_1 = 40.9$ and $R_2 = 10.1$ ohms. Therefore, m still equals 0.247, as in Example 7-5. From Eq. (7-8), the attenuation still equals 10.

Next, we observe from Eq. (7-7) that R_o is directly proportional to R_1. The value of m is still the same. Therefore, R_o equals one-tenth of 500, or 50 ohms.

Thus, by reducing all resistances by a factor of ten, we have reduced the characteristic resistance by ten, but the attenuation has remained the same.

7-5 Symmetrical T Design Formulas

In this section we develop design formulas for the symmetrical T attenuator. Equations (7-7) and (7-8) tell us how to find R_o and a, given the value of R_1 and R_2. If, on the other hand, we wish to design a T attenuator, we will be given the value of R_o and a and will need to find R_1 and R_2. We can find formulas for R_1 and R_2 by solving Eqs. (7-7) and (7-8) simultaneously. If this is done, we obtain

$$R_1 = \frac{a-1}{a+1} R_o \tag{7-9}$$

$$R_2 = \frac{2a}{a^2-1} R_o \tag{7-10}$$

These are very useful formulas for designing T attenuators. For instance, if the characteristic resistance is to be 50 ohms, and if the attenuation is to be 10, we would obtain

$$R_1 = \frac{10-1}{10+1} 50 = 40.9 \text{ ohms}$$

$$R_2 = \frac{2(10)}{10^2-1} 50 = 10.1 \text{ ohms}$$

From Eqs. (7-9) and (7-10) it should be clear that R_1 and R_2 are functions of a and R_o. Note especially that R_1 and R_2 are directly proportional to R_o. If we like, we can generate a table of design values for future reference. In order to simplify the table we may choose R_o equal to 50 ohms. (This value of R_o is one of the most widely used values in electronics.) With R_o equal to 50 ohms, R_1 and R_2 become functions of a only. To make a table we can select values of a and calculate the corresponding values of R_1 and R_2, as shown in Table 7-1.

Note that for any characteristic resistance not equal to 50 ohms, we need only multiply each value for R_1 and R_2 by $R_o/50$. For instance, if we need a 500-ohm 20-db attenuator, according to our table, the value of R_1 and R_2 should be 40.9 and 10.1 ohms, respectively, for a 50-ohm attenuator. For a 500-ohm attenuator we need only multiply each R_1 and R_2 value by $500/50$, or 10. Thus, we obtain $R_1 = 409$ and $R_2 = 101$ ohms for a 20-db 500-ohm attenuator.

Example 7-7

Design a 12-db 50-ohm T attenuator.

Solution

From Table 7-1 we find $R_1 = 29.9$ and $R_2 = 26.8$ ohms. Since the attenuator resistance is to be 50 ohms, these values are used as they are.

Table 7-1 Symmetrical T Design, $R_o = 50$

a_{db}	R_1	R_2
1	2.88	433
2	5.73	215
3	8.55	142
4	11.3	105
6	16.6	66.9
8	21.5	47.3
10	26	35.1
12	29.9	26.8
16	36.3	16.3
20	40.9	10.1
24	44.1	6.34
28	46.3	3.99
30	46.9	3.17
35	48.3	1.78
40	49	1.00

EXAMPLE 7-8

Design a 20-db 600-ohm T attenuator.

SOLUTION

From Table 7-1 we find $R_1 = 40.9$ and $R_2 = 10.1$ ohms. Since the characteristic resistance is to be 600 ohms, we must multiply R_1 and R_2 by $^{600}/_{50}$, or 12. If we do this, we obtain $R_1 = 490$ and $R_2 = 121$ ohms.

7-6 Cascading T Sections

Up to this time we have dealt only in basic T attenuators, that is, a single T composed of three resistors. Basic T sections may be cascaded,

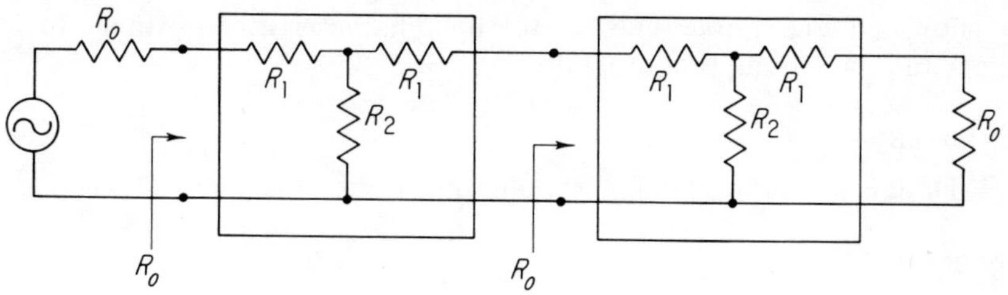

Fig. 7-9 Cascading symmetrical T sections.

as shown in Fig. 7-9. Note that the resistance level is preserved as we move from load to source. That is, starting from the load end, we see that the input resistance of the second attenuator is R_o. This means that the first attenuator is also loaded correctly in its characteristic resistance. As a result, the input resistance of the first attenuator is also equal to R_o. This useful property of attenuators allows us to cascade as many attenuators as we like. The R_o resistance is preserved throughout the entire system, with the result that a perfect impedance match occurs at all input and output terminals.

There is a good reason for wanting to cascade attenuator sections. From Table 7-1 note that as we approach higher values of attenuation, R_2 becomes very small. Because of this, values of attenuation above 40 db will require R_2 values that are impracticably small. Therefore, in the construction of, say, a 90-db attenuator, we can cascade three 30-db sections. For instance, if we wish a 90-db 50-ohm attenuator, we obtain $R_1 = 46.9$ ohms and $R_2 = 3.17$ ohms for each 30-db section. After cascading the 30-db sections, we have the circuit shown in Fig. 7-10*a*. The 46.9-ohm resistances can be lumped into a single 93.8-ohm resistor,

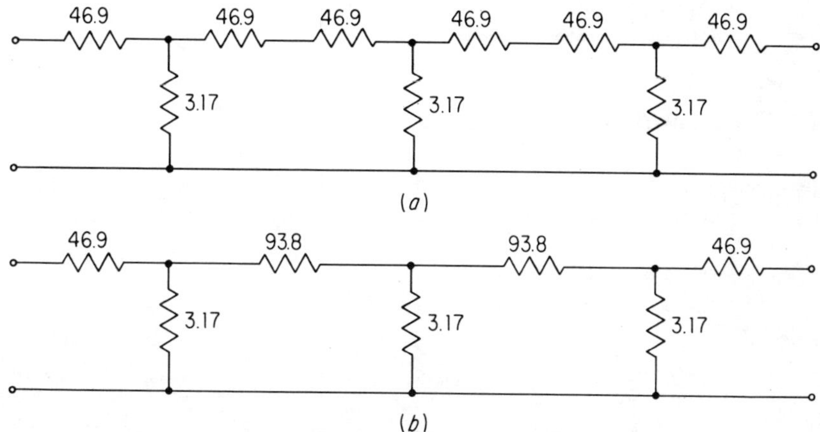

Fig. 7-10 (*a*) Three-section T attentuator. (*b*) Combining resistances.

as shown in Fig. 7-10*b*. This circuit has characteristic resistance of 50 ohms and an attenuation of 90 db.

EXAMPLE 7-9

Design a 50-db 500-ohm attenuator using three basic T sections.

SOLUTION

Arbitrarily, we can choose to use two 20-db sections and one 10-db section. For the 20-db section we obtain from Table 7-1

$$R_1 = 40.9 \qquad \text{and} \qquad R_2 = 10.1 \text{ ohms} \qquad \text{for } R_o = 50 \text{ ohms}$$

or

$$R_1 = 409 \qquad \text{and} \qquad R_2 = 101 \text{ ohms} \qquad \text{for } R_o = 500 \text{ ohms}$$

For the 10-db section we obtain

$$R_1 = 26 \qquad \text{and} \qquad R_2 = 35.1 \text{ ohms} \qquad \text{for } R_o = 50 \text{ ohms}$$

or

$$R_1 = 260 \qquad \text{and} \qquad R_2 = 351 \text{ ohms} \qquad \text{for } R_o = 500 \text{ ohms}$$

The final design is shown in Fig. 7-11.

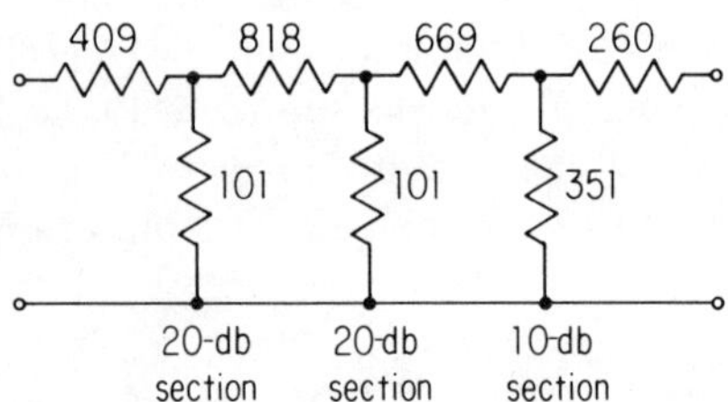

Fig. 7-11 Example 7-9.

7-7 The Symmetrical π Attenuator

The π section of Fig. 7-12*a* is as basic as the T section. Occasionally, the π section may be preferred to the T section. By defining *m* as the ratio

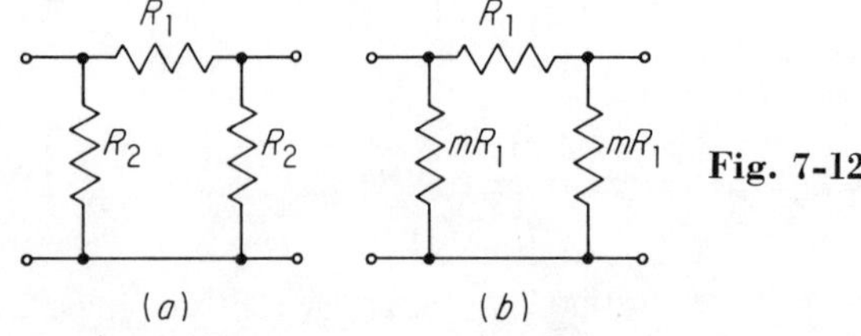

Fig. 7-12

of R_2 to R_1, we can relabel the values as shown in Fig. 7-12*b*. Proceeding as we did for the T section, we can find the following formulas for analysis and design:

Analysis
$$R_o = \frac{m}{\sqrt{1+2m}} R_1 \tag{7-11}$$
$$a = \frac{1 + m + \sqrt{1+2m}}{m} \tag{7-12}$$

Design
$$R_1 = \frac{a^2 - 1}{2a} R_o \tag{7-13}$$
$$R_2 = \frac{a+1}{a-1} R_o \tag{7-14}$$

As with the T section, we can generate a table for future reference. Table 7-2 gives the design values of R_1 and R_2 for a characteristic resistance of 50 ohms. For any other value of R_o, we need only multiply R_1 and R_2 by $R_o/50$.

Table 7-2 Symmetrical π Design, $R_o = 50$

a_{db}	R_1	R_2
1	5.77	870
2	11.6	436
3	17.6	292
4	23.8	221
6	37.4	150
8	52.8	116
10	71.2	96.2
12	93.2	83.5
16	154	68.8
20	248	61.1
24	395	56.7
30	790	53.3
40	2500	51

EXAMPLE 7-10

Design a 20-db 300-ohm π attenuator.

SOLUTION

From Table 7-2 we see that $R_1 = 248$ and $R_2 = 61.1$ ohms for an R_o of 50 ohms. For an R_o of 300 ohms we must multiply by 300/50, or 6. Hence, $R_1 = 1488$ and $R_2 = 366.6$ ohms.

7-8 The Bridged T Attenuator

The last specific type of attenuator we wish to study is the bridged T attenuator. The circuit for a bridged T is shown in Fig. 7-13. The reason

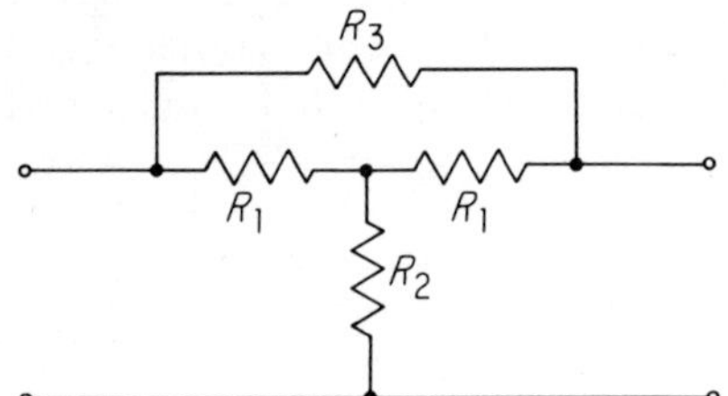

Fig. 7-13 Bridged T attenuator.

for the name *bridged T* should be clear. To an ordinary T attenuator is added a resistor that bridges from the input to the output. The analysis and design formulas for this important attenuator are as follows:

Analysis

$$R_o = R_1 \tag{7-15}$$

$$a = \frac{R_1}{R_2} + 1 \tag{7-16}$$

Design

$$R_1 = R_o$$

$$R_2 = \frac{R_o}{a - 1} \tag{7-17}$$

$$R_3 = (a - 1)R_o \tag{7-18}$$

Note carefully that the design formulas indicate that R_1 is not a function of a. Only R_2 and R_3 depend upon a. This is a very important property, as will be discussed in the next section.

EXAMPLE 7-11

Design a 20-db 50-ohm bridged T attenuator.

SOLUTION

$$R_1 = 50 \text{ ohms}$$

$$R_2 = \frac{50}{10 - 1} = 5.55 \text{ ohms}$$

$$R_3 = (10 - 1)50 = 450 \text{ ohms}$$

7-9 Variable Attenuators

Commercial instrument attenuators are often of the variable type to allow selection of different values of attenuation, while maintaining the resistance at the value of R_o. One way of building a continuously variable attenuator is by using ganged rheostats for the resistors in the attenuator. In either the T or the π attenuator all three resistances must be varied in accordance with the design equations. It is actually much easier to use a bridged T attenuator. Recall that the R_1 value does not depend upon the amount of attenuation. R_1 may be fixed at the value of characteristic resistance that is desired. We need only vary R_2 and R_3, as shown in Fig. 7-14. Note that R_2 and R_3 are ganged together. In order to work properly,

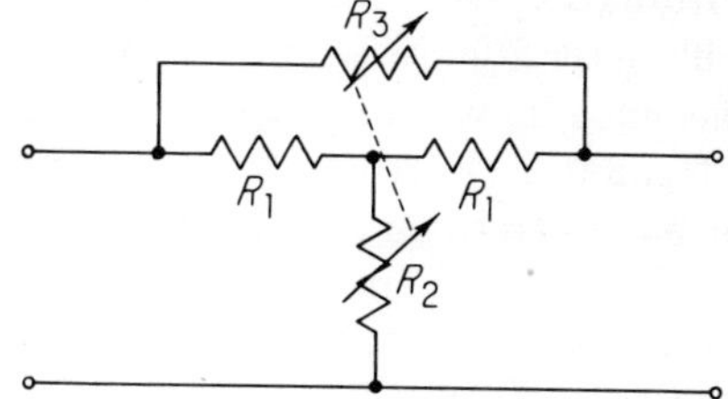

Fig. 7-14 Continuously variable attenuator.

these rheostats must track according to Eqs. (7-17) and (7-18). In these equations we note that R_2 is inversely proportional to a, whereas R_3 is directly proportional to a. A study of these equations shows that linear rheostats will not track properly. However, logarithmic rheostats can be ganged together, so that Eqs. (7-17) and (7-18) are satisfied. The result is then a continuously variable attenuator whose characteristic resistance remains constant.

Of course, the tracking of R_2 and R_3 cannot be made perfect. Some deviation in the value of R_o is to be expected. However, the variable bridged T attenuator provides a reasonably accurate value of R_o over its range of adjustment.

If more precise values of R_o and a are required, the usual procedure is to build a step attenuator, which is an attenuator varied in discrete steps. For instance, a step attenuator might be designed to cover from 0 to 10 db in steps of 1 db. We would then be able to select 0, 1, 2, 3, or any whole number of decibels up to 10 db.

One of the most popular ways of building a step attenuator is by building a number of simple T attenuators with different values of attenuation. By means of a proper switching arrangement, various combinations can be cascaded to produce the desired amount of attenuation. For example, suppose we desire to build a 0- to 10-db attenuator with 1-db steps. We could build four basic attenuators with values of 1, 2, 3, and

4 db. There are several switching arrangements that can be used to switch in any attenuation from 1 to 10 db, simply by using combinations of the four basic attenuators. To obtain 6 db, for example, the 2- and 4-db attenuators must be cascaded. To obtain 9 db, we must connect the 2-, 3-, and 4-db attenuators (see Prob. 7-16).

A 100-db attenuator with 1-db steps can be made by using two step attenuators in cascade. The first unit would be a 0- to 10-db step attenuator with 1-db steps. In cascade with this, we would use a 0- to 90-db attenuator with 10-db steps. Thus, any whole number of decibels between 0 and 100 db can be selected.

7-10 Padding Sources and Loads

Ordinarily we use source and load resistances that are equal to the characteristic resistance of the attenuator. Under this condition impedance matching occurs at the input and output terminals of the attenuator. Further, the signal is attenuated by a precise amount *a* as it passes from the input of the attenuator to the output.

However, there is a way of using an attenuator in a nonmatched situation. Assume that we have a signal source whose Thévenin resistance varies from 25 to 100 ohms because of temperature or aging or any number of reasons. In order to use this signal source in a 50-ohm system, we must stabilize its resistance to a value of 50 ohms. One way of fixing the source resistance at 50 ohms is by cascading an attenuator with a characteristic resistance of 50 ohms. If enough attenuation is present, the Thévenin resistance looking back into the attenuator will be very close to 50 ohms (see Fig. 7-15). The price we pay for stabilizing the source resistance

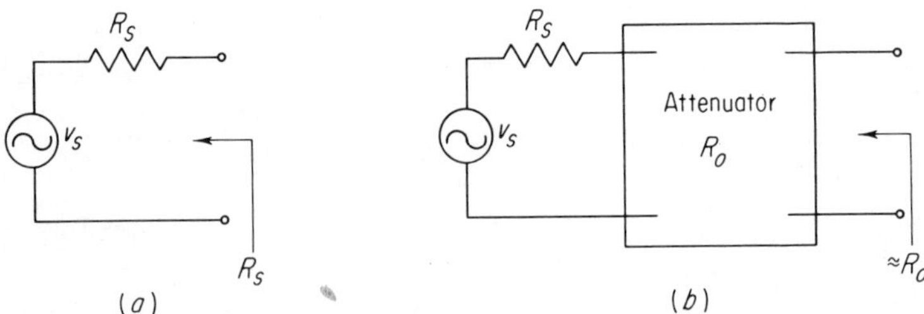

Fig. 7-15 (*a*) Unpadded source. (*b*) Padding a source.

is that we must give up some of the signal level. This is precisely what is normally done in good commercial signal sources. It is far better to have a fixed source resistance with less signal than to have more signal with an unreliable source resistance. The use of an attenuator in this way is commonly known as *padding* a source. Because of this, attenuators are often called pads.

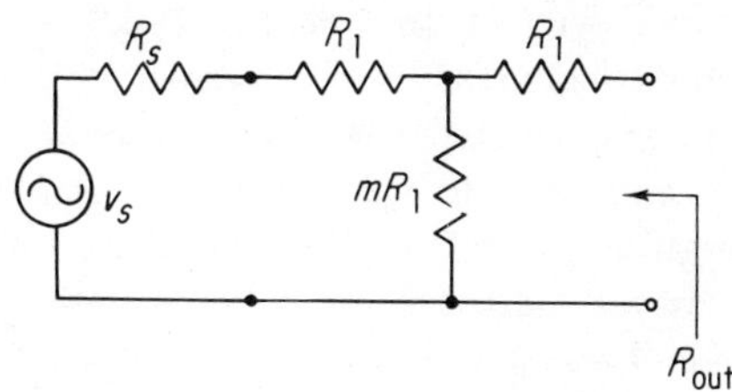

Fig. 7-16 Deriving the formula for a padded-source resistance.

We wish to obtain a formula for the resistance of a padded source (see Fig. 7-16). A simple T attenuator has been cascaded with a source whose resistance is R_s. The Thévenin resistance of this combination is

$$R_{\text{out}} = R_1 + mR_1 \| (R_1 + R_s) \tag{7-19}$$

By defining a new quantity k as the ratio of R_s to R_o we can manipulate Eq. (7-19) and obtain

$$R_{\text{out}} = R_o \left(1 + \frac{2}{a^2 \dfrac{k+1}{k-1} - 1} \right) \tag{7-20}$$

where $$k \triangleq \frac{R_s}{R_o}$$

This equation is useful if we wish to find the Thévenin resistance of a padded source. For instance, suppose we have $R_o = 50$, $R_s = 150$, and $a = 2$. Then,

$$k = {}^{150}\!/\!_{50} = 3$$

and
$$R_{\text{out}} = 50 \left(1 + \frac{2}{2^2 \dfrac{3+1}{3-1} - 1} \right)$$
$$= 50(1 + 0.286) = 64.3 \text{ ohms}$$

Note that the Thévenin resistance of the padded source is 64.3 ohms compared to 150 ohms for the unpadded source. If it is desired to have a value of resistance even closer to 50 ohms, more attenuation must be used. If, for example, the attenuation is increased to 10, we obtain

$$R_{\text{out}} = 50 \left(1 + \frac{2}{10^2 \dfrac{3+1}{3-1} - 1} \right)$$
$$= 50(1 + 0.01) = 50.5 \text{ ohms}$$

Note that the Thévenin resistance of the padded source is 50.5 ohms compared to 150 ohms for the unpadded source. The price paid for this is that the signal has been attenuated by a factor of ten.

Analysis shows that Eq. (7-20) is applicable to the π section as well as the T section. In fact, Eq. (7-20) is the same no matter what the form of the attenuator.

Suppose that the source resistance is completely unknown. How much attenuation do we need to stabilize the source resistance? We can obtain a guide in such a situation in the following way. First, we realize that the source resistance must be between zero and infinity. These extremes in possible resistance value bracket the possible range of R_{out}. For instance, if $R_s = 0$, then $k = 0$, and R_{out} reduces to

$$R_{out} = R_o\left(1 - \frac{2}{a^2 + 1}\right) \tag{7-21}$$

On the other hand, if $R_s = \infty$,

$$R_{out} = R_o\left(1 + \frac{2}{a^2 - 1}\right) \tag{7-22}$$

Equations (7-21) and (7-22) give the extreme values of R_{out}. For R_s between zero and infinity, R_{out} is between the values given by these two equations. For example, if $a = 10$ and $R_o = 50$ ohms, then for $R_s = 0$, we obtain from Eq. (7-21)

$$R_{out} = 50\left(1 - \frac{2}{10^2 + 1}\right) = 50(0.98) = 49 \text{ ohms}$$

At the other extreme, if $R_s = \infty$,

$$R_{out} = 50\left(1 + \frac{2}{10^2 - 1}\right) = 50(1.02) = 51 \text{ ohms}$$

Thus, we have the value of a padded source bracketed between 49 and 51 ohms. For any value of R_s between zero and infinity, the padded source has a Thévenin resistance between 49 and 51 ohms.

The situation described is often encountered in practice. Signal sources with unknown source resistances are used in systems where all loads and sources should be at a specified value of R_o. In order to make them compatible with the system, they must be padded heavily to ensure that the padded source has a Thévenin resistance that is very close to the value of R_o. Generally, if a 20-db pad is used, the padded-source resistance will be very close to the value of R_o.

Equations (7-21) and (7-22) can be tabulated as shown in Table 7-3, which will be useful for future reference. For example, it tells us that if a 20-db pad with a characteristic resistance of R_o is used to pad any source, the padded-source resistance must be between $0.98R_o$ and $1.02R_o$. Or, if only 10-db padding is used, the padded source resistance must lie between $0.82R_o$ and $1.22R_o$.

Table 7-3 Extremes of Padded-source Resistance

a_{db}	a	R_{out} for	
		$R_s = 0$	$R_s = \infty$
0	1	0	∞
6	2	$0.6R_o$	$1.67R_o$
8	2.51	$0.73R_o$	$1.38R_o$
10	3.16	$0.82R_o$	$1.22R_o$
12	4	$0.88R_o$	$1.13R_o$
16	6.3	$0.95R_o$	$1.05R_o$
20	10	$0.98R_o$	$1.02R_o$

EXAMPLE 7-12

A signal source with an unknown source resistance is to be used in a 600-ohm system. If a 12-db 600-ohm pad is used, what are the extreme values for the padded-source resistance?

SOLUTION

From Table 7-3 we find that R_{out} is between $0.88R_o$ and $1.13R_o$. Since R_o is 600 ohms, R_{out} must be between 528 and 678 ohms.

EXAMPLE 7-13

A crystal detector is to be used in a 50-ohm system. If a 16-db pad is used, what are the extremes on the padded resistance of the detector?

SOLUTION

From Table 7-3 we have R_{out} bracketed between $0.95R_o$ and $1.05R_o$. Since R_o is 50, R_{out} must be between 47.5 and 52.5 ohms.

SUMMARY

Attenuators are used to reduce the signal level by a precise amount. A very simple attenuator is the ordinary voltage divider. A voltage divider is usually found in the input stage of various measuring instruments. In order to extend its useful frequency range, the voltage divider is often compensated by means of a capacitor.

The characteristic resistance of an attenuator refers to that value of load resistance on the output terminals which produces the same value of resistance at the input terminals. The symmetrical T, π, and bridged T are some of the common attenuator circuits. These attenuators are generally used in matched systems, that is, where all load and source resistances are equal.

In telephone systems, 600 ohms is the resistance value normally used. In microwave systems, 50 ohms is the resistance value normally encountered. As a rule, all sources and loads should be equal to the characteristic resistance.

The bridged T section is often used in continuously variable attenuators. Because two logarithmic rheostats must be ganged together, only reasonably accurate performance can be attained with a bridged T variable attenuator.

For more precise variable attenuators, step attenuators are used. They consist of a few basic attenuators and a switching arrangement for cascading the basic sections in different combinations. The result is an attenuator that is variable in discrete steps.

Padding of sources and loads is a common practice in order to stabilize the resistance of a source or load. A 20-db pad will guarantee that the padded-source (or load) resistance is between $0.98R_o$ and $1.02R_o$.

GLOSSARY

attenuation The reciprocal of voltage gain. The ratio of the input voltage to the output voltage.

attenuator Any device that reduces the power level of a signal.

characteristic resistance When speaking of an attenuator, this is the value of load resistance on the attenuator that produces exactly the same value of input resistance when looking into the attenuator.

frequency compensation Extending the frequency range of an attenuator by adding a capacitance to offset the effects of stray and tube capacitance.

padding Using an attenuator in cascade with a source or load in order to obtain a resistance that is approximately equal to the characteristic resistance of the attenuator.

symmetrical attenuator An attenuator which is symmetrical about a vertical center line.

unbalanced Means that there is a common connection between the input and the output.

REVIEW QUESTIONS

1. What is an attenuator?
2. How is attenuation defined?
3. What is the voltage-gain formula for a simple voltage divider?
4. How can a voltage divider be compensated to improve high-frequency operation?
5. In adjusting the trimmer capacitor of a compensated voltage divider, what is the significance of a spiked square wave?
6. How is the characteristic resistance of an attenuator defined?
7. What does the word "unbalanced" mean?
8. How can the characteristic resistance be found experimentally?
9. The value of attenuation given by Eq. (7-8) is true under what load conditions?
10. In using Table 7-1, how do we convert the table values for characteristic resistances different from 50 ohms?
11. Why are attenuator sections sometimes cascaded?
12. How many resistors are there in a bridged T attenuator?
13. Why is the bridged T attenuator best suited for continuously variable attenuators?
14. Can linear rheostats be used in a continuously variable bridged T attenuator? If not, then what kind of rheostats must be used?
15. How can a 10-db step attenuator with 1-db steps be constructed?
16. What does padding a source mean?
17. In order to make the padded-source resistance approach R_o more closely, should more or less attenuation be used?
18. What characteristic resistance is commonly found in telephone systems? In microwave systems?

PROBLEMS

7-1 A simple voltage divider (Fig. 7-1) has $R_1 = 7$ kilohms and $R_2 = 1$ kilohm. Find the gain as an ordinary number and as a decibel equivalent. Also, find the attenuation in decibels.

7-2 In Fig. 7-17*a*, 100 volts is applied across the input to the voltage divider as shown. The voltage out of each tap point is shown. If the total resistance of the divider is 10 megohms, what are the values of the resistors in the divider?

7-3 In Fig. 7-17*b*, a two-position range switch is used to allow a step-down in voltage of either 10 or 100. If the capacitance across the 100-kilohm resistor is exactly 50 pf, to what values should the trimmers be adjusted in order to frequency-compensate this capacitance?

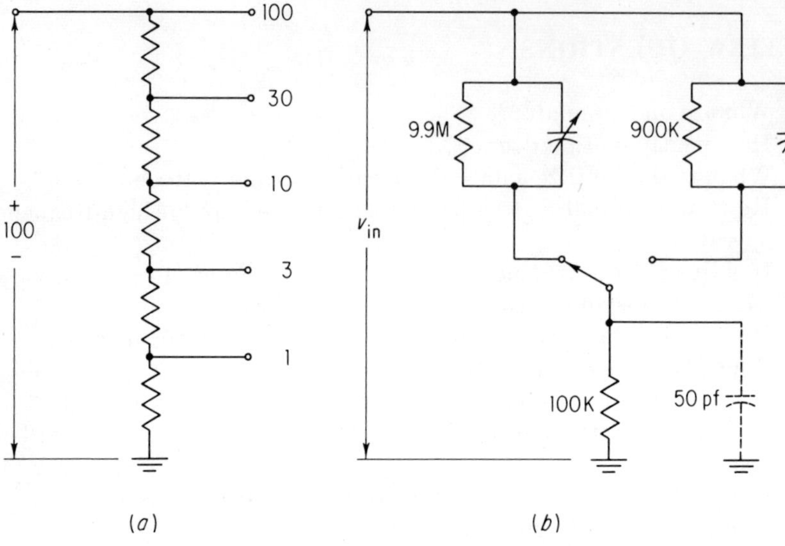

Fig. 7-17

7-4 A symmetrical T attenuator has R_1 equal to 320 ohms and R_2 equal to 75 ohms. What is the characteristic resistance of this attenuator? If the attenuator is loaded by its characteristic resistance, how much attenuation in decibels occurs from the input to the output of the attenuator?

7-5 What is the characteristic resistance and attenuation of a properly loaded T attenuator with $R_1 = 363$ ohms and $R_2 = 163$ ohms?

7-6 The characteristic resistance of a T attenuator with R_1 and R_2 equal to 21.5 and 47.3 ohms, respectively, is 50 ohms. Prove that $R_o = 50$ ohms by calculating the input resistance of such an attenuator loaded by 50 ohms.

7-7 A symmetrical T attenuator is made by using three 50-ohm resistors. What is the characteristic resistance and attenuation if the T is properly loaded?

7-8 A 50-ohm source with an open circuit voltage of 2 volts rms is connected to a T attenuator which has $R_o = 50$ ohms and $a_{db} = 18$ db. What is the Thévenin equivalent at the output terminals of the attenuator?

7-9 Design a 35-db 100-ohm T-section attenuator.

7-10 Design a 100-db 500-ohm attenuator using T sections.

7-11 Design a 30-db 600-ohm π-section attenuator.

7-12 Design a 25-db 50-ohm bridged T attenuator.

7-13 In Fig. 7-18*a*, two T sections have been cascaded. Find the characteristic resistance of the attenuator. If R_s and R_L are made equal to the characteristic resistance, what is the attenuation from the input to

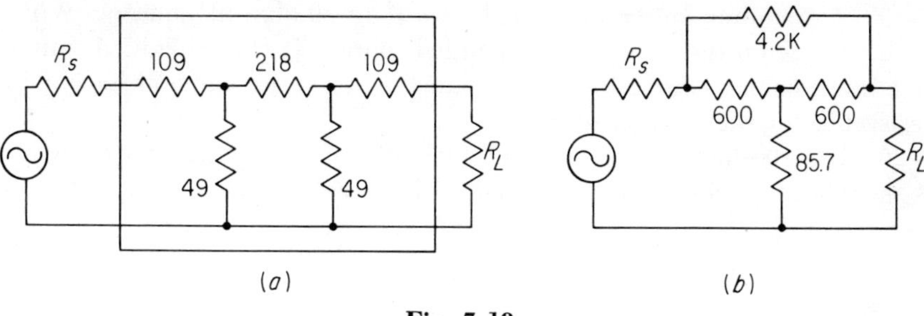

Fig. 7-18

the output of the attenuator? If the input voltage to the attenuator is 10 volts rms, what is the output voltage?

7-14 In the bridged T shown in Fig. 7-18*b*, what is the characteristic resistance of the attenuator? If the attenuator has been properly loaded, and if the input to the attenuator is 2 volts rms, what will the output voltage be?

7-15 For the bridge T section of Fig. 7-13, $R_1 = 600$ ohms. Make a table showing the values of R_2 and R_3 for the following values of a_{db}: 10, 20, 30, and 40 db.

7-16 In Fig. 7-19 a simple step attenuator is shown. What is the value of R_o and a_{db} for each section? (All switches are ganged together.) What is the value of attenuation in positions 1 to 4?

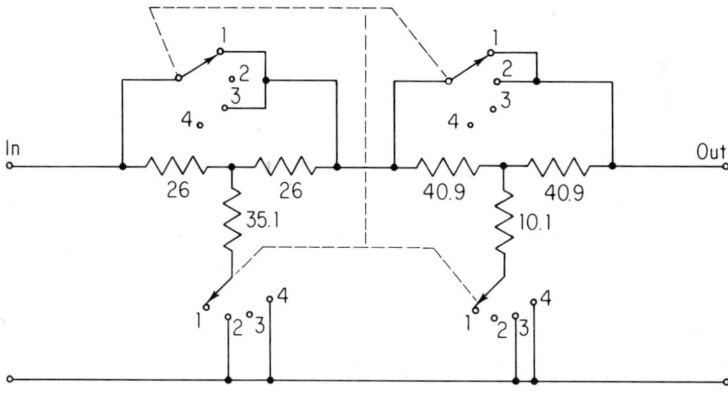

Fig. 7-19

7-17 A source with a Thévenin resistance of 300 ohms is to be used in a 50-ohm system. If the source is padded by a 12-db 50-ohm attenuator, what is the Thévenin resistance of the padded source?

7-18 An oscillator whose Thévenin resistance is unknown is padded by a 10-db 50-ohm attenuator. The Thévenin resistance of the padded source must lie between what two values?

7-19 A 100-ohm source is padded by a 6-db 50-ohm attenuator. What is the Thévenin resistance of the padded source? If the unpadded source resistance changes from 100 to 150 ohms, what is the value of Thévenin resistance for the padded source?

7-20 If a 10-ohm source is padded by a 10-db 50-ohm attenuator, what is the Thévenin resistance of the padded source?

8 Filters

There are many systems in which it is essential to attenuate sinusoidal signals whose frequencies lie outside a desired band. Telephone, television, and radar would be virtually impossible without a means of separating desired frequencies from undesired ones. Further, there are many complex instruments—receivers, oscillators, mixers, and frequency analyzers, to name but a few—that could not function properly without a means of frequency selection.

Filters are instruments whose function is to separate some sinusoidal frequencies from others. Because of their established importance to instrumentation, we will examine some of the basic filter types.

8-1 Ideal Filter Characteristics

A filter is normally inserted between a source and a load, as shown in Fig. 8-1. If the source is sinusoidal, we will find that some frequencies are passed from the input to the output of the filter with very little attenuation, whereas other frequencies are greatly attenuated.

The basic filter responses are shown in Fig. 8-2. These are ideal responses; they cannot be actually realized, although real filter responses can approach these ideal graphs.

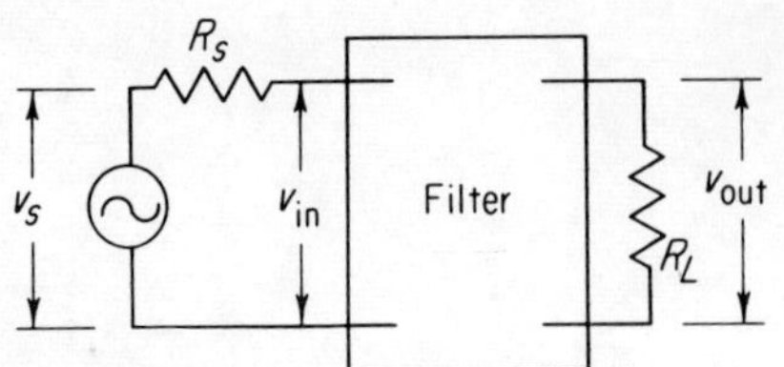

Fig. 8-1 Filter between source and load.

The ideal low-pass response is shown in Fig. 8-2*a*. The voltage gain A is defined as v_{out}/v_s. Thus, we see that the gain is constant from zero frequency up to a cutoff frequency f_c. Above the cutoff frequency the voltage gain drops to zero.

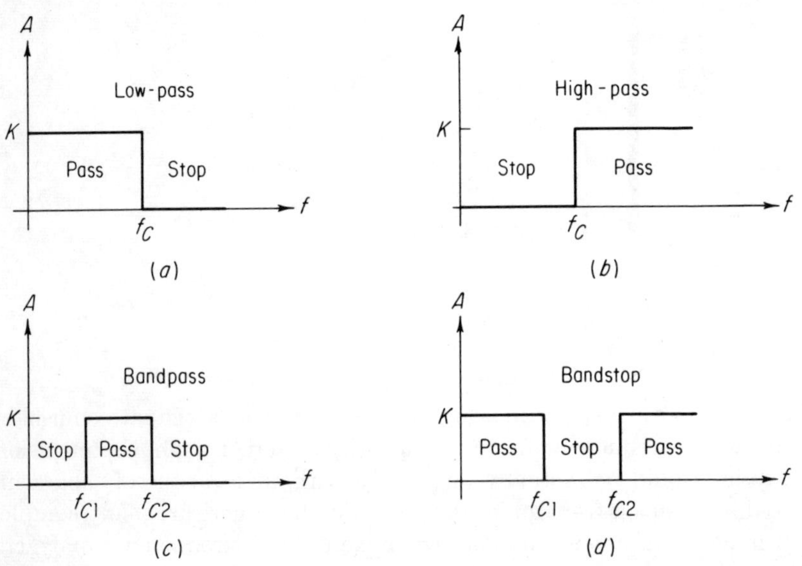

Fig. 8-2 Ideal filter responses. (*a*) Low-pass. (*b*) High-pass. (*c*) Bandpass. (*d*) Bandstop.

In a similar way, the high-pass filter has a gain of zero from zero frequency up to the cutoff frequency. Above the cutoff frequency the gain equals K (see Fig. 8-2*b*).

The bandpass and bandstop filters have two cutoff frequencies. In the passband the gain is K, and in the stopband the gain is zero (see Fig. 8-2*c* and *d*).

8-2 The Real Low-pass Response

The typical response of a real low-pass filter is shown in Fig. 8-3. The cutoff of the real filter is more gradual than the ideal filter. Because of this, the question naturally arises as to what the cutoff frequency is. This is a matter of definition. In other words, we simply have to agree upon a definition for cutoff frequency and then abide by that definition.

How shall we define the cutoff frequency? We could, if we liked, arbitrarily define the cutoff frequency as that frequency where the voltage gain drops to $0.9K$. Or, just as arbitrarily we could say that the cutoff frequency is that frequency where the voltage gain drops to $0.5K$.

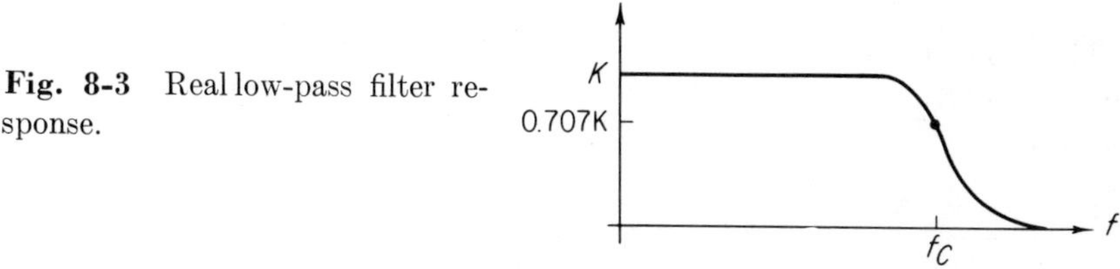

Fig. 8-3 Real low-pass filter response.

To keep in step with the rest of the electronics community we should use the definition that is commonly employed. Arbitrarily, the cutoff frequency is that frequency where the load power drops to one-half its passband value. In terms of voltage gain this is identical to saying that the cutoff frequency is that frequency where the voltage gain drops to 0.707 of the passband value, or -3 db.

The cutoff frequencies of the high-pass, bandpass, and bandstop filters are defined in the same way.

8-3 The Simple Low-pass Filter

In Fig. 8-4 the RC network inside the box is a simple low-pass filter. At very low frequencies the capacitive reactance is very high, so that

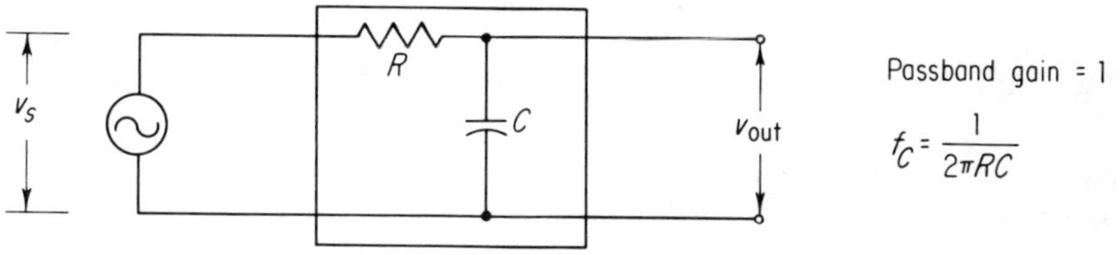

Fig. 8-4 Low-pass RC filter.

we can consider the capacitor as an open circuit. Under this condition, v_{out} equals v_s, and the voltage gain equals unity. At very high frequencies, the capacitive reactance is very low, so that v_{out} is much smaller than v_s. Under this condition, the filter is operating in its stopband, since the voltage gain is quite low.

To find an expression for the cutoff frequency we must use complex numbers. Recall that for sinusoidal signals, we can represent v_s and v_{out} by complex numbers. Also, the circuit elements can be represented by complex numbers. Therefore, we proceed as follows:

$$\mathbf{V}_{out} = \mathbf{I}(-jX_c) = \frac{\mathbf{V}_s}{R - jX_c}(-jX_c) = \frac{-jX_c}{R - jX_c}\mathbf{V}_s$$

or

$$\mathbf{A} = \frac{\mathbf{V}_{out}}{\mathbf{V}_s} = \frac{-jX_c}{R - jX_c} \tag{8-1}$$

This is not the most convenient formula for the gain. Recall that a complex number in rectangular form may be converted to the polar form as follows:

$$\mathbf{A} = \frac{-jX_c}{R - jX_c} = \frac{X_c\underline{/-90°}}{\sqrt{R^2 + X_c^2}\underline{/\arctan -X_c/R}} \tag{8-2}$$

This polar number has a magnitude

$$\frac{X_c}{\sqrt{R^2 + X_c^2}}$$

and an angle

$$\underline{/-90° + \arctan X_c/R}$$

The angle tells us how much phase shift takes place as the signal passes from input to output. For example, if $X_c/R = 1$, the angle becomes $-90 + 45°$, or simply $-45°$. This tells us that the output sinusoid is 45° behind the input sinusoid.

The angle formula is important in some studies, but we are more interested in the magnitude of the voltage gain

$$A = \frac{X_c}{\sqrt{R^2 + X_c^2}} = \frac{\text{rms output voltage}}{\text{rms source voltage}} \tag{8-3}$$

Basically, the magnitude of the voltage gain is the ratio of the rms value of the output voltage to the rms value of the source voltage. (Peak values may be used if more convenient.) For instance, if the input sinusoid has an rms value of 5 volts, and if the output has an rms value of 0.25 volts, the magnitude of the voltage gain is simply 0.25/5, or 0.05. There will be a phase angle between the input and output, but we are now interested only in rms values, and thus we obtain 0.05 for the voltage gain.

We can rearrange Eq. (8-3) into a simpler form by dividing numerator and denominator by X_c, obtaining

$$A = \frac{1}{\sqrt{1 + R^2/X_c^2}}$$

Finally, we observe that $X_c = 1/\omega C$. Substituting into the preceding equation, we obtain

$$A = \frac{1}{\sqrt{1 + (\omega RC)^2}} \tag{8-4}$$

Equation (8-4) is the equation for the voltage gain of a simple RC low-pass filter. Examine it carefully, and note the following. For very low frequency, ω approaches zero. As a result, ωRC must approach zero at low frequencies. Therefore, the voltage gain approaches unity. This confirms our earlier observation that the RC filter of Fig. 8-4 had unity gain for low frequencies. For very high frequencies, ωRC approaches infinity. As a result, the denominator of Eq. (8-4) is very large, so that A becomes very small. This too confirms our earlier observation that the gain should fall off at higher frequencies.

How can we find the cutoff frequency? By definition, the cutoff frequency is that frequency at which the gain is 0.707 of the passband value. If we substitute into Eq. (8-4), we have

$$0.707 = \frac{1}{\sqrt{1 + (\omega_c RC)^2}}$$

By squaring both sides we can find the value of ω_c, the radian cutoff frequency. However, we can avoid the algebra by using our common sense. By inspection, $\omega_c RC$ must equal 1 in order to satisfy the equation. Hence,

$$\omega_c RC = 1$$

or

$$2\pi f_c RC = 1$$

or

$$f_c = \frac{1}{2\pi RC} \tag{8-5}$$

Equation (8-5) is the formula for the cutoff frequency of a simple low-pass RC filter. Its use is straightforward. For instance, if the low-pass RC filter has $R = 10$ kilohms and $C = 1\ \mu$f, the cutoff frequency is

$$f_c = \frac{1}{2\pi(10)(10^3)(10^{-6})} = \frac{0.159}{10(10^{-3})} = 15.9 \text{ Hz}$$

At this frequency the low-pass filter has a gain of 0.707. Below this frequency the gain approaches unity, and above it the gain approaches zero.

Example 8-1

Find the cutoff frequency for a simple low-pass RC filter if $R = 1$ kilohm and $C = 0.01\ \mu$f.

Solution

$$f_c = \frac{0.159}{10^3(0.01)(10^{-6})} = 15.9 \text{ kHz}$$

8-4 Effects of Source and Load Resistance

Suppose we now consider the effects of adding a load resistor as shown in Fig. 8-5*a*. First, it should be clear that at very low frequencies the capacitor resembles an open circuit, so that the circuit becomes a simple resistive voltage divider. Hence, in the passband

$$A = \frac{R_L}{R + R_L} = \text{passband gain}$$

Second, it may or may not be clear that the cutoff frequency is different from that of an unloaded filter. The easiest way to see this is by using Thévenin's theorem. If we consider the capacitor as the load, then the Thévenin equivalent at the output terminals is the circuit shown in Fig. 8-5*b*. Note that this circuit is in the same form as the simple unloaded RC filter studied in the previous section, although we now have $R \| R_L$ instead of R. It follows that the cutoff frequency will therefore be

$$f_c = \frac{1}{2\pi(R \| R_L)C} \qquad \text{(8-6)}$$

In a similar fashion we can consider the effects of source resistance. In Fig. 8-5*c* it is probably clear that we can lump R_s and R together into a single resistance. It should also be clear that the low-frequency gain is unity.

For source and load resistance simultaneously applied, as in Fig. 8-5*d*, we merely add R_s and R to obtain the effective series resistance. Then we compute the value of this series resistance in parallel with the load resistance. We then have the effective resistance to use the cutoff-frequency formula. Some examples will illustrate.

EXAMPLE 8-2

In Fig. 8-5*a*, $R = 1$ kilohm, $C = 0.1\ \mu$f, and $R_L = 3$ kilohms. Find the value of the passband gain and the cutoff frequency.

SOLUTION

In the passband

$$A = \frac{R_L}{R + R_L} = \frac{3(10^3)}{10^3 + 3(10^3)} = 0.75$$

The cutoff frequency is

$$f_c = \frac{0.159}{[10^3 \| 3(10^3)](0.1)(10^{-6})} = 2.12 \text{ kHz}$$

Thus, the addition of load resistance has reduced the passband gain to 0.75 and also has changed the cutoff frequency to 2.12 kHz. At

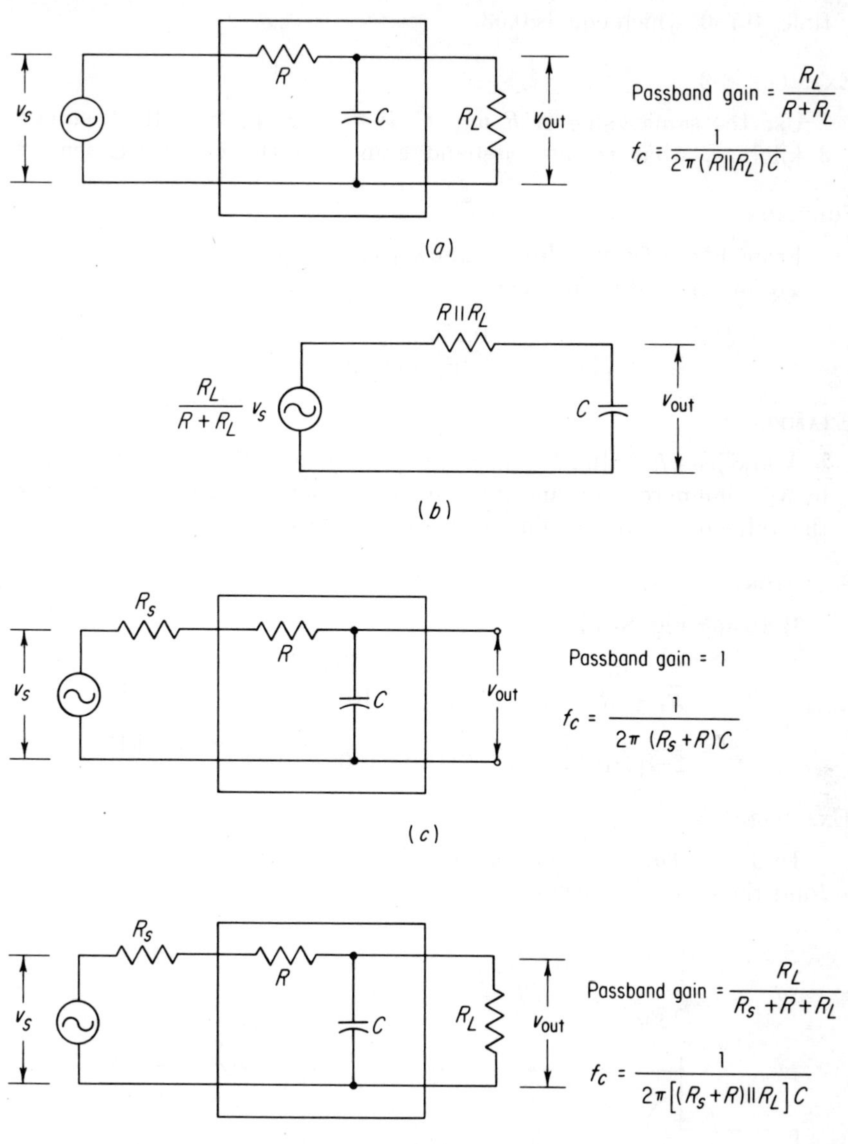

Fig. 8-5 Low-pass *RC* filter. (*a*) With load resistance. (*b*) Thévenin equivalent. (*c*) With source resistance. (*d*) With source and load resistance.

2.12 kHz the gain is equal to 0.707 of the passband value, or 0.707 times 0.750, which equals 0.53.

Example 8-3

Use the same value of R and C as in Example 8-2. If R_s equals 3 kilohms, what is the passband gain, and the cutoff frequency?

Solution

From Fig. 8-5*c*, we already know that the passband gain is unity. To find the cutoff frequency

$$f_c = \frac{0.159}{[3(10^3) + 10^3](0.1)(10^{-6})} = 398 \text{ Hz}$$

Example 8-4

A low-pass RC filter has $R = 1$ kilohm, $C = 1000$ pf. If it is loaded by a 7-kilohm resistor, and if the source resistance is 2 kilohms what is the value of passband gain and cutoff frequency?

Solution

By using Fig. 8-5*d*,

$$A = \frac{R_L}{R_s + R + R_L} = \frac{7(10^3)}{2(10^3) + 10^3 + 7(10^3)} = 0.7$$

$$f_c = \frac{1}{2\pi\{[2(10^3) + 10^3]\|7(10^3)\}(1000)(10^{-12})} = 75.7 \text{ kHz}$$

Example 8-5

In Fig. 8-6*a*, the tube has an a-c resistance of $r_p = 10$ kilohms. Find the cutoff frequency.

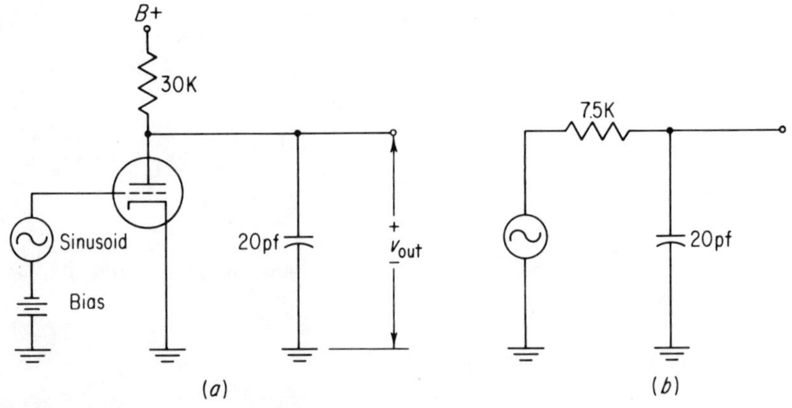

Fig. 8-6 Example 8-5.

Solution

The plate circuit of the tube is basically a low-pass RC filter. The Thévenin equivalent circuit looking back into the plate is an open-circuit voltage and a resistance. The resistance is the 30-kilohm load resistor in shunt with the 10 kilohms tube resistance, which is 7.5 kilohms. Figure 8-6b shows the Thévenin circuit with the 20-pf capacitor. Clearly, the plate circuit is equivalent to a low-pass RC filter.

The cutoff frequency is

$$f_c = \frac{0.159}{7.5(10^3)(20)(10^{-12})} = 1.06 \text{ MHz}$$

Example 8-6

Find the cutoff frequency and the output voltage in the passband of the circuit of Fig. 8-7.

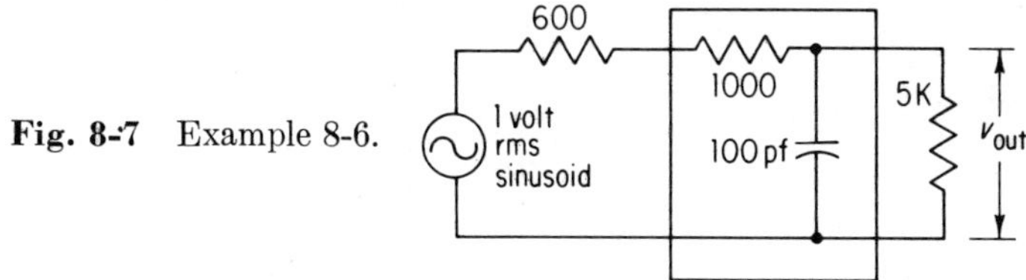

Fig. 8-7 Example 8-6.

Solution

In the passband the capacitor is considered open, so that

$$v_{out} = \frac{5000}{6600}\,1 = 0.757 \text{ volt rms}$$

The effective resistance to use in the cutoff formula is

$$(R_s + R)\|R_L = 1600\|5000 = 1210$$

and

$$f_c = \frac{0.159}{1.21(10^3)(100)(10^{-12})} = 1.31 \text{ MHz}$$

8-5 The Decibel Response of the Simple Low-pass RC Filter

Recall that the magnitude of the voltage gain for a simple low-pass RC filter is

$$A = \frac{1}{\sqrt{1 + (\omega RC)^2}}$$

This is the exact expression for gain. Note that if ωRC is much less than unity, the square of ωRC becomes negligible compared to unity, and the denominator becomes approximately the square root of 1. Further, if ωRC is much larger than unity, the denominator becomes approximately

ωRC. These observations prompt us to introduce the following rough approximation to the gain formula:

For $\omega RC \leq 1$ $$A \cong 1 \tag{8-7}$$

For $\omega RC > 1$ $$A \cong \frac{1}{\omega RC} \tag{8-8}$$

Admittedly, this is a very crude approximation to the gain, and the use of these approximations produces a large error in the vicinity of the cutoff frequency. However, for frequencies well above and below the cutoff, these formulas become quite accurate. For example, at $\omega RC = 0.1$, the approximate value of gain is unity, according to Eq. (8-7). The exact gain obtained from Eq. (8-4) is 0.995.

If we use these approximations in spite of their gross inaccuracy near cutoff, then the decibel gain is easily found.

Below cutoff $\omega RC < 1 \quad A \cong 1$

so that $A_{db} = 20 \log 1 = 0\ db$

Above cutoff $\omega RC > 1 \quad A \cong \dfrac{1}{\omega RC}$

so that $$A_{db} = 20 \log \frac{1}{\omega RC} = -20 \log \omega RC \tag{8-9}$$

It is instructive to make a short table of A_{db} and ωRC using these approximations (see Table 8-1). The cutoff frequency corresponds to $\omega RC = 1$. Note that up to the cutoff frequency the gain is 0 db (or unity). Above the cutoff frequency the gain begins dropping. Note that every time the frequency is doubled, the gain drops by 6 db. Further, every time the frequency increases by a factor of ten, the gain drops 20 db. (Factors of two correspond to 6 db, and factors of ten correspond to 20 db.)

An octave is defined as a 2:1 frequency ratio. Also, a decade is defined as a 10:1 frequency ratio. The behavior of the filter above cutoff is often described by saying that the gain of a low-pass *RC* filter rolls off at a rate of 6 db per octave. An equivalent statement is that the filter gain rolls off at a rate of 20 db per decade.

Both these expressions are commonly used in practice, and they should be clearly understood. For instance, if the gain is −6 db at 25 kHz, the gain will be −12 db at 50 kHz. If the frequency is again changed by an octave, that is, if the frequency changes to 100 kHz, the gain will be −18 db.

In a similar way, if the gain is −6 db at 25 kHz, the gain will be −26 db at 250 kHz. If we again change frequency by a decade, the gain will be −46 db at 2.5 MHz.

Table 8-1 can be graphed. If ordinary rectangular coordinate paper is used, nothing striking occurs, but if semilogarithmic paper is used, the

Table 8-1 *RC* Low-pass Response

ωRC or $\dfrac{f}{f_c}$	A_{db}
0.1	0
0.2	0
0.4	0
0.8	0
1	0
2	−6
4	−12
8	−18
10	−20
100	−40
1000	−60

graph will consist of two straight lines (see Fig. 8-8). (This occurs because of the logarithmic definition for decibels.)

The linear scale is along the vertical axis, and the log scale is along the horizontal. These straight-line graphs are convenient to read and very easy to construct. A horizontal line is drawn from the origin to the cutoff

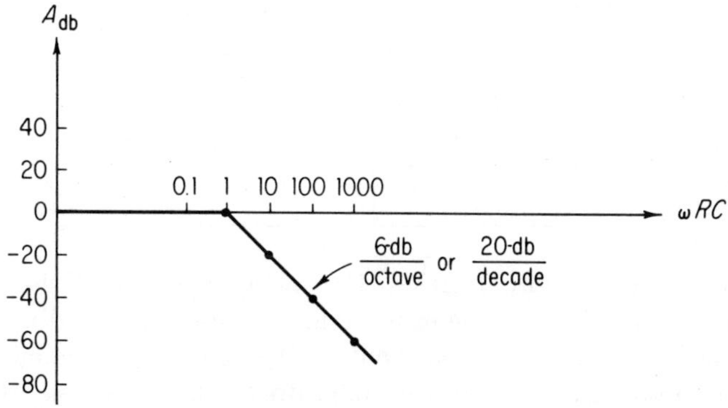

Fig. 8-8 Low-pass *RC* filter asymptotic response.

frequency. A second line is drawn from the cutoff frequency to any convenient point like (10, −20 db). The slope of the graph above cutoff is −6 db per octave, or −20 per decade.

Straight-line graphs of this type are very popular in spite of the fact that they are only an approximation of the exact response of a low-pass *RC* filter. The ease of construction far outweighs the loss of exactness. In any event, the largest error in the graph of Fig. 8-8 is 3 db at the cutoff frequency.

A study of the exact formula for gain compared to the approximate formulas allows us to generate a table of correction numbers, as shown in Table 8-2. The values in this table may be used to correct the value

Table 8-2 Asymptotic-response Correction Table

ωRC or f/f_c	Error, decibels
0.1	−0.04
0.2	−0.17
0.4	−0.64
0.5	−0.96
0.6	−1.34
0.8	−2.14
1.0	−3.01
1.25	−2.14
1.67	−1.34
2.0	−0.96
2.5	−0.64
5.0	−0.17
10.0	−0.04

of gain obtained by approximation. For instance, at cutoff the approximate gain is 0 db. To find the exact gain we subtract 3.01 db to obtain $A_{db} = -3.01$ db. One octave above cutoff, the approximate gain is −6 db. To find the exact gain we subtract 0.96 db to obtain $A_{db} = -6.96$ db.

The approximate graph of Fig. 8-8 is often called the *asymptotic re-*

sponse since the two straight lines are the asymptotes of the exact response. For practical purposes, we will sketch the asymptotic response instead of the exact response, always bearing in mind that the error at cutoff is actually 3 db and that this error rapidly diminishes as we move away from cutoff.

EXAMPLE 8-7

A simple low-pass RC filter has an R equal to 100 kilohms and a C equal to 500 pf. Sketch the asymptotic response.

SOLUTION

$$f_c = \frac{0.159}{100(10^3)(500)(10^{-12})} = 3.18 \text{ kHz}$$

We may show either ωRC or the cycle frequency f along the horizontal (see Fig. 8-9). We observe that the response drops 6 db per

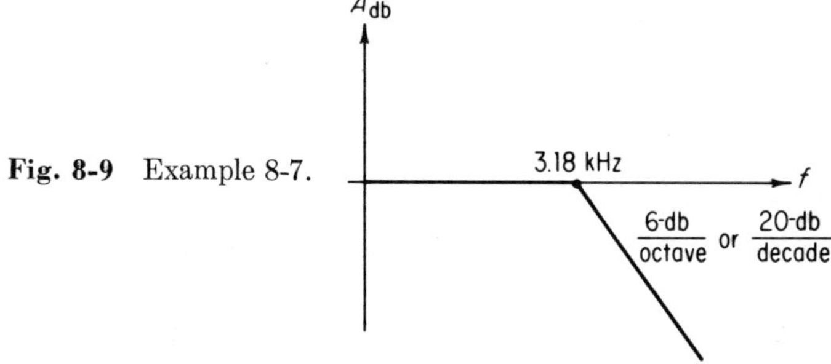

Fig. 8-9 Example 8-7.

octave, or 20 db per decade. Therefore, one octave above cutoff, $f = 6.36$ kHz, and $A_{db} = -6$ db. Also, one decade above cutoff, $f = 31.8$ kHz, and $A_{db} = -20$ db.

EXAMPLE 8-8

Find the exact response at 6.36 and 31.8 kHz for the filter of Example 8-7.

SOLUTION

The gains were -6 db at 6.36 kHz and -20 db at 31.8 kHz. From Table 8-2 we find that the correction numbers are -0.96 and -0.04 db. Therefore, the exact gains are -6.96 db at 6.36 kHz and -20.04 db at 31.8 kHz.

8-6 The Simple High-pass *RC* Filter

The simple high-pass RC filter is shown in Fig. 8-10. By analyzing this circuit using complex numbers, we find the magnitude of the voltage gain to be

$$A = \frac{1}{\sqrt{1 + 1/\omega RC)^2}} \tag{8-10}$$

Either from Eq. (8-10) or directly from Fig. 8-10 it should be clear that at high frequencies, the gain approaches unity, whereas at low frequencies the gain approaches zero. Hence, the filter is truly a high-pass one.

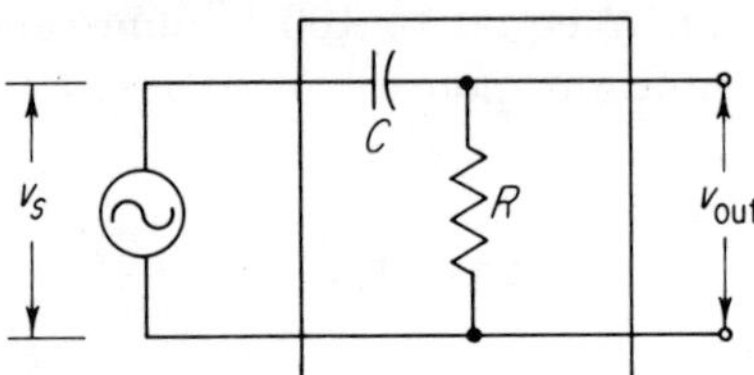

Fig. 8-10 High-pass *RC* filter.

The cutoff frequency is found by inspection. If $\omega RC = 1$, Eq. (8-10) tells us that the gain equals 0.707. Hence, as with the simple low-pass *RC* filter we find that the cutoff frequency is

$$f_c = \frac{1}{2\pi RC} \tag{8-11}$$

The effects of source and load resistance can be found in the manner used with the low-pass filter. The results of such an analysis are summarized by Fig. 8-11.

As far as the asymptotic response is concerned, we arrive at the following approximations:

Below cutoff $\quad A \cong \omega RC \quad$ and $\quad A_{db} \cong 20 \log \omega RC$

Above cutoff $\quad A \cong 1 \quad$ and $\quad A_{db} \cong 0$ db

The asymptotic graphs are constructed by drawing a horizontal line above cutoff and a line with a slope of 6 db per octave below cutoff.

To correct the asymptotic response in order to obtain the exact response, use Table 8-2.

Example 8-9

A simple high-pass *RC* filter has $R = 100$ kilohms and $C = 500$ pf. Sketch the asymptotic response.

Solution

$$f_c = \frac{1}{2\pi RC} = \frac{0.159}{100(10^3)(500)(10^{-12})} = 3.18 \text{ kHz}$$

The asymptotic sketch is shown in Fig. 8-12. Note that at 3.18 kHz, the gain is 0 db. One octave lower, at 1.59 kHz, the gain is −6 db. One decade below cutoff, at 318 Hz, the gain is −20 db.

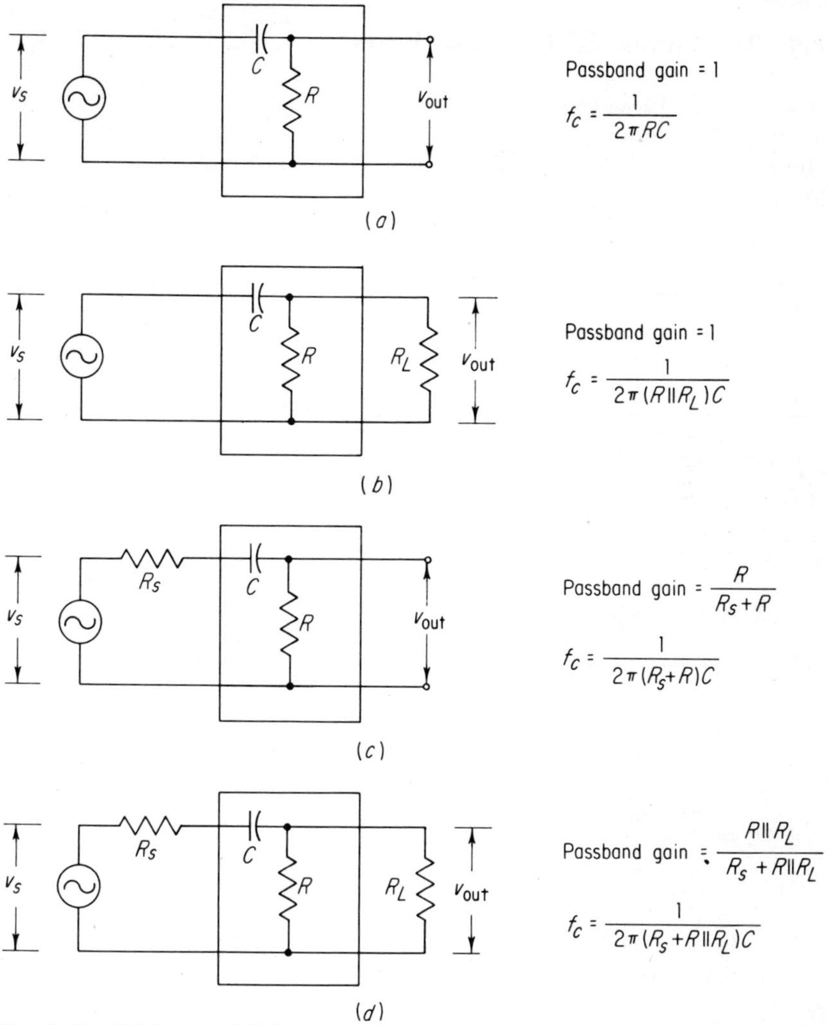

v_S
C
R
v_{out}
Passband gain = 1
$f_c = \frac{1}{2\pi RC}$
(a)
R_L
Passband gain = 1
$f_c = \frac{1}{2\pi(R \| R_L)C}$
(b)
R_S
Passband gain = $\frac{R}{R_S+R}$
$f_c = \frac{1}{2\pi(R_S+R)C}$
(c)
Passband gain ≑ $\frac{R \| R_L}{R_S + R \| R_L}$
$f_c = \frac{1}{2\pi(R_S+R \| R_L)C}$
(d)

Fig. 8-11 High-pass *RC* filters. (*a*) Unloaded. (*b*) With load resistance. (*c*) With source resistance. (*d*) With source and load resistance.

Fig. 8-12 Example 8-9.

A_{db}
3.18 kHz
f
$\frac{\text{6-db}}{\text{octave}}$ or $\frac{\text{20-db}}{\text{decade}}$

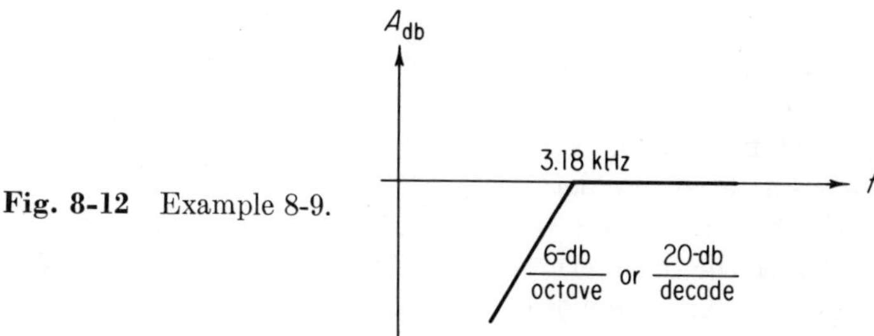

8-7 The Simple *RC* Bandpass Filter

A simple bandpass filter can be constructed by cascading a low-pass and a high-pass section as shown in Fig. 8-13*a*. If appropriate values are chosen, there will be a passband, with a lower cutoff frequency f_{c1} and an upper cutoff frequency f_{c2}. There are some precautions that must be

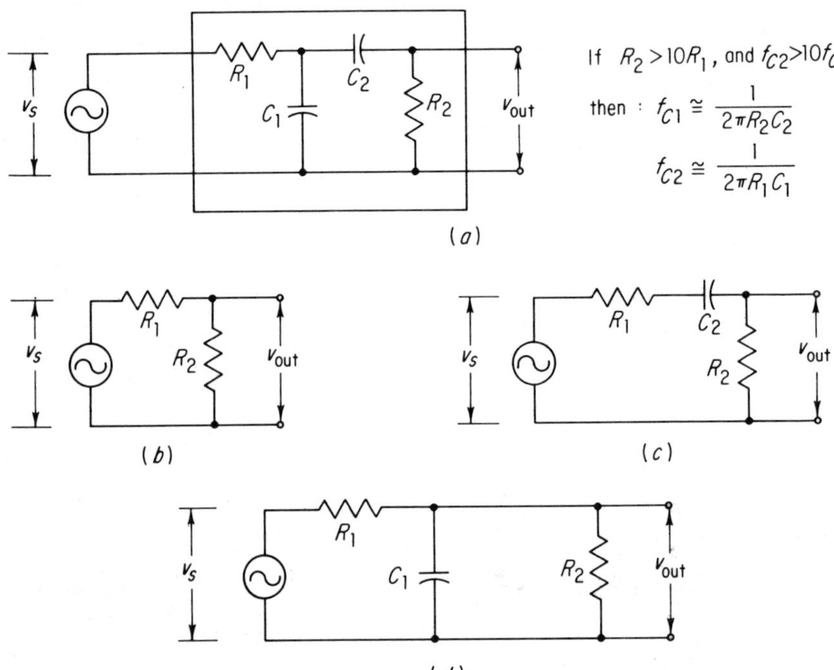

Fig. 8-13 *RC* bandpass filters. (*a*) Circuit. (*b*) Passband equivalent circuit. (*c*) Low-frequency equivalent circuit. (*d*) High-frequency equivalent circuit.

observed with this circuit. First, the circuit is not suitable for narrow-band applications because too much interaction takes place between the sections if the cutoff frequencies are close together. This results in a pass-band gain that is considerably less than unity. Hence, our first observation is that this circuit should be used only for wide-band applications, that is, in a situation where the upper cutoff frequency is much larger than the lower cutoff frequency. A reasonable rule would be to have the cutoff frequencies at least one decade apart.

Analysis of this circuit reveals that a great deal of interaction may occur between the two sections unless R_2 is much greater than R_1. Without stopping to analyze, we will merely indicate that R_2 should be at least 10 times greater than R_1.

Subject to the restrictions on cutoff frequencies and resistances, the formulas of Fig. 8-13 are reasonably good approximations.

It is helpful to visualize the circuit in the following way. In the passband the reactances are negligible, and the circuit behaves like the simple voltage divider shown in Fig. 8-13*b*. At frequencies below the passband the circuit behaves like a high-pass filter, as shown in Fig. 8-13*c*. (The reactance of C_1 is negligible.) For frequencies above the passband the circuit behaves like a low-pass filter, as shown in Fig. 8-13*d*. (The reactance of C_2 becomes negligible at high frequencies.) It must be kept in mind that these equivalent circuits are valid only if the restrictions on cutoff frequencies and resistances are observed.

A disadvantage of this simple bandpass filter is that the roll-off in the stop bands is only 6 db per octave. More sections may be cascaded to improve the roll-off, but in a situation where a sharper cutoff characteristic is required, the usual procedure is to use an inductive-capacitive filter.

Incidentally, the circuit of Fig. 8-13*a* is found in any typical amplifier stage. If the Thévenin equivalent of the vacuum tube (or transistor) is made, R_1 represents the r_p of the tube in shunt with the plate resistor. C_1 represents the tube capacitance and the stray wiring capacitance from plate to ground. C_2 is the coupling capacitor between stages, and R_2 is the input resistance of the next stage. Thus, we see that a typical amplifier stage will have an upper and lower cutoff frequency given by the formulas of Fig. 8-13.

EXAMPLE 8-10

In Fig. 8-13*a* let R_1 equal 10 kilohms, R_2 equal 1 megohm, C_1 equal 100 pf, and C_2 equal 0.01 μf. Find the lower and upper cutoff frequencies, and the passband gain.

SOLUTION

In the passband the equivalent circuit of Fig. 8-13*b* applies. Since it is a simple voltage divider,

$$A = \frac{10^6}{10(10^3) + 10^6} = 0.99 \cong 1 \qquad \text{in the passband}$$

The lower cutoff frequency can be found from the equivalent circuit of Fig. 8-13*c*. Since R_2 is much greater than R_1, we obtain

$$f_{c1} \cong \frac{0.159}{10^6(0.01)(10^{-6})} = 15.9 \text{ Hz}$$

The upper cutoff frequency can be found from the equivalent circuit of Fig. 8-13*d*. Since R_2 is much greater than R_1,

$$f_{c2} = \frac{0.159}{10(10^3)(100)(10^{-12})} = 159 \text{ kHz}$$

EXAMPLE 8-11

In Fig. 8-14*a* the r_p of the tube is 25 kilohms. Find the lower and upper cutoff frequencies. Assume that the cathode bypass capacitor is extremely large.

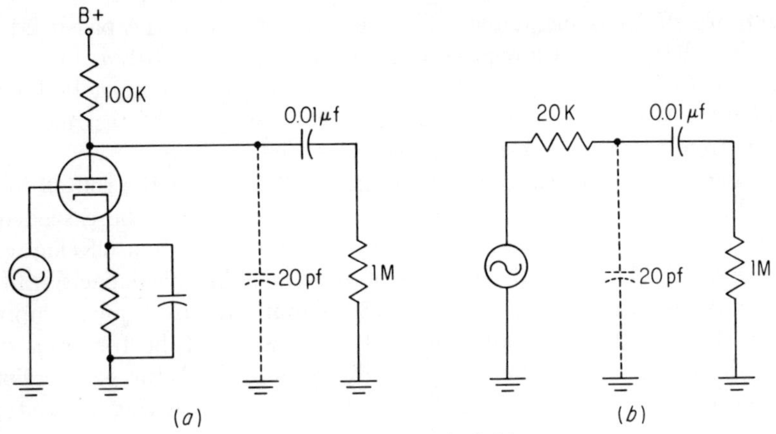

Fig. 8-14 Example 8-11.

SOLUTION

First, recognize that we can find the Thévenin equivalent looking back into the plate. We will see an open-circuit voltage and a resistance of 100 kilohms in parallel with 25 kilohms. The equivalent circuit is shown in Fig. 8-14*b*. This circuit is a cascade of low- and high-pass *RC* sections. Observe that R_2 is much larger than R_1. Therefore

$$f_{c1} \cong \frac{0.159}{10^6(0.01)(10^{-6})} = 15.9 \text{ Hz}$$

and

$$f_{c2} \cong \frac{0.159}{20(10^3)(20)(10^{-12})} \cong 398 \text{ kHz}$$

8-8 *RC* Bandstop Filters

Two popular methods of building simple *RC* bandstop filters are the use of a Wien bridge and what is known as a *twin T circuit.* A special form of the Wien bridge is shown in Fig. 8-15*a*. This bridge is actually a filter. At very low and very high frequencies the bridge is unbalanced. For instance, for very high frequency the capacitors resemble shorts, as shown in Fig. 8-15*b*. In this case, v_{out} is equal to the voltage across $R_1/2$, which is one-third of v_{in}. On the other hand, at very low frequency the capacitors resemble open circuits, as shown in Fig. 8-15*c*. In this case,

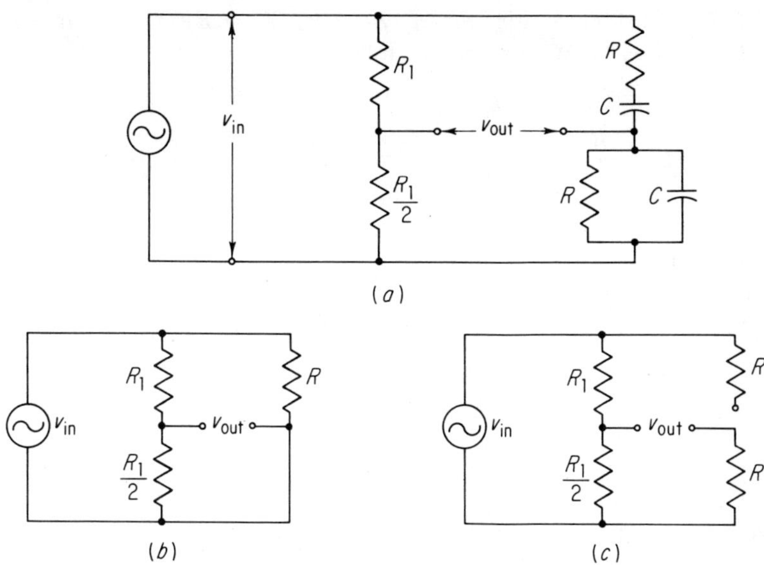

Fig. 8-15 Wien-bridge filter. (*a*) Circuit. (*b*) High-frequency equivalent circuit. (*c*) Low-frequency equivalent circuit.

v_{out} is still the voltage across the $R_1/2$ resistor. (There is no current through either R resistor.) Somewhere between very low and very high frequencies we will find a frequency where the bridge balances. In other words, v_{out} will equal zero for some specific frequency.

A sketch of v_{out} vs. frequency is shown in Fig. 8-16. Note carefully how the output voltage nulls out at f_o. This type of filter is often called

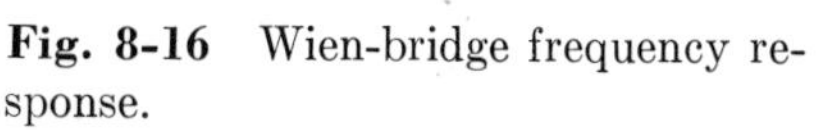

Fig. 8-16 Wien-bridge frequency response.

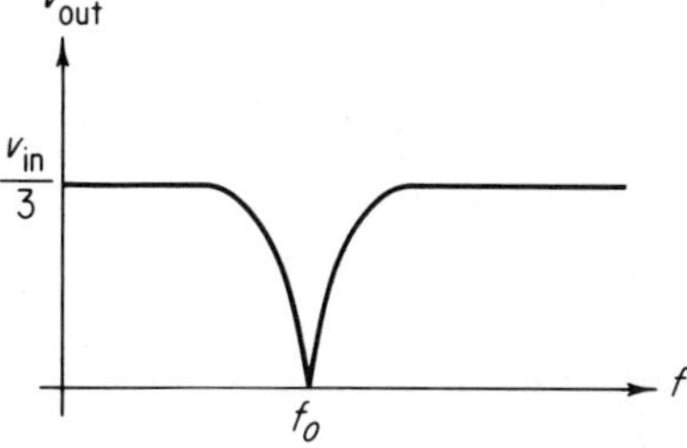

a *notch filter* because it completely rejects one particular frequency. We can find the value of f_o by applying the a-c bridge-balance condition. Recall that at balance

$$\frac{\mathbf{Z}_1}{\mathbf{Z}_2} = \frac{\mathbf{Z}_3}{\mathbf{Z}_4}$$

In the Wien bridge of Fig. 8-15*a*, $\mathbf{Z}_1 = R_1$, $\mathbf{Z}_2 = R_1/2$, $\mathbf{Z}_3 = R - jX_c$, and $\mathbf{Z}_4 = R \| -jX_c$. We proceed as follows:

$$\frac{R_1}{R_1/2} = \frac{R - jX_c}{R \| -jX_c}$$

$$2 = \frac{(R - jX_c)^2}{-jRX_c} = \frac{R^2 - X_c^2 - j2RX_c}{-jRX_c}$$

or

$$-j2RX_c = R^2 - X_c^2 - j2RX_c$$

From this last equation we see that the imaginary parts are equal for any frequency. However, the real parts are equal only if

$$0 = R^2 - X_c^2$$

or

$$R^2 = X_c^2$$

or

$$R = X_c = \frac{1}{2\pi f_o C}$$

Solving for the notch frequency f_o, we obtain

$$f_o = \frac{1}{2\pi RC} \tag{8-12}$$

This should be easy to remember since it is identical to the formula for for the cutoff frequency of the simple unloaded *RC* filters studied in preceding sections.

Equation (8-12) is equivalent to saying that the bridge is balanced at that frequency where the capacitive reactance equals the resistance *R*.

It can be shown in a straightforward manner that the magnitude of the voltage gain at any frequency is

$$A = \frac{1}{3} \frac{\omega RC - 1/\omega RC}{\sqrt{9 + (\omega RC - 1/\omega RC)^2}} \tag{8-13}$$

This is the exact expression for the magnitude of the voltage gain. Note that for very low or very high frequencies, ωRC approaches either zero or infinity. A study of Eq. (8-13) reveals that the gain then approaches one-third, or -9.5 db. At the notch frequency, ωRC equals one, and the numerator equals zero. Hence, the gain is zero at the notch frequency.

The Wien bridge is quite useful as a filter whenever it is desirable to notch out some particular frequency. When used in commercial instruments the notch is made sharper by using negative feedback. In other words, if we examine Eq. (8-13) we find that the gain at $2f_o$ is down about 7 db from the passband gain. This implies that the notch is broad. By using the Wien bridge in a negative-feedback amplifier, it is possible to sharpen the notch so that the gain at $2f_o$ is down only about 1.5 db from the passband gain. Also note that such a filter is easily tunable

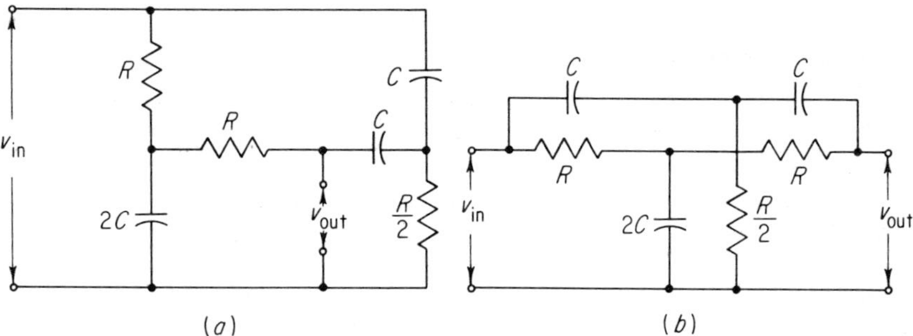

Fig. 8-17 Parallel T, or Twin T, notch filter.

by ganging either the R resistors or the C capacitors. We will examine the use of the Wien bridge in commercial instruments in later chapters.

An alternative to the Wien bridge is the circuit shown in Fig. 8-17*a*. The circuit can be redrawn as shown in Fig. 8-17*b*. Note that we have two T circuits in parallel. Because of this, the circuit is known as a twin T or a parallel T. Analysis shows that the circuit behaves very much the same as the Wien bridge. At very low and very high frequencies the gain approaches unity. Somewhere between these extremes in frequency there will be one frequency where the gain becomes zero. For the special form of the twin T shown in Fig. 8-17, the notch frequency is

$$f_o = \frac{1}{2\pi RC}$$

The twin T has a distinct advantage over the Wien bridge in that it has a common input and output terminal, which means that it is easier to connect into a practical system. However, note that to tune the twin T, three resistors or three capacitors must be ganged together, whereas only two elements need be ganged to make the Wien bridge tunable. Thus, in a system where a tunable notch filter is needed, the Wien bridge is still preferable in spite of the lack of a common input-output terminal. For those systems where a fixed notch filter is needed, the twin T is preferable because it has such a terminal.

Example 8-12

The Wien bridge of Fig. 8-15*a* has $R = 1$ megohm and $C = 500$ pf. Find the notch frequency.

Solution

$$f_o = \frac{0.159}{10^6(500)(10^{-12})} = 318 \text{ Hz}$$

Note that the notch frequency of a twin T with the same value of R and C is also 318 Hz.

8-9 *LC* Filters

The *RC* filters discussed so far are limited to those situations in which a gentle roll-off is acceptable. As we already know, the roll-off for a single low-pass or high-pass *RC* section is 6 db per octave. Sections may be added to steepen the roll-off, but this leads to more attenuation in the passband as well.

In order to increase the rate of roll-off and still keep the passband attenuation low, inductance-capacitance filters may be used. With properly designed *LC* filters a close approach to the ideal filter characteristics of Fig. 8-2 is possible.

Two basic approaches are currently used in the design of *LC* filters. The first method, commonly referred to as the *image-parameter design*, leads to simple, but approximate, design formulas. The second method, referred to as *modern network synthesis,* is a sophisticated mathematical approach which leads to complicated, but exact, design formulas. In the remaining sections of this chapter we will examine some of the simple *LC* filters using the image-parameter approach.

8-10 The Basic Low-pass *LC* Section

Figure 8-18 illustrates the basic configurations we will use for the low-pass filter. Note that the T section may be thought of as two back-to-back L sections, so that the shunt capacitor has a value of $2C$. In a similar way, the π section may be thought of as two L sections, connected in such a way that we obtain $2L$ for the inductance.

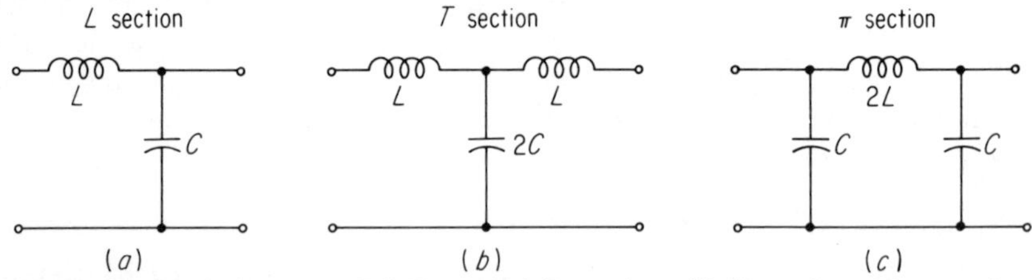

Fig. 8-18 Basic low-pass *LC* filters. (*a*) L section. (*b*) T section. (*c*) π section.

Observe that these basic sections are inherently low-pass. At very low frequencies the inductors resemble shorts and the capacitors seem open. Hence, low-frequency signals pass through without significant attenuation. On the other hand, at very high frequencies the inductors seem open and the capacitors appear shorted, so that very little signal appears at the output.

We will not actually derive the design equations for LC filters. Instead, we will merely summarize the results of the image-parameter theory. First, there is a resistance associated with the basic sections, whose value is

$$R_o = \sqrt{\frac{L}{C}} \tag{8-14}$$

where L and C are the values of the basic L section.

R_o, called the *characteristic resistance*, represents the value of source and load resistance that must be used for the filter to work properly. In other words, for the kind of LC filters we are studying, we must use the same value of source and load resistance, and this must equal R_o. Therefore, a filter whose R_o is 500 ohms must be used with a 500-ohm source and load if it is to work properly.

Second, there is a cutoff frequency associated with the basic sections, given by

$$f_c = \frac{1}{2\pi\sqrt{LC}} \tag{8-15}$$

where L and C are the values of the basic L section.

If a filter section like that in Fig. 8-18 is terminated in its characteristic resistance, there will be a passband and a stopband, and the cutoff frequency will be the f_c given by Eq. (8-15).

Example 8-13

Find the cutoff frequency and the characteristic resistance for the L section of Fig. 8-18*a* if $L = 1$ mh and $C = 1\ \mu$f.

Solution

$$R_o = \sqrt{\frac{10^{-3}}{10^{-6}}} = 31.6 \text{ ohms}$$

$$f_c = \frac{0.159}{\sqrt{10^{-3}(10^{-6})}} = 5.03 \text{ kHz}$$

Example 8-14

Find the R_o and the f_c for the basic T section of Fig. 8-18*b* if the inductors equal 1 mh and the shunt capacitor equals 1 μf.

Solution

Always remember that the L and C in Eqs. (8-14) and (8-15) refer to the values of the basic L section. The T section is composed of two back-to-back L sections. Therefore, the shunt capacitance of the T section is $2C$. Hence,

$$2C = 1\ \mu\text{f} \qquad \text{or} \qquad C = 0.5\ \mu\text{f}$$

We now proceed to calculate R_o and f_c.

$$R_o = \sqrt{\frac{10^{-3}}{0.5(10^{-6})}} = 44.7 \text{ ohms}$$

$$f_c = \frac{0.159}{\sqrt{10^{-3}(0.5)(10^{-6})}} = 7.1 \text{ kHz}$$

EXAMPLE 8-15

Find the R_o and f_c for the basic π section of Fig. 8-18c. The values of inductance and capacitance are 1 mh and 1 μf.

SOLUTION

Once more it is important to remember that the correct values of L and C to use in Eqs. (8-14) and (8-15) are the values of the basic L section. Since the π section has an inductance equal to $2L$,

$$2L = 1 \text{ mh} \qquad \text{or} \qquad L = 0.5 \text{ mh}$$

Hence, we may now calculate

$$R_o = \sqrt{\frac{0.5(10^{-3})}{10^{-6}}} = 22.4 \text{ ohms}$$

$$f_c = \frac{0.159}{\sqrt{0.5(10^{-9})}} = 7.1 \text{ kHz}$$

8-11 Cascading Basic T or π Sections

Another important result of the image-parameter theory is that any number of basic T sections (or π sections) can be cascaded, as shown in Fig. 8-19a and b. Note that it is permissible to lump elements together without changing the filter characteristics.

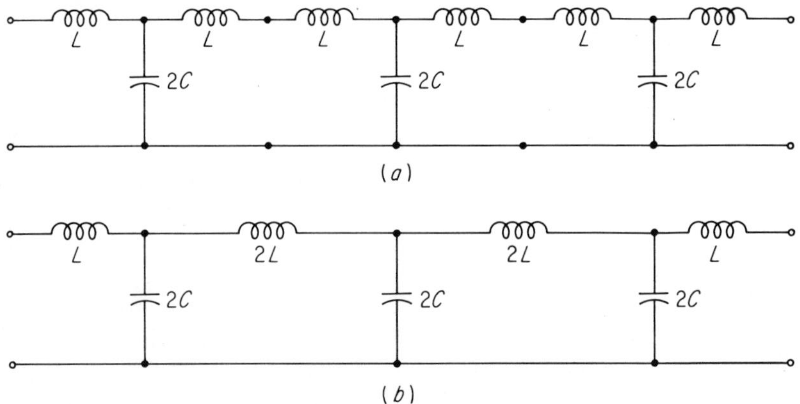

Fig. 8-19 Cascading T sections.

According to the image-parameter theory, the cutoff frequency and the characteristic resistance of the complete filter of Fig. 8-19*b* are the same as those of a single basic section.

For instance, if a basic T section has $R_o = 50$ ohms and $f_c = 20$ kHz, we can cascade as many of these basic T sections as we like. The resulting filter will still have an $R_o = 50$ ohms and a cutoff frequency of 20 kHz. If this filter is terminated by a 50-ohm source and load, it will be a low-pass filter with a cutoff frequency of 20 kHz.

8-12 Attenuation in the Stopband

Another important result of the image-parameter theory is that the attenuation in decibels in the stopband is given by

$$a_{db} \cong 8.7n\alpha \tag{8-16}$$

where n is the number of basic T or π sections and α is $2 \cosh^{-1} f/f_c$.

The α quantity involves hyperbolic functions, which may be unfamiliar to the reader and which we will bypass by using Table 8-3 directly.

Table 8-3

f/f_c	α
1.2	1.24
1.5	1.92
2.0	2.64
3.0	3.52
4.0	4.12
8.0	5.54

Our approach to finding the attenuation of a filter in its stopband is first to count the number of T or π sections. This gives us the value of n. Next, we compute the ratio of the signal frequency f to the cutoff frequency f_c. We can then find α from Table 8-3. Finally, we compute a_{db} using Eq. (8-16). The value obtained for the attenuation is an approximate answer with largest error in the vicinity of the cutoff frequency.

EXAMPLE 8-16

Find the value of R_o, f_c, and the attenuation at 45 kHz for the filter of Fig. 8-20.

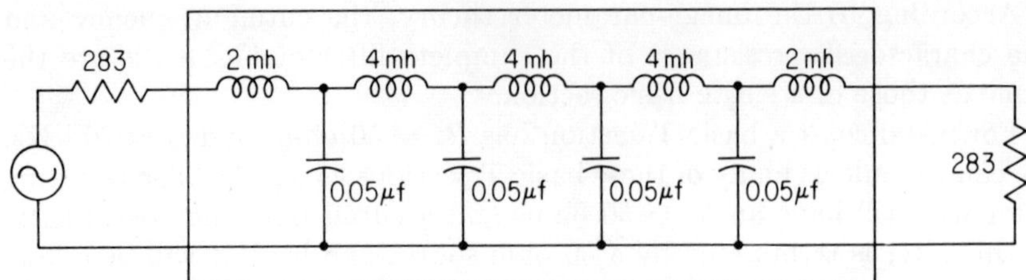

Fig. 8-20 Example 8-16.

Solution

The filter is a cascade of four T sections. The basic L section has $L = 2$ mh and $C = 0.025$ μf. Hence,

$$R_o = \sqrt{\frac{2(10^{-3})}{0.025(10^{-6})}} = 283 \text{ ohms}$$

$$f_c = \frac{0.159}{\sqrt{2(10^{-3})(0.025)(10^{-6})}} = 22.5 \text{ kHz}$$

At $f = 45$ kHz, $f/f_c = 45/22.5 = 2$. From Table 8-3 we find that $\alpha = 2.64$. Since there are four T sections we compute

$$a_{db} \cong 8.7(4)(2.64) = 92 \text{ db}$$

Hence, if the filter is properly loaded, as shown in Fig. 8-20, it will have a passband up to the cutoff frequency of 22.5 kHz. One octave above cutoff at 45 kHz, the attenuation will be 92 db.

Example 8-17

For the low-pass filter of Fig. 8-21 determine the values of source and load resistance that should be used for normal filter operation. Also, find the attenuation at $1.5f_c$.

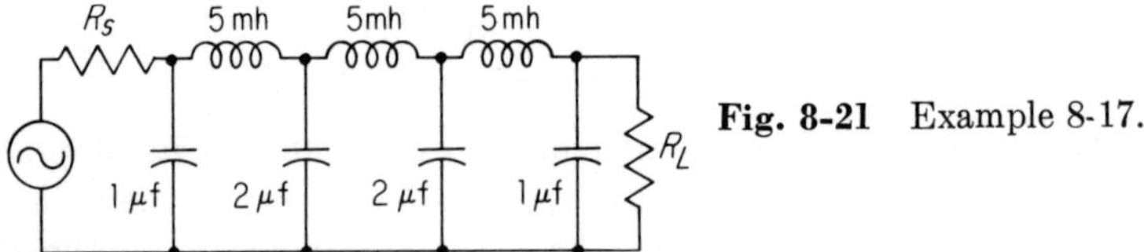

Fig. 8-21 Example 8-17.

Solution

To find the correct size of R_s and R_L we need only find the characteristic resistance of the filter.

$$R_o = \sqrt{\frac{2.5(10^{-3})}{10^{-6}}} = 50 \text{ ohms}$$

Thus, R_s and R_L must be 50 ohms for normal operation. If these values are not used, the filter will not cut off at the correct frequency.

To find the attenuation at 1.5 times cutoff, we need to find the α value corresponding to $f/f_c = 1.5$. From Table 8-3 we find $\alpha = 1.92$. Therefore,

$$a_{db} \cong 8.7(3)(1.92) = 50 \text{ db}$$

8-13 Design Formulas for the Low-pass *LC* Filter

The preceding sections dealt with the formulas for characteristic resistance, cutoff frequency, and stopband attenuation. These are useful formulas when we have the schematic of the filter and we wish to analyze its characteristics.

However, when we wish to design a filter, we will be given the value of R_o, f_c, and a_{db} in the stopband. For instance, we might wish to design a low-pass filter with a resistance of 50 ohms, a cutoff frequency of 1 MHz, and an attenuation of 60 db at 2 MHz. It will be useful, therefore, to have a set of design formulas. To obtain these we need to solve Eqs. (8-14) to (8-16) simultaneously for L, C, and n. If we do this, we obtain

$$L = \frac{R_o}{2\pi f_c} \tag{8-17}$$

$$C = \frac{1}{2\pi f_c R_o} \tag{8-18}$$

$$n = \frac{a_{db}}{8.7\alpha} \tag{8-19}$$

The use of these design formulas is straightforward and simple.

Example 8-18

Design a low-pass filter with a cutoff frequency of 20 kHz and an attenuation of at least 60 db at 40 kHz. The source and load resistance are 600 ohms.

Solution

$$L = \frac{600}{2\pi(20)(10^3)} = 4.78 \text{ mh}$$

$$C = \frac{1}{2\pi(20)(10^3)(600)} = 0.0132\ \mu\text{f}$$

Since the attenuation is to be at least 60 db at 40 kHz,

$$\frac{f}{f_c} = \frac{40(10^3)}{20(10^3)} = 2$$

From Table 8-3 we find that the corresponding value of α is 2.64.

Therefore,

$$n = \frac{60}{8.7(2.64)} = 2.6 \text{ sections}$$

or

$$n = 3 \text{ sections}$$

We round n off to the next higher whole number to ensure that there will be at least 60 db of attenuation at 40 kHz.

We may use either T or π sections. Arbitrarily, let us choose T sections. Bearing in mind that the L and C values are for the basic L section, we arrive at the final filter shown in Fig. 8-22. This filter

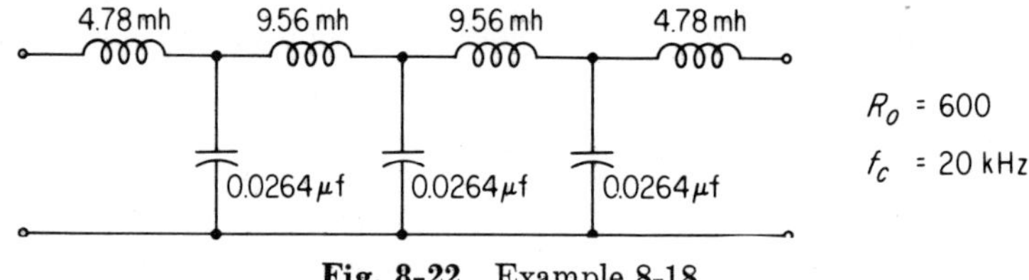

Fig. 8-22 Example 8-18.

must be used with a 600-ohm source and load. Under these conditions it will behave like a low-pass filter with a cutoff frequency of 20 kHz and an attenuation of more than 60 db at 40 kHz.

8-14 The High-pass *LC* Filter

The basic sections for the high-pass LC filter are shown in Fig. 8-23. Note carefully how the T section has a shunt inductance of $L/2$, and how the π section has a series capacitance of $C/2$.

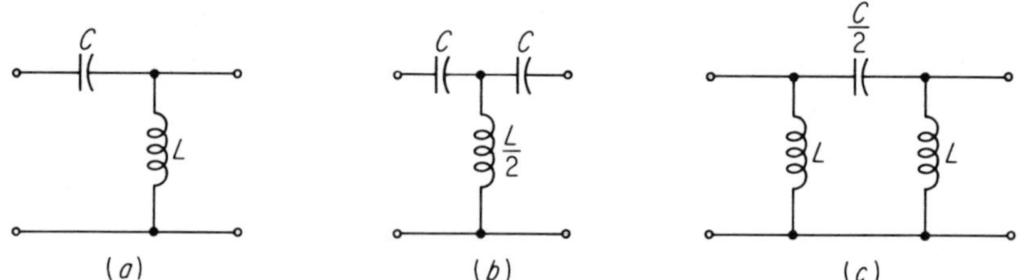

Fig. 8-23 Basic high-pass LC filter. (*a*) L section. (*b*) T section. (*c*) π section.

The analysis and design formulas Eqs. (8-14) to (8-19) for the low-pass filter apply to the high-pass filter also. Table 8-3 also may be used for the high-pass filter provided that instead of using f/f_c, we use f_c/f. For instance, if a high-pass filter has cutoff frequency of 1 kHz, its stopband lies below 1 kHz. To find the α value corresponding to 500 Hz, we must use f_c/f, which is $^{1000}\!/_{500}$, or 2. Then, from Table 8-3 we find that α equals 2.64.

EXAMPLE 8-19

Design a high-pass filter with a characteristic resistance of 50 ohms, a cutoff frequency of 20 MHz, and an attenuation of 80 db at 5 MHz.

SOLUTION

$$L = \frac{R_o}{2\pi f_c} = \frac{50}{2\pi(20)(10^6)} = 0.398\ \mu\text{h}$$

$$C = \frac{1}{2\pi f_c R_o} = \frac{1}{2\pi(20)(10^6)(50)} = 159\ \text{pf}$$

Since $f_c/f = 20(10^6)/5(10^6) = 4$, then $\alpha = 4.12$, and

$$n = \frac{80}{8.7(4.12)} = 2.23$$

or

$$n = 3$$

Bearing in mind that the values of L and C refer to the basic L section, we can arrive at the T filter shown in Fig. 8-24.

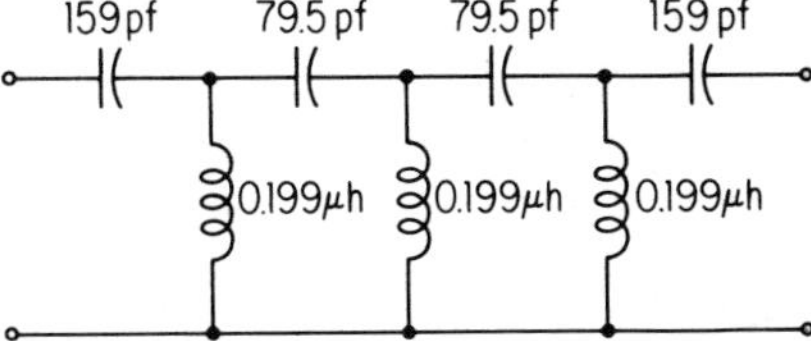

Fig. 8-24 Example 8-19.

8-15 *M*-Derived Sections

Ideally, we would like to have a passband response that is flat up to the cutoff frequency and a stopband response that rolls off rapidly beyond cutoff. The LC filters discussed thus far do roll off rapidly beyond cutoff, but in the passband the response is not flat up to the cutoff frequency. The reason for this is that there is an impedance mismatch between the filter and its terminations, which becomes pronounced as the cutoff frequency is approached. In other words, for frequencies well within the passband, the match between the filter and its terminations is excellent. However, as cutoff is approached, the match deteriorates, leading to a response that is not so flat throughout the passband as we would like it to be.

The standard method of improving the flatness of passband response is the use of *m-derived sections*. These special sections are used on the source and load ends of the filter in order to maintain the impedance match almost all the way to cutoff, with the result that the response of the filter in the passband remains flat up to the cutoff frequency.

Figure 8-25 illustrates the m-derived section used for a low-pass T filter. The L and the C in this figure are the values of the basic L section.

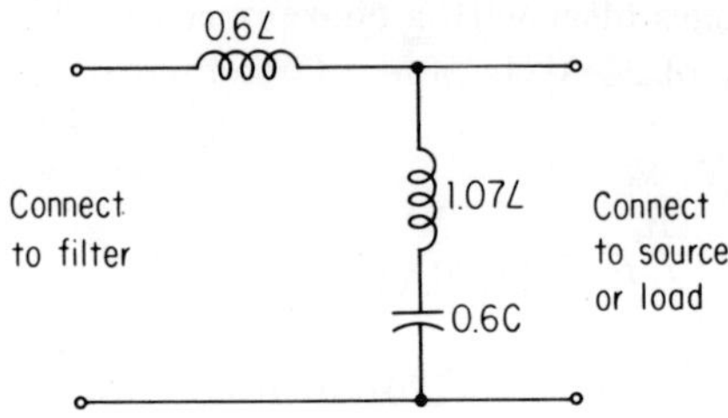

Fig. 8-25 m-Derived section for use with low-pass T filter.

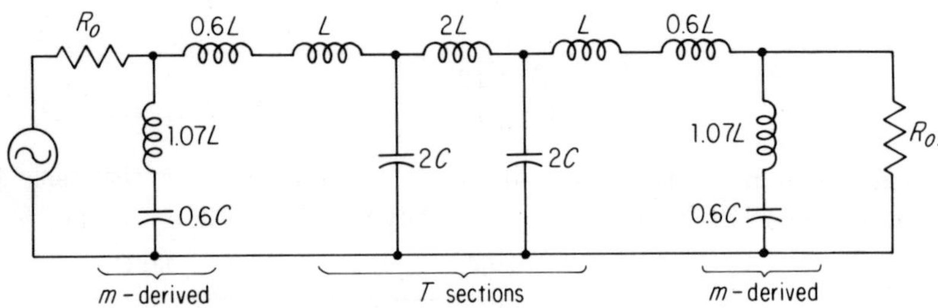

Fig. 8-26 Low-pass filter with m-derived end sections.

The m-derived section must be connected as indicated in order to work properly. For example, given a two-section low-pass T filter, the correct orientation of the m-derived sections is shown in Fig. 8-26. Note that an m-derived section is used on each end of the filter. Note especially the orientation of the m-derived sections. The m-derived sections to use for the various types of filters are summarized by Fig. 8-27.

The use of m-derived sections is not essential in filters. Satisfactory filters can be built without them. However, if the best performance possible is desired, the m-derived sections should be used on each end of the filter.

Example 8-20

Design m-derived sections for use with the filter of Fig. 8-22.

Solution

By inspection of Fig. 8-22, this is a low-pass T filter. Hence, we must use the m-derived section shown in Fig. 8-27a. We now compute

$$0.6L = 0.6(4.78)(10^{-3}) = 2.87 \text{ mh}$$
$$1.07L = 1.07(4.78)(10^{-3}) = 5.11 \text{ mh}$$
$$0.6C = 0.6(0.0132)(10^{-6}) = 0.00792\ \mu\text{f}$$

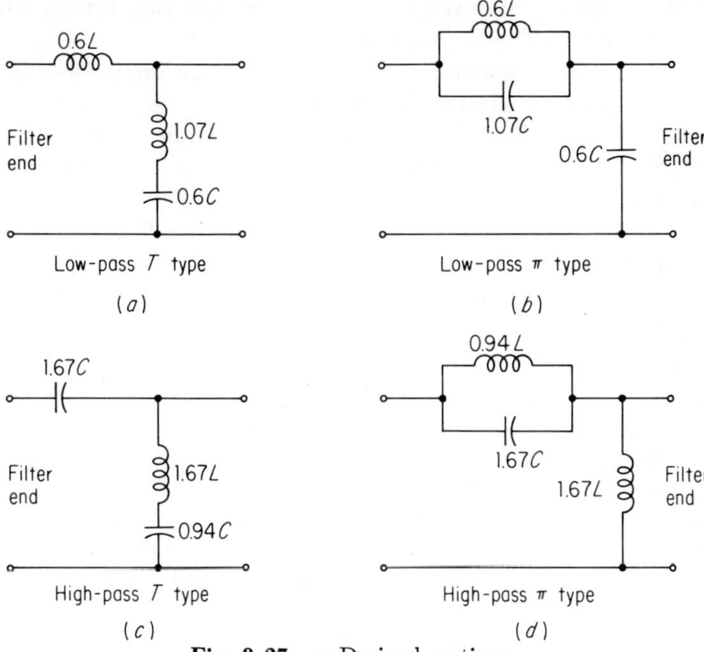

Fig. 8-27 *m*-Derived sections.

The final filter design with *m*-derived sections is shown in Fig. 8-28. Note that the 2.87 mh of the *m*-derived section has been lumped with the 4.78 mh of the T section to obtain 7.65 mh.

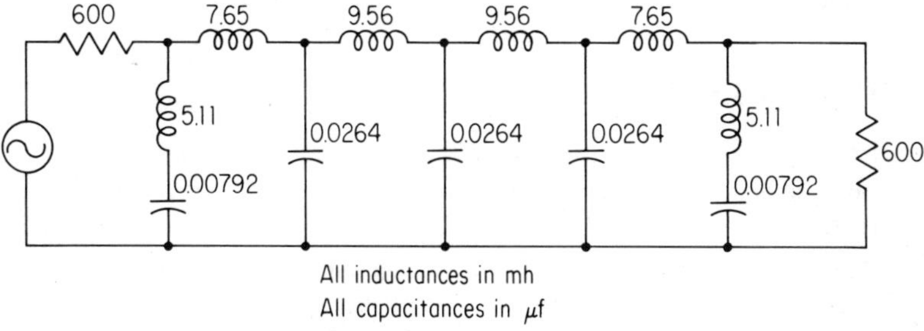

Fig. 8-28 Example 8-20.

SUMMARY

The *RC* filters are usable in some situations. The low-pass and high-pass types roll off at a rate of 6 db per octave for a single section. The simple *RC* bandpass filter is a cascade of a low-pass and a high-pass *RC* section. The roll-off rates are 6 db per octave.

The Wien bridge and the twin T are *RC* rejection filters. They can be used to notch out an unwanted frequency.

Asymptotic responses are generally used more often than exact responses because they are much easier to use.

For filters where a sharper roll-off characteristic is desired, the *LC* filters are generally used. These filters have important quantities like characteristic resistance and cutoff frequency. The *LC* filters studied in this chapter must be used with sources and loads whose resistances equal the characteristic resistance of the filter.

m-Derived sections are used at each end of an *LC* filter in order to flatten the passband response up to the cutoff frequency. They are not essential but are generally used whenever top filter performance is desired.

GLOSSARY

asymptotic response The approximate response of a filter. The error is largest in the vicinity of the cutoff frequency but rapidly diminishes as the frequency goes above and below the cutoff frequency.

characteristic resistance The value of source and load resistance that must be used with *LC* filters using the image-parameter approach.

cutoff frequency That frequency where the filter response drops down 3 db from the value of the passband response.

decade A frequency ratio of 10:1.

octave A frequency ratio of 2:1.

roll-off Refers to the rate at which a filter's attenuation is increasing in the stopband of a filter.

sinusoidal Any waveform which has the classical sine-wave shape.

REVIEW QUESTIONS

1. How is the cutoff frequency of a filter defined?
2. What is the circuit arrangement for a simple low-pass *RC* filter?
3. If the gain of an *RC* filter is expressed in polar form, what is the significance of the magnitude and angle of the gain?
4. What does the magnitude of the voltage gain mean?
5. What is the formula for the cutoff frequency of a simple low-pass *RC* filter?
6. Does load resistance reduce or increase the cutoff frequency of a low-pass *RC* filter?
7. How do we account for resistance in the source when dealing with a low-pass *RC* filter?
8. To what does the asymptotic response refer?
9. How much error is there at cutoff when using the asymptotic response?

10. What is an octave? A decade?
11. What kind of paper must be used when graphing the asymptotic response?
12. How does the formula for cutoff frequency of a simple high-pass *RC* compare to the formula for the low-pass *RC* cutoff?
13. What is the formula for the cutoff frequency of a simple low-pass or high-pass filter?
14. How can we correct the asymptotic response to obtain the exact response?
15. What is the roll-off rate of a simple low-pass filter?
16. If a low-pass and high-pass *RC* filter are cascaded as in Fig. 8-13*a*, what conditions concerning frequencies and resistances should we observe in order for the low-pass and high-pass filters to act independently of each other?
17. Why is the simple *RC* bandpass filter not suited to narrow-band applications?
18. For a simple *RC* bandpass filter what is the rate of roll-off above and below the passband?
19. How is the simple *RC* bandpass filter related to a typical amplifier stage?
20. What are two popular *RC* circuits used to reject a single frequency?
21. In the special form of the Wien bridge studied, what is the formula for the notch frequency? What is the ratio of the resistive arms of the bridge?
22. In the Wien bridge what is the value of ωRC at the notch frequency? At twice the notch frequency?
23. How can the notch filter response be made sharper?
24. Why is the twin T also called a parallel T?
25. What advantage does the twin T have over the Wien bridge? What advantage does the Wien bridge have over the twin T?
26. How is the characteristic resistance of an *LC* filter related to the source and load resistance?
27. What are the three basic *LC* sections?
28. What are the formulas for R_o and f_c for low-pass *LC* filters?
29. For a cascade of basic T sections what is the characteristic resistance and the cutoff frequency of the entire *LC* filter?
30. How are the design formulas for the high-pass *LC* filter related to formulas for the low-pass *LC* filter?
31. Why are *m*-derived sections often used in filters?

PROBLEMS

8-1 Prove that the voltage gain drops to 0.707 of its passband value if the power gain drops to 0.5. Use Fig. 8-1.

8-2 In Fig. 8-1, the input voltage equals 2 volts rms, and the output equals 0.5 volt rms. Calculate the voltage gain and the attenuation, both in ordinary numbers and in decibels.
8-3 Using Eq. (8-4), calculate the gain for $\omega = 1/RC$, $2/RC$, $10/RC$.
8-4 A simple RC low-pass filter like that shown in Fig. 8-4 has $R = 100$ kilohms and $C = 500$ pf. Find the cutoff frequency.
8-5 A loaded RC filter as in Fig. 8-5a has the following values: $R = 100$ kilohms, $C = 500$ pf, and $R_L = 50$ kilohms. Compute the passband voltage gain and the cutoff frequency.
8-6 In the circuit of Fig. 8-5c, the values are $R_s = 500$, $R = 1$ kilohm, and $C = 2000$ pf. Compute the passband voltage gain from the input of the filter to the output. Compute the cutoff frequency. Also, if the generator voltage is 1 volt rms, what is the output voltage in the passband?
8-7 A vacuum-tube amplifier like that in Fig. 8-6a has a load resistance of 100 kilohms instead of 30 kilohms, and an r_p of 10 kilohms. If the total capacitance from the plate to ground (tube capacity and stray wiring capacity) is 50 pf, what is the cutoff frequency of the amplifier? If the load resistance is changed from 100 to 10 kilohms what is the new cutoff frequency? Why is the frequency response better for a 10-kilohm load than for a 100-kilohm load?
8-8 A low-pass filter like that shown in Fig. 8-4 has $R = 30$ kilohms and $C = 0.001$ μf. Sketch the asymptotic response.
8-9 A low-pass filter like that shown in Fig. 8-5a has $R = 100$ kilohms, $C = 1000$ pf, and $R_L = 400$ kilohms. Sketch the asymptotic response. What is the approximate value of gain at 2 times cutoff frequency? At 10 times cutoff?
8-10 A simple low-pass RC filter has a gain of -10 db at 5 kHz. What is the gain at 10, 20, 40, 100, and 200 kHz and at 1 MHz?
8-11 A simple RC high-pass filter has $R = 10$ kilohms and $C = 50$ pf. Sketch the asymptotic response.
8-12 In Fig. 8-29, the r_p of the tube is 10 kilohms, R is 10 kilohms, R_L is 100 kilohms, and C is 0.1 μf. Sketch the asymptotic response of the amplifier. If the coupling capacitor is changed to 1 μf, what is the cutoff frequency of the amplifier?
8-13 In Fig. 8-29, $r_p = 20$ kilohms, $R = 10$ kilohms, $R_L = 90$ kilohms, and $C = 0.1$ μf. Suppose that the tube capacitance and the stray capacitance from the plate to ground is 50 pf. Sketch the asymptotic response. (*Hint:* There will be an upper and a lower cutoff frequency.)
8-14 In Fig. 8-13a, the following values apply: $R_1 = 500$, $R_2 = 100$ kilohms, $C_1 = 680$ pf, and $C_2 = 0.1$ μf. Find the approximate passband gain and the cutoff frequencies.
8-15 In Fig. 8-29, the following values apply: $R = 40$ kilohms, $R_L = 100$ kilohms, $r_p = 10$ kilohms, $C = 0.1$ μf, and the tube and stray capacitance from plate to ground is 50 pf. The voltage gain in the pass-

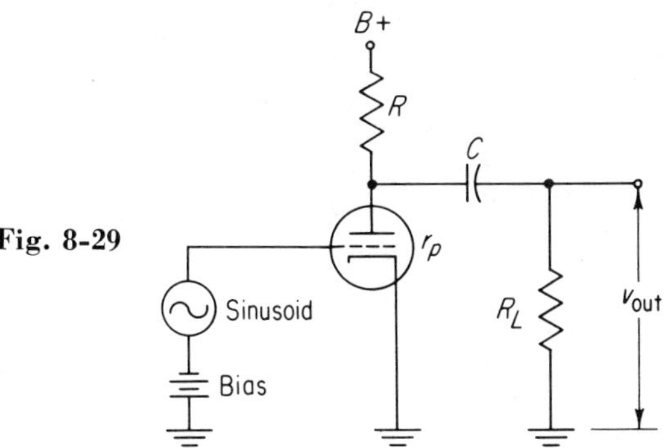

Fig. 8-29

band is 20 db. Sketch the asymptotic response. From the asymptotic response determine the frequencies at which the gain is 0 db.

8-16 In Fig. 8-15*a*, $R = 100$ kilohms, and $C = 300$ pf. Find the notch frequency.

8-17 Compute the voltage gain of the Wien bridge at 2 times the notch frequency. Express this gain in decibels.

8-18 Find the notch frequency of the twin T of Fig. 8-17*b* for $R = 50$ kilohms and $C = 2000$ pf.

8-19 The parallel T shown in Fig. 8-17*b* has R equal to 1 megohm. For what value of C is the notch frequency equal to 10 kHz?

8-20 A basic low-pass T section uses an inductance of 100 mh and a capacitance of 5000 pf. Find the size load and source resistance that should be used with this filter. What is the cutoff frequency of this filter?

8-21 A three-section filter like that in Fig. 8-19*b* has L's of 200 and 400 mh. The shunt capacitors equal 6800 pf. Find the value of characteristic resistance and cutoff frequency. What is the attenuation at 1.5 and $2f_c$?

8-22 What is the attenuation of a low-pass LC filter with three T sections at 4 times cutoff frequency? At 1.5 times cutoff frequency?

8-23 Design a low-pass LC filter to the following specifications: source and load resistances will be 100 ohms; cutoff frequency is to be 5 MHz, and the attenuation at 7.5 MHz is to be 70 db.

8-24 Design a high-pass filter with $R_o = 500$ ohms, $f_c = 20$ kHz, and an attenuation of 40 db at 10 kHz.

8-25 Design the m-derived sections for the filter of Fig. 8-24. Show the final design.

8-26 Design a low-pass LC filter using π sections with the following characteristics: $R_o = 50$ ohms, $f_c = 10$ MHz, and an attenuation of 80 db at 1.5 times cutoff frequency. Include m-derived sections in the design.

9 Transistors

This chapter is a brief study of transistors. Although normally an entire book should be devoted to them, we must limit our discussion to a simple introduction. We emphasize those aspects of transistors which will be most useful in our later work on amplifiers, oscillators, multivibrators, and logic circuits. In order to cover transistors simply and briefly we must rely heavily upon approximations. Further, we limit our discussion to the common-emitter connection and consider only low-frequency operation, which is adequate for our purposes.

9-1 Real Transistors

A transistor is a three-terminal device made of germanium or silicon. By a special process known as doping, the transistor takes on several interesting properties. The two common types of transistors are the *n-p-n* transistor and the *p-n-p* transistor. The schematic symbol for the *n-p-n* is shown in Fig. 9-1*a*. Note that the terminal with the arrow has been labeled the *emitter*. The uppermost terminal is the *collector*, and the other terminal is called the *base*. Similarly, the schematic symbol for the *p-n-p* transistor is shown in Fig. 9-1*b*.

Fig. 9-1 Transistor schematic symbols. (*a*) *n-p-n*. (*b*) *p-n-p*.

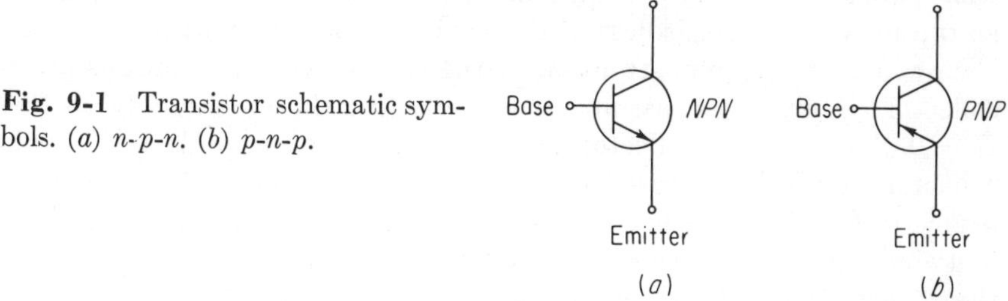

If voltages are applied to the transistor terminals, currents will flow. How are these voltages and currents related?

To answer this question, let us engage in a hypothetical experiment. We connect an *n-p-n* transistor as shown in Fig. 9-2. There are two adjustable power supplies, and there are three currents flowing. Suppose that we adjust the collector supply V_{cc} to some arbitrary value like 5 volts.

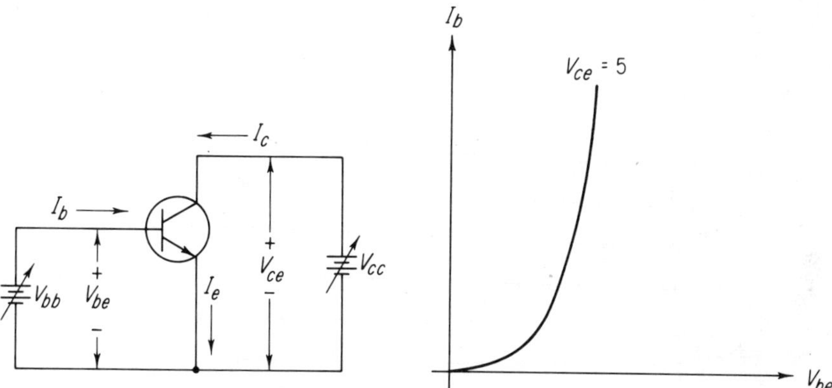

Fig. 9-2 Circuit for obtaining the *iv* characteristics.

Fig. 9-3 Base current versus base voltage.

Now, let us turn our attention to the current and voltage in the base circuit, namely, I_b and V_{be}. As we adjust the base power supply, we find that different values of base current flow. Typically, the graph of I_b vs. V_{be} would resemble that shown in Fig. 9-3. This shape is very much the same as an ordinary diode current-voltage graph. And indeed it should be, because the base-emitter part of a transistor is basically the same as any *p-n* diode.

We now return to the collector power supply and change the setting from 5 to 10 volts. Back in the base circuit we find that as we adjust the base supply to different values of voltage, the base current still varies *approximately* as indicated by the graph of Fig. 9-3. In other words, the base-emitter section of a transistor behaves approximately the same as an ordinary diode, regardless of the value of collector voltage.

Now, let us turn our attention to the current-voltage relations in the collector circuit. First, assume that we adjust the base supply so that $I_b = 0.01$ ma. In the collector circuit this is what we would find: as the collector supply is increased from zero volts to higher values, a current begins to flow in the collector. The current will increase very rapidly at first, but after the collector supply has reached a few tenths of a volt, the collector current will practically reach a fixed value (see Fig. 9-4*a*).

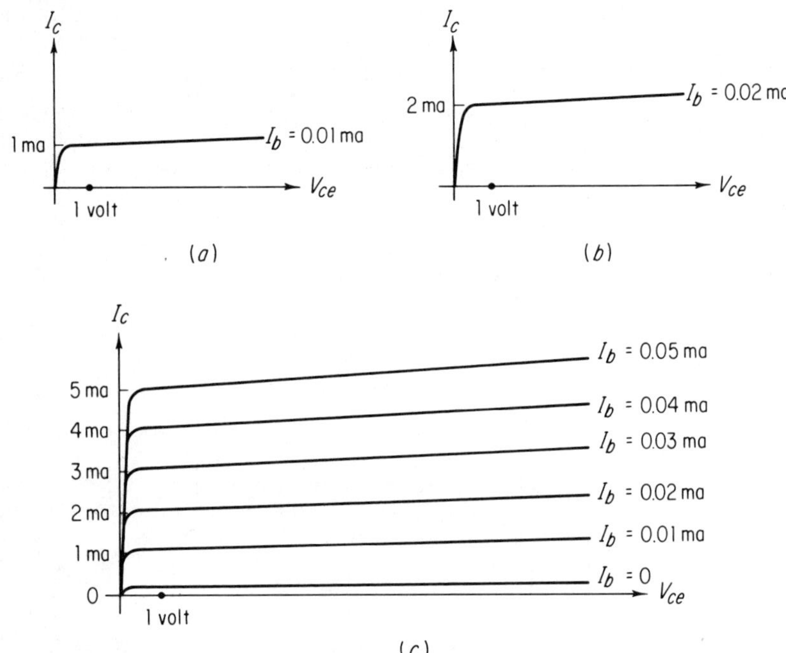

Fig. 9-4 Collector *iv* characteristics. (*a*) $I_b = 0.01$ ma. (*b*) $I_b = 0.02$ ma. (*c*) Family of curves.

Note carefully how the collector current rises rapidly but soon reaches an almost fixed value of approximately 1 ma. Once above the knee of the curve, any further change in collector voltage produces only a small increase in collector current. Note that in this typical experiment the collector current is around 1 ma compared to a base current of 0.01 ma. Hence, the collector current is about 100 times larger than the base current.

Suppose that we now readjust the base supply so that 0.02 ma of base current flows. What happens in the collector circuit?

As we increase the collector voltage from zero, we find that the collector current rises sharply until a knee is reached and then increases only slightly as the collector voltage is increased further (see Fig. 9-4*b*). In this case, note that the collector current reaches a value of about 2 ma above the knee of the curve. Once again, note that collector current is about 100 times larger than the base current.

If we repeat the experiment for several values of base current and draw all graphs on the same set of axes, we obtain the overall graph shown in Fig. 9-4*c*. Note how the collector current reaches an almost fixed value above the knee of each curve. Also, note how the ratio of collector current to base current remains at approximately 100.

The ratio of collector current to base current is a very important transistor quantity and is commonly referred to as the β (beta) of the transistor. There are actually two definitions for the β of a transistor. The first, the d-c β, is defined as the total collector current divided by the total base current.

$$\beta_{dc} \triangleq \frac{I_c}{I_b} \tag{9-1}$$

Note that the d-c β is a point function; that is, its value depends upon which point on the I_c vs. V_{ce} graph is chosen. For instance, if we pick any point above the knee on the graph for $I_b = 0.01$ ma, the d-c β equals approximately 100. If we pick a point below the knee, the d-c β will be less than 100. At the origin the d-c β is zero. Generally, we will be interested in the value of the d-c β above the knee of each curve.

If we examined a large number of transistors of different types, we would find a wide variation in the values of the d-c β. Typically, we would find variations from about 20 to about 200, and β's of 50 to 100 are very common.

The second, the a-c β, is defined as the change in collector current about a given operating point divided by the corresponding change in base current. The a-c β is also a point function, meaning that its value depends upon which point on the collector characteristics is chosen. To bring out the meaning of the a-c β more clearly, consider the circuit in Fig. 9-5. Suppose that we adjust the value of V_{cc} to 5 volts. Further, let us adjust V_{bb} so that 0.1 ma of base current flows. Suppose that we measure the

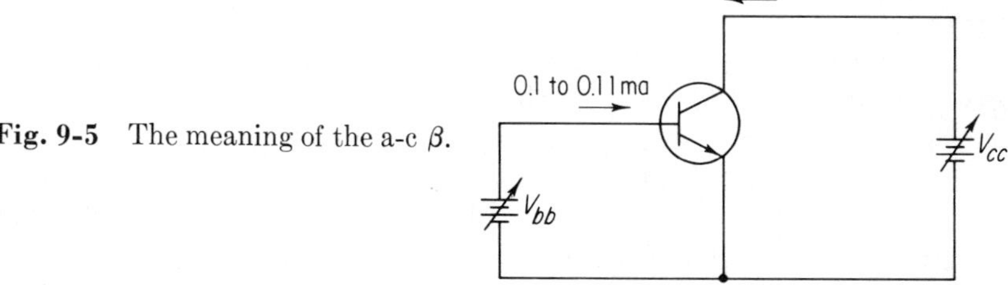

Fig. 9-5 The meaning of the a-c β.

collector current and find that it equals 10 ma. Then the operating point of the transistor is (10 ma, 5 volts).

Next, let us change the base supply as needed to produce a base current of 0.11 ma. Suppose that the collector current changes to 10.9 ma. The change in the collector current is 0.9 ma, and the change in the base current is 0.01 ma. The a-c β is the ratio of these changes.

$$\beta \triangleq \frac{\Delta I_c}{\Delta I_b} = \frac{0.9 \text{ ma}}{0.01 \text{ ma}} = 90$$

The a-c β and the d-c β are not the same. The d-c β is the ratio of total currents, whereas the a-c β is the ratio of changes in currents. We would find that if we changed the operating point, the a-c β would change slightly.

Another approach to transistors involves the use of what are called h parameters. On transistor data sheets the quantity h_{FE} is sometimes used instead of the d-c β. The two quantities are equal. Also, data sheets sometimes give the value of h_{fe} instead of the a-c β. Once again, these two quantities are equal.

In summarizing our hypothetical experiments we conclude:

1. The base-emitter section of the transistor behaves approximately like an ordinary diode.
2. Above the knee of any given collector curve, the collector current does not change appreciably for an increase in collector voltage.
3. The total collector current equals the d-c β times the total base current.
4. A small change in collector current equals the a-c β times the change in the base current.

9-2 The Ideal Transistor

Just as we idealized the ordinary diode in Chap. 3, so too is it possible to idealize the transistor. For example, we already know that the base-emitter part of the transistor behaves approximately like an ordinary diode. Therefore, as a first approximation we can use an ideal diode for the base emitter, and we can draw the ideal base-emitter characteristic as shown in Fig. 9-6*a*. As far as the collector is concerned, we note from Fig. 9-4 that the collector current is almost constant above the knee of each curve. Therefore, as an approximation we can show the ideal collector characteristics as in Fig. 9-6*b*. According to this figure, the collector current is constant for a fixed value of base current. In fact, the collector is a slave to the base current. For any value of base current, the collector current is simply the d-c β times the base current. For instance, if the d-c

β is 100, then for a base current of 10 μa the collector current is 1000 μa. If the base current is changed to 1 ma, the collector current changes to 100 ma.

We already have decided that as an approximation the base-emitter section behaves like an ideal diode. What shall we use to represent the collector-emitter section of the transistor?

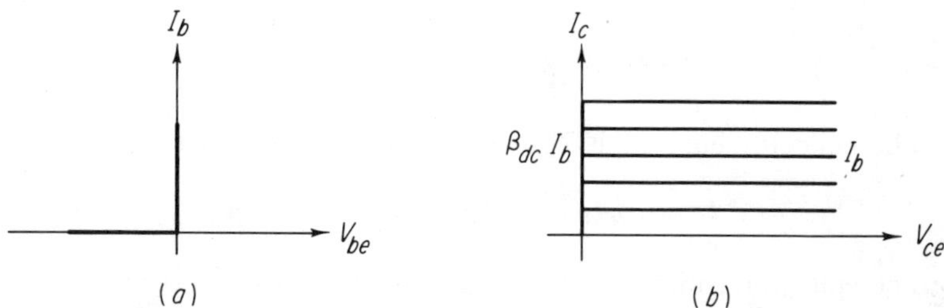

Fig. 9-6 The ideal transistor. (*a*) Base characteristics. (*b*) Collector characteristics.

Recall that a current source is a device whose current is independent of the voltage across it. The collector behaves basically as a current source because its value does not depend upon the voltage across the collector-emitter terminals but only upon the value of base current and the d-c β.

The equivalent circuit for an ideal transistor is shown in Fig. 9-7. There is an ideal diode in the base circuit, and an ideal current source in the collector. The value of the current source is equal to the d-c β times the base current. This model is valid as long as the collector current is greater than zero and the collector-emitter voltage is greater than zero.

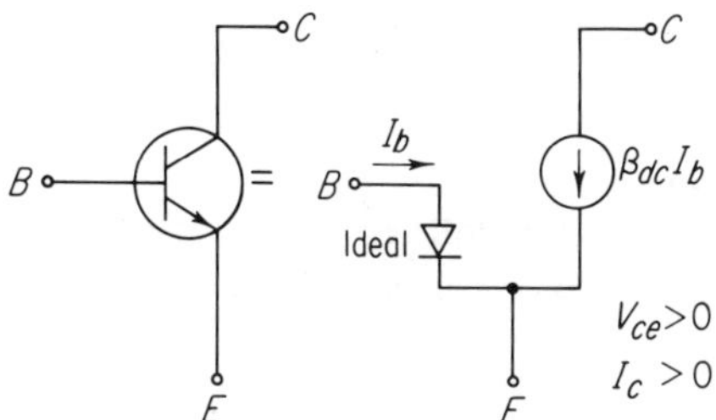

Fig. 9-7 Equivalent circuit of the ideal transistor.

The ideal *n-p-n* transistor equivalent circuit shown in Fig. 9-7 will allow us to analyze some transistor circuits rapidly. A word of caution is appropriate, however. This model will give gross errors in some circuits. Whether or not it is a good approximation to a real transistor will depend upon the external circuitry connected to the transistor.

Example 9-1

Find the collector-to-emitter voltage in the circuit of Fig. 9-8. Assume that the transistor is ideal and has a d-c β of 100.

Solution

The base-emitter diode is ideal. Therefore, the base current is

$$I_b = \frac{5}{100(10^3)} = 0.05 \text{ ma}$$

The collector current is controlled by the base current and equals

$$I_c = \beta_{dc} I_b = 100(0.05 \text{ ma}) = 5 \text{ ma}$$

The collector-emitter voltage V_{ce} is equal to the power supply voltage minus the voltage across the 1-kilohm load resistor. Since the collector current of 5 ma must flow through the 1-kilohm load resistor, there is a 5-volt drop across this resistor. Hence,

$$V_{ce} = 20 - 5 = 15 \text{ volts}$$

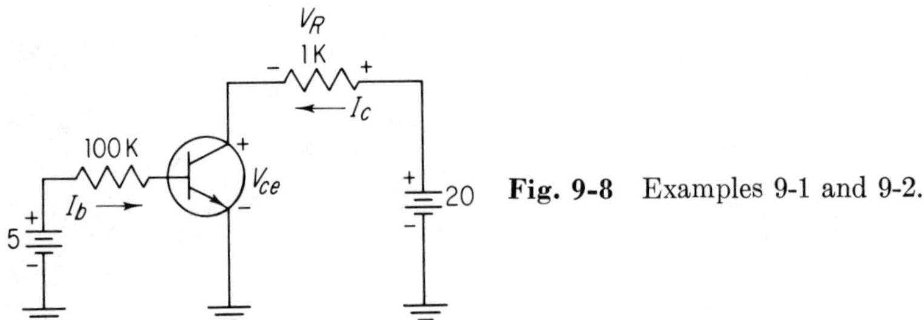

Fig. 9-8 Examples 9-1 and 9-2.

Example 9-2

In Fig. 9-8 the collector voltage V_{ce} equals 10 volts. Find the approximate value of the d-c β. Assume an ideal transistor.

Solution

In order for V_{ce} to be 10 volts, there must be a 10-volt drop across the 1-kilohm load resistor. This means that the collector current must be 10 ma. Further, since the transistor is assumed ideal, the base-emitter diode is ideal. Therefore, the base current is 0.05 ma. As a result, the d-c β is

$$\beta_{dc} = \frac{I_c}{I_b} = \frac{10 \text{ ma}}{0.05 \text{ ma}} = 200$$

9-3 The Second Approximation of the Transistor

The results obtained by the ideal transistor will be adequate for some circuits but grossly inaccurate for others. For example, if the power supply in the base circuit is comparable to the knee voltage of a typical diode (0.3 volts for germanium and 0.7 volt for silicon), we can expect to have errors when using an ideal diode to represent the base-emitter diode. To improve our approximation of a real transistor we may then think of the base-emitter diode as a real diode and use the higher approximations of a real diode that were developed in Chap. 3. In other words, for low base-supply voltages we can allow 0.3 volt for germanium transistors and about 0.7 volt for silicon. Once again, we can expect to obtain only approximate answers with these higher approximations. Better answers are to be had only by applying graphical techniques directly to graphs of I_b vs. V_{be} and I_c vs. V_{ce}.

There is also a source of error in the collector of the ideal transistor. Note that the curves of Fig. 9-4*c* actually slope upward, instead of being horizontal as shown in Fig. 9-6*b*. To account for this we could shunt a resistor across the current source, but for our purposes this will be unnecessary.

Our second approximation of a transistor will be to view the transistor as having a real diode in the base circuit and a current source in the collector whose value is equal to the d-c β times the base current.

Example 9-3

Find the value of I_b, I_c, and V_{ce} in the transistor circuit of Fig. 9-9*a*. The transistor is made of germanium and has a d-c β of 100.

Solution

By using the ideal-transistor approach we obtain

$$I_b = \frac{5}{100(10^3)} = 0.05 \text{ ma}$$
$$I_c = 100(0.05)(10^{-3}) = 5 \text{ ma}$$
$$V_{ce} = 20 - 5(10^{-3})(10^3) = 15 \text{ volts}$$

By using the second approximation

$$I_b = \frac{5 - 0.3}{100(10^3)} = \frac{4.7}{100(10^3)} = 0.047 \text{ ma}$$
$$I_c = 100(0.047)(10^{-3}) = 4.7 \text{ ma}$$
$$V_{ce} = 20 - 4.7(10^{-3})(10^3) = 15.3 \text{ volts}$$

Note that the results obtained are practically the same by either approximation.

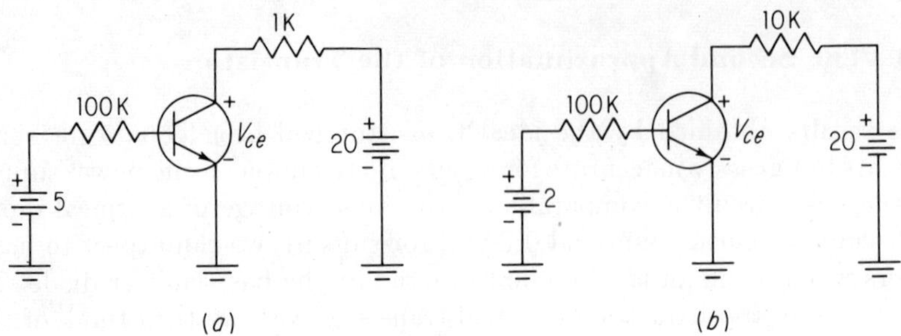

Fig. 9-9 Examples 9-3 and 9-4.

EXAMPLE 9-4

Find the value of I_b, I_c, and V_{ce} for the transistor circuit of Fig. 9-9*b*. Use a silicon transistor with a d-c β of 50.

SOLUTION

By the ideal-diode approach

$$I_b = \frac{2}{100(10^3)} = 0.02 \text{ ma}$$
$$I_c = 50(0.02)(10^{-3}) = 1 \text{ ma}$$
$$V_{ce} = 20 - 10^{-3}(10)(10^3) = 10 \text{ volts}$$

By the second approximation

$$I_b = \frac{2 - 0.7}{100(10^3)} = 0.013 \text{ ma}$$
$$I_c = 50(0.013)(10^{-3}) = 0.65 \text{ ma}$$
$$V_{ce} = 20 - 0.65(10^{-3})(10)(10^3) = 13.5 \text{ volts}$$

Actually, an exact analysis of the transistor will show that less than 0.7 volt is needed to produce 0.013 ma of current in the base. Hence, the exact answer will lie somewhere between the answer obtained by the ideal transistor and the second approximation of the transistor. In other words, by using the ideal and the second approximation, we can bracket the exact answer. In this case, the exact value of V_{ce} must lie somewhere between 10 and 13.5 volts. Thus, for preliminary analysis of a transistor circuit, or for troubleshooting purposes, the use of the ideal and second approximations are entirely adequate.

9-4 The Transistor Used as a Switch

The transistor can be used as an electronic switch. Consider the circuit of Fig. 9-10*a*. In many circuits we will study later (multivibrators, Schmitt triggers, etc.) we will need to short terminal A to terminal B.

The transistor may be used for this purpose by using the circuit of Fig. 9-10*b*. If the voltage driving the base circuit is properly controlled, the transistor can be made to resemble either a short or an open from the collector to the emitter. For instance, assuming an ideal transistor with a d-c beta of 100, it should be clear that if V_{bb} equals zero, the collector current equals zero. If there is no collector current, the transistor is the same as an open circuit. Hence, the *A* and *B* terminals are not connected.

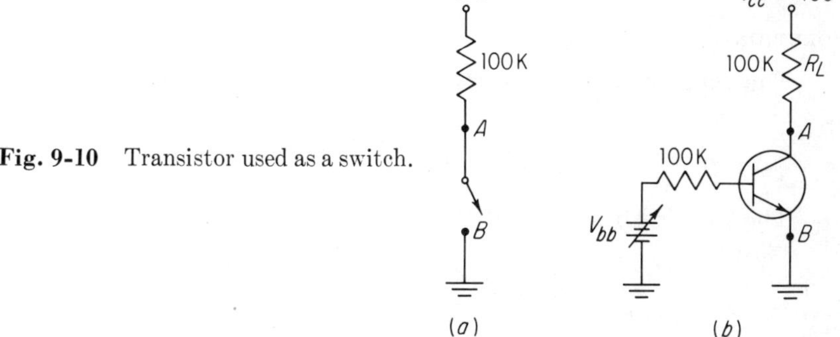

Fig. 9-10 Transistor used as a switch.

On the other hand, if V_{bb} equals 1 volt, ideally the base current equals approximately 0.01 ma. The collector current is 100 times greater than this, or 1 ma. With 1 ma current through the 100-kilohm load resistor, the voltage across the load resistor is 100 volts. Therefore, the value of V_{ce} is zero. But this is equivalent to saying that the transistor is a short from collector to emitter. If V_{bb} is greater than 1 volt, no further change takes place in the collector voltage since the transistor is saturated.

Figure 9-11 graphically illustrates what is taking place. For V_{bb} equals zero, the transistor is operating at the *open* point on the load line. For

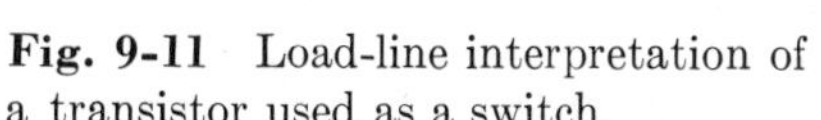

Fig. 9-11 Load-line interpretation of a transistor used as a switch.

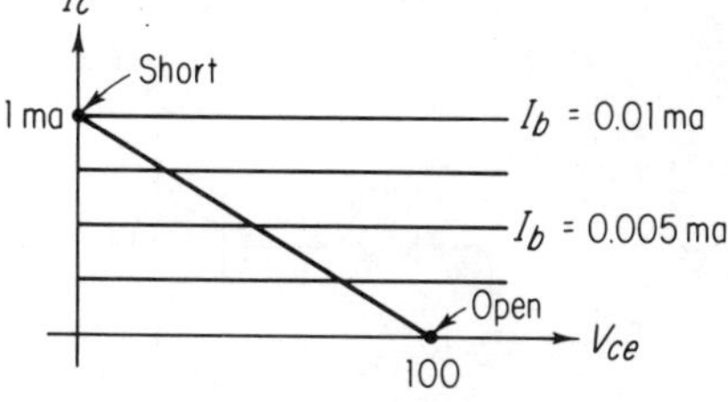

V_{bb} equals 1 volt, the transistor is operating at the *short* point on the load line. For V_{bb} greater than 1 volt, the transistor remains at the *short* point since it is saturated, much the same as a vacuum tube is saturated.

The value of collector current required to saturate the transistor in Fig. 9-10*b* is

$$I_{c(\text{sat})} = \frac{V_{cc}}{R_L} \tag{9-2}$$

Also, the value of base current required to produce saturation must be at least equal to, or greater than, the value given by Eq. (9-3)

$$I_{b(\text{sat})} = \frac{I_{c(\text{sat})}}{\beta_{dc}} \tag{9-3}$$

Example 9-5

In the circuit of Fig. 9-12*a*, determine whether or not the transistor is saturated. Use a d-c β of 50.

Solution

The value of collector current that saturates the transistor is

$$I_{c(\text{sat})} = \frac{20}{10(10^3)} = 2 \text{ ma}$$

The value of base current that produces saturation is

$$I_{b(\text{sat})} = \frac{2(10^{-3})}{50} = 0.04 \text{ ma}$$

Using the ideal-transistor approach, the actual base current is

$$I_b = \frac{10}{100(10^3)} = 0.1 \text{ ma}$$

The actual base current is 0.1 ma, which is more than enough to saturate the transistor. Thus, the transistor resembles a short from collector to emitter.

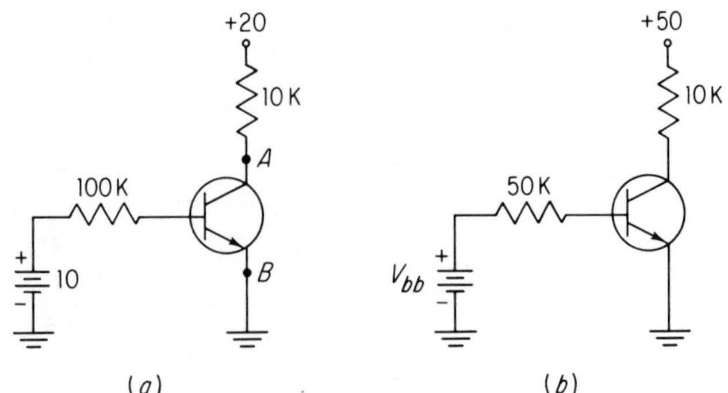

Fig. 9-12 (*a*) Examples 9-5 and 9-6. (*b*) Example 9-7.

Example 9-6

For the circuit of Fig. 9-12*a*, what is the minimum value of d-c beta that just saturates the transistor?

SOLUTION

The value of collector current required to saturate the transistor is still 2 ma. The actual value of base current is still 0.1 ma. Hence, the minimum d-c β required to saturate is

$$\beta_{dc} = \frac{2 \text{ ma}}{0.1 \text{ ma}} = 20$$

EXAMPLE 9-7

In the circuit of Fig. 9-12*b*, what is the minimum value of V_{bb} required to saturate the transistor? Use a d-c β of 50.

SOLUTION

$$I_{c(\text{sat})} = \frac{50}{10(10^3)} = 5 \text{ ma}$$

$$I_{b(\text{sat})} = \frac{5 \text{ ma}}{50} = 0.1 \text{ ma}$$

Using the ideal-transistor approach we have

$$V_{bb} = 50(10^3)(0.1)(10^{-3}) = 5 \text{ volts}$$

If a silicon transistor is used, we can allow 0.7 volt for the base-emitter diode. In this case, the minimum V_{bb} to saturate would be about 5.7 volts. The exact answer will lie between 5 and 5.7 volts.

9-5 Biasing the Common-emitter Transistor

Recall that with a vacuum tube operated as class A it is necessary to establish a d-c operating point. Then an a-c signal can be applied to the tube, and it will cause excursions from the operating point. As long as the a-c signal is not too large, the tube is approximately linear, so that no clipping takes place at either extreme of the a-c signal.

In a class A transistor amplifier we must likewise establish an operating point before applying an a-c signal. Establishing the d-c operating point is commonly known as *biasing* the transistor. There are many ways of biasing a transistor, only a few of which are practical. We will limit our discussion to what are probably the two most widely used forms of common-emitter bias.

In Fig. 9-13*a*, recall the common form of bias used for the common-cathode tube connection. A bypass capacitor is often used to prevent excessive degeneration. In Fig. 9-13*b*, the transistor is biased in a similar way. However, note that an additional power supply is needed. This V_{ee} supply must be used in order to forward-bias the base-emitter diode. Without this supply there would be essentially zero base current and therefore no collector current (except for leakage current).

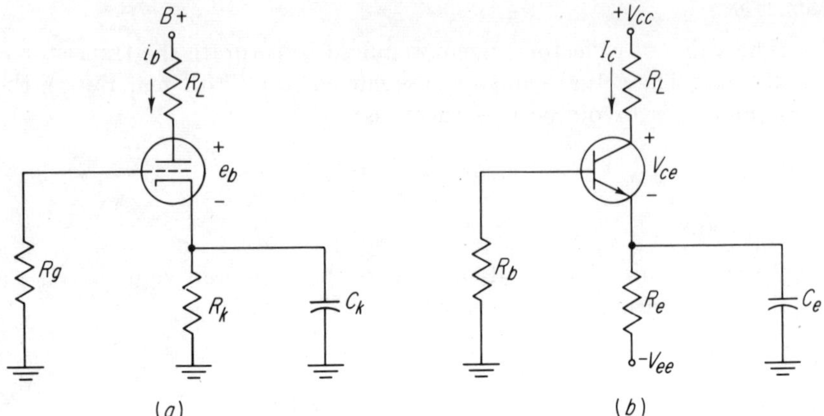

Fig. 9-13 Biasing. (*a*) Cathode bias. (*b*) Emitter bias.

It can be shown that the approximate formulas for the collector current and collector-emitter voltage are

$$I_c \cong \frac{V_{ee}}{R_e} \tag{9-4}$$

$$V_{ce} = V_{cc} - I_c R_L \qquad \text{provided that } V_{ee} \gg V_{be},\ \beta_{dc} R_e \gg R_b \tag{9-5}$$

Both of the above formulas are approximations, but they give reasonably accurate results if the conditions for approximation are satisfied. In most practical circuits, the conditions for approximation are easily satisfied.

As an example of the use of Eqs. (9-4) and (9-5) consider the circuit of Fig. 9-14*a*. The collector current equals the emitter supply voltage divided

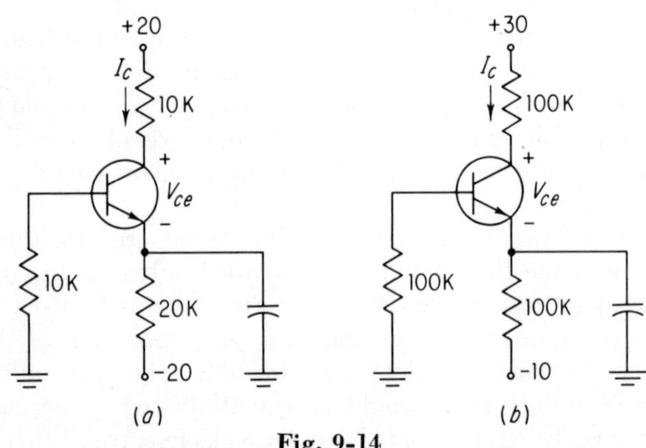

Fig. 9-14

by the emitter resistance

$$I_c \cong \frac{V_{ee}}{R_e} = \frac{20}{20(10^3)} = 1 \text{ ma}$$

The collector-emitter voltage equals the collector supply voltage minus the drop across the load resistor

$$V_{ce} \cong V_{cc} - I_c R_L = 20 - 10^{-3}(10)(10^3) = 10 \text{ volts}$$

Hence, the operating point (I_c, V_{ce}) equals (1 ma, 10 volts). Note also that the conditions of approximation are easily satisfied.

As another example, consider the circuit in Fig. 9-14*b*. The collector current is

$$I_c \cong \frac{10}{100(10^3)} = 0.1 \text{ ma}$$

and $$V_{ce} = 30 - 0.1(10^{-3})(100)(10^3) = 20 \text{ volts}$$

Hence, the operating point is (0.1 ma, 20 volts).

The second popular way of biasing a common emitter transistor is shown in Fig. 9-15*a*. It can be shown that the values of I_c and V_{ce} are given by

$$I_c \cong \frac{R_2}{R_1 + R_2} \frac{V_{cc}}{R_e} \qquad \text{(9-6)}$$

$$V_{ce} \cong V_{cc} - I_c(R_L + R_e)$$ provided that

$$\frac{R_2}{R_1 + R_2} V_{cc} \gg V_{be}, \; \beta_{dc} R_e \gg R_1 \| R_2 \qquad \text{(9-7)}$$

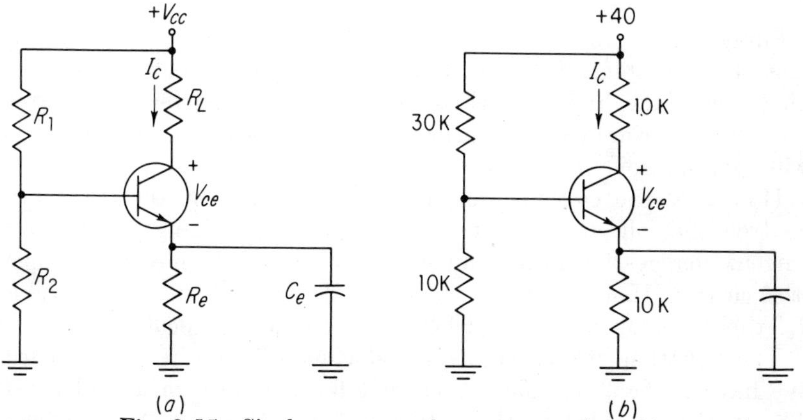

Fig. 9-15 Single-power-supply common-emitter bias.

As an example of using these equations to find the d-c operating point, consider Fig. 9-15*b*.

$$I_c = \frac{10(10^3)}{30(10^3) + 10(10^3)} \frac{40}{10(10^3)} = 1 \text{ ma}$$

and $$V_{ce} \cong 40 - 10^{-3}[10(10^3) + 10(10^3)] = 20 \text{ volts}$$

Hence, the operating point is (1 ma, 20 volts).

9-6 A Typical Transistor Amplifier Stage

We wish to now consider the a-c operation of a transistor. Figure 9-16*a* and *b* show typical transistor amplifier stages for low-frequency operation. The stages are biased in the two ways discussed in the preceding section.

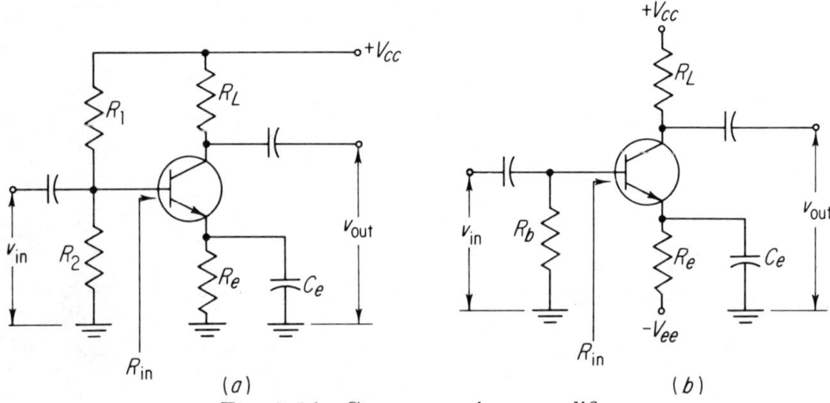

Fig. 9-16 Common-emitter amplifiers.

Suppose that a small sinusoidal signal is coupled into the input terminals of either stage. This signal appears directly across the base-emitter diode, since the bypass capacitor C_e makes the emitter an a-c ground point. Since we are varying the base voltage sinusoidally, the base current will vary sinusoidally.

How does the collector current vary? Recall that the base current controls the collector current. If the base current changes, the collector current changes by an amount equal to the a-c β times the change in base current. Hence, if the base current is a sinusoid with a peak value of I_p, the collector current will be a sinusoid with a peak value of βI_p.

The situation at this point is analogous to that in a vacuum tube. We have a changing collector current flowing through a load resistor. The voltage coupled to the output will be the a-c voltage developed across the load resistor. Just as with a vacuum tube, phase inversion takes place. In other words, the output signal is 180° out of phase with the input signal.

We can show that the voltage gain in the circuits of Fig. 9-16 is approximately given by

$$A = \frac{v_{\text{out}}}{v_{\text{in}}} \cong \beta \frac{R_L}{R_{\text{in}}} \tag{9-8}$$

As indicated in Fig. 9-16, R_{in} is the a-c resistance looking into the base. Remember that the bypass capacitor is an a-c short from the emitter to ground. Therefore, when we look into the base, the only resistance we see is the a-c resistance of the base-emitter diode. The exact value of this a-c resistance depends upon the d-c operating point, the transistor itself, and the value of the load resistance. This a-c input resistance of the transistor is a highly unreliable quantity in the sense that it will change with temperature, humidity, and so on. Further, R_{in} takes on a wide variety of different values as we change transistors. Hence, for any given transistor it is virtually impossible to know the exact value of R_{in} without measuring it experimentally.

For our purposes we will use a rough, but simple, approximation for the value of R_{in}.

$$R_{\text{in}} \cong \beta \frac{25 \text{ mv}}{I_c} \tag{9-9}$$

where I_c is the bias value of collector current. Equation (9-9) should be used with caution. It leads to large errors in some circuits. However, as a rough guide, it is quite useful. For instance, suppose that the a-c β of a transistor is 100 and that in either of the circuits of Fig. 9-16, the d-c value of collector current is 1 ma. Then, the a-c resistance looking into the base will be

$$R_{\text{in}} \cong 100 \frac{25 \text{ mv}}{1 \text{ ma}} = 2500 \text{ ohms}$$

If we change the circuit values so that there is a new bias current of $I_c = 2$ ma, the a-c input resistance becomes

$$R_{\text{in}} \cong 100 \frac{25 \text{ mv}}{2 \text{ ma}} = 1250 \text{ ohms}$$

Example 9-8

In Fig. 9-16*a*, the circuit values are as follows: $V_{cc} = 30$, $R_1 = 20$ kilohms, $R_2 = 10$ kilohms, $R_e = 5$ kilohms, $R_L = 5$ kilohms, and the a-c $\beta = 50$. Find the approximate input resistance looking into the base.

SOLUTION

$$R_{\text{in}} \cong \beta \frac{25 \text{ mv}}{I_c} = \frac{1.25}{I_c}$$

$$I_c = \frac{R_2}{R_1 + R_2} \frac{V_{cc}}{R_e} = \frac{10(10^3)}{30(10^3)} \frac{30}{5(10^3)} = 2 \text{ ma}$$

Hence, $$R_{\text{in}} \cong \frac{1.25}{2(10^{-3})} = 625 \text{ ohms}$$

EXAMPLE 9-9

Find the voltage gain in the circuit of Example 9-8.

SOLUTION

$$A \cong \beta \frac{R_L}{R_{\text{in}}} = 50 \frac{5(10^3)}{625} = 400$$

9-7 Single-stage Feedback

In Fig. 9-13*a*, the purpose of the cathode bypass capacitor is to prevent excessive degeneration. The voltage gain in such a circuit is heavily dependent upon the μ and the r_p of the tube. If these quantities change with temperature or with time, the voltage gain of the stage changes. Recall that by bypassing only part of the cathode resistance some degeneration occurs and stabilizes the voltage gain against changes in the tube parameters.

In a similar way, a change in the transistor parameters will change the voltage gain of the circuits of Fig. 9-16. To overcome this, we can use local feedback by bypassing only part of the emitter resistance, as shown in Figs. 9-17*a* or 9-17*b*. It can be shown that the voltage gain in either circuit is

$$A \cong \frac{R_L}{R'_e} \tag{9-10}$$

where R'_e is the unbypassed emitter resistance. This voltage-gain formula is very important and should be remembered. Equation (9-10) tells us that the voltage gain of either of the two typical transistor circuits shown in Fig. 9-17 is merely the ratio of the load resistance to the unbypassed emitter resistance. For example, if R_L = 10 kilohms and R'_e = 1 kilohm, the voltage gain is 10. This means that an input signal with a value of 1 mv rms will produce an output signal of 10 mv rms.

The use of local feedback as shown in Fig. 9-17 greatly improves the gain stability of the stage. In other words, the voltage gain will not change significantly with temperature changes, or transistor replacement, and so on. This is very important in most applications.

Another useful approximation for the circuits of Fig. 9-17 is that the a-c input resistance looking into the base is equal to the a-c β times the unbypassed emitter resistance. That is,

$$R_{\text{in}} \cong \beta R'_e \tag{9-11}$$

Note that the R_{in} for the circuits of Fig. 9-17 is different from the circuits of Fig. 9-16, where R_{in} was equal to the value given by Eq. (9-9). The reason for this is that the emitter is no longer an a-c ground. The a-c ground has been moved to the bottom of the R'_e resistor. Because of this, when we look into the base, we effectively see the R'_e resistor transformed by the current factor of β. In any event, Eq. (9-11) is quite useful and generally quite accurate as long as R'_e is much larger than 25 mv/I_c.

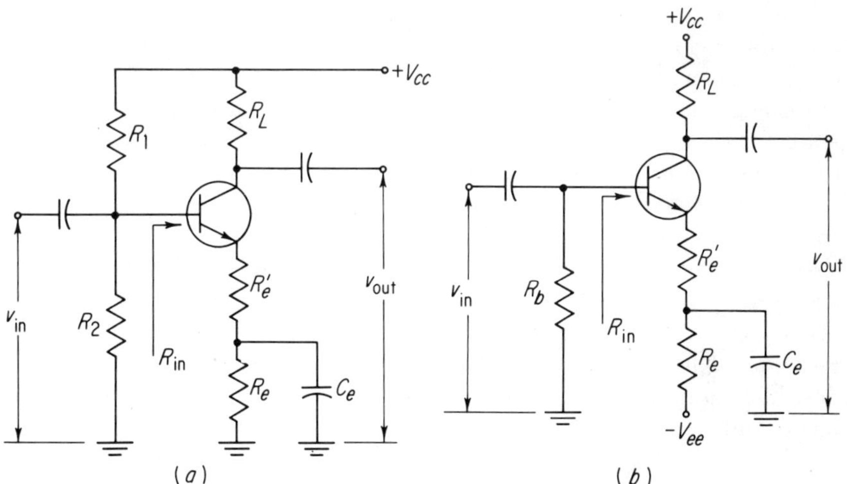

Fig. 9-17 Common-emitter amplifiers with local degeneration.

Example 9-10

In Fig. 9-17*a* or *b*, $R_L = 10$ kilohms, $R'_e = 500$, and the a-c β equals 100. Find the approximate voltage gain and the a-c input resistance looking into the base.

Solution

$$A \cong \frac{R_L}{R'_e} = \frac{10(10^3)}{500} = 20$$

and

$$R_{\text{in}} \cong \beta R'_e = 100(500) = 50 \text{ kilohms}$$

The value of R_{in} does not include the resistances that are part of the bias network. To find the input resistance at the input terminals of the stage, we need to calculate the 50 kilohms looking into the base in parallel with the biasing resistors.

SUMMARY

The transistor is a complicated device. As an approximation we can think of the base-emitter part as an ordinary diode and the collector-emitter part as a current source. The base current controls the collector current. The total collector current equals the d-c β times the total base current. Any change in the base current produces a change in the collector current. The change in collector current equals the a-c β times the base-current change.

The transistor may be used as a switch. In this case, the transistor is operated at either the cutoff point on the load line or at the saturated point on the load line. When the transistor is cut off, it resembles an open circuit. When it is saturated, it resembles a short circuit.

Biasing the transistor refers to establishing a d-c operating point. Unlike the vacuum tube, which has no grid current under normal conditions, the transistor must have base current in order to operate as class A.

After biasing the transistor to an operating point, it is then possible to couple in an a-c signal to obtain amplification. If the emitter resistance is completely bypassed, a voltage gain is obtained which depends a great deal upon the type of transistor used, the temperature, and several other factors. In order to stabilize the voltage gain, some of the emitter resistance is left unbypassed. This leads to less voltage gain, but the value does not change appreciably with temperature changes, transistor replacement, and so on.

GLOSSARY

a-c β The ratio of a change in the collector current to the change in base current under the condition of a fixed collector-to-emitter voltage.

a-c resistance In reference to the common-emitter connection this is the resistance seen by a-c signal when driving the base of a transistor.

biasing A term analogous to that used with vacuum tubes. Refers to setting the operating point of collector voltage and current.

d-c β The ratio of the total collector current to the total base current.

ideal transistor A transistor which is represented by an ideal diode in the base and by an ideal current source in its collector.

saturation A condition whereby the collector current produces enough voltage drop in the external circuitry to reduce the collector-emitter voltage essentially to zero.

REVIEW QUESTIONS

1. What are the two materials commonly used in transistors?
2. What are the schematic symbols for the *n-p-n* and *p-n-p* transistors?
3. Above the knee, what can be said about the collector current as the collector voltage increases?
4. How is the d-c β of a transistor defined? The a-c β?
5. How does the size of the base current compare to the collector current?
6. The collector current is controlled by what?
7. In the ideal approximation of a transistor how do we view the base-emitter part of the transistor? The collector?
8. In the second approximation of a transistor, how do we account for the base-emitter voltage for a germanium and a silicon transistor?
9. When the transistor is used as an electronic switch, as in the circuit of Fig. 9-10*b*, what is the value of collector current that saturates the transistor?
10. How do you find the value of base current that just saturates a transistor for a typical switching circuit? What happens to the collector voltage if the base current is greater than the value required to saturate?
11. Draw the schematic of the two circuits that are widely used to bias a common-emitter transistor.
12. In the two-power-supply common-emitter biasing circuit, what is the approximate value of collector current?
13. What is one way of stabilizing the voltage gain of a common-emitter amplifier?
14. What is the value of the input resistance of a common-emitter transistor if there is an unbypassed emitter resistance of R_e'?

PROBLEMS

9-1 Measurements made on a transistor show that the collector current equals 50 ma and the base current equals 1 ma. What is the value of the d-c β? Suppose that the base current is reduced to 0.02 ma. If the d-c β has remained constant, what is the value of the collector current?
9-2 A transistor has a collector current of 20 ma and a base current 0.4 ma. What is the d-c β? If the base current is increased to 0.45 ma, the collector current is found to be 23 ma. What is the value of the a-c β?
9-3 In Fig. 9-18*a*, R_L equals 10 kilohms. Assuming an ideal transistor with a d-c β of 100, what value of R_b produces a collector current of 0.5 ma? What value of R_b produces a V_{ce} of 2 volts?

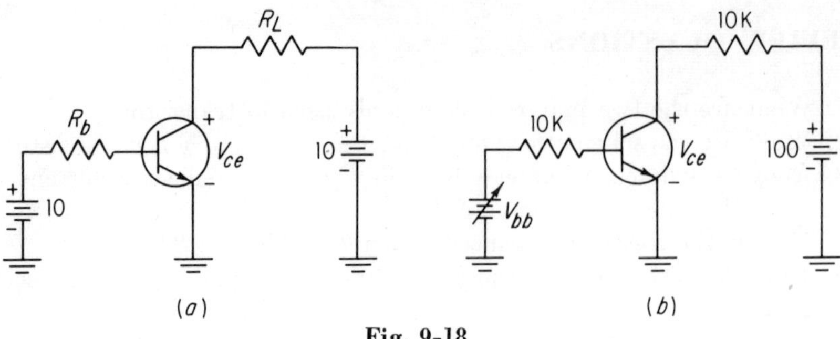

Fig. 9-18

9-4 In Fig. 9-18*a*, $R_L = 5$ kilohms, and $R_b = 1$ megohm. Assuming an ideal transistor with a d-c β of 50, what is the value of V_{ce}? If R_b is reduced to 250 kilohms, what is the value of V_{ce}?

9-5 In Fig. 9-18*b*, compute the value of V_{ce} if $V_{bb} = 1$ volt. Assume an ideal transistor with a d-c β of 50. Compute the value of V_{ce} for $V_{bb} = 2$ volts. How much change takes place in the value of V_{ce} as V_{bb} changes from 1 to 2 volts?

9-6 In Fig. 9-19*a*, the d-c β of the transistor is 50. Find the value of I_b. Is the transistor saturated? What is the value of V_{ce} and I_c?

9-7 In Fig. 9-19*a*, what is the minimum value of d-c β required to saturate the transistor?

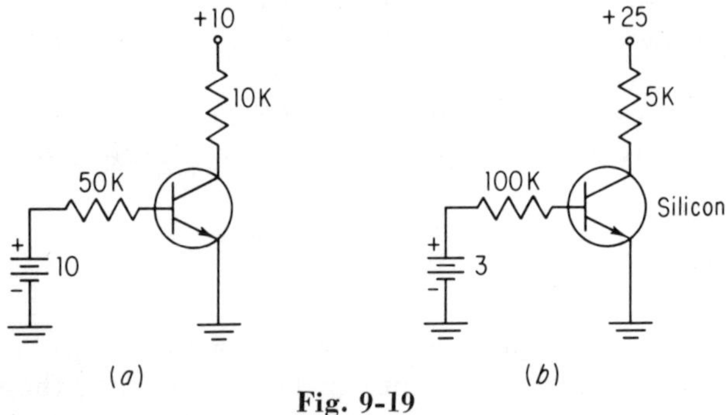

Fig. 9-19

9-8 In Fig. 9-19*b*, the d-c β is 100. Find the base current, the collector current, and the voltage from collector to ground. Use the ideal-transistor approximation and compare these answers to those obtained by using the second approximation.

9-9 In Fig. 9-19*b*, what is the minimum value of d-c β required to saturate the transistor?

9-10 In Fig. 9-19*b*, use an ideal transistor with a d-c β of 100. Calculate the change that takes place in the collector voltage if the base supply voltage is changed from 3 to 4 volts.

9-11 In Fig. 9-20*a*, V_{cc} and V_{ee} equal 10 volts, R_L and R_b equal 1 kilohm, and R_e equals 2 kilohms. Find I_c and V_{ce} approximately. If the d-c β equals 100, what is the voltage across R_b?

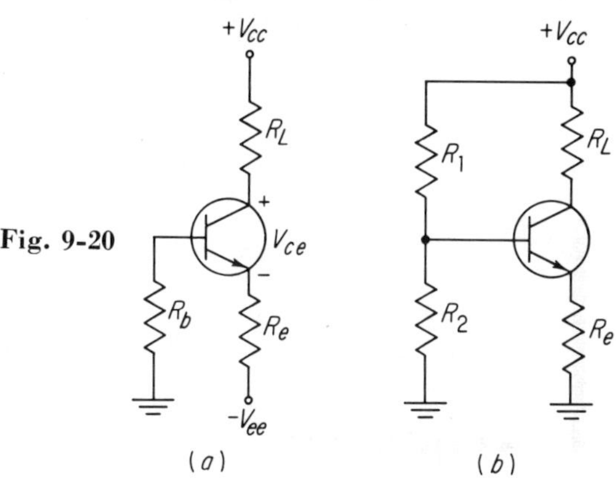

Fig. 9-20

9-12 In Fig. 9-20*a*, $V_{cc} = 50$, $V_{ee} = 25$, R_L and $R_b = 10$ kilohms. What value of R_e produces a V_{ce} of approximately 25 volts? And what value of R_e will cause V_{ce} to equal zero?

9-13 In Fig. 9-20*b*, $V_{cc} = 30$, R_L and $R_e = 10$ kilohms, $R_1 = 40$ kilohms, and $R_2 = 20$ kilohms Find I_c and V_{ce}.

9-14 In Fig. 9-20*b*, $V_{cc} = 30$, $R_L = 5$ kilohms, $R_1 = 10$ kilohms, $R_2 = 5$ kilohms. What value of R_e produces an I_c of 1 ma? What value of R_e produces a V_{ce} of zero volts?

9-15 In Fig. 9-16*a*, the d-c value of collector current is 0.5 ma. The a-c β of the transistor is 75, and the value of R_L is 5 kilohms. Find the approximate voltage gain from input to output. If the input signal is 1 mv rms, what is the approximate value of output voltage?

9-16 In the circuit of Fig. 9-16*b*, $V_{ee} = 15$ volts, and $R_e = 10$ kilohms. The a-c β is 150, and the value of R_L is 3 kilohms. Find the approximate value of voltage gain.

9-17 In Fig. 9-17*a*, R_L is 5 kilohms, and R_e' is 750. The a-c β is 120. Find the voltage gain and the input resistance looking into the base.

9-18 In Fig. 9-17*b*, R_b and $R_L = 1$ kilohm, $R_e = 2$ kilohms, and $R_e' = 100$. V_{cc} and V_{ee} equal 20 volts, and the a-c β is 100.

(*a*) Find the approximate value of the d-c collector current.
(*b*) Find the value of the collector-to-ground d-c voltage.
(*c*) What is the voltage gain of the stage?
(*d*) What is the a-c input resistance looking into the base?
(*e*) What is the a-c input resistance looking into the input terminals?

10 Amplifiers

The main function of an amplifier is to produce an enlarged version of an input signal. Tubes and transistors are the most frequently used amplifying devices, although some newer devices, such as tunnel diodes and variable-capacitance diodes, are being used in special situations.

In this chapter we examine some of the important features of amplifiers, such as input and output impedance, frequency response, and impedance matching. We will also examine some special amplifying circuits, which are not ordinarily covered in a basic electronics course.

10-1 A-C Amplifiers

An a-c amplifier is designed to amplify sinusoidal signals whose frequencies lie within a prescribed frequency range. Ideally, the graph of voltage gain versus frequency is the response shown in Fig. 10-1*a*. Note that the voltage gain equals A_{mid} over the passband of the amplifier. There is a lower and an upper cutoff frequency. In effect, the a-c amplifier is a bandpass filter.

Of course, the ideal response shown in Fig. 10-1*a* cannot be attained in practice. What we actually can obtain is the typical response shown

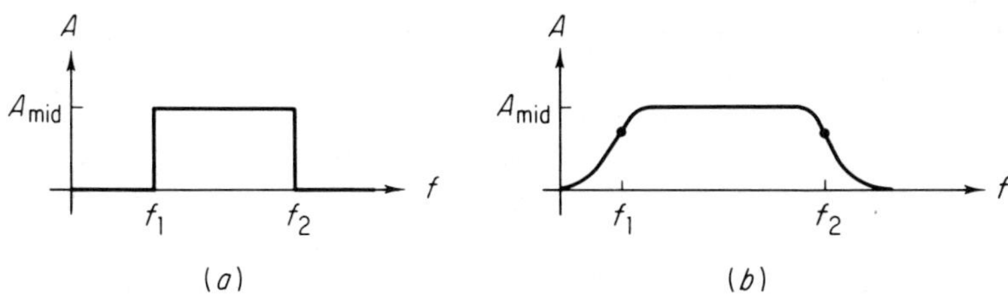

Fig. 10-1 A-c amplifier response. (*a*) Ideal. (*b*) Typical.

in Fig. 10-1*b*. There is a passband where the voltage gain equals A_{mid}, and there are lower and upper cutoff frequencies where the gain has dropped to $0.707A_{\text{mid}}$.

The roll-off that takes place above and below the cutoff frequencies is usually caused by the presence of capacitance. The lower cutoff frequency depends upon the size of the coupling capacitors and the cathode (or emitter) bypass capacitors used in the amplifier stages. The upper cutoff frequency depends primarily on the amount of shunt capacitance from each plate (or collector) to ground. This shunt capacitance is composed of tube (or transistor) capacitance and wiring capacitance.

Most amplifier stages may be thought of simply as a combination of a low-pass and high-pass *RC* filters with a tube or transistor providing gain in the passband. If an amplifier consists of several stages in cascade, the cutoff frequencies will represent the cumulative effect of all stages. For instance, suppose that each identical stage shown in Fig. 10-2 has

In → A → A → A → Out

Fig. 10-2 Cascade of identical amplifier stages.

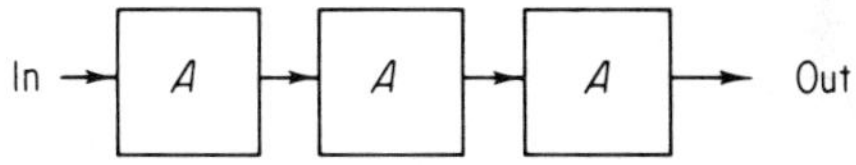

an upper cutoff frequency of 100 kHz. Then each stage is down 3 db from its passband value, and the overall amplifier is down 9 db. It should be clear that the cutoff frequency for the overall amplifier is considerably less than 100 kHz. In this case, the cutoff frequency of the amplifier will occur at that frequency where each stage is down 1 db from its passband response. From Table 8-2 we see that the response of each stage will be down about 1 db at one-half the cutoff frequency of the stage. Hence, for a cascade of three identical stages the overall cutoff frequency will occur at one-half the cutoff frequency of a stage. In our example, the cutoff frequency would be 50 kHz.

A useful *approximation* for the upper cutoff frequency of several identical stages in cascade is given by

$$f_2 \cong \frac{f_c}{1.1\sqrt{n}} \tag{10-1}$$

where f_c is the upper cutoff frequency of a single stage
f_2 is the upper cutoff frequency of the overall amplifier
n is the number of stages

Equation (10-1) is an approximation which becomes more accurate for higher values of n. (Note that for $n = 1$ the answer is off by about 10 percent.)

For nonidentical stages the exact formula for the cutoff frequency is quite complicated. We will only observe that if the cutoff frequencies of the stages are reasonably close together, Eq. (10-1) may still be used as an approximation. On the other hand, if one of the stages has a cutoff frequency that is much lower than the others, that stage predominates, and the overall cutoff frequency will approximately equal the cutoff frequency of the dominant stage.

The lower cutoff frequency of a cascade of stages will likewise be the cumulative effect of all stages. As an *approximation* of the lower cutoff frequency for a cascade of identical stages we may use

$$f_1 \cong 1.1 \sqrt{n}\, f_c \tag{10-2}$$

where f_c is the lower cutoff frequency of a single stage
f_1 is the lower cutoff frequency of a cascade of identical stages
n is the number of stages

EXAMPLE 10-1

Five identical stages are cascaded. The lower cutoff frequency of each stage is 100 Hz, and the upper cutoff frequency is 100 kHz. Find the lower and upper cutoff frequencies for the overall amplifier.

SOLUTION

The approximate value of the lower cutoff frequency may be obtained by using Eq. (10-2)

$$f_1 \cong 1.1 \sqrt{5}\,(100) = 250 \text{ Hz}$$

The approximate upper cutoff frequency may be found by using Eq. (10-1)

$$f_2 \cong \frac{100(10^3)}{1.1 \sqrt{5}} = 40 \text{ kHz}$$

Thus, we see that the passband of a single stage extends from 100 Hz to 100 kHz, whereas a cascade of five such stages has a passband from about 250 Hz to about 40 kHz.

10-2 D-C Amplifiers

The need often arises for an amplifier whose frequency response extends down to zero frequency, or direct current. At other times there may be a need for an amplifier whose frequency response extends to extremely low frequencies. For instance, we may need an amplifier whose passband is from 0.001 Hz to some upper cutoff frequency. In such a case, the size of the coupling and bypass capacitors becomes prohibitively large.

For either requirement, the type of amplifier used is what is commonly known as a d-c amplifier. The response for such an amplifier is shown in Fig. 10-3. The response extends all the way down to direct current, or zero frequency. Note that this response is basically that of a low-pass filter.

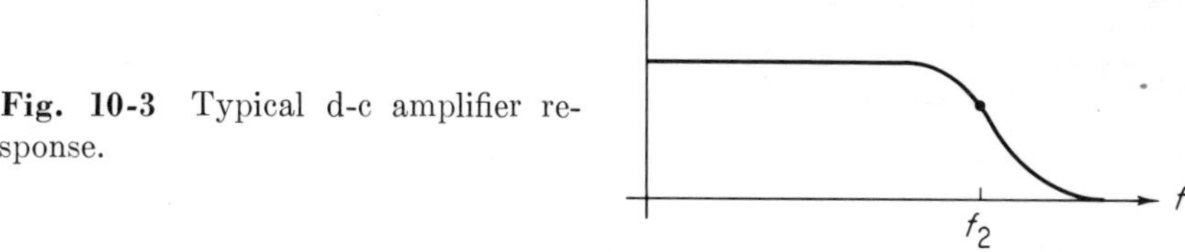

Fig. 10-3 Typical d-c amplifier response.

To achieve this type of response either of two basic approaches is generally used. First, an amplifier can be designed with no coupling or bypass capacitors. Second, the d-c or low-frequency input can be first converted to a higher frequency. This higher frequency can then be amplified in an ordinary a-c coupled amplifier, and then the signal can be converted back to the original lower-frequency signal. We will discuss both of these basic methods in detail in later sections.

10-3 A Useful Amplifier Equivalent Circuit

The majority of amplifiers can be represented by the equivalent circuit shown in Fig. 10-4, which is applicable in the passband of the amplifier.

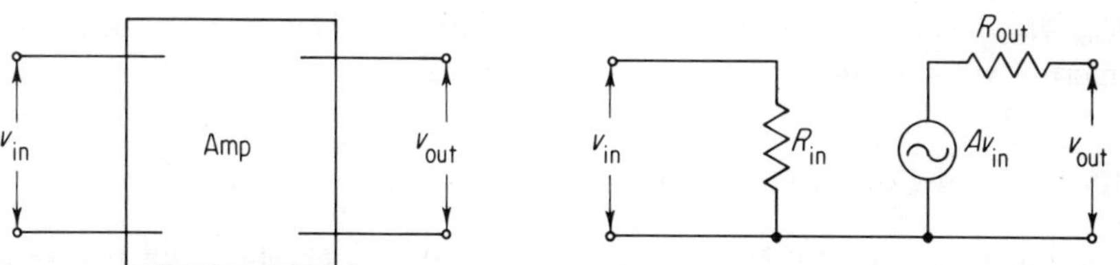

Fig. 10-4 Equivalent circuit for an amplifier operating in its passband.

Note carefully the various quantities. The amplifier has an input resistance R_{in}. The size of this input resistance will determine how much loading takes place when a signal source is connected to the input terminals.

On the output side of the amplifier we have a Thévenin equivalent consisting of an open-circuit voltage generator and an output resistance. The value of the open-circuit voltage generator is A times v_{in}, where A is the open-circuit voltage gain of the amplifier.

As an example of how to use the equivalent circuit, consider the situation depicted in Fig. 10-5*a*. The amplifier has an input resistance of 10-kilohms, an output resistance of 1 kilohm, and an open-circuit voltage

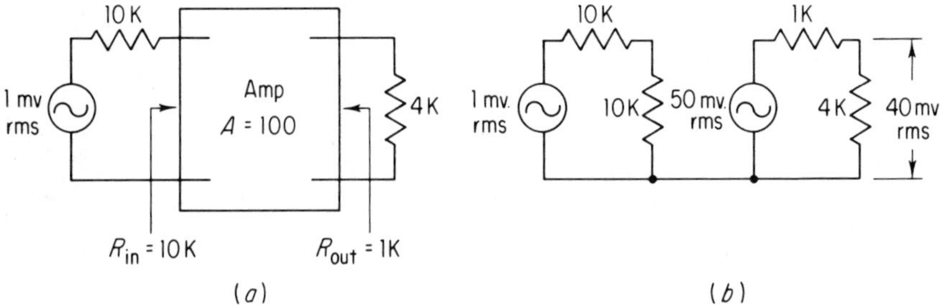

Fig. 10-5

gain of 100. We can replace the amplifier by its equivalent circuit as shown in Fig. 10-5*b*. Since the source resistance equals the input resistance, the actual signal at the input terminals of the amplifier is 0.5 mv. Since the open-circuit voltage gain is 100, the value of the generator on the output side is 100(0.5 mv), or 50 mv. The output circuit is a simple voltage divider, so that four-fifths of the voltage is actually delivered to the 4-kilohm load resistor. Hence, the load voltage is 40 mv.

In dealing with any amplifier, whether it is a single stage or a cascade of several stages, it is essential to know the value of input and output resistance, as well as the value of the open-circuit voltage gain. It is not enough to merely know the value of amplifier gain. We must know the value of input and output resistance in order to determine how much loading will take place when a source and load are connected. Hence, whenever selecting or using an amplifier we must specify or know the values of R_{in}, R_{out}, and A in order to know beforehand how the amplifier will operate when connected to a source or load.

10-4 Gain Formulas for Special Cases

Amplifiers are often used in either of two ways. First, the input resistance of the amplifier is often much larger than the source resistance. Second, the load resistance is often much larger than the output resistance of the amplifier (see Fig. 10-6).

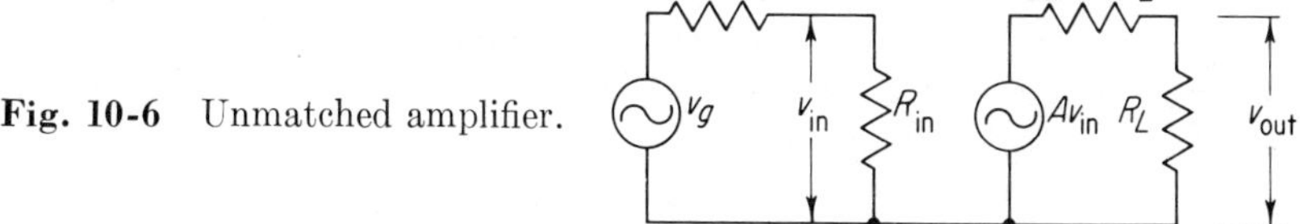

Fig. 10-6 Unmatched amplifier.

Note that since R_{in} is much greater than R_o, the value of input voltage to the amplifier is essentially equal to the generator signal. That is,

$$v_{in} = v_g$$

Further, since $v_{in} = v_g$, the output generator equals Av_g. Finally, since R_{out} is much smaller than R_L, all the generator voltage is delivered to R_L. In other words,

$$v_{out} = Av_g$$

or

$$\frac{v_{out}}{v_g} = A \qquad (10\text{-}3)$$

Thus, we see that under the special conditions indicated, the voltage gain from the generator to the load is simply equal to the open-circuit voltage gain of the amplifier.

We will refer to Eq. (10-3) as the *voltage gain for the completely unmatched case.* This special case is often encountered in practice because many amplifiers are deliberately designed with very high input resistances and very low output resistances.

As an example, consider the situation in Fig. 10-7*a*. The amplifier has an input resistance of 100 kilohms, an output resistance of 200 ohms,

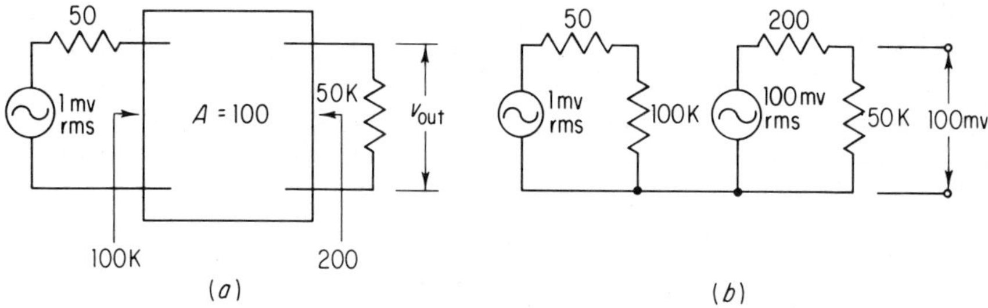

Fig. 10-7 Example of an unmatched amplifier.

and an open-circuit voltage gain of 100. With the given source resistance, it is clear that the entire 1-mv-rms signal appears at the input terminals of the amplifier. Furthermore, on the output side it should also be clear that the entire output generator signal is delivered to the load resistor.

Hence, the load voltage will be 100 mv rms. Figure 10-7*b* illustrates the equivalent circuit in case there are any doubts.

Figure 10-6 represents the completely unmatched situation. However, the need often arises for impedance matching an amplifier, whether it is a single stage or a cascade of stages. Impedance matching is often used when the signal is very weak, the reason being that the signal may be approaching the noise level of the amplifier. If this is the case, all the signal power that is available in the source should be delivered to the amplifier input terminals in order to improve the signal-to-noise ratio.

Figure 10-8 illustrates an amplifier that has been impedance-matched on both the input and output sides. The matching devices are used to transform the impedances so that a match occurs. For example, a transformer may be used to impedance-match the input resistance of the amplifier to the source resistance. If the correct turns ratio is used, then looking into the transformer the source will see a resistance of R_o. Similarly, on the output side a transformer with the correct turns ratio will make the load resistance appear to be a resistance of R_{out} when viewed from the left side of the transformer.

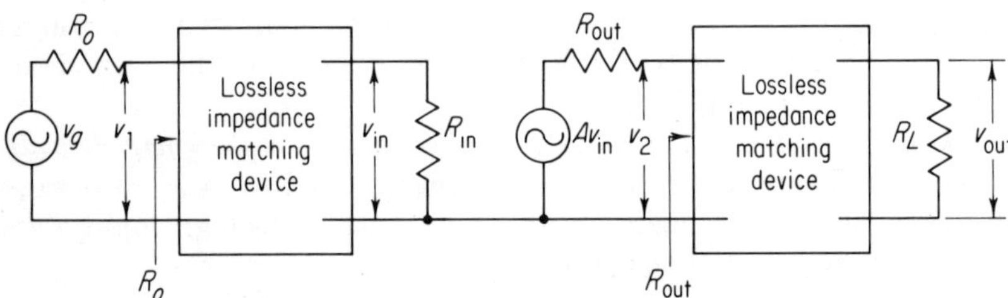

Fig. 10-8 Impedance-matching the amplifier.

What is the formula for the overall voltage gain from the input generator to the load resistance; in other words, what is the formula for v_{out}/v_g?

First, note that the power delivered to the lossless matching device on the input side is

$$p_1 = \frac{v_1^2}{R_o}$$

Since v_1 equals $v_g/2$ under matched conditions,

$$p_1 = \frac{(v_g/2)^2}{R_o} = \frac{v_g^2}{4R_o}$$

The impedance-matching device is lossless (or very low loss), meaning that all the power delivered to the device is passed on to the amplifier input. In other words,

$$p_{\text{in}} = p_1$$

or

$$\frac{v_{\text{in}}^2}{R_{\text{in}}} = \frac{v_g^2}{4R_o}$$

If we now solve for v_{in}, we obtain

$$v_{\text{in}} = \frac{v_g}{2}\sqrt{\frac{R_{\text{in}}}{R_o}} \tag{10-4}$$

This formula is very useful. It tells us the value of v_{in} under matched conditions on the input side. Further, it should be clear that v_{in} can be larger than v_g for high values of R_{in}/R_o. (Recall that for the completely unmatched case, $v_{\text{in}} = v_g$.) For example, suppose that $R_{\text{in}} = 100$ kilohms and $R_o = 1$ kilohm. If we use a transformer, or some other impedance matching device, Eq. (10-4) applies. Since $R_{\text{in}}/R_o =$ (100 kilohms)/(1 kilohm), or 100,

$$v_{\text{in}} = \frac{v_g}{2}\sqrt{100} = 5v_g$$

In other words, by impedance-matching the input, we have increased the input voltage to the amplifier from v_g for the unmatched case to $5v_g$ for the matched case. We have, in effect, delivered five times more voltage (or 14 db) to the amplifier by impedance matching. This represents a substantial improvement in the performance of a receiver used in television or radar.

If the output is also impedance-matched, then from Fig. 10-8 we can see that the power delivered to the left side of the impedance-matching device is

$$p_2 = \frac{v_2^2}{R_{\text{out}}} \tag{10-5}$$

Since the output is matched, one-half the output generator voltage is delivered to the left side of the output impedance-matching device. That is,

$$v_2 = \frac{Av_{\text{in}}}{2}$$

If we now substitute this value of v_2 into Eq. (10-5), we obtain

$$p_2 = \frac{(Av_{\text{in}}/2)^2}{R_{\text{out}}} = \frac{A^2v_{\text{in}}^2}{4R_{\text{out}}}$$

Since the matching device is lossless, all this power is delivered to the load resistance. Hence,

$$p_L = p_2$$

or

$$\frac{v_L^2}{R_L} = \frac{A^2v_{\text{in}}^2}{4R_{\text{out}}}$$

If we solve this equation for v_L, we obtain

$$v_L = \frac{A}{2} v_{\text{in}} \sqrt{\frac{R_L}{R_{\text{out}}}} \tag{10-6}$$

Finally, to obtain an expression for v_{out}/v_g, we need only substitute Eq. (10-4) into (10-6). We then obtain an expression for the voltage gain from the input generator to the load.

$$\frac{v_{\text{out}}}{v_g} = \frac{A}{4} \sqrt{\frac{R_{\text{in}}}{R_o}} \sqrt{\frac{R_L}{R_{\text{out}}}} \tag{10-7}$$

Equation (10-7) is quite useful when dealing with amplifiers that have been impedance-matched on both the input and output sides. Recall that for the completely unmatched case of Fig. 10-6, $v_{\text{out}}/v_g = A$. It should be clear that in the matched case we can obtain a considerable improvement in the voltage gain. Some examples will illustrate.

Example 10-2

Find the output voltage in the circuit of Fig. 10-9.

Solution

Since the input resistance is much larger than the source resistance, it is clear that $v_{\text{in}} = 1$ mv. The value of the output generator is then 100 mv. Since R_L is much larger than R_{out}, the entire 100 mv is delivered to the load. Hence, $v_{\text{out}} = 100$ mv.

It should have been clear from the outset that the situation in Fig. 10-9 represents the completely unmatched case. The gain from the input generator to the load is then simply A, or 100. Since v_g equals 1 mv, v_{out} equals 100 mv.

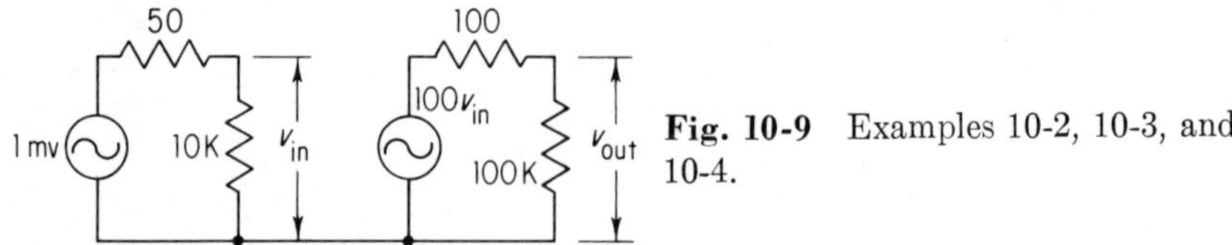

Fig. 10-9 Examples 10-2, 10-3, and 10-4.

Example 10-3

If ideal transformers are used to impedance-match the input and output of the amplifier shown in Fig. 10-9, what are the correct turns ratios?

Solution

Recall from basic electronics courses that impedances are transformed according to the turns ratio squared.

$$\left(\frac{N_2}{N_1}\right)^2 = \frac{Z_2}{Z_1}$$

or

$$\frac{N_2}{N_1} = \sqrt{\frac{Z_2}{Z_1}}$$

Hence, on the input side the turns ratio should be

$$\frac{N_2}{N_1} = \sqrt{\frac{10(10^3)}{50}} \cong 14$$

On the output side the turns ratio should be

$$\frac{N_2}{N_1} = \sqrt{\frac{100(10^3)}{100}} \cong 32$$

Example 10-4

If the amplifier of Fig. 10-9 is impedance-matched on the input and output sides, what is the value of v_{out}?

Solution

Since both the input and output are matched, Eq. (10-7) applies.

$$\frac{v_{out}}{v_g} = \frac{100}{4}\sqrt{\frac{10(10^3)}{50}}\sqrt{\frac{100(10^3)}{100}} = 11{,}200$$

Since v_g equals 1 mv, $v_{out} = 11.2$ volts.

Note the tremendous improvement in the voltage gain of this matched case compared to the unmatched case of Example 10-2. In the former example, the voltage gain is 100. In the matched case, the gain is 11,200.

One should not jump to the conclusion that all amplifiers ought to be impedance-matched. Such impedance-matching devices as transformers are relatively expensive, and they have definite frequency limits which may reduce the passband response of an unmatched amplifier. However, in those cases where signals are near the noise level, or where large amounts of power must be efficiently amplified, the use of impedance matching is standard procedure.

10-5 Direct-coupled Amplifiers

In the construction of a d-c amplifier one approach is to eliminate the causes of the lower cutoff frequency. Basically, the cutoff frequency of an a-c amplifier is produced by the coupling capacitors between stages and by the cathode or emitter bypass capacitors.

Figure 10-10 shows a typical three-stage amplifier. The d-c voltage on each plate is 100 volts. A 5-volt bias is being produced by each cathode resistor.

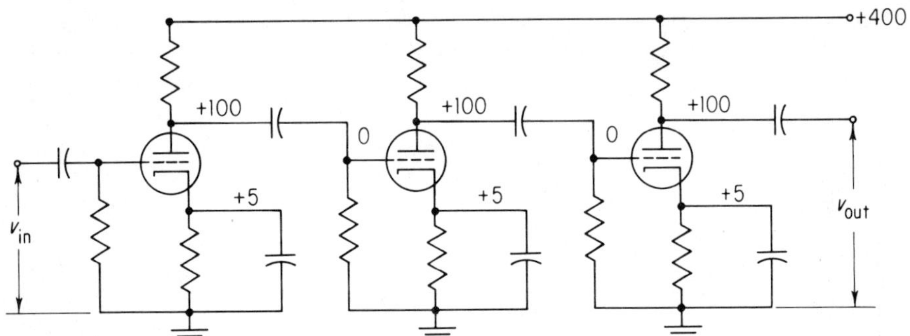

Fig. 10-10 Typical three-stage a-c amplifier.

Recall the basic purpose of the capacitors. The coupling capacitors isolate the plate voltage of one stage from the grid of the next stage. Also, the cathode bypass capacitors prevent excessive degeneration. How can we eliminate these capacitors?

We will discuss three different methods. First, the coupling capacitors are eliminated. This means that the plate voltage of any one tube will appear directly on the grid of the next stage, as shown in Fig. 10-11. In order to prevent excessive grid current, the cathodes of each stage must then be made positive, as shown.

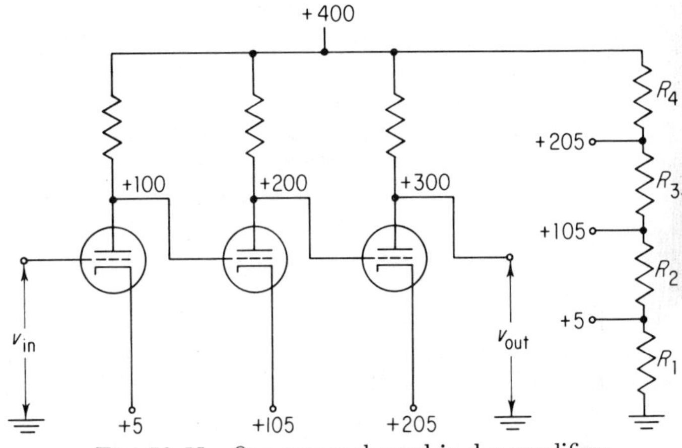

Fig. 10-11 One approach used in d-c amplifiers.

The cathode voltages of 5, 105, and 205 can be obtained from separate positive power supplies or from a single power supply with a voltage divider and appropriate tap points. The resistances in the voltage divider must be low in order to prevent excessive degeneration in each stage. The need for increasingly higher voltages as we add stages is the main disadvantage of this system.

Another approach is to use the two power supplies, one positive and the other negative (see Fig. 10-12). In this system, voltage dividers are

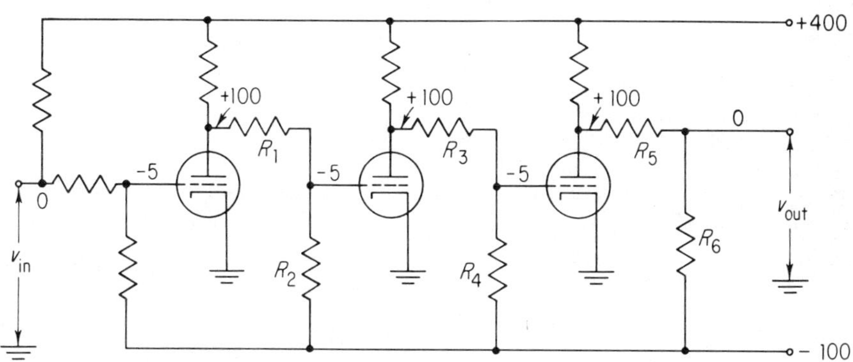

Fig. 10-12 A second approach used in d-c amplifiers.

used between stages to produce a suitable bias for each stage. This system has the disadvantage that the voltage gain is reduced, since the voltage dividers between stages attenuate the signal. Hence, the gain of this system is less than that of Fig. 10-11.

Another basic approach sometimes used involves zener diodes. Recall that the zener diode behaves like a battery when it is operating in the breakdown region. We can take advantage of this fact by using a system like that in Fig. 10-13.

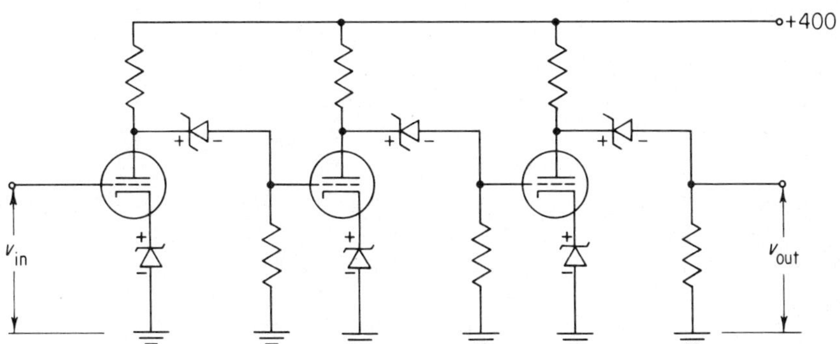

Fig. 10-13 A third approach used in d-c amplifiers.

All these methods have one common weakness. Any change in power-supply voltages or tube parameters will produce a change in the output voltage. Since these circuits are d-c amplifiers, ideally only an input d-c signal should change the output d-c voltage. Hence, any drift in power-supply voltages or tube parameters will be indistinguishable from a genuine input d-c signal. Drift in amplifiers of this type is especially critical in the first stage, since any change in the voltages in the first stage is amplified in the succeeding stages. Hence, amplifiers of this type are suitable as d-c amplifiers only in those situations where the true input d-c voltages are much larger than the drift voltages of the first stage.

10-6 Chopped and Modulated D-C Amplifiers

Another approach used to build a d-c amplifier is that of first converting the d-c to an a-c signal, which is then amplified in a standard a-c amplifier and finally converted back to a d-c signal. We will discuss two basic methods. First, there is the system shown in Fig. 10-14. Assume

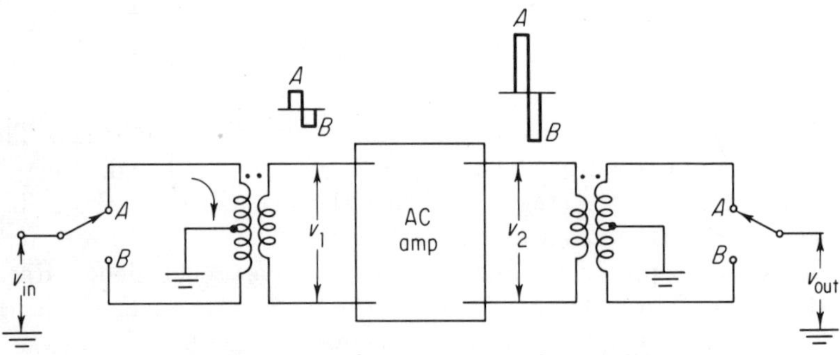

Fig. 10-14 A chopper type of d-c amplifier.

that v_{in} is a d-c voltage. The switch on the input moves back and forth between A and B. When the switch is in position A, the current in the primary flows in one direction. When the switch is in position B, the current flows in the opposite direction. This means that an a-c voltage will be induced in the secondary. Ideally, with a perfect transformer and zero switching time, the signal to the amplifier will be a perfect square wave, as shown in Fig. 10-15a. With a real transformer and a finite switching time between A and B, we can expect the vertical parts of the square wave to have slope and the horizontal parts of the wave to have a sag.

The basic idea should be clear. A d-c signal is converted to an a-c signal. The peak value of this a-c signal will be proportional to the d-c input.

The a-c signal is then amplified in a standard a-c amplifier. Finally, the amplified signal is converted back to a d-c signal. The output switch is ganged to the input switch, so that the signal is converted back to a d-c voltage, as indicated in Fig. 10-15*b*. In practice, the actual output is not a perfect d-c voltage. It will be a d-c signal with ripple. If necessary, this can be filtered, much the same as an ordinary power supply is filtered.

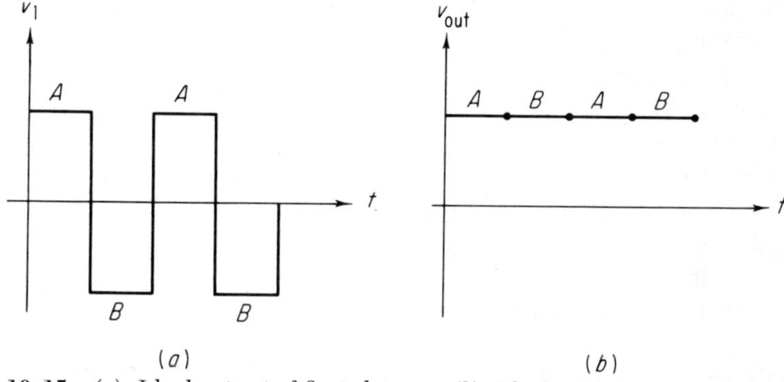

Fig. 10-15 (*a*) Ideal output of first chopper. (*b*) Ideal output of second chopper.

The amplifier of Fig. 10-14 is generally referred to as a *chopper* type of amplifier. It is well named since the input d-c signal is literally chopped to produce an a-c signal. The chopping action can be done either by mechanical means, such as a vibrating reed, or by electronic means, one system being that shown in Fig. 10-16. The oscillator signal enters the input modulator and is modulated by the input signal. The output of the modulator is a signal of the same frequency as the oscillator, but the peak value of this signal is proportional to the size of the d-c input. For a zero d-c input, there is *no* modulator output. (This is different from the

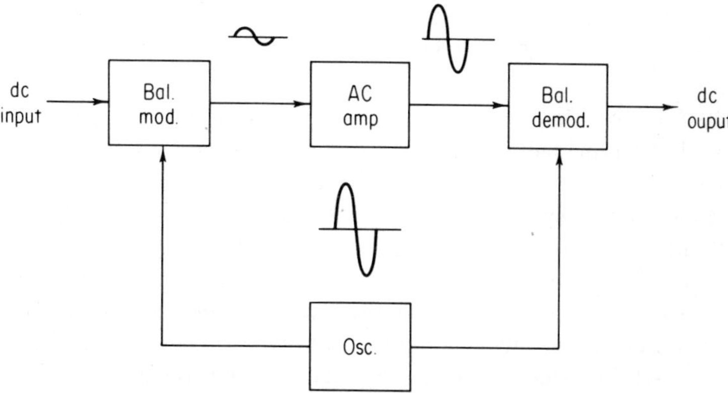

Fig. 10-16 Electronic chopper type of d-c amplifier.

common type of modulator, in which a continuous-wave output occurs for a zero modulating signal.) The modulator of Fig. 10-16 is said to be balanced because there is no output unless an input modulating signal is present. The modulator output is now amplified in a conventional a-c amplifier and then demodulated to recover the d-c signal.

The system can also handle low-frequency input signals. In this case, the oscillator signal is modulated by the low-frequency input. The output of the modulator is amplified and then demodulated to recover the original input frequency.

The chopped amplifier of Fig. 10-14 or the modulated type of Fig. 10-16 has the decided advantage of far less drift than the direct-coupled amplifiers of Sec. 10-5. The only sources of drift are in the input chopper or modulator. The drift in these units is much smaller than the drift in the first stage of a direct-coupled amplifier.

10-7 One Type of Input Modulator

In this section we examine one popular type of input modulator. Figure 10-17 shows the schematic of a typical input modulator suitable for use

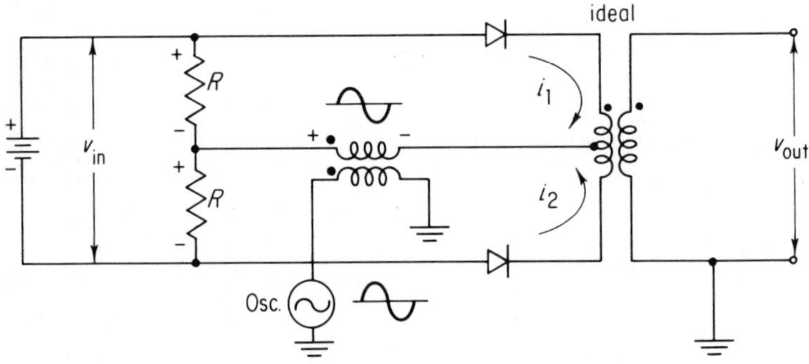

Fig. 10-17 An input modulator.

in a system like that of Fig. 10-16. A battery is shown across the input terminals to represent the input d-c signal. Note that for a *zero* input d-c signal both diodes are being driven only by the oscillator signal. Assuming that both diodes are identical and that the primary is tapped exactly at the center, there will be no output. We can see this by analyzing the circuit action over one complete cycle. For instance, during the positive half cycle of the oscillator input, both diodes are being turned on. The current i_1 and i_2 will be equal, and since these currents flow in opposite directions, the net flux in the primary will be zero. Therefore, no signal is induced in the secondary. During the negative half cycle of oscillator input, both diodes are off, and once again there is no output signal. Hence, the modulator is balanced because with no input, there is no output.

The waveforms for the currents under the zero-input-signal condition are shown in Fig. 10-18*a*. Note that the currents are essentially half-wave-rectified sinusoids with equal peak values.

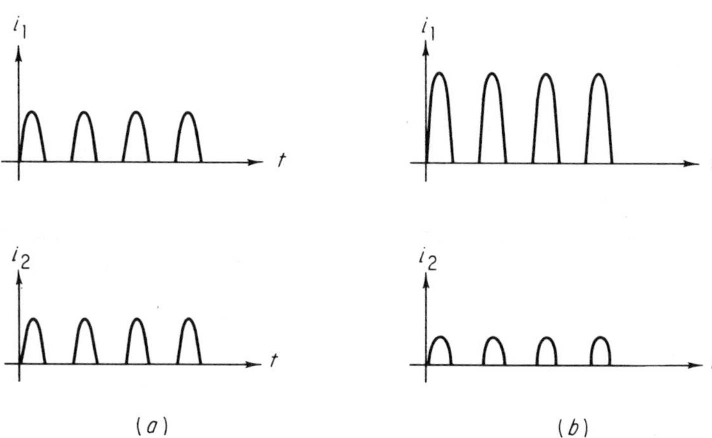

Fig. 10-18 Input modulator currents. (*a*) For zero input signal. (*b*) For d-c input signal.

Suppose that we now consider the circuit action for a d-c input signal. A positive d-c voltage at the input terminals will produce plus-minus d-c voltages across the R resistors, as shown in Fig. 10-17. During the positive half cycle of the oscillator signal, a plus-minus voltage appears across the oscillator secondary. By inspection of the upper diode loop we see that the d-c voltage across R aids the oscillator signal, whereas in the lower loop the voltages are in opposition. Because of this, the upper diode conducts more heavily than the lower diode, with the result that i_1 is greater than i_2.

Figure 10-18*b* illustrates the current waveforms for a positive d-c input signal. Since i_1 is greater than i_2, there is a net flux in the primary which induces an output voltage in the secondary. The output voltage will be proportional to the difference of i_1 and i_2 and therefore has the shape illustrated in Fig. 10-19*a*. The size of v_{out} is proportional to the size of the d-c input signal. If the d-c signal is reduced to zero, v_{out} becomes zero.

If the battery of Fig. 10-17 is reversed, the voltages across the R resistors are reversed. In this case, the lower diode conducts more heavily than the upper diode, so that a negative-going output is obtained, as shown in Fig. 10-19*b*.

The modulator of Fig. 10-17 will also accommodate low-frequency input signals. In fact, we may think of a low-frequency sinusoid as a battery whose value is being varied, first positively, and then negatively. With this viewpoint, the modulator output resembles the waveshape of Fig. 10-19*c*.

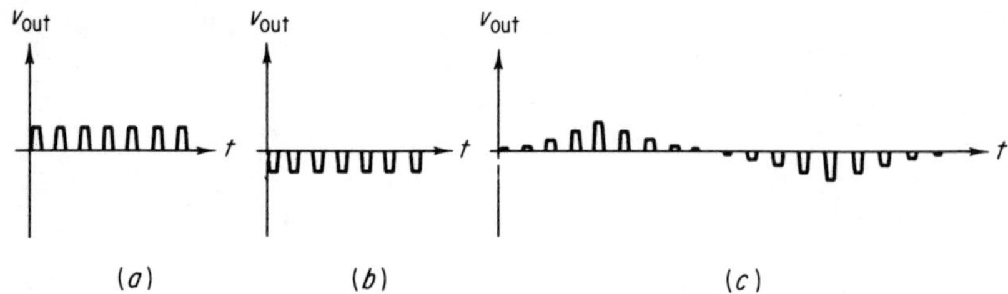

Fig. 10-19 Modulator output voltages. (*a*) For positive d-c input. (*b*) For negative d-c input. (*c*) For low-frequency a-c input.

Even though the ideal waveforms of Fig. 10-19 are not the same as the ones in Fig. 10-16, nevertheless, they are a-c signals and can be amplified prior to demodulation.

The circuit of Fig. 10-17 will actually have unbalance between the two diode loops. In other words, both diodes will not be exactly identical, and the transformer cannot be conveniently tapped at the exact electrical center. Because of this, there will be a residual output signal for a zero-input condition. Further, there are two transformers.

More practical versions of a balanced modulator are shown in Fig. 10-20. Note that only one transformer is required, and an adjustment has been added to allow balancing the demodulator under the zero-input-signal condition. The circuits of Fig. 10-20 and variations are quite popular in practice. The waveforms obtained are essentially the same as those of Fig. 10-19.

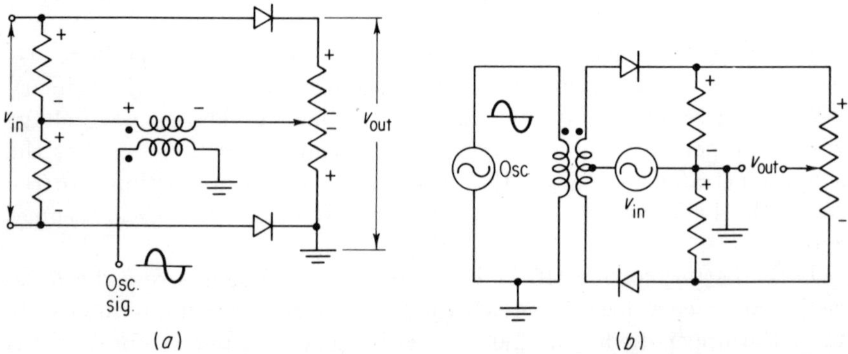

Fig. 10-20 Practical versions of balanced modulators.

10-8 A Basic Demodulator

We now examine a simple demodulator that is suitable for a system like that of Fig. 10-16. In Fig. 10-21 we have a typical demodulator. The same oscillator signal used for the modulator is applied to the demodulator. Let us first consider the case of zero input signal. With no input, only the oscillator signal is driving the diodes. Recall the peak detectors studied in Chap. 4. In the circuit of Fig. 10-21, the RC time constants

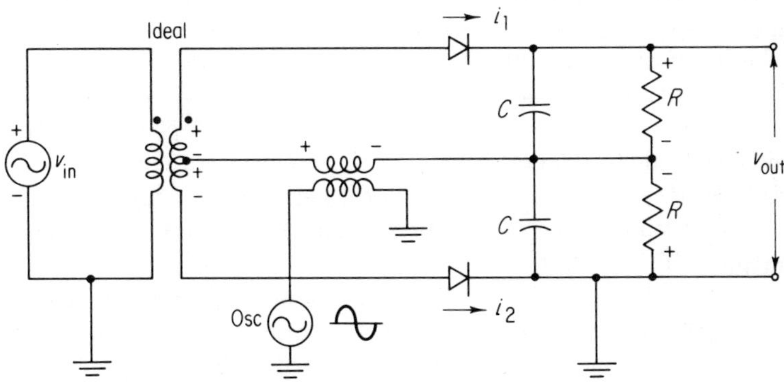

Fig. 10-21 A balanced demodulator.

are chosen large enough so that peak detection occurs. The upper diode is part of one peak detector, and the lower diode is part of a second peak detector. With an oscillator signal driving the diodes, the capacitors charge to the peak value of the oscillator signal. However, the voltages across the capacitors are of opposite polarity, so that the output voltage is zero. Hence, for zero input there is zero output.

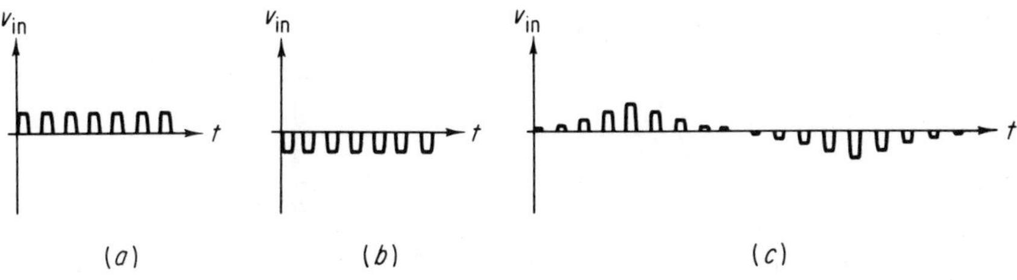

Fig. 10-22 Input signals to the demodulator.

What happens if we now have an input signal as shown in Fig. 10-22a? This input signal will induce voltages across the secondary with the polarity indicated. Note that the first half cycle of input signal is in phase with the first half cycle of oscillator signal. Because of this, the voltages in the upper loop are aiding, whereas they are opposing in the lower loop. This means that a larger peak voltage is detected in the upper loop than in the lower loop. As a result, the d-c voltage across the upper capacitor is larger than the d-c voltage across the lower one. The output voltage is the difference of the two capacitor voltages. Therefore, v_{out} will be a positive d-c voltage.

Suppose that the input voltage is the waveform of Fig. 10-22*b*. In this case, the polarities on the secondary winding of Fig. 10-21 are reversed, and a larger peak voltage is detected by the lower diode. The effect is that the d-c voltage across the lower capacitor is larger than that across the upper capacitor, so that v_{out} becomes a negative d-c voltage.

If the input signal to the demodulator is the waveform shown in Fig. 10-22*c*, the output voltage will merely follow the envelope of this waveform, provided that the *RC* time constants of the peak detectors are correctly chosen. In general, the *RC* time constant in each peak detector should be large compared to the oscillator period time but small compared to the period time of the modulating signal. If this condition is satisfied, the output will be able to follow the envelope of the waveform shown in Fig. 10-22*c*, and the original modulating signal will be recovered.

A more practical version of the basic demodulator is shown in Fig. 10-23. Note that one of the diodes has been reversed and the oscillator signal is driving the primary. The input signal is capacitively coupled, thus eliminating a transformer. A balance adjustment has been added to eliminate any unbalance between the two peak detectors.

The circuit operation of Fig. 10-23 is still essentially the same as before. There are two peak detectors. The input signal aids the oscillator on one side and opposes it on the other. As a result, the output signal obtained is directly proportional to the input signal provided that the input signal is small compared to the oscillator signal.

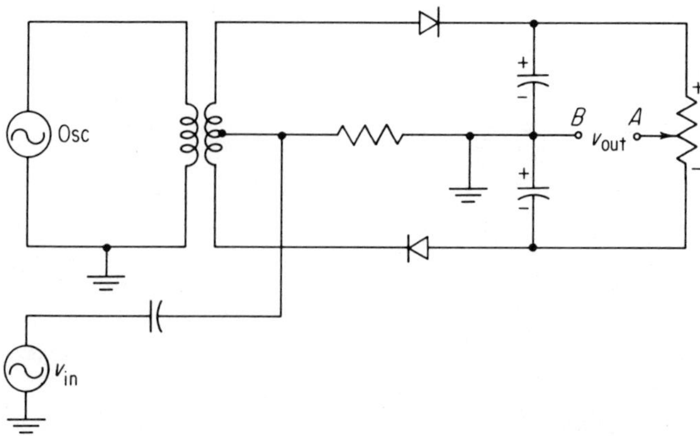

Fig. 10-23 Practical version of demodulator.

10-9 A Phase Detector

It is worthwhile mentioning at this time that the demodulator of Fig. 10-21 or 10-23 can also be used in another way. Suppose that the oscillator signal and the input signal are both sinusoidal, as shown in Fig. 10-24*a*. The frequencies are equal, but the input signal is out of phase with the oscillator signal by an angle of ϕ.

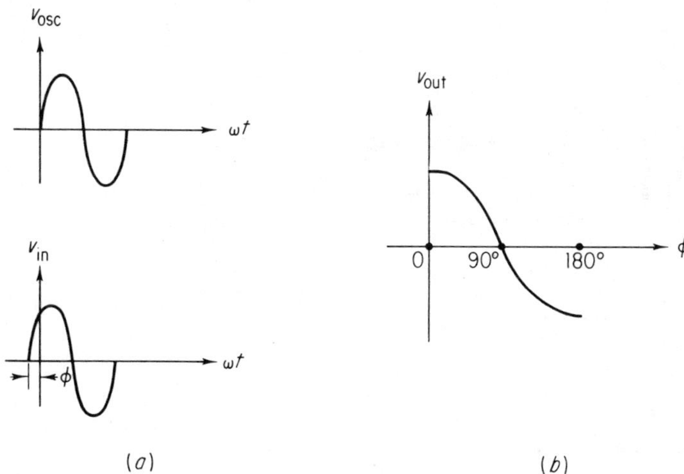

Fig. 10-24 Phase detector. (*a*) Input signals. (*b*) D-c output voltage versus phase angle.

We already know from the preceding section that if ϕ is zero, the signals are in phase, and v_{out} equals a positive d-c voltage. On the other hand, if ϕ equals 180°, v_{out} equals a negative d-c voltage.

It can be shown either mathematically or experimentally that for ϕ equals 90°, the value of v_{out} is zero. This result makes sense. Since 90° is midway between an angle of 0 and 180°, we would expect the output d-c voltage to be between the positive d-c voltage obtained for 0° and the negative d-c voltage obtained for 180°. In other words, as the phase angle ϕ between the two sinusoidal signals changes from 0 to 180°, the output voltage must change from a positive d-c value to a negative d-c value. This implies that the output voltage must pass through a zero value, and this zero value occurs when ϕ equals 90°.

Furthermore, it can be shown that for intermediate angles, the output d-c voltage is proportional to the cosine of the phase angle ϕ.

Figure 10-24*b* illustrates the relation between the output d-c voltage and the phase angle. The shape is that of a cosine function and indicates that the demodulators studied in the preceding section can be used to detect the phase angle.

EXAMPLE 10-5

A phase detector has a characteristic as shown in Fig. 10-24*b*. The maximum positive value is 2 volts. Find the output d-c voltage if the phase angle between two sinusoids is 60°.

SOLUTION

The output voltage is a cosine function with a peak value of 2. Hence,

$$v_{out} = 2 \cos \phi$$
$$v_{out} = 2 \cos 60° = 1 \text{ volt d-c}$$

10-10 The Difference Amplifier

One more special type of amplifier will be studied in this chapter, the so-called *difference amplifier*, or differential amplifier. Let us first discuss

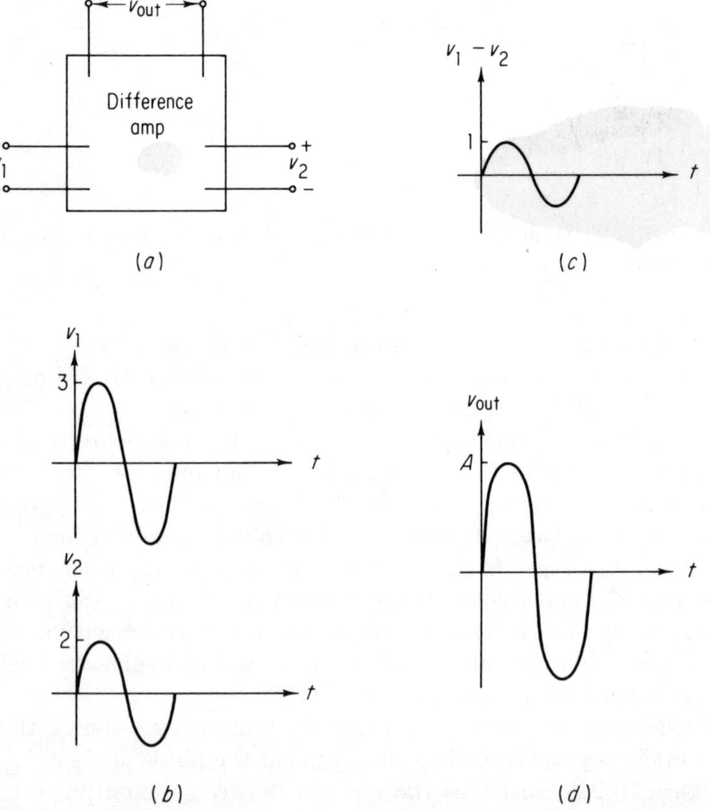

Fig. 10-25 Difference amplifier. (*a*) Block diagram. (*b*) Input signals. (*c*) Difference of input signals. (*d*) Output of difference amplifier.

the basic purpose of this amplifier, a block diagram of which is shown in Fig. 10-25*a*. Note that it has two inputs and one output. It is designed in such a way as to subtract v_2 from v_1 and then amplify this difference, $v_1 - v_2$. By way of illustration, suppose that v_1 and v_2 are sine waves, as shown in Fig. 10-25*b*. The frequencies are equal, but the peak value of v_1 is 3 volts while the peak value of v_2 is 2 volts. Since the frequencies are equal and in phase, $v_1 - v_2$ is simply a new sine wave with a peak value of 1 volt, as shown in Fig. 10-25*c*. The final output signal is then the amplified version shown in Fig. 10-25*d*.

As another example, consider the waveforms of Fig. 10-26*a*. The frequencies are equal but are 180° out of phase. The algebraic difference of v_1 and v_2 is a sine wave with a peak value of $3 - (-2)$, or 5 volts, as shown in Fig. 10-26*a*. This difference is then amplified.

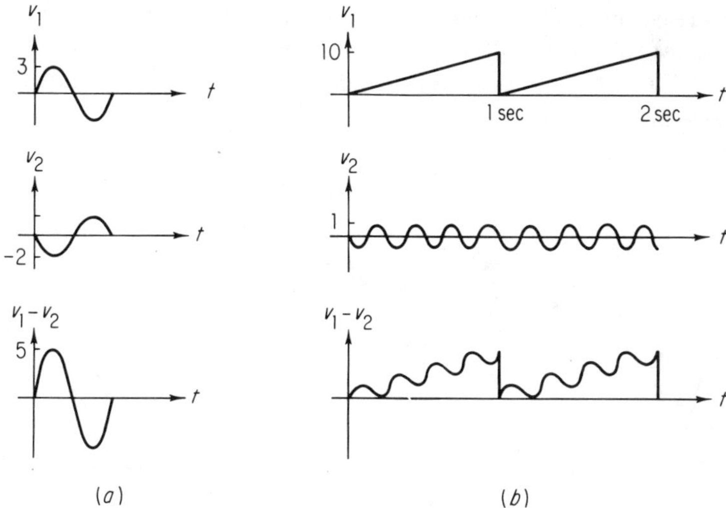

Fig. 10-26 Example of difference-amplifier signals.

As a final example, consider the waveforms shown in Fig. 10-26*b*. The v_1 signal is a sawtooth with a period time of 1 sec. The v_2 signal is a sine wave with a period time of 0.25 sec. At any one instant in time, we must subtract the value of v_2 from the value of v_1, obtaining a waveform as shown in Fig. 10-26*b*. The output of the difference amplifier is simply an amplified version of $v_1 - v_2$.

A tube version of the difference amplifier is shown in Fig. 10-27. There are two inputs, v_1 and v_2. There is one output, v_{out}, taken from the AB terminals. Two power supplies are needed for this circuit, a positive $B+$ and a negative $B-$ supply.

Let us obtain a qualitative feel for what this circuit does by considering a specific example. Suppose that v_1 is a 1-volt-peak sine wave and that v_2 is zero, as shown in Fig. 10-28. During the positive half cycle of v_1,

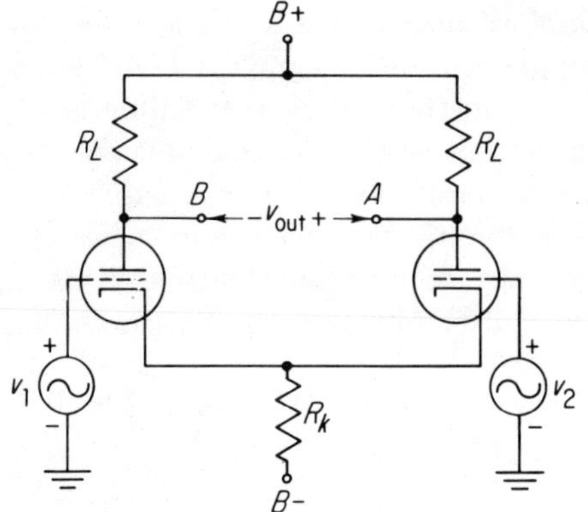

Fig. 10-27 Vacuum-tube difference amplifier.

the grid of the *left* tube is going positive, so that plate current increases. This increase in plate current produces a larger drop across the plate load resistor so that the plate voltage is negative-going, as shown. (This action is the same as in a single-stage amplifier, where a 180° phase shift occurs.)

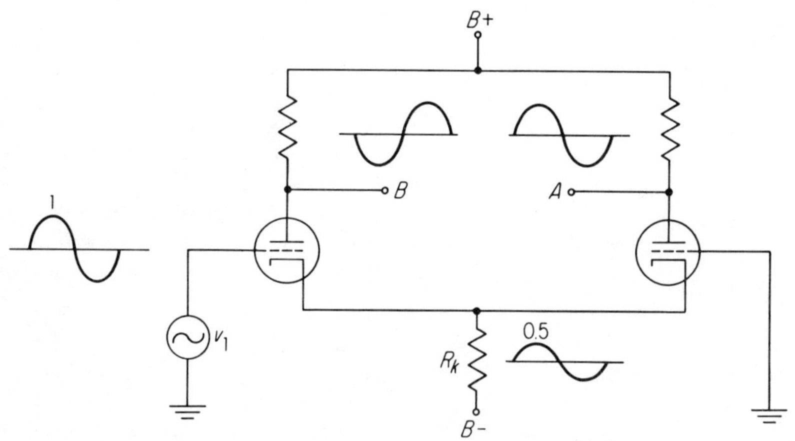

Fig. 10-28 Difference amplifier with one input.

What happens at the cathode? During the positive half cycle of v_1, the plate current in the left tube is increasing, so that more current flows through the common cathode resistor R_K. This will produce a positive-going signal, as shown. The size of this signal is about one-half the size of v_1, that is, about 0.5 volt. Because the cathode signal is going positive during the first half cycle, the current in the right tube is reduced. With less plate current in the right tube, the voltage drop across the plate resistor is less, and we obtain a positive-going signal from the plate of the right tube to ground.

The signals shown on each plate of Fig. 10-28 are equal in magnitude but 180° out of phase. The output voltage from A to B will then be a sine wave with a peak value of twice the size of either plate signal.

What happens if v_1 is a 1-volt-peak sine wave and v_2 is also a 1-volt-peak in-phase sine wave? It should be clear that if both sides of the difference amplifier are identical, the net effect will be a zero output signal.

Sometimes, it is helpful to visualize this circuit as a bridge, as shown in Fig. 10-29. Each tube represents a d-c resistance which is controlled

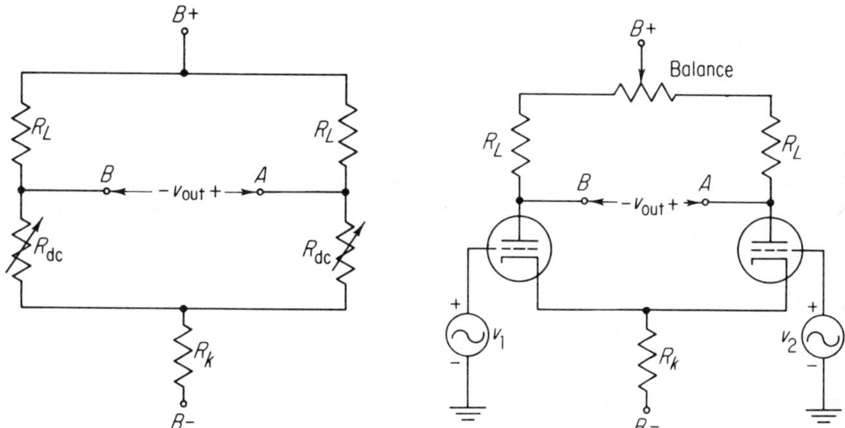

Fig. 10-29 Interpretation of difference amplifier as a bridge.

Fig. 10-30 Difference amplifier with balance adjustment.

by the input signals. If both input signals are equal, each tube resistance is equal, and the bridge remains balanced. If signals are unequal, then of course the bridge is unbalanced, and an output is obtained from the AB terminals.

It can be shown using equivalent circuits for the tubes that the output voltage of a difference amplifier such as shown in Fig. 10-27 is approximately

$$v_{\text{out}} = \frac{\mu}{1 + r_p/R_L}(v_1 - v_2) \tag{10-8}$$

This equation should be easy to remember since the coefficient of $v_1 - v_2$ is the voltage gain of a single common-cathode stage. Equation (10-8) tells us that the output voltage of a difference amplifier is the algebraic difference of v_1 and v_2 multiplied by a constant.

Since we cannot expect both sides of the difference amplifier to be exactly identical, we cannot expect a perfect balance with a zero input unless we add an adjustment. This adjustment may be placed in any number of points in the circuit. A typical circuit with such an adjustment is shown in Fig. 10-30. To balance the difference amplifier, we merely adjust the potentiometer until v_{out} is zero under the no-input-signal condition.

A transistorized version of the difference amplifier is shown in Fig. 10-31*a*. For identical transistors, analysis shows that the output voltage

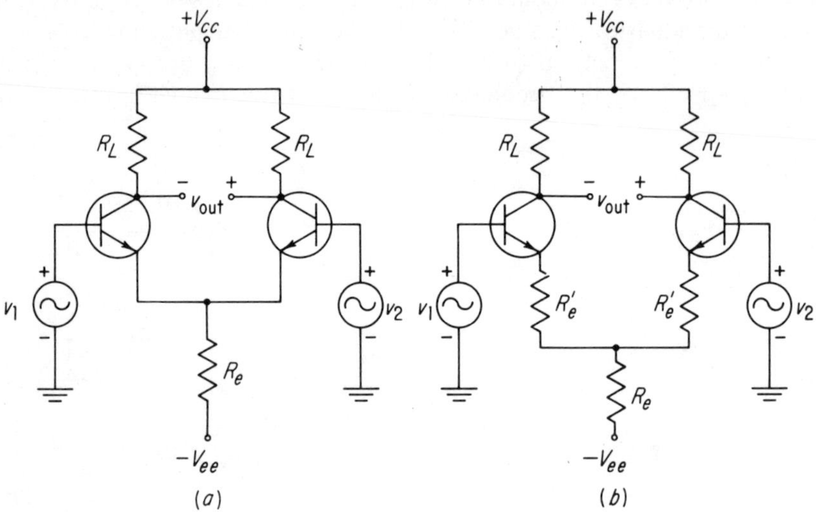

Fig. 10-31 Transistorized difference amplifiers. (*a*) Without degeneration. (*b*) With degeneration.

equals the voltage gain of a single common-emitter stage times the difference of the input voltages. That is,

$$v_{out} \cong \beta \frac{R_L}{R_{in}} (v_1 - v_2) \tag{10-9}$$

If the transistors are not identical, average values may be used for β and R_{in}. Also, a balance adjustment may be added.

The voltage gain of the circuit of Fig. 10-31*a* depends upon the β and R_{in} of the transistors. To improve the voltage-gain stability, resistors are often added in each emitter as shown in Fig. 10-31*b*. With this circuit the output voltage is

$$v_{out} \cong \frac{R_L}{R'_e} (v_1 - v_2) \tag{10-10}$$

The difference amplifier is an important circuit and finds application in many systems where it is necessary to subtract two signals, as in analog computers, oscilloscopes, radar, etc.

Example 10-6

In Fig. 10-27, the μ of each tube is 50, r_p is 10 kilohms, and R_L is 40 kilohms. Find the voltage gain.

SOLUTION

$$A = \frac{v_{out}}{v_1 - v_2} = \frac{\mu}{1 + r_p/R_L} = \frac{50}{1 + 10(10^3)/40(10^3)} = 40$$

EXAMPLE 10-7

In Example 10-6, what is the output voltage if v_1 is a sine wave with a 0.1-volt peak and v_2 is an in-phase equal-frequency sine wave with a 0.07-volt peak?

SOLUTION

The algebraic difference, $v_1 - v_2$, will be a sine wave with a peak value of 0.1 − 0.07, or 0.03 volt. Hence, the output will be an amplified sine wave with a peak value of 40(0.03), or 1.2 volts.

EXAMPLE 10-8

For the transistor circuit of Fig. 10-31*a*, the β is 50, R_{in} is 1 kilohm, and R_L is 10 kilohms. Find the approximate voltage gain.

SOLUTION

$$\frac{v_{out}}{v_1 - v_2} = \beta \frac{R_L}{R_{in}} = 50 \frac{10(10^3)}{10^3} = 500$$

EXAMPLE 10-9

In Example 10-8, v_1 and v_2 have the same frequency but are 180° out of phase. If the rms value of v_1 is 100 μv and the rms value of v_2 is 60 μv, find the output rms voltage.

SOLUTION

The algebraic difference of the two 180° out-of-phase sine waves is

$$100\ \mu\text{v} - (-60\ \mu\text{v}) = 160\ \mu\text{v rms}$$

Hence $$v_{out} = 500(160)(10^{-6}) = 80\ \text{mv rms}$$

SUMMARY

An a-c amplifier may be thought of as an active bandpass filter that provides gain in the passband. The upper and lower cutoff frequencies are defined as those frequencies at which the voltage gain has dropped to 0.707 of the passband value.

A d-c amplifier may be thought of as a low-pass filter. The frequency response extends down to zero frequency.

In dealing with amplifiers operating in the passband, three important characteristics emerge: the input resistance, the output resistance, and the value of open-circuit voltage gain. It is essential to know the value of these quantities in order to predict how the amplifier will operate when connected to a source and load.

For an unmatched amplifier where the input resistance is much larger than the source resistance and where the load resistance is much greater than the output resistance of the amplifier, the voltage gain from source to load is equal to the open-circuit voltage gain of the amplifier. A considerable improvement in voltage gain can be made by matching the amplifier on the input and output sides.

A d-c amplifier may be constructed in either of two basic ways. First, all capacitors are removed to allow operation down to zero frequency. This creates drift problems. Second, the d-c signal can be converted to an a-c signal, then amplified, and finally converted back to a d-c signal.

A balanced demodulator can also be used as a phase detector. In this application the output voltage of the balanced demodulator is proportional to the phase angle between the sinusoids.

The difference amplifier takes the algebraic difference of two input signals and amplifies this difference. Vacuum-tube and transistor versions are widely used.

GLOSSARY

a-c amplifier An amplifier with a lower and upper cutoff frequency.

cascade Stages connected together so that the output of one stage is used as the input to the next stage.

chopped d-c amplifier An amplifier which first converts the d-c input to an a-c signal before amplification. After amplifying, the a-c signal is demodulated to recover an amplified version of the d-c input.

completely unmatched amplifier An amplifier whose input resistance is much larger than the source resistance and whose output resistance is much smaller than the load resistance.

d-c amplifier An amplifier with no lower cutoff frequency.

difference amplifier An amplifier with two inputs. The output is an amplified version of the algebraic difference of the two input signals.

impedance-matched amplifier An amplifier whose input resistance equals the source resistance and whose output resistance equals the load resistance.

phase detector A balanced mixer or demodulator with two input signals of equal frequency. The output is a d-c voltage determined by the phase angle between the two input signals.

tube parameters These are the g_m, r_p, and μ of a tube.

REVIEW QUESTIONS

1. What is the usual cause of the lower cutoff frequency in an a-c amplifier? The upper cutoff frequency?
2. What are the approximations for finding the lower and upper cutoff frequencies of a cascade of identical amplifier stages?
3. To amplify extremely low frequencies what kind of amplifier is used?
4. What is the equivalent circuit for an amplifier in its passband?
5. In the amplifier equivalent circuit developed in this chapter what is the meaning of A?
6. For the completely unmatched case where $R_{\text{in}} \gg R_o$ and $R_L \gg R_{\text{out}}$, what is the value of voltage gain from the generator to the load?
7. When is it generally necessary to match an amplifier to the source and load resistance?
8. Since matching an amplifier improves the voltage gain, explain why not all amplifiers are matched.
9. Describe three methods for building a direct-coupled amplifier.
10. In a chopped d-c amplifier, why is it impossible to obtain a perfect square wave from the input chopper?
11. What does the word "balanced" mean when speaking of a balanced modulator or demodulator?
12. What advantage does a chopper type of d-c amplifier have over the direct-coupled amplifier?
13. If the demodulator of Fig. 10-21 is to recover the modulating signal, what must be true about the value of the RC time constant in each peak detector?
14. What effect does the use of nonidentical diodes have on the performance of the demodulator shown in Fig. 10-21?
15. What is the output d-c voltage of a balanced demodulator if the input signal is 90° out of phase with the oscillator signal?
16. Why is a balanced demodulator also called a phase detector?
17. What is a difference amplifier?
18. Why is an adjustment usually necessary in a difference amplifier?

PROBLEMS

10-1 An amplifier consists of four identical stages of gain. If the lower cutoff frequency of each stage is 20 Hz and the upper cutoff frequency is 20 kHz, what are the lower and upper cutoff frequencies of the four-stage amplifier?

10-2 An amplifier consists of six stages of gain. The first two stages have cutoff frequencies of 20 Hz and 20 kHz. The next two stages have cutoff frequencies of 15 Hz and 25 kHz. The last two stages have cutoff frequencies of 25 Hz and 15 kHz. What are the approximate values of cutoff frequencies for the six-stage amplifier?

10-3 An amplifier has an input resistance of 50 kilohms, an output resistance of 50 ohms, and an open-circuit voltage gain of 75. If this amplifier is driven by a 600-ohm source and is loaded by a 10 kilohm resistor, what is the exact value of voltage gain from generator to load? What is the approximate value using the unmatched-case approach?

10-4 If the amplifier of Problem 10-3 is matched to the source and load resistances, what is the voltage gain from generator to load? If ideal transformers are used for matching, what are the correct turns ratios?

10-5 If the amplifier of Problem 10-3 is matched only on the input side, what is the voltage gain from source to load? Express the answer in decibels.

10-6 In Fig. 10-11 the voltages for the cathodes are obtained from a tapped voltage divider, as shown. If the total resistance of the voltage divider is 2000 ohms, what sizes should be used for R_1 to R_4?

10-7 In Fig. 10-12, the correct voltage for each grid is obtained by means of voltage dividers between stages. What are the correct sizes of R_1 to R_6 if the total resistance in any one voltage divider is 100 kilohms?

10-8 In Fig. 10-14, the input chopper uses a transformer with a one-to-one turns ratio and v_{in} equals 0.05 volt d-c. Assuming the ideal square wave out of the amplifier, what will the peak value of this square wave be if the amplifier voltage gain is 100?

10-9 A phase detector has a characteristic as shown in Fig. 10-24*b*. The maximum positive value of this cosine function is 10 volts.

(*a*) What is the output d-c voltage for a phase angle of 180°?

(*b*) What is the d-c output for $\phi = 60°$?

10-10 A difference amplifier has a voltage gain of 10. If one input is a 10-mv sawtooth and the other is a 10-mv-peak sine wave, sketch the output voltage. Assume that both signals start to rise at zero time and are equal in frequency.

10-11 In the circuit of Fig. 10-27, $\mu = 30$, $r_p = 15$ kilohms, and $R_L = 30$ kilohms. If v_1 is a 50-mv-peak sine wave and v_2 is zero, what is the output voltage?

10-12 In Fig. 10-31*a*, $V_{cc} = 30$ volts and $-V_{ee} = -30$ volts; $R_L = 10$ kilohms. What size should R_e be in order to produce a d-c collector voltage of 15 volts?

10-13 In Fig. 10-31*a*, $R_L = 20$ kilohms, $R_{in} = 1$ kilohm, and $\beta = 40$. Find the voltage gain of the stage.

10-14 In Fig. 10-31*b*, $R_L = 20$ kilohms, $R'_e = 2$ kilohms, and $\beta = 75$. Find the voltage gain.

11 Electronic Voltmeters

The simple voltmeters studied in earlier chapters have two basic disadvantages: they tend to load the circuit under test, especially on lower ranges, and they cannot be used to measure extremely low d-c or a-c voltages in the millivolt or microvolt region.

In this chapter we examine some basic ideas behind electronic voltmeters. We will see that considerable improvement can be made both in reducing the loading error and in improving sensitivity. We will also examine one of the basic methods used in making true rms voltage measurements.

11-1 The Difference-amplifier Type of VTVM

To increase the input resistance of a d-c voltmeter we can use vacuum tubes between the circuit under test and the d-c meter, the idea being to isolate the relatively low meter resistance from the circuit being tested.

One of the basic circuits used in building a vacuum-tube voltmeter (VTVM) is shown in Fig. 11-1. Note that this circuit is the difference amplifier studied in the last chapter. An ammeter is connected across the AB terminals of the amplifier. How does the circuit operate?

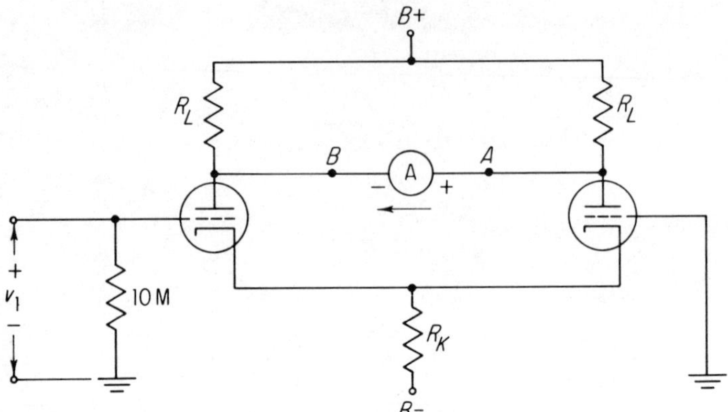

Fig. 11-1 The difference-amplifier type of VTVM.

Clearly, with identical triodes, the circuit is balanced, so that for a zero input, there is no current through the ammeter. If the grid of the left tube is connected to a circuit so that a positive d-c voltage appears across the input, a current will flow through the ammeter in the direction shown. The size of this current will be a function of the input voltage. By properly designing the circuit, the ammeter current will be directly proportional to the value of d-c voltage across the input. As a result, the ammeter can be calibrated in volts so as to indicate the input voltage.

The relation between the ammeter current and the input d-c voltage can be found by using Thévenin's theorem, where the ammeter is considered the load. If we remove the ammeter, the circuit of Fig. 11-2*a* is the difference amplifier studied in the last chapter. Recall that the out-

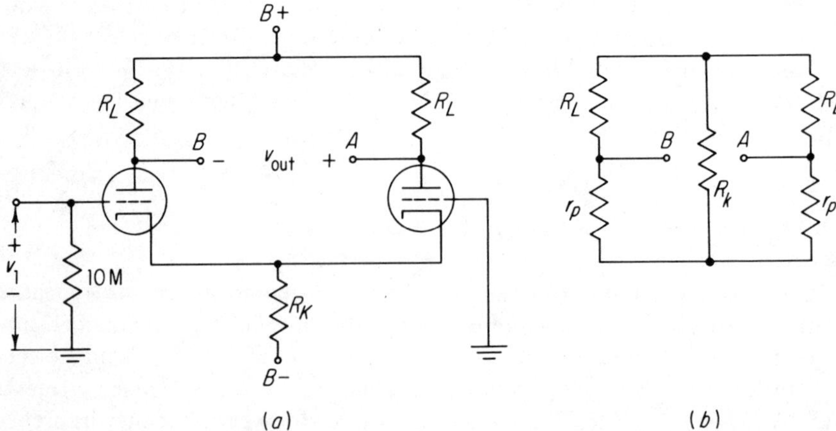

Fig. 11-2 Applying Thévenin's theorem to the VTVM. (*a*) Removing the load to find V_{oc}. (*b*) Setting all voltages equal to zero to find R_o.

put voltage is the voltage gain of a single tube times the difference of v_1 and v_2. Since v_2 is zero, the output voltage under open-circuit conditions is

$$v_{\text{out}} = \frac{\mu}{1 + r_p/R_L} v_1$$

To find the Thévenin resistance looking back into the AB terminals, we first set v_1 and the d-c supplies equal to zero. Under this condition both tubes have a resistance of r_p, as shown in Fig. 11-2*b*. From this balanced circuit we see that the resistance between the A and B terminals is

$$R_o = 2r_p \| 2R_L = 2(r_p \| R_L)$$

We may now show the Thévenin equivalent circuit with the ammeter connected as a load (see Fig. 11-3). From this circuit it is clear that the ammeter current is

$$i = \frac{\mu}{1 + r_p/R_L} \frac{v_1}{2(r_p \| R_L) + R_m} \qquad (11\text{-}1)$$

Equation (11-1) relates the ammeter current to the input d-c voltage. As already indicated, it assumes that both triodes are identical. For nonidentical tubes, an approximate relation can be obtained by using the average values of μ and r_p.

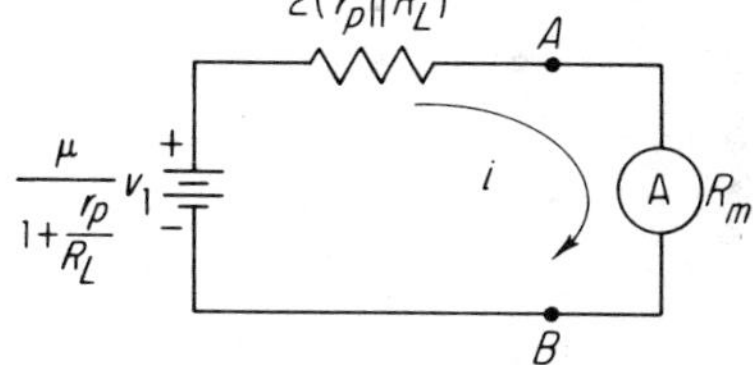

Fig. 11-3 Equivalent circuit for the difference-amplifier type of VTVM.

As an example of using Eq. (11-1), let us assume the following set of values: $\mu = 20$, $r_p = 10$ kilohms, $R_L = 10$ kilohms, and $R_m = 50$ ohms. Substituting these values in Eq. (11-1), we obtain

$$i = \frac{20}{1 + 10(10^3)/10(10^3)} \frac{v_1}{2[10(10^3) \| 10(10^3)] + 50} = \frac{10v_1}{10(10^3) + 50}$$
$$\cong 10^{-3}v_1$$

Note what this final result indicates. First, it tells us that the ammeter current is directly proportional to the input voltage. Hence, the ammeter may be marked off in uniform divisions. Second, an input of 1 volt yields a current of 1 ma. Thus, if we wish to have a 0- to 1-volt indicator, we would mark 1 volt at full scale on an ammeter with a full-scale current of 1 ma. The remainder of the scale would be marked off in a linear manner.

The circuit of Fig. 11-1 can be made practical by adding certain adjustments and switches, as shown in Fig. 11-4. First, note the addition of a zero adjustment, the purpose of which is to equalize both halves of the difference amplifier so that there is no current through the ammeter under zero-signal conditions.

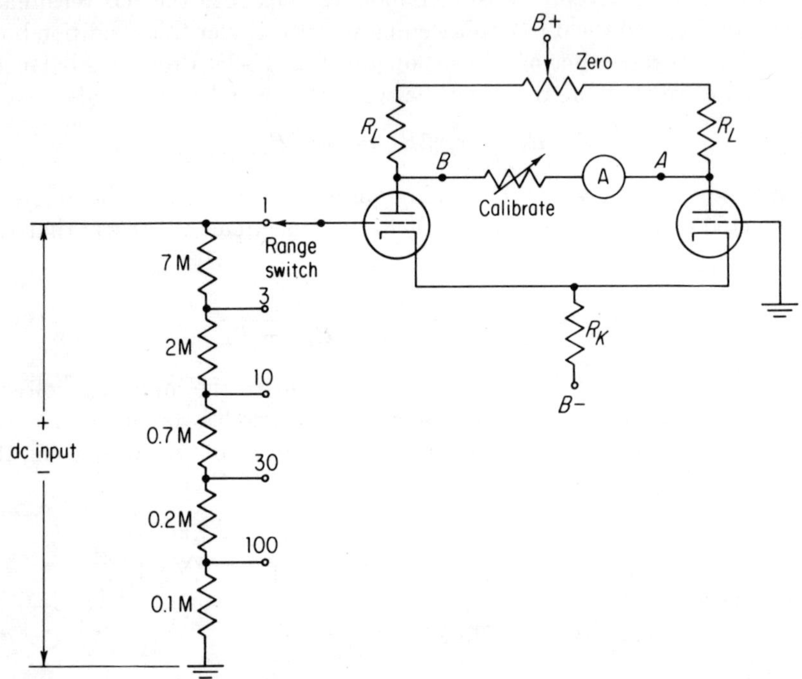

Fig. 11-4 A practical version of the difference-amplifier type of VTVM.

Second, there is a calibration adjust for the purpose of accurately setting the full-scale reading of the ammeter. This adjustment is necessary because μ and r_p are different from tube to tube. From Eq. (11-1) it should be clear that for a fixed value of v_1, different values of current will flow if μ and r_p change from tube to tube. Hence, by adding an adjustable resistance in series with the ammeter, we can adjust the full-scale reading for different tubes. For example, if the ammeter is marked 1 volt at full scale, we would calibrate by measuring an input that is exactly 1 volt. The calibration adjust would be set to give a reading of exactly 1 volt.

Third, there is a range switch on the input to allow several different full-scale ranges. The input resistance is 10 megohms on any position. With the switch in the position shown, the voltmeter is on its most sensitive range and will read up to 1 volt at full scale. For higher input voltages, the range switch is moved to a lower tap point. For example, if the input voltage is 50 volts, the range switch must be moved to the lowest tap point, which corresponds to the 100-volt range. The voltmeter would then read midscale 50 volts.

The VTVM of Fig. 11-4 is a vast improvement over the simple d-c voltmeters discussed in earlier chapters. The very high input impedance of 10 megohms that is typical (it can be made even higher) is undoubtedly the principal advantage of a VTVM. When using the VTVM we are virtually assured that loading effects are negligible for most typical circuits.

The lowest range for the circuit of Fig. 11-4 is the 1-volt range. We do not attempt to go any lower because the drift in this circuit is a limiting factor.

11-2 The Cathode-follower Type of VTVM

Another of the basic VTVM circuits is the circuit shown in Fig. 11-5. The ammeter has been moved so that it bridges the two cathodes. For identical tubes it is clear that the circuit is balanced, so that for zero signal input, there is no ammeter current. If v_1 is a positive input voltage, current flows through the ammeter in the direction indicated.

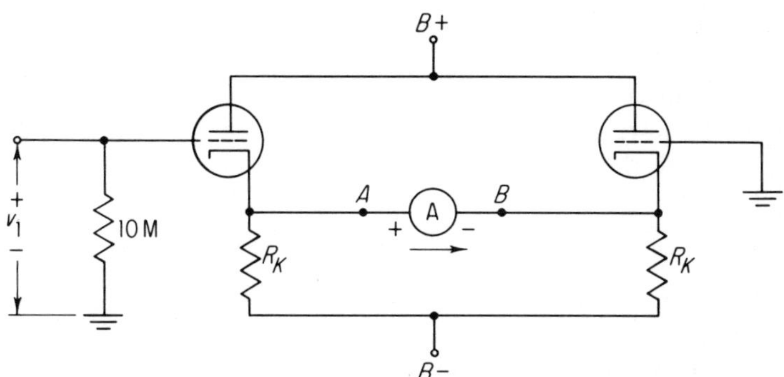

Fig. 11-5 The cathode-follower VTVM.

We can find the relation between the ammeter current and the input voltage by using Thévenin's theorem at the AB terminals. To find the open-circuit voltage, we remove the ammeter, as shown in Fig. 11-6*a*. Under this condition, the grid of the right tube is grounded, and therefore no signal appears at terminal B. The left tube, however, is a cathode follower. Recall from basic electronics courses that the output voltage from a cathode follower is

$$v_{\text{out}} = \frac{\mu}{\mu + 1} \frac{R_K}{R_K + r_p/(\mu + 1)} v_1$$

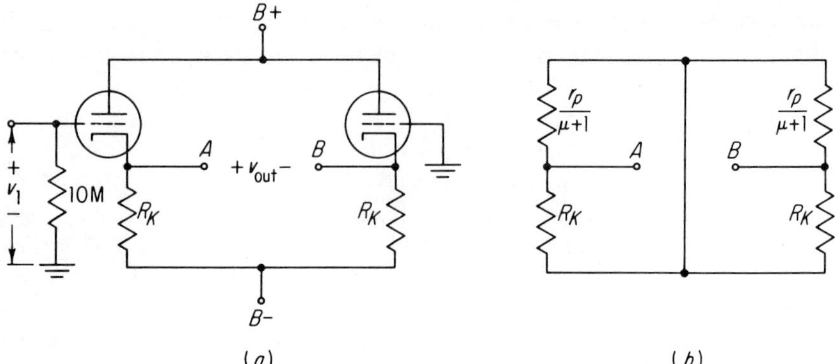

Fig. 11-6 Applying Thévenin's theorem to the cathode-follower VTVM. (*a*) Removing the ammeter to find V_{oc}. (*b*) Setting all voltages equal to zero to find R_o.

To find the Thévenin resistance looking back into the *AB* terminals, recall that because of the degeneration taking place in the cathode follower, the resistance seen looking into the cathode is $r_p/(\mu + 1)$, as shown in Fig. 11-6*b*. From this circuit we can see that the Thévenin resistance is

$$R_o = R_K \left\| \frac{r_p}{\mu + 1} + R_K \right\| \frac{r_p}{\mu + 1} = 2\left(R_k \left\| \frac{r_p}{\mu + 1}\right.\right)$$

The Thévenin equivalent with the ammeter connected across the *AB* terminals is shown in Fig. 11-7. From this circuit we can see that the current through the ammeter is

$$i = \frac{\mu}{\mu + 1} \frac{R_K}{R_K + r_p/(\mu + 1)} \frac{v_1}{2[R_K \| r_p/(\mu + 1)] + R_m} \tag{11-2}$$

To obtain an approximation we observe that μ is much greater than unity for most vacuum tubes. Further, R_K is often much larger than $r_p/(\mu + 1)$. Under these conditions, Eq. (11-2) can be simplified to

$$i \cong \frac{v_1}{2r_p/\mu + R_m} \tag{11-3}$$

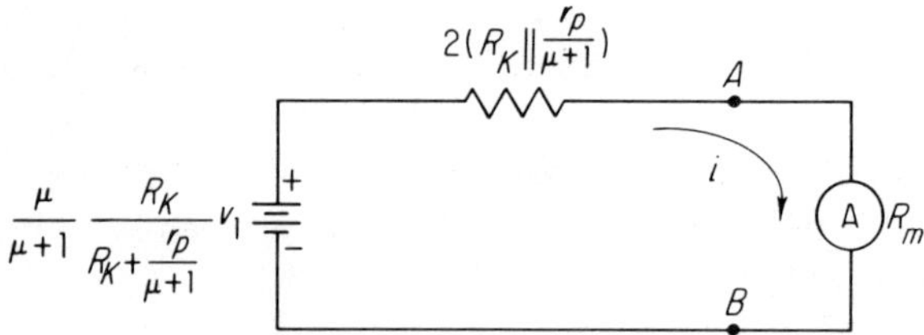

Fig. 11-7 Equivalent circuit for cathode-follower VTVM.

As an example, suppose that $r_p = 10$ kilohms, $\mu = 20$, and the ammeter is a 1-ma 50-ohm movement. Then, by substituting into Eq. (11-3) we obtain

$$i \cong \frac{v_1}{2(10)(10^3)/20 + 50} = \frac{v_1}{10^3 + 50} \cong 10^{-3}v_1$$

From this result, we see once again that the ammeter current in a VTVM is directly proportional to the input voltage. In this example, the ammeter has a full-scale current of 1 ma, so that a 1-volt input would produce full-scale current. This ammeter would then be marked 1 volt at full scale, 0.5 volt at midscale, 0.25 volt at quarter scale, and so on, in a linear fashion.

Equations (11-2) and (11-3) were found on the basis that both tubes are identical. Usually, a dual triode is used, so that both halves have almost the same characteristics.

The circuit of Fig. 11-5 can be made practical by adding a zero adjust, a calibration adjust, and a voltage divider on the input, as shown in Fig. 11-8. The purpose of the adjustments and the voltage divider is the same as in our discussion of Sec. 11-1.

Note that the input resistance seen from the measuring terminals is 10 megohms on any position of the range switch. This is typical of most VTVM's although even higher input resistances are possible.

Many variations of the VTVM shown in Fig. 11-8 appear in commercial instruments. Nevertheless, the circuit of Fig. 11-8 represents the basic

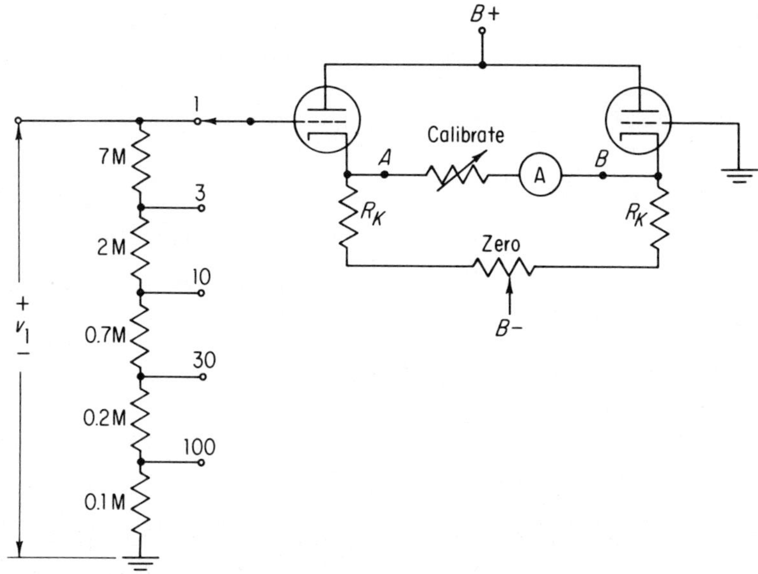

Fig. 11-8 A practical version of the cathode-follower VTVM.

idea behind the cathode-follower type of VTVM. The lowest range is the 1-volt range because in going any lower the drift in the zero setting becomes a problem. If we want more sensitivity, an entirely different approach must be used, as will be discussed in later sections.

EXAMPLE 11-1

The VTVM of Fig. 11-8 has the following values: $R_K = 50$ kilohms, $r_p = 5$ kilohms, $\mu = 20$, and a 50-ohm ammeter with a full-scale current of 1 ma. If the input voltage is exactly 1 volt, what value of calibration resistance will produce full-scale current?

SOLUTION

First, note that $r_p/(\mu + 1)$ is much smaller than R_K, so that we can use the approximation given by Eq. (11-3). Substituting into Eq. (11-3), we get

$$i = \frac{1}{2(5)(10^3)/20 + R_m} = \frac{1}{500 + R_m}$$

The value of R_m *includes* the calibration resistance as well as the meter resistance. In order to have 1 ma, R_m must equal 500 ohms. Hence, the calibration resistance must be 450 ohms.

Note that a 1-kilohm rheostat may be used in this circuit. Then, as tubes are changed, the rheostat may be adjusted to take care of variations in μ and r_p.

EXAMPLE 11-2

In Example 11-1, suppose that the tubes are changed and that μ now is 22 and r_p is 8 kilohms. Find the value of calibration resistance that produces 1 ma of current for a 1-volt input.

SOLUTION

$$i = \frac{1}{2(8)(10^3)/22 + R_m} = \frac{1}{726 + R_m}$$

Hence, in order to have 1 ma, R_m must be 274 ohms. Since the meter resistance is 50 ohms, the calibration resistance must be changed to 224 ohms. Thus, we see that the voltmeter can be calibrated to read correctly at full scale in spite of the change in tubes.

11-3 A D-C–A-C Vacuum-tube Voltmeter

The d-c VTVM discussed in preceding sections may be used to measure a-c voltages by first detecting or rectifying the alternating voltage, as shown in Fig. 11-9. The a-c detector may be any of the types studied in Chap. 4, such as an average detector, a peak detector, or a peak-to-peak detector. As an example, consider the circuit shown in Fig. 11-10. A clamping circuit clamps the input signal above the zero line as shown. A lowpass filter then removes the a-c component, so that only a pure direct voltage is applied to the VTVM. Since the average, or d-c value of the clamped signal is V_p, the VTVM reads the peak value of the input signal.

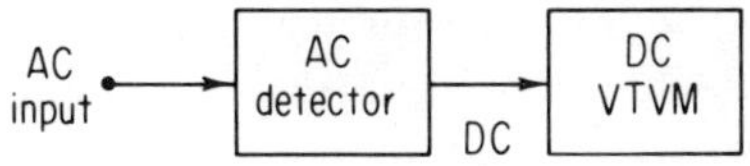

Fig. 11-9 An a-c VTVM.

AC input → AC detector → DC → DC VTVM

The ammeter in the VTVM may be calibrated in peak or in rms values. If peak values are used, the input signal being measured may be any kind of waveshape, such as a square wave, sawtooth wave, sinusoid, etc. The ammeter will indicate the peak value.

If the ammeter is marked off in rms values, the shape of the input waveform must be known. Usually voltmeters are marked in rms values, assuming that the input signal is a pure sinusoid. In other words, with the sinusoid we know that the rms value is 0.707 times the peak value. For almost all other waveforms a number different from 0.707 is used. Because of this, the rms scale of most voltmeters is valid only for an input sinusoidal signal.

The low-pass filter shown in Fig. 11-10 will pass the average voltage but will stop the alternating voltage provided that the cutoff frequency of

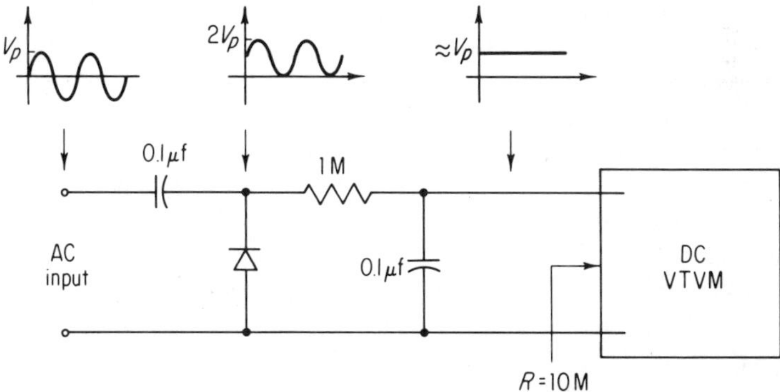

Fig. 11-10 An a-c VTVM using a d-c clamping circuit for a detector.

the filter is much lower than the lowest frequency to be measured. For instance, if the VTVM is to be used for frequencies as low as 20 Hz, the filter should have a cutoff frequency much lower than 20 Hz. In Fig. 11-10 the cutoff frequency has been arbitrarily chosen as

$$f = \frac{1}{2\pi RC} \cong \frac{0.159}{10^6(0.1)(10^{-6})} = 1.59 \text{ Hz}$$

The cutoff frequency is down about one decade from 20 Hz, so that we can expect an attenuation of around 20 db at 20 Hz. Hence, only the d-c, or average, value of the clamped waveform passes through the filter. The d-c value will be reduced slightly because there is a 1-megohm resistor in series with the 10-megohm input resistance of the VTVM. But this difference can be compensated by a calibration adjustment in the VTVM.

Another detector used is the peak-to-peak detector shown in Fig. 11-11. The signal is first positively clamped, and then peak-detected. The direct

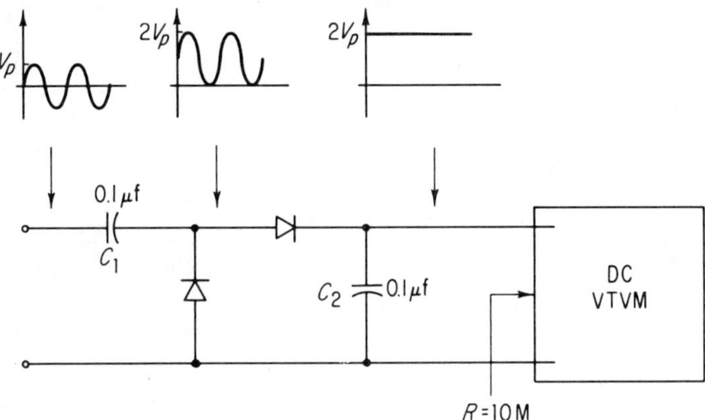

Fig. 11-11 An a-c VTVM using a peak-to-peak detector.

voltage out of the peak detector equals the peak-to-peak value of the input waveform. If the ammeter is marked in peak-to-peak values, any kind of waveform can be measured. The capacitors must be chosen large enough to ensure that the RC time constant is much larger than the period of the lowest frequency to be measured. For instance, in Fig. 11-11 the product of RC_2 is 1 sec. If the lowest frequency to be measured has a period of 0.05 sec (20 Hz), the RC time constant is 20 times larger, so that good peak detection occurs at 20 Hz. Similarly, the product of RC_1 is also 1 sec, so that good clamping action will occur at 20 Hz.

A d-c–a-c VTVM can be made by using a suitable arrangement like that shown in Fig. 11-12. Note the addition of a separate calibration adjustment for a-c operation. An exact a-c voltage can be applied to the input to allow calibrating the VTVM for a-c operation. It should be remembered that the VTVM must be calibrated whenever changing tubes. In fact, it should be calibrated periodically, since the tube characteristics change with time.

The lowest voltage range with the VTVM of Fig. 11-12 is typically around 1 volt. The reason for this is that on d-c measurements the drift problem may become quite serious if the VTVM is too sensitive. Further, on a-c operation the knee voltages of the diodes become a limiting factor.

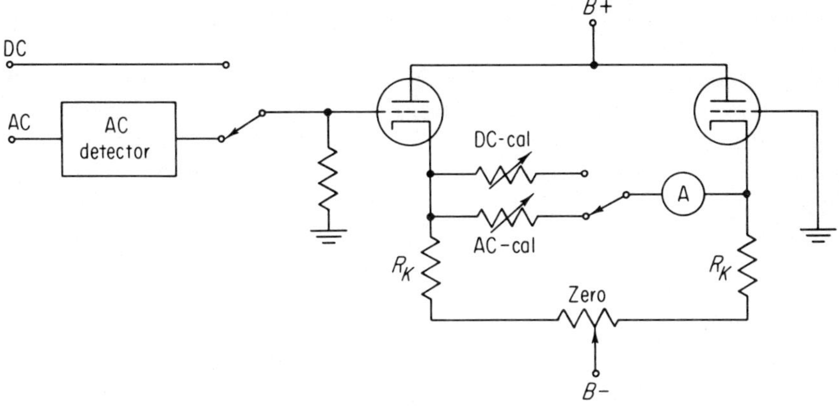

Fig. 11-12 A d-c–a-c VTVM.

Commercial instruments generally go as low as a 1-volt range but no lower because of the drift-voltage and knee-voltage limitations.

11-4 A Sensitive A-C Vacuum-tube Voltmeter

If the signal to be measured is an a-c signal, it may be amplified before detection, instead of first detecting, as was done in the preceding section. Figure 11-13 conveys the essential idea behind this approach. A conventional a-c amplifier is used to amplify the input signal. Then, the a-c signal is detected by any of our basic methods. The indicator is marked to read rms, peak, or peak-to-peak values.

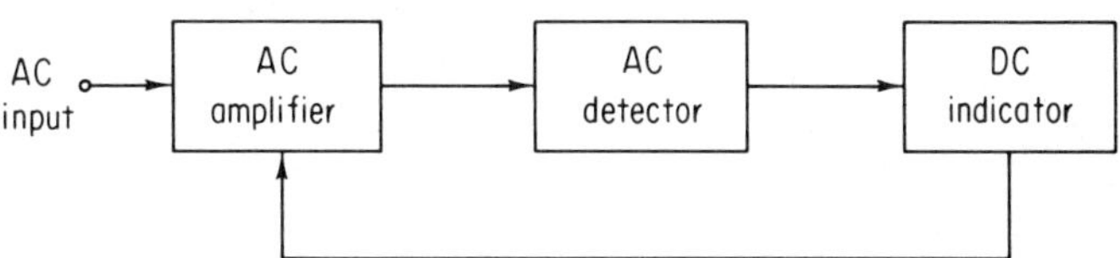

Fig. 11-13 Block diagram for a sensitive a-c VTVM.

Various voltage ranges can be provided by using a voltage divider or an attenuator either on the front end of this system or at an intermediate point in the a-c amplifier.

In order to stabilize the gain of the system against tube changes, negative feedback is often employed by feeding a signal from the output back to the input. This has the effect of holding the gain constant, as well as improving the frequency response.

As an example of the use of negative feedback, consider the simple two-stage system shown in Fig. 11-14. The amplifier is the conventional two-stage feedback arrangement that is often used in practice. The gain in such a system is approximately equal to the ratio of the feedback resistor to the cathode resistor, that is, R_F/R_K. The meter circuit is a standard full-wave bridge rectifier. Calibration is performed by applying an exact a-c voltage across the input and adjusting the feedback resistor. Figure 11-14 conveys the essential idea. Of course, many variations appear in practice.

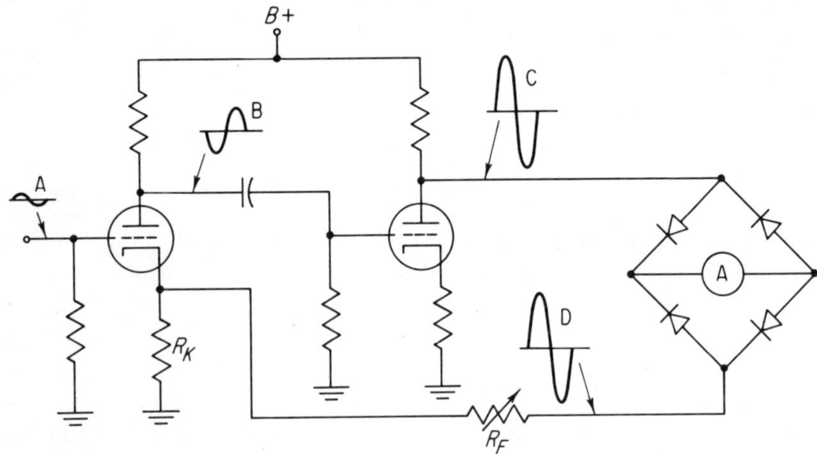

Fig. 11-14 Schematic of a simple a-c VTVM with negative feedback.

11-5 A Sensitive D-C Voltmeter

In order to overcome the drift limitation imposed by a simple d-c VTVM, we must resort to a different approach. One very popular method for building extremely sensitive d-c voltmeters is the use of a chopped d-c amplifier (see Fig. 11-15).

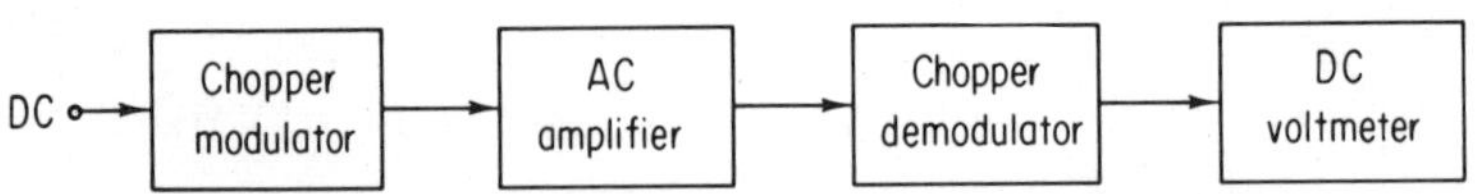

Fig. 11-15 Block diagram for a sensitive d-c VTVM.

As was indicated in our discussion of amplifiers, the choppers may be mechanical or electronic. Among the more interesting electronic choppers are those which use photocells. One type of photocell available shows a marked change in resistance as the light striking it changes. In other words, it is a resistance that is extremely sensitive to intensity of the light striking. Figure 11-16*a* is a sketch of a typical variation. Note that the resistance decreases with the amount of light striking the photocell.

This effect can be exploited by using photocells for modulators and demodulators.

As a simple example of how photocells may be used to convert direct to alternating voltage, consider the circuit of Fig. 11-16*b*. A flashing light

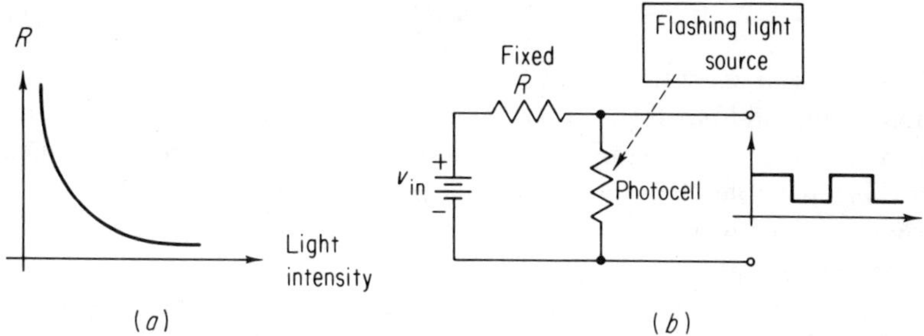

Fig. 11-16 Use of a photocell for a chopper. (*a*) Photocell characteristic. (*b*) Simple photocell chopper.

source causes the photocell to change from a high to a low resistance. As a result, the output of the voltage divider is an a-c signal. Of course, the output will not be a perfect square wave, but it will be an a-c signal which we can amplify and demodulate.

The chopper type of d-c voltmeter can be made extremely sensitive. D-c voltages in the microvolt region can be measured with this approach.

11-6 True RMS Voltmeters

Most a-c voltmeters have an rms scale which is valid only if the input signal being measured is a sinusoid. As indicated earlier, this restriction arises because average or peak detectors are used. In order to build a voltmeter that will indicate the true rms value of any waveform (sine wave, square wave, sawtooth, etc.), it is necessary to use an rms detector, that is, a detector that responds *directly* to the heating value of the input signal.

One approach to measuring the rms value of an arbitrary waveform is to use thermocouples. Recall that a thermocouple is a junction of dissimilar metals and that a voltage is obtained which is proportional to the temperature of the junction. To measure the heating effect of an input signal we may use a heater in close proximity to a thermocouple, as shown in Fig. 11-17. The input signal is applied to the heater. This raises the temperature of the thermocouple and produces an output d-c voltage of v. Since the thermocouple is basically a power-responding

Fig. 11-17 An rms detector using a thermocouple.

device, the voltage v is proportional to the power delivered to the heater by the signal. Since the power delivered to the heater is equal to the square of rms value divided by the heater resistance, we can say that the output voltage of the thermocouple is proportional to the square of the rms value. That is,

$$v = KV_{\text{rms}}^2 \tag{11-4}$$

where K is the constant of proportionality.

The value of K in Eq. (11-4) depends upon the distance between the heater and the thermocouple and upon the materials used in the heater and thermocouple. The important relation to notice in Eq. (11-4) is that the voltage out of the thermocouple is proportional to the square of the rms voltage input.

A crude but simple system for measuring the rms voltage of an arbitrary waveform is shown in Fig. 11-18*a*. The voltage out of the thermocouple

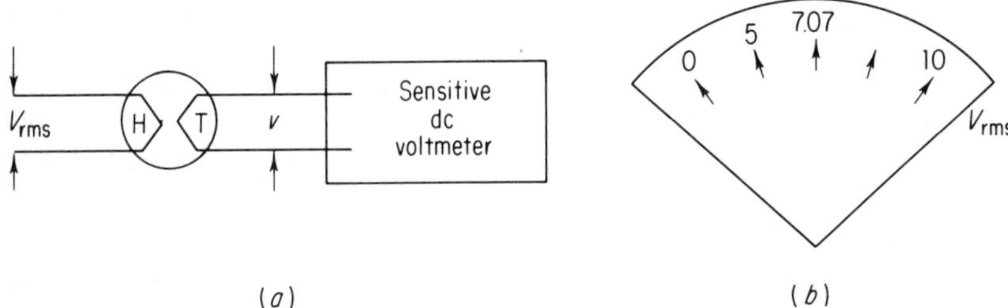

Fig. 11-18 A simple true-rms voltmeter. (*a*) Diagram. (*b*) Nonlinear scale.

can be read by a d-c voltmeter. The indicator of the d-c voltmeter must be marked according to the square relation given by Eq. (11-4). This results in a nonlinear scale, as illustrated by Fig. 11-18*b*, where 10 volts has been arbitrarily shown as the full-scale value. Because of the square relation between v and V_{rms} the 5-volt mark is not at half scale, but at quarter scale. This is one of the serious disadvantages of this system.

The system often used in practice is the two-thermocouple circuit shown in Fig. 11-19. Basically, this is a feedback arrangement where the

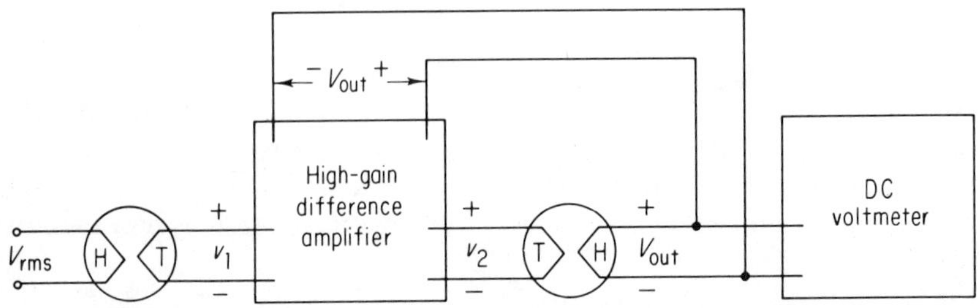

Fig. 11-19 A true-rms voltmeter with linear response.

output of the difference amplifier is fed back to a second thermocouple. The chief advantage of this system is that the output voltage measured by the voltmeter is equal to the rms voltage. That is,

$$V_{out} = V_{rms} \tag{11-5}$$

Since V_{out} equals V_{rms}, an ordinary voltmeter with a linear scale can be used to indicate the rms value of the input voltage.

To prove Eq. (11-5) we first observe that

$$V_{out} = A(v_1 - v_2) \tag{11-6}$$

where A is the voltage gain of the difference amplifier. We can rearrange Eq. (11-6) to get

$$v_1 - v_2 = \frac{V_{out}}{A} \tag{11-7}$$

Note that for a high-gain amplifier A is a very large number, so that the right side of Eq. (11-7) is approximately zero. Therefore, $v_1 - v_2$ is approximately zero, or

$$v_1 \cong v_2 \tag{11-8}$$

From Eq. (11-8) it is immediately clear that

$$KV_{rms}^2 \cong KV_{out}^2$$

or

$$V_{rms} \cong V_{out}$$

This last result tells us that the voltage measured by the d-c voltmeter is approximately equal to the rms value of the input signal. The waveform of the input signal is immaterial, since the heater responds directly to the rms value of waveform. Hence, we have a true-rms voltmeter.

If the input signal being measured is very small, an a-c amplifier may be used to increase the signal level before applying it to the input thermocouple. Sensitivities in the millivolt region are possible with such an arrangement.

SUMMARY

Simple d-c vacuum tube voltmeters may be made by using either a difference-amplifier type of VTVM or a cathode-follower type of VTVM. A zero adjustment is required to equalize both halves of the VTVM. Further, calibration adjustment is necessary to offset the variation in tube parameters. Calibration should be done periodically, and certainly whenever tubes are changed.

A simple a-c VTVM is made by detecting the a-c signal before applying it to the VTVM. Average or peak detection may be used. If only sinusoidal signals are measured, then the scale may be marked in rms values. Most a-c voltmeters with an rms scale assume that the input signal is sinusoidal.

To obtain extremely sensitive voltmeters, it is necessary to change the basic approach. For a-c measurements, the a-c signal is first amplified before detection. For d-c measurements, the d-c input is first converted to alternating voltage so that the signal can be easily amplified before demodulating to recover the direct voltage. Photocell choppers are often used in the construction of sensitive d-c voltmeters.

To measure the true rms value of any waveform, thermocouples may be used. By means of a difference amplifier and a feedback arrangement, the rms value can be measured on a linear scale.

GLOSSARY

calibration adjustment A rheostat in series with the ammeter of a VTVM used to adjust the full-scale reading of the VTVM. This adjustment is periodically checked to take care of changes caused by tube aging.

negative feedback Feeding part of the output signal of an amplifier back to the input (180° out of phase) in order to stabilize the voltage gain.

sensitivity In regard to a VTVM this simply refers to the smallest signal that can be reliably measured on the VTVM. The sensitivitity of a VTVM bears no relation at all to the concept of the reciprocal of the full-scale current of a VOM.

thermocouple A device made out of two dissimilar metals. A contact potential is developed across the junction of the two metals. This potential is a function of the temperature of the junction.

true rms detector A detector that responds to the rms value (heating value) of the signal being detected.

zero adjust In a VTVM the zero adjust is used to balance both halves of the difference amplifier or cathode-coupled amplifier.

REVIEW QUESTIONS

1. What are the two basic VTVM circuits used for measuring d-c voltages?
2. Why is it possible to mark the ammeter scale linearly in the basic VTVM circuits discussed in this chapter?
3. What is the purpose of the zero adjust in a difference-amplifier or cathode-follower type of VTVM?
4. What is the purpose of the calibration adjust in a difference-amplifier or cathode-follower type of VTVM?

5. Why is a voltage divider used on the input of a VTVM?
6. How is a d-c VTVM like that of Fig. 11-8 modified to allow a-c voltage measurements?
7. Why is the rms scale of most voltmeters valid only for sinusoidal signals?
8. How can a d-c VTVM be modified to allow peak-to-peak voltage measurements?
9. Why are the simple VTVMs discussed in Sec. 11-3 limited to about 1-volt ranges?
10. What approach can be used to build a very sensitive a-c VTVM?
11. Why is negative feedback often used in voltmeters?
12. What approach is generally used in the construction of a very sensitive d-c voltmeter?
13. What is a thermocouple?
14. What is the disadvantage of a single-thermocouple system?
15. In the two-thermocouple system used for measuring true rms voltages, why is the voltage gain of the amplifier made very high?

PROBLEMS

11-1 For the basic VTVM of Fig. 11-1, assume the following values: $R_L = 15$ kilohms, $r_p = 5$ kilohms, and $\mu = 20$. If the meter has a resistance of 50 ohms and a full-scale current of 1 ma, what value of v_1 produces full-scale current?

11-2 If the VTVM of Prob. 11-1 is to have full-scale current for v_1 equal to 1 volt, what size resistance must be added in series with the ammeter?

11-3 In the circuit of Fig. 11-4, if a 300-volt range is to be added to the voltage divider, show the new voltage divider with appropriate resistances. The total resistance of the divider is to be 10 megohms.

11-4 In Fig. 11-5 find the relation between ammeter current and input voltage if $\mu = 20$, $r_p = 5$ kilohms, $R_K = 250$, and $R_m = 50$. Use Eq. (11-2).

11-5 In Fig. 11-5, $r_p = 10$ kilohms, $\mu = 50$, $R_K = 20$ kilohms, and $R_m = 50$. How much current flows for a 1-volt input? What size resistance must be added in series with the ammeter in order to have 1 ma of current for a 1-volt input?

11-6 In Fig. 11-11, the clamping circuit works into a peak detector. At what frequency will the discharge between cycles in the peak detector be about 1 percent of the maximum capacitor voltage?

11-7 In the circuit of Fig. 11-12, $R_K = 15$ kilohms, $\mu = 20$, $r_p = 10$ kilohms, and a 50-ohm 1-ma meter is used. The a-c detector is an ideal peak-to-peak detector. If the input signal to the a-c detector is a 1-volt rms sine wave, what value of a-c calibration adjust produces full-scale current?

11-8 In Fig. 11-14, assume that the voltage gain from the input to the bridge rectifier (point A to point C) is given by R_F/R_K. If R_F is 10 kilohms, and if R_K is 100, what is the rms value of an input sinusoid if it produces full-scale current in a 1-ma ammeter? (Assume ideal diodes and an ideal ammeter.)

11-9 In the simple photocell chopper of Fig. 11-16, v_{in} equals 1 mv, and R equals 100 kilohms. Assume that the photocell changes between resistance values of 10 and 500 kilohms. What are the maximum and minimum values of the output voltage?

12 Oscilloscope Fundamentals

The oscilloscope is so common in electrical measurements that a study of its basic principles and circuits is well worth the effort. We can expect to benefit in at least two ways from such a study: we will be able to operate the oscilloscope more intelligently if we have a knowledge of the basic ideas behind it, and we will find that many of the principles and circuits used in an oscilloscope are also used in other electronic instruments and systems.

12-1 The Cathode-ray Tube

The cathode-ray tube, (CRT) is normally covered in basic electronics courses. We will merely review a few of the ideas that are essential in our study of the oscilloscope. The construction of the CRT is shown schematically in Fig. 12-1. Recall that the cathode is a source of electrons which are accelerated toward the screen by means of the first and second anodes. The control grid determines the number of electrons that pass through it. Unlike the triode, however, the electrons are focused into a beam as they pass through the region between the first and second anodes. After leaving this focusing region, the electrons enter the region between the deflection plates, where they may be deflected either vertically or horizontally. Finally, the beam strikes the screen and causes a small spot of light to appear at the impact point.

Very important is the fact that the amount of deflection is directly proportional to the size of the voltage applied to the deflection plates. For instance, in Fig. 12-1, let us assume that for $V_u = 10$ volts there is

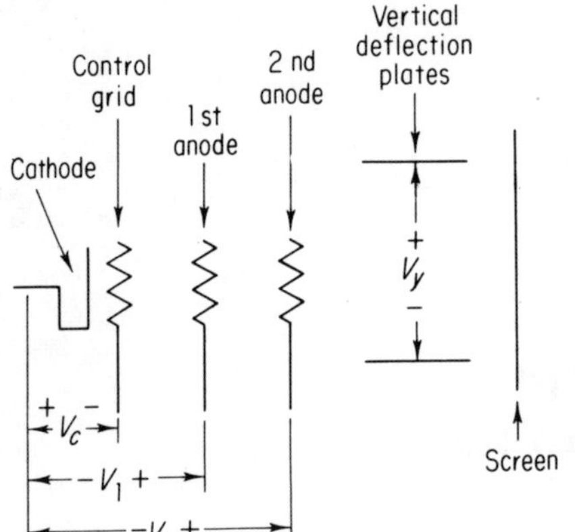

Fig. 12-1 Schematic of the cathode-ray tube.

a deflection of exactly 1 in. If V_y is then doubled, the deflection will double to 2 in. Hence, the deflection is directly proportional to the deflection voltage.

12-2 Basic Oscilloscope Controls

When the CRT is used in an oscilloscope, a number of typical adjustments are used to control the beam characteristics. There is always an *intensity control,* which adjusts the brightness of the spot by changing the voltage on the control grid. The *focus control* focuses the beam of electrons onto a small spot on the screen by changing the voltage between the first and second anodes.

Sometimes there is an *astigmatism control.* Generally, a beam that is focused at the center of the screen will be defocused at the edges of the screen because the lengths of the electron paths are different. Adjusting the astigmatism control gives a sharp focus over the entire screen.

The horizontal and vertical *position controls* are standard adjustments. By applying d-c voltages to either the vertical or horizontal deflection plates, the beam can be moved to any part of the screen. The remaining controls on a typical oscilloscope will be discussed in later sections.

12-3 Basic Oscilloscope Patterns

In this section we determine the kind of patterns that result from applying sinusoidal voltages to the deflection plates. Let us begin by considering the special case of applying a sine wave of voltage to the horizontal deflection plates but no voltage to the vertical deflection plates. Specifically,

$$V_x = V_p \sin \omega t \qquad \text{and} \qquad V_y = 0$$

The V_x voltage is a pure sine wave with a peak value of V_p and a radian frequency of ω. What is the resulting pattern?

Figure 12-2 illustrates the position of the spot at various times throughout the cycle. At point A in time, both voltages are zero, so that the

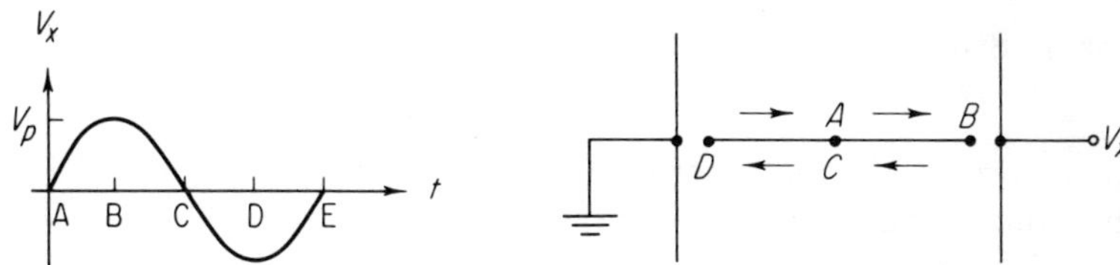

Fig. 12-2 Spot deflection for a sine wave on the horizontal deflection plates.

spot remains undeflected at the center of the screen. As the V_x voltage becomes positive, the deflection plate on the right attracts the electron beam, causing the spot to move to the right of center. At point B in time, V_x is at its maximum positive value, and the spot is at the extreme right of the screen. At point C in time, the voltages are once again zero, and the spot returns to the center. During the negative half cycle, the spot moves to the left, reaching a maximum deflection at point D in time. The spot then returns to the center, and the cycle repeats. Thus, we obtain a horizontal line.

It should be evident that if we now apply a sine wave to the vertical deflection plates and apply no voltage to the horizontal deflection plates, a vertical line is obtained. Specifically,

$$V_x = 0 \qquad \text{and} \qquad V_y = V_p \sin \omega t$$

Figure 12-3 illustrates the resulting pattern.

What would happen if we applied sine-wave signals to both the horizontal and vertical deflection plates?

Let us begin with the case of

$$V_x = V_p \sin \omega t \qquad \text{and} \qquad V_y = V_p \sin \omega t$$

In this case, both signals are equal-frequency equal-amplitude in-phase sine waves. Figure 12-4 shows the signals and the resulting pattern. At point A in time, both voltages are zero, and the spot is undeflected at the center. At point B in time, both voltages are maximum positive, and the spot is deflected a maximum distance to the right, and a maximum

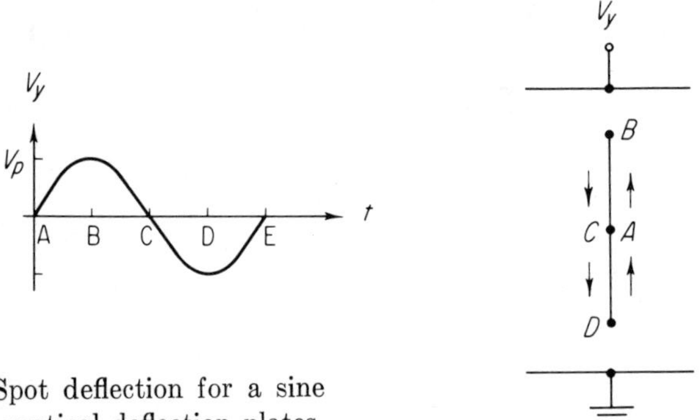

Fig. 12-3 Spot deflection for a sine wave on the vertical deflection plates.

distance upward. For any intermediate point in time, the spot is deflected by the same amount in x and y directions. Hence, we will get a straight line tilted 45° to the positive x axis.

It is very helpful in analyzing oscilloscope patterns to realize that the position of the spot is the vector sum of the horizontal and vertical deflection. Thus, for the case of two in-phase sine waves, we have the

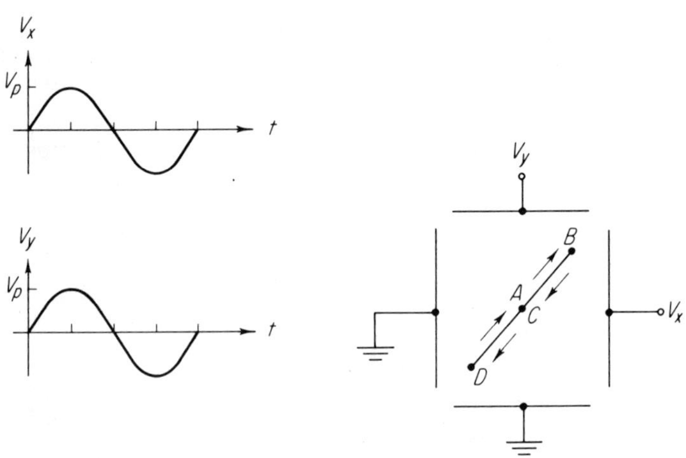

Fig. 12-4 Spot deflection for equal-amplitude equal-frequency in-phase sine waves on the vertical and horizontal deflection plates.

vector diagram of Fig. 12-5*a*. During the positive half cycle, there is a deflection to the right, plus an equal deflection upward. These vectors change their lengths during the positive half cycle, but at any one instant in time they are equal in magnitude, so that the spot must move along a line tilted 45° to the positive real axis. During the negative half cycle, both vectors reverse directions as shown in Fig. 12-5*b*. The vector sum still implies that the spot moves along a 45° line.

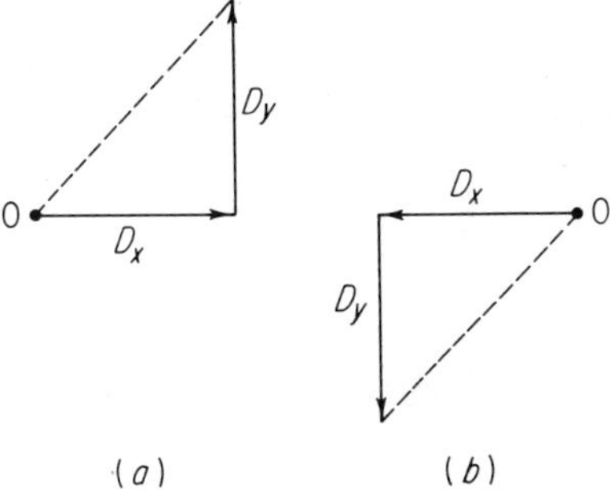

Fig. 12-5 Vector diagrams for in-phase sine waves. (*a*) During the positive half cycle. (*b*) During the negative half cycle.

Referring to Fig. 12-4, we see that for equal amplitudes, the line forms a 45° angle with the horizontal axis. It should be evident that if we now reduce the amplitude of the V_y signal, the line will form less than a 45° angle with the horizontal. Conversely, if we increase the amplitude of V_y, the angle between the line and the horizontal will be larger than 45°. (See Fig. 12-6.)

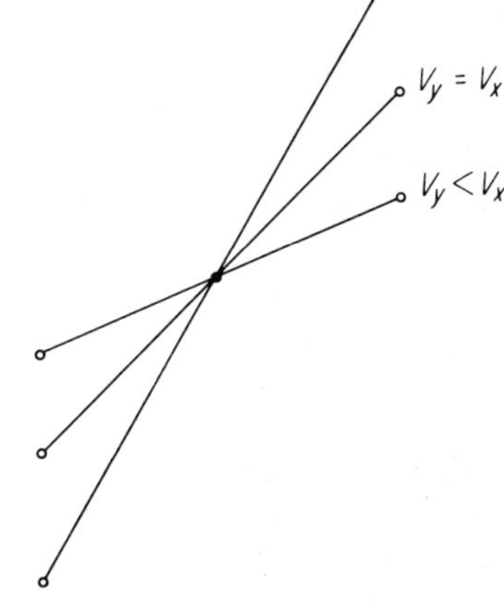

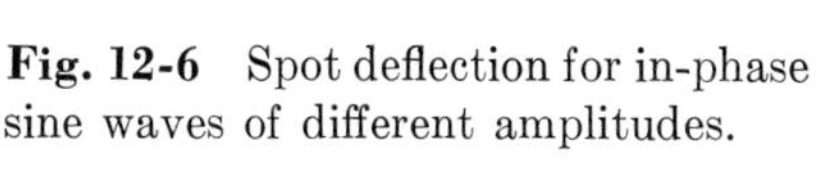
Fig. 12-6 Spot deflection for in-phase sine waves of different amplitudes.

Suppose that both sinusoids have equal amplitude and equal frequency but are 180° out of phase, as shown in Fig. 12-7*a*. At point *A* in time, both voltages are zero, and the spot is at the center. At point *B* in time V_y is maximum positive, and V_x is maximum negative. Hence, the spot is

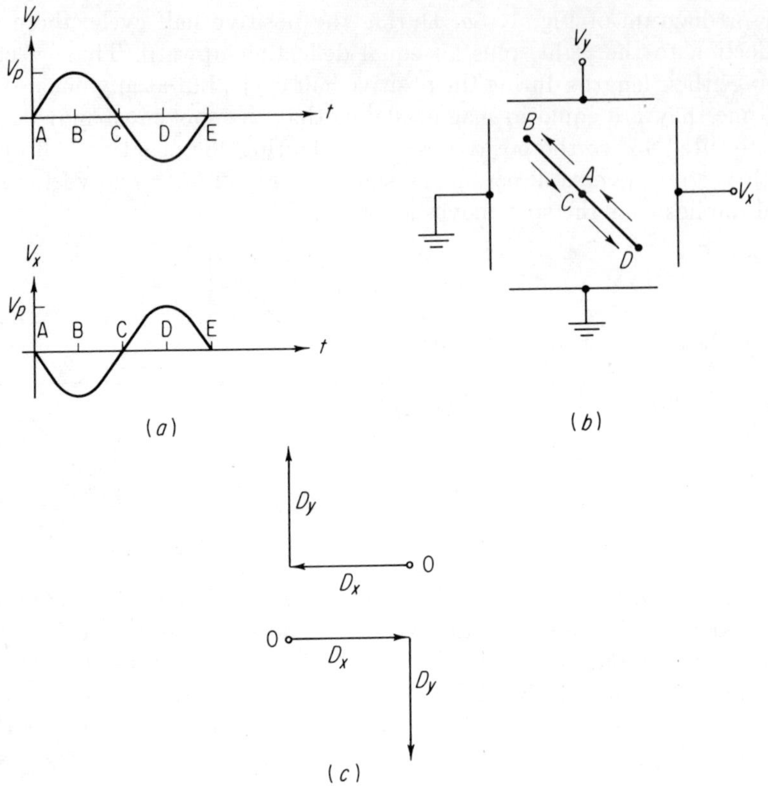

Fig. 12-7 Spot deflection for 180° out-of-phase sinusoids. (*a*) 180° out-of-phase. (*b*) Scope pattern. (*c*) Vector diagrams.

deflected a maximum distance to the left and upward, as shown in Fig. 12-7*b*. Similarly, at point *D* in time, the spot is deflected to the extreme right and downward. The vector diagrams are shown in Fig. 12-7*c*.

Suppose we now consider the pattern that results from the application of equal-frequency equal-amplitude 90° out-of-phase sinusoids. Specifically, consider

$$V_x = V_p \cos \omega t \qquad \text{and} \qquad V_y = V_p \sin \omega t$$

The graphs of these waveforms are shown in Fig. 12-8*a*.

At point *A* in time, there is maximum deflection to the right and zero deflection in the vertical direction, as shown in Fig. 12-8*b*. At point *B* in time, there is zero deflection horizontally and maximum deflection upward. The remaining points *C* and *D* are easily found, and are shown in Fig. 12-8*b*.

During one complete cycle, the spot traces out a circle on the screen of the CRT. To prove that the shape is actually a circle, we need only

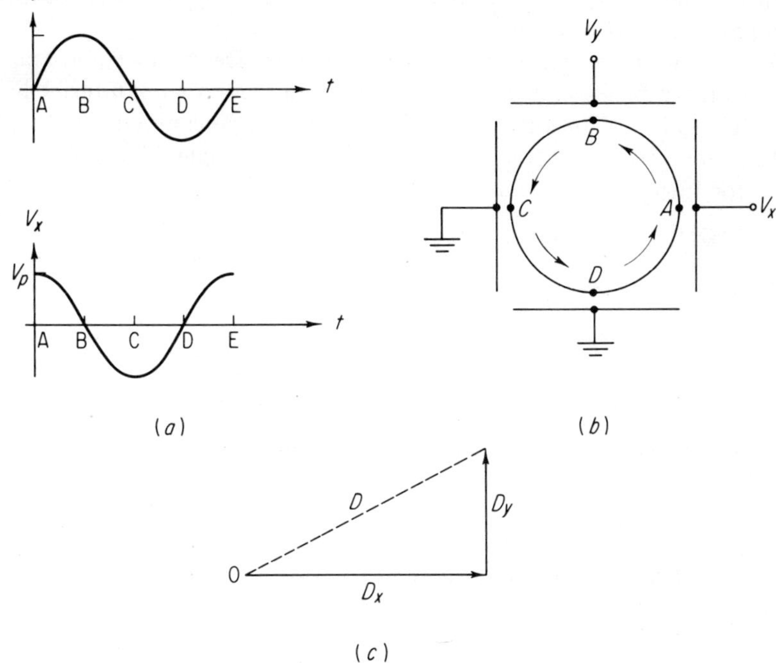

Fig. 12-8 Spot deflection for 90° out-of-phase sinusoids. (*a*) Waveforms. (*b*) Scope pattern. (*c*) Vector diagram.

prove that the distance of the spot from the center of the screen is a constant. This is easily done in the following manner. Note from the vector diagram in Fig. 12-8*c* that the distance of the spot from the center is equal to the length of D. We can find this length by using the Pythagorean theorem.

$$D = \sqrt{D_x^2 + D_y^2} \tag{12-1}$$

Since deflection is directly proportional to the applied voltage,

$$V_x = V_p \cos \omega t \quad \text{implies that} \quad D_x = D_p \cos \omega t$$

and

$$V_y = V_p \sin \omega t \quad \text{implies that} \quad D_y = D_p \sin \omega t$$

The value of D_p is simply the peak deflection in either the x or y direction. If we substitute these expressions into Eq. (12-1), we get

$$D = \sqrt{D_p^2 \sin^2 \omega t + D_p^2 \cos^2 \omega t}$$

or

$$D = D_p \sqrt{\sin^2 \omega t + \cos^2 \omega t} = D_p$$

(Recall from trigonometry that the sine squared plus the cosine squared of an angle are equal to one.)

Since D equals D_p (a constant), the spot must trace a circle as it moves from point A to B to C and so on.

Thus far, we have considered the cases of equal-frequency equal-amplitude arbitrary-phase sinusoids. There is an infinite number of intermediate cases. The pattern for any intermediate phase angle is an ellipse. Figure 12-9 summarizes the patterns for arbitrary phase angle. These are quite useful for future reference, and should be memorized.

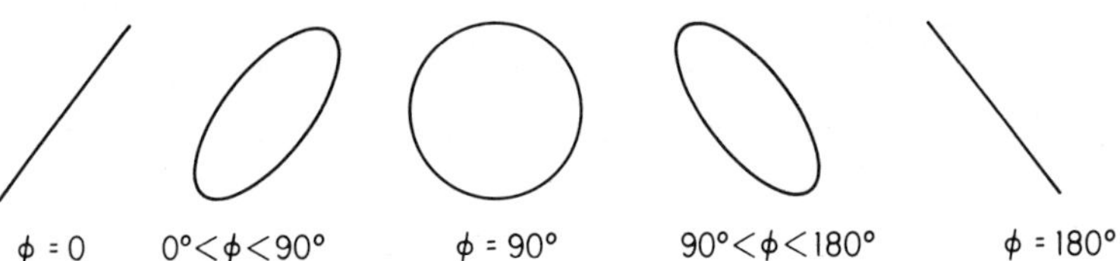

Fig. 12-9 Scope patterns for equal-amplitude equal-frequency arbitrary-phase sinusoids.

12-4 The Phase Angle between Sinusoids

Sometimes it is useful to be able to determine the phase angle between equal-frequency sinusoids. Let us consider the case of equal-frequency equal-amplitude out-of-phase sinusoids, as shown in Fig. 12-10*a*. The equations for these waveforms are

$$V_x = V_p \sin \omega t \qquad \text{and} \qquad V_y = V_p \sin (\omega t + \phi)$$

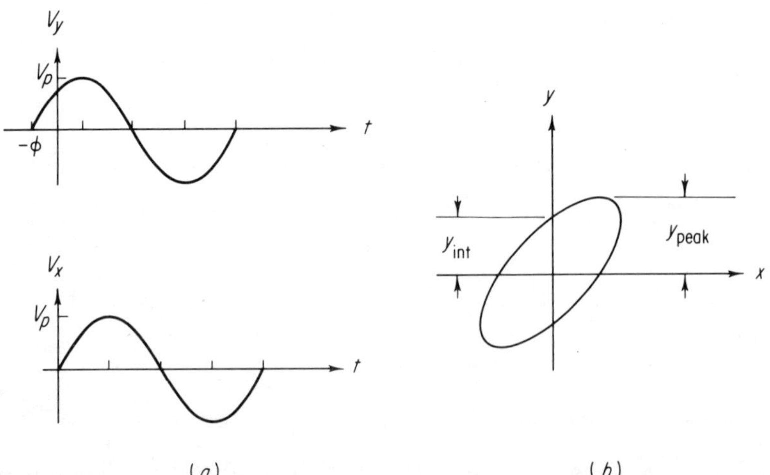

Fig. 12-10 Out-of-phase sinusoids. (*a*) Waveforms. (*b*) Elliptical pattern.

Since deflection is directly proportional to voltage, we can write

$$D_x = D_p \sin \omega t \qquad \text{and} \qquad D_y = D_p \sin (\omega t + \phi)$$

We can find a formula for the phase angle by observing that at $t = 0$ we get

$$D_x = 0 \qquad \text{and} \qquad D_y = D_p \sin \phi$$

These equations tell us that for zero x deflection, the y deflection equals the peak y deflection times the sine of the phase angle. To make this relation easier to remember we can rewrite it as

$$\sin \phi = \frac{y_{\text{intercept}}}{y_{\text{peak}}} \tag{12-2}$$

The graphical meanings of y intercept and y peak are shown in Fig. 12-10*b*.

In Fig. 12-10*a*, V_y leads V_x by an angle of ϕ. If the situation is reversed, so that V_x leads V_y by ϕ, the exact same ellipse occurs. Because of this, Eq. (12-2) can only give us the phase angle between the two sinusoids. It does not tell us whether V_x leads V_y or vice versa.

Example 12-1

For the ellipse shown in Fig. 12-11*a*, find the phase angle between the sinusoids producing it.

Solution

$$\sin \phi = \frac{2.5}{5} = 0.5$$

From trigonometry tables, or by using a slide rule, we get

$$\phi = 30 \text{ or } 150°$$

Referring to Fig. 12-9, we see that ϕ must equal 30°.

Hence, we know that the phase angle between the two sinusoidal signals is 30°. (We cannot say whether V_y leads or lags V_x.)

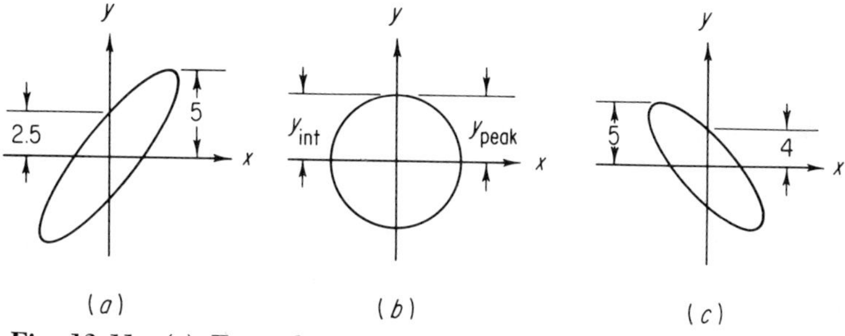

Fig. 12-11 (*a*) Example 12-1. (*b*) Example 12-2. (*c*) Example 12-3.

EXAMPLE 12-2

Use the formula for the phase angle to show that the phase angle is 90° for a circular pattern.

SOLUTION

Referring to Fig. 12-11*b*, it is clear that

$$\sin \phi = 1$$

or

$$\phi = 90°$$

EXAMPLE 12-3

Find the phase angle between the sinusoids that produce the ellipse of Fig. 12-11*c*.

SOLUTION

$$\sin \phi = \frac{4}{5} = 0.8$$

From tables or from the slide rule we find

$$\phi = 53 \text{ or } 127°$$

Referring to Fig. 12-9, we see that the only applicable value of ϕ is 127°. Hence, the phase angle between the sinusoids is 127°.

12-5 Lissajous Patterns

The oscilloscope patterns discussed in preceding sections fall in the general category of what are called *Lissajous patterns*. Simply stated, a Lissajous pattern is a steady pattern. If we look at an oscilloscope and see a picture that is standing still, we are looking at a Lissajous pattern.

It should be immediately evident that in order for a pattern to be steady, the spot must be tracing out the same pattern cycle after cycle. It can be shown that the same pattern is traced only if the ratio of the vertical frequency to the horizontal frequency is a rational (fractional) number. Specifically,

$$\frac{f_y}{f_x} = \frac{m}{n} \tag{12-3}$$

where m and n are whole numbers. As an example, suppose that the vertical frequency is 4 kHz and the horizontal frequency is 2 kHz. Then,

$$\frac{f_y}{f_x} = \frac{4 \text{ kHz}}{2 \text{ kHz}} = \frac{2}{1} = 2$$

Since the ratio is a rational or fractional number, the resulting pattern will be stationary.

As another example, let f_y equal 3.2 kHz and f_x equal 2.4 kHz. Then,

$$\frac{f_y}{f_x} = \frac{3.2 \text{ kHz}}{2.4 \text{ kHz}} = \frac{4}{3}$$

Once again the ratio is a rational number, so that a steady pattern must result.

Lissajous patterns may be divided into two general classes. First, there is the closed Lissajous pattern. Basically, this is a pattern that has no breaks or discontinuities. In other words, there are no loose or free ends. Some examples of closed Lissajous patterns are given in Fig. 12-12*a*. Second, there is the open Lissajous pattern. This is simply a steady pattern that has free ends. Examples of open Lissajous patterns are given in Fig. 12-12*b*.

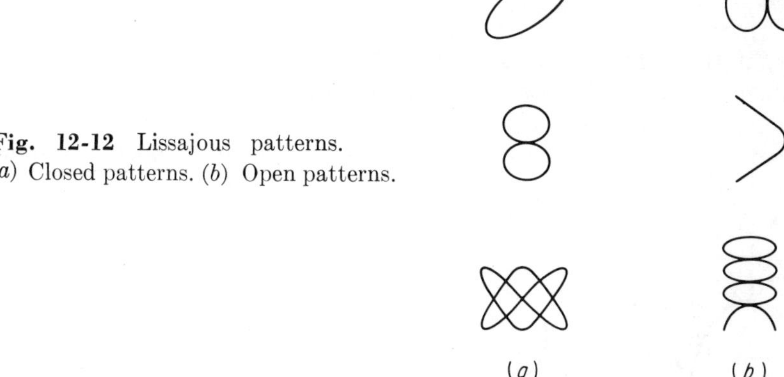

Fig. 12-12 Lissajous patterns. (*a*) Closed patterns. (*b*) Open patterns.

When dealing with *closed patterns*, we can find the ratio of vertical to the horizontal frequency by counting the number of positive y peaks and dividing by the number of positive x peaks. That is,

$$\frac{f_y}{f_x} = \frac{\text{number of } +y \text{ peaks}}{\text{number of } +x \text{ peaks}} \tag{12-4}$$

As an example of how to use Eq. (12-4), consider the closed Lissajous pattern of Fig. 12-13*a*. We count one y peak since there is only one maximum positive y value. We count two x peaks since there are two points that represent maximum x deflection. Hence, the ratio of the frequencies is

$$\frac{f_y}{f_x} = \frac{1}{2}$$

Hence, if the x frequency is 2 kHz, the y frequency must be one-half of this, or 1 kHz.

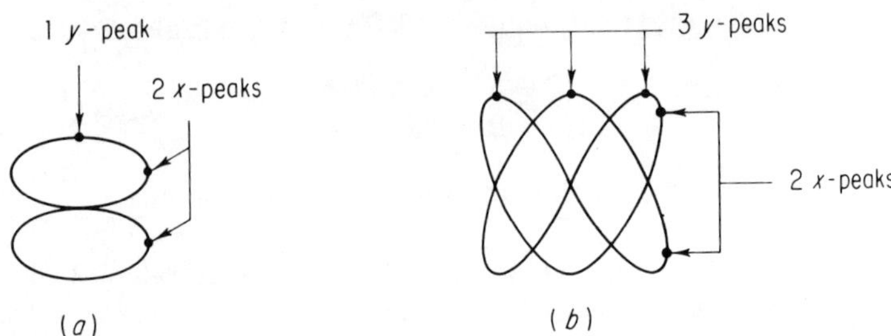

Fig. 12-13 Examples of counting peaks on closed Lissajous patterns.

As another example, consider the closed Lissajous pattern of Fig. 12-13*b*. Clearly, there are three y peaks and two x peaks. Hence,

$$\frac{f_y}{f_x} = \frac{3}{2}$$

Thus, if the x frequency is 2 kHz, the y frequency must be 3 kHz.

When dealing with *open patterns*, we can still find the ratio of frequencies by using Eq. (12-4), provided that we count free ends as ½ instead of 1. For instance, in Fig. 12-14*a* we have an open Lissajous

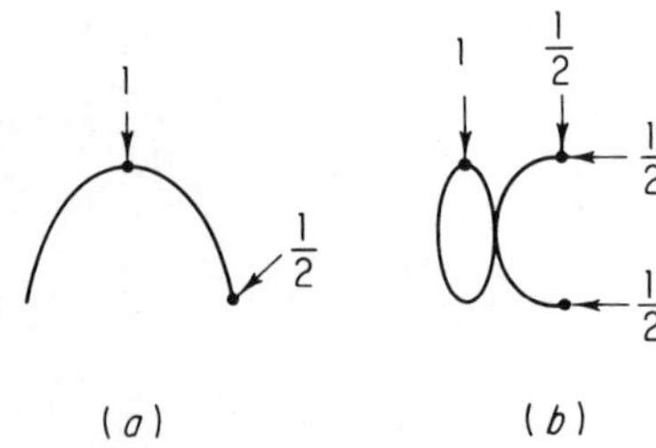

Fig. 12-14 Examples of counting peaks on open Lissajous patterns.

pattern. We count the positive y peak as 1, but the positive x peak is counted as ½ because it is a free end. Hence, for Fig. 12-14*a*, we get

$$\frac{f_y}{f_x} = \frac{1}{1/2} = 2$$

As another example, consider the open pattern of Fig. 12-14*b*. In this case,

$$\frac{f_y}{f_x} = \frac{1 + 1/2}{1/2 + 1/2} = \frac{3}{2}$$

Example 12-4

An upright figure eight appears on a CRT. If the x frequency is 1 kHz, find the y frequency.

Solution

The upright figure eight is a closed pattern, so we would count one y peak and two x peaks. Hence,

$$\frac{f_y}{f_x} = \frac{1}{2}$$

or

$$f_y = \tfrac{1}{2} f_x = \tfrac{1}{2}(1000) = 500 \text{ Hz}$$

Example 12-5

The pattern of Fig. 12-14*b* appears on a CRT. If the x frequency is 1 kHz, find the y frequency.

Solution

This is an open Lissajous pattern, so we count a free end as $\frac{1}{2}$ instead of 1. Hence,

$$\frac{f_y}{f_x} = \frac{1.5}{1} = \frac{3}{2}$$

or

$$f_y = \tfrac{3}{2} f_x = \tfrac{3}{2}(1000) = 1500 \text{ Hz}$$

12-6 Linear-time-base Patterns

There are special types of Lissajous patterns known as *linear-time-base patterns*. Basically, these are patterns obtained when the horizontal deflection voltage is a sawtooth waveform.

Let us begin our discussion by considering the effect of applying an ideal sawtooth to the horizontal deflection plates and zero voltage to the vertical deflection plates. In Fig. 12-15 we see that at point A in

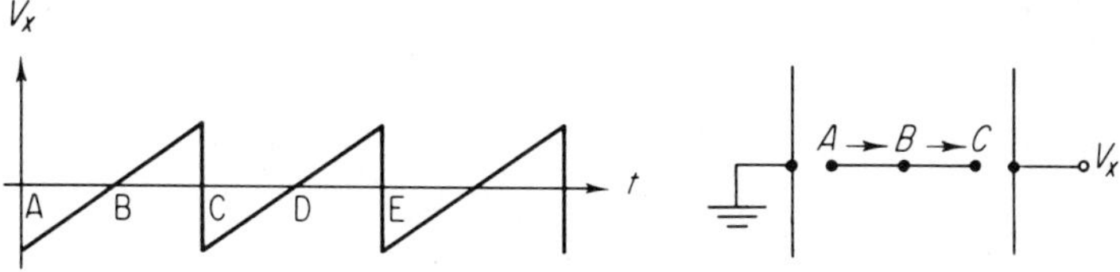

Fig. 12-15 Linear time base.

time, the sawtooth voltage is maximum negative. Therefore, the spot will be deflected to the extreme left of center. At point B in time, the voltage is zero, and the spot is at the center. Just before point C in time, the voltage is maximum positive, and the spot is at the extreme right of the screen. At point C in time the voltage flies back to maximum negative, and the spot goes from the extreme right to the extreme left in zero time. During the next cycle, the spot traces from left to right over the same path. Thus, a horizontal line appears on the CRT.

There is an extremely important aspect of this horizontal trace, and that is that the spot moves across the screen at uniform speed. For instance, suppose that the ideal sawtooth has a period of 10 sec, as shown in Fig. 12-16. Then the spot will trace out the horizontal line shown.

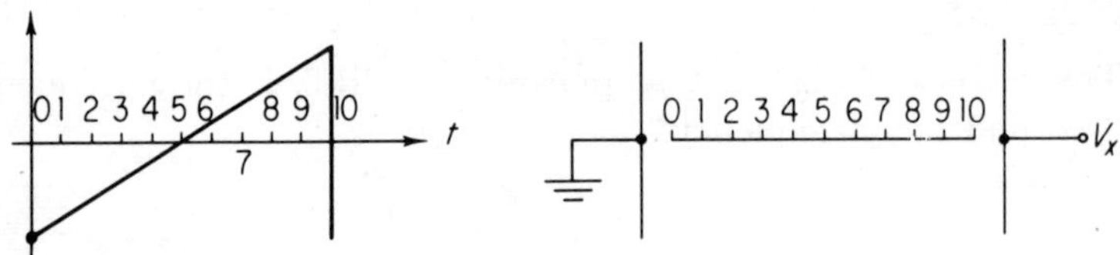

Fig. 12-16 Example of linear time base with period time of 10 sec.

Note carefully how the spot moves the same distance during each second of time. We speak of this trace as being a linear time base because the deflection of the spot from the extreme left is directly proportional to the amount of time that has elapsed since the beginning of the trace.

The importance of the linear time base is that functions of time can be displayed on the face of the CRT. For instance, suppose that V_y is a sine wave with a period of 10 sec and that V_x is an ideal sawtooth with a period of 10 sec, as shown in Fig. 12-17. At zero time, the spot is at the extreme left. At the end of 2.5 sec, the spot is one-quarter of the way across the screen in the horizontal direction and at maximum deflection in the vertical direction, as shown. At the end of 5 sec, the spot is at the center of the screen. At the end of 7.5 sec, the spot is three-fourths of the

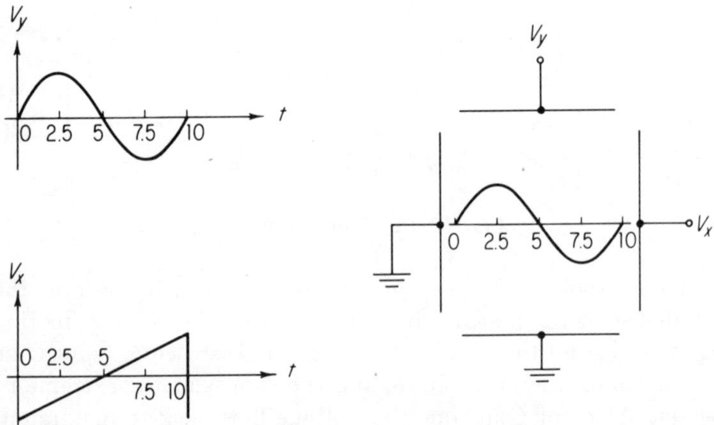

Fig. 12-17 A linear-time-base pattern.

way across the screen in the horizontal direction and at maximum negative deflection. Finally, at the end of 10 sec, the spot is at the extreme right, and then it flies back to begin a new trace.

If the period of the sine wave is reduced to 5 sec, exactly two sine-wave cycles appear on the CRT.

For any real sawtooth wave, it will take a finite amount of time for the spot to fly back to the starting point. Because of this, the pattern of Fig. 12-17 is a closed Lissajous pattern, and we would count one y peak and one x peak. As a result, the frequency ratio for the signals of Fig. 12-17 is unity.

We already know from our earlier discussion of Lissajous patterns that in order for a pattern to be stationary, the ratio of the frequencies must be a rational or fractional number. This represents one of the more difficult problems in the design of an oscilloscope. Given any repetitive signal on the vertical deflection plates, it is necessary to apply a sawtooth whose frequency exactly satisfies the rational-number condition required for a Lissajous pattern. How this sawtooth is generated and synchronized with the vertical input signal is discussed in later sections.

12-7 A Block Diagram of an Oscilloscope

In order to gain an initial understanding of how an oscilloscope works, let us use the much simplified block diagram of Fig. 12-18. Note that there are vertical and horizontal amplifiers so that signals can be amplified before being applied to the deflection plates. There is a two-position switch on the input side of the horizontal amplifier so that either an internally generated sawtooth or an external signal can be applied to the horizontal deflection plates.

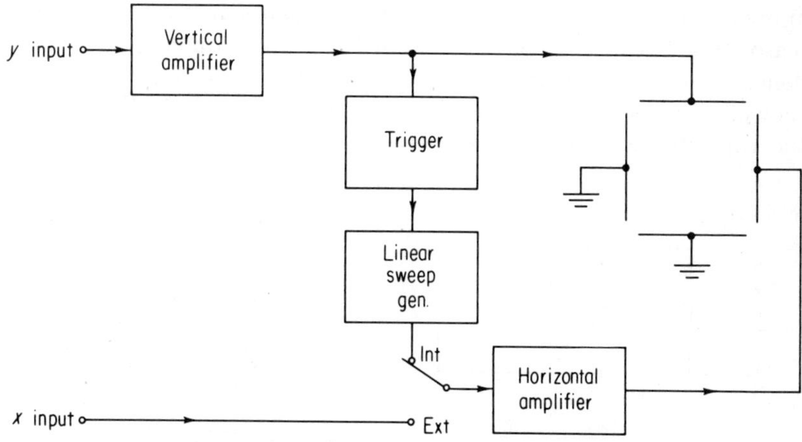

Fig. 12-18 Simplified block diagram of oscilloscope.

The operation of the oscilloscope is as follows. The y input signal is amplified and then applied to the vertical deflection plates. The linear sweep generator produces a sawtooth voltage. On the INT position of the switch this sawtooth is amplified by the horizontal amplifier and then applied to the horizontal deflection plates. On the EXT position of the switch, the signal on the x input terminals is used to drive the horizontal amplifier. In either INT or EXT position a steady pattern can result only if the ratio of the vertical frequency to the horizontal frequency is a rational number.

The frequency response of the oscilloscope is primarily determined by the response of the vertical amplifier. Most oscilloscopes use d-c amplifiers, so that no restriction exists on the frequency response at the low end. However, there is a limit to the high-frequency response determined by the upper cutoff frequency of the amplifier.

Two types of linear sweep generators are commonly used. First, there is a free-running type, which generates a sawtooth whether or not there is a y input signal. With this type of generator it is necessary to adjust the frequency of the sawtooth so that the pattern is almost stationary. Then, by feeding the y signal into the sweep generator, it is possible to pull the sweep frequency into synchronism with the y input signal. The second type of sweep generator does not free-run. A sawtooth is generated only if a y input signal is present. The start of the sweep is triggered by the y signal so that synchronization is assured. Both of these sweeps will be discussed in later sections.

12-8 The Free-running Sweep Generator

One of the earliest methods used to obtain a sawtooth waveform is the approach of charging and discharging a capacitor in such a way that a reasonably linear sawtooth is obtained. As an example of how this is done, consider the circuit of Fig. 12-19a. With the switch in the position shown, v equals zero. Suppose that the switch is opened. We know that the capacitor will charge. Furthermore, we know from our studies of

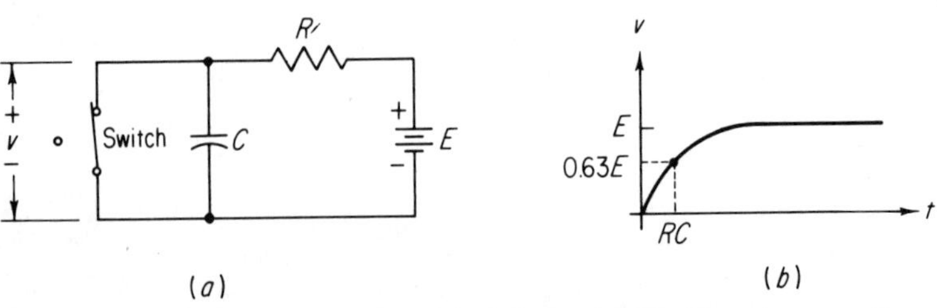

Fig. 12-19 Capacitor charging. (a) RC circuit. (b) Charging waveform.

transients that the final capacitor voltage is equal to the battery voltage E. With the switch open, we have a single-loop circuit, and it is clear that the time constant is simply RC. Hence, the formula for the voltage v is

$$v = v_f + (v_i - v_f)\,\epsilon^{-t/RC} = E + (0 - E)\epsilon^{-t/RC}$$

or

$$v = E(1 - \epsilon^{-t/RC}) \tag{12-5}$$

The graph of Eq. (12-5) is shown in Fig. 12-19*b*. This is the usual exponential curve starting at the initial voltage and asymptotically approaching the final voltage.

The early portion of the charging curve is almost linear. If we close the switch soon after the capacitor starts charging, we can obtain the waveform of Fig. 12-20*a*. Furthermore, if we close and open the switch

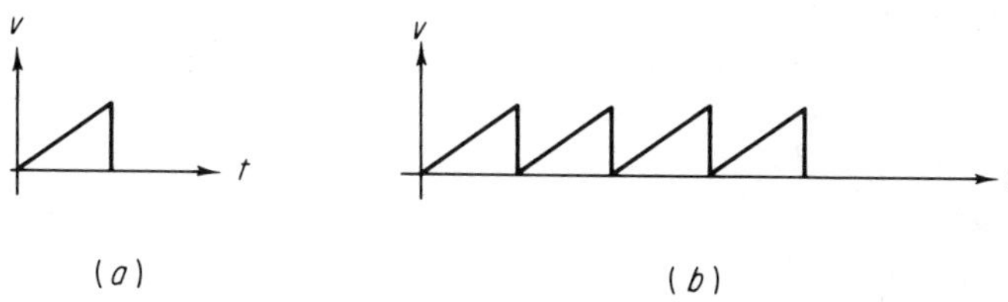

Fig. 12-20 Obtaining the sawtooth waveform.

at just the right instants in time, we can obtain a repetitive sawtooth, as shown in Fig. 12-20*b*. This is the waveform we require for the horizontal deflection plates. The rising part is not perfectly linear, but it will do for practical purposes. To improve the linearity, we need only close the switch earlier during the charging cycle.

The exact formula for the charging portion of the sawtooth of Fig. 12-20*a* is given by Eq. (12-5). A very useful approximation of Eq. (12-5) can be obtained in the following manner. Since we are interested in the early portion of the charging curve, in effect, the amount of charging time must be kept much smaller than one RC time constant. This is equivalent to saying that

$$\frac{t}{RC} \ll 1$$

In our study of peak detectors in Chap. 4, we learned that

$$\epsilon^{-t/RC} \cong 1 - \frac{t}{RC} \qquad \text{if } \frac{t}{RC} \ll 1$$

If we substitute this expression into Eq. (12-5) we obtain

$$v \cong E\left(1 - 1 + \frac{t}{RC}\right)$$

or

$$v \cong \frac{E}{RC}\,t \tag{12-6}$$

Equation (12-6) immediately confirms the fact that the early portion of the charging curve is linear. Recall that any equation of the form $y = mx$ graphs as a straight line through the origin with a slope of m. In our case, the graph of v vs. t is a straight line through the origin with a slope of E/RC. Of course, Eq. (12-6) is only an approximation, but it is quite accurate if t/RC is much less than unity. A careful mathematical analysis shows that Eq. (12-6) is accurate to within 5 percent if t/RC is less than 0.1.

In practice, a thyratron is often used for the switch that discharges the capacitor. Basically, a thyratron is a triode that is filled with gas. If there is no current in the tube, the gas has no effect. However, if there is current in the tube, the gas ionizes, and the tube then has a very low resistance.

The way in which the thyratron is used for switching is brought out by considering Fig. 12-21. The control grid is negatively biased, so that

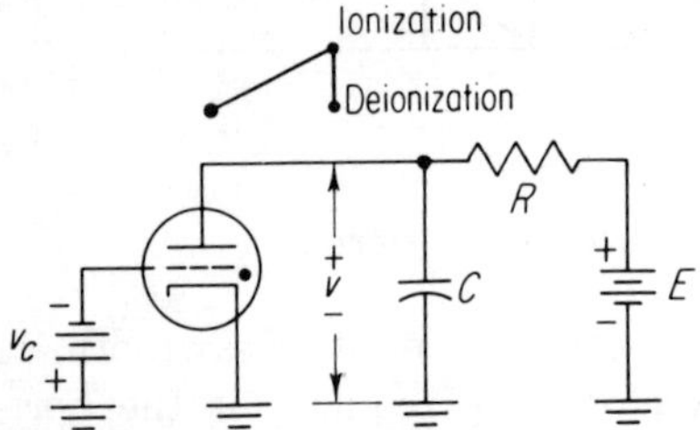

Fig. 12-21 Thyratron sawtooth generator.

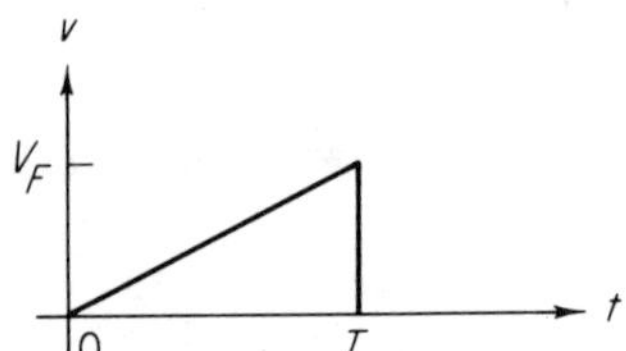

Fig. 12-22 One cycle of sawtooth voltage.

the thyratron is cut off during the early portion of charging curve. As the capacitor voltage builds up, however, a point is eventually reached where current just begins to flow in the thyratron. Collisions between the electrons and the gas molecules cause the gas to ionize. Once this happens, the tube has a very low resistance between the plate and the cathode. In effect, the tube becomes a short. This discharges the capacitor until the voltage drops almost to zero, at which time the tube deionizes or shuts off. The charging cycle then repeats.

The point at which the thyratron conducts heavily is called the *ionization voltage* or the *firing potential* of the thyratron. The firing potential of the thyratron can be controlled by changing the bias on the tube. In order to ensure a linear sawtooth the tube must be biased so that the firing potential is much smaller than the power-supply voltage E. Typically, the firing potential should be at least 10 times smaller than E. Thus, if E is 300 volts, the firing potential should be less than 30 volts. The grid of the thyratron is μ times more effective than the plate voltage in determining the cut off point of the thyratron. Thus, if a tube has

$\mu = 20$, and if the firing potential of the thyratron is to be 30 volts, the grid should be set at approximately $^{30}\!/_{20}$, or 1.5 volts negative.

The period of the sawtooth can be found by considering Fig. 12-22. Note that the sawtooth flies back at the instant in time that v reaches the firing potential V_F. Hence, when $t = T$, $v = V_F$. Substituting into Eq. (12-6) we get

$$V_F = \frac{E}{RC} T$$

or

$$T = \frac{V_F}{E} RC \qquad \text{provided that } V_F \ll E \qquad (12\text{-}7)$$

From Eq. (12-7) it is immediately clear that the period of the sawtooth waveform can be controlled by changing any of the quantities on the right-hand side of the equation. We will discuss this further in the next section.

EXAMPLE 12-6

In Fig. 12-21 R equals 100 kilohms and C equals 1000 pf. The power-supply voltage E is 400 volts, and the thyratron has a firing potential of 10 volts. Find the period of the sawtooth generated by this circuit.

SOLUTION

$$T = \frac{V_F}{E} RC = {}^{10}\!/_{400}(100)(10^3)(1000)(10^{-12}) = 2.5\ \mu\text{sec}$$

12-9 Synchronizing a Free-running Sawtooth Generator

A more practical version of the sawtooth generator is shown in Fig. 12-23. The cutoff bias for the thyratron is provided by the voltage divider formed by R_2 and R_3. Thus, the cathode is positive with respect

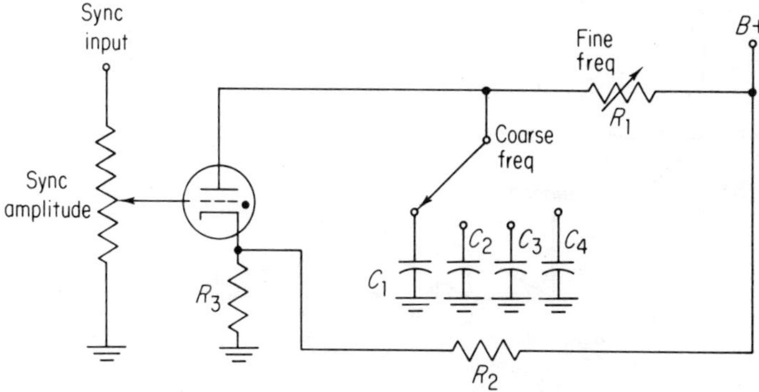

Fig. 12-23 Variable-frequency sawtooth generator.

to the grid, and the tube remains cut off until the plate voltage reaches the firing potential. There is a coarse frequency switch to allow changing the time constant in large steps. There is also a fine frequency control R_1, which allows us to change the frequency of the sawtooth continuously.

When using an oscilloscope with a free-running sweep circuit like that of Fig. 12-23, it is necessary to adjust the coarse and fine frequency until the sawtooth frequency is almost equal to the y input frequency or until it is a submultiple of the y frequency. Under this condition the pattern on the CRT will be almost stationary. Normally, to really lock in the picture so that it remains stationary, it will be necessary to synchronize the sawtooth frequency with the y input signal. This is usually accomplished by feeding the y signal into the grid of the thyratron. This has the effect of lowering the firing potential during the positive half cycle of the y signal and raising the firing potential during the negative half cycle. By adjusting the size of the y input to the grid, it is possible to pull the sawtooth frequency into synchronism with the y signal.

To bring the synchronization out more clearly, let us idealize the situation by assuming that the y signal has been processed to obtain a train of narrow pulses, as shown in Fig. 12-24*a*. The time interval between these pulses exactly equals the period of the y signal. These narrow pulses are the sync signal that is applied to the grid of the thyratron. At the instant in time that one of these pulses appears, the firing potential of the thyratron is lowered (see Fig. 12-24*b*). Note that the firing potential is momentarily lowered *each* time a sync pulse appears at the grid. The

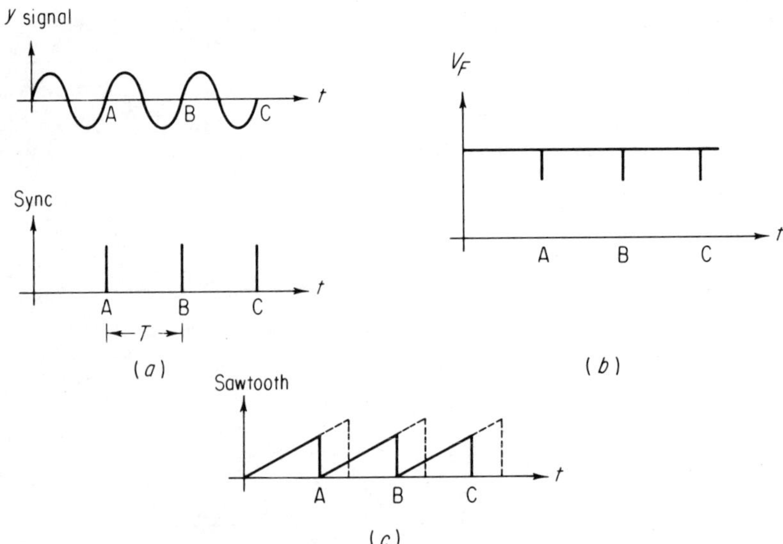

Fig. 12-24 Ideal synchronization of sawtooth generator.

way in which these pulses synchronize the sawtooth is shown in Fig. 12-24*c*. During the first sawtooth cycle, the sawtooth voltage is increasing toward the firing potential of the tube. With no sync signal, the sawtooth would follow the dashed lines until it reached the firing potential. With a sync signal the firing potential is lowered at times A, B, and C. Hence, the thyratron fires slightly earlier in time with the sync signal present. As a result, the sawtooth flies back at times A, B, and C. In effect, the period of the sawtooth equals the period of the y input signal. Hence, a steady pattern appears on the CRT.

The y signal can be injected directly into the grid without first processing it into narrow pulses. In this case, the synchronizing action is similar to that for ideal pulses. The y signal lowers the firing potential of the tube and causes the sawtooth to fly back slightly sooner than it would without a sync signal.

Note that the period of the unsynchronized sawtooth must be slightly larger than the period of the y signal. As a result, when we use an oscilloscope with this type of sweep generator, we first turn the sync amplitude down to zero. Then the coarse and fine frequency are adjusted so that the pattern is almost stationary. In order to ensure that the sawtooth period is slightly longer than when synchronized, we should have a pattern that is drifting to the left. (This implies that the sawtooth period is larger than the period of the y signal.) Finally, we increase the sync amplitude until the pattern just locks in.

Up to now, we have made the period of the sawtooth exactly equal to the period of the signal. This means that we would obtain one cycle of the signal on the CRT. If the period of the sawtooth is a multiple of the y signal period, more than one cycle is obtained on the CRT. The synchronization is similar, except that instead of each sync pulse triggering the sawtooth, every second, or every third, or every nth pulse may trigger the sawtooth.

Synchronizing a free-running sawtooth generator is only one of the approaches used in oscilloscopes. Clearly, this particular approach is far from ideal. There are many disadvantages in this system. For instance, adjusting the fine frequency control until the pattern drifts slowly to the left requires a certain amount of time and patience. Further, after increasing the sync amplitude to lock in the picture, we will find that if for some reason the y amplitude changes, the pattern may drop out of synchronism.

12-10 The Miller Sweep Generator

In this section we examine another approach in generating the sawtooth waveform required for linear-time-base patterns. In discussing a simple form of the Miller sweep generator, we will obtain a basic understanding of how a linear sawtooth can be generated in a manner fundamentally different from that discussed in the preceding sections.

Consider the circuit of Fig. 12-25. This is an elementary form of the Miller sweep generator and works as follows. Before point A in time,

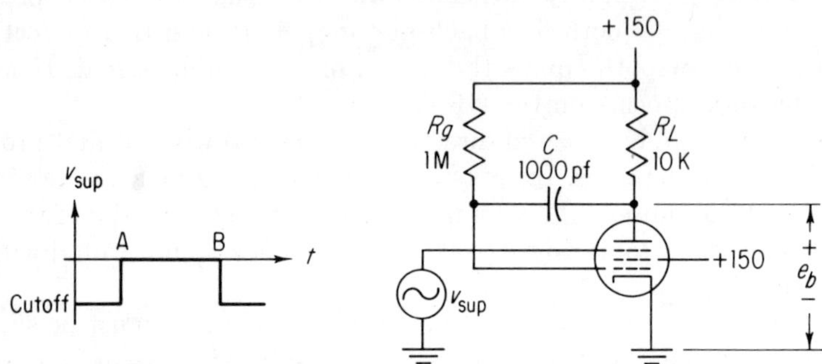

Fig. 12-25 Elementary form of Miller sweep generator.

the suppressor voltage is negative enough to prevent plate current. Under this condition the only current in the tube is the screen current and the grid current. Note that there is grid current because the grid is returned through a 1-megohm resistor to the +150-volt supply. The grid-cathode part of the tube behaves essentially like a diode, so that there is a small positive voltage from grid to cathode. Since there is no plate current, the voltage from the plate to ground is +150 volts.

Let us assume that the tube has the characteristics shown in Fig. 12-26*a*. A 10-kilohm load line has been drawn on the tube characteristics. Before point A in time, there is no plate current, and the operating point is at the bottom of the load line. At point A in time the signal on the suppressor suddenly changes from a large negative value to zero volts. Immediately, plate current flows, and the plate voltage drops. This negative-going voltage drop is coupled through the capacitor back to the control grid. Since the control grid has been driven negatively, it tends to prevent the plate voltage from dropping too far. A compromise occurs such that the plate voltage stops dropping after a few volts. Specifically, on the load line of Fig. 12-26*a* the operating point suddenly goes from the cutoff point to the point labeled A. Note that at this point the plate voltage is 147 volts and the grid voltage is −3 volts. These sudden changes in grid and plate voltage take place in a very short time, and are illustrated in the waveforms of Fig. 12-26*c* and *d*. Note that at point A in time the plate suddenly drops from +150 to +147 volts. This change is coupled back to the grid, and it suddenly drops from about 0 to −3 volts, as shown.

After this initial drop has occurred, the tube acts as an amplifier and will amplify the signal that is on the grid.

What signal will we have on the grid? Recall that whenever a capacitor is connected from the plate back to the grid, a phenomenon known as the Miller effect takes place. The Miller effect basically means that a capacitor connected from the plate to the grid of a tube will resemble a capacitor whose size is $(1 + A)C$ when observed from the grid side of the tube. (A is the voltage gain from grid to plate.) In other words, we can redraw the circuit as shown in Fig. 12-26*b*.

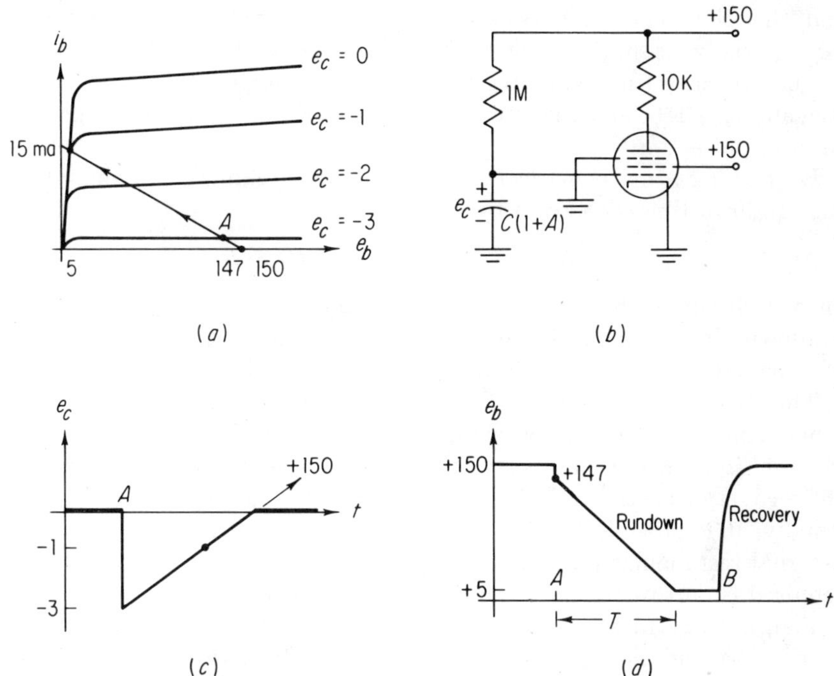

Fig. 12-26 Miller-sweep-generator operation. (*a*) Load line. (*b*) Equivalent circuit during rundown. (*c*) Grid voltage. (*d*) Plate voltage.

In the equivalent circuit of Fig. 12-26*b*, the initial value of e_c at point A in time is -3 volts. Clearly, the capacitor voltage cannot remain at -3 volts. The capacitor is connected to the $+150$-volt supply through a 1-megohm resistor. Hence, the capacitor must charge exponentially toward a final voltage of $+150$ volts. The early part of the charging curve is shown in Fig. 12-26*c*. The voltage on the capacitor starts to rise toward a target voltage of $+150$ volts. Since the grid voltage is rising, the plate current is increasing, and the operating point of the tube moves from point A on the load line toward the saturation point.

The plate-voltage variation is shown in Fig. 12-26*d*. Note that during the rundown, the plate voltage is dropping linearly from $+147$ volts to

+5 volts. At +5 volts the voltage can drop no further because the tube has saturated. In Fig. 12-26*a*, we can see that the tube saturates when the grid voltage has reached about −1 volt. The plate voltage is an amplified version of the change in grid voltage. Only the earliest part of the charging curve on the grid is being amplified. Because of this we obtain an output from the plate that is extremely linear.

Once the plate voltage bottoms, it merely holds until point B in time. At point B in time the suppressor is once again driven beyond cutoff, and the plate current goes to zero. The plate voltage then recovers exponentially, as shown in Fig. 12-26*d*. This exponential recovery is caused by the capacitor from plate to grid. Once it has charged, the plate voltage is again at +150, and the circuit is ready to receive another suppressor turn-on pulse.

By making a mathematical analysis of this circuit we can show that the rundown time T is given by

$$T \cong R_g C \qquad \text{provided that } R_g \gg R_L \tag{12-8}$$

In our circuit we have $R_g = 1$ megohm and $C = 1000$ pf, so that the rundown time is about $10^6(1000)(10^{-12})$, or 1 msec. It takes the plate approximately 1 msec to drop linearly from +147 to +5 volts.

The Miller circuit of Fig. 12-25 is only an elementary form. Many refinements are possible. For instance, it is possible to eliminate the initial voltage drop on the plate that occurs at point A in time. Furthermore, the recovery time shown in Fig. 12-26*d* at point B can be greatly reduced. Finally, it is possible to make the Miller sweep self-gating, so that an external rectangular pulse is not required for the suppressor. All that is required is narrow trigger pulse to initiate the sweep.

Figure 12-27 illustrates the input-output signals that are possible if more tubes and diodes are added to the basic Miller sweep circuit. Note

Fig. 12-27 Diagram of modified Miller sweep generator.

that in the modified Miller sweep we require only narrow input-trigger pulses. For each trigger received there is one sawtooth. There will be a sawtooth output only if an input trigger is received. Thus, at point A in time the first trigger is received, and the sawtooth starts. The next sawtooth occurs at point B in time. Then, there is a holding period until the C trigger arrives. The third sawtooth then starts.

The advantage of an oscilloscope using a modified Miller sweep is that the input triggers can be derived from the y signal. In effect, the y signal controls the starting point of the sweep, so that reliable sychronization is possible. This will be discussed in later sections.

Example 12-7

In Fig. 12-28 find the minimum and maximum value of rundown time on each range.

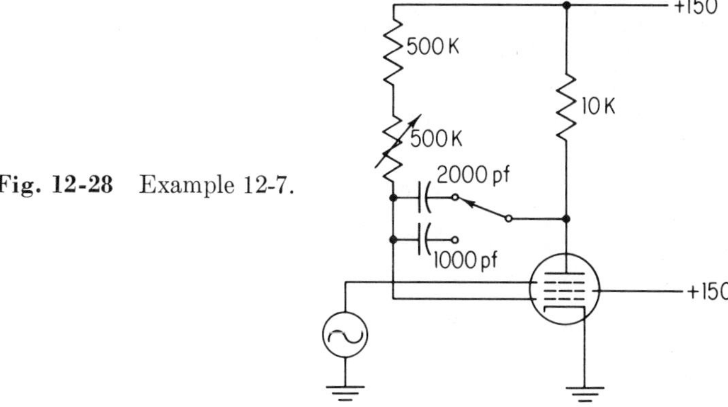

Fig. 12-28 Example 12-7.

Solution

The minimum value of the rheostat is zero, and the maximum value is 500 kilohms. Hence, R_g varies from 500 kilohms to 1 megohm. On the 1000-pf position

$$T \cong 500(10^3)(1000)(10^{-12}) = 500\ \mu\text{sec minimum}$$
$$T \cong 10^6(1000)(10^{-12}) = 1000\ \mu\text{sec maximum}$$

On the 2000-pf position

$$T \cong 500(10^3)(2000)(10^{-12}) = 1000\ \mu\text{sec mimimum}$$
$$T \cong 10^6(2000)(10^{-12}) = 2000\ \mu\text{sec maximum}$$

12-11 The Schmitt Trigger

An extremely important circuit in oscilloscopes and other areas of electronics is the Schmitt trigger. This is a binary type of circuit in that its output is either a low voltage or a high voltage. Whether the Schmitt-trigger output is in the low or high state depends upon the value of the input voltage.

In order to see how a typical Schmitt-trigger circuit works, let us analyze the operation of the circuit shown in Fig. 12-29a. It has been designed in such a way that one of the transistors is saturated, and the other one is cut off. The input voltage has been represented by a battery to simplify our preliminary analysis. Let us begin by adjusting the input battery voltage to zero. Under this condition there is no base current in Q1; therefore, there is no collector current in Q1. The base of Q2 is connected to a voltage divider formed by the 100-kilohm resistors. The voltage at the top of the voltage divider is approximately 10 volts. In this circuit the base current is more than enough to saturate Q2. With Q2 saturated, the collector and emitter are effectively shorted together, as shown in Fig. 12-29*b*. As a result, the voltage from the emitter to ground is 2 volts.

Thus, with the input battery at zero volts, we have Q1 cut off and Q2 saturated. Under this condition the output voltage of the Schmitt trigger is about 2 volts, which is evident from an inspection of Fig. 12-29*b*.

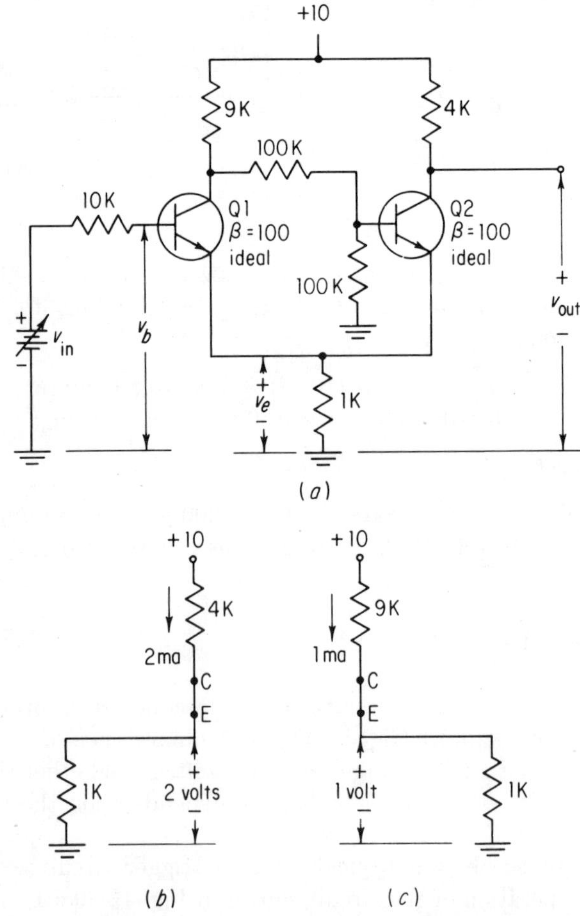

Fig. 12-29 Transistorized Schmitt trigger. (*a*) Circuit. (*b*) Q2 saturated. (*c*) Q1 saturated.

Since the emitter voltage is 2 volts, it should be clear that for any value of input voltage less than 2 volts, there can be no base current in Q1 because the base-emitter diode of Q1 remains back-biased. Therefore, for any input less than 2 volts, the output voltage of the Schmitt trigger remains at 2 volts since Q2 stays saturated.

If we raise the input voltage above 2 volts, base current flows in Q1. Once this happens, the collector current increases, and the voltage at the Q1 collector decreases. This drop in collector voltage is coupled into the base of Q2, bringing Q2 out of saturation. The reduced Q2 current now reduces the voltage from emitter to ground. Since v_e has been reduced, Q1 is turned on harder. The increase in the Q1 current drops the collector voltage of Q1 even further, and we have what is commonly known as *regeneration*. This regeneration continues until Q1 becomes saturated and Q2 is cutoff. With Q2 cutoff, the output voltage is 10 volts, since there is no current through the 4-kilohm load resistor. The regenerative switching action takes place very quickly, so that we may think of v_{out} as suddenly having gone from 2 to 10 volts.

Any further increase in input voltage will certainly increase the Q1 base current. However, since Q2 is already cut off, the output voltage must remain at 10 volts.

Note that with Q1 saturated the emitter voltage to ground is only 1 volt, as shown in Fig. 12-29*c*.

With the output voltage at 10 volts, the only way of bringing the output voltage back to 2 volts is by reducing the input voltage driving Q1. Since the emitter voltage is only 1 volt, as shown in Fig. 12-29*c*, the input voltage must be reduced to about 1 volt. At this point Q1 comes out of saturation. The collector voltage of Q1 increases, and this in turn causes Q2 to conduct. With Q2 conducting, the emitter voltage increases, causing the current in Q1 to decrease further. This raises the collector voltage of Q1, and once again we have regenerative action. The regeneration continues until Q1 is cut off and Q2 is saturated. The circuit is then back in the original condition with an output voltage of 2 volts.

The circuit action of the Schmitt trigger can be conveniently summarized by drawing a graph of the output voltage versus the input voltage (see Fig. 12-30*a*). Note that the output voltage is either 2 or 10 volts. When v_{out} is in the low state, it is necessary to raise v_{in} to slightly more than 2 volts in order to cause v_{out} to jump into the higher state. Once in the high state, v_{out} remains at 10 volts until v_{in} is reduced to slightly less than 1 volt. The output then jumps back to the low state of 2 volts. The rapid switching action is indicated by the dashed lines.

In general, any Schmitt trigger is characterized by a graph like that in Fig. 12-30*b*. The value of v_{in} that causes the output to jump from a low to a high state is called the upper trip point (UTP). The value of

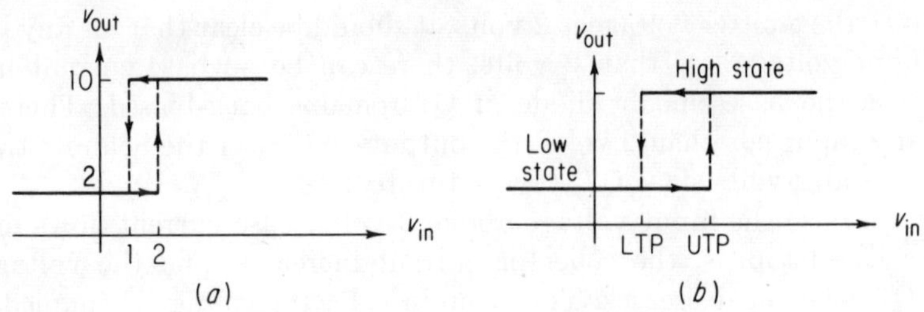

Fig. 12-30 Schmitt-trigger input-output characteristics. (*a*) Specific example. (*b*) General.

v_{in} that causes the output to go from the high to the low state is called the lower trip point (LTP).

The Schmitt trigger can also be built using vacuum tubes.

Example 12-8

A Schmitt trigger has the following characteristics:

$$\text{UTP} = 3 \text{ volts} \qquad \text{LTP} = 1 \text{ volt}$$
$$\text{High state} = 20 \text{ volts} \qquad \text{low state} = 2 \text{ volts}$$

Sketch the output voltage of the Schmitt trigger if it is driven by a sinusoidal voltage with a peak value of 6 volts.

Solution

Let us sketch the Schmitt-trigger characteristic and the input sinusoid as shown in Fig. 12-31*a*. As the sinusoid increases above 3 volts, the Schmitt trigger changes from a low to a high state. This occurs at point *A* in time. The output remains in the high state until

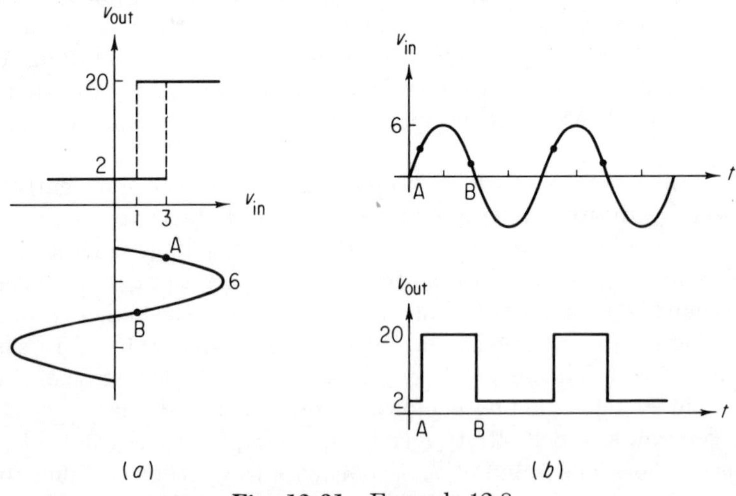

Fig. 12-31 Example 12-8.

the input sinusoid drops below 1 volt. Then the output drops back to low state at point B in time. Hence, we can sketch the input and output as shown in Fig. 12-31*b*. Note that the output is a rectangular pulse.

EXAMPLE 12-9

The Schmitt trigger of the preceding example is driven by a sawtooth voltage with a peak value of 10 volts. Sketch the Schmitt-trigger output.

SOLUTION

The Schmitt characteristic and the sawtooth are shown in Fig. 12-32*a*. It should be clear that the Schmitt trigger trips as the sawtooth

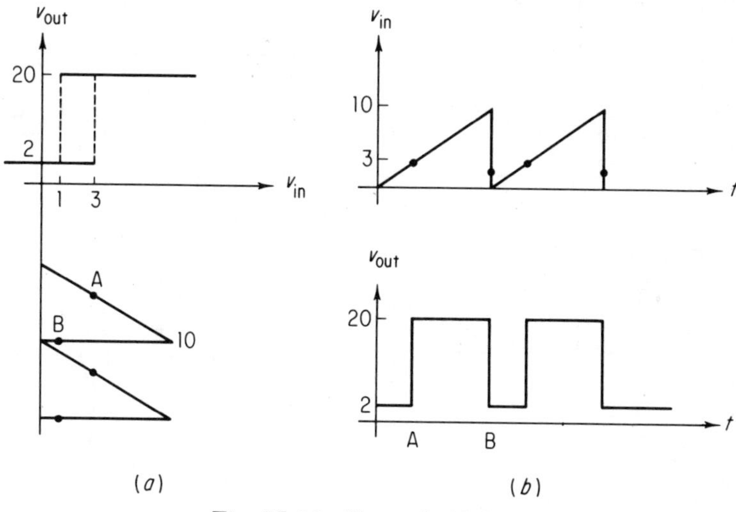

Fig. 12-32 Example 12-9.

passes through the 3-volt level. On the sawtooth flyback, the Schmitt trigger trips at 1 volt. The output voltage is shown in Fig. 12-32*b*. In general, we may note that whenever a Schmitt trigger is driven by a periodic signal whose peak value is greater than the UTP, the output of the Schmitt trigger will be a rectangular waveform.

12-12 A Simple *RC* Differentiator

One more circuit must be discussed before we describe how an oscilloscope using a Miller sweep generator is synchronized. Consider the circuit of

Fig. 12-33*a*. If the capacitor is very large, we can expect the square wave to be coupled to the output. Specifically, in order for the square wave to be well coupled to the output, the RC time constant must be much larger than the period of the square wave, as shown in Fig. 12-33*b*.

On the other hand, if the RC time constant is very short compared to the period of the square wave, the capacitor will actually have time to charge and discharge during each half cycle. Because of this, the square wave is not coupled to the output. Instead, a so-called differentiated wave appears at the output, as shown in Fig. 12-33*c*.

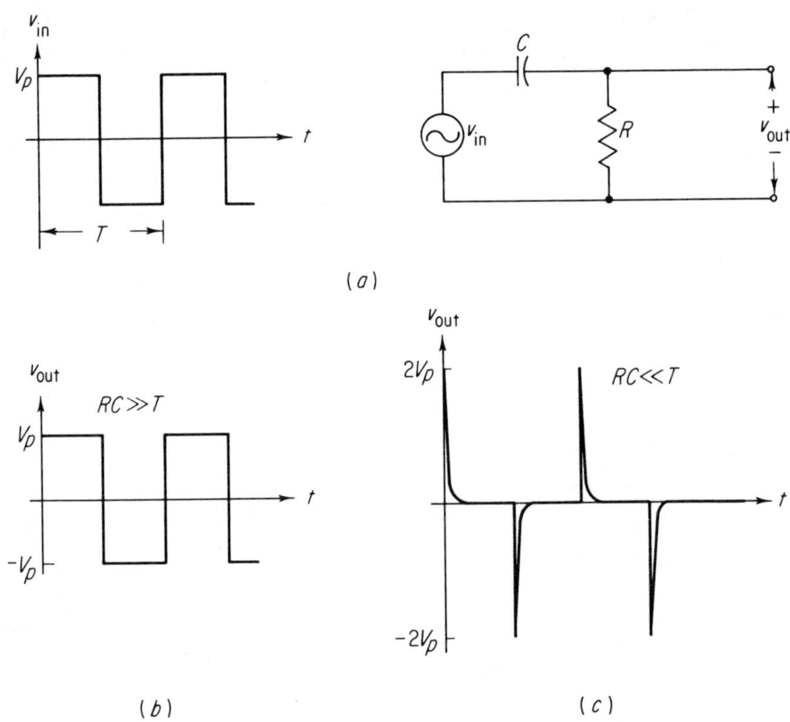

Fig. 12-33 RC differentiation. (*a*) Circuit. (*b*) Output for RC much greater than T. (*c*) Output for RC much less than T.

A mathematical analysis using the transient equation of Chap. 1 allows us to use the following two rules as guides in designing good coupling or good differentiating circuits:

For good coupling

$$RC > 100T$$

For good differentiation

$$T > 100RC$$

Example 12-10

A square wave with a period of 1 msec is to be coupled into a load resistor of 100 kilohms. Find the size of the coupling capacitor needed for good coupling.

Solution

$$RC > 100T \qquad \text{or} \qquad RC > 100(10^{-3})$$

or

$$RC > 0.1$$

Hence, the minimum value of C should be

$$C = \frac{0.1}{100(10^3)} = 1\ \mu\text{f}$$

Example 12-11

In the preceding example, what size should the capacitor be if we desire to differentiate the square wave to obtain narrow pulses?

Solution

$$T > 100RC \qquad \text{or} \qquad 0.001 > 100(100)(10^3)C$$

Hence, the capacitor should be no larger than

$$C = \frac{0.001}{100(100)(10^3)} = 100\ \text{pf}$$

12-13 Automatic Synchronization

A simplified block diagram of a modern oscilloscope is shown in Fig. 12-34. The y input signal may be a-c or d-c coupled into the vertical amplifier. There is an attenuator to allow different measuring sensitivities. The output of the vertical amplifier is applied to the vertical deflection plates and to a Schmitt trigger. The output of the Schmitt trigger is a rectangular pulse whose leading edge coincides with the same voltage on each cycle of the y signal. This rectangular pulse is differentiated to obtain narrow pulses. These pulses are then negatively clipped to obtain a train of positive pulses. The Miller sweep circuit is driven by these narrow pulses. The first pulse into the Miller sweep initiates the sweep. As the first sawtooth builds up, another trigger pulse appears. The Miller sweep does not respond to any pulses once the rundown has begun. The sweep continues until the end of the rundown time and then flies back. The Miller circuit is then ready to be triggered by the next input trigger.

The Miller sweep time can be changed so that it is longer or shorter. We have arbitrarily shown it as being long enough to be triggered by

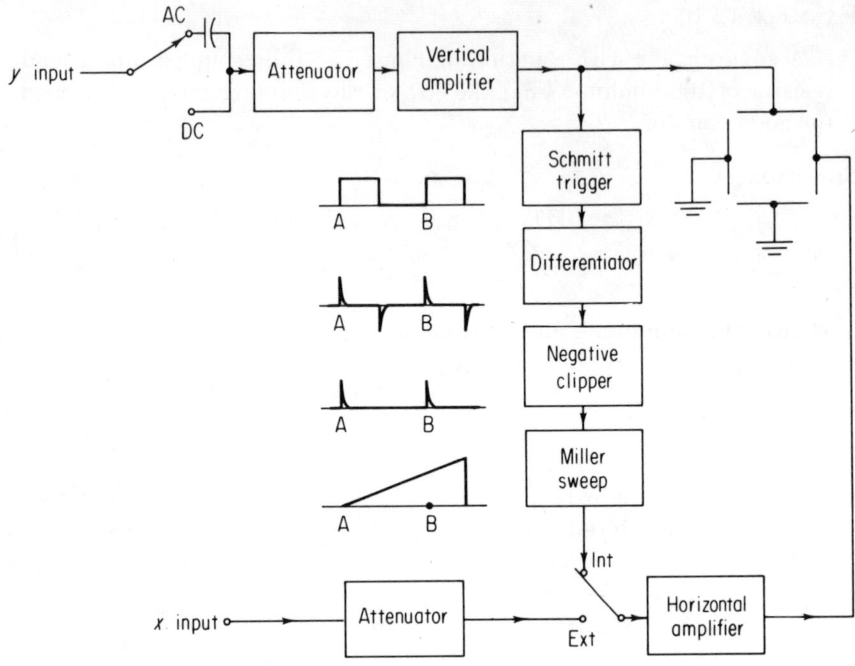

Fig. 12-34 Block diagram for automatic synchronization.

every other trigger pulse. As already indicated, once the rundown begins, the Miller circuit does not respond to intermediate triggers.

The sweep voltage is then amplified in the horizontal amplifier before being applied to the horizontal deflection plates. If we wish to use an x signal input, the switch on the horizontal amplifier input is changed to EXT.

The various waveforms are shown in Fig. 12-35. Once again, note that the leading edge of each rectangular pulse out of the Schmitt trigger occurs at the same voltage for each cycle of the y signal. After the Schmitt-trigger output is differentiated and clipped, we have a train of narrow trigger pulses. In this case, we have arbitrarily shown the Miller sweep time of such a duration that it responds to every other trigger. The important thing to notice is that the start of the sweep is synchronized with a fixed voltage level on the y signal. As a result, the same pattern is traced on the CRT for each sweep.

There is one more item to be mentioned. During the flyback time, it is normal procedure to apply a large negative voltage to the control grid of the CRT in order to cut off the electron beam. This is known as *blanking* and is done simply to prevent a confusing retrace line from appearing on the CRT.

There are many details involved in a modern oscilloscope; however, the block diagram of Fig. 12-34 conveys many of the essential ideas.

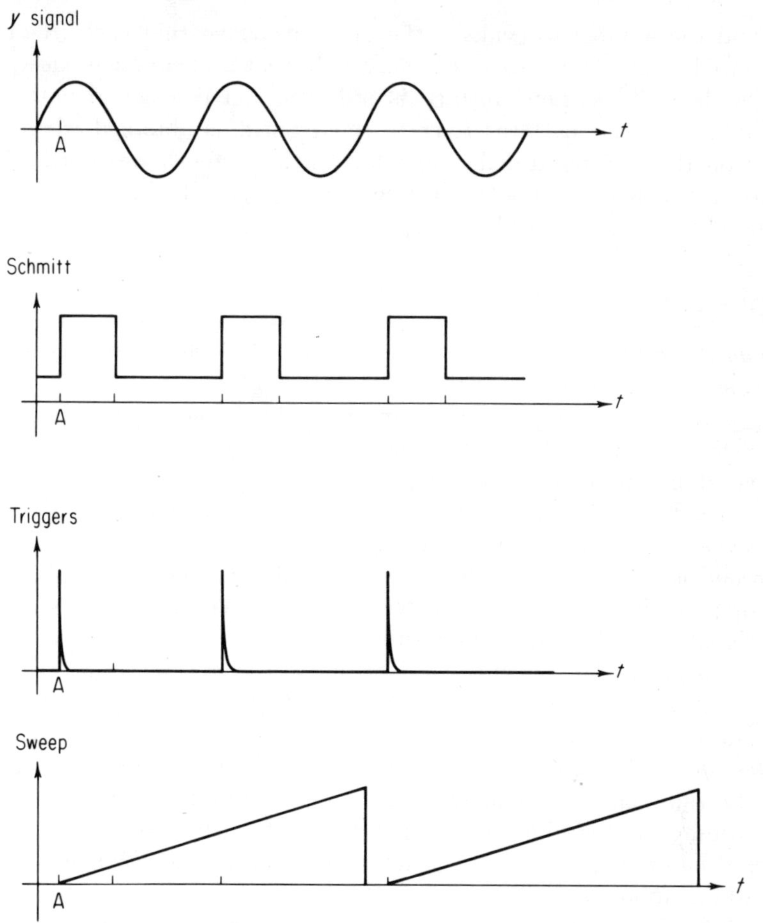

Fig. 12-35 Waveforms involved in synchronization. (*a*) Input signal. (*b*) Output of Schmitt trigger. (*c*) Sync triggers. (*d*) Synchronized sweep.

SUMMARY

If the ratio of the frequencies applied to the x and y inputs of an oscilloscope is a rational number, a steady pattern results. With equal-frequency equal-amplitude sinusoids the result will be a straight line, a circle, or an ellipse, depending upon the phase angle between the sinusoids. The sine of the phase angle between these sinusoids is equal to the ratio of the y intercept to the y peak.

When dealing with closed Lissajous patterns the ratio of the y and x frequencies is equal to the ratio of the number of y peaks to the number of x peaks. For open Lissajous patterns the relation between the frequencies and the number of peaks is the same, provided that each free end is counted as one-half instead of one. (Note that a linear-time-base pattern with a blanked-out retrace is still considered a closed pattern.)

Linear-time-base patterns refer to those patterns obtained when the signal on the horizontal deflection plates is a sawtooth waveform. The sawtooth is generated in either a free-running type of generator or in a triggered type like the Miller sweep generator.

GLOSSARY

astigmatism control Used in conjunction with the focus control to obtain a sharp trace over the entire face of the CRT.

firing potential In speaking of a thyratron this is the value of plate-to-cathode voltage that causes the gas to ionize. The firing potential is a function of the grid voltage.

linear time base A horizontal trace produced by a spot moving across the screen with a constant velocity.

Lissajous patterns Stationary patterns resulting from the application of periodic signals to the deflection plates. The frequencies of the signals must be rationally related.

lower trip point In reference to a Schmitt trigger this is the value of input voltage that causes the Schmitt trigger to go from the high state into the low state.

Miller effect Refers to the fact that the grid-plate capacitance produces the same effect as a much larger capacitance from grid to ground whose value is given by $A + 1$ times the grid-plate capacitance.

rational number Any number that can be expressed as the ratio of two whole numbers.

Schmitt trigger A circuit whose output is either a low or a high voltage. The state of the circuit is controlled by the input voltage.

thyratron A triode filled with gas. The tube acts as either a very low or very high resistance, depending upon the values of grid and plate voltage.

upper trip point The value of input voltage to a Schmitt trigger that causes the output to change from a low to a high voltage.

REVIEW QUESTIONS

1. What is the purpose of the astigmatism control in an oscilloscope?
2. If equal-frequency equal-amplitude in-phase sinusoids are applied to the deflection plates, what pattern results? If the sinusoids are 180° out of phase, what pattern results?
3. What pattern results from applying equal-frequency equal-amplitude 90° out-of-phase sinusoids to the deflection plates?
4. If an ellipse is the pattern on the face of a CRT, how can you find

the phase angle between the sinusoids being applied to the deflection plates?

5. In order for a stationary pattern to exist on the face of a CRT, what is the necessary relation between the x and y frequency?
6. What is an open Lissajous pattern? A closed Lissajous pattern?
7. How can we find the ratio of the y and x frequencies if a closed Lissajous pattern appears on a CRT?
8. What kind of signal must be applied to the horizontal deflection plates to obtain a linear-time-base pattern?
9. In an oscilloscope what is the purpose of the INT-EXT switch in the horizontal section?
10. What kind of tube is sometimes used as a switch in a free running type of sawtooth generator?
11. When charging and discharging a capacitor to produce a sawtooth waveform, how is it possible to obtain a linear sawtooth?
12. How can the linearity of a sawtooth be improved in the free-running type of sawtooth generator?
13. Name some of the quantities that control the period of the sawtooth generated by a free-running generator.
14. When using an oscilloscope with a free-running type of sawtooth generator, which way should the pattern drift before the sync amplitude is turned up?
15. If a positive pulse is applied to the grid of a thyratron, does this lower or raise the firing potential of the thyratron?
16. In the Miller sweep circuit of Fig. 12-25 how can you find the approximate value of the rundown time?
17. In Fig. 12-26*d* there is a small drop in plate voltage before the rundown. What causes this drop?
18. In Fig. 12-26*d* the plate voltage returns exponentially at point B in time to +150 volts. Why does it take time for the plate to recover to +150 volts?
19. Describe the operation of a Schmitt trigger in terms of its input and output voltage.
20. How is the upper trip point of a Schmitt trigger defined?
21. What is an RC differentiating circuit? What effect does it have on a square-wave input?
22. With automatic triggering why does the pattern remain stationary?

PROBLEMS

12-1 Two equal-frequency sinusoids are applied to the deflection plates of a CRT. The sinusoids are in phase, but the peak value of V_y is only one-half the peak value of V_x. Sketch the resulting waveform.

12-2 Two equal-frequency sinusoids are applied to the deflection plates. The sinusoids are 90° out of phase.

(*a*) Sketch the pattern if the peak value of V_x is twice as large as the peak value of V_y.
(*b*) Sketch the pattern if the peak value of V_y is twice as large as the peak value of V_x.

12-3 An ellipse like that in Fig. 12-10*b* appears on the screen of a CRT. The y intercept is 3.5 cm, and the y peak is 5 cm. Find the phase angle between the sinusoids.

12-4 A figure eight lying on its side appears on a CRT. If the vertical frequency is 250 Hz, what is the horizontal frequency?

12-5 Refer to Fig. 12-12*a*. In each of these patterns the horizontal frequency is 5 kHz. Find the vertical frequency for each pattern.

12-6 Refer to Fig. 12-12*b*. In each of these patterns the vertical frequency is 1 MHz. Find the horizontal frequency for each pattern.

12-7 An ideal sawtooth voltage (zero flyback time) with a period of 1 msec is applied to the horizontal deflection plates. Sketch the patterns that result from applying:
(*a*) A sine wave with a period of 0.25 msec.
(*b*) A sine wave with a period of 2 msec.
(*c*) A cosine wave with a period of 0.5 msec.
(*d*) A sawtooth wave with a period of 0.25 msec.

12-8 In the circuit of Fig. 12-19, the value of R is 50 kilohms, and the value of C is 500 pf. The power supply has a value of 300 volts. Sketch the transient that occurs after the switch is opened.

12-9 In the circuit of Fig. 12-21, the firing potential of the tube equals μv_c, where $\mu = 20$. If $v_c = 2$, $R = 100$ kilohms, $C = 2000$ pf, and $E = 250$ volts, what is the period of the sawtooth?

12-10 In the preceding problem what value of C changes the period to 1 msec?

12-11 In Fig. 12-25, if the capacitor is changed to 200 pf, what will the value of the rundown time be? If the capacitor is changed to 10,000 pf, what is the value of the rundown time?

12-12 A Schmitt trigger has a low state of 5 volts, a high state of 50 volts, an LTP of 3 volts, and a UTP of 5 volts. If the Schmitt trigger is driven by a sine wave with a peak value of 10 volts, sketch the output waveform.

12-13 If the Schmitt trigger of Prob. 12-12 is driven by a 1-kHz sine wave whose peak value just reaches the upper trip point, a rectangular pulse is obtained. What is the time duration of this pulse? (*Hint:* Use trigonometry.)

12-14 A Schmitt trigger has the following characteristics:

High state = 10 volts   low state = 2 volts
UTP = 2 volts   LTP = 1 volt

Sketch the output waveforms for each of the following inputs:

(*a*) A square wave with a positive peak of 10 volts and a negative peak of -10 volts.

(*b*) A sawtooth with a positive peak of 10 volts and a minimum value of zero.

(*c*) A half-wave-rectified sine wave with a peak value of 10 volts.

12-15 Refer to the differentiating circuit of Fig. 12-33*a*. If the square wave has a frequency of 10 kHz, what size should the capacitor be in order to ensure narrow pulses into a 100-kilohm resistance?

13 Harmonics

The sinusoid is undoubtedly the most common waveshape in electronics. We already know that if the voltages and currents in a circuit are sinusoidal, Ohm's law is applicable provided that we use complex numbers to represent voltage, current, and impedance. However, there are many waveshapes that are not sinusoidal. How then do we solve a circuit problem involving nonsinusoidal quantities?

This is one of the questions we wish to answer in this chapter, in which we also discuss harmonic theory in detail in order to be able to understand how harmonic and spectrum analyzers operate.

13-1 The Basic Idea

Fourier discovered that any *periodic* waveform can be expressed as the sum of a series of *harmonically* related *sinusoids*. Let us discuss each of the important words in the last sentence. By a periodic waveform is meant a waveform that repeats its pattern after a fixed time interval. For instance, consider the various waveforms shown in Fig. 13-1. Note that each waveform is cyclical; that is, it repeats after a fixed time interval T. The interval of time T is called the period of the waveform. The waveform

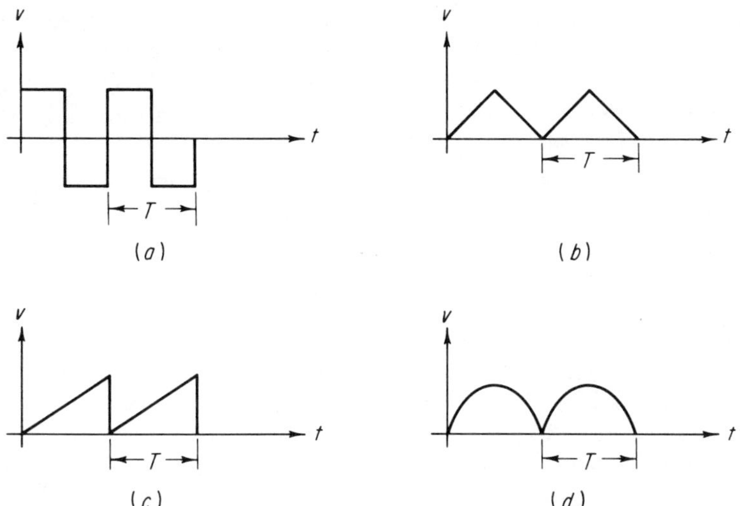

Fig. 13-1 Period of nonsinusoidal waveforms. (*a*) Square wave. (*b*) Triangular wave. (*c*) Sawtooth wave. (*d*) Full-wave-rectified sinusoid.

traces out some pattern during the period, and then it merely repeats the pattern during each new period.

A sinusoid is any waveform that has the *shape* of the ordinary sine wave. Recall that a sine wave begins to rise from the origin as shown in Fig. 13-2*a*. On the other hand, a cosine wave starts falling at zero

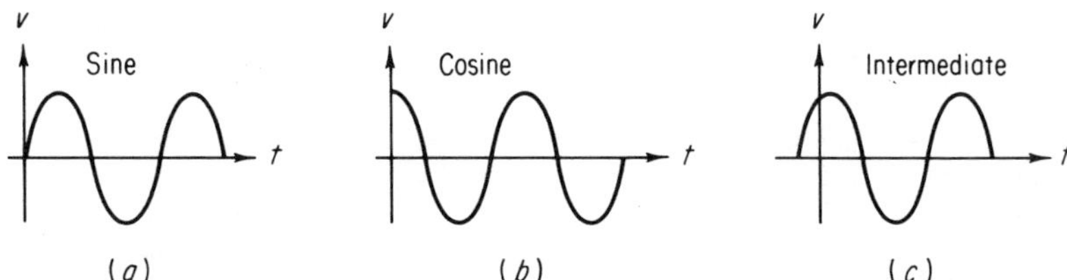

Fig. 13-2 Sinusoids. (*a*) Sine wave. (*b*) Cosine wave. (*c*) Sinusoid.

time as shown in Fig. 13-2*b*. A sinusoid is a waveshape that is either a sine wave, a cosine wave, or any intermediate waveshape such as shown in Fig. 13-2*c*. The sinusoid has the shape of a sine wave, but it has an arbitrary phase angle between 0 and 360°.

Harmonically related sinusoids are sinusoids whose frequencies are multiples of some basic frequency. For example, consider a group of five sinusoids with frequencies of 1, 2, 3, 4, and 5 kHz. The lowest frequency is called the *fundamental frequency*, or the first harmonic. In the given group, 1 kHz is the fundamental frequency. The remaining frequencies are multiples, or harmonics, of 1 kHz. Thus, 2 kHz is the second harmonic of 1 kHz, 3 kHz is the third harmonic of 1 kHz, and so on. We would then say that these sinusoids are harmonically related.

To state Fourier's theory more fully: any periodic waveform of period T is equal to the sum of a d-c term plus a series of harmonically related sinusoids. The fundamental frequency for the group of harmonically related sinusoids is equal to the reciprocal of the period T.

A word equation for Fourier's theory is

Periodic wave = d-c term + first harmonic
+ second harmonic + third harmonic + · · ·

Physically, Fourier's theory tells us that any voltage source that is generating a periodic waveform is equivalent to a battery in series with harmonically related sinusoidal generators. For instance, suppose that there is a generator like that in Fig. 13-3*a*. The voltage across the generator terminals is a periodic waveshape. According to Fourier's theory,

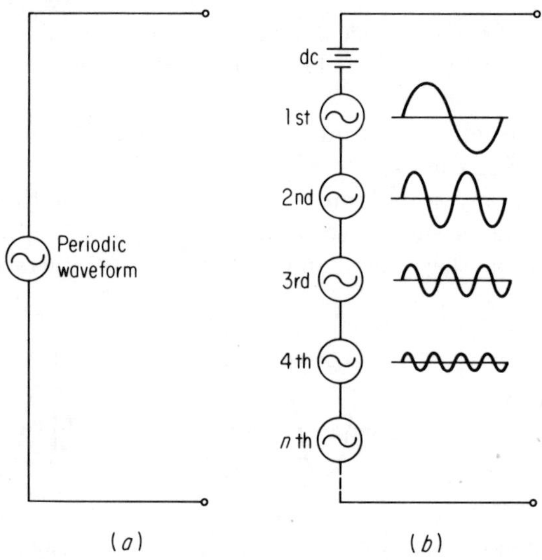

Fig. 13-3 Physical meaning of Fourier's theory. (*a*) Periodic waveform generator. (*b*) Equivalent circuit.

this generator can be replaced by a battery and a group of harmonically related sinusoids, as shown in Fig. 13-3*b*. This is a very important result, since it means that any nonsinusoidal a-c circuit problem can be solved by applying Ohm's law to each individual harmonic.

Fourier's theory is more than a mere mathematical curiosity. The harmonics are very real in the sense that they can be removed by using filters. For instance, suppose that we have a sawtooth wave with a period of 1 msec. According to Fourier's theory, this sawtooth has a fundamental sinusoid with a frequency of $1/T$, or 1 kHz. Furthermore, it has harmonics which are multiples of 1 kHz. Therefore, the harmonics are 2, 3, 4 kHz, and so on. If this sawtooth is the input to bandpass filters, as shown in Fig. 13-4, each harmonic can be removed as indicated. The outputs will actually be pure sinusoids of 1, 2, and 3 kHz, as shown.

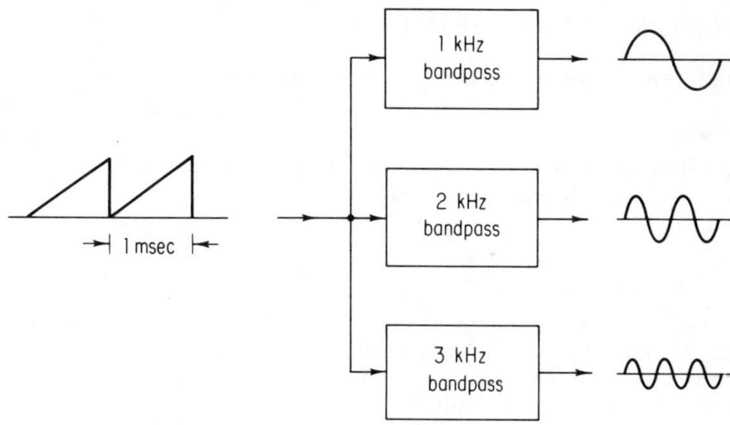

Fig. 13-4 Decomposing a sawtooth into harmonics.

Example 13-1

A periodic nonsinusoidal waveform has a period of 50 μsec. Find the frequencies of the first four harmonics.

Solution

To find the frequency of the fundamental, or the first harmonic, we take the reciprocal of the period.

$$f_1 = \frac{1}{T} = \frac{1}{50(10^{-6})} = 20 \text{ kHz}$$

The harmonics are simply the multiples of 20 kHz. Hence, $f_2 = 40$ kHz, $f_3 = 60$ kHz, $f_4 = 80$ kHz.

13-2 The Formal Expression of Fourier's Theory

Fourier's theory is usually expressed in mathematical symbols as follows:

$$y(t) = C_0 + C_1 \sin (\omega t + P_1) + C_2 \sin (2\omega t + P_2) + \cdots$$

where $y(t)$ is a function of time representing the periodic waveshape
C_0 is a constant representing the d-c term
C_1 is the peak value of the first harmonic

C_2, C_3, C_4, and so on represent the peak values of the higher harmonics
P_1 is the phase angle of the first harmonic
P_2, P_3, P_4, and so on represent the phase angles of the higher harmonics
ω is the radian frequency of the first harmonic

This expression merely says that

Periodic waveform = d-c term + first harmonic + second harmonic + · · ·

Another mathematical expression for Fourier's theory which is often used is the following compact notation:

$$y(t) = C_0 + \sum_{n=1}^{\infty} C_n \sin (n\omega t + P_n) \tag{13-1}$$

where $\sum_{n=1}^{\infty}$ indicates that we must add the sinusoids by first letting $n = 1$, then $n = 2$, and so on to infinity.

Equation (13-1) may look formidable at first, but it is only a shorthand way of writing Fourier's theory. C_0 is the d-c term, and C_n is the peak value of the nth harmonic, where n can take on any value from 1 to ∞. The phase angle P_n of the nth harmonic is important in some studies but not for the instrument studies with which we are concerned. Our main concern in the remainder of this chapter will be with C_0 and C_n.

13-3 The Sawtooth Wave

The sawtooth wave often occurs in practice. For instance, the voltage on the horizontal deflection plates of a television picture tube is approximately a sawtooth waveform.

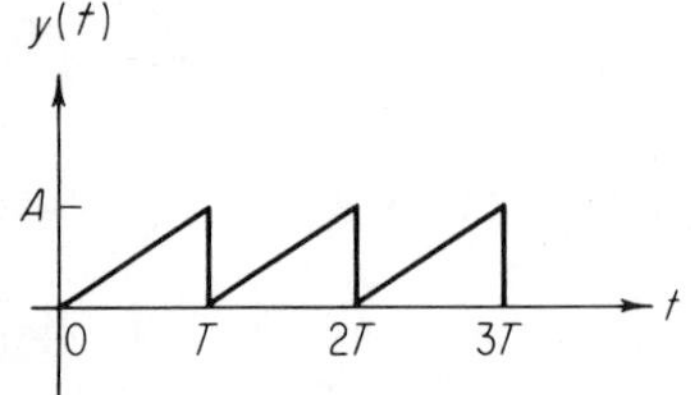

Fig. 13-5 Ideal sawtooth waveform.

The ideal sawtooth wave with zero flyback time is shown in Fig. 13-5. The amplitude of the sawtooth is designated by A, and the period by T.

What are the formulas for the d-c term and for the peak value of the nth harmonic? In advanced mathematics and engineering courses, calculus is used to prove that

$$C_0 = \frac{A}{2} \tag{13-2}$$

$$C_n = \frac{A}{n\pi} \tag{13-3}$$

Equation (13-2) says that the d-c value of the sawtooth of Fig. 13-5 is simply one-half of the sawtooth amplitude. Equation (13-3) says that the peak value of the nth harmonic is the sawtooth amplitude divided by n times π.

As an example of how to use the formulas, let us assume that the sawtooth of Fig. 13-5 has an amplitude of 10 volts. Then, according to Eq. (13-2), the d-c value of this sawtooth is $^{10}/_2$, or 5 volts. If this sawtooth is measured with a d-c voltmeter, the voltmeter will read 5 volts.

The peak value of the nth harmonic is $10/n\pi$. If we wish to find the peak value for any specific harmonic we need only substitute the value of n corresponding to that harmonic. For instance, the peak value of the fifth harmonic is

$$C_5 = \frac{10}{5\pi} = 0.636$$

To repeat, the harmonics are real, and can be separated by means of filters. In this case, if the 10-volt sawtooth is the input to a bandpass filter that passes only the fifth harmonic, the output will be a pure sinusoid, as shown in Fig. 13-6.

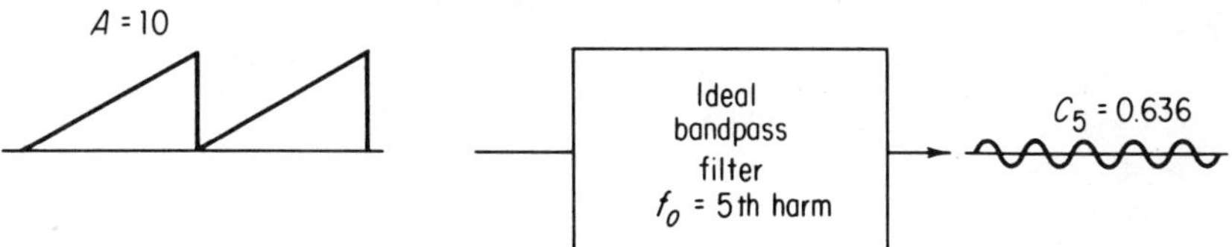

Fig. 13-6 Removing the fifth harmonic from a sawtooth waveform.

Note in Eq. (13-3) that the peak value of the nth harmonic becomes smaller for higher values of n. As n approaches infinity, the peak value approaches zero.

Example 13-2

It the sawtooth of Fig. 13-5 has an amplitude of 50 volts, what reading will it produce on a d-c voltmeter?

Solution

The d-c value of the sawtooth is given by

$$C_0 = {}^{50}/_2 = 25$$

Hence, the d-c voltmeter will read 25 volts.

EXAMPLE 13-3

If the sawtooth of Fig. 13-5 has an amplitude of 50 volts, what is the peak value of the fundamental? Of the second harmonic?

SOLUTION

The peak value of the fundamental is

$$C_1 = \frac{A}{n\pi} = \frac{50}{\pi} = 15.9$$

The peak value of the second harmonic is

$$C_2 = \frac{50}{2\pi} = 7.95$$

EXAMPLE 13-4

A sawtooth with an amplitude of 25 volts and a period of 1 msec is passed through an ideal bandpass filter tuned to the tenth harmonic. Find the rms value of the filter output and its frequency.

SOLUTION

$$C_{10} = \frac{25}{10\pi} = 0.795$$

To find the rms value of the tenth harmonic we multiply the peak value by 0.707 to obtain

$$0.707(0.795) = 0.562 \text{ volt rms}$$

The frequency of the tenth harmonic is simply 10 times the fundamental frequency. The fundamental is

$$f_1 = \frac{1}{10^{-3}} = 1 \text{ kHz}$$

Therefore, the filter output has a frequency of 10 kHz, and an rms value of 0.562 volt.

13-4 The Frequency Spectrum of a Sawtooth Wave

We know that the peak value of the nth harmonic of the ideal sawtooth wave shown in Fig. 13-5 is

$$C_n = \frac{A}{n\pi}$$

If we like, we can graph C_n vs. n. Be aware, however, that only whole numbers may be used for n. No fractional values are permitted, since the harmonics are whole-number multiples of the fundamental frequency.

For example, if n equals 1, then $C_n = A/\pi$. If $n = 2$, then $C_n = A/2\pi$. If we continue in this fashion, we will have enough values to construct a line graph like that in Fig. 13-7.

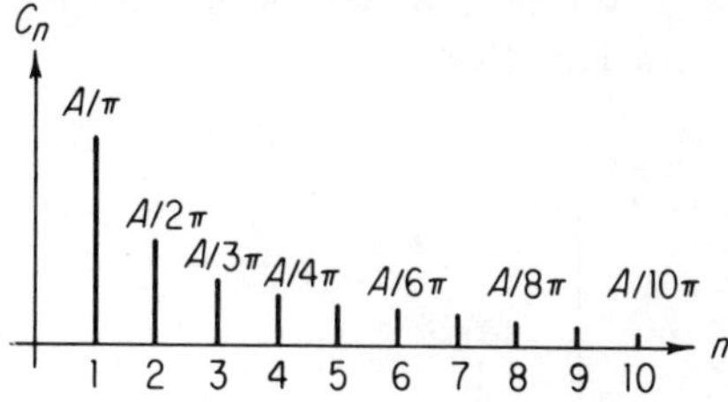

Fig. 13-7 The spectrum of a sawtooth waveform.

Figure 13-7 is an interesting picture. It tells us a great deal about the sawtooth. For instance, it is immediately clear that the peak values of the higher harmonics approach zero. Further, we see that all harmonics are present.

A graph like that shown in Fig. 13-7 is called a *frequency spectrum* or simply a spectrum. As we study different waveforms, we will see that each new waveform has a spectrum of its own. In fact, one of the most interesting measuring devices is what is known as a *spectrum analyzer*. This instrument displays a graph of C_n vs. n on the face of a cathode-ray tube. Thus, if we look at a sawtooth with a spectrum analyzer, we will see a picture like the spectrum shown in Fig. 13-7.

Example 13-5

If a sawtooth is passed through an ideal bandpass filter tuned to the third harmonic, what will be the spectrum of the output of the filter?

Solution

The filter will remove all harmonics except the third. As a result, the spectrum will consist of a single line located at $n = 3$.

Example 13-6

A pure sine wave with a peak value of 10 mv is passed through an amplifier with a 40-db voltage gain. The amplifier introduces some distortion. Assume that the amplifier introduces a second-harmonic output of 0.1 volt, and a third-harmonic output of 0.05 volt. Sketch the spectrum of the original input sine wave and the spectrum of the output.

Solution

The voltage gain of 40 db is equivalent to two factors of 10, or 100. Hence, the first-harmonic output of the amplifier is

$$C_1 = 100(10)(10^{-3}) = 1 \text{ volt}$$

We are given the distortion components

$$C_2 = 0.1 \qquad \text{and} \qquad C_3 = 0.05$$

We may now sketch the spectra of the input and output as shown in Fig. 13-8.

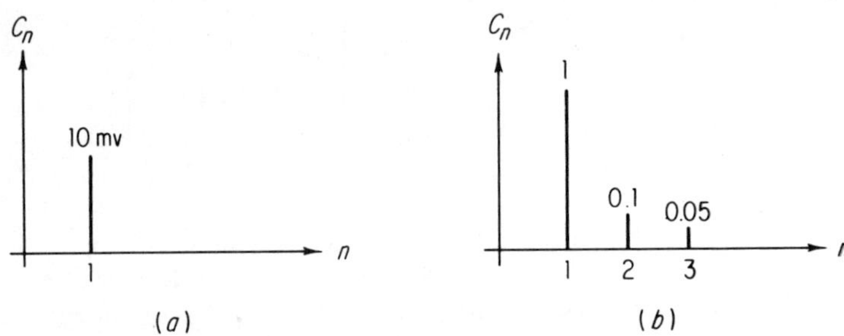

Fig. 13-8 Example 13-6.

13-5 Application of Ohm's Law to Nonsinusoidal Problems

If a linear circuit is driven by a periodic voltage source which is nonsinusoidal, how do we solve for the voltages and currents in various parts of the circuit? (A linear circuit is one that contains only linear elements; see Sec. 1-2.)

One method of solving such problems is to first replace the nonsinusoidal generator by its Fourier equivalent generator: a battery in series with harmonically related sinusoidal generators. Once this is done, it is permissible to use the superposition theorem, which says that in a linear circuit we may consider one generator at a time and compute the effect it produces. The sum of all the effects produced by the generators will be the total effect in the circuit.

As an example, consider the circuit shown in Fig. 13-9*a*. A sawtooth generator is driving a high-pass *RC* filter. The cutoff frequency of the high-pass filter is

$$f_c = \frac{1}{2\pi RC} = \frac{0.159}{10^6(0.1)(10^{-6})} = 1.59 \text{ Hz}$$

We note that the sawtooth has a fundamental frequency of $1/T$. In this case, the fundamental frequency is 1 kHz. The second harmonic is 2 kHz, and so on.

We can replace the sawtooth generator by its Fourier equivalent generator as shown in Fig. 13-9*b*. Now, we can consider the effect of each generator, one at a time. First, we note that the battery will produce no direct current in the circuit because of the capacitor. Hence, there will be no d-c voltage in the output.

Next, we consider the effect of the first-harmonic generator. The frequency is 1 kHz. Since the cutoff frequency of the filter is 1.59 Hz, we immediately know that the first harmonic is well in the passband of the filter, and therefore the first-harmonic voltage appears across the output terminals. In a similar way, we see that all the harmonics are well into the passband of the filter, and therefore they appear at the output terminals.

The net effect of the circuit is simply to remove the d-c component from the sawtooth wave. The output is then the waveshape shown in Fig. 13-9*c*.

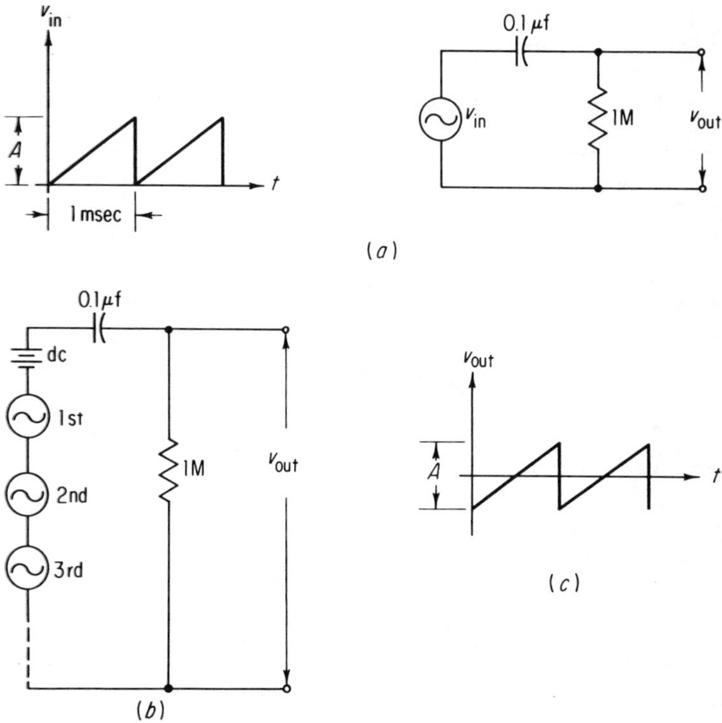

Fig. 13-9 Applying Ohm's law to a nonsinusoidal waveform. (*a*) Circuit. (*b*) Fourier equivalent circuit. (*c*) Output.

Since the harmonic content of the input or output is the same, it should be clear that the formulas for C_0 and C_n are

$$C_0 = 0 \qquad \text{and} \qquad C_n = \frac{A}{n\pi}$$

The C_n formulas for Figs. 13-5 and 13-9*c* are the same, provided we interpret A as the peak-to-peak value of the sawtooth.

13-6 The Square Wave

Another very common waveform in electronics is the square wave, shown in Fig. 13-10. Note that A is the peak-to-peak value. It should be clear that the d-c or average value of this square wave is zero. Hence, $C_0 = 0$.

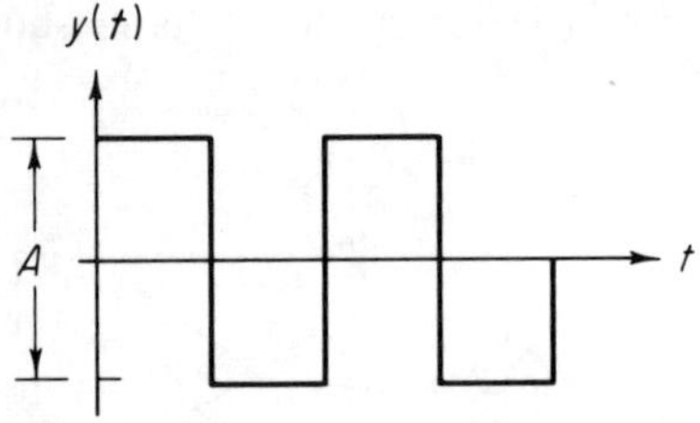

Fig. 13-10 Square wave.

By applying calculus it can be shown that the C_n formula is

$$C_n = A \left| \frac{\sin (n\pi/2)}{n\pi/2} \right| \tag{13-4}$$

The vertical bars are the usual notation indicating that only the positive or absolute value of the quantity inside the bars is used. In other words, if we compute a value of -1 for the numerator, we use the absolute value, which is $+1$.

To illustrate the use of Eq. (13-4), let us calculate the peak values of the first four harmonics.

$$C_1 = A \left| \frac{\sin (\pi/2)}{\pi/2} \right| = A \left| \frac{1}{\pi/2} \right| = \frac{2A}{\pi}$$

$$C_2 = A \left| \frac{\sin (2\pi/2)}{2\pi/2} \right| = A \left| \frac{\sin (\pi)}{\pi} \right| = 0$$

$$C_3 = A \left| \frac{\sin (3\pi/2)}{3\pi/2} \right| = A \left| \frac{-1}{3\pi/2} \right| = \frac{2A}{3\pi}$$

$$C_4 = A \left| \frac{\sin (4\pi/2)}{4\pi/2} \right| = A \left| \frac{\sin (2\pi)}{2\pi} \right| = 0$$

Note from this progression that whenever n is an even number, we will be taking the sine of a multiple of π (or 180°). The sine of any multiple of π is zero. Therefore, the peak value of any even harmonic is zero. Further, whenever n is odd, we will be taking the sine of an odd multiple of $\pi/2$ (or 90°). Hence, this results in either a plus or minus one in the numerator.

Equation (13-4) may now be simplified as follows:

$$C_n = 0 \qquad \text{for } n \text{ even} \tag{13-5}$$

$$C_n = \frac{2A}{n\pi} \qquad \text{for } n \text{ odd} \tag{13-6}$$

These last two equations for the peak value of the nth harmonic should be easy to remember. The peak value of any even harmonic is zero; that is, the ideal square wave has no even harmonics. The peak value for any odd harmonic is given by Eq. (13-6). Note that this formula is almost the same as that for the sawtooth, except that a factor of two appears in the numerator.

Example 13-7

Find the peak values of the first three harmonics of a square wave with a peak-to-peak value of 10 volts.

Solution

$$C_1 = \frac{2(10)}{\pi} = 6.36$$

$$C_2 = 0$$

$$C_3 = \frac{2(10)}{3\pi} = 2.12$$

Example 13-8

A square wave with a peak value of 50 volts is the input to an ideal bandpass filter which passes only the ninth harmonic. Find the output of the filter.

Solution

The value of A to use in the formula for C_n is the peak-to-peak value. Since the peak value of the square wave is 50 volts, A is 100 volts.

$$C_9 = \frac{2(100)}{9\pi} = 7.06$$

Example 13-9

A square wave (Fig. 13-10) with a peak-to-peak value of A is the input to a positive d-c clamping circuit. Find the formula for the d-c value and the peak value of the nth harmonic for the output of the clamping circuit.

Solution

Recall that a clamping circuit does not change the shape of the waveform. It only shifts the waveform vertically. The output of the clamping circuit is shown in Fig. 13-11. All the clamping circuit has

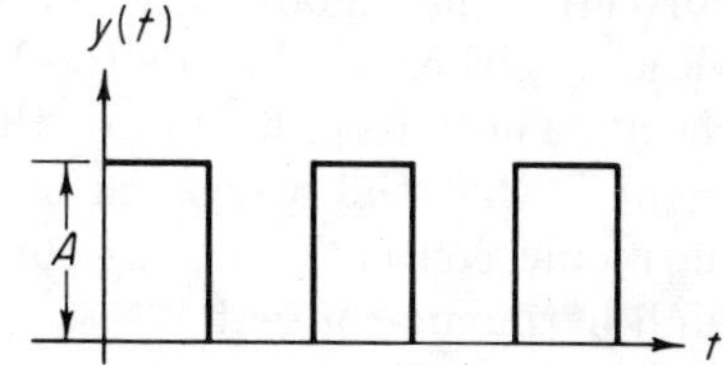

Fig. 13-11 Positively clamped square wave of Example 13-9.

done is to change the d-c, or average, value of the square wave from zero to $A/2$. Since the shape of the square wave has not changed, the harmonic content in the output is the same as in the input. Therefore, for the square wave of Fig. 13-11 the appropriate formulas are

$$C_0 = \frac{A}{2}$$

$$C_n = 0 \qquad \text{for } n \text{ even}$$

$$C_n = \frac{2A}{n\pi} \qquad \text{for } n \text{ odd}$$

13-7 The Spectrum of a Square Wave

The spectrum of a square wave is easily constructed. We already know that the square wave has no even harmonics. Therefore, there will be no spectral lines for even values of n. The peak values for the odd harmonics are given by $C_n = 2A/n\pi$. Therefore, if we pick $n = 1, 3, 5, \ldots$, we can compute the corresponding values of C_n.

The spectrum of the square wave is shown in Fig. 13-12. This is the kind of picture we will see if the square wave is measured by a spectrum

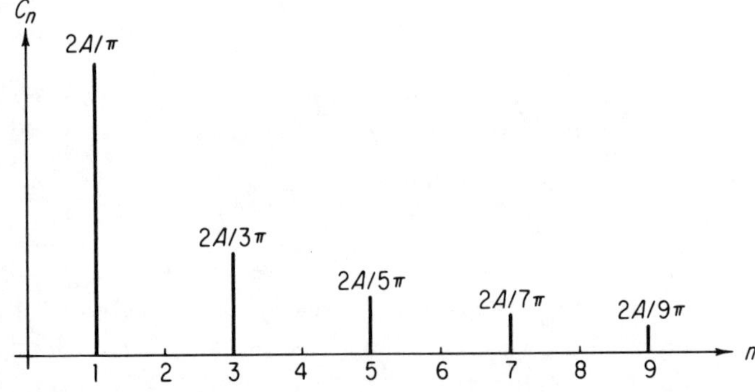

Fig. 13-12 The spectrum of a square wave.

analyzer. Note that the peak values become smaller as we approach higher values of n.

Recall that in the chapter on attenuators we discussed frequency-compensating a voltage divider. If the compensating capacitor is adjusted correctly, the square wave of Fig. 13-13*a* results. But if the capacitor value is either too low or too high, the waveforms of Fig. 13-13*b* and *c* result. The interpretation of these waveforms from the spectrum viewpoint is that the waveform of Fig. 13-13*b* does not have enough high-harmonic content, whereas the waveform of Fig. 13-13*c* has too much high-harmonic content.

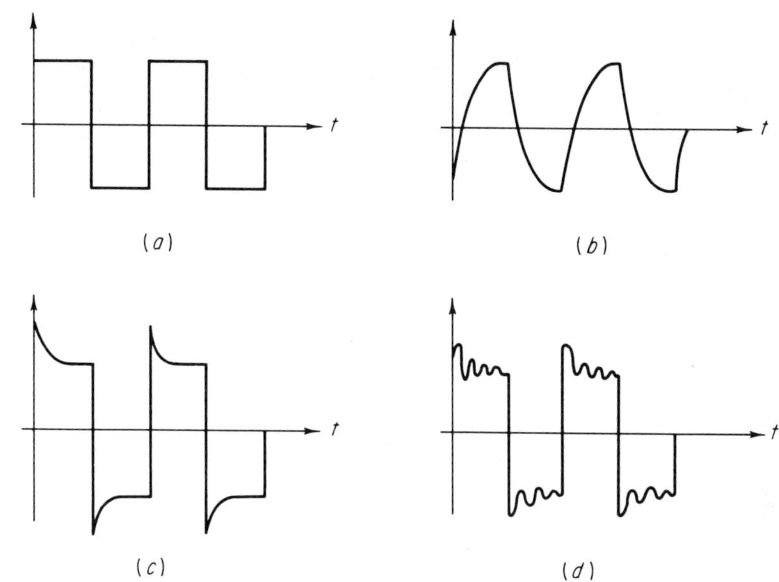

Fig. 13-13 Square-wave interpretation. (*a*) Correct proportion of low- and high-frequency components. (*b*) High-frequency components too small. (*c*) High-frequency components too large. (*d*) A particular frequency component too large.

A similar interpretation from the spectrum viewpoint can be made when square-wave-testing amplifiers. For instance, if an amplifier is driven by a square-wave input, then, in effect, the amplifier is driven by a series of harmonically related sinusoidal generators. The peak values of these sinusoids are given by the spectrum of the square wave shown in Fig. 13-12. If the amplifier response is not flat over a broad frequency range, some of the harmonics are amplified more than others. The output spectrum will then be different from the input, which is the same as saying that the square wave is distorted as it passes through the amplifier. Figure 13-13*b* illustrates a poor high-frequency response, whereas Fig. 13-13*c* indicates too much high-frequency response. Many other waveforms can occur. If, for example, the amplifier is resonant at a particular frequency because of lead inductances and stray capacitances, the output spectrum will be peaked in the vicinity of the resonant frequency. This results in a ringing effect on the square wave, as shown in Fig. 13-13*d*.

13-8 The Full-wave-rectified Sine Wave

Recall that if a sinusoid is the input to a full-wave rectifier, the output is the familiar full-wave-rectified signal shown in Fig. 13-14*a*. The formulas for C_0 and C_n are readily derived with calculus, and are

$$C_0 = \frac{2A}{\pi} \tag{13-7}$$

$$C_n = \frac{4A}{\pi}\frac{1}{4n^2 - 1} \tag{13-8}$$

As an example of using these formulas, let us find the d-c value and the peak values of the first three harmonics of a full-wave-rectified signal with an amplitude of 10 volts.

$$C_0 = \frac{2(10)}{\pi} = 6.36$$

$$C_1 = \frac{4(10)}{\pi}\frac{1}{4 - 1} = 4.24$$

$$C_2 = \frac{4(10)}{\pi}\frac{1}{4(2)^2 - 1} = 0.848$$

$$C_3 = \frac{4(10)}{\pi}\frac{1}{4(3)^2 - 1} = 0.364$$

The spectrum of the full-wave-rectified sinusoid is shown in Fig. 13-14*b*. Note that all harmonics are present.

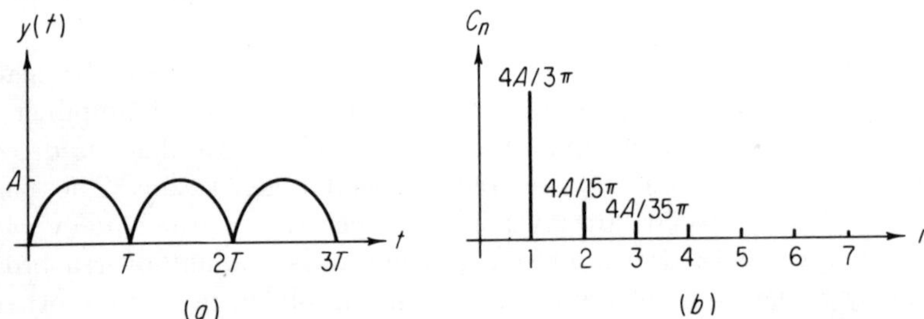

Fig. 13-14 Full-wave-rectified sine wave. (*a*) Waveform. (*b*) Spectrum.

Example 13-10

A sinusoid with a frequency of 1 kHz is full-wave-rectified. Find the frequencies of the first three harmonics.

Solution

The 1-kHz sinusoid is shown in Fig. 13-15*a*. Note that it has a period of 1 msec. After rectification, the waveform has a period of 0.5 msec (see Fig. 13-15*b*). Therefore, the fundamental frequency is

$$f_1 = \frac{1}{0.5(10^{-3})} = 2\text{ kHz}$$

The second and third harmonic frequencies are 4 and 6 kHz.

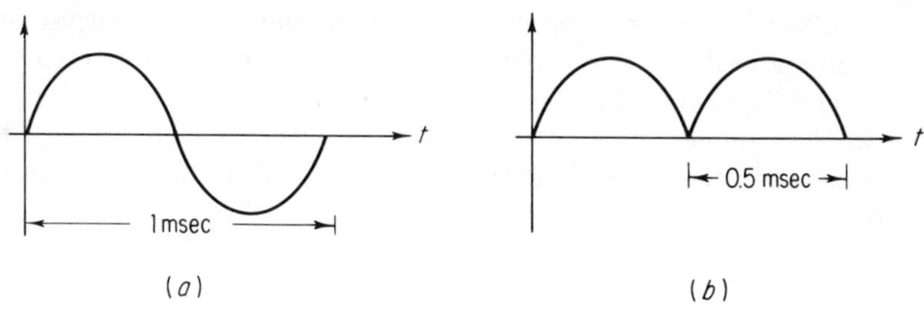

Fig. 13-15 Example 13-10. (*a*) Input. (*b*) Rectified signal.

Note carefully the significance of what is happening. The input 1-kHz sinusoid is full-wave-rectified. The output signal then contains only 2, 4, 6 kHz, and so on. In other words, the lowest frequency in the output of a full-wave-rectified signal is twice as high as the input frequency.

EXAMPLE 13-11

A power supply uses a full-wave rectifier. If the line voltage has a frequency of 60 Hz, what is the lowest frequency that needs to be filtered?

SOLUTION

In Example 13-10 we saw that the period of the full-wave-rectified signal is one-half of the period of the input. This means that the lowest frequency in the output will be twice the input frequency, or 120 Hz. In fact, the frequencies in the output will be 120, 240, 360, and so on. The spectrum of the output is shown in Fig. 13-16*a*.

Of course, in practice we would not expect to have a full-wave-rectified signal that is *perfectly* balanced on both halves of the input, simply because the diodes in the rectifier are not identical. This means that one peak of the signal of Fig. 13-14*a* will not exactly equal the next adjacent peak. Because of this, the period of the output is still equal to the period

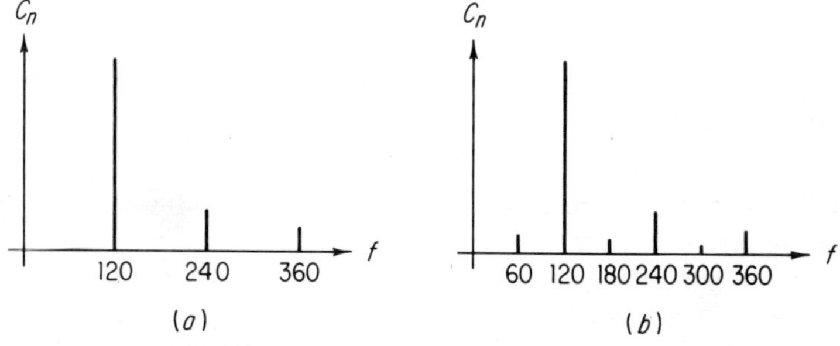

Fig. 13-16 Spectrum for a full-wave-rectified sinusoid. (*a*) Balanced rectification. (*b*) Slightly unbalanced rectification.

of the input signal. Therefore, the lowest frequency in the output of a slightly unbalanced full-wave rectifier will equal the input frequency. The more closely balanced the two halves are, the smaller the peak value of this lowest frequency. A sketch of the spectrum as in Fig. 13-16*b* conveys the essential idea. For perfect balance, the harmonics at 60, 180, 300, etc., will disappear.

13-9 The Flip Test for Odd Harmonics

Many waveforms contain only odd harmonics. We recall that the square wave is an example of a waveform with odd harmonics only. Very often, it will be helpful to be able to glance at a waveform and quickly determine whether it contains only odd harmonics.

There is a very useful rule, which can be proved with calculus, for testing waveforms in order to find whether they contain only odd harmonics. The rule is given by the following three steps:

1. If the waveform under consideration does not have an average value of zero, then shift it mentally or on paper until it does.
2. Next, flip the negative parts of the waveform so that they become positive.
3. Now, determine whether the resulting waveform has a period equal to one-half of the original period. If it does, the original waveform has odd harmonics only.

As an example of applying the flip test, let us test the waveform in Fig. 13-17*a*.

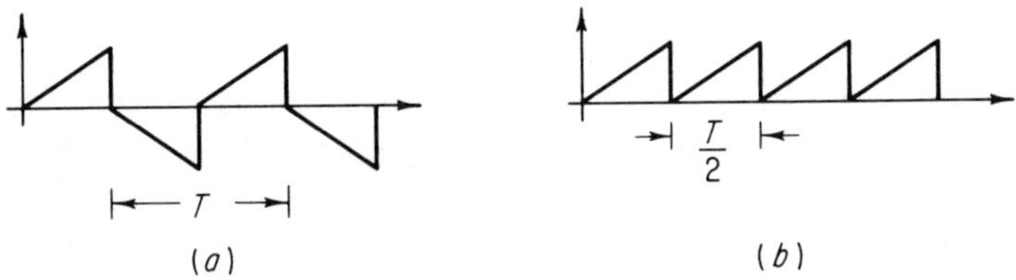

Fig. 13-17 Testing a waveform for odd harmonics. (*a*) Given waveform. (*b*) After flipping negative portions.

Step 1: The waveform already has an average value of zero, so we proceed directly to step 2.

Step 2: Flip the negative parts so that they become positive. The resulting waveform is shown in Fig. 13-17*b*.

Step 3: The period of the resulting waveform is one-half of the original period. Therefore, the original waveform has only odd harmonics.

As another example, let us consider the sawtooth of Fig. 13-18*a*. Does this contain only odd harmonics? We already know that the sawtooth contains even as well as odd harmonics. Nevertheless, for practice, let us apply the flip test to the sawtooth.

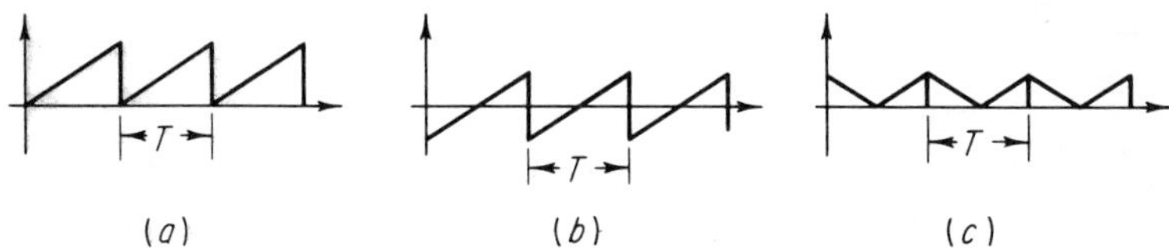

Fig. 13-18 Applying the flip test to a sawtooth.

Step 1: The waveform does not have an average value of zero. Hence, we shift it until it does, as shown in Fig. 13-18*b*.

Step 2: Flip the negative parts to obtain the waveform of Fig. 13-17*c*.

Step 3: The period of the resulting waveform is still the same as the original period. Therefore, the original waveform has more than just the odd harmonics. The original waveform must contain at least one even harmonic. This is the strongest statement we can make about the original waveform when the period remains the same, as in this example. That is, when the period remains the same, we cannot say that the waveform contains all the even harmonics. All we can say is that the waveform contains at least one even harmonic.

When the flip test succeeds, that is, when the new waveform has a period equal to one-half of the original period, we know that the original waveform contains only odd harmonics. We are *not* allowed to say that the waveform contains *all* the odd harmonics. The strongest statement we can make is that the waveform contains only odd harmonics (not necessarily all).

In conclusion, with some practice it is possible to perform the flip test mentally, so that many waveforms can be quickly analyzed to determine whether or not they are composed entirely of odd harmonics. In practice, this is sometimes very useful.

Example 13-12

Test the waveform shown in Fig. 13-19*a* to determine whether it contains only odd harmonics.

Solution

Step 1: We shift the waveform until it has an average value of zero as shown in Fig. 13-19*b*.

Step 2: We flip the negative parts to obtain the waveform of Fig. 13-19*c*.

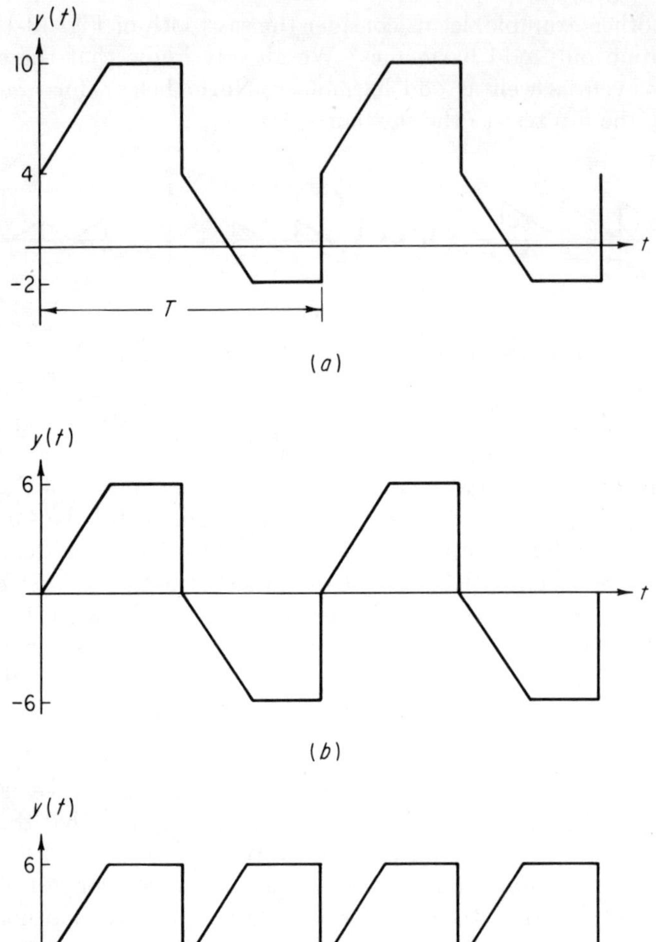

Fig. 13-19 Example 13-12.

Step 3: We observe that the period of the new waveform is one-half of the original period. Therefore, the original waveform contains only odd harmonics.

SUMMARY

Fourier's theory tells us that a periodic nonsinusoidal waveform is equivalent to a d-c term plus a series of harmonically related sinusoids.

Table 13-1

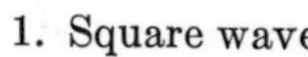

1. Square wave

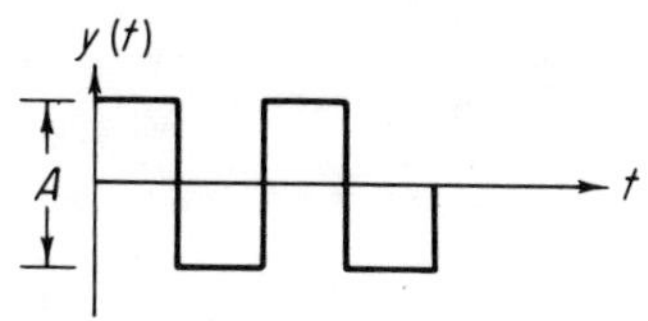

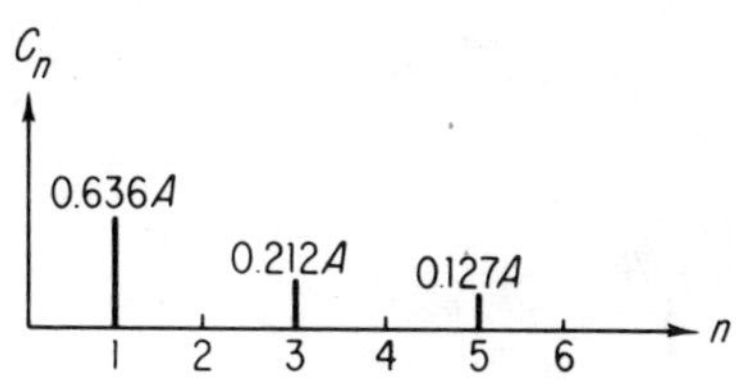

$$\text{rms} = \frac{A}{2} \qquad C_n = 0 \quad \text{for } n \text{ even}$$

$$C_0 = 0 \qquad C_n = \frac{2A}{n\pi} \quad \text{for } n \text{ odd}$$

2. Clamped square wave

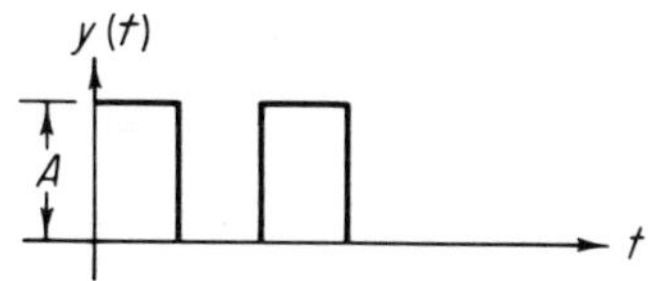

C_n

The spectrum is the same as in 1

n

$$\text{rms} = \frac{A}{\sqrt{2}} \qquad C_n = 0 \quad \text{for } n \text{ even}$$

$$C_0 = \frac{A}{2} \qquad C_n = \frac{2A}{n\pi} \quad \text{for } n \text{ odd}$$

3. Rectangular wave

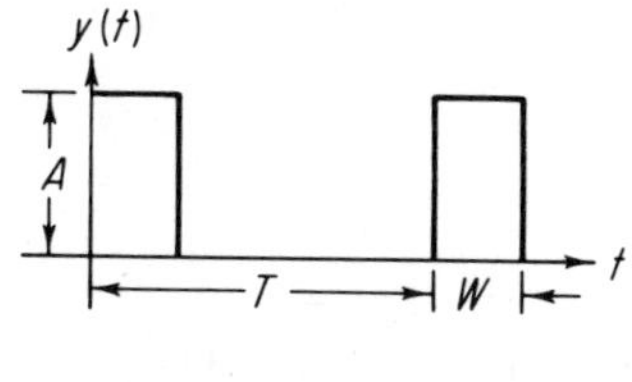

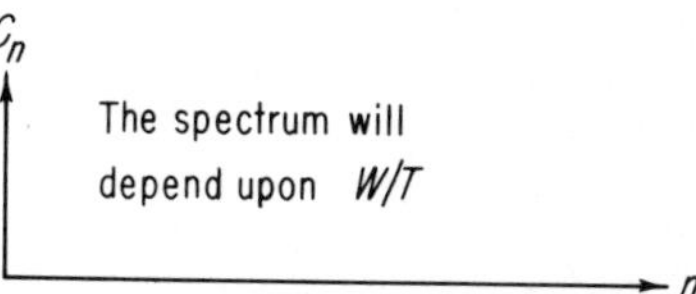

$$\text{rms} = A\sqrt{\frac{W}{T}} \qquad C_n = \frac{2AW}{T}\left|\frac{\sin(n\pi W/T)}{n\pi W/T}\right|$$

$$C_0 = A\frac{W}{T}$$

Table 13-1 (*Continued*)

4. Full-wave-rectified sinusoid

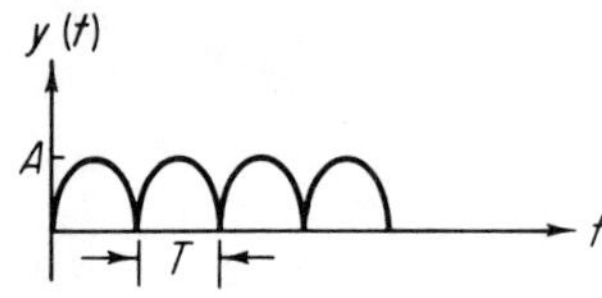

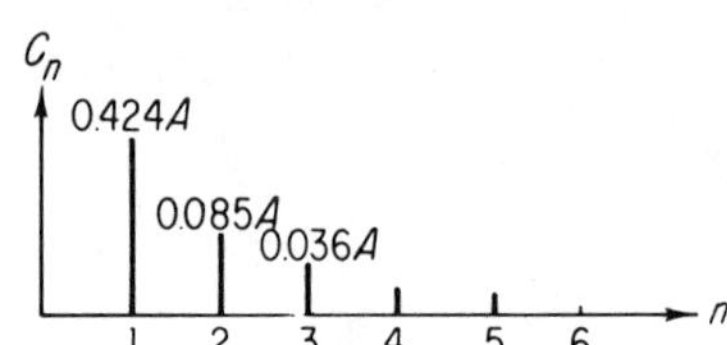

$$\text{rms} = \frac{A}{\sqrt{2}} \qquad C_n = \frac{4A}{\pi}\frac{1}{4n^2 - 1}$$

$$C_0 = \frac{2A}{\pi}$$

5. Half-wave-rectified sinusoid

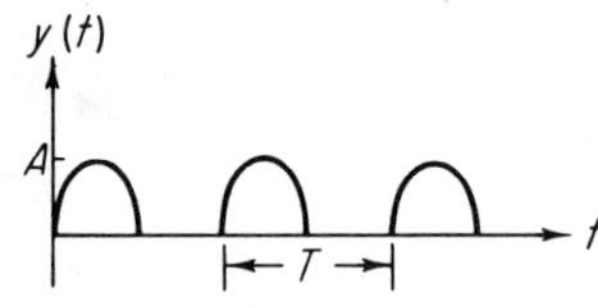

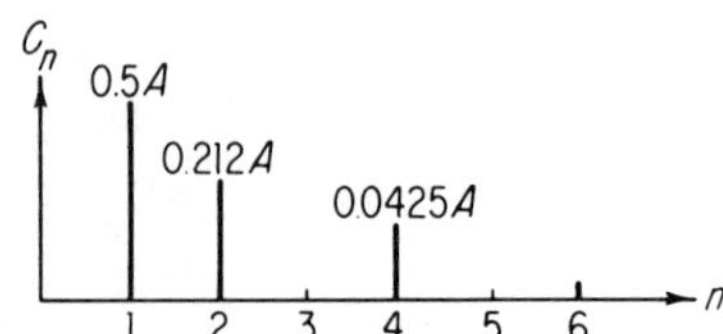

$$\text{rms} = \frac{A}{2}$$

$$C_0 = \frac{A}{\pi}$$

$C_n = 0$ for all odd values of n, except $n = 1$

For $n = 1$: $C_1 = \dfrac{A}{2}$

For n even: $C_n = \dfrac{2A}{\pi}\dfrac{1}{n^2 - 1}$

Table 13-1 (*Continued*)

6. Sawtooth wave

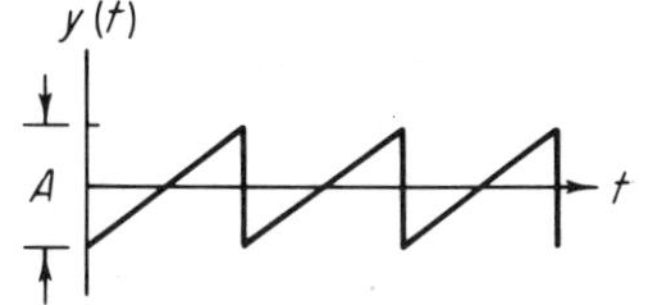

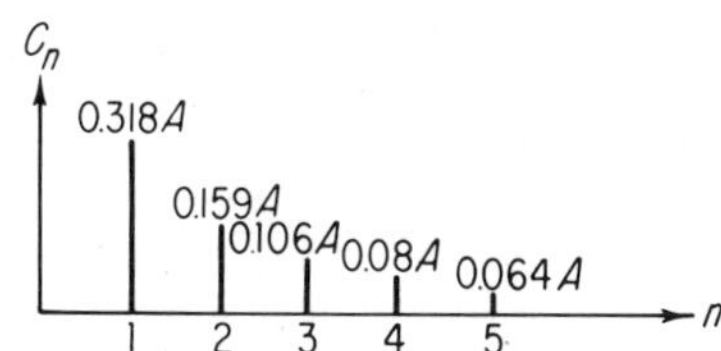

$$\text{rms} = \frac{A}{2\sqrt{3}} \qquad C_n = \frac{A}{n\pi}$$

$$C_0 = 0$$

7. Clamped sawtooth wave

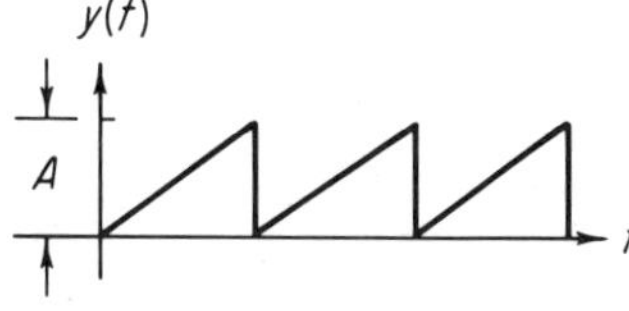

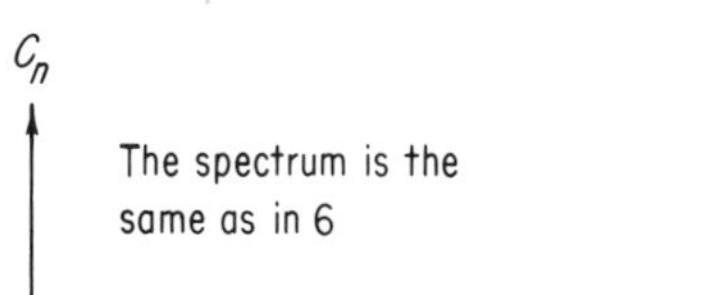

$$\text{rms} = \frac{A}{\sqrt{3}} \qquad C_n = \frac{A}{n\pi}$$

$$C_0 = \frac{A}{2}$$

Table 13-1 (*Continued*)

8. Sawtooth with flyback

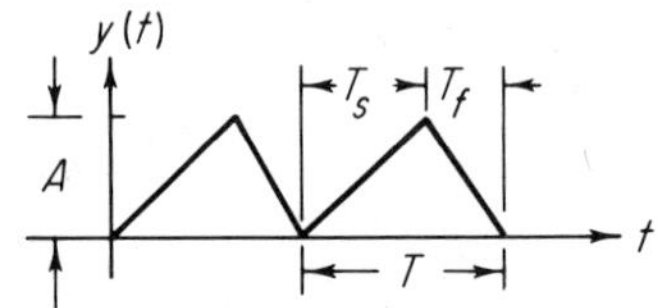

C_n

The spectrum depends upon the value of T_s/T

n

$$\text{rms} = \frac{A}{\sqrt{3}}$$

$$C_0 = \frac{A}{2}$$

$$C_n = \frac{AT^2}{\pi^2 n^2 T_s T_f} \sin\left(n\pi \frac{T_s}{T}\right)$$

9. Triangular wave

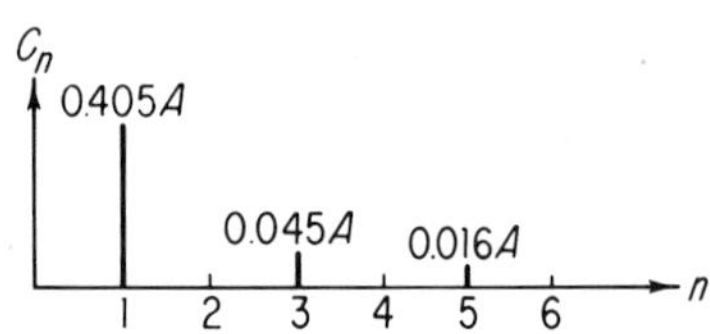

$$\text{rms} = \frac{A}{2\sqrt{3}}$$

$$C_0 = 0$$

For n even: $C_n = 0$

For n odd: $C_n = \dfrac{4A}{n^2\pi^2}$

Table 13-1 *(Continued)*

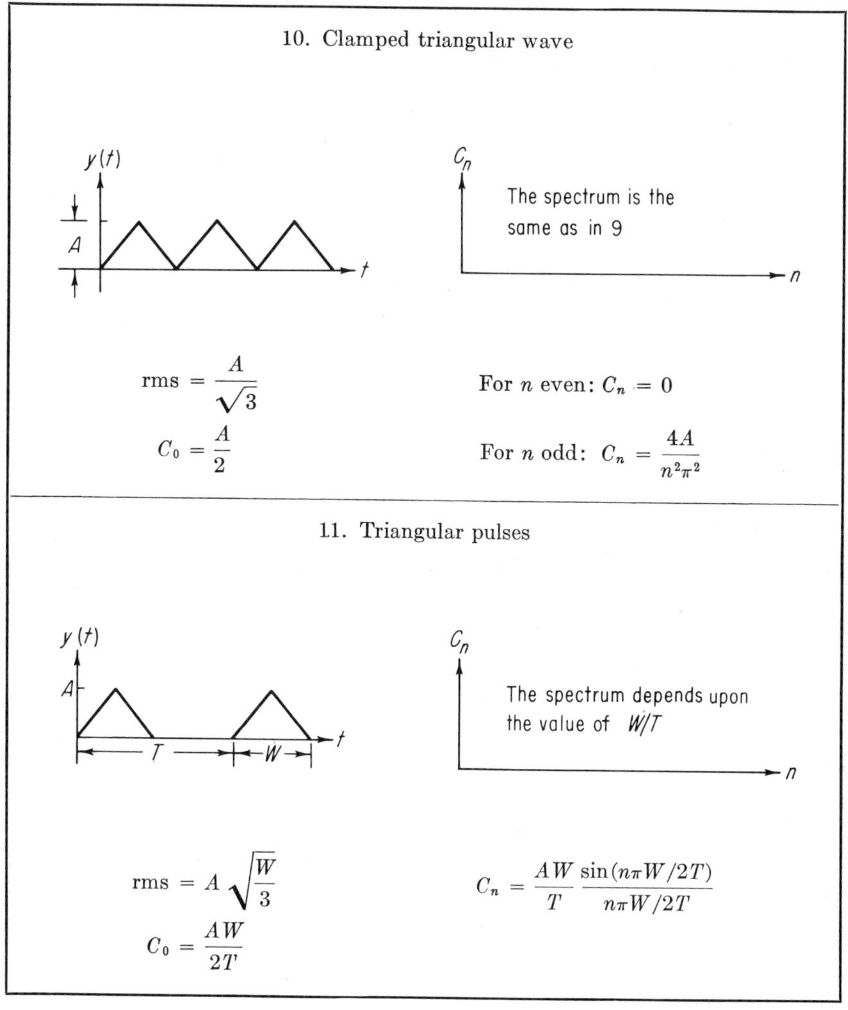

The fundamental frequency is given by the reciprocal of the period of the waveform.

The harmonics are unquestionably real, since they can be separated by means of filters.

The sawtooth is a very common waveshape. It contains all the harmonics. The perfect square wave, however, contains only the odd harmonics.

The spectrum of a waveform refers to the line graph of C_n vs. n. An instrument known as the spectrum analyzer is often used to display the spectrum of a waveform. Thus, we can see at a glance which harmonics are present and what the peak values are.

One approach to solving a linear circuit problem involving nonsinusoidal voltage sources is to consider one harmonic at a time and determine the effect it has. Then, by adding all the effects of the harmonics, the total effect is obtained.

Square waves are often used to test amplifier response, since the use of a square wave is equivalent to using many sinusoidal generators simultaneously. If the amplifier response is not flat, the output spectrum will be different from the input. The result is a distorted square wave whose shape can be interpreted in terms of amplifier response.

The flip test is useful in ascertaining whether a waveform is composed entirely of odd harmonics. There are many situations where such information will be useful.

As a convenient reference, Table 13-1 lists some of the common nonsinusoidal waveforms. The rms value of the waveforms is also included, as well as the C_0 and C_n formulas.

GLOSSARY

balanced full-wave rectification Rectification in which both halves of the full-wave-rectified sine wave are identical in amplitude and shape.

clamping circuit A circuit that changes the average or d-c value of a signal without changing the shape of the signal.

harmonics Sinusoidal signals whose frequencies are multiples of the fundamental frequency of a nonsinusoidal signal.

impedance A mathematical concept using complex numbers in order to account for opposition offered by circuit elements to a sinusoidal current.

periodic An adjective describing a waveform that repeats its shape after a fixed amount of time.

sinusoid A general term describing any signal that has the sine-wave shape but whose phase angle is any angle between 0 and 360°.

spectrum A line graph of the harmonic amplitudes versus the harmonic number or frequency.

REVIEW QUESTIONS

1. What does Fourier's theory tell us about periodic waveforms?
2. What are sinusoids? What are harmonics?
3. How do you find the fundamental frequency of a periodic waveform?
4. Does the sawtooth contain all harmonics?
5. What is the d-c value of a positively clamped sawtooth wave?
6. What is a frequency spectrum? What does the frequency spectrum of a sawtooth look like? Of a pure sine wave?
7. What is a spectrum analyzer?

8. How is Fourier's theory used to solve circuit problems involving nonsinusoidal voltage sources?
9. Which harmonics are missing from the square wave?
10. What effect does positively clamping a square wave have on the harmonic content?
11. How can a square wave be used to check the frequency response of an amplifier?
12. For a full-wave-rectified sinusoid, what is the lowest frequency in the waveform compared to the input frequency, assuming that both halves of the rectified signal are identical? What happens to the spectrum if the two halves are not identical?
13. Describe the flip test for testing nonsinusoidal waveforms.
14. If after applying the flip test the resulting waveform still has a period equal to the original waveform, what can be said about the even-harmonic content of the original waveform?

PROBLEMS

13-1 A nonsinusoidal waveform has a period of 10 μsec. If this waveform contains all harmonics, what are the frequencies of the first five harmonics?

13-2 A nonsinusoidal waveform with a period of 50 μsec is the input to an ideal bandpass filter that has a lower cutoff frequency of 50 kHz and an upper cutoff of 111 kHz. What are the only frequencies that appear in the output if the original waveform has all harmonics?

13-3 A sawtooth wave has a minimum value of zero and a maximum value of 75 volts. What are the d-c value and the peak values of the first four harmonics?

13-4 A sawtooth has a peak-to-peak value of 20 volts. What is the rms value of the fiftieth harmonic?

13-5 Sketch the spectrum of a sawtooth with a peak-to-peak value of 20 volts. Show the first 10 harmonics.

13-6 A sawtooth with a peak-to-peak value of 10 volts and a period of 1 msec is the input to the *RC* filter shown in Fig. 13-20*a*. Find the peak value of the first and tenth harmonics at the input and the output of the filter.

13-7 A square wave with a peak-to-peak value of 25 volts has a period of 20 μsec. Find the rms value of the 150-kHz component.

13-8 A square wave with a peak-to-peak value of 50 volts and a period of 1 msec is the input to the *RC* filter of Fig. 13-20*a*. Find the approximate value of the fifth harmonic at the output of the filter.

13-9 A full-wave-rectified sinusoid has a peak value of 100 volts. Find the d-c value and the peak values of the first four harmonics. Also, what is the peak value of the one-hundredth harmonic?

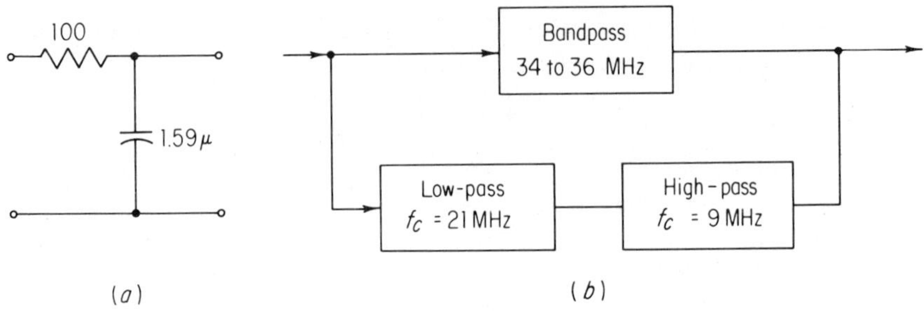

Fig. 13-20

13-10 A square wave with a period of 0.2 μsec is the input to the filter system shown in Fig. 13-20*b*. What frequencies appear in the output? Assume ideal filters.

13-11 Apply the flip test to a pure sine wave and state why the result makes sense.

13-12 Do the waveforms shown in Fig. 13-21*a* and *b* contain only odd harmonics?

13-13 Using Table 13-1, find the rms value of a sawtooth wave with a minimum value of zero and a maximum value of 50 volts.

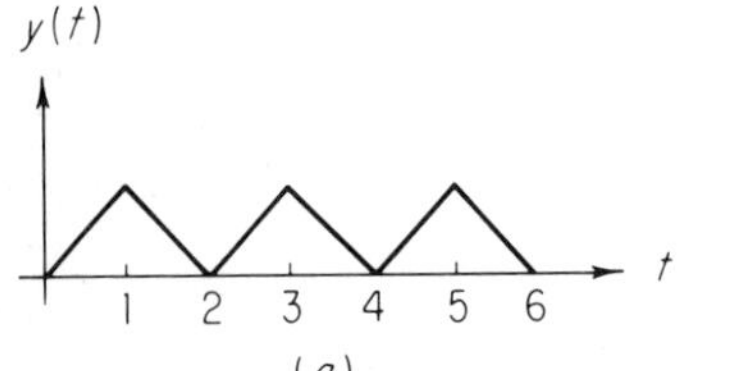

y(t)
t
3 4 7 8 11 12
(b)

Fig. 13-21

13-14 A triangular wave has a minimum value of zero and a maximum value of 25 volts. Find the rms value of this wave and find the rms value of the first three harmonics.

13-15 A sawtooth with a period of 1 msec has a flyback time of 0.25 msec. Which harmonics are missing in this sawtooth? Use Table 13-1.

13-16 A positively clamped rectangular wave has a period of 1 msec and a peak value of 20 volts. The pulse width is 0.25 msec. Find the rms value of the wave and the peak value of the first three harmonics. Use Table 13-1. Which harmonics will be missing from such a wave?

14 Harmonic Analyzing Instruments

In dealing with a periodic nonsinusoidal signal we know that we can think of this signal as a combination of a fundamental sinusoid plus its higher harmonics. In this chapter we examine three basic instruments used to measure the size of these harmonics. (1) The *distortion analyzer* measures the total rms value of all higher harmonics simultaneously. Thus, with a distortion analyzer we are measuring the total higher harmonic content of a signal. (2) The *wave analyzer* differs from the distortion analyzer in that it measures each harmonic individually and presents its value on a voltmeter. Thus, if we wish to know the value of a specific harmonic, such as the tenth harmonic, we can use a wave analyzer. (3) The *spectrum analyzer* is a very complex instrument that actually displays the spectrum of the signal on the face of a CRT.

14-1 Harmonic Distortion

Whenever a pure sinusoid is amplified, harmonics of this signal appear at the output of the amplifier. These harmonics exist because the signal is distorted as it passes through the amplifier. The amount of distortion may be very small, but nevertheless, some distortion always occurs in any amplifier.

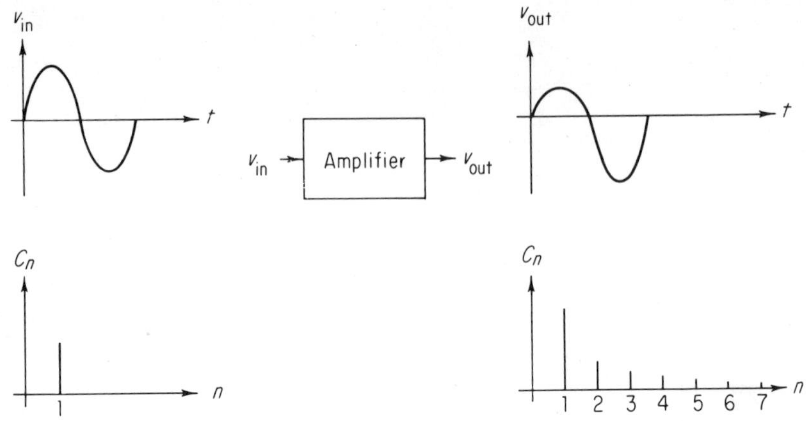

Fig. 14-1 Spectrum interpretation of harmonic distortion.

To bring the idea out more clearly, consider Fig. 14-1. The input to the amplifier has been shown as a pure sinusoid. Therefore, the spectrum of the input signal is a single line at $n = 1$. As the signal passes through the amplifier, the shape of the signal is distorted, because amplifying devices such as tubes or transistors have some degree of nonlinearity. As a result, the output shape is nonsinusoidal. In Fig. 14-1 we have exaggerated the output shape to bring out the fact that the positive half cycle has been flattened and the negative half cycle has been peaked. This is just one type of distortion that may occur. The point is that the output signal is nonsinusoidal and therefore must contain harmonics as shown in its spectrum.

The distortion shown in Fig. 14-1 is commonly known as *amplitude distortion* or *harmonic distortion*. Of course, it is possible to design amplifiers so that very little harmonic distortion occurs. Nevertheless, any real amplifier or, for that matter, any device that has nonlinear characteristics will introduce harmonics of the input signal.

We now have a qualitative concept of harmonic distortion; that is, we know that harmonic distortion refers to the amount of harmonic content above the fundamental frequency. How can we obtain a formula for the harmonic distortion?

We are now in an area of definition, and as before, we must agree on a definition. Historically, the numerical definition is

$$\text{Harmonic distortion} \triangleq \frac{\text{rms value of all higher harmonics}}{\text{rms value of fundamental}}$$

The rms value of the fundamental presents no problem, since we know that it has an rms value of 0.707 times the peak value. But how do we find the rms value of all the higher harmonics lumped together?

By using calculus it can be shown that any signal containing different frequency components has an rms value equal to the square root of the sum of the squares of each harmonic rms value. In other words,

$$\text{rms value of a signal} = \sqrt{V_a^2 + V_b^2 + V_c^2 + \cdots}$$

where V_a, V_b, V_c, etc., are the rms values of each sinusoid in the signal.

Thus, we can rewrite the formula for the harmonic distortion of a signal as:

$$\text{Harmonic distortion} \triangleq \frac{\sqrt{V_2^2 + V_3^2 + V_4^2 + \cdots}}{V_1} \tag{14-1}$$

where V_1 is the rms value of the first harmonic
V_2 is the rms value of the second harmonic
V_3 is the rms value of the third harmonic
and so on

As an example of using Eq. (14-1) to compute harmonic distortion, suppose that the signal out of an amplifier contains a fundamental with an rms value of 1 volt, a second harmonic with an rms value of 0.2 volt, and a third harmonic with an rms value of 0.1 volt. Let us assume that there are no harmonics above the third. Then, we calculate using Eq. (14-1) as follows:

$$\text{Harmonic distortion} = \frac{\sqrt{0.2^2 + 0.1^2}}{1} = \frac{\sqrt{0.05}}{1}$$

$$= 0.224 = 22.4\%$$

Equation (14-1) gives us a way of specifying the amount of harmonic distortion in a signal. If there are no higher harmonics present in a signal, the signal has a harmonic distortion of zero, since the numerator of Eq. (14-1) is zero. On the other hand, if the harmonics are *extremely* large compared to the fundamental, then theoretically the harmonic distortion can be as high as infinity. As a practical matter, when a sine wave is amplified, the amount of distortion is usually small, so that most of the time we will be dealing with harmonic-distortion values that are considerably less than unity. For example, a good high-fidelity amplifier typically has less than 1 percent of harmonic distortion. In other words, the rms value of all higher harmonics lumped together is less than 1 percent of the rms value of the fundamental.

14-2 The Ideal Harmonic-distortion Analyzer

How can we build an instrument that measures the harmonic distortion of a signal? According to Eq. (14-1), we must measure the rms value of all the higher harmonics lumped together, and then compare this value to the rms value of the fundamental.

An ideal system for measuring harmonic distortion is shown in Fig. 14-2*a*. It works as follows. The input signal to be analyzed is first passed through a bandpass filter tuned to the fundamental. Hence, only the fundamental frequency is measured when the switch is in the reference position. The attenuator is adjusted to give a reference reading on the voltmeter. For convenience, let us adjust the attenuator so that we read 1 volt in the reference position. Under this condition, V_1 equals 1 volt. With the true rms voltmeter on the 1-volt range we would have a meter deflection as shown in Fig. 14-2*b*.

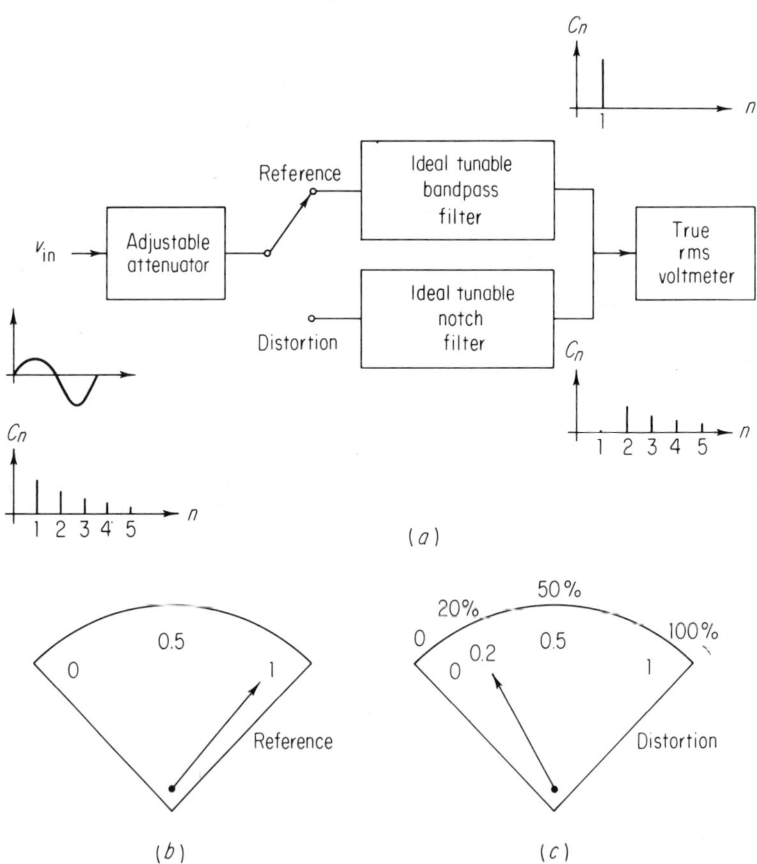

Fig. 14-2 Ideal harmonic-distortion analyzer. (*a*) Block diagram and spectra. (*b*) Reference reading on fundamental. (*c*) Distortion reading on higher harmonics.

The switch is next changed to the distortion position. The notch filter is then tuned to notch out the fundamental frequency. Thus, only the higher harmonics are passed on to the true rms voltmeter. The voltmeter now reads the rms value of all higher harmonics lumped together. Let us assume that we have a meter deflection as shown in Fig. 14-2*c*. In this case, the rms value of all higher harmonics is 0.2 volt. It should be immediately clear that

$$\text{Harmonic distortion} = \frac{\sqrt{V_2^2 + V_3^2 + V_4^2 + \cdots}}{V_1} = \frac{0.2}{1} = 0.2 = 20\%$$

The ideal system of Fig. 14-2 conveys the essential ideas behind commercial harmonic-distortion analyzers. First, a reference reading is made where we are measuring the value of the fundamental. Second, a distortion reading is made where we are measuring the rms value of all the higher harmonics. The meter face may be marked directly in volts, or in percent, as shown in Fig. 14-2*c*.

EXAMPLE 14-1

A signal is analyzed in the system of Fig. 14-2*a*. Suppose that the reference reading on the fundamental is 10 volts instead of 1 volt. If the reading in the distortion position is 0.25 volt, then what is the harmonic distortion?

SOLUTION

$$\text{Harmonic distortion} = \frac{0.25}{10} = 0.025 = 2.5\%$$

14-3 Other Forms of the Distortion Analyzer

The ideal distortion analyzer of the preceding section is not normally used in commercial distortion analyzers. In this section we examine some alternative systems for measuring harmonic distortion. Let us first consider the system shown in Fig. 14-3. In this system, the total distorted signal is measured on the reference position. As a result, instead of measuring V_1, the rms value of the fundamental, we are actually measuring

$$V_{\text{ref}} = \sqrt{V_1^2 + V_2^2 + V_3^2 + \cdots} \tag{14-2}$$

When we set the reference, the attenuator must be adjusted to a slightly higher value than it would be if only the fundamental were measured.

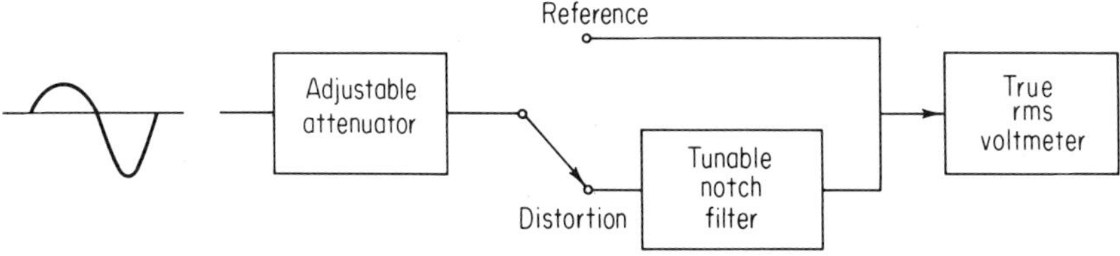

Fig. 14-3 Harmonic-distortion analyzer without bandpass filter on reference reading.

Therefore, when we switch to the distortion position we obtain a lower distortion reading than we would with the ideal system of Fig. 14-2*a*. How much lower will the distortion reading be?

This depends upon the size of the higher harmonics. By an inspection of Eq. (14-2) it should be clear that if the harmonics are small compared to the fundamental, the reference voltage will be approximately equal to V_1. Under this condition, the distortion readings are very close to the true values.

An analysis of Eq. (14-1) and (14-2) allows us to construct the following table:

True distortion, %	Actual reading, %
∞	100
100	70.7
30	28.7
10	9.95

Note from this table that if the true distortion is 10 percent, the reading obtained with the system of Fig. 14-3 is extremely close to the true value. Even for a true distortion of 30 percent, the actual reading obtained is only 1.3 percent lower than the true value. However, for a 100 percent true distortion, the actual reading is only 70.7 percent.

As a practical matter, most distortion measurements involve distortions of less than 30 percent, so that the error produced by not using a bandpass filter in the reference position becomes negligible. Thus, in a practical distortion analyzer, where distortions are normally much less than 30 percent, the system of Fig. 14-3 is entirely adequate.

Another system that is often used is that shown in Fig. 14-4. In this case, not only is the bandpass filter omitted, but the voltmeter is the average-detector type discussed in Chap. 4. Typically, this average detector is a full-wave-rectifier bridge type. Recall that the average

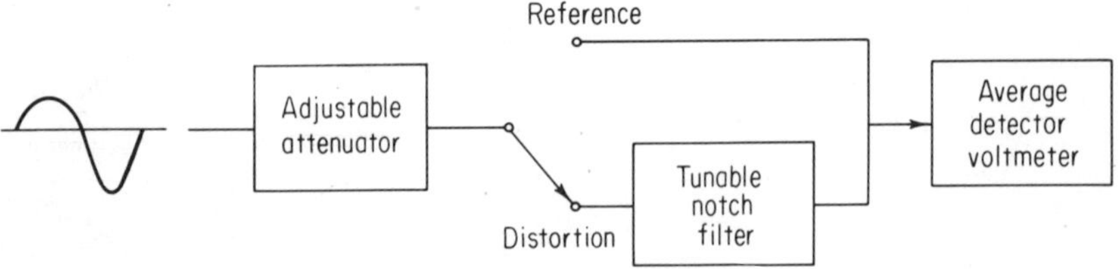

Fig. 14-4 Harmonic-distortion analyzer with average detector instead of true rms detector.

value of a full-wave-rectified sine wave is 0.636 times the peak value, whereas the rms value is 0.707 times the peak value. Thus, the ratio of the rms to the average value is 0.707/0.636, or 1.11. When an average detecting type of voltmeter is used to make voltage measurements on a sine-wave signal, the needle actually points to the average value, but the marks on the meter face are 1.11 times higher than the average value. As a result, we *read* the rms value of the sine-wave signal. This reading is valid as long as the signal is a pure *sinusoid*. In general, the ratio of the rms value to the average value of rectified *nonsinusoidal* signals is not 1.11. Therefore, we have a calibration error whenever we measure a nonsinusoidal signal on a voltmeter calibrated for sinusoidal signals.

In Fig. 14-4 the signal out of the notch filter may be an extremely complex waveform. The ratio of the rms value to the average value of the rectified version of this complex wave may be far different from 1.11. Therefore, a considerable error may arise, especially in those cases where the input signal being analyzed is a pulsed waveform.

In most typical distortion measurements, the signal being analyzed is recognizable as a distorted sine wave. It may be flattened on one side and peaked on the other side, but it still is recognizable as a distorted sine wave. In such cases, the errors produced by the use of an average detector voltmeter are not large, and the distortion readings are adequate for most measurements.

The tunable notch filter used in either Fig. 14-3 or 14-4 is usually a Wien-bridge notch filter. Normally, the notch is made extremely sharp by using a Wien bridge and an amplifier with negative feedback.

14-4 The Wave Analyzer

A distortion analyzer measures all the higher harmonics simultaneously. A wave analyzer is designed to measure one harmonic at a time. Most wave analyzers are based upon the idea of filtering out the desired harmonic from the complex waveform and measuring this component on an ordinary voltmeter. There are several ways of filtering out the desired component, perhaps the most popular being that of heterodyning the signal under test with an internal oscillator.

For the sake of illustration, let us consider the system of Fig. 14-5. There is an oscillator that we can manually tune from 50 to 70 kHz. There is a mixer whose output is applied to a narrow-band amplifier tuned to 50 kHz. The bandwidth of the amplifier is only 10 Hz. Finally, there is an a-c voltmeter to read the output of the narrow-band amplifier.

Let us assume that the input signal to be analyzed is a 100-Hz square wave. We already know that the square wave has only odd harmonics. Therefore, the spectrum shown correctly indicates that the sinusoidal com-

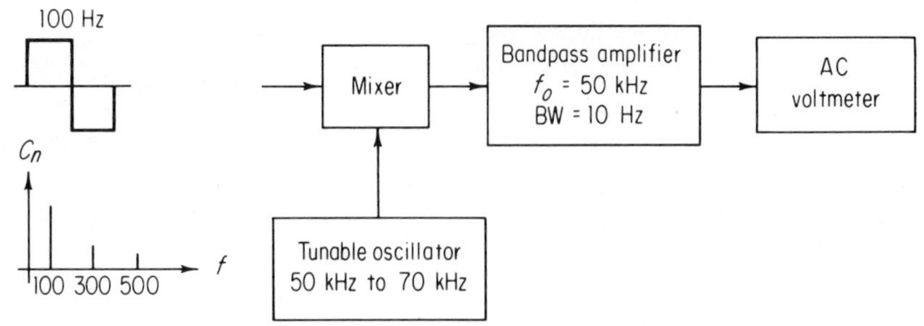

Fig. 14-5 Wave-analyzer block diagram.

ponents of the square wave occur at frequencies of 100, 300, 500, ... Suppose that we adjust the oscillator to 50.1 kHz. The output of the mixer contains the sum and difference of each harmonic beating against the oscillator frequency. The only mixer output signal that can pass through the narrow-band amplifier is the 50-kHz component. This component is the result of 100 Hz beating with 50.1 kHz. All other mixer products are above or below 50 kHz. Therefore, the only signal that can pass through the narrow-band amplifier is the difference signal produced by 100 Hz and 50.1 kHz. This difference signal has an rms value that is proportional to the size of the 100-Hz fundamental of the square wave. The a-c voltmeter then reads the rms value of the 50-kHz signal, but since this voltage is in direct proportion to the size of the 100-Hz signal, we can calibrate the meter face to read the rms value of the 100-Hz fundamental.

The next beat note that can pass through the amplifier occurs for an oscillator frequency of 50.3 kHz. In this case, the third harmonic, 300 Hz, beats against the 50.3 kHz to produce a 50-kHz signal that can pass through the narrow-band amplifier. The reading we now obtain on the voltmeter is an rms value proportional to the 300-Hz component.

By progressively adjusting the oscillator frequency, each harmonic can be separated from the other harmonics. The a-c voltmeter indicates the rms value of each harmonic. To indicate the frequency of the harmonic producing the beat note, the oscillator may be ganged to a dial that reads the frequency of the harmonic.

The wave analyzer can be used to analyze many waveforms. Sawtooth waves, triangular waves, distorted sine waves, even noise can be easily analyzed. For example, if there is more noise in one part of the frequency spectrum than in another, the wave analyzer will indicate this as we scan through the spectrum.

A wave analyzer is sometimes called a movable window since it allows us to look at a small part of the input spectrum. In the system of Fig. 14-5 the window is approximately 10 Hz. Tuning the oscillator merely moves the window over a large frequency range. It should be clear that the total scanning range of a wave analyzer is equal to the tuning range of the oscillator. In the system of Fig. 14-5 the scanning range of the wave analyzer is 20 kHz.

The system of Fig. 14-5 conveys the essential ideas behind most commercial wave analyzers. The size of the window may differ from one wave analyzer to another, as well as the scanning range.

Example 14-2

A wave analyzer similar to that of Fig. 14-5 has an amplifier with a bandwidth of 20 Hz, and an oscillator with a range of 75 to 150 kHz. What is the approximate size of the window, and what is the total scanning range?

Solution

The window is approximately equal to the bandwidth of the amplifier. Therefore, the window is about 20 Hz.

The total scanning range is equal to the tuning range of the oscillator, which is 75 kHz in this problem.

Example 14-3

If the wave analyzer of Fig. 14-5 is used to measure the harmonics of a sawtooth, for what fundamental frequency of the sawtooth will two adjacent harmonics produce beat notes that fall within the bandwidth of the amplifier?

Solution

Since the bandwidth is 10 Hz, the window is 10 Hz. Thus, if the harmonics of the sawtooth are within 10 Hz of each other, they will produce beat notes that fall within the 3-db bandwidth of the amplifier. Therefore, a sawtooth with a fundamental frequency of 10 Hz has harmonics of 20, 30, 40 Hz, etc., and any two adjacent harmonics can produce beat notes that fall within the 3-db bandwidth of the amplifier.

14-5 The Spectrum Analyzer

Undoubtedly, the spectrum analyzer is the ultimate tool in measuring harmonics and spectra. This instrument displays the spectrum of an input signal on the face of a CRT. The kinds of patterns that are obtained are extremely interesting and informative in that we can see at a glance the location and strength of all the frequency components of the input signal.

There are many types of commercial spectrum analyzers, but the majority seem to be based upon a system similar to that used for the wave analyzer. The frequency components of the input signal are mixed with an internal oscillator signal, and the mixer products are then filtered in a narrow-band amplifier. The output of this amplifier is then detected and applied to the vertical deflection plates of a CRT.

In order to illustrate how a typical spectrum analyzer works, consider the system of Fig. 14-6. There is a sawtooth generator whose output is

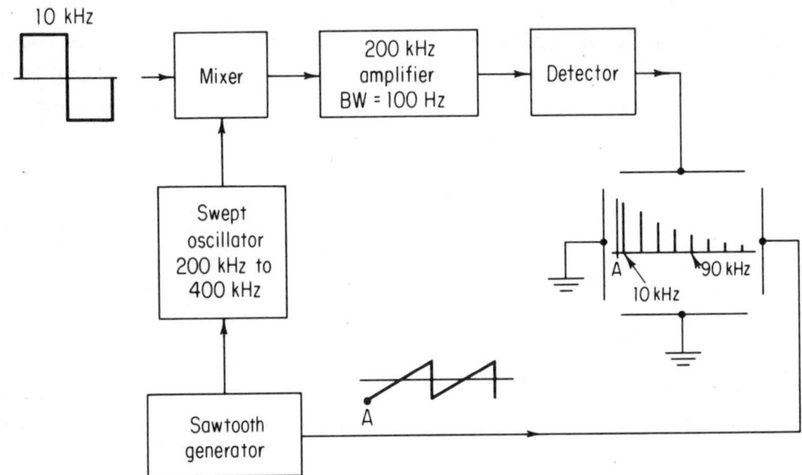

Fig. 14-6 Spectrum-analyzer block diagram.

applied to the horizontal deflection plates of a CRT. The sawtooth signal is also applied to the internal oscillator. This oscillator differs from that of a wave analyzer in that the frequency is electronically controlled by the instantaneous value of the sawtooth voltage. When the sawtooth voltage is just starting to rise, the oscillator frequency is 200 kHz. As the sawtooth voltage increases, the oscillator frequency increases. When the sawtooth has reached its midvalue, the oscillator frequency is at 300 kHz. Finally, when the sawtooth voltage is at its peak value, the oscillator frequency is at 400 kHz. There are several ways of building electronically controlled oscillators, and we will examine some of these ways in the next chapter. For the moment, it is sufficient to realize that the oscillator frequency is linearly swept from 200 to 400 kHz as the sawtooth voltage goes from its minimum to its maximum value.

Let us use a square wave with a fundamental frequency of 10 kHz as the input to the spectrum analyzer. The spectrum of this square wave contains frequency components of 10, 30, 50 kHz, and so on.

At point A in time the sawtooth voltage begins to rise. The oscillator frequency at this instant in time is 200 kHz. The output of the mixer contains the original frequencies and the sum and difference frequencies.

With the oscillator at 200 kHz, we have the following mixer outputs:

Original frequencies: 200, 10, 30, 50, . . . kHz
Sum frequencies: 210, 230, 250, . . . kHz
Difference frequencies: 190, 170, 150, . . . kHz

In this case the only signal that can pass through the narrow-band amplifier is the 200-kHz oscillator signal. This signal is detected and applied to the vertical deflection plates of the CRT. Thus, at point A in time, the spot is deflected to the left and upward, as shown in Fig. 14-6.

As the sawtooth voltage builds up, the oscillator frequency changes. When the oscillator frequency is at 210 kHz, the mixer outputs are

Original frequencies: 210, 10, 30, 50, . . . kHz
Sum frequencies: 220, 240, 260, . . . kHz
Difference frequencies: 200, 180, 160, . . . kHz

In this case, the only signal that can pass through the narrow-band amplifier is the 200-kHz mixer output that is obtained from beating the 210-kHz oscillator signal with the 10-kHz fundamental. The size of this 200-kHz difference frequency is proportional to the size of the 10-kHz fundamental. This signal is detected and applied to the vertical deflection plates. In the meantime the spot has moved to the right, so that we obtain a line at 10 kHz, as shown in Fig. 14-6.

The oscillator continues to change its frequency, and each time the oscillator frequency is 200 kHz greater than one of the harmonics, a 200-kHz difference frequency occurs. The 200-kHz signal, which is proportional to the harmonic involved, is detected and applied to the vertical deflection plates. Thus, the entire spectrum is displayed on the CRT.

In the system of Fig. 14-6, the scanning range of the spectrum analyzer equals the tuning range of the oscillator. Hence, with this system we can scan through a 200-kHz range. The bandwidth of the amplifier is 100 Hz, so that we may think of looking at the spectrum of the input signal through a window of 100 Hz. In this particular example, we are looking at a square wave with harmonics that are 20 kHz apart. Therefore, there is no problem in separating the harmonics. It should be clear, however, that if we look at a signal with harmonics that are only 100 Hz apart, the window is not narrow enough to separate the harmonics. In any event, as long as we look at input signals whose frequency components are far enough apart compared to the bandwidth of the amplifier, we will obtain clear sharp lines on the CRT.

Commercial spectrum analyzers are far more complicated than the simple system of Fig. 14-6. The scanning ranges and the size of the window may differ considerably from one spectrum analyzer to another. Nevertheless, our simple system conveys most of the basic ideas on how a spectrum analyzer works.

SUMMARY

The harmonic-distortion analyzer measures the total harmonic content above the fundamental frequency. When taking a reference reading, only the fundamental is measured in an ideal distortion analyzer. However, in most commercial distortion analyzers the total distorted signal is measured in the reference position. This leads to some error in the distortion measurement, but for distortions of less than 30 percent, we may consider the error as negligible. Another source of error in some commercial distortion analyzers is the use of an average-detector voltmeter instead of a true rms voltmeter. The size of the error depends upon the exact shape of the wave being measured. For some waveshapes, the error can become quite large; however, for most typical distortion measurements the size of the error is acceptable for approximate distortion readings.

The wave analyzer is a manually operated instrument that measures each harmonic individually. This is accomplished by beating the spectrum of the input signal with an internal oscillator and then filtering the mixer products to obtain a signal voltage that is proportional to the harmonic voltage being measured. The signal voltage is then measured on an a-c voltmeter calibrated to read the rms value of the harmonic being measured. The scanning range of a wave analyzer equals the tuning range of the internal oscillator, and the window of the wave analyzer equals the bandwidth of the filter amplifier. We may think of a wave analyzer as an instrument that allows us to look at the input spectrum through a narrow window.

The spectrum analyzer is similar to the wave analyzer, except that the internal oscillator is electronically swept through the scanning range, and the final indication appears on a CRT instead of a simple voltmeter. At any one instant in time, the spectrum analyzer is looking at some part of the input spectrum through a narrow window. If there is a signal in that part of the spectrum, a vertical line appears on the face of the CRT. The position of this vertical line along the base line is an indication of the frequency component involved.

GLOSSARY

distortion analyzer An instrument for measuring the amount of harmonic distortion.

harmonic distortion Defined as the ratio of the rms value of all higher harmonics to the rms value of the fundamental.

heterodyning Mixing two or more signals in order to obtain sum and difference frequencies.

rms value of a signal The value of a d-c signal that would produce exactly the same heating effect as the signal.

spectrum analyzer An instrument that displays the spectrum of an input signal on the screen of a CRT.

wave analyzer Basically a narrow tunable bandpass filter followed by a voltmeter. Used in measuring the various frequency components of a signal.

window In a wave analyzer or a spectrum analyzer this refers to effective bandwidth of the overall system.

REVIEW QUESTIONS

1. Why does any amplifier introduce harmonics of the input signal?
2. How is the harmonic distortion of a signal defined?
3. What are the maximum and minimum possible values of harmonic distortion?
4. If a signal contains several sinusoidal frequencies, how do we find the total rms value of the signal?
5. In the ideal harmonic distortion analyzer calibrated in percent why is it necessary first to adjust the voltmeter to a reference?
6. What are two sources of error in using a nonideal distortion analyzer?
7. How does a wave analyzer differ from a distortion analyzer?
8. What determines the size of the window in a wave analyzer?
9. What determines the total scan range of a wave analyzer?
10. How does a spectrum analyzer differ from a wave analyzer?
11. In a spectrum analyzer what determines the size of the window? What determines the scanning range of the spectrum analyzer?
12. Why should the size of the window of a spectrum analyzer be much smaller than the spacing between the frequency components of the signal being analyzed?

PROBLEMS

14-1 A sinusoidal signal is amplified by a device that introduces all harmonics of the signal. If the input signal has a period of 50 μsec, what frequencies appear in the output signal?

14-2 A signal contains sinusoidal frequencies of 1, 2, 3, 4, and 5 kHz. The respective peak values are 10, 5, 7, 2, and 3 volts. Find the rms value of the signal.

14-3 A signal has a fundamental with an rms value of 5 volts. The signal also contains a second, third, and fourth harmonic with rms values of 1, 0.5, and 0.3 volt, respectively. Find the harmonic distortion.

14-4 The system of Fig. 14-3 is used to measure the distortion of a signal. If the reading is 70.7 percent, what is the true harmonic distortion? If the reading is 30 percent, approximately what is the true harmonic distortion?

14-5 Prove that the system of Fig. 14-3 actually reads 70.7 percent for a true harmonic distortion of 100 percent.

14-6 A wave analyzer is needed that has a scanning range from 0 to 50 kHz and a window of 30 Hz. Referring to Fig. 14-5, change the block diagram as needed to meet the specifications.

15 Signal Sources

In this chapter we turn our attention to some of the basic circuits and techniques used to generate sine-wave and square-wave signals.

15-1 Producing Oscillations

One of the most fundamental methods of producing sine-wave oscillations is that of coupling the output of an amplifier back to its input through a filter so that the amplifier oscillates at only one frequency.

In order to convey the basic idea behind this approach, consider the system of Fig. 15-1. A signal generator is driving the amplifier. The output of the amplifier is therefore an enlarged version of the input sine wave. In this case, we are arbitrarily showing the output sine wave as being in phase with the input. This signal is then fed back to a filter so that the output v_f of the filter is a sine wave whose magnitude and phase depend upon the frequency of the signal.

Suppose that we adjust the frequency of the input signal generator so that the feedback signal v_f is exactly in phase with the generator signal. Let us now consider what happens if we connect the feedback signal to the amplifier, and at the same time remove the generator. There

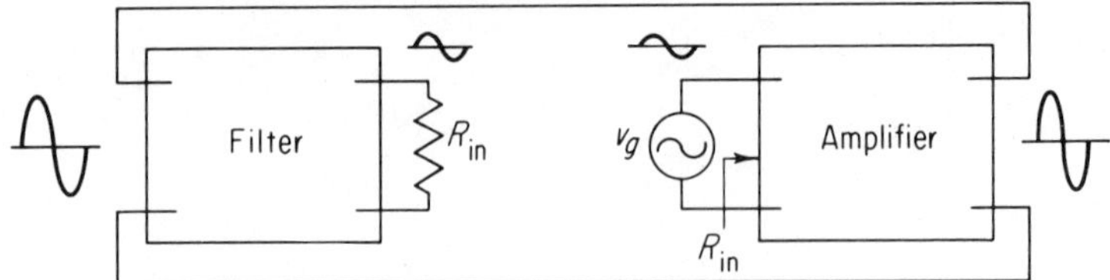

Fig. 15-1 The positive-feedback method of producing oscillations.

are three possibilities. First, if the feedback signal has a peak value equal to that of the generator signal, the system remains in equilibrium, with the filter output supplying the necessary input signal. Figure 15-2*a* indicates that the amplitude of the signal is constant. Second, if the feedback signal is smaller than the generator signal, then substituting the smaller feedback signal for the generator signal means that the output signal must be reduced. If the output is reduced, the feedback signal is reduced, and the signal decays to zero, as shown in Fig. 15-2*b*. Third,

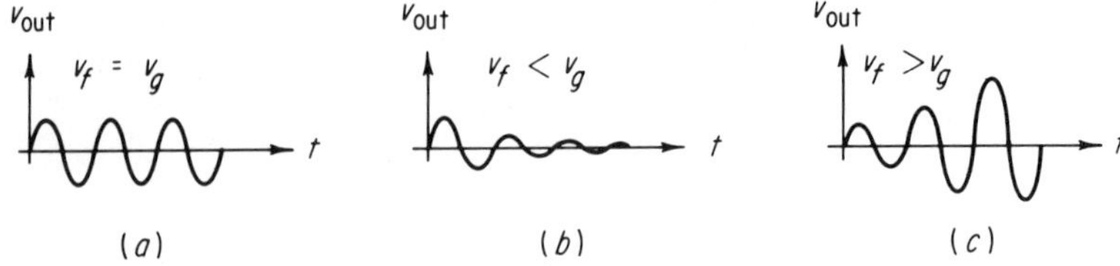

Fig. 15-2 Output waveforms. (*a*) Stable oscillations. (*b*) Decaying oscillations. (*c*) Increasing oscillations.

if the feedback signal is larger than the generator signal, the output voltage will actually increase, as shown in Fig. 15-2*c*.

The general idea in building an oscillator using positive feedback is clear. We must design an amplifier and a feedback network so that at the desired frequency of oscillation the feedback signal is in phase and larger than the amplifier input signal. Then, in order to obtain oscillations we need only connect the feedback signal to the amplifier input as shown in Fig. 15-3.

It is reasonable to ask at this time how oscillation begins without a signal generator to initially drive the amplifier. One explanation is that

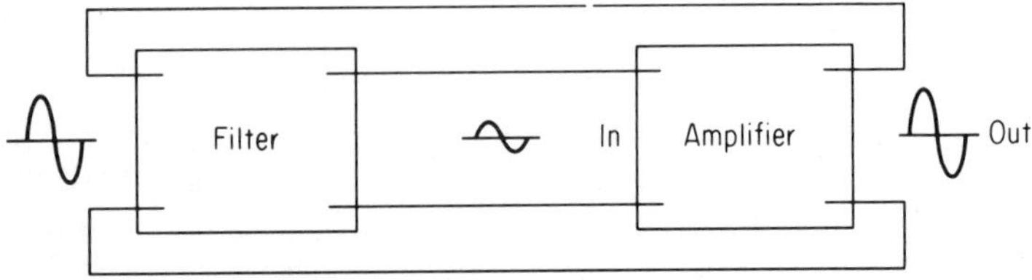

Fig. 15-3 Oscillator block diagram.

the amplifier noise starts the oscillations. Recall that any resistor is generating noise voltages because of the thermal agitation of its free electrons. The spectrum of this noise covers all frequencies. In other words, we may think of the input resistor associated with the first stage of the amplifier as being a source of all sinusoidal frequencies. These sinusoidal signals are amplified and fed back to the filter. Only one of these sinusoidal frequencies returns to the amplifier input with exactly the correct phase required to reinforce the signal producing it. If this feedback signal is larger than the original sinusoid in the noise spectrum, the oscillations will build up at this frequency until the amplifier or the filter saturates. The output of the amplifier then levels off, and we have a fixed-amplitude sine wave. (A different explanation of how oscillations begin is sometimes given in terms of transients.)

Here are the essential ideas behind any oscillator using positive feedback:

1. The phase shift through the amplifier and the filter must be exactly zero degrees at the frequency of oscillation.
2. In order for the oscillations to start, the voltage gain of the amplifier and the filter must be greater than unity at the frequency of oscillation.
3. After the oscillations have reached a certain amplitude, the voltage gain of the amplifier and the filter will drop to unity.

15-2 The Wien-bridge Oscillator

Undoubtedly, the Wien-bridge oscillator is the most widely used oscillator circuit in commercial signal generators operating in the frequency range 5 Hz to 500 kHz.

To understand the theory of this type of oscillator, consider the system of Fig. 15-4. The A and B terminals of the Wien bridge are connected to

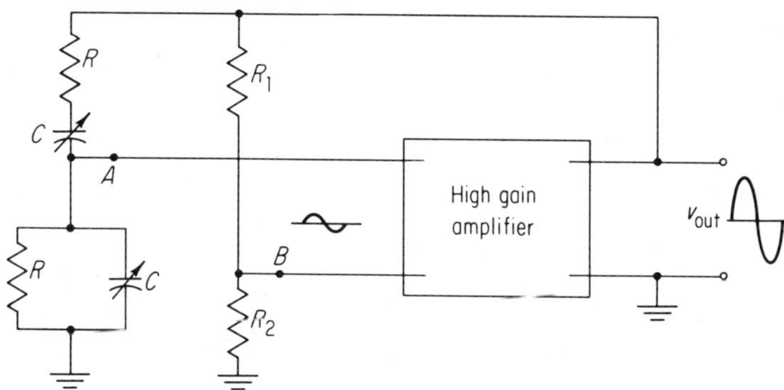

Fig. 15-4 Wien-bridge oscillator.

the amplifier input. The output of the amplifier is fed back to the Wien bridge. It can be shown that the output of the Wien bridge is of the correct phase required to sustain oscillations only if the bridge is near the balance condition. This implies that the frequency of oscillation is approximately given by $1/2\pi RC$.

In order to explain the operation of the Wien-bridge oscillator in detail, let us consider the system of Fig. 15-5*a*. In this circuit R_2 is a tungsten lamp. Recall that the resistance of a tungsten lamp depends upon the voltage applied to it. As the lamp heats up, its resistance increases. A typical variation of resistance versus the rms voltage across the lamp is shown in Fig. 15-5*b*. In the vicinity of zero volts, the lamp resistance is

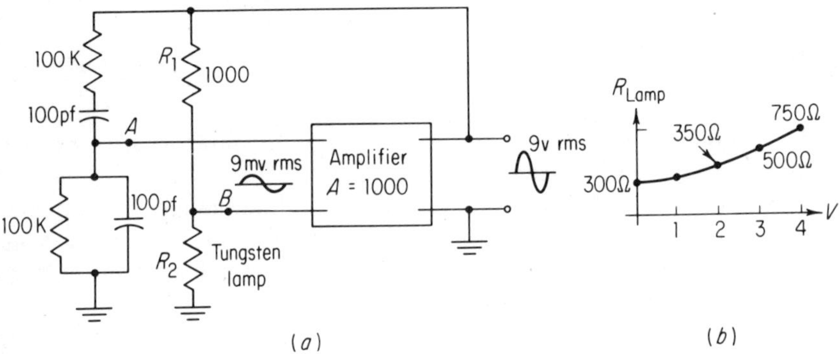

Fig. 15-5 Wien-bridge oscillator. (*a*) Block diagram. (*b*) Tungsten-lamp characteristics.

about 300 ohms, whereas at 3 volts rms, the resistance is 500 ohms. Recall that one of the conditions of bridge balance is that R_2 equal $R_1/2$. In this case, R_2 must equal 500 ohms in order for the bridge to balance. When the oscillations are just starting, the lamp resistance is only 300 ohms, and the bridge is unbalanced. This means that the amplifier input signal is quite large, and as a result, the oscillations will build up. However, as the oscillations increase in size, the voltage fed back to the bridge increases, causing a larger voltage across the lamp. This means that the lamp resistance will increase. Eventually, the lamp resistance becomes almost 500 ohms, and the bridge is almost balanced. The lamp resistance will approach 500 ohms as closely as required to reduce the overall loop gain to unity. When this happens, the output of the amplifier becomes a fixed-amplitude sine wave. Note carefully that there is no need at all for the amplifier to saturate in order to reduce the loop gain to unity. This is accomplished by the tungsten lamp. The importance of this is simply that since the amplifier is not saturated, a reasonably low-distortion sine wave can be obtained from the amplifier.

It should be clear that the amplifier output is around 9 volts rms. The reason for this is as follows. We know that the voltage across the lamp is about 3 volts rms. Since the lamp resistance is equal to one-half of R_1, the voltage across R_1 must be about 6 volts rms. Therefore, the voltage across R_1 and R_2 (the output voltage) is 9 volts rms.

Also note that the voltage gain of the amplifier has been shown as 1000. As a result, the input to the amplifier must be 9 mv. This confirms the notion that the bridge is only slightly unbalanced. This also means that the voltage from terminal B to ground is only 9 mv less than the voltage from terminal A to ground.

We may summarize the operation of the Wien-bridge oscillator by noting that:

1. The bridge is almost balanced.
2. The frequency of oscillation is $f \cong 1/2\pi\, RC$.
3. The output voltage is about 3 times larger than the voltage across the tungsten lamp.

The Wien-bridge oscillator may be built using either tubes or transistors. A common tube version is shown in Fig. 15-6.

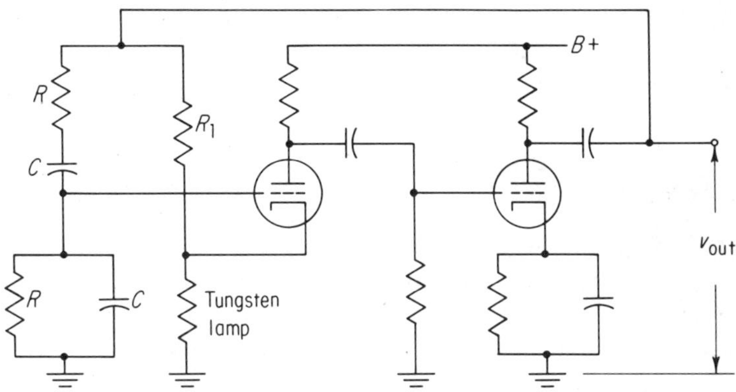

Fig. 15-6 A vacuum-tube version of the Wien-bridge oscillator.

Example 15-1

In Fig. 15-4, the value of R is 100 kilohms, and the value of C is 500 pf. What is the approximate frequency of oscillation?

Solution

$$f = \frac{1}{2\pi RC} = \frac{0.159}{100(10^3)(500)(10^{-12})} = 3.18 \text{ kHz}$$

Example 15-2

In the oscillator of Fig. 15-5 what change may be made in order to increase the output from 9 to 12 volts rms?

Solution

One possible change is to make R_1 a 1500-ohm resistor instead of a 1000-ohm resistor. In this way, the tungsten-lamp resistance must be around 750 ohms in order to balance the bridge. From the graph of Fig. 15-5*b* it is clear that the lamp voltage will then be about 4 volts rms, and therefore the output must be 3 times larger, or 12 volts.

Example 15-3

In Fig. 15-4, the tuning range of the capacitors is from 50 to 500 pf.
(*a*) What is the frequency range if the value of R is 159 kilohms?
(*b*) What is the frequency range if the value of R is 15.9 kilohms?

Solution

For R = 159 kilohms:

$$f_{\text{min}} = \frac{0.159}{159(10^3)(500)(10^{-12})} = 2 \text{ kHz}$$

$$f_{\text{max}} = \frac{0.159}{159(10^3)(50)(10^{-12})} = 20 \text{ kHz}$$

For R = 15.9 kilohms, the minimum and maximum frequencies are increased by a factor of ten. Hence, $f_{\text{min}} = 20$ kHz, and $f_{\text{max}} = 200$ kHz.

15-3 The Colpitts Oscillator

The Colpitts oscillator is widely used in signal generators operating in the frequency range of about 100 kHz to 500 MHz. A basic Colpitts oscillator is shown in Fig. 15-7. The circuit action is as follows. When the d-c power is applied, noise in the R_g resistor is amplified in the triode.

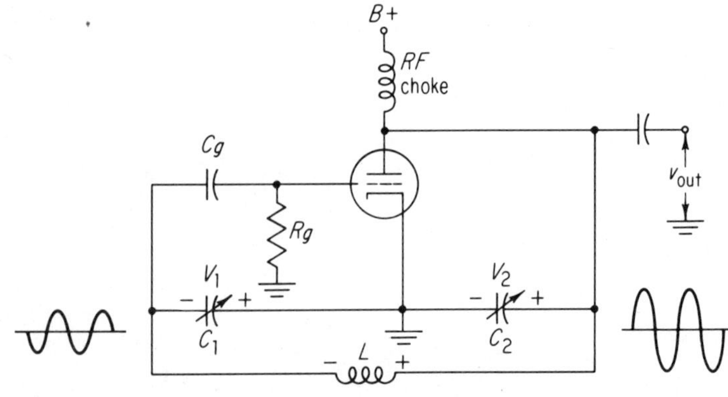

Fig. 15-7 Colpitts oscillator.

This noise is coupled into the tank circuit consisting of L, C_1, and C_2. This tank circuit is resonant at only one of the sinusoidal frequencies present in the noise. The polarity of the voltages across the capacitors is shown during the positive half cycle. (These polarities reverse during the negative half cycle.) It should be clear from these polarities that the signal fed back to the grid is 180° out of phase with the signal on the plate. Since there is already 180° of phase inversion in the tube, the phase shift around the entire feedback loop is zero at the resonant frequency of the tank circuit.

The size of the signal on the grid compared to the size of the signal on the plate is determined by the ratio of C_1 to C_2. Specifically, since the same circulating current is flowing through C_1 and C_2,

$$\frac{V_2}{X_2} = \frac{V_1}{X_1} \qquad \text{or} \qquad \frac{V_2}{V_1} = \frac{X_2}{X_1}$$

or

$$\frac{V_2}{V_1} = \frac{C_1}{C_2} \tag{15-1}$$

where V_1 is the peak value of the sinusoid across C_1 and V_2 is the peak value of the sinusoid across C_2.

In effect, Eq. (15-1) determines the feedback factor. As an example of using Eq. (15-1), suppose that $C_1 = 100$ pf and $C_2 = 50$ pf. Then, the ratio of V_2 to V_1 must be

$$\frac{V_2}{V_1} = \frac{100(10^{-12})}{50(10^{-12})} = 2$$

Thus, the sine wave across C_2 has a peak value that is twice as large as the sine wave across C_1.

Recall that an oscillator can start to oscillate only if the loop gain is greater than unity. In the circuit of Fig. 15-7 this means that the voltage gain of the tube from grid to plate must be greater than the reduction in signal that is given by Eq. (15-1). Specifically, oscillations can start only if

$$A > \frac{C_1}{C_2} \tag{15-2}$$

where A is the voltage gain from grid to plate. As an example, if $C_1 = 100$ pf, and if $C_2 = 50$ pf, the voltage gain from the grid to the plate must be greater than 2; otherwise, oscillations cannot start.

After the oscillations build up, there must be some means of reducing the loop gain to unity. This is accomplished by the grid-leak-bias network consisting of R_g, C_g, and the grid-cathode part of the tube. As the oscillations build up, the bias on the tube increases, causing the tube to cut off during part of the cycle. This in effect reduces the gain of the tube so that the loop gain becomes unity.

One way of understanding how the grid leak bias is established is to visualize R_g, C_g, and the grid-cathode part of the tube as a negative clamping circuit (see Fig. 15-8*a*). This is basically the clamping circuit that was studied in Chap. 4. To operate normally, we need only choose the values of R_g and C_g so that the RC time constant is much greater than the period of the sine-wave signal being clamped. As the oscillations build up, the signal at the input to the negative clamping circuit builds up as shown in Fig. 15-8*b*. This signal is clamped at the grid, resulting in the

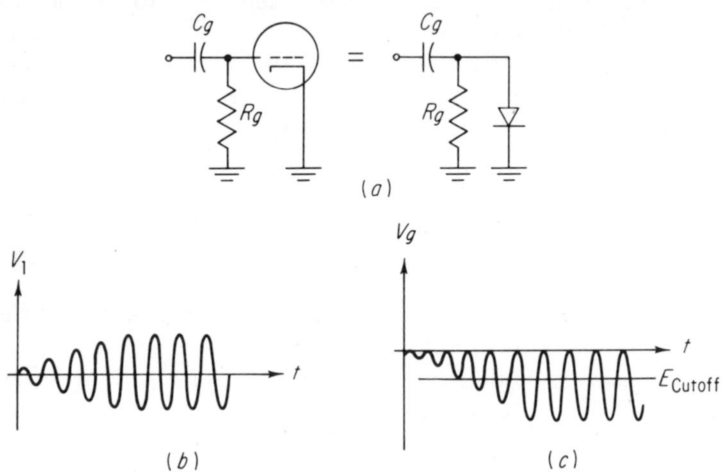

Fig. 15-8 Grid leak bias. (*a*) Equivalent of grid circuit. (*b*) Input to clamping circuit. (*c*) Clamped waveform on the grid.

signal of Fig. 15-8*c*. Note that eventually the signal exceeds the cutoff voltage of the tube, so that current is flowing only for part of a cycle. This effectively reduces that voltage gain of the tube. The correct bias level is automatically adjusted since the signal will continue to build up until the overall loop gain becomes unity.

The frequency of oscillation is approximately equal to the resonant frequency of the tank circuit. That is,

$$f_o \cong \frac{1}{2\pi\sqrt{LC}} \tag{15-3}$$

where

$$C = \frac{C_1C_2}{C_1 + C_2}$$

The Colpitts oscillator is normally tuned by ganging C_1 and C_2 together.

Example 15-4

In Fig. 15-7, $C_1 = 300$ pf, and $C_2 = 60$ pf. What is the minimum voltage gain required of the tube to guarantee that the oscillations start?

Solution

From inequality (15-2) we know that the voltage gain must be greater than the ratio of C_1 to C_2. Hence,

$$A_{\min} = \frac{C_1}{C_2} = \frac{300(10^{-12})}{60(10^{-12})} = 5$$

Example 15-5

In Fig. 15-7, $C_1 = 600$ pf, $C_2 = 300$ pf, and $L = 1$ mh. What is the approximate frequency of oscillation?

Solution

$$C = \frac{C_1C_2}{C_1 + C_2} = \frac{600(10^{-12})(300)(10^{-12})}{600(10^{-12}) + 300(10^{-12})} = 200 \text{ pf}$$

and

$$f \cong \frac{1}{2\pi\sqrt{10^{-3}(200)(10^{-12})}} = 356 \text{ kHz}$$

15-4 Typical Sine-wave Generators

The block diagram for a typical low-frequency generator is shown in Fig. 15-9. In order to prevent excessive loading of the oscillator, a cathode

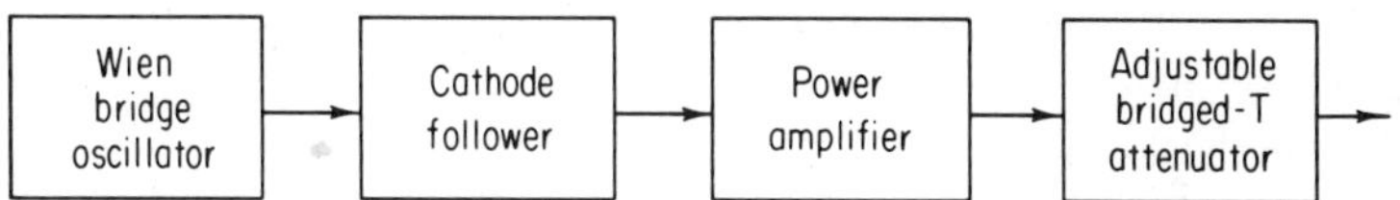

Fig. 15-9 Typical low-frequency generator block diagram.

follower is normally used as a buffer stage. The use of a power amplifier makes it possible to deliver large amounts of power to the final load. A bridged T attenuator is often used to control the signal level and at the same time provide the signal generator with a fixed Thévenin resistance. In many low-frequency generators a Thévenin resistance of 600 ohms is used. Of course, there are many variations of the block diagram of Fig. 15-9, which, it should be understood, is typical only of low-frequency generators.

The block diagram of a typical r-f signal generator is shown in Fig. 15-10. The Colpitts oscillator is often found in r-f generators operating in the range of about 100 kHz to 500 MHz. Note that provision has been made for modulating the signal if this is desired. Usually the attenuator is designed to have a characteristic resistance of 50 ohms.

Signal generators are usually straightforward instruments to operate. Most of the knobs are self-explanatory, and there are few difficulties encountered in using these instruments. However, there is one problem that almost everyone will encounter at some time or other when using a signal generator to drive diode circuits such as rectifiers, peak detectors,

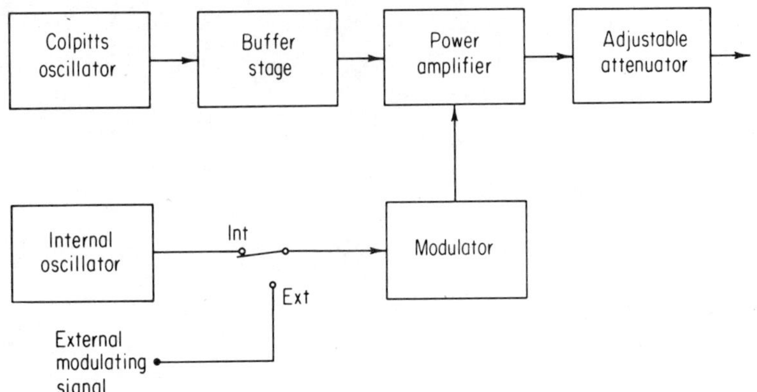

Fig. 15-10 Typical r-f signal generator block diagram.

mixers, and so on. This is the famous problem of the d-c return. To understand the problem, it is necessary first to be aware of the fact that some signal generators are capacitively coupled to the output, as shown in Fig. 15-11*a*. Here we have represented the signal generator by an open-circuit voltage generator, a Thévenin resistance, and a capacitor. The capacitor is often added to the signal generator in order to allow coupling the signal into the loads which may be operating at a high d-c voltage. For instance, in troubleshooting an amplifier, we may wish to couple a signal into the plate of one of the amplifier stages. The capacitor thus prevents the d-c voltage on the plate from being shorted through the relatively low generator resistance.

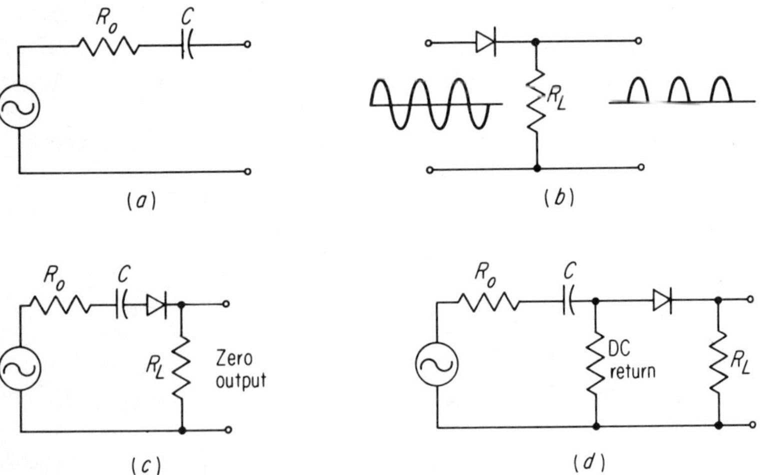

Fig. 15-11 The problem of the d-c return. (*a*) Capacitively coupled signal generator. (*b*) Half-wave rectifier. (*c*) Diode circuit with no d-c return. (*d*) Diode circuit with d-c return.

Now consider the simple half-wave rectifier of Fig. 15-11*b*. We know that if we drive this circuit with a sine-wave voltage, the output voltage will be the usual half-wave-rectified sine wave. The diode current, of course, is also a half-wave-rectified sine wave. A critical point about this current through the diode is that it flows in only one direction. Further, we know that the d-c, or average, value of this diode current is $0.636I_p$.

Suppose that we use a signal generator with a d-c blocking capacitor to drive the rectifier circuit (see Fig. 15-11*c*). From this circuit, it should be immediately obvious that we cannot possibly have a d-c current through the diode because direct current cannot flow through a capacitor indefinitely. As a result, the rectifier simply does not work, and we have no output at all. In order to use the signal generator to drive our diode circuit, we must add a d-c return resistor, as shown in Fig. 15-11*d*. If possible, this resistor should have a value that is greater than R_o but less than R_L. In this way, the signal generator is not loaded down excessively by the d-c return resistor, and the rectifier is still driven from a low source resistance.

The problem of the d-c return can occur in any diode circuit, especially detectors, mixers, clipping circuits. Therefore, the safest course to follow when checking diode circuits of any kind is automatically to add a d-c return across the signal-generator terminals unless it is a known fact that the generator does not have a blocking capacitor.

Example 15-6

A transistor amplifier has an input impedance of 1200 ohms. If a signal generator with a Thévenin resistance of 600 ohms and an open-circuit voltage of 1 volt rms drives the amplifier, how much voltage appears across the amplifier input terminals?

Solution

This is a simple voltage-divider problem as depicted by Fig. 15-12*a*. Obviously, the value of v_{in} is

$$v_{in} = \frac{1200}{600 + 1200} 1 \cong 0.667 \text{ volts rms}$$

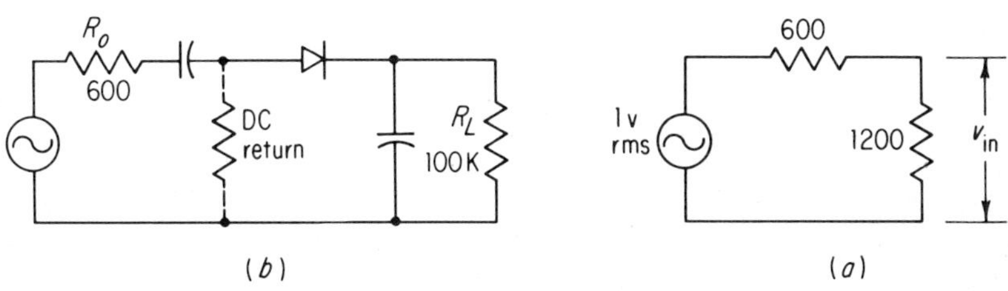

Fig. 15-12 Example 15-6.

Example 15-7

For the peak detector of Fig. 15-12*b* to operate normally, a d-c return must be added to the circuit. What size d-c return can we use?

Solution

The general guide in such cases is to choose a value of d-c return that is greater than R_o but less than R_L. Hence, a reasonable value for the d-c return might be around 6000 to 10,000 ohms.

15-5 Electronically Tunable Oscillators

Recall in our discussion of the spectrum analyzer that we used a swept oscillator. This was an oscillator whose frequency was controlled by the voltage applied to it. In this section we wish to examine some of the ways of controlling the frequency of an oscillator by electronic means.

When a diode is reverse-biased, it has a reverse resistance. In addition to this reverse resistance, there is a diode capacitance, as indicated by the equivalent circuit of a back-biased diode shown in Fig. 15-13*a*. At very low frequency, the reactance of the capacitance is much larger than the reverse resistance, and we think of a back-biased diode as simply a high resistance. At very high frequencies the reactance of the diode capacity becomes much smaller than the reverse resistance, and we may think of the back-biased diode as primarily a capacitor, as shown in Fig. 15-13*b*.

The capacity of a diode is not fixed; it depends upon the value of the reverse voltage across the diode. Figure 15-13*c* shows a typical variation

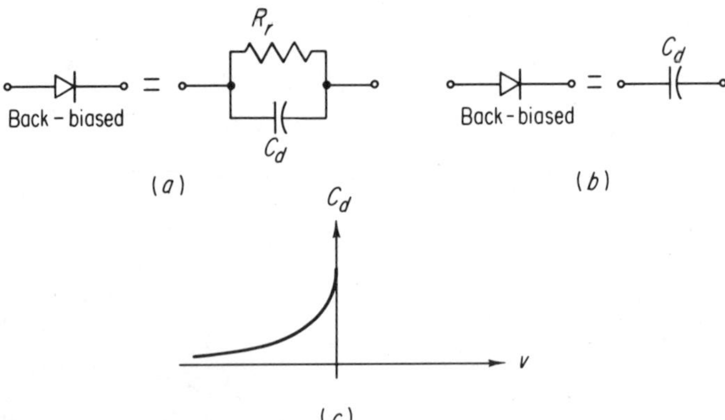

Fig. 15-13 Variable-capacitance diode. (*a*) Equivalent of back-biased diode. (*b*) High-frequency equivalent of back-biased diode. (*c*) Small signal capacitance versus back-bias voltage.

of capacitance versus voltage. Note that the capacitance decreases for an increase in the reverse voltage.

Diodes that are manufactured to take advantage of this capacitance effect are known as variable-capacitance diodes. Usually, only silicon is used in these diodes, in order to have extremely low reverse current. It can be shown that for some silicon diodes the capacitance in the reverse direction is approximately

$$C_d \cong \frac{K}{\sqrt{V + 0.7}} \tag{15-4}$$

where C_d is the diode capacitance
K is a constant
V is the magnitude of reverse voltage

The value of K can be controlled in the manufacturing process so that a variety of different capacitance ranges are commercially available. As an example of using Eq. (15-4), let us suppose that the value of K is given as 100 pf. Then, we have

$$C \cong \frac{100(10^{-12})}{\sqrt{V + 0.7}}$$

Hence, if the reverse voltage equals 3.3 volts, the diode capacitance is

$$C \cong \frac{100(10^{-12})}{\sqrt{3.3 + 0.7}} = 50 \text{ pf}$$

If the reverse voltage is 24.3 volts,

$$C \cong \frac{100(10^{-12})}{\sqrt{24.3 + 0.7}} = 20 \text{ pf}$$

To make an electronically tunable oscillator we need only use a variable-capacitance diode in the filter circuit of an oscillator. An example of how this is done is the tunable oscillator of Fig. 15-14. The oscillator is a tuned-plate type, where the frequency of oscillation is determined by the resonant frequency of the tank circuit in the plate. Note that

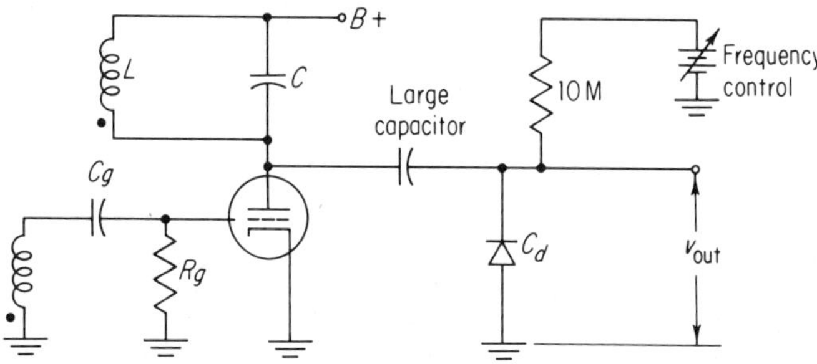

Fig. 15-14 Electronically tunable oscillator.

included in the tank-circuit capacitance is C_d, the value of diode capacitance. The approximate frequency of oscillation is

$$f = \frac{1}{2\pi \sqrt{L(C + C_d)}} \tag{15-5}$$

It should be clear that the battery can be used to change the reverse voltage across the diode. This of course changes C_d, which changes the frequency of oscillation. The 10-megohm resistor is used to prevent the a-c signal from being shorted by the battery.

Instead of using a battery to control the frequency of oscillation, we can use a signal, such as a sawtooth voltage. This means that the frequency of oscillation is swept through a band of frequencies. From Eqs. (15-4) and (15-5) it should be clear that the frequency of oscillation cannot be directly proportional to the reverse voltage across the diode. However, if we restrict the change in diode capacity to a very small range, we can obtain approximately a linear relation between the oscillation frequency and the control voltage. For example, suppose that the oscillator is designed to operate from 100 to 100.2 MHz. Clearly, we are talking about a very small change in the diode capacity. Thus, if a sawtooth controls the diode capacity, we find that at the start of the sawtooth the frequency of oscillation is 100 MHz. At the midpoint of the sawtooth the frequency is 100.1 MHz. At the end of the sawtooth the frequency is 100.2 MHz. The frequency is linearly related to the sawtooth voltage. On the other hand, if we tried to change the frequency over a large range like 100 to 200 MHz, we would definitely find that the frequency and the sawtooth voltage are by no means linearly related.

One method of obtaining relatively large ranges of frequency while still maintaining a linear relation between the frequency and the control voltage is conveyed by the system of Fig. 15-15. The sawtooth input sweeps the voltage-controlled oscillator linearly from 100 to 100.2 MHz. A fixed-frequency oscillator beats against the swept-oscillator signal. The

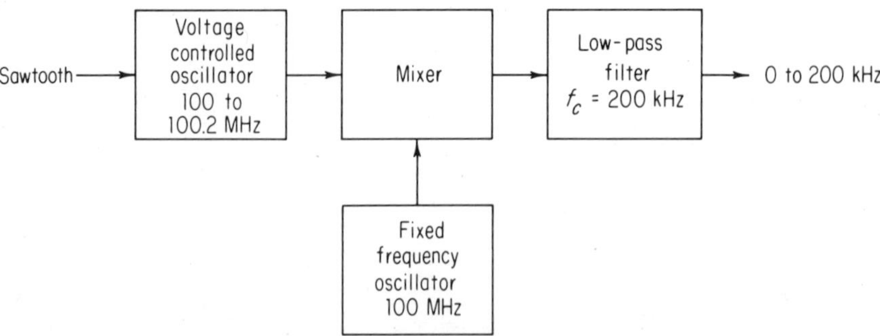

Fig. 15-15 Linearly swept frequency oscillator.

only mixer product that can pass through the low-pass filter is the difference frequency. Hence, as the oscillator sweeps from 100 to 100.2 MHz, the difference frequency changes from 0 to 200 kHz. Thus, we obtain a final output frequency that is linearly related to the sawtooth input.

If we change the fixed-frequency oscillator to operate at 99.8 MHz, the difference frequency sweeps linearly from 200 to 400 kHz. This would be one way of obtaining the 200 to 400 kHz swept oscillator for the spectrum analyzer discussed in the preceding chapter.

Example 15-8

In the oscillator of Fig. 15-14, $L = 100\ \mu$h and $C = 200$ pf. The variable-capacitance diode has $K = 100$ pf. Compute the oscillation frequency for a reverse voltage of 3.3 volts and for a reverse voltage of 24.3 volts.

Solution

We must use Eqs. (15-4) and (15-5). From Eq. (15-4)

$$C_d = \frac{100(10^{-12})}{\sqrt{V + 0.7}}$$

If $V = 3.3$, then $C_d = 50$ pf. If $V = 24.3$, then $C_d = 20$ pf.

Now, we use Eq. (15-5) to find the approximate oscillation frequencies. For $V = 3.3$ volts,

$$f = \frac{0.159}{\sqrt{100(10^{-6})(250)(10^{-12})}} \cong 1.01 \text{ MHz}$$

For $V = 24.3$ volts,

$$f = \frac{0.159}{\sqrt{100(10^{-6})(220)(10^{-12})}} = 1.07 \text{ MHz}$$

15-6 Frequency Multipliers and Dividers

In many situations it is desirable to take a given frequency sinusoid and use this frequency to generate a higher or lower frequency. The most common way of building a frequency multiplier is to generate harmonics of the input sinusoid and then filter out the desired harmonic by means of a bandpass filter. For instance, in Fig. 15-16 the input sinusoid has a frequency of 1 MHz. This signal is half-wave-rectified by the diode circuit, and by using a bandpass filter, we can filter out the nth harmonic.

Any circuit that takes the input sinusoid and distorts it into a nonsinusoidal waveform can be used in a frequency multiplier. Thus, any type of rectifier circuit, or an overdriven amplifier, or a Schmitt trigger, etc., can be used to generate harmonics of the input signal.

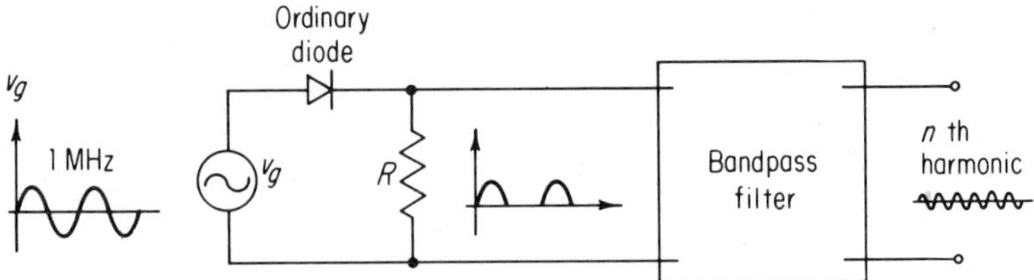

Fig. 15-16 Frequency multiplier (harmonic generator).

One of the more interesting devices that can be used in generating harmonics is the *step-recovery diode.* This is a special type of diode that takes advantage of the charge stored at the junction of a forward-biased diode. If the diode is suddenly reverse-biased, the stored charges can flow for a while, but when they terminate, the current stops abruptly. To convey the idea, consider Fig. 15-17. During the positive half cycle the diode is

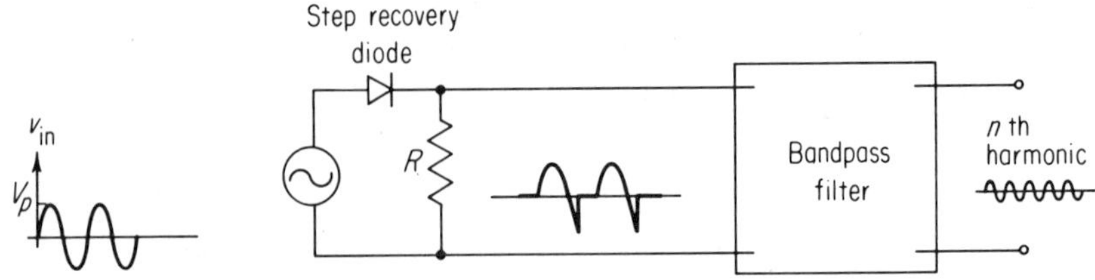

Fig. 15-17 Frequency multiplier using step-recovery diode.

forward-biased, and some charge is stored at the *p-n* junction of the diode. During the reverse half cycle, the charge stored at the junction can actually let reverse current flow for a while. However, in these specially processed diodes, when the stored charge is depleted, the reverse current abruptly drops to zero, as indicated by the waveform of Fig. 15-17. This abrupt step is very rich in higher harmonics, and as a result, large harmonic voltages can be obtained with such diodes.

It is also possible to build a frequency divider. One type of frequency divider is the regenerative system shown in Fig. 15-18*a*. The only input to this system is the 5-MHz input sinusoid. This 5-MHz signal mixes with the 4-MHz signal, producing a 1-MHz difference frequency. This is the only mixer product that can pass through the bandpass filter. This 1-MHz signal is amplified and fed back to a frequency multiplier that generates the fourth harmonic of the 1-MHz signal. This 4-MHz signal beats against the incoming 5-MHz signal, and we have a regenerative action.

There may be some question as to how such a system starts. As we observed in studying oscillators, one explanation is that a regenerative system can start on noise, provided that the loop gain is greater than unity. Thus, the voltage gain of the amplifier must be greater than the attenuation of the mixer, the filter, and the frequency multiplier.

A general representation of the regenerative frequency divider is shown in Fig. 15-18*b*.

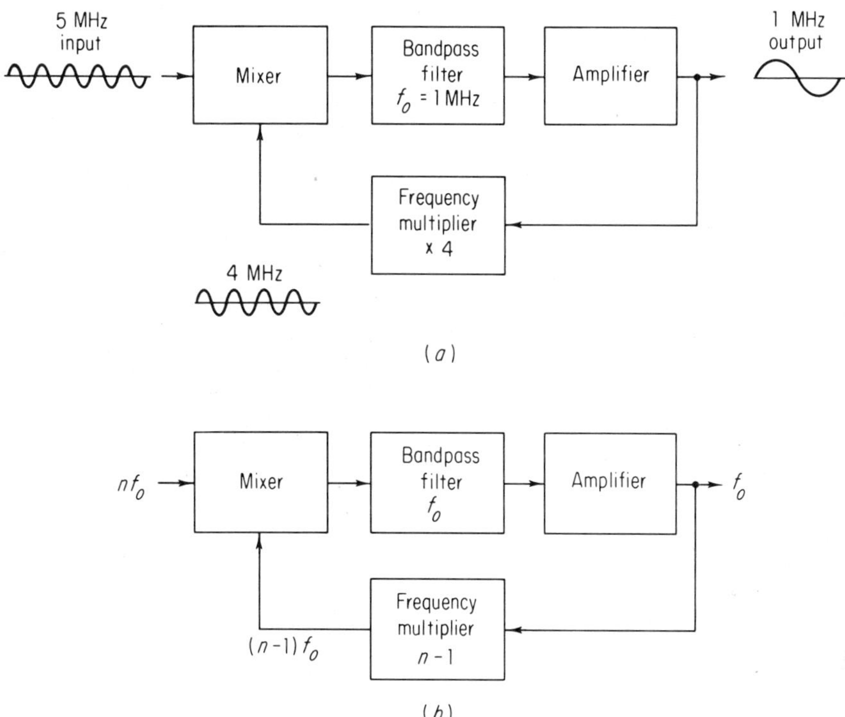

Fig. 15-18 Frequency dividers. (*a*) Divide by five. (*b*) Divide by *n*.

EXAMPLE 15-9

In the harmonic generator of Fig. 15-16 the bandpass filter passes only the tenth harmonic of 1 MHz. If the input sine wave has a peak value of 10 volts, what is the approximate peak value of the 10-MHz output of the filter?

SOLUTION

From Table 13-1

$$C_n = \frac{2A}{\pi} \frac{1}{n^2 - 1} \qquad \text{for } n \text{ even}$$

Hence

$$C_{10} = \frac{20}{\pi} \frac{1}{100 - 1} = 0.0644 \text{ volts peak}$$

15-7 Square Waves Derived from Sine Waves

One of the ways of obtaining square waves is the method of clipping a sine wave. Several circuits we have already studied accomplish this clipping action. For instance, the simple diode clipper of Fig. 15-19 clips

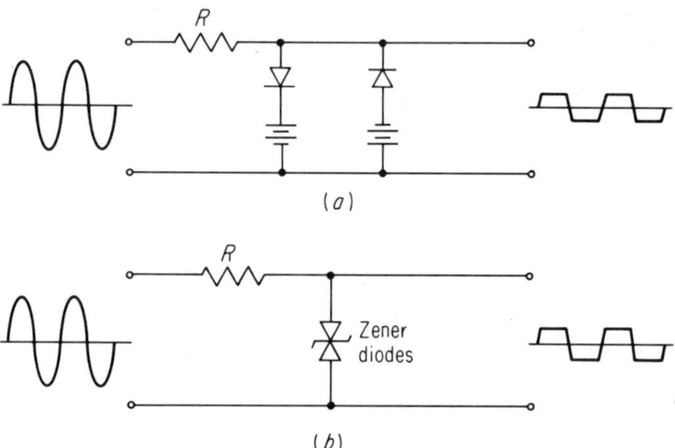

Fig. 15-19 Deriving square waves from sine waves using diodes. (*a*) Conventional positive-negative clipper. (*b*) Zener-diode clipper.

the top and bottom of the input sine wave to obtain a reasonably good square wave. Alternatively, this clipping may be done by the zener-diode clipper of Fig. 15-19*b*.

An overdriven amplifier can also clip a sine wave on both half cycles. For instance, the transistor amplifier of Fig. 15-20 will certainly saturate

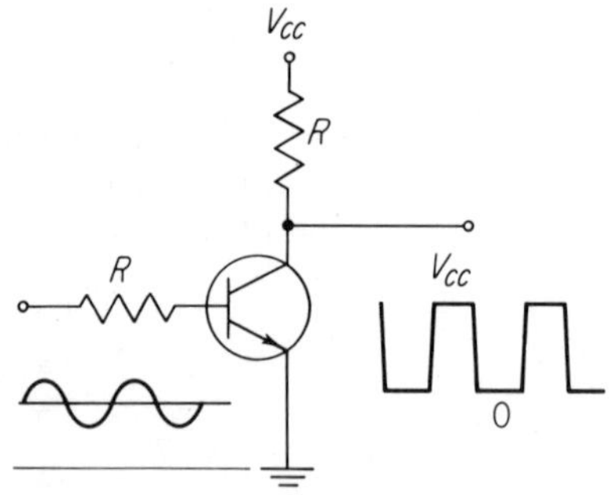

Fig. 15-20 Deriving square waves from sine waves by overdriving an amplifier.

and cut off if the input sine wave is large. During the positive half cycle, the transistor saturates almost immediately, and during the negative half cycle the transistor cuts off. Hence, we can obtain a good square-wave output.

Another way of deriving square waves from sine waves is to use a Schmitt trigger with very low trip points compared to the peak value of the input sine wave. During the positive half cycle the Schmitt trigger trips almost immediately, and the output is the fixed voltage associated with the high state. During the negative half cycle the output is the fixed voltage associated with the low state.

In order to improve the quality of the square wave, we can progressively amplify and clip, as shown in Fig. 15-21. In this way reasonably good square waves can be obtained.

Fig. 15-21 Progressive amplifying and clipping to obtain square waves.

15-8 The Flip-flop

In this section we discuss a circuit that is very important in digital types of instruments. The *flip-flop* is a circuit whose output can be either a low or a high voltage. The circuit is driven by narrow trigger pulses, and the output of the flip-flop changes from low to high, or vice versa, as each trigger pulse arrives. The general idea of a flip-flop is conveyed by Fig. 15-22. At the instant that the first trigger appears at point A in

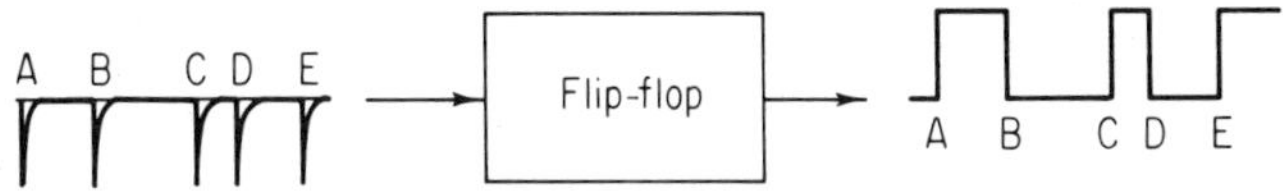

Fig. 15-22 Flip-flop signals.

time, the output of the flip-flop changes from a low to a high voltage. The output remains at a high voltage until the next trigger arrives at point B in time. Thus, the basic idea of the flip-flop circuit is that it changes from one state to another as each trigger arrives.

The flip-flop is sometimes called the Eccles-Jordan multivibrator, the binary multivibrator, or the bistable multivibrator.

There are many circuit arrangements using vacuum tubes or transistors that accomplish the flip-flop action of Fig. 15-22. We will discuss one of the basic transistor flip-flop circuits in order to demonstrate how such circuits operate. Consider the circuit of Fig. 15-23. This is designed in such a way that if one transistor is cut off, the other is saturated. For example, if Q1 is saturated, it is approximately a short circuit from collector to ground. Therefore, the collector of Q1 is about zero volts with respect to ground. As a result, the base of Q2 is almost zero volts, so that Q2 is cut off. With Q2 cut off, the collector of Q2 is approximately 10 volts with respect to ground. This voltage is applied to the voltage divider consisting of the 20-kilohm resistors. The result is that there is enough base current to saturate the Q1 transistor.

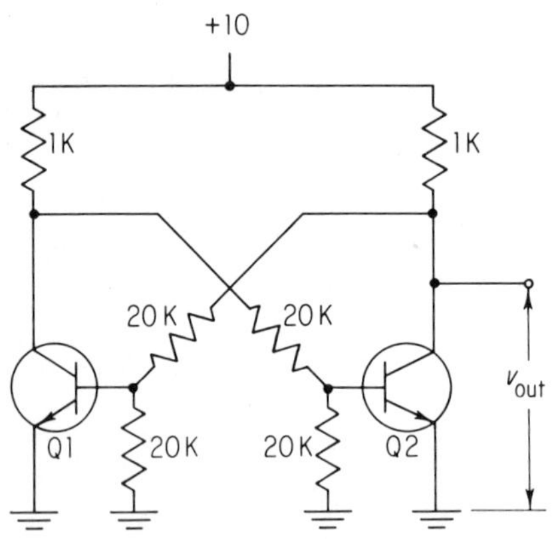

Fig. 15-23 Transistorized flip-flop circuit.

The circuit will remain in this condition indefinitely with Q1 saturated and Q2 cut off unless disturbed by an external trigger. This trigger is usually fed into the circuit in such a way as to cause regeneration to occur, so that the flip-flop changes states. For instance, suppose that a negative trigger is fed into the base of Q1, the saturated transistor. This causes Q1 to come out of saturation. As a result, the collector voltage of Q1 rises from zero volts to some higher positive voltage. This voltage rise is coupled through the voltage divider to the base of Q2 and turns Q2 on. The collector voltage of Q2 then drops from about 10 volts to a lower voltage. This negative-going change is coupled into the base of Q1, reinforcing the original negative trigger. Thus, we have a regenerative action that continues until Q1 is cut off and Q2 is saturated. The flip-flop remains in this new state until a negative trigger is fed into Q2, causing the flip-flop to revert to the original state with Q1 saturated and Q2 cut off.

In the circuit of Fig. 15-23, the output voltage is taken from the collector of Q2. Note that the output voltage is approximately 0 or 10 volts. For convenience, we will speak of the output as being in the 0 state if the output voltage is low, and as being in the 1 state if the output voltage is high.

A practical version of the flip-flop is shown in Fig. 15-24. The diodes in this circuit are often called *steering diodes* because they literally steer the negative trigger into the base of the saturated transistor via the voltage divider consisting of the 20-kilohm resistors. The capacitors that are shunted across the 20-kilohm resistors are often called speed-up capacitors. The basic purpose of these capacitors is to compensate the voltage divider at higher frequencies. This is necessary because the negative trigger is a sharp pulse with many higher harmonics. In order to ensure that it is coupled into the base of the saturated transistor, it is necessary to compensate the voltage divider. (See Sec. 7-2 if in doubt.)

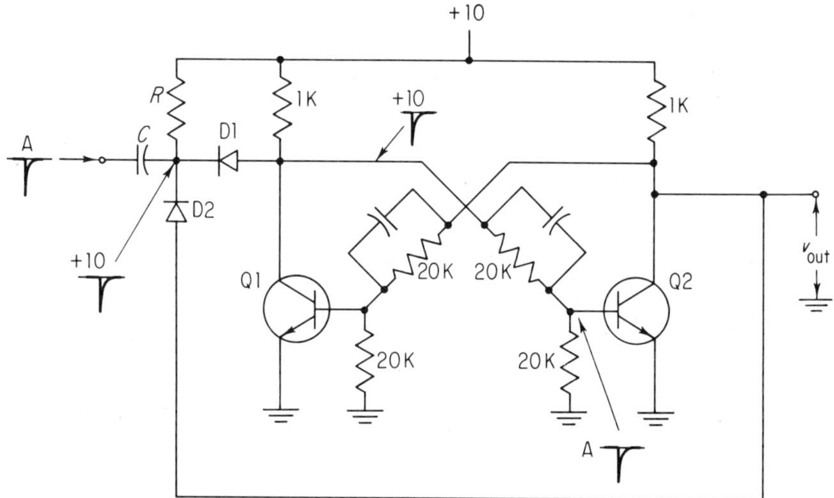

Fig. 15-24 Transistorized flip-flop with steering diodes and speedup capacitors.

In order to describe the operation of the steering diodes let us assume that the output of the flip-flop is in the 0 state. This means that the collector of Q2 is almost zero, and the collector of Q1 is about 10 volts with respect to ground. At point A in time the negative trigger appears. This is coupled through the capacitor into the junction of the two diodes, as shown in Fig. 15-24. Note that this pulse drops from 10 volts downward. Diode D2 does not conduct, because with the collector of Q2 at zero volts, D2 remains back-biased. Diode D1 does conduct because the collector of Q1 is initially at 10 volts. Since the trigger applied to D1 goes from 10 volts downward, D1 is forward-biased. The diode is therefore turned on, and the negative trigger is coupled into the voltage divider, as shown. With the speedup capacitor in the circuit, the negative trigger appears at the base of Q2 and brings Q2 out of saturation. The flip-flop then regenerates, driving Q1 into saturation and Q2 into a cutoff condition. The output is now in the 1 state and remains in this state until another trigger appears. When the next trigger appears, D2 will conduct and D1 will remain off. Thus, the trigger is automatically coupled into the base of the saturated transistor.

The circuit of Fig. 15-24 responds only to negative triggers. If positive triggers are used, both diodes remain back-biased, and therefore the flip-flop simply does not respond.

Very often, it is desirable to drive the flip-flop with a square-wave input. This is possible if we deliberately use a small coupling capacitor so that the square wave is differentiated to produce narrow positive and negative triggers. Figure 15-25 illustrates the situation. By using an *RC*

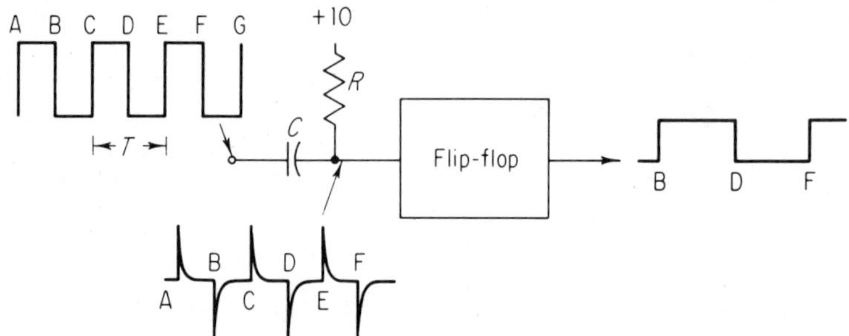

Fig. 15-25 *RC* differentiation at the input of the flip-flop.

time constant that is small compared to the period of the input square wave, we obtain the positive and negative triggers shown. The flip-flop responds only to the negative triggers. Because of this, the output of the flip-flop is a square wave with one-half the frequency of the input square wave. In effect, a flip-flop represents a divide-by-two circuit.

Example 15-10

The flip-flop of Fig. 15-24 is driven by the waveshape shown in Fig. 15-26*a*. The *RC* network at the input of the flip-flop differentiates to produce positive and negative triggers. Sketch the output waveform of the flip-flop, assuming that the flip-flop is initially in the 0 state.

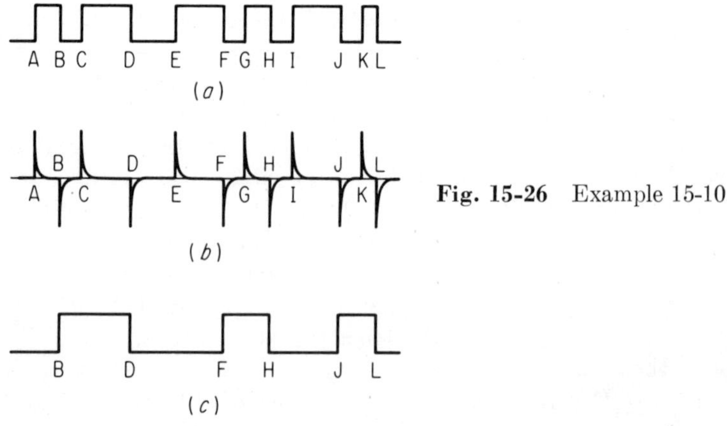

Fig. 15-26 Example 15-10.

SOLUTION

After differentiation we obtain the triggers shown in Fig. 15-26*b*. Since the flip-flop responds only to negative triggers, we can sketch the output as shown in Fig. 15-26*c*.

15-9 The Free-running Multivibrator

A circuit often used in the generation of square waves is the free-running multivibrator. This type of multivibrator does not require an input signal. It simply free-runs, producing a square-wave output signal.

A transistorized version of the free-running multivibrator is shown in Fig. 15-27. We will not delve into the details of the circuit operation

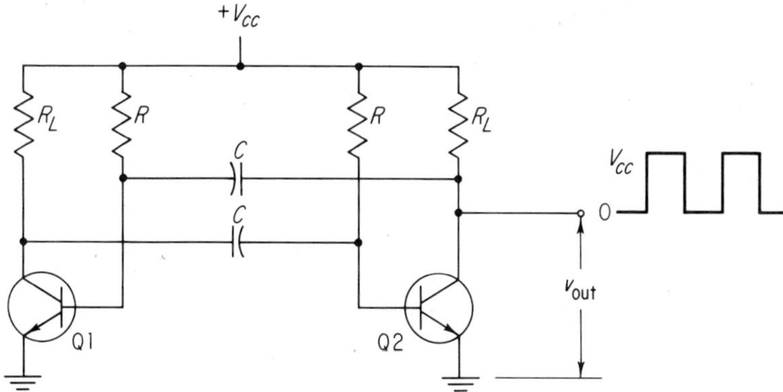

Fig. 15-27 Free-running multivibrator.

except to say that the circuit is designed so that each transistor is alternately saturated and cut off. The amount of time that a transistor is cut off is determined by the *RC* time constant of the circuit. It can be shown that the period of the output square wave is

$$T \cong 1.4RC \tag{15-6}$$

or

$$f \cong \frac{0.7}{RC} \tag{15-7}$$

where T is the period of the square wave
f is the fundamental frequency
R is the value of the base resistor
C is the value of the coupling capacitor

If a variable-frequency multivibrator is desired, variable capacitors can be ganged together. In this way the frequency of the output square wave can be controlled by changing the value of C.

Another method used to control the frequency of the square wave is shown in Fig. 15-28. In this circuit the base resistors are returned to a separate power supply. By changing the value of V_{bb} the frequency of the square wave can be changed. In fact, the multivibrator can be swept through a range of different frequencies by using a sawtooth wave for V_{bb}.

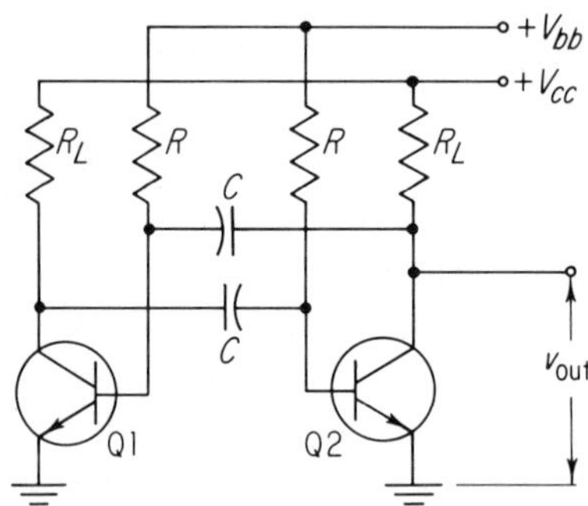

Fig. 15-28 Free-running multivibrator with voltage-frequency control.

For the reader acquainted with natural logarithms

$$T \cong 2RC \ln \left(1 + \frac{V_{cc}}{V_{bb}}\right) \tag{15-8}$$

Example 15-11

In the multivibrator of Fig. 15-27, R has a value of 100 kilohms and C has a value of 1000 pf. Find the approximate frequency of the square-wave output.

Solution

Using Eq. (15-7),

$$f \cong \frac{0.7}{RC} = \frac{0.7}{100(10^3)(1000)(10^{-12})} = 7 \text{ kHz}$$

SUMMARY

Sine-wave oscillators may be built using an amplifier with positive feedback. A filter is normally used in either the amplifier or the feedback loop to permit oscillations at only one frequency. In order for oscillations to start, the loop voltage gain must be greater than unity. After the oscillations build up, the loop gain drops to unity.

For low-frequency oscillators in the frequency range of about 5 Hz to 500 kHz, the most widely used oscillator is the Wien-bridge oscillator. Oscillations occur at a frequency where the bridge is almost balanced. A tungsten lamp is used to reduce the loop gain to unity after the oscillations have attained the desired amplitude.

For oscillators operating in the frequency range of about 100 kHz to 500 MHz, the most popular circuit is the Colpitts oscillator. The frequency of oscillation is approximately equal to the resonant frequency of the tank circuit. After the oscillations have built up, the loop gain is reduced to unity by means of the grid-leak-bias network. Basically, this is a negative clamping circuit.

Whenever a commercial signal generator is used to drive a circuit containing diodes, one should be aware of the problem of the d-c return path. It may be necessary to shunt a resistor across the terminals of the signal generator if the generator is capacitively coupled.

A swept-frequency oscillator may be built by using variable-capacitance diodes. A sawtooth voltage may be used to sweep the oscillator through some frequency range. In order to obtain a relatively large sweep range, a swept r-f generator can be mixed with a fixed-frequency oscillator to obtain the difference frequency.

Frequency multipliers refer simply to harmonic generators. An input sine wave is distorted by a nonlinear device such as a diode. Harmonics are then generated and can be filtered to obtain the desired harmonic. Step-recovery diodes are very efficient harmonic generators.

Frequency dividers can be built using a regenerative system.

Square waves can be derived from sine waves by using a clipping type of circuit, such as a diode clipper, an overdriven amplifier, or a Schmitt trigger.

The flip-flop is an important circuit often used in digital types of instruments. It is a two-state circuit whose output is either a low voltage or a high voltage. Narrow triggers fed into the flip-flop cause it to change states. If a square wave is used for an input, it is first differentiated into a train of positive and negative triggers. The flip-flop responds to only one of these polarities, and as a result, the square-wave output of the flip-flop has a frequency equal to one-half of the input frequency.

A free-running multivibrator is basically a square-wave generator. Its frequency can be controlled by changing the RC time constant of the multivibrator. Alternately, the base resistors may be returned to a separate supply, whose value controls the frequency of the output square wave.

GLOSSARY

Colpitts oscillator A basic oscillator circuit widely used in radio-frequency signal generators. Recognizable by the use of a capacitive divider in the parallel resonant LC tank.

d-c return Refers to having a complete path for d-c current when looking back into a signal generator.

flip-flop A circuit with either a low or high output voltage. The output voltage changes from one state to the other as each input trigger occurs.

grid leak bias A form of bias developed by the clamping action at the grid of a vacuum tube.

1 state The high-voltage output of a two-state circuit such as a flip-flop or a Schmitt trigger.

oscillator A circuit that generates an a-c signal, often by means of positive feedback.

step-recovery diode A specially manufactured diode that utilizes stored charge in order to produce very sharp pulses during reverse conduction.

swept-frequency oscillator An oscillator that is electronically swept through a range of frequencies.

variable-capacitance diode A back-biased diode which behaves like a capacitance and whose value can be controlled by the amount of reverse voltage.

Wien-bridge oscillator A basic oscillator widely used in low-frequency generators. Consists of a Wien bridge, an amplifier, and a feedback path.

0 state The low-voltage output of a two-state circuit such as a flip-flop or a Schmitt trigger.

REVIEW QUESTIONS

1. What is the basic idea behind an oscillator using the positive-feedback approach?
2. What initially causes oscillations?
3. What must be true about the phase shift and the voltage gain in an oscillator?
4. In a Wien-bridge oscillator what is the approximate value of the oscillation frequency?
5. In a Wien-bridge oscillator what is the purpose of the tungsten lamp? How is the output voltage of the oscillator related to the voltage across the lamp?
6. What is the condition required for oscillations to begin in a Colpitts oscillator?
7. How is the grid leak bias developed in a Colpitts oscillator? What must be true about the *RC* time constant of the grid-leak-bias network?
8. What is the approximate formula for the oscillation frequency of a Colpitts oscillator?
9. What is the typical value of Thévenin resistance for a low-frequency signal generator? For a high-frequency generator?

10. Why is a buffer stage normally used after the oscillator stage in a typical signal generator?
11. Why is a blocking capacitor used in some signal generators?
12. Why does a blocking capacitor in a signal generator prevent some diode circuits from operating normally?
13. What is a variable-capacitance diode? How does the capacity vary with reverse voltage?
14. How can the frequency of a swept oscillator be made approximately linear with respect to the diode control voltage?
15. What is the basic idea behind a frequency multiplier?
16. Draw the block diagram of a regenerative frequency divider. How does this system start?
17. Name some of the methods used to obtain a square wave from a sine-wave input.
18. If a flip-flop is to be driven by a square-wave input, what must be done to the square wave? How is the output frequency of the flip-flop related to the frequency of the input square wave?

PROBLEMS

15-1 Refer to Fig. 15-4. R equals 300 kilohms, and C equals 250 pf. The amplifier voltage gain is 2000, and R_1 equals 700 ohms.

(*a*) At what frequency do oscillations occur?

(*b*) What is the value of the amplifier input voltage after the oscillations have become stable? Use the tungsten characteristics of Fig. 15-5*b*.

15-2 Refer to Fig. 15-4. If R equals 1 megohm, and if C has a tuning range of 50 to 500 pf, what is the frequency range of oscillations? If the value of R_1 is 1500 ohms, what is the output voltage of the oscillator? Use the tungsten curve of Fig. 15-5*b*.

15-3 In Fig. 15-7, let $L = 100\ \mu$h, $C_1 = 250$ pf, and $C_2 = 100$ pf. What is the approximate value of the oscillation frequency?

15-4 In the circuit of Fig. 15-7, suppose that the frequency of oscillation is 1 MHz. If R_g is 100 kilohms, then in order to have a time constant that is equal to 100 times the period, what size should C_g be?

15-5 A variable-capacitance diode has a K constant of 50 pf. Compute the capacitance of the diode for reverse voltages of 1, 2, 4, 8, 16, and 32 volts.

15-6 In the circuit of Fig. 15-14, the variable-capacitance diode has a K constant of 200 pf. The value of L is 500 μh, and the value of C is 10 pf. Compute the frequency of oscillation for reverse voltages of 9, 10, and 11 volts. Would you say that the oscillation frequency is linearly related to the control voltage?

15-7 In the system of Fig. 15-16 assume that the input signal has a peak value of 5 volts. What is the approximate value of the output signal if the filter passes only the eighth harmonic? What is the output if the filter is tuned to the seventh harmonic frequency?

15-8 In Fig. 15-17 let us assume that the peak value of the nth harmonic is equal to the peak value of the input signal divided by n. The generator peak value is 10 volts. Find the peak value of the output of the filter if the filter passes only the tenth harmonic. What is the output if the filter passes only the one-hundredth harmonic?

15-9 Referring to Fig. 15-18*b*, suppose that the input is a 1-MHz signal and we wish to obtain a 100-kHz output.

(*a*) What frequency should the filter pass?

(*b*) What harmonic should the frequency multiplier generate?

(*c*) Will the system work if the frequency multiplier generates the eleventh harmonic?

15-10 Refer to Fig. 15-19*a*. The batteries have a potential of 5 volts, and the input sine wave has a peak value of 50 volts. Sketch the output waveform.

15-11 In the circuit of Fig. 15-20, assume that the base-emitter drop in the forward direction is 0.7 volt. Let R equal 10 kilohms, and let V_{cc} = 10 volts. The input sine wave has a peak value of 10 volts.

(*a*) What value of collector current saturates the transistor?

(*b*) If the d-c β is 50, what value of base current saturates the transistor?

(*c*) What value of input voltage causes saturation?

15-12 Refer to Fig. 15-23. What value of collector current saturates Q2? If the d-c β of Q2 is 100, how much base current causes saturation? What is the approximate value of the actual base current in Q2 if Q1 is cut off?

15-13 In Fig. 15-24, a square-wave input is to be used. The period of the square wave is 1 msec. If R equals 1 kilohm, what value of C is required to have an RC time constant that is equal to $T/100$? Describe the signal appearing at the junction of D1 and D2.

15-14 In the circuit of Fig. 15-27 the value of R is 50 kilohms, and the value of C is 0.005 μf. What is the approximate frequency of the output square wave? What is the period?

15-15 Refer to Fig. 15-27. If R equals 20 kilohms, and if the capacitors are adjustable from 50 to 500 pf, what is the frequency range of the free-running multivibrator?

15-16 In the circuit of Fig. 15-28, V_{cc} equals 10 volts, R equals 100 kilohms, and C equals 500 pf. If V_{bb} is swept from 5 to 10 volts, over what frequency range does the multivibrator operate?

16 Digital Principles

Many electronic instruments, such as computers, frequency counters, and digital voltmeters, use circuits that are basically two-state, that is, circuits that are either *on* or *off*. For such two-state circuits it is possible to employ a new number system as well as a new kind of algebra. In this chapter we become acquainted with binary numbers, Boolean algebra, and logic circuits so that we may better understand how two-state circuits are used to count and compute.

16-1 The One-to-one Correspondence

In mathematics the term *set* means a collection of distinct objects that have something in common with one another. For instance, we may speak of the set of all human beings. Clearly, each human being is distinct from any other, and yet we have humanity in common. Therefore, it is quite correct to speak of the set of all human beings. In a similar way we may speak of the set of all trees, or the set of all positive numbers, or the set of all books.

One of the most important concepts in mathematics is that of the one-to-one correspondence. This concept is the basis of all number systems, and perhaps even more important, it is the basis of all thought and communication. Stated simply, a one-to-one correspondence is a relation between two sets whereby each object in one set is related to one and only one object in the other set.

To understand this important idea more clearly, consider Fig. 16-1. Suppose that the objects in set A and set B are somehow related. This

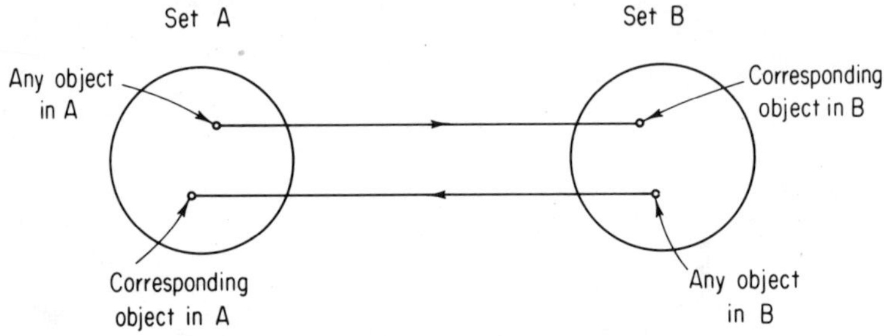

Fig. 16-1 One-to-one correspondence.

relation is a one-to-one correspondence if both of the following conditions are met:

1. For any object that we select in set A, we find that there is only one corresponding object in set B.
2. For any object that we select in set B, there is only one corresponding object in set A.

As an example, let set A be the English alphabet, and let set B be the Morse-code letter symbols. For any alphabet letter there is only one Morse-code symbol, and for any Morse-code letter symbol there is only one corresponding letter of the alphabet. Therefore, the relation between these two sets is a one-to-one correspondence.

Example 16-1

The set of Arabic numerals (1, 2, 3, . . .) and the set of Roman numerals (I, II, III, . . .) are in a one-to-one relation with each other.

Example 16-2

As an example of a correspondence between sets that is *not* a one-to-one relation let set A be the set of all human beings, and let set B be the set of all first names. Clearly, if we select almost any name in set B, we find that there are many persons in set A with this name. Therefore, the relation between the two sets is not a one-to-one correspondence.

16-2 Counting

The way we count objects involves the use of a one-to-one correspondence. For instance, suppose we have three pebbles in hand. We see something like

●●●

We have a written symbol that we use to indicate this amount. The symbol is 3. We also have a sound that we use to indicate this amount. The sound is *three*. If we pick a different amount of pebbles, there are a different symbol and sound used to represent the amount. In short, somewhere in history our decimal number system was invented. This system spread throughout most of the world and is now commonly accepted by almost everyone. For convenience in our discussion we will represent quantity by means of pebbles. Hence, we may say that our decimal number system represents a one-to-one correspondence between a set of distinct pebble quantities and a set of decimal numerals. This one-to-one correspondence is shown in Table 16-1. Note that there are ten basic symbols, 0 to 9.

Table 16-1

Pebbles	Basic symbol
None	0
●	1
●●	2
●●●	3
●●●●	4
●●●●●	5
●●●●●●	6
●●●●●●●	7
●●●●●●●●	8
●●●●●●●●●	9

The decimal number system is quite familar to all of us. In fact, it is so thoroughly ingrained in our minds that we may rebel at the idea of using a different number system. However, we should realize that there is nothing sacred about using ten basic symbols. Why not use only eight basic symbols, or perhaps only two basic symbols? There is absolutely no reason at all why we cannot count using a different number system.

Undoubtedly, the use of ten basic symbols, 0 to 9, evolved because a man has ten fingers. In order to convey the idea that another number system is possible, let us assume that somewhere in this large universe there exists a creature with only two fingers. What kind of a number system would such a creature devise? If this creature makes decisions similar to those that man made in devising the decimal number system, we will find that there are only two basic symbols. These two basic symbols can be any two distinct characters such as A and B, — and /, or 0 and 1. For convenience, we will use 0 and 1. In this new number system the correspondence between pebbles and basic symbols would look like this:

Pebbles	Basic symbols
None	0
•	1

Such a number system is referred to as a binary number system.

The question naturally arises as to how the two-fingered creature counts above one. What does he use to represent the following amount of pebbles: ••? (Remember that this new system can use only 0 and 1. Numbers like 2, 3, 4, etc., do not exist in a binary number system.) We answer this question by examining what we do in the decimal number system after we reach 9. For ten pebbles we use 10. We have formed a combination of two basic symbols by taking our second basic symbol, 1, followed by our first basic symbol, 0, to get 10. For eleven pebbles we use a combination of 1 followed by 1 to get 11, and for twelve pebbles we use a combination of 1 followed by 2 to get 12. (Strictly speaking, these are permutations of basic symbols rather than combinations.) Following the same pattern of construction in the binary number system results in the correspondence shown in Table 16-2. Note carefully that

Table 16-2

Pebbles	Binary number
None	0
•	1
••	10
•••	11

the binary number corresponding to •• is 10. As we did in the decimal number system, we have taken our second basic symbol, 1, followed by our first basic symbol, 0, to get 10. To avoid confusion, it is helpful to read 10 as *one-zero*, and not as *ten*. The binary symbol corresponding to ••• is 11. Read this as *one-one*.

What binary number corresponds to ••••? Once again, we are momentarily stopped, since we have run out of two-symbol combinations. As before, we follow the pattern established in the decimal number system. In the decimal number system we have the following combinations using two basic symbols: 10, 11, 12, 13, . . . , 98, 99. After reaching 99 we have exhausted all the possibilities. What do we do? We now form combinations with three basic symbols to get 100, 101, 102, 103, ... Following this same pattern in the binary number system means that we will use three basic symbols at a time. Table 16-3 illustrates the relations

Table 16-3

Pebbles	Binary number	Decimal number
None	0	0
•	1	1
••	10	2
•••	11	3
••••	100	4
•••••	101	5
••••••	110	6
•••••••	111	7

between pebbles, binary numbers, and decimal numbers for counting to seven.

A memory aid for the binary number system is the following. First, think of the decimal number system. Second, cross out all decimal numbers that contain a basic symbol that is not 0 or 1. What remains is the binary number system. For example, if we think of the decimal number system and cross out all numbers containing basic symbols other than 0 or 1, we obtain

0, 1, ~~2~~, ~~3~~, ~~4~~, . . . , ~~9~~, 10, 11, ~~12~~, ~~13~~, . . . , ~~98~~, ~~99~~, 100, 101, ~~102~~, ~~103~~, . . . , ~~109~~, 110, 111, ~~112~~, ~~113~~, . . .

Collecting the numbers that remain, we have the binary number system:

0, 1, 10, 11, 100, 101, 110, 111, . . .

The reader should be able to count to seven using binary numbers.

16-3 Binary Arithmetic

In this section we determine how to add binary numbers, but before we can do this, we must realize that addition is an operation on numbers that reflects how physical quantities are combined. In other words, when we write $2 + 3 = 5$, we are writing a coded message for the physical act of combining •• with ••• to obtain a total of •••••.

This → ••	2	+
combined with → •••	3	
gives → •••••	5	=

Loosely speaking, addition is a shadowlike operation that traces out what happens in the physical world when quantities are combined.

When we turn our attention to binary addition, we must make sure that addition of binary numbers still accurately reflects the act of combining physical quantities.

The one-to-one correspondence between pebbles and binary numbers is repeated for convenience.

Pebbles	Binary
None	0
•	1
••	10

Let us now determine how to add binary numbers. There are four different cases to be analyzed.

Case 1: In the physical world no pebbles combined with no pebbles gives no pebbles. The binary message for this is $0 + 0 = 0$.

Case 2: In the physical world *none* combined with • gives •. The binary message is $0 + 1 = 1$.

Case 3: If we combine • with *none,* we get •. The binary equivalent is $1 + 0 = 1$.

Case 4: If we combine • with •, we obtain ••. The binary equivalent is $1 + 1 = 10$.

To summarize the results for binary addition:

$$0 + 0 = 0$$
$$0 + 1 = 1$$
$$1 + 0 = 1$$
$$1 + 1 = 10$$

There should be nothing disturbing about the last result since 10 does not mean decimal number ten. It means binary number *one-zero.*

EXAMPLE 16-2

We know that in the decimal system, $2 + 2 = 4$. Convert to binary numbers and perform binary addition.

SOLUTION

Using Table 16-3,

$$\begin{array}{rr} 2 & 10 \\ +2 & +10 \\ \hline 4 & 100 \end{array}$$

The binary addition is as follows:

First column: zero plus zero is zero.
Second column: one plus one is zero, carry one.

EXAMPLE 16-3

Add the following binary numbers:
(*a*) $101 + 110$
(*b*) $111 + 110$
(*c*) $1010 + 1101$
(*d*) $1011 + 1010$

SOLUTION

(*a*) $\begin{array}{r} 101 \\ +\ 110 \\ \hline 1011 \end{array}$ first column: $1 + 0 = 1$; second column: $0 + 1 = 1$; third column: $1 + 1 = 10$ (zero, carry one)

(*b*) $\begin{array}{r} 111 \\ +\ 110 \\ \hline 1101 \end{array}$ first column: $1 + 0 = 1$; second column: $1 + 1 = 10$ (zero, carry one); third column: $1 + 1 + 1 = 10 + 1 = 11$

(*c*) $\begin{array}{r} 1010 \\ +\ 1101 \\ \hline 10111 \end{array}$

(*d*) $\begin{array}{r} 1011 \\ +\ 1010 \\ \hline 10101 \end{array}$

16-4 Decimal-to-binary Conversion

With the aid of Table 16-3 we can count to seven using binary numbers. What we really need, however, is a method for quickly converting from decimal numbers to binary numbers and vice versa. In this section we examine the technique used to convert from decimal to binary.

The most popular method in converting from decimal to binary is known as the *double-dabble method.* It involves the progressive division of the given decimal number by 2, writing down the quotient and remainder of each division. The remainders taken in reverse order then form the binary equivalent of the original decimal number. The double-dabble method is best illustrated by a series of examples, which should be carefully read and understood before going on to the next section.

Example 16-4

Convert decimal number 2 into its binary equivalent using the double-dabble method.

Solution

Step 1: Divide 2 by 2 to get 1 with a remainder of 0.

```
2 |2
  |__
    1    0    Remainder
```

Step 2: Divide the quotient of the first division, 1, by 2 to get 0 with a remainder of 1.

```
2 |2
  |__
   |1    0
   |__
    0    1    Remainder
    ↑
    └──────────────────┘
```

In this method you stop when a zero appears here.

Step 3: Take the remainders in reverse order to get the binary equivalent.

```
0 ↑
1 |
```

The binary equivalent of 2 is 10, which checks with Table 16-3.

Example 16-5

Find the binary equivalent of decimal number 5.

SOLUTION

```
2 | 5
  |__
   | 2       1  ↑
   |__          |
     | 1     0  |
     |__        |
       0     1  |
```

Step 1: 5 divided by 2 is 2 with a remainder of 1.
Step 2: 2 divided by 2 is 1 with a remainder of 0.
Step 3: 1 divided by 2 is 0 with a remainder of 1.
Step 4: The remainders taken in reverse order form the binary equivalent of 5. Hence, the answer is 101.

EXAMPLE 16-6

Find the binary equivalent of 12 using the double-dabble method.

SOLUTION

```
2 | 12
  |___
   | 6       0  ↑
   |__          |
     | 3     0  |
     |__        |
       | 1   1  |
       |__      |
         0   1  |
```

The answer is 1100.

EXAMPLE 16-7

Find the binary equivalent of 25.

SOLUTION

```
2 | 25
  |___
   | 12        1  ↑
   |___           |
     | 6       0  |
     |__          |
       | 3     0  |
       |__        |
         | 1   1  |
         |__      |
           0   1  |
```

The answer is 11001.

16-5. Binary-to-decimal Conversion

In this section we learn how to convert binary numbers to decimal numbers. Recall that any decimal number can be expressed in units, tens, hundreds, etc. For instance, 2745 can be expressed as

$$2745 = 2000 + 700 + 40 + 5$$

In a similar way, any binary number can be decomposed into its constituent parts. For instance, binary number 111 can be expressed as

$$111 = 100 + 10 + 1 \tag{16-1}$$

This decomposition is permissible since the right side of the equation adds up to the left side.

$$\begin{array}{r} 100 \\ 10 \\ +\ \ 1 \\ \hline 111 \end{array}$$

Something interesting occurs if we convert Eq. (16-1) into its decimal counterpart. Using Table 16-3,

$$\begin{array}{ccccccccl} 111 & = & 100 & + & 10 & + & 1 & & \text{Binary} \\ \downarrow & & \downarrow & & \downarrow & & \downarrow & & \\ 7 & = & 4 & + & 2 & + & 1 & & \text{Decimal} \end{array}$$

Decomposing a binary number into its constituent parts is equivalent to decomposing the decimal equivalent into units, twos, fours, and so on. Some examples will illustrate how we can exploit this property.

Example 16-8

Convert 1111 into its decimal equivalent.

Solution

$$\begin{array}{ccccccccc} 1111 & = & 1000 & + & 100 & + & 10 & + & 1 \\ \downarrow & & \downarrow & & \downarrow & & \downarrow & & \downarrow \\ ? & = & 8 & + & 4 & + & 2 & + & 1 \end{array}$$

Obviously, ? = 15. Hence, the decimal equivalent of 1111 is 15.

Example 16-9

Convert 101 into its decimal equivalent.

Solution

$$\begin{array}{ccccccc} 101 & = & 100 & + & 0 & + & 1 \\ \downarrow & & \downarrow & & \downarrow & & \downarrow \\ ? & = & 4 & + & 0 & + & 1 \\ ? & = & 5 & & & & \end{array}$$

Hence, 5 is the decimal equivalent of 101.

We can streamline our conversion method by the following procedure:

1. Write the binary number.
2. Directly under the binary number write 1, 2, 4, 8, 16, . . . , working from right to left.
3. If a zero appears in the binary number, cross out the decimal number directly below this zero.
4. Add the remaining decimal numbers to obtain the decimal equivalent.

EXAMPLE 16-10

Convert 101 to its decimal equivalent.

SOLUTION

Step 1: 101
Step 2: 421
Step 3: 4~~2~~1
Step 4: 4 + 1 = 5
Hence, 5 is the decimal equivalent of 101.

EXAMPLE 16-11

Convert 1011 into its decimal equivalent.

SOLUTION

1011
8~~4~~21
8 + 2 + 1 = 11 (Answer)

EXAMPLE 16-12

Convert 10101 to its decimal equivalent.

SOLUTION

10101
16~~8~~4~~2~~1
16 + 4 + 1 = 21 (Answer)

16-6 Basic Logic Circuits

At this point we know that binary numbers are a code for decimal numbers. Further, we know how to add binary numbers so that the answers agree with the decimal answers. We now turn our attention to some circuits that we will eventually use to perform binary addition.

The first basic logic circuit that we will study is the OR circuit shown in Fig. 16-2. Let us analyze its operation. We know that if the diodes are forward-biased, they are like short circuits. If they are back-biased, they are like open circuits. The battery voltages A and B are the inputs, and C is the output of the OR circuit. We will go through all the possible input-output conditions with one restriction. The input voltages are either 0 or 1 volt. No other inputs will be allowed.

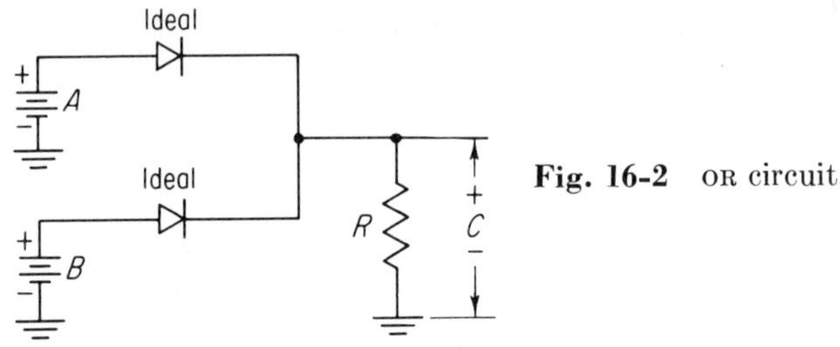

Fig. 16-2 OR circuit.

Case 1: $A = 0$, $B = 0$. With zero volts applied to each input, we get zero volts out, so that $C = 0$.

Case 2: $A = 0$, and $B = 1$. The diode connected to the B input is forward-biased, so it acts like a short. Therefore, $C = B = 1$. (Note that the A diode is back-biased.)

Case 3: $A = 1$, and $B = 0$. The argument here is similar to case 2. We get $C = 1$.

Case 4: $A = 1$, and $B = 1$. Both diodes are forward-biased, or shorted. Therefore, $C = 1$.

We may summarize the input-output conditions of the OR circuit as shown in Table 16-4. Any table like Table 16-4 where all the input-output possibilities are displayed is called a *truth table*.

The OR circuit is so named because from the truth table we note that if A *or* B is 1, then C is 1.

Table 16-4 The OR Truth Table

A	B	C
0	0	0
0	1	1
1	0	1
1	1	1

Another of the basic logic circuits is the AND circuit shown in Fig. 16-3. We can find the truth table for the AND circuit by determining the value of C for all the different input conditions under the restriction that the inputs are either 0 or 1.

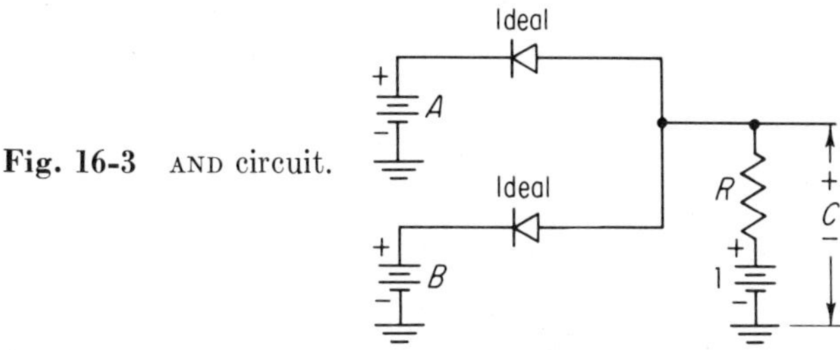

Fig. 16-3 AND circuit.

Case 1: $A = 0$, and $B = 0$. Note that both diodes are forward-biased, or shorted. Therefore, the diodes are shorted to ground, and C must equal 0.

Case 2: $A = 0$, and $B = 1$. In this case, the A diode is shorted to ground through the A battery. Therefore, $C = 0$.

Case 3: $A = 1$, and $B = 0$. The argument is similar to case 2, and therefore $C = 0$.

Case 4: $A = 1$, and $B = 1$. There is no current in any part of the circuit because all batteries are at the same potential. With no current through the R resistor, C must equal the voltage across the 1 volt battery. Therefore, $C = 1$.

The truth table for the AND circuit is given by Table 16-5.

Table 16-5 The AND Truth Table

A	B	C
0	0	0
0	1	0
1	0	0
1	1	1

The AND circuit is so named because C equals 1 only if A *and* B equal 1.

There is one more basic logic circuit to be considered in this section. It is known as the NOT circuit. Figure 16-4 illustrates one way of building a NOT circuit. There is only one input and one output.

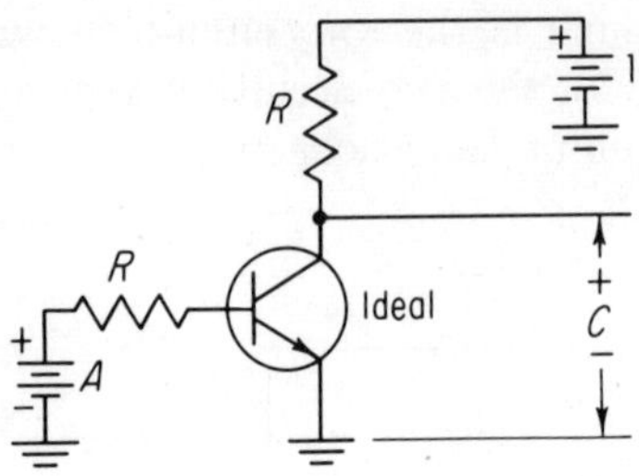

Fig. 16-4 NOT circuit.

Case 1: $A = 0$. If we assume an ideal transistor, there is no base current. Therefore, there is no collector current, and C equals the power supply voltage, that is, 1 volt.

Case 2: $A = 1$. Assuming a d-c β greater than unity, the transistor is saturated, or shorted. Hence, $C = 0$.

Table 16-6 is the truth table for the NOT circuit.

Table 16-6 The NOT Truth Table

A	C
0	1
1	0

The NOT circuit is called a NOT circuit because the output is *not* the same as the input.

EXAMPLE 16-13

In Fig. 16-2 the input batteries may be set at either 2 or 10 volts. Construct a table showing the actual input and output voltages.

SOLUTION

A	B	C
2	2	2
2	10	10
10	2	10
10	10	10

The entries in this table should be obvious. If both inputs are at 2 volts, the output must be 2 volts. If either input is at 10 volts, the output must be 10 volts.

EXAMPLE 16-14

In Example 16-13 call 2 volts the low state, and call 10 volts the high state. Construct a table with the words low and high. Construct a second table where 0 represents the low state, and 1 represents the high state.

SOLUTION

A	B	C
Low	Low	Low
Low	High	High
High	Low	High
High	High	High

A	B	C
0	0	0
0	1	1
1	0	1
1	1	1

The point is that in logic circuits the absolute value of the voltage is irrelevant. What matters is whether the voltage is low or high. Most of the circuits used in digital instruments are two-state circuits, meaning that the output voltage is either low or high. We will generally use 0 to represent the low voltage and 1 to represent the high voltage.

16-7 Boolean Algebra

It is possible to use a new kind of algebra to describe the behavior of logic circuits. This new kind of algebra is called *Boolean algebra* in honor of the inventor (George Boole, 1815–1864). Boolean algebra is different from the ordinary algebra, in which the set of numbers used includes all real numbers. Thus, when we solve an ordinary algebraic equation, we may get positive or negative numbers, fractional or irrational numbers, in short, any real number. In Boolean algebra, when we solve an equation we can get either a 0 or a 1. No other answers are possible, because the set of numbers in Boolean algebra is restricted to 0 and 1.

Another startling difference in Boolean algebra is the meaning of the plus sign and the multiplication sign. Let us first discuss the meaning of the plus sign. Consider the OR circuit of Fig. 16-5. A and B are the inputs, and C is the output. In Boolean algebra the $+$ sign is used to represent the action of the OR circuit. In other words, we may think of an

OR circuit as a device that combines A with B to give C. Thus, in Boolean algebra when we write $C = A + B$, we mean that the A and B inputs are to be combined in the same way that an OR circuit combines A and B. The expression, $C = A + B$, should be read as C equals A *or* B. The

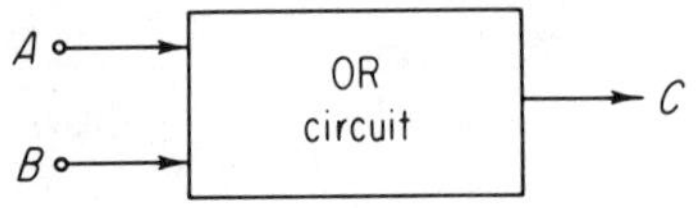

A
B
OR circuit
C

Fig. 16-5 OR block diagram.

+ sign means OR addition, and not ordinary addition. The following example should be read carefully.

EXAMPLE 16-15

Solve the Boolean expression, $C = A + B$, for the following inputs:
(*a*) $A = 0, B = 0$
(*b*) $A = 1, B = 0$
(*c*) $A = 1, B = 1$

SOLUTION

(*a*) $C = A + B = 0 + 0 = 0$ because an OR circuit combines 0 with 0 to give 0.
(*b*) $C = A + B = 1 + 0 = 1$ because an OR circuit combines 1 with 0 to give 1.
(*c*) $C = A + B = 1 + 1 = 1$ because an OR circuit combines 1 with 1 to give 1.

This last result is sometimes very disturbing because of our built-in understanding of the + sign. We simply must realize that the + sign has several meanings. When dealing with decimal numbers, it has the ordinary conventional meaning of adding decimal numbers. When dealing with binary numbers, it has the meaning of binary addition. When dealing with Boolean algebra, it has the meaning of OR addition as defined by an OR circuit. To illustrate the three different meanings:

Decimal addition

$$1 + 1 = 2$$

Binary addition

$$1 + 1 = 10$$

Boolean algebra

$$1 + 1 = 1$$

In Boolean algebra the multiplication sign also has a different meaning from ordinary multiplication. Consider the AND circuit shown in Fig. 16-6. As we did with the OR circuit, we may think of the AND circuit

Fig. 16-6 AND block diagram.

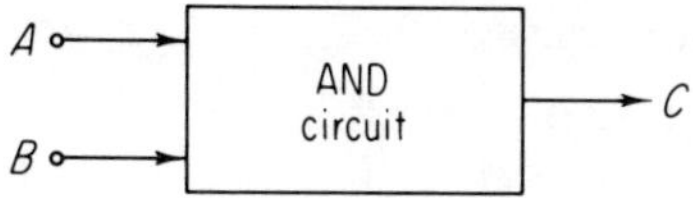

as a device that combines A with B to give C. Thus, in Boolean algebra when we write

$$C = A \cdot B$$

or

$$C = AB$$

we mean that A and B are to be combined in the same way that an AND circuit combines A with B. Therefore, it is helpful to read $C = AB$ as C equals A *and* B. The following example should be carefully read.

EXAMPLE 16-16

Solve the Boolean expression, $C = AB$, for the following inputs:
(*a*) $A = 0, B = 0$
(*b*) $A = 1, B = 0$
(*c*) $A = 1, B = 1$

SOLUTION

(*a*) $C = AB = 0 \cdot 0 = 0$
(*b*) $C = AB = 1 \cdot 0 = 0$
(*c*) $C = AB = 1 \cdot 1 = 1$

None of these results is disturbing, because even though the dot does not mean multiplication in the ordinary sense, the results are the same as for ordinary multiplication.

There is one more operation in Boolean algebra that we need to know. Consider the NOT circuit shown in Fig. 16-7. The NOT circuit operates on

Fig. 16-7 NOT block diagram.

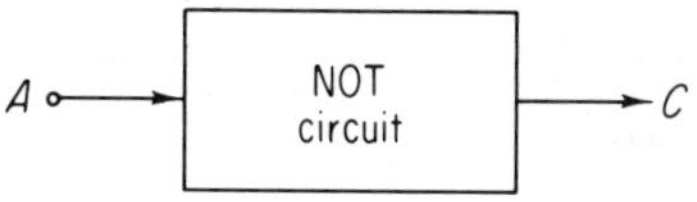

the input to give an output. In Boolean algebra the expression

$$C = \bar{A}$$

means that we are to operate on A in the same way that a NOT circuit operates on A. We read the expression as C equals *not* A.

EXAMPLE 16-17

Solve $C = \bar{A}$ for $A = 0$ and for $A = 1$.

Solution

For $A = 0$

$$C = \bar{A} = \bar{0} = 1 \qquad \text{because } not \text{ zero is one}$$

For $A = 1$

$$C = \bar{A} = \bar{1} = 0 \qquad \text{because } not \text{ one is zero}$$

It will be convenient in our discussion of logic circuits to use the block diagrams of Fig. 16-8 to represent the OR, AND, and NOT circuits.

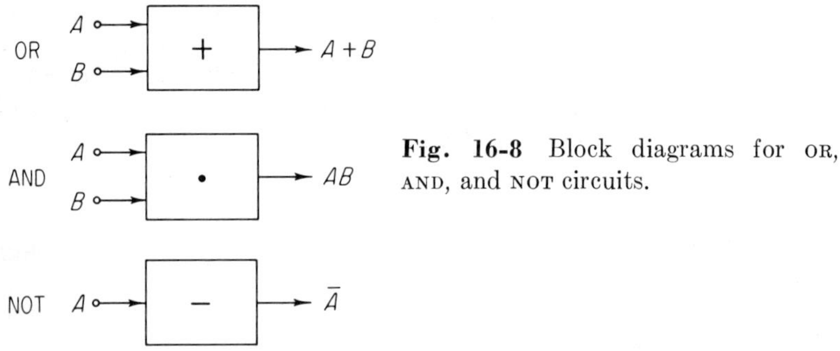

Fig. 16-8 Block diagrams for OR, AND, and NOT circuits.

There are other differences between ordinary algebra and Boolean algebra, but for our purposes the foregoing discussion is sufficient.

Example 16-18

Write the Boolean equation for the output of the logic system shown in Fig. 16-9.

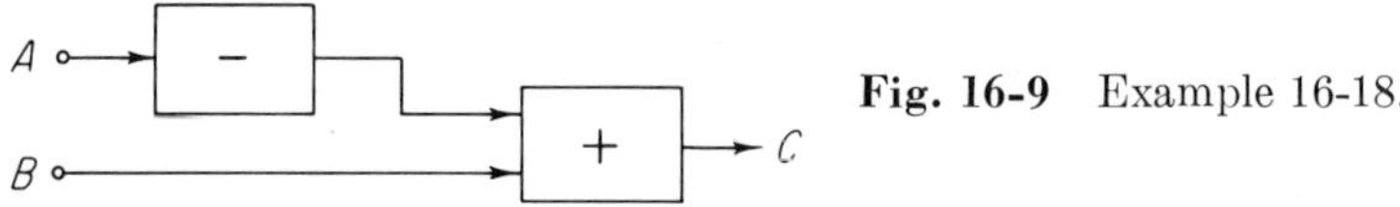

Fig. 16-9 Example 16-18.

Solution

The OR circuit has two inputs. One of them is $\bar{A}$, and the other is B. Hence, the output of the system is

$$C = \bar{A} + B$$

Example 16-19

Solve the Boolean equation of the preceding example for

(a) $A = 0, B = 0$

(b) $A = 1, B = 0$

Solution

(a) $C = \bar{A} + B = \bar{0} + 0 = 1 + 0 = 1$

(b) $C = \bar{A} + B = \bar{1} + 0 = 0 + 0 = 0$

EXAMPLE 16-20

Write the Boolean expression for the system of Fig. 16-10*a*.

SOLUTION

C equals the *not* of the input to the last block. The input to the last block is $A + B$. Thus,

$$C = \overline{A + B}$$

Note carefully that we must take the *not* of the entire input to the last block.

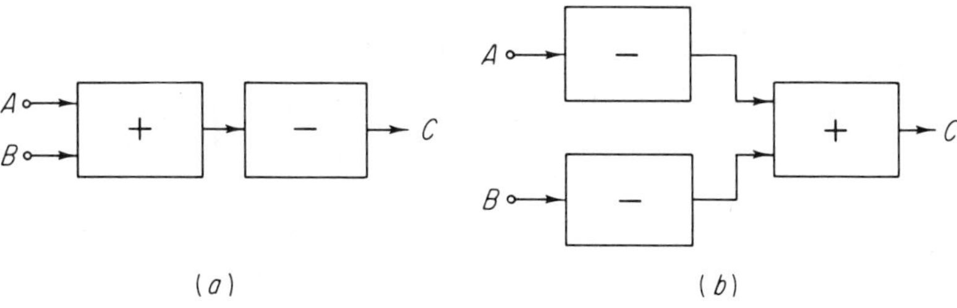

Fig. 16-10 Examples 16-20 and 16-21.

EXAMPLE 16-21

Find the Boolean equation for the system of Fig. 16-10*b*.

SOLUTION

One of the inputs to the OR circuit is $\bar{A}$, and the other input is $\bar{B}$. Hence, the final output is

$$C = \bar{A} + \bar{B}$$

EXAMPLE 16-22

Work out the truth table of $C = \overline{A + B}$ and the truth table of $C = \bar{A} + \bar{B}$.

SOLUTION

First, we work out all possible cases for $C = \overline{A + B}$.

$$C = \overline{0 + 0} = \bar{0} = 1$$
$$C = \overline{0 + 1} = \bar{1} = 0$$
$$C = \overline{1 + 0} = \bar{1} = 0$$
$$C = \overline{1 + 1} = \bar{1} = 0$$

Second, we work out all possible cases for $C = \bar{A} + \bar{B}$.

$$\begin{aligned} C &= \bar{0} + \bar{0} = 1 + 1 = 1 \\ C &= \bar{0} + \bar{1} = 1 + 0 = 1 \\ C &= \bar{1} + \bar{0} = 0 + 1 = 1 \\ C &= \bar{1} + \bar{1} = 0 + 0 = 0 \end{aligned}$$

The truth table for each system of Fig. 16-10 is

$C = \overline{A + B}$		
A	B	C
0	0	1
0	1	0
1	0	0
1	1	0

$C = \bar{A} + \bar{B}$		
A	B	C
0	0	1
0	1	1
1	0	1
1	1	0

Since the truth tables are different, $\overline{A + B} \neq \bar{A} + \bar{B}$. In other words, since the truth tables are different, the two systems of Fig. 16-10 are not equivalent. Sometimes, two systems which have different block diagrams have the same truth table. In this case, the systems are equivalent and may be interchanged.

Incidentally, the logic circuit of Fig. 16-10*a* is very popular in practice and is known as a NOR circuit. Note that the NOR circuit is an OR followed by a NOT circuit. Another popular logic circuit is the NAND circuit. The NAND circuit is an AND circuit followed by a NOT circuit, as shown in Fig. 16-11.

A, B → [•] → [–] → $C = \overline{AB}$

Fig. 16-11 NAND circuit.

EXAMPLE 16-23

Write the Boolean expression for the system of Fig. 16-12.

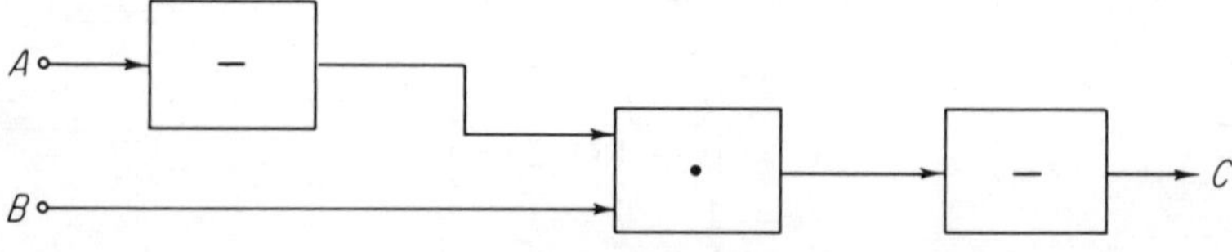

Fig. 16-12 Example 16-23.

SOLUTION

Working from the input to the output we see that the two inputs to the AND circuit are $\bar{A}$ and B. Therefore, the input to the NOT circuit is $\bar{A}B$. Hence, the final output is

$$C = \overline{\bar{A}B}$$

16-8 The Exclusive-OR Circuit

Recall from Sec. 16-3 that $1 + 1 = 10$, where the + sign indicates binary addition. One of the aims of this chapter is to show how logic circuits can be used to perform binary addition.

In Sec. 16-6 we saw that in the OR circuit, $1 + 1 = 1$, where the + sign means OR addition. What we need to do now is to find a combination of OR, AND, and NOT circuits that yields $1 + 1 = 10$. Before we can achieve this result, we must discuss the special logic circuit shown in Fig. 16-13. The input and output of each block have been worked out. Note that the final output is

$$C = A\bar{B} + \bar{A}B$$

Any logic system with this Boolean expression is called an *exclusive*-OR circuit.

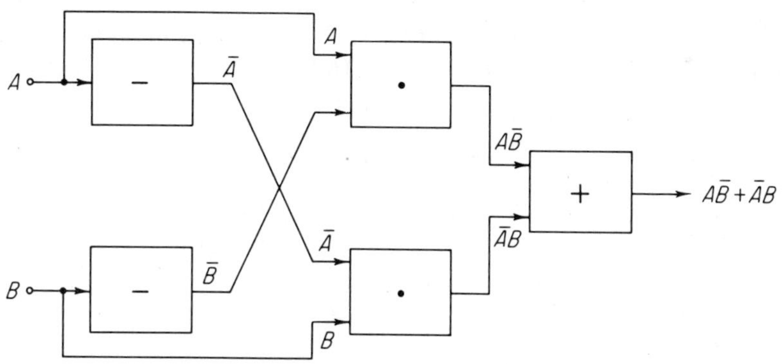

Fig. 16-13 Exclusive-OR circuit.

We can find the truth table for the system of Fig. 16-13 by considering four possible input conditions, namely, $A, B = 0, 0; 0, 1; 1, 0;$ and $1, 1$. For instance,

When $A = 0, B = 0$

$$C = 0 \cdot \bar{0} + \bar{0} \cdot 0 = 0 \cdot 1 + 1 \cdot 0 = 0$$

When $A = 0, B = 1$

$$C = 0 \cdot \bar{1} + \bar{0} \cdot 1 = 0 \cdot 0 + 1 \cdot 1 = 1$$

After working out the two remaining possibilities, we can construct the truth table shown in Table 16-7. Notice the last entry in Table 16-7. In the exclusive-OR circuit 1 is combined with 1 to give a 0 output. The exclusive-OR is so named because the output is 1 if either A or B is 1, but not both.

Table 16-7 The Exclusive-OR Truth Table

A	B	C
0	0	0
0	1	1
1	0	1
1	1	0

16-9 The Half-adder

We now have enough logic circuits for a system that will perform binary addition. The system shown in Fig. 16-14 is known as a half-adder.

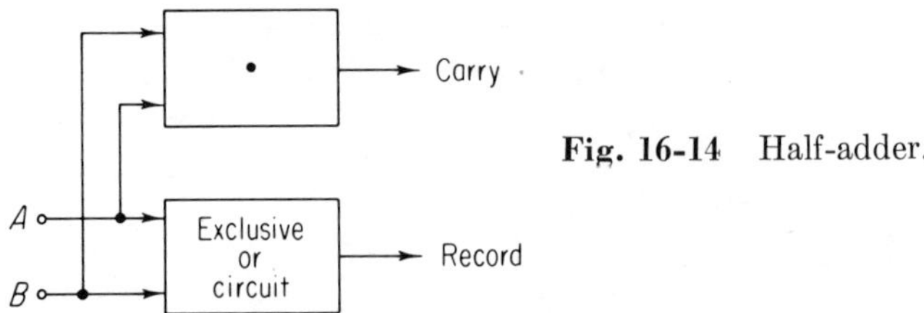

Fig. 16-14 Half-adder.

This system has two inputs and two outputs. The Boolean equations of the two outputs are

$$\text{Record} = A\bar{B} + \bar{A}B$$
$$\text{Carry} = AB$$

The truth table for this system is given by Table 16-8.

We have passed a major milestone. We now have a system that performs simply binary addition. The half-adder does what we do mentally when we perform binary addition. In the first row of the truth table, 0 combined with 0 gives 0 carry a 0. In the last row 1 combined with 1 gives 0 carry a 1.

Table 16-8 Half-adder Truth Table

A	B	Carry	Record
0	0	0	0
0	1	0	1
1	0	0	1
1	1	1	0

The half-adder represents only a simple step toward more complex logic systems that are capable of more difficult arithmetic.

16-10 The Binary Adder

Another of the basic adding circuits is the binary adder, shown in Fig. 16-15. The binary adder has three inputs and two outputs. We wish to

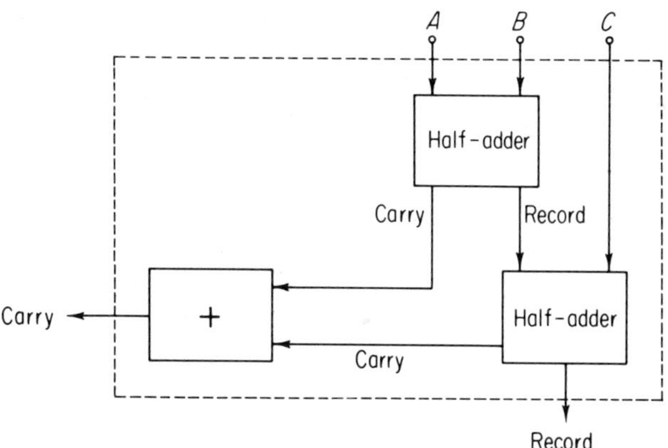

Fig. 16-15 Binary adder.

obtain the truth table for the binary adder. Instead of writing the Boolean equation for the final outputs, we will use an easier approach in finding the truth table. Since we have an ABC input, we have eight possible input conditions: 000, 001, 010, 011, 100, 101, 110, 111. (Note that these inputs are the permutations of two things taken three at a time.) To get the truth table we can take one input condition at a time and work our way through the system, labeling each block with its input and output. For instance, take the input condition: $A = 1$, $B = 0$, and $C = 1$. We know

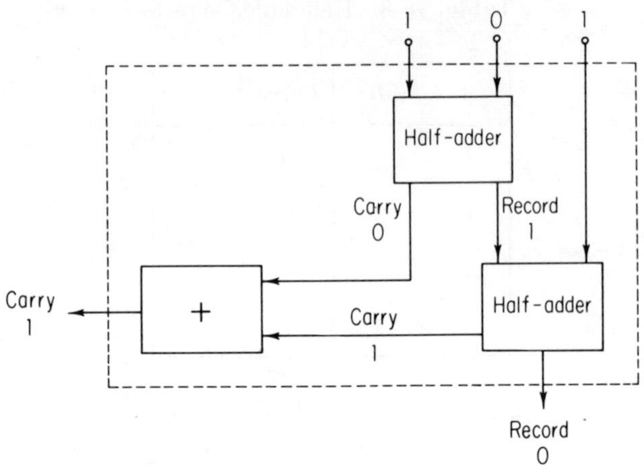

Fig. 16-16 Binary adder values for $A = 1$, $B = 0$, $C = 1$.

how the half-adder operates, so we work our way through the system, labeling each block as shown in Fig. 16-16.

If we work out the final record and carry outputs in a similar fashion for the seven remaining input conditions, we can construct the truth table of Table 16-9. (The reader should work out the remaining possibilities.)

Table 16-9 Binary-adder Truth Table

A	B	C	Carry	Record
0	0	0	0	0
0	0	1	0	1
0	1	0	0	1
0	1	1	1	0
1	0	0	0	1
1	0	1	1	0
1	1	0	1	0
1	1	1	1	1

The purpose of the binary adder is to allow the binary addition of three numbers at a time. This is important because sometimes in performing binary addition there is a carry from one column to another, as in

$$\begin{array}{r} 11 \\ +\ 11 \\ \hline 110 \end{array}$$

After adding the first column we have 0 carry a 1. In adding the second column, we must be able to add three 1s. The half-adder only handles two inputs, but the binary adder can handle three inputs.

16-11 A Simple Arithmetic Unit

By connecting binary adders and half-adders we will have a system that is capable of doing binary addition of two rows of binary numbers. Figure 16-17 illustrates such a system. One of the binary-number inputs

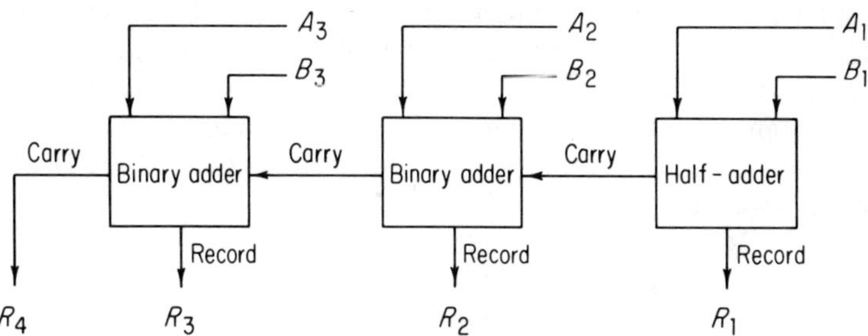

Fig. 16-17 A simple arithmetic unit.

is $A_3A_2A_1$. The other binary-number input is $B_3B_2B_1$. The system will add these inputs to obtain an answer of $R_4R_3R_2R_1$. In effect,

$$\begin{array}{r} A_3A_2A_1 \\ +\ \ B_3B_2B_1 \\ \hline R_4R_3R_2R_1 \end{array}$$

In the first column we are adding only two digits; therefore, to handle the first column we only require a half-adder. For any column above the first, there is the possibility of having a carry from the preceding column. Hence, we must use a binary adder for each column above the first column.

As a numerical example, let us add 2 + 2 to get 4. The $A_3A_2A_1$ input is 010, the binary equivalent of 2. Similarly, the $B_3B_2B_1$ input is 010. We already know that the answer should be 0100, the binary equivalent of 4. Let us check the operation of the system of Fig. 16-17 by working our way through the system, labeling each block with its correct input and

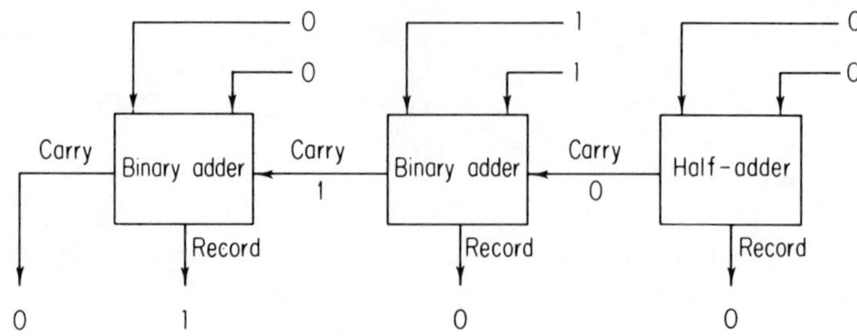

Fig. 16-18 Adding 010 to 010 to obtain 0100.

output (see Fig. 16-18). In the first column, the input to the half-adder is 0 and 0. Hence, the output of the half-adder is 0, carry a 0. The binary adder of the second column now adds 1 + 1 + 0 to give a record of 0 and a carry of 1. The binary adder of the third column adds 0 + 0 + 1 to give a record of 1 and a carry of 0. Hence, the final output, $R_4R_3R_2R_1$ is 0100, which is the binary equivalent of 4. (The reader should work out a few other cases to convince himself that the system does add binary numbers.)

The system of Fig. 16-17 has a limited capacity for addition. The largest binary numbers that can be added are 111 and 111. Hence, the maximum capacity is

$$\begin{array}{r} 111 \\ +\ 111 \\ \hline 1110 \end{array} \qquad \begin{array}{r} 7 \\ +\ 7 \\ \hline 14 \end{array}$$

It should be obvious that to increase the capacity we need only cascade more binary adders to the left end of the system.

The system of Fig. 16-17 gives us only a glimpse into the field of digital computers. There are many other ways of doing binary arithmetic. There are also many other aspects of digital computers that we have not discussed, such as storing numbers, bringing the numbers out of storage to be added, putting the answer back in storage, and so on. However, our simple system has at least removed some of the mystery of how a computer can duplicate the mental processes of man in solving problems.

SUMMARY

The decimal number system represents a one-to-one correspondence between quantity and decimal symbols. The binary number system represents a one-to-one correspondence between quantity and binary symbols. Either system can be used for counting as long as we understand the meaning of the symbols.

Binary arithmetic is an operation with binary numbers that reflects the action of combining physical quantities. In binary arithmetic, $1 + 1 = 10$, because we are combining • with • to obtain a total of ••.

The basic logic circuits are the OR, the AND, and the NOT circuits. A truth table is simply a table listing all the possible input and output conditions for a logic circuit.

In Boolean algebra there are only two numbers, 0 and 1. Further, the + and · sign take on new meanings given by the OR and the AND circuits. In addition, there is an operation in Boolean algebra known as the NOT operation. Boolean equations algebraically describe logic systems. Sometimes it is convenient to work directly with the logic system, whereas at other times it is more convenient to work with the Boolean equation for the logic system.

By combining half-adders and binary adders it is possible to perform binary arithmetic.

GLOSSARY

binary arithmetic The arithmetic of a number system with only two basic symbols such as 0 and 1.

Boolean algebra The algebra of logic circuits; an algebra on a set with only two elements: 0 and 1.

double dabble A method for converting from decimal to binary numbers involving progressive division by 2.

half-adder A logic circuit for performing binary addition of two basic binary numbers.

one-to-one correspondence A relation between the objects of one set and the objects of another set whereby each object in one set is related to only one object in the other set and vice versa.

set A collection of similar but distinct objects.

truth table An exhaustive table showing all the input and output possibilities of a logic circuit.

REVIEW QUESTIONS

1. What is a set? What is a one-to-one correspondence?
2. What is a binary number system? Count to seven using binary numbers.
3. Why does $1 + 1 = 10$ in the binary number system?
4. Describe the double-dabble method for converting from decimal to binary numbers. What is the method for converting from binary to decimal numbers?

5. Draw the schematic of an OR circuit using diodes. What is the truth table for this circuit?
6. Draw the schematic for the AND circuit and give the truth table for the AND circuit.
7. What is the set of numbers used in Boolean algebra? What is the meaning of the + sign and the · sign?
8. In Boolean algebra why does $1 + 1 = 1$?
9. What is the Boolean equation for the output of an exclusive-OR circuit? What is the truth table for this circuit?
10. Draw the block diagram for a half-adder. What is the truth table for a half-adder?
11. What advantage does a binary adder have over a half-adder? What is the truth table for a binary adder?
12. Draw the block diagram of a system similar to that of Fig. 16-17 that has the capacity to add 11101 and 10011.

PROBLEMS

16-1 Write the binary numbers for counting from 0 to 31.

16-2 Add the following using binary addition:

(*a*) 10101 + 11011.

(*b*) 11101011 + 10011001.

(*c*) 1111 + 1001 + 1101 + 1110.

16-3 Convert the following decimal numbers into their equivalent binary forms: 12, 17, 26, 56, and 127.

16-4 Convert the following binary numbers into equivalent decimal numbers: 1011, 1001, 1110101, 11101100101.

16-5 The circuit of Fig. 16-19*a* is an OR circuit with three inputs. Work out the truth table for this circuit. Also, what is the Boolean expression for the output of this circuit?

16-6 The circuit of Fig. 16-19*b* is an AND circuit with four inputs. Find the Boolean expression for the output and construct the truth table.

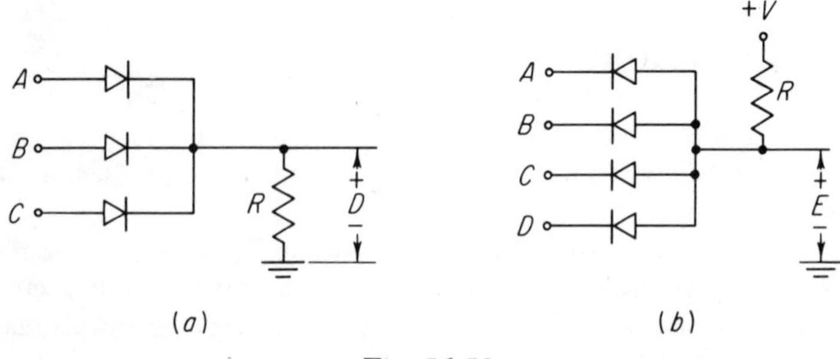

Fig. 16-19

16-7 Prove that $\overline{A + B} = \bar{A} \cdot \bar{B}$ by constructing the truth tables of each expression.

16-8 Prove that $\overline{AB} = \bar{A} + \bar{B}$ by constructing the truth table of each expression.

16-9 A system has three inputs: A, B, and C. Find the truth table if the output of the system is

(a) $D = (A + B)(A + C)$.

(b) $D = A + BC$.

16-10 Draw the block diagram for each of the following Boolean equations:

(a) $D = (A + B)(A + C)$.

(b) $D = A + BC$.

16-11 In Fig. 16-20*a*, what is the Boolean equation for the output? What is the truth table of this system?

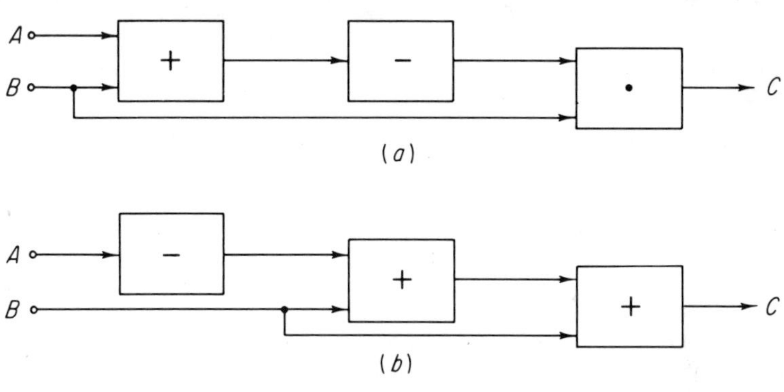

Fig. 16-20

16-12 In Fig. 16-20*b*, what is the Boolean equation of the output, and what is the truth table?

16-13 Show a circuit layout of diodes, transistors, and resistors for the system of Fig. 16-20*b*.

16-14 Given that $C = A\bar{B} + \bar{A}B$, show the block diagram and the circuit layout for this Boolean equation.

17 Electronic Counters

There is a large body of instruments whose main purpose is to count electronically the number of pulses received in a given period of time. These instruments are generally known as *electronic counters,* and as a rule they use two-state circuits such as flip-flops to perform the counting function.

In this chapter we study the principles behind electronic counters. We examine binary counters first, and after understanding their operation, discuss how they can be modified to obtain decimal counters. Finally, we examine how counters are used in various instruments.

17-1 The Binary Counter

Recall that the flip-flop is a two-state circuit that remains in one state (low or high output) until triggered into the alternate state. Several flip-flops can be cascaded to produce a system capable of counting. For instance, consider the system of Fig. 17-1. A train of triggers is fed into the right end of the system. The output of the first flip-flop drives the second flip-flop. The second flip-flop drives the third, and so. These flip-flops are designed to change states on negative triggers only. The points A, B, C, and D are the outputs of the flip-flops.

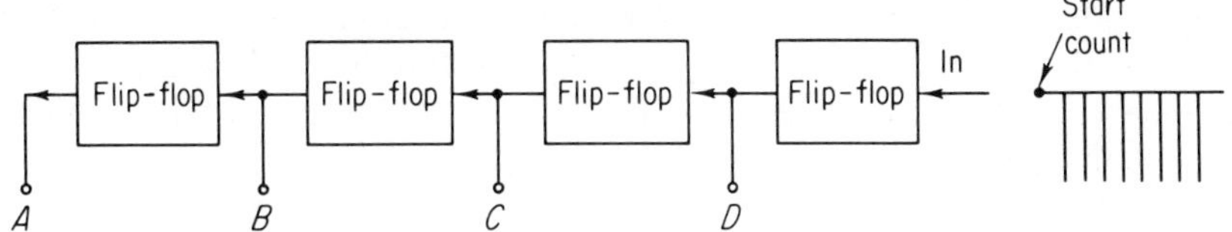

Fig. 17-1 A binary counter using flip-flops.

How can this system be used to count the number of triggers in the train of input pulses?

Suppose we begin by saying that all flip-flops are in the 0 state. In other words, $A = 0$, $B = 0$, $C = 0$, and $D = 0$. We can write this simply as $ABCD = 0000$. After the first trigger occurs, D changes from 0 to 1. This positive step is coupled into the second flip-flop from the right. A differentiating circuit in the second flip-flop produces a narrow positive trigger. Since the flip-flops respond only to negative triggers, the second flip-flop remains in the *zero* state. Since the second flip-flop remains in the *zero* state, no change is coupled into the remaining flip-flops. Hence, after the first trigger, $ABCD$ equals 0001.

When the second negative trigger arrives at the input, the D flip-flop changes from the 1 state back to the 0 state. This is a negative change. When this negative step is coupled into the C flip-flop, it is differentiated to produce a narrow negative trigger. This negative trigger causes C to change from the 0 state to the 1 state. This positive step is coupled into the B flip-flop, but since it is positive, the B flip-flop will not respond. As a result, after the second input trigger has arrived, $ABCD$ equals 0010.

When the third input trigger arrives, the D flip-flop changes from the 0 state to the 1 state. This is a positive step, and therefore the C flip-flop will not respond. Since the C flip-flop does not respond, the A and B flip-flops cannot respond. Hence, after the arrival of the third input trigger, $ABCD$ equals 0011.

We can summarize the operation of the system as follows:

1. The D flip-flop changes states as each negative input trigger arrives.
2. Any of the succeeding flip-flops (A, B, or C) will change states only if the flip-flop directly to the right has changed from the 1 state to the 0 state.

It is highly instructive to make a truth table showing the various flip-flop states (see Table 17-1). Note the progression. After the first trigger arrives, D changes from 0 to 1. This a positive change, so that all other flip-flops remain at 0. After the second trigger arrives, D changes from 1 to 0. This negative change causes C to change from 0 to 1. A and B remain at 0. After the third trigger, D changes from 0 to 1, and all other flip-flops remain in their previous states. After the fourth trigger, D changes from 1 to 0. This changes C from 1 to 0. This in turn changes B from 0 to 1. A remains at 0. Continuing in this fashion, we can construct the entire table. (The reader should work out this table to his satisfaction.)

Table 17-1 Binary-counter Truth Table

Number of triggers	A	B	C	D
0	0	0	0	0
1	0	0	0	1
2	0	0	1	0
3	0	0	1	1
4	0	1	0	0
5	0	1	0	1
6	0	1	1	0
7	0	1	1	1
8	1	0	0	0
9	1	0	0	1
10	1	0	1	0
11	1	0	1	1
12	1	1	0	0
13	1	1	0	1
14	1	1	1	0
15	1	1	1	1
16	0	0	0	0

Here is the point. We may think of the $ABCD$ entry as a binary number since it is composed of 0s and 1s. Further, we note that the progression in $ABCD$ is the binary-number code studied in Chap. 16. In effect, the value of $ABCD$ tells us how many input triggers have occurred, provided we interpret $ABCD$ as a binary number. Thus, we see that after four triggers have occurred, $ABCD$ equals 0100, the binary equivalent of 4. After eight triggers have occurred, the value of $ABCD$ is 1000, the binary equivalent of 8.

The system of Fig. 17-1 is a binary counter. Note that the capacity of this system is 15. On the sixteenth trigger, $ABCD$ returns to a value of 0000. If a greater capacity is desired, we need only add more flip-flops to the left end of the system.

For a visual readout of the binary count we could use four lamps, one connected to each flip-flop. If a flip-flop is in the 1 state (high-voltage output), its lamp is lit. In the 0 state (low voltage) the lamp is out. Thus, after receiving a train of triggers we could glance at the light bulbs and read the binary equivalent of the number of triggers.

The binary counter has many uses in counting. What we really prefer, however, is a system that reads the count as a decimal number. In other words, it would be much more convenient if we had a group of lamps, numbered 0 through 9, so that we could read the number without having to convert mentally from a binary number to a decimal number. The next section is devoted to this problem.

Example 17-1

If the capacity of the system of Fig. 17-1 is increased by adding three more flip-flops, what is the maximum number of triggers that can be counted?

Solution

With a total of seven flip-flops the largest binary number that we can obtain is 1111111. The decimal equivalent is obtained in the usual way.

$$1111111$$

or

$$64 + 32 + 16 + 8 + 4 + 2 + 1 = 127$$

On the 128th trigger the system resets to 0000000.

17-2 The Decimal Counter

The binary counter of the preceding section counts up to 15 and then resets on the sixteenth trigger. We now wish to modify the binary counter so that after reaching a count of 9, it will reset on the tenth trigger.

One method of accomplishing the reset on the tenth trigger is depicted by the system of Fig. 17-2. We have modified the binary counter by feeding the output of the A flip-flop back to a NOT circuit. The output of the NOT circuit is then used to drive the B and C flip-flops.

How does the use of feedback alter the counting pattern of the binary counter?

Let us begin with all flip-flops reset to the zero state. Hence, *ABCD* equals 0000. Clearly, no feedback signal occurs until the *A* flip-flop changes states. From Table 17-1 we know that the *A* flip-flop does not change states until the eighth trigger comes in. Thus, the system of Fig. 17-2 acts as an ordinary binary counter for the first seven triggers. The

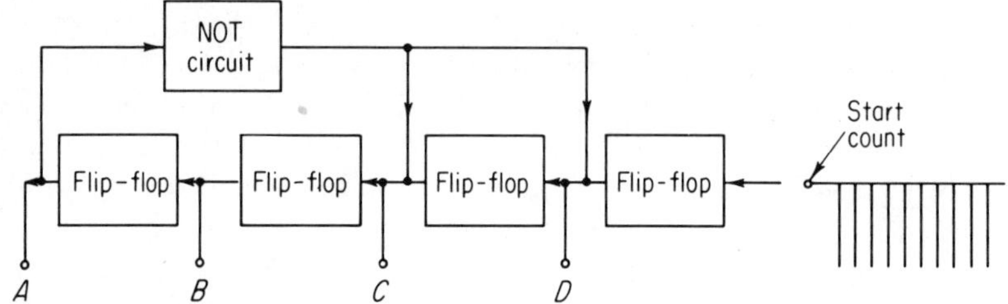

Fig. 17-2 Modifying the binary counter to reset after 10 input triggers.

progression in *ABCD* would be the usual pattern: 0000, 0001, 0010, 0011, 0100, 0101, 0110, and 0111. On the eighth trigger, however, *B* changes from a 1 to a 0. This causes the *A* flip-flop to change from a 0 to a 1. This positive step is fed back to the NOT circuit, so that the output of the NOT circuit changes from a 1 to a 0. This negative step is then applied to the *B* and *C* flip-flops and causes these flip-flops to change states. Here is what happens after the eighth trigger.

$$ABCD = 1000 \qquad \textit{before} \text{ feedback}$$
$$ABCD = 1110 \qquad \textit{after} \text{ feedback}$$

The feedback simply changes *B* and *C* from 0s to 1s.

On the ninth trigger, *D* changes to 1, so that *ABCD* equals 1111.

On the tenth trigger, all flip-flops reset to the zero states, so that *ABCD* equals 0000. Note that the *A* flip-flop has changed from 1 to 0. The output of the NOT circuit changes from 0 to 1, and therefore, the *C* and *D* flip-flops do not respond.

Thus, we see that the feedback has an effect only on the eighth trigger. Instead of obtaining *ABCD* equals 1000 after eight triggers, we obtain *ABCD* equals 1110. Further, on the tenth trigger the system resets to 0000.

The truth table for our modified counter is shown in Table 17-2. It should be clear that when we memorize this truth table, the system of Fig. 17-2 can be used to count from 0 to 9.

17-3 Decimal Readout for the Modified Counter

With the modified counter of Fig. 17-2, we can count from 0 to 9. If we like, we can attach lamps to each flip-flop output, and we will be

Table 17-2 Decimal-counter Truth Table

Number of triggers	A	B	C	D
0	0	0	0	0
1	0	0	0	1
2	0	0	1	0
3	0	0	1	1
4	0	1	0	0
5	0	1	0	1
6	0	1	1	0
7	0	1	1	1
8	1	1	1	0
9	1	1	1	1
10	0	0	0	0

able to read the decimal count, provided that we use the modified code of Table 17-2.

Most of us are not so accustomed to working with binary numbers as we are to working with decimal numbers. Therefore, a practical counter should have a decimal readout. Instead of having to look at four lamps and mentally convert to a decimal equivalent, we prefer to look at one numbered lamp directly marked in the decimal equivalent. What we need is a circuit that converts $ABCD$ into its decimal equivalent. There are many such binary-to-decimal converters. For purposes of illustration, we will discuss one of the more straightforward ways in which this can be accomplished.

Consider Fig. 17-3. The problem of binary-to-decimal conversion by electronic means boils down to the problem of finding logic circuits that we can place between the flip-flop outputs and 10 lamps numbered 0 through 9. For any one value of $ABCD$, only one lamp can be lit, and this lamp must be the decimal equivalent of $ABCD$.

Let us begin with an $ABCD$ value of 0000. Suppose that we use a logic circuit as shown in Fig. 17-4*a*. The output of the NOT circuits is 1111. This is fed into an AND circuit, and therefore the output of

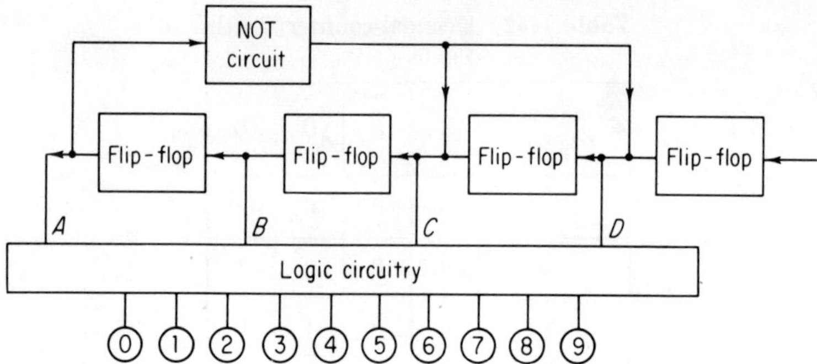

Fig. 17-3 Converting from binary to decimal readout.

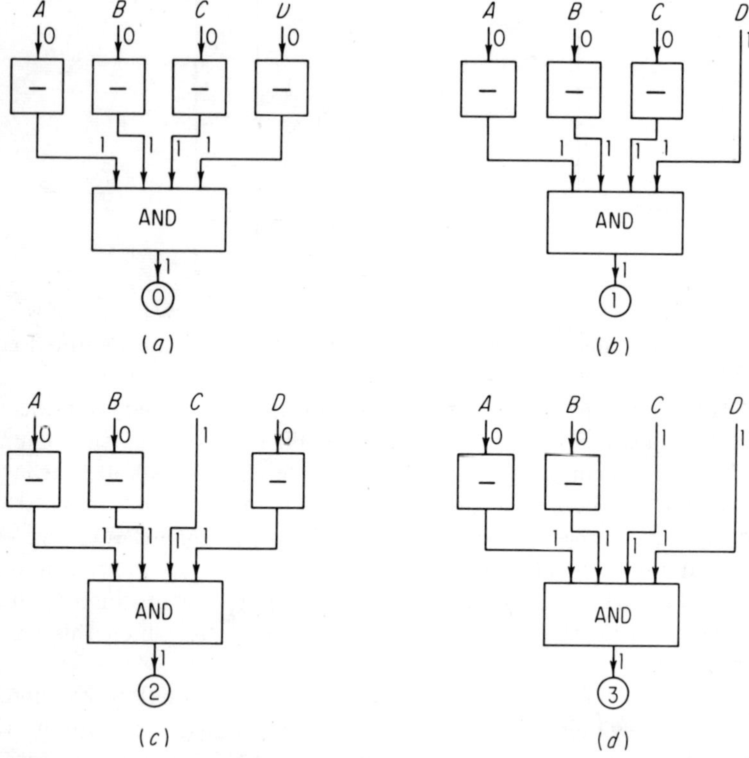

Fig. 17-4 Logic circuits for binary-to-decimal conversion. (*a*) Logic for lighting the zero lamp. (*b*) Logic for lighting lamp 1. (*c*) Logic for lighting lamp 2. (*d*) Logic for lighting lamp 3.

the AND circuit is 1. The output of the AND circuit drives the lamp labeled 0. Hence, the lamp labeled 0 is lit, and we read the decimal equivalent of *ABCD*.

Suppose the value of *ABCD* is 0001. This corresponds to a decimal equivalent of 1. The logic circuit used for this is shown in Fig. 17-4*b*. The 0s are inverted to get 1s. Hence, the input to the AND circuit is 1111. Again, we have a 1 output to drive the lamp labeled 1. This lamp is lit, and we read the decimal equivalent of 0001. Note in Fig. 17-4*a* that the lamp labeled 0 does not light if the value of *ABCD* is 0001, because the input to the AND circuit is 1110. This results in an output of 0 from the AND circuit.

Suppose that the value of *ABCD* is 0010, the binary equivalent of 2. The logic for this is shown in Fig. 17-4*c*. With *ABCD* equal to 0010, the output of the AND circuit is a 1, which lights the lamp labeled 2. Note that the lamps labeled 0 and 1 cannot be lit if *ABCD* equals 0010.

The logic used for lamp 3 is shown in Fig. 17-4*d*. Again, note that with an *ABCD* value of 0011, the only lamp that is lit is the 3 lamp. All others are off.

Thus, each numbered lamp has an appropriate logic circuit. With 10 different lamps, there are 10 different logic circuits. The 10 logic circuits are all in parallel on their input sides, and are all being driven by *ABCD*. For each *ABCD* value, only one logic circuit is delivering a 1 to the appropriate lamp. Thus, we have a system that electronically converts from binary to decimal equivalents.

There is no need to actually use NOT circuits in each of the logic circuits, since each flip-flop consists of two transistors, one on and one off. Thus, if the output of a flip-flop is 0, this means that the other transistor associated with that flip-flop is in the 1 state. From now on, we may think of a flip-flop as having two outputs: the regular output and the *not* of this output. Hence, the *D* flip-flop has a normal output of *D* from one transistor and an output of $\bar{D}$ from the other transistor.

The circuit connection for lamp 3 is shown in Fig. 17-5*a*. Note that

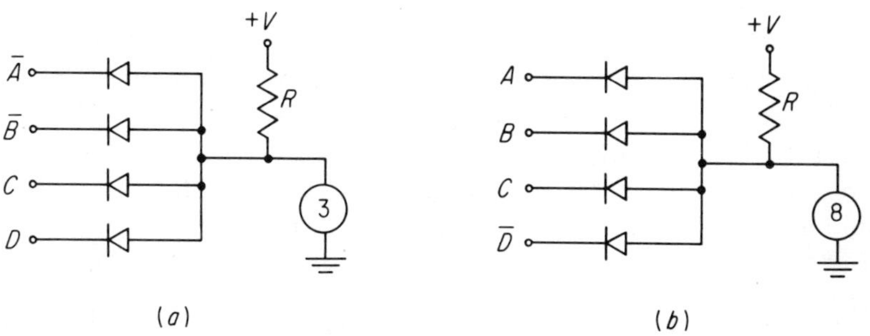

Fig. 17-5 Logic circuits for binary-to-decimal conversion.

the binary equivalent of 3 is 0011. Hence, we must return the two upper diodes to the $\bar{A}$ and $\bar{B}$ sides of the A and B flip-flops, respectively. In a similar way the *modified* binary equivalent of 8 is 1110. The logic circuit is shown in Fig. 17-5*b*.

Thus, to have a decimal readout of the $ABCD$ value stored in the flip-flops, we would use 10 AND circuits, one for each lamp. With four diodes per AND circuit, there would be a total of 40 diodes.

It should be understood that we have discussed only the most straightforward type of binary-to-decimal converter. There are other approaches. For instance, by using neon lamps and the proper circuit arrangement, it is possible to eliminate the diodes used in the AND circuits.

Very often, instead of using 10 separate lamps, a single lamp known as the *nixie tube* is used. It is basically a lamp in which the numbers 0 through 9 are stacked on top of each other. There are 10 input leads to this lamp. If a voltage is applied to one of these inputs, the decimal number associated with that input is lit.

Finally, in some applications the flip-flops can be replaced by a beam-switching tube. This is an electronic tube that acts as a 10-position switch. It may be used to count from 0 to 9.

In any event, we now have a method for counting the number of triggers from 0 to 9 with a direct decimal readout. In order to increase the capacity of our counter, we need only cascade several decimal counters together, as shown in Fig. 17-6. The first counter on the right counts

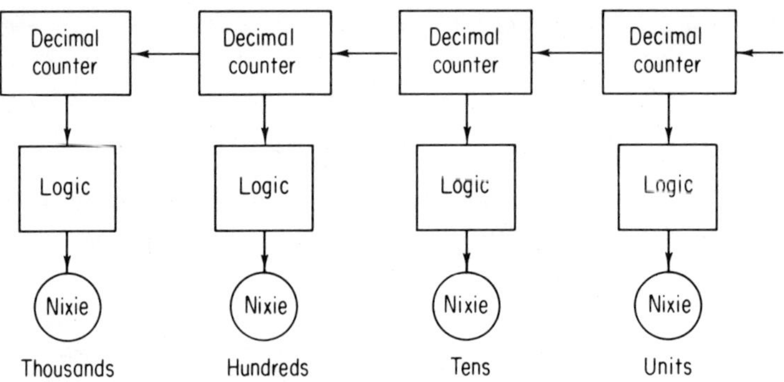

Fig. 17-6 An electronic counter with a capacity of 9,999.

from 0 to 9. The tenth trigger causes the units counter to reset to the zero state. This means that a negative step is coupled into the tens counter, and it then advances one count. After the tens counter has received ten triggers, it resets and causes the hundreds counter to advance one count. In this way, the counters continue until a count of 9999 is reached. The entire system resets after 10,000 triggers. If more capacity is required, additional counters are added to the system.

17-4 Gating the Decimal Counter

The system of Fig. 17-6 can be used to count the number of triggers occurring in a given period of time. This implies the necessity of resetting the counter to zero at the beginning of the count time. Further, there must be a way of limiting the number of triggers counted.

Figure 17-7 illustrates some of the basic ideas behind gating a decimal counter system so that it will count the number of triggers occurring in

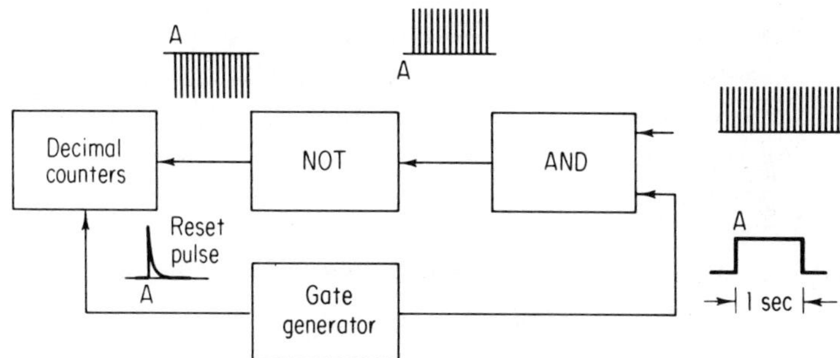

Fig. 17-7 Gating a decimal counter.

a given time period. The gate generator is a circuit that delivers a reset pulse to the decimal counters at point A in time. Therefore, at point A in time all counters are returned to zero. The gate generator also delivers a rectangular pulse to the AND circuit. For convenience, we are showing the width of this pulse as 1 sec. The input trigger train is the other input to the AND circuit. Since the AND circuit has an output only when both inputs are positive, we obtain the number of triggers that occur in a 1-sec interval of time. This 1-sec sample of triggers is inverted by the NOT circuit and is then counted by the decimal counters. Thus, at the end of the counting time, the decimal counters indicate the number of triggers that have occurred in 1 sec. The count registered on the decimal counters holds until the next reset pulse occurs, and the counting process begins again.

The accuracy of the system of Fig. 17-7 is limited by the accuracy of the gating pulse. Ideally, we have shown it as a 1-sec pulse. The amount of error in this 1-sec pulse depends upon how it is derived. Usually, this pulse is derived from an accurate r-f generator whose frequency has been divided down to 1 Hz. For instance, the most accurate crystal oscillators generally operate around 1 MHz and can be built with an accuracy of better than 1 part in 10^8. In other words, for a 1-MHz oscillator, the frequency is within 0.01 Hz of 1 MHz. This accurate 1-MHz signal can then be divided down to a 1-Hz signal, as shown in

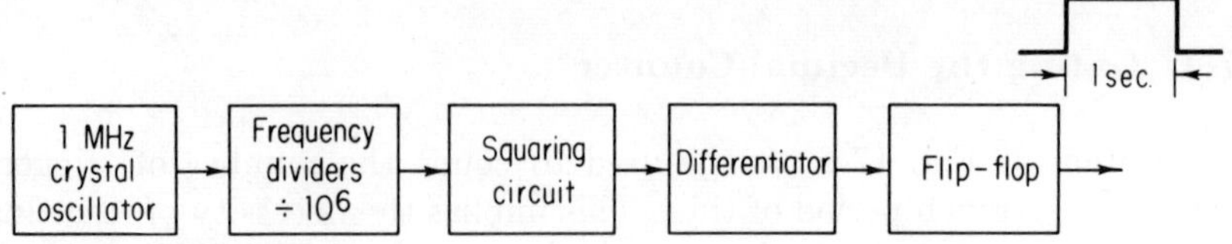

Fig. 17-8 Obtaining an accurate 1-sec gate.

Fig. 17-8. This 1-Hz signal is processed by squaring and differentiating. A flip-flop can then be used to generate an accurate 1-sec-wide gate, as shown.

Note that we can obtain different gating times by changing the amount of frequency division. For instance, if we need a 0.1 sec gating time, we can change the frequency division to 10^5. The output of the frequency dividers will then be a 10-Hz signal with a period of 0.1 sec.

Example 17-2

In the system of Fig. 17-8, what values of frequency division correspond to gating times of 0.01, 0.1, 1, and 10 sec?

Solution

For a 1-sec gating time we already know that the frequency division must be 10^6. Hence, the frequency-division values are 10^4, 10^5, 10^6, and 10^7, respectively.

17-5 Some Applications of Counters

One of the most widespread uses of decimal counters is that of measuring frequency. The basic idea behind a frequency counter is simply to change the input signal under test into a train of narrow triggers, which are then counted. For instance, in Fig. 17-9 the 1-kHz input signal is squared, differentiated, and clipped to obtain a positive-trigger train. There will

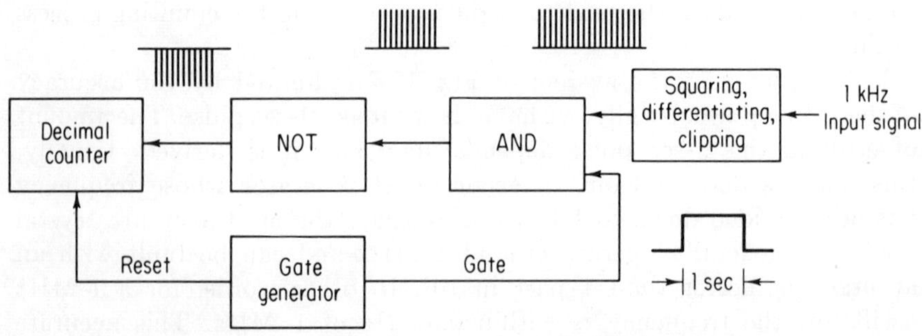

Fig. 17-9 A simple frequency-counter block diagram.

be one positive trigger for each cycle of the input signal. With a 1-sec gate time, the output of the AND circuit is a train of 1000 triggers. These are counted and registered on the decimal counters. The reading obtained is clearly the frequency of the input signal.

Another application of a decimal counter is the digital voltmeter. The voltmeters we have studied up to now have indicated the voltage on a meter face. The accuracy in such readings has been limited to a few percent. A digital voltmeter, however, displays the voltage by means of a decimal counter. With a digital voltmeter it is possible to read voltages with an accuracy in the range of 0.01 to 0.1 percent.

We will discuss only one of the possible approaches used in digital voltmeters, merely to demonstrate how such voltmeters are possible. Consider the system of Fig. 17-10. A d-c voltage V is to be measured. The

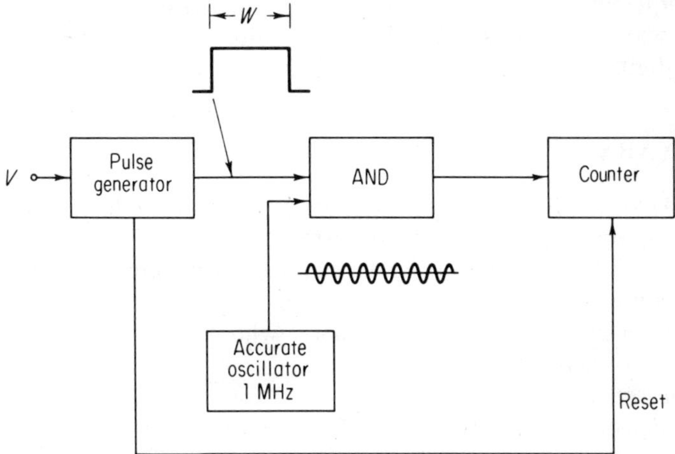

Fig. 17-10 A simple digital-voltmeter block diagram.

block labeled *pulse generator* consists of whatever circuits are necessary to generate a rectangular pulse whose width is directly proportional to the input voltage. To make this discussion concrete, suppose we say that

$$W = \frac{V}{10}$$

Hence, if the input voltage V is 1 volt, the pulse width is 0.1 sec. If the input voltage is 10 volts, the pulse width is 1 sec.

Note that the pulse is one of the inputs to the AND circuit. The other input is an accurate 1-MHz signal. Thus, the 1-MHz signal is gated by the pulse, and as a result, the counter reads the number of cycles that occur during the gating time. Because of this, the counter reading is directly proportional to the input voltage to be measured. Hence, the counter can be calibrated to read the input voltage.

The system of Fig. 17-10 can be modified to allow a-c voltage measurements.

SUMMARY

The typical binary counter consists of several flip-flops in cascade. The *ABCD* output is the binary equivalent of the number of triggers received.

The binary counter can be modified by means of feedback so as to obtain a decimal counter. In such a system a modified binary code is used. Logic circuits can be used to convert the *ABCD* value into its decimal equivalent. Nixie tubes are often used to display this decimal equivalent.

Accurate gating times are usually obtained by using a crystal oscillator and frequency-dividing its output to obtain more-suitable frequencies.

Two widespread uses of the decimal counter are in frequency counters and in digital voltmeters.

GLOSSARY

binary counter A device using binary numbers to indicate the number of input triggers that have occurred.

decimal counter A device using decimal numbers to indicate the number of input triggers that have occurred.

digital voltmeter An accurate voltmeter whose reading is given directly as a decimal number.

gating a counter Turning the counter on for a fixed amount of time to allow counting the triggers that occur during this time.

nixie tube A lamp in which transparent numbers 0 to 9 are stacked on top of each other; by applying voltage to one of the 10 input pins the number corresponding to that pin is lit.

REVIEW QUESTIONS

1. How many flip-flops are used in a binary counter with a capacity for counting to 15 before reset?
2. Count from 0 to 15 using binary numbers.
3. How is the binary counter modified to allow reset after 10 triggers have been received?
4. Why is a NOT circuit used in the feedback line of a modified binary counter?
5. On a modified binary counter the *ABCD* value equals 0111 after seven triggers are received. What is the *ABCD* value after the eighth trigger occurs?

6. Refer to Fig. 17-4. What logic circuit is used for lamp 7? For lamp 8?
7. Refer to Fig. 17-5. What circuit is used for lamp 5? For lamp 9?
8. What is a nixie tube? A beam-switching tube?
9. In Fig. 17-7 how is the very accurate 1-sec gating pulse obtained?
10. How can different gating times be obtained in the system of Fig. 17-7?
11. What is the basic idea behind the frequency counter?
12. Describe the operation of the digital voltmeter discussed in this chapter.

PROBLEMS

17-1 Construct the truth table for a binary counter that uses five flip-flops.
17-2 What is the maximum number of triggers that can be counted with a binary counter that uses nine flip-flops?
17-3 Construct the truth table for the modified binary counter shown in Fig. 17-11. Start with an *ABCD* value of 0010.

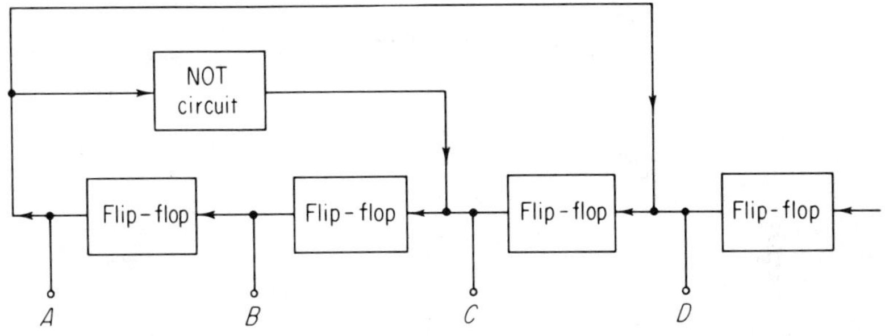

Fig. 17-11

17-4 Refer to Fig. 17-5. Draw the circuit diagrams for the logic circuits of lamps 1, 4, 6, and 9. Use Table 17-2.
17-5 In the system of Fig. 17-8, suppose that we use a 5-MHz crystal oscillator instead of a 1-MHz oscillator. What amount of frequency division is required to obtain a 0.01-sec output pulse?
17-6 In the frequency counter of Fig. 17-9, suppose that the input frequency is 24.6 kHz instead of 1 kHz. How many cycles are counted if the gating time is 0.1 sec? If the gating time is 10 sec?
17-7 In the system of Fig. 17-10 the relation between W and V is $W = V/10$. How many cycles are counted if V equals 5 volts? If V equals 3.27 volts?
17-8 In Fig. 17-10 suppose that we change the oscillator frequency from 1 to 5 MHz, and suppose that $W = V/5$. How many cycles are counted if V equals 7.5 volts? If V equals 2.23 volts?

18 Transducers

From our study of instruments we have become aware of the versatile nature of an electric signal. It is easily amplified, attenuated, filtered, detected, analyzed, modulated, transmitted, recorded, and so on. In order for electronics to have any practical value this versatility must be brought to bear on some of the problems encountered in our environment. In other words, electronics must help us handle such nonelectrical quantities as temperature, sound, light, humidity, velocity, force, radioactivity, displacement, and pressure. To accomplish this, we need devices that can bridge the gap between the electrical and the nonelectrical. Such devices are known as *electric transducers*. Basically, an electric transducer is a device that allows a nonelectrical quantity to control the value of an electrical quantity or vice versa. Because of this, it is possible to measure and control many of the nonelectrical quantities in our environment. In a wider sense this means that with electronics we can improve the world in which we live.

In this chapter we examine some transducers in order to gain an awareness of what they can do. Although our discussion is limited to only a few types of transducers, we should realize that there is a transducer for almost any nonelectrical quantity.

18-1 The Transfer Function

Transducers are devices that relate the electrical to the nonelectrical. A convenient way to summarize the behavior of a transducer is with a transfer function, which is simply a mathematical relation between the electrical quantity and the nonelectrical quantity. In general, the relation is

$$y = f(x)$$

An input transducer is one in which x is a nonelectrical quantity and y is an electrical quantity. A familiar example of an input transducer is a microphone. The x quantity for a microphone would be pressure variations in the surrounding air. The y quantity would be voltage or resistance, depending upon the type of microphone.

An output transducer is one in which the x quantity is electrical and the y quantity is nonelectrical. A simple example of an output transducer is a light bulb.

The point is that electrical and nonelectrical quantities are mathematically related to one another in a transducer. If one of the quantities changes, the other will change.

18-2 Photocells

Photocells are an interesting class of transducers in which light intensity controls the value of an electrical quantity. There are three general types of photocells: the photoemissive, the photoconductive, and the photovoltaic type.

The photoemissive transducer is basically a *diode* whose cathode is coated with a material such as potassium or cesium oxide. As light strikes the cathode, electrons are emitted and may be collected by a positive plate. No filament power is required because the emission is produced solely by the impinging light. Figure 18-1 illustrates the basic idea. A current I is flowing. In the normal operating range of the diode, this

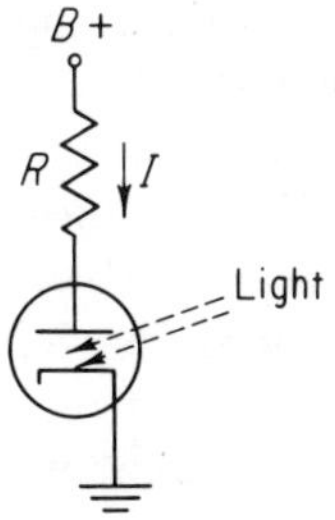

Fig. 18-1 Photoemissive diode.

current is proportional to the amount of light striking the cathode, and is given by

$$I = KF \tag{18-1}$$

where I is the current

K is a constant of proportionality

F is the amount of light striking the cathode (usually measured in lumens)

This equation tells us that the diode current is a function of the amount of light involved. As a result, it is clear that by measuring the current we are indirectly measuring the amount of light. It would be possible therefore to calibrate an ammeter to read the value of light in some convenient unit such as lumens.

Materials such as selenium, germanium, silicon, and metal sulfides are used in photoconductive transducers. Basically, we can think of a photoconductive transducer as a *resistor* whose value is controlled by the amount of light striking it. A typical sketch of resistance versus light is shown in Fig. 18-2. As the amount of light increases, the resistance

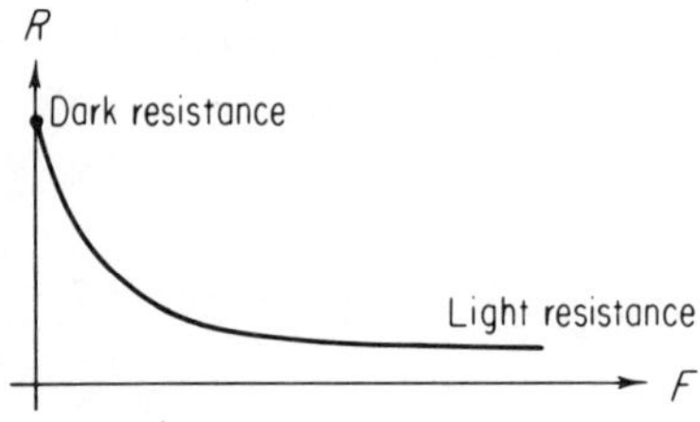

Fig. 18-2 Resistance variation of photoconductive transducer.

decreases. With enough light, the device saturates, in the sense that no further change takes place in resistance. The value of resistance with no light is simply referred to as the dark resistance, whereas the value of resistance with high light intensity is called the light resistance. Between the limits of dark and light resistance a number of interesting applications are possible. These will be discussed shortly.

The photovoltaic transducer may be thought of as a *voltage source* whose value depends upon the amount of light striking it. Such devices have been made of materials like cuprous oxide, selenium, germanium, and silicon. Photovoltaic transducers are often called *solar cells*, and are commonly used as power supplies on satellites and other extraterrestrial spacecraft.

The three types of photocells provide us with a variety of possible applications. For instance, lights can be turned on and off automatically with a system like that shown in Fig. 18-3. The photocell used is a photoconductive type. It is chosen so that its dark resistance is greater than R and so that its light resistance is less than R. Thus, during the daytime the resistance of the photocell is low, and the voltage applied to the base of the transistor is negative. This back-biases the base, and there is no collector current. The relay is therefore open, and the lights remain off. At night, the photocell resistance is greater than R. A positive voltage is applied to the base, and this causes the relay to close. The lights then come on.

In Fig. 18-3 we may use any number of different loads. Instead of turning on lights, we could open doors, turn on water faucets, dim headlights, and so on. The number of applications is infinite.

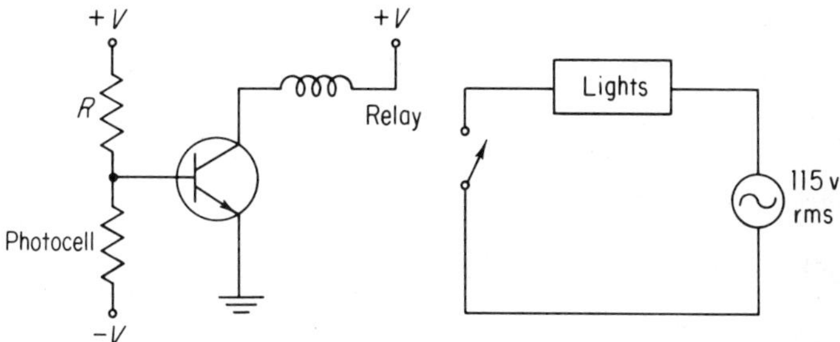

Fig. 18-3 A system for automatically turning lights on at night.

Another possible use of photocells is in counting. In Fig. 18-4 we have a photoemissive diode driven by a light source. If an object passes in front of the light beam, the diode current decreases and causes a positive pulse to appear at the plate. This pulse can be coupled into a decimal counter.

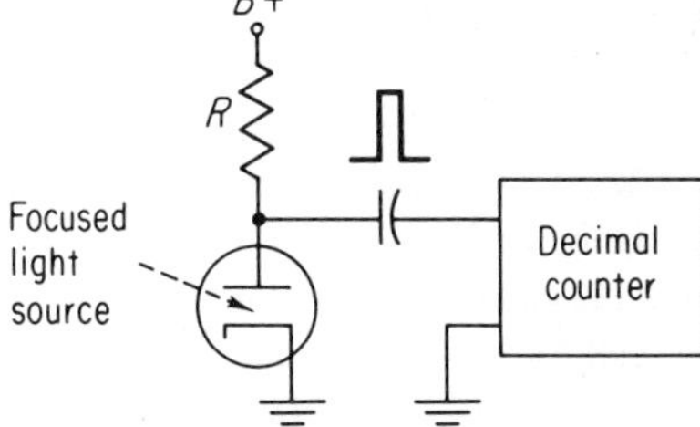

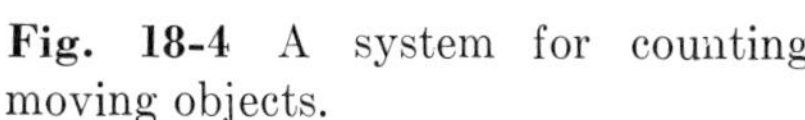

Fig. 18-4 A system for counting moving objects.

Each time the light beam is interrupted, the counter registers an additional count. We may use this system to count. For instance, on a production line objects moving down a conveyor belt can be counted as they pass through the light beam.

Example 18-1

In Fig. 18-1 the photoemissive diode has a K value of 30 μa per lumen. The power-supply voltage equals 100 volts, and the value of R is 1 megohm. Find the voltage across the diode and the current that is flowing if the amount of light striking the cathode is 2 lumens.

SOLUTION

Using Eq. (18-1) we can calculate the current.

$$I = KF = 30(10^{-6})(2) = 60\ \mu a$$

With 60 μa of current there is a 60-volt drop across the 1-megohm resistor. Hence, the voltage across the diode is

$$V = 100 - 60 = 40 \text{ volts}$$

EXAMPLE 18-2

An ammeter with a full-scale deflection of 50 μa is used to measure the current in the circuit of Fig. 18-1. If the value of K for the diode is 20 μa per lumen, what amount of light causes full-scale deflection? Half-scale deflection?

SOLUTION

$$I = KF$$

or $$F = \frac{I}{K} = \frac{50(10^{-6})}{20(10^{-6})} = 2.5 \text{ lumens} \qquad \text{for full-scale}$$

and $$F = 1.25 \text{ lumens} \qquad \text{for half-scale}$$

Note that the entire meter face can be marked to read the amount of light directly.

18-3 Temperature Transducers

In a variety of transducers temperature is the nonelectrical quantity. There are both input and output types. Among the input types is the familiar bimetallic strip. This consists of two strips of different materials, such as brass and steel, that have been welded together, as shown in Fig. 18-5*a*. The thermal rate of expansion is greater for brass than for steel. As a result, when the temperature is increased above the initial temperature T_i, the bimetallic strip bends downward. On the other hand, if the temperature is lowered, the strip bends upward (see Fig. 18-5*b* and 18-5*c*). The most common use of the bimetallic strip is as a thermal switch, as illustrated in Fig. 18-5*d*. As the temperature increases, the bimetallic strip bends downward enough to open the switch. This interrupts the current to the load. The load is often an output temperature transducer such as a heater. The system of Fig. 18-5*d* is then the familiar thermostatically controlled heater.

Another of the important temperature transducers is the resistance thermometer. This is basically a resistor whose value is controlled by temperature. Resistance thermometers are usually made out of metals

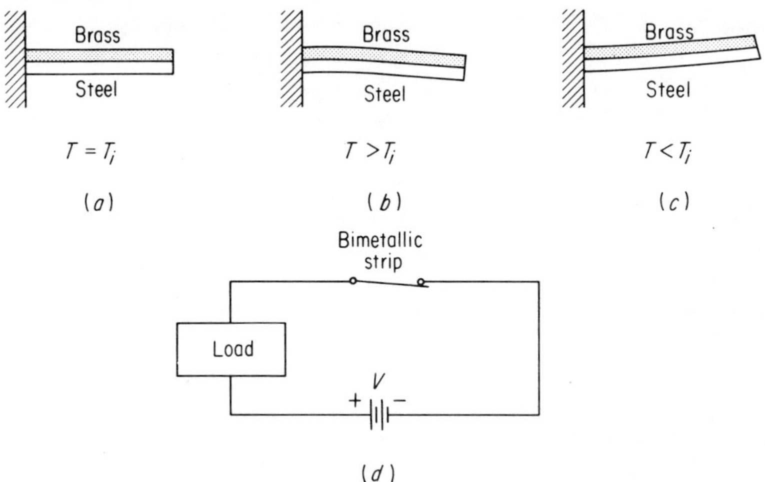

Fig. 18-5 Bimetallic strip. (*a*) $T = T_i$. (*b*) $T > T_i$. (*c*) $T < T_i$. (*d*) Thermostatic-regulated oven.

or semiconductors. In the metallic class, platinum is most often used because it has stable properties over a very large temperature range. Typically, a resistance thermometer made out of platinum wire obeys Eq. (18-2) over a temperature range of several hundred centigrade degrees.

$$R = R_o\,[1 + K\,\Delta T] \tag{18-2}$$

where R is the resistance at the actual temperature
R_o is the resistance at a reference temperature
K is the temperature coefficient
ΔT is the change or difference between the actual and the reference temperatures

If the temperature is measured in degrees centigrade, the value of K to use in Eq. (18-2) is 0.00392 (pure platinum).

Resistance thermometers made out of semiconductor materials are called *thermistors*. The temperature coefficient of thermistors is usually negative and has a typical value of about -5 percent per degree centigrade; however, this value of K changes over a wide temperature range. Equation (18-2) can be used as an approximation of the thermistor resistance over a *narrow* range if the average value of K over this range is used.

A *thermocouple* is another type of temperature transducer. This is a device formed by joining two dissimilar metals. The contact potential between the two metals is a function of the temperature at the junction of the metals. Thus, we may think of the thermocouple as a voltage source whose value depends upon the junction temperature.

The various temperature transducers find a wide variety of uses. The platinum resistance thermometer is the most accurate temperature transducer and is generally used as a temperature standard. With a platinum resistance thermometer it is possible to measure temperature with accuracies of better than 10^{-3}°C.

Thermocouples are widely used in r-f voltmeters. The r-f signal is applied to a heater that is in close proximity to the thermocouple junction. The voltage produced is then easily measured with a d-c voltmeter, which may be calibrated in rms values.

Thermistors are widely used in electronic-circuit design because of their small size and because of the large variety of nominal resistances available. As an example of using a thermistor, let us consider the temperature-regulated oven shown in Fig. 18-6. The dashed lines represent the insulated walls of the oven. When properly designed, the circuit holds the

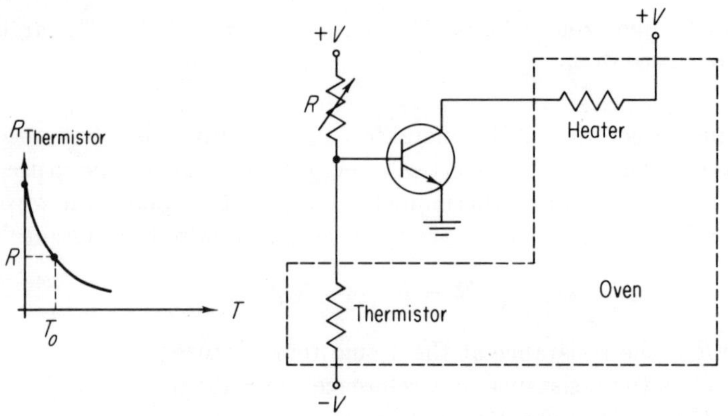

Fig. 18-6 Temperature-regulated oven.

temperature inside the oven almost constant even though the ambient temperature (temperature outside the oven) changes over a wide range. It is possible to maintain the oven temperature within a degree or two for an ambient temperature change of about 50 to 100°C. (This narrow temperature range inside the oven is essential for any kind of oscillator whose frequency must be held constant.)

The operation of the system of Fig. 18-6 is as follows. When the power is first applied to the system, the oven temperature is equal to the ambient temperature. The thermistor resistance is high, and therefore a positive voltage is applied to the base. This produces a collector current causing the heater to raise the temperature of the oven. As the temperature inside the oven increases, the thermistor resistance decreases, approaching a value of R. This reduces the base current, which in turn, reduces the heater current. Eventually, the system reaches an equilibrium whereby the potentiometer bridge is almost balanced. The heater is generating a very small amount of heat, just equal to the heat loss through the oven walls. Under this condition the temperature inside the oven is almost equal to T_o, the temperature at which the thermistor balances the bridge. If the ambient temperature should increase for some reason, then there would be less heat loss through the oven walls. This would cause the temperature inside the oven to increase. The thermistor resistance then decreases, thereby reducing the heater current. This in turn tends to compensate for the increase in oven temperature caused by the ambient-temperature change. It can be shown using a feedback analysis that the change in the oven temperature is given by

$$\Delta T = \frac{\Delta T_a}{1 + BA} \tag{18-3}$$

where ΔT is the change in oven temperature

ΔT_a is the change in ambient temperature

B is a constant of proportionality

A is the voltage gain of the transistor

The purpose of the rheostat R in Fig. 18-6 is to allow setting the oven temperature to different values. For instance, if the value of R is decreased, the thermistor must approach a lower value of resistance to almost balance the bridge. This implies that the equilibrium takes place at a higher temperature.

Example 18-3

A platinum resistance thermometer has a resistance of 100 ohms at 25°C. What is the resistance at 65°C?

Solution

Using Eq. (18-2),

$$R = 100[1 + 0.00392(65 - 25)] = 115.7 \text{ ohms}$$

Example 18-4

If the platinum resistance thermometer of the preceding example has a resistance of 150 ohms, what is the temperature?

Solution

Solving Eq. (18-2) for ΔT, we obtain

$$\Delta T = \frac{R - R_o}{R_o K} = \frac{150 - 100}{100(0.00392)} = 127.5°\text{C}$$

The reference temperature is 25°C. Hence, the actual temperature is

$$T = 25 + 127.5°\text{C} = 152.5°\text{C}$$

Example 18-5

Over the temperature range of 25 to 50°C, a thermistor has a temperature coefficient K of -5 percent per degree centigrade. If the thermistor resistance is 100 ohms at 25°C, what is its resistance at 30°C?

Solution

Using Eq. (18-2) we obtain the approximate solution

$$R \cong 100[1 + (-0.05)(30 - 25)] = 75 \text{ ohms}$$

Example 18-6

In the system of Fig. 18-6 the thermistor has a resistance of 2000 ohms at 70°C. If the rheostat is adjusted to a value of 1800 ohms, what is the approximate temperature of the oven under equilibrium conditions? Use $K = -0.05$.

Solution

The oven will reach an equilibrium approximately at that temperature where the thermistor resistance balances the potentiometer bridge. Since the voltage at each end of the bridge has the same magnitude, balance occurs for

$$R_{\text{thermistor}} = R = 1800 \text{ ohms}$$

We now can use Eq. (18-2) to find the change in temperature from the given value of 70°C. As we saw in Example 18-4,

$$\Delta T = \frac{R - R_o}{R_o K} = \frac{1800 - 2000}{2000(-0.05)} = 2°\text{C}$$

In other words, the temperature must rise 2°C above the 70°C reference in order for the thermistor resistance to change from 2000 to 1800 ohms. Hence, the oven temperature will be 72°C.

Example 18-7

In Fig. 18-6 the oven temperature is 80°C when the ambient temperature is 25°C. If the ambient temperature changes to 75°C, what is the new value of oven temperature? The voltage gain A of the transistor is 200, and the constant B for the system is 0.15.

Solution

We may use Eq. (18-3) to find the change in oven temperature.

$$\Delta T = \frac{\Delta T_a}{1 + BA} = \frac{75 - 25}{1 + 0.15(200)} = \frac{50}{31} = 1.61°\text{C}$$

The change in oven temperature is only 1.61°C. Hence, the new oven temperature is

$$T = 80 + 1.61 = 81.61°\text{C} \cong 81.6°\text{C}$$

Realize what this means. While the outside temperature has changed from 25 to 75°C, the regulated oven temperature has only changed from 80 to 81.6°C.

18-4 The Strain Gage

Strain, in the engineering sense, refers to the percentage change in the dimensions of an object. For instance, consider the metal bar shown in Fig. 18-7*a*. The bar has a length of L. If the ends of the bar are pulled

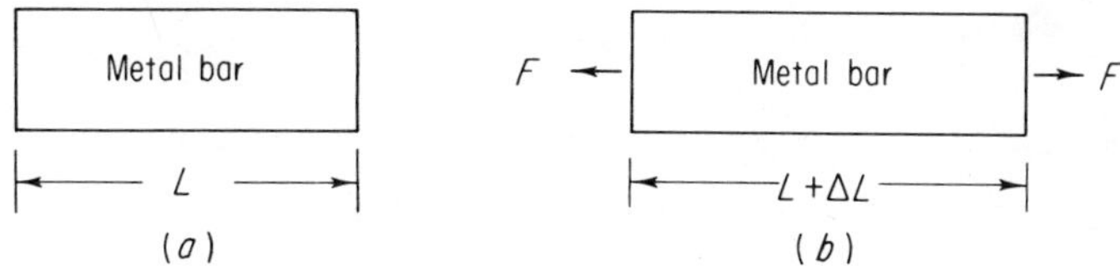

Fig. 18-7 Concept of strain. (*a*) Unstrained bar. (*b*) Strained bar.

by a force F, the bar stretches. It then has a new length of $L + \Delta L$, as shown in Fig. 18-7*b*. The quantity ΔL represents the change in length that has taken place. Strain is defined as

$$S \triangleq \frac{\Delta L}{L} = \frac{\text{new length} - \text{original length}}{\text{original length}} \tag{18-4}$$

where S is the strain
ΔL is the change in length
L is the original length

As an example, suppose that the bar of Fig. 18-7 has an original length of 10 in. After being stretched it may have a new length of 10.1 in. Hence, we would say that the strain, or percentage change, is

$$S = \frac{10.1 - 10}{10} = \frac{0.1}{10} = 0.01 = 1\%$$

A negative strain refers to compression rather than elongation. For instance, if the bar is compressed by pushing on the ends, we might find that the 10-in. bar has a new length of 9.8 in. In this case,

$$S = \frac{9.8 - 10}{10} = -2\%$$

A strain gage is a transducer that can be used to measure the amount of strain that an object undergoes. The simplest form of a strain gage is shown in Fig. 18-8*a*. A fine wire is bonded to a piece of insulating material. The resistance of the wire is a function of its length, its diameter, and the type of metal used. Various resistances may be obtained by increasing the wire length, as shown in Fig. 18-8*b*. The strain gage can then be

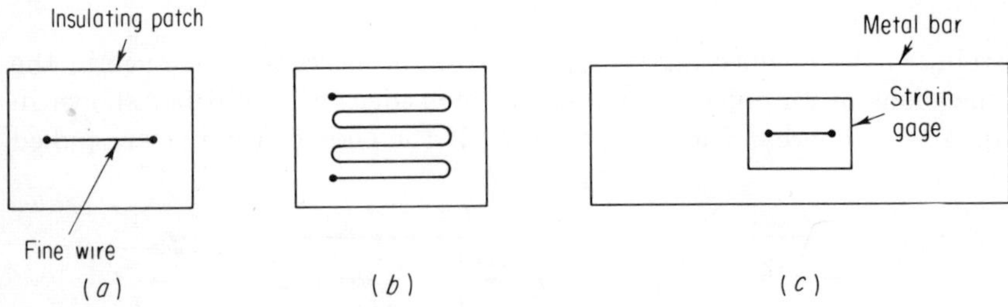

Fig. 18-8 Strain gage. (*a*) Simple wire strain gage. (*b*) Alternate form of strain gage. (*c*) Strain gage bonded to specimen.

bonded to an object such as a metal bar, as shown in Fig. 18-8*c*. With no force applied to the bar, the strain-gage resistance is equal to some initial value. As the bar is strained, however, the resistance of strain gage changes. It can be shown that the percentage change in resistance is

$$\frac{\Delta R}{R} = K \frac{\Delta L}{L} \tag{18-5}$$

where ΔR is the change in resistance
R is the original value of resistance
K is a constant of proportionality (called the *gage factor*)

The value of K in Eq. (18-5) takes on a variety of positive or negative values, depending upon the type of wire material used. For a typical strain gage made of constantan the value of K is about 2.

The point of Eq. (18-5) is that the resistance of the strain gage is a function of the amount of strain that has taken place. By measuring the change in resistance, we are in effect measuring the amount of strain. The changes that take place in resistance, however, are small. For instance, if we use a K value of 2, a strain of 1 percent gives us a percentage change in resistance of 2 percent. If we try to use an ohmmeter to measure the resistance, an almost imperceptible change in the reading takes place. As a rule, the strain gage is used in conjunction with a d-c bridge, where it is possible to measure small changes accurately. Figure 18-9 illustrates one system for measuring strain. The procedure for making a strain measurement is straightforward. We first balance the bridge before any strain has occurred. After the bar is strained, we rebalance the bridge. The change in the setting of the rheostat indicates the amount of strain.

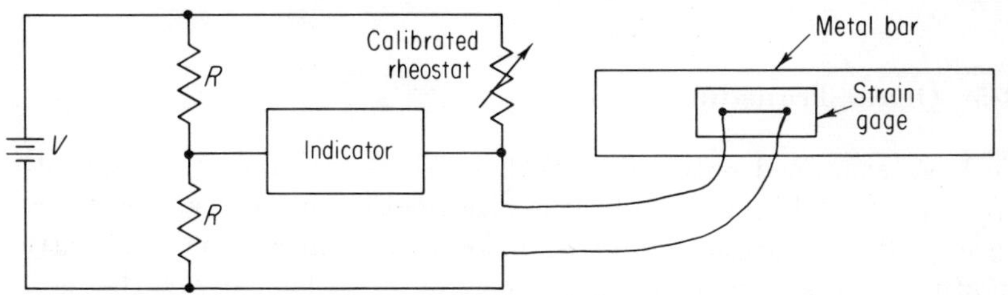

Fig. 18-9 Measuring strain using Wheatstone bridge.

This rheostat may be calibrated to read the strain directly instead of the resistance change.

Example 18-8

A strain gage has a gage factor K of 4. If this strain gage is attached to a metal bar that stretches from 10 to 10.2 in., what is the percentage change in resistance? If the unstrained value of resistance is 120 ohms, what is the value after strain?

Solution

Using Eq. (18-4), we find that the strain is

$$S = \frac{10.2 - 10}{10} = 2\%$$

From Eq. (18-5),

$$\frac{\Delta R}{R} = 4(2\%) = 8\%$$

Hence,

$$\Delta R = 0.08(120) = 9.6 \text{ ohms}$$

and the value of resistance after strain is

$$120 + 9.6 = 129.6 \text{ ohms}$$

Example 18-9

In Fig. 18-9 the value of the rheostat that balances the bridge before strain has taken place is 100 ohms. After straining the metal bar, the rheostat must be adjusted to 110 ohms. If the gage factor is 2, what is the value of the strain?

Solution

$$\frac{\Delta R}{R} = \frac{110 - 100}{100} = 0.1 = 10\%$$

With a gage factor K of 2 the value of strain is

$$S = \frac{10\%}{2} = 5\%$$

18-5 Other Transducers

We have examined only a few of the various transducers. Many other types are available. Generally, the electrical quantity involved is resistance, voltage, current, inductance, or capacitance. The nonelectrical quantity covers a wide range of possibilities. To convey the notion of how broad the range of nonelectrical quantities is, consider the following incomplete list: acceleration, acidity, air flow, air velocity, blood pressure, compression, corrosion, density, displacement, drag, elasticity, evaporation, force, gravity, hardness, heartbeat, heat, humidity, impact, light, liquid level, magnetic field strength, position, pressure, purity of solutions, radiation, roughness, sound, speed, strain, temperature, tension, thickness, thrust, torque, turbulence, vibration, viscosity, weight, and yaw. The point is that there is a large number of input transducers that allow indirect measurement of nonelectrical quantities. There are also a number of output transducers that allow us to control nonelectrical quantities with our electronic instruments.

In closing, we may observe that without transducers, electronics could not have attained the important role that it plays in our lives. Our electronic instruments would be nothing more than laboratory phenomena. But with transducers, we can use our electronic instruments to measure, modify, and improve the world in which we live.

GLOSSARY

ambient temperature The surrounding temperature.

bimetallic strip Two strips of dissimilar metals bonded together. As the temperature changes, the bimetallic strip bends either way, depending upon the rates of thermal expansion of the metals.

photocell A transducer sensitive to light.

resistance thermometer An accurate resistance whose value may be used for indirect measurement of the temperature.

strain The percentage change in the dimensions of an object caused by force or temperature.

strain gage A resistive transducer for measuring strain.

thermistor A resistance whose value is very sensitive to temperature.

REVIEW QUESTIONS

1. Why are transducers important in electronic instrumentation?
2. How does an input transducer differ from an output transducer? Give some examples of each type.
3. Name the three different types of photocells. What three common circuit elements are equivalent to the three types of photocells?
4. What is the basic idea behind the bimetallic strip? How is it used in a thermostatically controlled oven?
5. What is a resistance thermometer? Which metal is often used because of its stable properties?
6. What is a thermistor? What is a typical value for the thermal coefficient of a thermistor?
7. What is a thermocouple? Name one of its uses.
8. In the system of Fig. 18-6, what effect does changing the value of the rheostat have? Why is there a small amount of current through the heater even when the oven temperature has reached an equilibrium condition?
9. What is a strain gage? What is the gage factor?
10. Name some of the nonelectrical quantities that are transducible to electrical quantities.

PROBLEMS

18-1 A photoemissive diode has a K value of 50 μa per lumen. Graph the current versus the amount of light for a range of 0 to 5 lumens.
18-2 In Fig. 18-1 an ammeter with a full-scale deflection of 50 μa is to be used to measure the amount of light striking the cathode. If 5 lumens of light causes full-scale deflection, what is the value of K for the diode?
18-3 In the circuit of Fig. 18-3 the value of R is 10 kilohms, V is 10 volts, and the transistor has a d-c β of 50. Allow 0.7 volt drop for the base-emitter diode. If the relay closes when the current through it is 1 ma, what value of photocell resistance just closes the relay?
18-4 A solar cell has an open-circuit voltage of 300 mv and a Thévenin resistance of 200 ohms. If 20 of these cells are placed in series, what is the Thévenin equivalent?
18-5 In the system of Fig. 18-4 the amount of light striking the cathode is 1.5 lumens. The power supply voltage is 100 volts, and the value of the load resistor is 1 megohm. The input impedance of the decimal counter is 1 megohm, and the K value of the diode is 25 μa per lumen. If the light beam is interrupted, the value of light striking the cathode drops to 0.25 lumen. How large is the pulse appearing at the input to the decimal counter? Assume a large coupling capacitor.

18-6 A resistance thermometer made out of platinum has a resistance of 150 ohms at 0°C. What is the resistance at 200°C? At what temperature does the thermometer have a resistance of 400 ohms?

18-7 In the bridge of Fig. 18-10, the ammeter reads 250 μa. The meter resistance is 50 ohms. If the thermistor has a thermal coefficient of -5 percent per degree centigrade, and if the resistance is 1000 ohms at 35°C, what is the temperature of the thermistor?

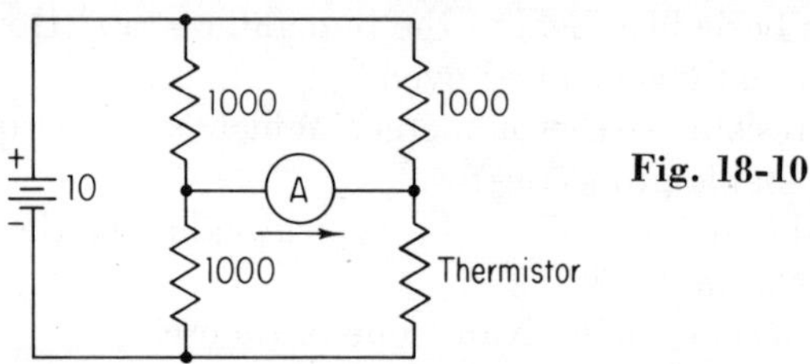

Fig. 18-10

18-8 A thermistor has a resistance of 10 kilohms at 25°C and K value of -5 percent. A Wien-bridge oscillator uses two identical thermistors in the frequency-determining part of the bridge. The value of C used in the bridge is 500 pf. What is the frequency of oscillation for the following temperatures: 20, 25, and 30°C?

18-9 A strain gage has a resistance of 120 ohms unstrained and a gage factor of -12. What is the resistance value if the strain is 1 percent?

18-10 In Fig. 18-9 a strain gage with a gage factor of 2 is used. If the unstrained value of resistance is 120 ohms, what is the value of the rheostat at balance if the strain is:

(*a*) 0?

(*b*) -1.5 percent?

References for Further Reading

Burroughs Corporation: "Digital Computer Principles," McGraw-Hill Book Company, New York, 1962.

Jackson, H. W.: "Introduction to Electric Circuits," Prentice-Hall, Inc., Englewood Cliffs, N.J., 1963.

Lion, K. S.: "Instrumentation in Scientific Research," McGraw-Hill Book Company, New York, 1959.

Lurch, E. N.: "Fundamentals of Electronics," John Wiley & Sons, Inc., New York, 1964.

O'Higgins, P. J.: "Basic Instrumentation," McGraw-Hill Book Company, New York, 1966.

Partridge, G. R.: "Principles of Electronic Instruments," Prentice-Hall, Inc., Englewood Cliffs, N.J., 1960.

Philco Technological Center Staff: "Electronic Precision Measurement Techniques and Experiments," Prentice-Hall, Inc., Englewood Cliffs, N.J., 1964.

Prensky, S. D.: "Electronic Instrumentation," Prentice-Hall, Inc., Englewood Cliffs, N.J., 1963.

Ramey, R. L.: "Electronics and Instrumentation," Wadsworth Publishing Co., Belmont, Calif., 1963.

Slurzberg, M., and W. T. Osterheld: "Essentials of Radio-electronics," 2d ed., McGraw-Hill Book Company, New York, 1961.

Soisson, H. E.: "Electronic Measuring Instruments," McGraw-Hill Book Company, New York, 1961.

Terman, F. E., and J. M. Pettit: "Electronic Measurements," 2d ed., McGraw-Hill Book Company, New York, 1952.

Answers to Odd-numbered Problems

CHAPTER 1

1-1 (*a*) $V_{oc} = 30$, and $R_o = 2.2$ kilohms (*b*) 13.6 ma (*c*) 4.16 ma **1-3** 1 ma **1-5** (*a*) $V_{oc} \cong 20.3$ and $R_o \cong 100$ (*b*) $V \cong 20.3$ **1-7** 1.11 ohms **1-9** Exponential curve starting at zero and approaching 50 volts; time constant is 1 msec. **1-11** $100(1 - \epsilon^{-t/0.1})$ **1-13** $100 + 50\epsilon^{-t/0.1}$ **1-15** 19.5 volts **1-17** $v = 300 - 200\epsilon^{-t/250\text{ nsec}}$ **1-19** The capacitor charges from 0 to about 6.67 volts with a time constant of 66.7 sec. **1-21** 67 db, approximately 2200 **1-23** 0.25 mv rms

CHAPTER 2

2-1 0.30 to 0.40 ma **2-3** 0.922 to 0.982 ma **2-5** Less than 30 ohms **2-7** 100 μa, 92.6 μa, 250 ohms **2-9** 222 ohms, 200 ohms **2-11** 0.98 ohm, 51 ma, 50 mv **2-13** 70 kilohms, 245 kilohms, 745 kilohms, 2.45 megohms, 7.45 megohms, 25 megohms **2-15** 50 μa **2-17** 8 volts, 5.45 volts, 2.86 volts **2-19** 9 volts **2-21** 25 megohms **2-23** 5950 ohms **2-25** 7.2 kilohms **2-27** 23%

CHAPTER 3

3-1 (*a*) 5 ma (*b*) 4.97 ma (*c*) 4.95 ma **3-3** Half-wave-rectified sine wave with a positive peak of 40 volts and a negative peak of 0 volts **3-5** The output is the input with the negative portions clipped off. **3-7** A sine wave clipped at 10 volts on the positive half cycle and clipped at -5 volts on the negative half cycle **3-9** The output stays at 20 volts with the switch open or closed. **3-11** (*a*) 20 kilohms (*b*) 5 kilohms **3-13** (*a*) 6 kilohms (*b*) 35 ma **3-15** 5 ma **3-17** A square wave with positive and negative peak values of 10.7 and -10.7 volts, respectively **3-19** The voltage will charge exponentially from 0 toward 100 volts, but once the 60-volt level is reached, the zener diode breaks down, thus holding the output voltage at 60 volts.

CHAPTER 4

4-1 4.77 ma **4-3** Approximately 900 kilohms **4-5** 5.75 volts rms **4-7** 45 volts peak **4-9** 12.5 kilohms, 1.88 volts rms **4-11** 750 kilohms **4-13** 0.5 μf

4-15

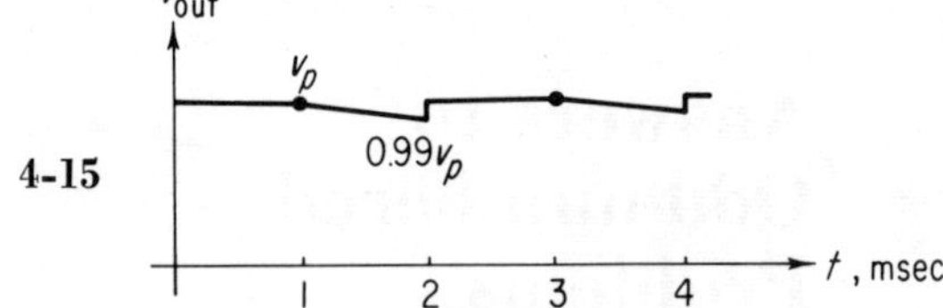

4-17 The output is a positively clamped sawtooth with a peak value of 75 volts. **4-19** The output is a square wave with a positive peak of $+90$ volts and a negative peak of -50 volts. **4-21** The first waveform is a negatively clamped sawtooth with a negative peak of -30 volts and a positive peak of 0 volts. The second waveform is essentially a d-c voltage of -30 volts.

CHAPTER 5

5-1 (*a*) Yes (*b*) Yes (*c*) No **5-3** 10 ohms **5-5** $V_{oc} = 7.15$ and $R_o =$ 3.14 kilohms **5-7** 20 ma **5-9** 12.5 kilohms **5-11** 0.25 volts **5-13** 0.45 volts **5-15** 1%

CHAPTER 6

6-1 $R_p = 850$, $X_p = 212$ **6-3** (*a*) $R_s = 0.005$, $X_s = 100$ (*b*) $R_s = 0.5$, $X_s = 1000$ **6-5** $R_s = 4$, $X_s = 200$ **6-7** $R_s = 1.59$, $R_p = 1.59$ megohms **6-9** $R_p = 2.5$, $X_p = 5$ **6-13** 7.95 kHz **6-15** $R_p = 200$, $L_p = 1$ mh, $D = 0.157$, $Q = 6.36$ **6-19** $f = 15.9$ kHz

CHAPTER 7

7-1 $A = 0.125$, $A_{db} = -18$ db, $a_{db} = 18$ db **7-3** $C_{\text{left}} = 0.505$ pf, $C_{\text{right}} =$ 5.55 pf **7-5** $R_o = 500$, $a = 6.29$, or $a_{db} = 16$ db **7-7** $R_o = 86.6$, $a =$ 3.73 or $a_{db} = 11.4$ db **7-9** $R_1 = 96.6$, $R_2 = 3.56$ **7-11** $R_1 = 9480$, $R_2 = 640$ **7-13** $R_o = 150$, $a = 6.3$ or $a_{db} = 16$ db, $v_{out} = 1.59$ **7-15** R_2,

R_3 progressively equal: (278, 1300), (66.7, 5400), (19.6, 18.4 kilohms), (6.06, 59.4 kilohms) **7-17** $R_{out} = 54.7$ **7-19** $R_{out} = 59.2$, and 64.3

CHAPTER 8

8-3 $A = 0.707, 0.447, 0.0995$ **8-5** Passband gain = 0.333, $f_c = 9.55$ kHz **8-7** $f_c = 350$ kHz, 636 kHz **8-9** (*a*) Low-pass response: approx. -2 db in passband, and a cutoff frequency of 1.97 kHz (*b*) -8 db (*c*) -22 db **8-11** High-pass response with cutoff of 318 kHz **8-13** Bandpass response: $f_{c1} =$ 16.4 Hz, $f_{c2} = 512$ kHz **8-15** (*a*) Bandpass response: 20 db in passband with cutoff frequencies of 14.7 Hz and 430 kHz (*b*) Gain is 0 db at 1.47 Hz and 4.3 MHz **8-17** $A = 0.150$ or $A_{db} = -16.4$ db **8-19** 15.9 pf **8-21** $R_o = 7.65$ kilohms, $f_c = 6.1$ kHz, $a_{db} = 50$ db at $1.5f_c$, and $a_{db} = 69$ db at $2f_c$ **8-23** $L = 3.18$ μh, $C = 318$ pf, $n = 5$ **8-25** $1.67C = 266$ pf, $1.67L =$ 0.665 μh, $0.94C = 150$ pf

CHAPTER 9

9-1 (*a*) d-c beta = 50 (*b*) $I_c = 1$ ma **9-3** (*a*) $R_b = 2$ megohms (*b*) $R_b = 1.25$ megohms **9-5** (*a*) $V_{ce} = 50$ (*b*) $V_{ce} = 0$ (*c*) Change = 50 **9-7** Minimum beta is 5 **9-9** Approximately 167 by ideal-transistor approach **9-11** $I_c = 5$ ma, $V_{ce} = 5$ volts, and 50 mv across R_b **9-13** $I_c =$ 1 ma, $V_{ce} = 10$ volts **9-15** $A = 100$, $v_{out} = 100$ mv **9-17** $A = 6.67$, $R_{in} = 90$ kilohms

CHAPTER 10

10-1 $f_1 = 44$ Hz, $f_2 = 9.1$ kHz **10-3** 73.7; 75 **10-5** 50.7 db **10-7** $R_1 = 21$ kilohms, $R_2 = 79$ kilohms, $R_3 = 34.2$ kilohms, $R_4 = 65.8$ kilohms, $R_5 = 42.9$ kilohms, $R_6 = 57.1$ kilohms **10-9** (*a*) -10 volts d-c (*b*) 5 volts d-c **10-11** 1-volt-peak sine wave **10-13** 800

CHAPTER 11

11-1 0.5 volts **11-3** From the bottom: 30 kilohms, 70 kilohms, 200 kilohms, 700 kilohms, 2 megohms, and 7 megohms **11-5** 2.22 ma; 550 ohms **11-7** 1780 ohms **11-9** $v_{max} = 0.833$ mv: $v_{min} = 0.091$ mv

CHAPTER 12

12-1 A line with a slope of ½ **12-3** 44.5° **12-5** Top: 5 kHz; middle: 2.5 kHz; bottom: 7.5 kHz **12-7** (*a*) Four cycles of a sine wave (*b*) Positive half cycle on top of negative half cycle (*c*) Two cycles of a cosine wave (*d*) Four cycles of a sawtooth **12-9** 32 μsec **12-11** 200 μsec; 10 msec **12-13** 147 μsec **12-15** 10 pf

CHAPTER 13

13-1 100 kHz; 200 kHz; 300 kHz; 400 kHz; 500 kHz **13-3** $C_o = 37.5$; $C_1 = 23.8$; $C_2 = 11.9$; $C_3 = 7.95$; $C_4 = 5.96$

13-5

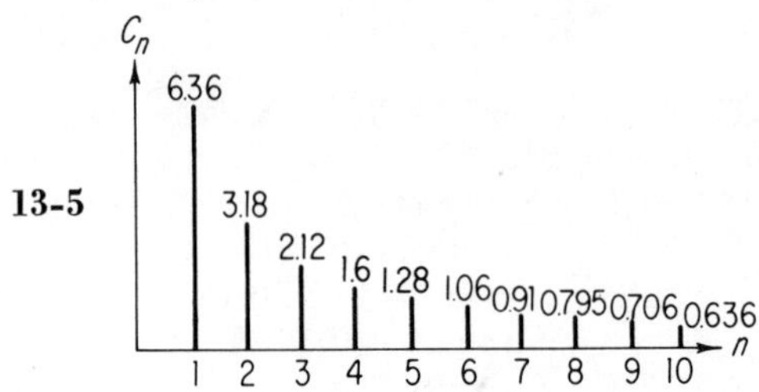

13-7 3.75 volts rms **13-9** $C_0 = 63.6$; $C_1 = 42.4$; $C_2 = 8.48$; $C_3 = 3.6$; $C_4 = 2.02$; $C_{100} = 0.00318$ **13-11** The flip test indicates that a pure sine wave contains only odd harmonics. This makes perfect sense because a pure sine wave has only a fundamental, which is an odd harmonic. **13-13** 28.8 volts rms **13-15** $n = 4, 8, 12, 16$, etc.

CHAPTER 14

14-1 20 kHz; 40 kHz; 60 kHz; 80 kHz, etc. **14-3** 0.232, or 23.2%

CHAPTER 15

15-1 (*a*) 2.12 kHz (*b*) 3 mv rms **15-3** 1.88 MHz **15-5** 38.4 pf; 30.4 pf; 23 pf; 16.9 pf; 12.2 pf; 8.75 pf **15-7** $C_8 = 50.5$ mv; $C_7 = 66.2$ mv **15-9** (*a*) 100 kHz (*b*) Ninth harmonic, or 900 kHz (*c*) Yes **15-11** (*a*) 1 ma (*b*) 20 μa (*c*) 0.9 volt (*d*) An almost square wave with a maximum of 10 volts and a minimum of almost zero **15-13** 0.01 μf; narrow positive and negative triggers **15-15** 7 to 70 kHz

CHAPTER 16

16-1 0, 1, 10, 11, 100, 101, 110, 111, 1000, 1001, 1010, 1011, 1100, 1101, 1110, 1111, 10000, 10001, 10010, 10011, 10100, 10101, 10110, 10111, 11000, 11001, 11010, 11011, 11100, 11101, 11110, 11111 **16-3** 1100; 10001; 11010; 111000; 1111111 **16-5** Truth table: $D = 0$ for $ABC = 000$, and $D = 1$ for all other ABC inputs; Boolean expression is $D = A + B + C$

16-7

A	B	$\overline{A+B}$	$\overline{A} \cdot \overline{B}$
0	0	1	1
0	1	0	0
1	0	0	0
1	1	0	0

16-9 (*a*) $D = 0$ for the following three ABC values: 000, 001, 010, and $D = 1$ for the remaining ABC values (*b*) Same truth table as part *a* **16-11** $C = (\overline{A + B})B$; truth table: $C = 0$ for all ABC entries **16-13** One possible circuit arrangement is the following:

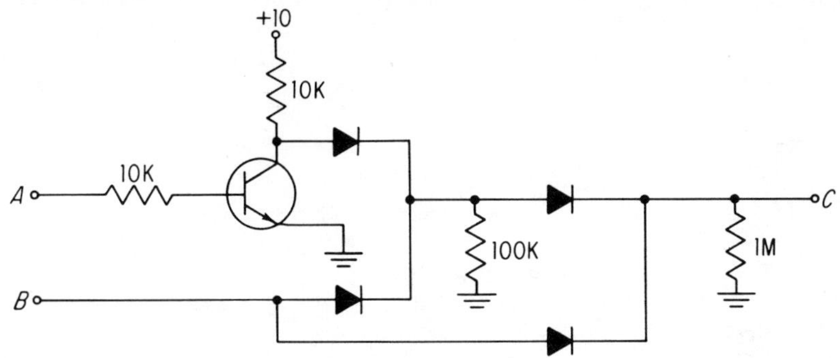

CHAPTER 17

17-1 The truth table for $ABCDE$ should be a binary progression from 00000 to 11111

17-3

Number of triggers	A	B	C	D
0	0	0	1	0
1	0	0	1	1
2	0	1	0	0
3	0	1	0	1
4	0	1	1	0
5	0	1	1	1
6	1	1	0	0
7	1	1	0	1
8	1	1	1	0
9	1	1	1	1
10	0	0	1	0

17-5 $5(10^4)$ **17-7** 500,000; 327,000

CHAPTER 18

18-1 A straight line passing through the origin and the point $I = 250\ \mu a$, $F = 5$ lumens **18-3** 11.6 kilohms **18-5** About 15.6 volts peak **18-7** Approximately 37°C **18-9** 106 ohms

Index